An Army of Phantoms

ALSO BY J. HOBERMAN

Bridge of Light: Yiddish Film Between Two Worlds
The Dream Life: Movies, Media, and the Mythology of the Sixties
Entertaining America: Jews, Movies, and Broadcasting
(co-edited with Jeffrey Shandler)
The Magic Hour: Film at Fin de Siècle
Midnight Movies (with Jonathan Rosenbaum)
On Jack Smith's "Flaming Creatures" (and Other Secret-Flix of Cinemaroc)
The Red Atlantis: Communist Culture in the Absence of Communism
Vulgar Modernism: Writing on Movies and Other Media

An Army of Phantoms

AMERICAN MOVIES
AND THE MAKING OF THE COLD WAR

J. Hoberman

THE NEW PRESS

NEW YORK
LONDON

Requests for permission to reproduce selections from this book should be mailed
to: Permissions Department, The New Press, 38 Greene Street, New York, NY 10013.

Published in the United States by The New Press, New York, 2011
Distributed by Perseus Distribution

LIBRARY OF CONGRESS CATALOGING-IN-PUBLICATION DATA

Hoberman, J.
    An army of phantoms : American movies and the making of the Cold War /
J. Hoberman.
        p.   cm.
    Includes bibliographical references and index.
    ISBN 978-1-59558-005-4 (hc.)
    1. Motion pictures—Political aspects—United States.   2. Motion pictures—United
States—History—20th century.   3. Cold War in motion pictures.   4. Communism
and motion pictures—United States.   I. Title.
    PN1995.9.P6H62   2011
    791.43'6582825—dc22

                                                                    2010049107

The New Press was established in 1990 as a not-for-profit alternative to the
large, commercial publishing houses currently dominating the book publishing
industry. The New Press operates in the public interest rather than for private
gain, and is committed to publishing, in innovative ways, works of educational,
cultural, and community value that are often deemed insufficiently profitable.

www.thenewpress.com

Composition by Westchester Book Composition

Printed in the United States of America

10   9   8   7   6   5   4   3   2   1

For Norma Jean Baker (1926–1962)
and Jacob Julius Garfinkle (1913–1952)

An army of phantoms vast and wan
Beleaguer the human soul.
—HENRY WADSWORTH LONGFELLOW, *"The Beleaguered City" (1839)*

CONTENTS

ACKNOWLEDGMENTS

An Army of Phantoms is the first installment of a projected three-volume chronicle of American movies in the light of American politics, during the period of the Cold War. Roughly covering the years between V-J Day and Dwight Eisenhower's reelection, *An Army of Phantoms* is the prequel to *The Dream Life: Movies, Media, and the Mythology of the Sixties*, published by The New Press in 2003. A final volume picking up the story on the eve of the Bicentennial and taking it just past the fall of the Berlin Wall is in preparation.

The dust had barely settled in Berlin when I began work on this project and I have many people to thank. In New York, my research was conducted at the New York Public Library: Library for the Performing Arts, the Celeste Bartos International Film Study Center at the Museum of Modern Art, the Paley Center for Media, and New York University's Elmer Holmes Bobst Library, particularly the Tamiment Library and Robert F. Wagner Labor Archives. In Los Angeles, I was privileged to work at the Margaret Herrick Library of the Academy of Motion Picture Arts and Sciences, the University of California Los Angeles Library—Performing Arts Special Collections, the University of Southern California's Warner Bros. Archives, and the Southern California Library for Social Studies and Research. This book would not have been possible without these institutions and their dedicated staffs.

Thanks to the Freedom of Information Act, I have also had the benefit of the records kept by the Federal Bureau of Investigation. Like many researchers I owe a debt of gratitude to Daniel Leab for requesting and organizing an extensive dossier of excerpts from the FBI's massive "Communist Infiltration—Motion Picture Industry (Compic)" files. In addition, I requested and received FBI files on William Alland, Ben Barzman, Martin Berkeley, Cecil B. DeMille, Hanns Eisler, Carl Foreman, Samuel Fuller, Mikhail Kalatozov, Elia Kazan, Stanley Kramer, Nicholas Ray, Dore Schary, John Wayne, and the Motion Picture Alliance for the Preservation of American Ideals. Although often heavily redacted, these files were never less than interesting—not least because the FBI agents so diligently clipped and preserved articles from the Communist press.

In addition to Professor Leab, a number of historians blazed a trail that I might follow. These guides include Thomas Doherty (whose interests have anticipated many of mine), Gerald Horne, Joseph McBride (author of *Searching for John Ford*, the finest Hollywood biography I have ever read), Greg Mitchell, Lawrence Suid, and the exemplary cultural historian Richard Slotkin. Published thirty years ago, Larry Ceplair and Steve Englund's *The Inquisition in Hollywood* remains the definitive work in the field. I'd also like to salute oral historians Paul Buhle and Patrick McGilligan for their truly invaluable work, as well as Michel Ciment for his unmatched book-length interviews with Elia Kazan and Joseph Losey, and beg the pardon of all those I've forgotten.

Friends who provided crucial assistance include Steve Anker, Danny Czitrom, Eva Forgacs, Ken and Flo Jacobs, Bob Schneider, and Art Spiegelman; I'm particularly appreciative of Manohla Dargis, Mel Gordon, and Dave Kehr for taking time from their own work to help me track down and retrieve specific material. Thanks also to Tom Brueggemann, who was kind enough to send me a number of key DVDs. Finally, I had the benefit of many resourceful research assistants, most of them students from NYU. While these are too numerous to thank individually, I'll cite the last three (Vadim Rizov, Violet Lucca, and Anna Bak-Kvapil) for their heroic efforts, tracking down stray Hedda Hopper columns and scanning the *Daily Worker*, during the book's final push to completion.

Over the decades, fragments of what would be *An Army of Phantoms* appeared in a number of publications, including the *American Prospect*, *Arcade*, *Artforum*, the *New York Times*, the *Virginia Quarterly Review*, and the *Village Voice*; my appreciation to their editors for giving me the opportunity to follow my interests. Finally, a shout-out to Sarah Fan, who edited my manuscript at The New Press and to copy editor Aja Pollock; to Andy Hsiao, no longer at The New Press but nevertheless responsible for rescuing this project during its darkest hour; to my invariably supportive agent Jim Rutman; and to my beloved lifelong helpmeet Shelley Hoberman.

INTRODUCTION:
FROM GOD'S MOUTH TO YOUR EAR

Probably, we will never be able to determine the psychic havoc of
the concentration camps and the atom bomb upon the unconscious mind of almost everyone alive in these years.
—NORMAN MAILER, "The White Negro" (1957)

For collective problems only collective remedies suffice . . .
—JACQUES ELLUL, *Propaganda: The Formation of
Men's Attitudes* (1962)

There are movies that alter one's perspective and movies designed to do that
very thing. *The Next Voice You Hear*, an MGM film directed by William Wellman in 1950, is one such manufactured revelation. (Among other things, it inspired this book.)

The transmission reached me via television on a Christmas morning, some
twenty years after its theatrical release—an unexpected discovery, comparable, in
its way, to stumbling upon the Taj Mahal or the Grand Canyon. Not that *The
Next Voice* is, as a movie, particularly grandiose. The perfection of this dowdy
black-and-white production derives from its premise—so simple as to be nearly
elegant and so cosmic as to appear certifiably insane. Can any movie top it?
Framed by two biblical citations representing the Old and New Testaments, the
movie practices a unique form of direct address. For six consecutive nights,
the Creator of the Universe commandeers the airwaves to personally talk to the
American people.

The implications of such divine intervention are vast, but God's audience is
essentially reduced to a single family living in a modest home in suburban Los
Angeles. Joe Smith (James Whitmore) is a mechanic in the Ajax Aircraft Plant;
his pregnant wife, Mary (Nancy Davis), is a gracious, super-nurturing mother

to their ten-year-old son, Johnny (Gary Gray). Initially, *The Next Voice You Hear* appears as an unfunny situation comedy with Joe both compliant wage slave and household tyrant: "Don't do like I do—do like I tell you to do," he instructs Johnny even as he chafes under authority (defined as "everybody telling you what to do"), resenting most particularly his acerbic foreman (Art Smith) and the neighborhood cop who regularly chastises him for heedlessly backing his heap out of the driveway.

God enters history, although—as if in accordance with the Old Testament ban on representation—only by hearsay. One night, puzzled Joe tells Mary that the radio show to which he had been listening was interrupted by a self-identified Voice of God informing listeners, "I'll be with you for the next few days." Charles Schnee's rigorously schematic script ensures that, on each of the six evenings that God addresses the public, the movie audience will miss the divine performance. Evidently producer Dore Schary feared that patrons would react with laughter—as well they might have, if perhaps a bit nervously.

Despite its bland, earnest, self-congratulatory corn, *The Next Voice You Hear* is a study in terror; it acknowledges an actual anxiety and, however piti-fully, responds to a real sense of helplessness. "You're not supposed to worry about the fate of the world until you're big enough to shave," Joe tells Johnny after God's second broadcast—or should we say, civil defense warning. If (or rather, when) there's another war, the battlefield will be everywhere. When Johnny expresses his apprehension, Joe blames God: "Scaring kids—it's gone too far." Terrorizing Johnny is Joe's job, as is made clear when the boy breaks the radio plug just before the Voice's third scheduled appearance and Joe predict-ably flies into a rage.

Truly, *The Next Voice You Hear* has many lessons to teach. On the third night, God goes to the interpersonal, asking if His listeners are afraid of Him and wondering, "Why should children be afraid of their father?" (Why indeed, when He is omniscient and holds the power of life and death?) A hard rain be-gins to fall as the broadcast ends, causing normally placid Mary to scream in terror. But, as this is a movie, there is nothing that can't be resolved—it was Schary, in fact, who famously called America a "happy ending nation." Thus, a quick cut: instead of the end of the world, day four brings sunshine, and, for once, Joe's jalopy starts up without a problem. But that night, after the Voice has taken credit for certain large miracles and asked listeners to reciprocate with their own small miracles of love and kindness, God gives Joe Smith a test: Mary goes into false labor and her annoying Aunt Ethel becomes hysterical, prompt-ing jumpy Joe to further panic and shake the silly woman.

Day five falls on a Saturday. Mary is angry with her husband for his brutish behavior, so he storms out of the house to a neighborhood tavern. "If God stays on the radio, these joints will close down!" somebody can be heard slurring. (If only! Hadn't movie mogul Samuel Goldwyn only recently maintained that TV was "little more than a gimmick used by tavern-keepers to induce patrons to linger over another drink"?) Sure enough, Joe meets Satan in the form of a feckless war buddy with a female familiar. Joe is ready to take off for the South Seas, fleeing the Voice of God like a latter-day Jonah, until the buddy and the barfly make light of his family. Suddenly, it's as if Joe had sulked off to a movie that caused him to think! Reacquainted with his responsibilities, he turns lugubriously lachrymose and staggers home (again frightening Johnny, albeit inadvertently) to bury his head in Mary's lap.

That night God tells His listeners (or so we are told) that they are like schoolchildren: "You've forgotten your lessons. I ask you to do your homework." On day six, it's Johnny's turn to run away. Unbeknownst to Joe, the boy is a friend to his nemesis, the curmudgeonly foreman at his factory. Just before the Voice's nightly address, Joe discovers Johnny at the foreman's house, happily building a model airplane. (This demonstration of workplace harmony is not intended as ironic.) Manager and managed are reconciled; they exchange first names and bless each other. Monday evening finds the entire community expectantly gathered in church, eyes fixed on the cathedral-style radio that's been placed on the pulpit: "Ladies and gentlemen of the universe," the announcer solemnly begins, "the next voice you hear . . ."

But the radio is silent. As the minister steps into the breach, Mary goes into labor. Celestial music heralds the conclusion of the movie. Heavenly clouds fill the screen. There is no end title, save perhaps for the viewer's soft, incredulous "Wow."

"The heaviest movie Hollywood ever made," I wrote then in my film journal. "Slow-motion situation comedy alternates with accelerated soap opera. The iconography of American unconscious/alienated suffering—the workers' suburbs—is as strong as Crumb's best. . . . Fantastically symptomatic of Hollywood's impending nervous breakdown in the face of TV." Here are some more recent notes:

- *The Next Voice You Hear* appeared at a moment of crisis for the nation as well as the movie industry. The United States and Hollywood were both dazed, if not traumatized, by the loss of a significant monopoly—the United

States was no longer the world's sole nuclear power, and the studios had been compelled to divest themselves of their theater chains. Each entity was threatened by an alien threat (Communism, television).

- *The Next Voice You Hear* addresses this crisis in part by projecting a situation in which everyone can receive the same divine message. For Hollywood, this doubles as a form of self-celebration. What is a movie if not an idea—or a dramatized scenario—that is pictured and played out in millions of minds? *The Next Voice You Hear* is a mass-produced idea in praise of mass-produced ideas. (Published shortly before the movie opened, Hortense Powdermaker's anthropological study *Hollywood, the Dream Factory* put this in both business and ideological terms: Hollywood "tries to adapt the American dream, that all men are created equal, to the view that all men's dreams should be made equal.") But if an idea is pictured by a million minds simultaneously, it is called television—which, unlike radio, does not exist in this particular utopia.

- *The Next Voice You Hear* is self-serving not just in its mission but by its affirmation of the Hegelian notion that history is a rational force with a definite goal. The invention of radio, if not television, is part of an ongoing divine plan—as is, at least implicitly, Dore Schary's ascension to the MGM front office. A studio promotional release articulated the producer's point of view: "May I suggest that, while you do not hear God's voice, you go to see *The Next Voice You Hear* accepting the premise that God would use the radio much as at an earlier date He used the burning bush." But why radio and why not the burning bush? The earth was not yet denuded of foliage.

- *The Next Voice You Hear* maintains that, as the French social philosopher Jacques Ellul wrote of propaganda a decade after the movie's release, God cannot exist in a mass society without access to the mass media. Indeed, the unheard Voice of God in *The Next Voice You Hear* is the essence of what Ellul termed "sociological propaganda"—a vague, spontaneous, all-pervasive, yet half-conscious form of social bonding and ideological proselytizing advanced by advertising, newspaper editorials, social service agencies, patriotic speeches, and anything else that might use the phrase "way of life." (The concept of freedom is to America as entertainment is to Hollywood.)

- *The Next Voice You Hear*, which might be alternately titled "Dore Schary's Mission," was intended as something more than entertainment. But is it entertainment as propaganda or propaganda as entertainment? Perhaps we should think of it as an illustration of an idea willing itself into history. The main thing, Ellul would argue, is that *The Next Voice You Hear* (as well as the Next

Voice that is unheard) responds to actual problems—a state of national insecurity—and that it also proposes itself as a solution to these problems.

- Thus, *The Next Voice You Hear* upholds motherhood and the family and asserts that neighborly neighbors and responsible policemen are necessary, that suburbia, "honest" work, school, and a vague nondenominational Protestantism are both the natural order of things and the greatest good. "The original affinity of business and amusement is shown in the latter's special significance: to defend society." So wrote the social philosophers Theodor Adorno and Max Horkheimer from their wartime refuge in Los Angeles. "To be pleased means to say Yes."

- *The Next Voice You Hear* defines the nation as an audience. In the second broadcast, God had been heard to complain that people wanted miracles. According to Mary, who recounts this message to Joe (who missed it, Wednesday being his bowling night), "the Voice said He was going to think about that." (Humanity being His focus group.) But, of course, fantastic miracles were precisely what Dore Schary did not want in his movie; he wanted naturalized, everyday miracles, like *The Next Voice You Hear* itself.

- *The Next Voice You Hear* is deliberately unprepossessing as cinema precisely because it strives to locate eternity in the familiar—just as a Renaissance painting of the Annunciation might be set in a fifteenth-century Florentine courtyard. "Naturalism" is vouchsafed by offhand references to the Federal Communications Commission, Nielsen ratings, and Orson Welles, who had panicked the nation—or at least some members of the radio-listening public—with his 1938 Halloween eve broadcast, *The War of the Worlds*. Natural skeptics, Joe Smith and his fellow workers initially theorize that the alien Voice speaking through their radio sets may be Welles practicing some newfangled form of "mass suckerology." This is an inoculation for the audience—the acknowledgment of a historical hoax to conceal the greater ahistorical hoax that is this movie.[1]

- *The Next Voice You Hear* is of 1950 but not in it: the Smiths do not own a television set because, like God, TV cannot be shown on the screen. Nor is this the only absence. No one refers to the atomic bomb, let alone the recent loss of America's nuclear monopoly. The Russians are furtively mentioned (but not China). The words "Communism" and "fascism" are never whispered;

---

1. Similarly, while *The Next Voice* is careful to note that everyone in the world can hear the Voice in their own language, it is taken for granted that the Voice broadcasts when it's prime time in L.A.—after all, that's where dreams are born.

neither is the name "Jesus." Thus, *The Next Voice You Hear* is set in a fantastic parallel universe that rigorously works to exclude, conceal, or deny that which it might actually be about. Let's call that imaginary world the Movies.

If one movie is a manufactured fantasy, a year's worth of movies—or a decade's—becomes an instrumentalized stream of consciousness that insinuates itself into a shared national narrative. As Thomas Mann wrote in *The Magic Mountain*, "a human being lives out not only his personal life as an individual, but also, consciously or subconsciously, the lives of his epoch and contemporaries." As suggested by *The Next Voice You Hear*, that second, dream life is lived through the mass media.

However much the product of particular forces at a specific moment, a mass-consumed idea like *The Next Voice* draws on preexistent fantasies and contributes to an ongoing, collective drama. In some respects, *The Next Voice*'s scenario was fulfilled in 1952 with the election of a God-fearing yet soothing Christian soldier to the presidency. (Dore Schary had campaigned for General Dwight D. Eisenhower as early as 1948.) James Whitmore, the movie's designated everyman, grew up to play two presidents, including the actual everyman writ large who occupied the White House when *The Next Voice* was made; even better, his onscreen spouse was elevated to the White House itself, in a move that suggests a logic beyond all logic operating in the Dream Life: marrying a fellow movie actor who would be elected president—*the* president.[2]

Schary mobilized the shadows; *The Next Voice You Hear* had assigned itself a mission, just as Hollywood assumed one during the last war. It was made to demonstrate that, certain technological developments notwithstanding, movies remained a powerful, positive, necessary force in American society. In this, *The Next Voice* may have been shameless but hardly unique. Evoking extraterrestrial invasion, mind control, national insecurity, and even Armageddon, Schary presents themes common to Cold War Hollywood, albeit in a more comforting sociological-propagandist form.[3]

In 1950, *New York Times* film critic Bosley Crowther bracketed *The Next*

---

2. Whitmore received an Oscar nomination in 1975 for *Give 'Em Hell, Harry!* and, three years later, played Theodore Roosevelt in the made-for-television movie *Bully*. Nancy Davis married Ronald Reagan in 1952.

3. As the issues of the 1950s were revived in the 1970s, *The Next Voice You Hear* is a prototype for *Close Encounters of the Third Kind*; despite the absence of dramatic special effects, the movie's reassuring construction of the spectator as a child mark it as a primitive example of Spielbergism.

Voice with the near simultaneous Eagle-Lion release *Destination Moon* as an instance of "stimulating movie fantasy." *Destination Moon*, produced by George Pal and directed by Irving Pichel, also insisted on its verité. *Life* magazine's production story absurdly maintained that the movie was so realistic that it "met its chief obstacle in the form of important scientific visitors who poked around the painted craters just to get an idea of what a trip to the moon might really be like." But *Destination Moon*—its title unavoidably echoing the wartime hit *Destination Tokyo* (1943)—was far more concerned with geopolitical danger than extraterrestrial exploration.

Crowther's review cited the Soviet threat in its lead paragraph, noting that no one had yet reached the moon unless "the Russians have pulled a fast one on us," and musing that it was "arresting to hear an eloquent scientist proclaim that the first nation which can use the moon for launching missiles will control the earth." *Destination Moon* addressed the very national security problem that the Truman administration had grappled with for the past three years: how to prepare for war and prepare the people for war when, as yet, there was no war.

One mission stood in for another. Opening at the White Sands military installation, site of the original atomic bomb tests and the present home to the von Braun rocket team (which had been largely transplanted from Germany in 1945), *Destination Moon* immediately evokes the notion of top secret technology, the specter of enemy sabotage, and the necessity of a lunar military base in no uncertain terms: "There is no way to stop a missile launched from outer space. That is the most important military fact of this century." This hard sell echoes the rhetoric of NSC-68, the U.S. National Security Council report that advocated massive rearmament in the aftermath of the Soviet atomic bomb and, like *Destination Moon,* was in production in early 1950.[4]

As *The Next Voice* imagines God as the miracle of television without TV, *Destination Moon* conceives of national security as a Hollywood super-production and assigns the leading role to private industry. "If we want to stay in business we have to build this ship," one visionary plutocrat tells a conclave of his tuxedo-clad peers. (If anything, the government is an impediment. The expedition blasts off in defiance of a court order, one step ahead of the police—which is to say, reality. *Destination Moon* anticipates the "space race" by the better part of a decade and Ronald Reagan's "Star Wars" program by some thirty-three years.) As the Cold War heated up, Hollywood naturally sought the divine guidance of an earlier

---

4. Released a month earlier (and discussed in chapter 2), *Rocketship X-M* was *Destination Moon*'s "progressive" equivalent.

mission. Underlying the stimulating fantasies of *The Next Voice You Hear* and *Destination Moon* was the movie industry's unprecedented World War II mobilization and sense of purpose.

The actor James Whitmore was not just Joe Smith but, for the audience of 1950, an Oscar-winning supporting actor in a previous Dore Schary production, *Battleground* (1949), and thus an iconic GI Joe. Indeed, for Schary, *The Next Voice* was a sequel to if not a remake of *Joe Smith, American*, a patriotic morale booster that helpfully propagandized President Franklin D. Roosevelt's preparedness program; it was produced by Schary's old MGM B-movie unit and released four months into World War II. In the apocalyptic glow of the Soviet atomic bomb, Schary had the idea of letting God, rather than FDR, speak directly to Joe Smith, American.

If *The Next Voice You Hear* imagined a cosmic fireside chat, the scenario projected by *Destination Moon* seemingly took its cues from the novelist Ayn Rand, an influential right-wing critic of liberal Hollywood, in promoting an anti–New Deal plutocracy to safeguard America. Despite their ideological differences, both movies took it for granted that fantasy could be instrumentalized, and both celebrated Hollywood's capacity to change the world. War included a war of images. Entertainment had a vital social function: just as Joe Smith is instructed by the radio, so the industrialists are educated in the principles of rocketry by a specially prepared Woody Woodpecker cartoon.

The Next Voice You Hear and *Destination Moon* suggest that Hollywood's World War II mobilization, along with the belief that the people who made movies were not just professional entertainers but politically aware culture workers, continued after the war ended, through the Truman presidency and into Eisenhower's first term. Hollywood accepted a new mission and assigned itself a role, albeit a largely unofficial one, in the new war—both in terms of movies made and careers unmade.

An Army of Phantoms: American Movies and the Making the Cold War initiates a three-part chronicle of American politics from 1945 through 1990, as filtered through the prism of Hollywood movies—their scenarios, backstories, and reception. The middle part has already been published as *The Dream Life: Movies, Media, and the Mythology of the Sixties*; the conclusion, *Found Illusions: The Romance of the Remake and the Triumph of Reaganocracy*, is in progress. This chronicle makes no pretense to providing a comprehensive history of Hollywood during this period. The movies discussed are not necessarily the most critically prized, nor even the most popular with audiences; their makers are not always Hollywood's greatest artists, some of whom may be conspicuous by their absence. Rather, these are individuals responsible for those movies that best crystallize, address, symptomize, or exploit their historical moment—or, just as importantly, were understood to do so at the time.

The collective drama that *An Army of Phantoms* recounts was not restricted to America's movie theaters but played out in the press, comic books, popular music, ongoing FBI investigations, congressional hearings, and political campaigns. Thanks to the movies, however, this drama was elevated to a cosmic struggle against National Insecurity for possession of the Great Whatzit. The war was waged in the desert surrounding Fort Apache and in the streets of Hadleyville, as well as the hills of Korea and the halls of Washington, DC, and invoked all manner of imaginary beings. In the national Dream Life, this war was fought by archetypal figures: the Christian Soldier and the Patriot Roughneck were pitted against an Implacable Alien Other, as well as the Wild One, and sometimes themselves.

PROLOGUE:
MISSION FOR HOLLYWOOD—STALINGRAD TO V-J DAY

The world at war; Americans at the movies. "Every night is Saturday Night!" Variety declares exultantly. Ticket sales and domestic rentals nearly double between 1939 and 1946. Hollywood has never been more important to America, and America's Communists have never been more important to Hollywood—or so they think.

November 10, 1942, a few weeks from Pearl Harbor's first anniversary, two months into the Battle of Stalingrad, another day that will live in infamy: behind their studio gates, Warner Bros. begins production on its patriotic superspectacle *Mission to Moscow*.

The project, based on the bestselling memoir by America's envoy to the Soviets, Joseph E. Davies, is enthusiastically supported by the Office of War Information and looked upon with favor by President Franklin D. Roosevelt. Throughout production, Ambassador Davies, who has script approval, will keep Roosevelt apprised of the movie's progress.

Mission to Moscow is shooting even as *Time* magazine declares Joseph Stalin the Man of the Year, the United States engages Japan at Guadalcanal, and atomic physicist Enrico Fermi orchestrates the first self-sustained nuclear chain reaction beneath the football stadium at the University of Chicago. In Washington, the Committee to Investigate the National Defense Program, chaired by Senator Harry Truman (Democrat of Missouri), is holding hearings on irregularities in Hollywood's military contracts, including alleged favoritism on the part of Twentieth Century-Fox chieftain Darryl Zanuck, accused of taking home $5,000 per week for four months while on active duty, as well as failing to put his Fox stock in trust.

Must have slipped his mind: Zanuck is already pondering the peace and planning a colossal tribute to America's last war president, Woodrow Wilson. Elsewhere in Hollywood, an old nightclub on Cahuenga, near Sunset, has been transformed into a star-spangled USO center—the Hollywood Canteen, brain-stormed into existence by Bette Davis and John Garfield in the exclusive, stars-only Green Room of the Warner Bros. commissary. The Canteen was the Green Room at war: servicemen on leave might dance a dance with a visiting glamour gal while volunteer starlets served coffee and sandwiches made in a kitchen run by John Ford's wife, Mary—the director, having organized a navy photographic unit, is also on a patriotic mission.

Taking advantage of Zanuck's absence, Fox producer-director (and European refugee) Otto Preminger is planning a movie focused on another U.S. diplomat, William Dodd, ambassador to Nazi Germany from 1933 through 1937; the source is daughter Martha Dodd's book *Through Embassy Eyes*, recounting her life among the Nazis—or at least part of her life. Martha is both a sexual adventuress and an enthusiastic Soviet spy. Preminger has hired Communist screenwriter Ring Lardner Jr., fresh from the Army Signal Corps, to work on the script. Over at Paramount, Communist director Frank Tuttle is filming *Hostages*, a tale of the Czech underground adapted by Communist writer Lester Cole from the newly published, well-received antifascist novel by the young German-Jewish (and Communist) exile Stefan Heym.

Formerly with Paramount, independent producer (and Comintern agent) Boris Morros has planted a story that Ingrid Bergman, Swedish star of two current Popular Front dramas, *Casablanca* and Paramount's upcoming adaptation of Ernest Hemingway's Spanish Civil War romance *For Whom the Bell Tolls*, has been approached to star in a movie based on *The Russian People*—the Konstantin Simonov play recently adapted by Communist playwright Clifford Odets. Morros and fellow independent Sam Spiegel have engaged Lewis Milestone to direct, just as soon as the ultraliberal, Russian-born Milestone finishes *The North Star*, a big-budget Samuel Goldwyn production set in a miraculously uncollectivized Ukrainian "farming village," with an original screenplay by noted playwright (and fellow traveler) Lillian Hellman. Soon after *The North Star* goes into production, the Los Angeles office of the Federal Bureau of Investigation presents director J. Edgar Hoover with the comprehensive report on Communist activity in Hollywood that Hoover had requested the previous summer.[1]

---

1. A unique entity in the annals of proletarian internationalism, the Hollywood Communist Party (CP) received direction not from local Party officials but, via cultural apparatchik V.J. Jerome, directly from the New York–based national leadership. John Howard Lawson, instrumental in founding the Screen Writers Guild, was the movie industry's foremost Communist ("the grand Poo-Bah" in Martin Berkeley's sarcastic formulation); other members of the lead-

The talk of the industry is the box-office success of RKO's lurid cheapster *Hitler's Children*, made for less than $190,000 and predicted by the trades to gross a million or more. The movie was adapted by the liberal, politically ambitious playwright Emmet Lavery from Gregor Ziemer's *Education for Death: The Making of a Nazi* and directed by Edward Dmytryk, who, the following year, would be invited to a small gathering at Frank Tuttle's mansion in the hills beneath the Hollywood sign, there recruited into the Communist Political Association by screenwriter Alvah Bessie—a veteran of the *New Masses* and (exotic for Hollywood) the Spanish Civil War.

Exposing the indoctrination of German youth, as well as Nazi labor camps and eugenic breeding, *Hitler's Children* centers on the doomed romance between an American-born, German-raised, true-believing Nazi boy (Tim Holt) and a German-born, freedom-loving American girl (Bonita Granville); the latter is prominently featured in the movie's ads submitting to a ritualized flogging. Despite concerns expressed by Hollywood's internal censor Joseph Breen, the movie more than fulfills the Office of War Information's mandate to depict the Nature of the Enemy.

On February 2, the Germans surrender to the Red Army at Stalingrad, and, five weeks later, MGM's *Song of Russia* swings into production. The studio's most handsome leading man, Robert Taylor, plays an American conductor who falls for and marries a fetching young Russian pianist and *traktorist*. Like *The North Star*, *Song of Russia* depicts the horror of the German invasion as experienced by glamorous ordinary Russians. The screenplay is by two members of the CP's writer-enriched Northwest Section, Richard Collins and Paul Jarrico,

---

ership committee included screenwriters Herbert Biberman, Richard Collins, and Lester Cole, as well as talent agent John Weber. According to the FBI, the Communist Party of Los Angeles had 2,491 members in 1944, nearly a fifth of whom belonged to the Northwest Section, which encompassed Hollywood, Brentwood, and Beverly Hills. Individual branches were organized by profession and professional status. High-salaried screenwriters like Dalton Trumbo and Ring Lardner Jr. were in an elite branch; lower-paid writers like Alvah Bessie and Albert Maltz were attached to a lesser one, along with script readers and secretaries. Gender discrimination existed as well. Jean Rouverol Butler remembered that "the men were always working in a group in the Beverly Hills area, and the wives were sent out to the San Fernando Valley with the dentists' and doctors' wives." Still, benefits, rallies, and other gatherings provided a good deal of mixing. The CP was "the best social club in Hollywood," according to Abraham Polonsky, who jokingly compared the Party to the Sunset Strip: "Thousands of people used to go there, hang around a few days and then pass on to someplace else." The CP provided friendly outreach and professional guidance in the form of writing clinics, film classes, and, most notably, the Actors Laboratory Theater. There were also connections to be made. Max Benoff, a young radio gagman anxious to break into pictures, would later testify that "top writer" Robert Rossen encouraged him to join the Party for the sake of his career: "He said, 'You will meet big people.'"

who inherited this dream job from a gaggle of other Reds—including German refugee Victor Trivas, veteran screenwriter Guy Endore, and journalist Anna Louise Strong.

Within a few days, Hearst columnist (and Hoover informant) Hedda Hopper issues a warning: "Those communistic directors who talk openly on the sets at various studios better pipe down. They've been reported to the FBI—and about time." To whom does she refer? The Commies are everywhere; *People's World* is available on street corners from Long Beach to Burbank. The action is frantic. Party leader Collins will remember attending three, four, sometimes five evening meetings a week. *Life's* March 23 issue is entirely devoted to the USSR, with Joseph Stalin the beaming cover boy.

Antifascist heroism is ubiquitous onscreen: Fox's *Chetniks!*, a celebration of the Yugoslav partisans, opens at the Globe New York on March 19—the same day a gang of Chicago mobsters, including Frank Nitti and "Handsome Johnny" Roselli, are indicted down at Foley Square for using the International Alliance of Theatrical Stage Employees (IATSE), the stage handlers' and projectionists' union, to extort hundreds of thousands of dollars from frightened Hollywood studios. The Globe's next attraction will be the indie cheapster *Hitler—Dead or Alive*, wherein a band of gangsters led by Ward Bond, bellicose pal of Republic Pictures' cowboy star John Wayne, take a million-dollar contract on the führer and, as sarcastically noted by *New York Times* critic Bosley Crowther, are hailed as "towering heroes" in the sacrificial fade-out.

Fritz Lang's *Hangmen Also Die*, a United Artists production celebrating the assassination of Czechoslovakia's Nazi ruler Reinhard Heydrich, opens in New York on March 24 ("America's finest artistic comment on the war," per Joy Davidman in the *New Masses*); it is followed two days later by *The Moon Is Down*, a story of Norway under the Nazi jackboot, directed by Irving Pichel for Twentieth Century-Fox from John Steinbeck's novel. Some suspect Pichel might be a Red, but the FBI is more interested in *Hangmen*, directed by an alleged Commie from a script by two known Reds—John Wexley and German refugee Bertolt Brecht—with music supplied by possible Comintern agent Hanns Eisler.[2]

Director-producer Cecil B. DeMille, an FBI special service contact since December 1941, has been furnishing the bureau's Los Angeles office with infor-

---

2. A prominent member of the Hollywood Anti-Nazi League in the late 1930s, Lang was named as a Communist—along with a number of well-known antifascist actors—before a Los Angeles grand jury during the summer of 1940 and placed under FBI surveillance throughout World War II because of his association with Brecht and Eisler. (The FBI's voluminous Eisler file identifies Lang as a "known Communist.")

mation on Lang and his associates. DeMille secures an advance screening of
Hangmen, for which an internal FBI memo will praise him as "the most all-
around valuable contact in this field."

After months of publicity, *Mission to Moscow* is set to open.

Back in New York, the Trotskyist *New Leader* has been agitating against
what they call "Submission to Moscow" since December, but although the *New
Leader* had hoped that the Office of War Information would ensure that *Mission*
"not be shaped to the grotesque pattern of Comintern propaganda," the agency
could hardly be more enthusiastic. An internal OWI memo, dated April 29, terms
the movie "a magnificent contribution." President Roosevelt is shown precogni-
tive in his wisdom, past boldly scripted to serve the present, all ambiguity liqui-
dated: the three purge trials Ambassador Davies saw as evidence of a Kremlin
power struggle are compressed into one super trial, exposing the heinous guilt
of a Nazi-sponsored "Trotskyite" treason conspiracy.

Lavish, polished, and—once shown in the Soviet Union—a model for Soviet
social realist spectaculars, *Mission to Moscow* screens at the White House on
April 21 with a gala Washington, DC, premiere the following week. Guests include cabinet members, senators, and congressmen. The *Washington Post* reports a profound, "almost reverent" silence until the final scene provokes a
torrent of applause so sustained it nearly drowns out the orchestral finale. Mission accomplished!

Warners has spent a record $250,000 to establish that "The Story of Two
Guys Named Joe!" is "as American as YANKEE DOODLE DANDY!" Sockeroo
in Los Angeles, *Mission* opens at three local theaters, setting a house record at
Warner Bros.'s Hollywood. For the *Daily Worker*, *Mission to Moscow* exceeds all
expectation—"a great political document and an event in the history of the
American screen," per critic David Platt, "brilliantly acted, directed and produced, bold and lucid in its presentation of the facts." Still, Hollywood's *Mission* is attacked from the right by the Hearst press and from the left by the
Socialist Workers Party.

The *New York Times* publishes a letter from philosopher John Dewey denouncing "the first instance in our country of totalitarian propaganda for mass
consumption." Trotskyist-pacifist Dwight Macdonald initiates a letter-writing
campaign against the movie. Republicans demand a congressional investigation. Defending *Mission* with regular updates, the *Worker* will report endorsements not just from Red unions but from the Legion of Decency, the National
Board of Review, former presidential candidate Al Smith, the National Maritime

and Transit Workers unions, *Variety*, Eleanor Roosevelt, and comedian Milton Berle. Praising *Mission*'s "skill," "sentiments," and "nerve," director Elia Kazan calls the movie "a hell of a step forward."

Variety notes that *Mission* has generated more ink than any film since *Gone with the Wind*. Still, box office soon drops off everywhere outside New York (where *Mission* runs ten weeks on Broadway and has placards throughout the city's subway system as part of its abbreviated tenure as Department of Transportation "Motion Picture of the Month") and Washington, DC. *Variety* sagely attributes credible evening grosses to speechifying politicians looking for something to attack in the *Congressional Record*.

May 21, the same day that the National Council of American-Soviet Friendship rallies at Carnegie Hall to support *Mission to Moscow* and less than a week after the Soviet Union announced the dissolution of the Comintern, Warner Bros. celebrates the National Maritime Union—by way of merchant marine assistance to our Soviet allies—in the Humphrey Bogart vehicle *Action in the North Atlantic*. The movie is produced by Jerry Wald and written by Hollywood's arch-Communist, John Howard Lawson. "Of all the film studios in Hollywood, only one has a consistent record for outstanding achievement," Platt writes. "That studio is the 100% New Deal Warner Brothers"—producer of *Casablanca*, *Air Force*, *Watch on the Rhine*, *Edge of Darkness*, *Mission to Moscow*, and now, *Action in the North Atlantic*.

Scarcely has *Action* opened in Los Angeles than the city is convulsed. Thursday, June 3, a sailor on shore leave is stabbed in a brawl with a group of zoot-suit-wearing so-called pachucos. The next day, sailors, marines, and off-duty policemen organize a brigade of thirty taxis, driving from downtown to the East L.A. barrio, attacking random zoot-suiters en route. Saturday's newspaper predictions of a pachuco counterattack inspire hundreds of sailors and marines to spend their weekend on zoot suit patrol. The downtown becomes a war zone, with military mobs assaulting anything be-zooted, halting streetcars to eject Mexicans and other dark-skinned passengers, and invading the sanctuary of darkened movie houses. Community activist Josefina Fierro de Bright, wife of Communist screenwriter John Bright, tells the press that throughout the beatings, police stood by joking. Hearst dailies commend the servicemen for "cleansing" Los Angeles; *People's World* accuses Hearst of acting like a fifth columnist, sabotaging the war effort by fomenting a lynch-mob atmosphere.

June 21, the state legislature's Fact-Finding Committee on Un-American Activities in California, chaired by Senator Jack B. Tenney, opens hearings.

Tenney is particularly concerned about what seems to him a new Communist front, the Citizens' Committee for the Defense of Mexican American Youth, whose Hollywood sponsors include Bright and actress Dorothy Comingore. Meanwhile, five studios announce plans for feature films on the problem of juvenile violence, although these are dropped after an unofficial warning from the OWI. In the middle of the Tenney hearings, the Southern California division of Russian War Relief marks the second anniversary of the Nazi invasion musically with "Tribute to Russia" at the Hollywood Bowl. Leopold Stokowski conducts the Los Angeles Symphony Orchestra in a program produced by Boris Morros, the only bona fide Soviet spy operating in Hollywood.

The Communists should be happy but . . .

June 28, David Platt informs his readers of two reliable reports that Paramount's upcoming *For Whom the Bell Tolls* will emphasize the worst aspects of Ernest Hemingway's novel. Hollywood's version of the Spanish Civil War "depicts the Republicans as barbarians, distorts the role of the Soviet Union, . . . handles Franco with kid gloves and is definitely pro-fascist."

On the other hand, an exciting development: big-time director Frank Tuttle has closed a deal with Communist novelist Howard Fast for the movie rights to Fast's bestselling *Citizen Tom Paine*, with John Bright working on the adaptation and former Group Theater member Franchot Tone set to star. "A great motion picture is in the making!" Platt predicts. As the independent *Three Russian Girls*—a remake of the Soviet film *Girl from Leningrad*, to feature battlefield footage furnished by Artkino—goes into production, the Red Army begins a major offensive. Moscow greets *Mission to Moscow* in late July, around the time that Warner Bros.'s musical extravaganza *This Is the Army* opens—"buoyant, captivating, as American as hot dogs or the Bill of Rights," per the *New York Times*, and "a great democratic musical show," according to the *Daily Worker*, which praises Lieutenant Ronald Reagan for holding up "the heart interest in the best Hollywood tradition."[3]

---

3. A member of the cavalry reserve, Reagan was assigned to the Army Air Corps training-film facility at the nine-acre Hal Roach studio in Culver City. Screenwriter Alfred Lewis Levitt, also "stationed" at Fort Roach, recalled Reagan reporting for duty in costume, if not character, wearing jodhpurs and a campaign hat. Communist director Bernard Vorhaus, who served with Reagan as well, remembers the actor as "anxious to attend left-wing functions," such as the weekly current affairs discussions hosted by Communist writers Sam Ornitz and Guy Endore. Unbeknownst to Vorhaus, Reagan had been recruited as an FBI informer in September 1941; on November 18, 1943, he met with an FBI agent at Fort Roach to report that he nearly had a fistfight with an unidentified drunken anti-Semite, possibly on the set of *This Is the Army*.

In other musical news, Allan Jones's version of the Jerome Kern–E.Y. Harburg ballad "And Russia Is Her Name"—premiered at the Hollywood Bowl "Tribute to Russia" concert and soon to be featured in *Song of Russia*—is the second-most popular tune on the radio during the first week of August, at least according to the *Daily Worker*. A few weeks later, the Benny Goodman orchestra releases a swing ditty called "Mission to Moscow." Are they dancing to it at the Hollywood Canteen? Edward Dmytryk is set to direct a new home-front movie with Ginger Rogers and the astonishing title *Tender Comrade*—scripted by newly enlisted gung-ho Communist Dalton Trumbo.

Platt sees signs that the House Committee on Un-American Activities (HUAC) is planning a "comic opera" probe of Hollywood for the fall; meanwhile, the movie industry happily welcomes Stalin's ambassador to Hollywood, Soviet director and administrator Mikhail Kalatozov. Scarcely has Comrade Kalatozov arrived than Communist screenwriter Herbert Biberman is eagerly pestering a comrade Northwest Section member (and secret FBI informant) for an introduction.

Around a week later, Kalatozov is feted by five hundred guests on a Sunday afternoon at Mocambo, the swanky Latin-themed Sunset Strip nightclub where the walls are lined by glass-caged tropical birds. The reception is organized by the National Council of American-Soviet Friendship; sponsors include the writer of *Mission to Moscow* and director of *The North Star*, then in postproduction, as well as directors Fritz Lang, Leo McCarey, Jean Renoir, Orson Welles, and Frank Tuttle; cinematographer James Wong Howe; writers Dudley Nichols, Sidney Buchman, John Wexley, Clifford Odets, and Robert Rossen; plus Pop Front icons Paul Robeson, John Garfield, and Charles Chaplin, not to mention Confidential Source A-2 (using an invite she got from Confidential Source A-1). The forty-year-old Kalatozov, who speaks no English (but, as Communist screenwriter Alvah Bessie will note, has an "astounding" capacity for vodka), smiles politely.

August: The Red Army engages the Nazis in the Battle of Kursk and Walt Disney's animated documentary *Victory Through Air Power* is playing at theaters, along with *The City That Stopped Hitler: Heroic Stalingrad*. Columbia's *None Shall Escape*, another occupation drama with a script by comrade Lester Cole, is in production. In mid-September, Herman Shumlin's film version of the Lillian Hellman antifascist drama *Watch on the Rhine* follows *This Is the Army* into Warner's Hollywood Downtown. Guests at the gala premiere include distinguished émigrés Thomas Mann and Bertolt Brecht, as well as two radical social theorists, Theodor Adorno and Max Horkheimer, busily working on their analysis of the culture industry *Dialectic of Enlightenment*.[4]

The first weekend of October, as the Red Army crosses the Dnieper (and despite a preemptive attack launched by Senator Tenney), the Writers' Congress opens. Not just writers but directors, musicians, animators, publicists, and even producers have gathered on the University of California's beautiful Los Angeles campus. The mood is excited, resolute, and militant. The conclave is, as one participant puts it, barely "a cannon shot" from the studios where they work: Hollywood in the crosshairs! Organized by the Hollywood Writers Mobilization ("a clearing house for Communist propaganda," per Tenney) and officially greeted by President Roosevelt, Vice President Henry Wallace, and—through Comrade Kalatozov—the fraternal Writers and Artists of the Soviet Union, the Congress is dedicated to the proposition that, as its chairman, Comrade Rossen, declares, movies have the power to influence human behavior, defeat the Axis, and shape the postwar world.

Dressed in his specially tailored uniform, Lieutenant Colonel (Ret.) Darryl F. Zanuck provides the keynote for a Saturday morning panel on the "responsibility of the industry." Unable not to cite the unprecedented undertaking that is *Wilson*, Zanuck declares that Hollywood is obliged to accept its mission: "We must begin to deal realistically in film with the causes of wars and panics, with social upheavals and depression, with starvation and want and injustice and barbarism under whatever guise." Zanuck is not the only producer at the congress. Walter Wanger serves alongside him on the Advisory Committee; Dore Schary, himself an erstwhile screenwriter, is a member of the Continuations Committee. That spring, Schary had resigned as head of MGM's B-unit to work on personal productions—and anticipate Zanuck's agenda by commissioning Nobel laureate Sinclair Lewis to write an allegorical Western explaining world events since 1938.

Realistical madness in Western guise: *Storm in the West* would open with the murder of rancher Chuck Slattery (might that be "Czechoslovakia"?), who has been set up by a Mr. Chambers to be slaughtered by the outlaws Hygatt,

---

4. Among other things, *Dialectic of Enlightenment* predicts the mission to follow: "Culture monopolies are weak and dependent [on the most powerful sectors of industry]. They cannot afford to neglect their appeasement of the real holders of power if their sphere of activity in mass society (a sphere producing a specific type of commodity which anyhow is still too closely bound up with easygoing liberalism and Jewish intellectuals) is not to undergo a series of purges."

Gribble, Gerrel, and Mullison (call them Hitler, Goebbels, Goering, and Mussolini) and trigger total range war. Eventually, Joel Slavin, a Civil War veteran from Georgia (*sic*) who's taken over the "old Nicholas place," joins Ulysses Saunders (note initials) and Walter Chancel (as in Winston Churchill) to defeat the outlaw axis. In a June 9 memo, Schary described *Storm in the West* as "the story of the world history of the last ten years in terms of what we might call a realistic allegory . . . people must be told again the methods of Nazism and how best we can by collective security hang on, not desperately, but triumphantly to what we know is the way of life we want to live."

Zanuck identifies screenwriters as a vanguard: "If you have something worthwhile to say, dress it in the glittering robes of entertainment. . . . No producer who is worthy of the name will reject entertainment, and without entertainment no propaganda film is worth a dime." Young screenwriter Ben Barzman tackles the propaganda issue head-on, declaring that "the full importance of the motion picture as a social factor is attested by the constant attacks on it by partisan groups outside the motion picture industry [whose] obvious preoccupation is to hamper the full prosecution of the war." Moreover, and "contrary to popular motion picture trade opinion, pictures with social ideas have been successful out of all proportion to the number produced." Recruiting drive director for Branch A, Group 2, Northwest Section, Los Angeles County Communist Party, Barzman can't help but single out *Mission to Moscow*—"a new kind of dramatized chronicle [that] like all important experimental films . . . has indicated a new area of motion picture ideas."

Comrade Barzman fixes his gaze on the radiant future: "The distribution of our motion pictures will be global. The freedom that has been won with blood will mean not only milk and bread for the stomach, but motion pictures for the eye, the heart, and the mind." His optimistic rhetoric is echoed by Comrade Lawson: "Cultural democracy is as essential as political and economic democracy. The flowering of popular culture is the best guarantee of a peaceful and prosperous future." Soon after the conference, Lawson is hauled before the Tenney Committee, along with Comrades Albert Maltz and Waldo Salt. All deny membership in the CP, which, according to another witness, has been organizing mixed-race parties on the Santa Monica beach, operating a "prostitution squad," and using marijuana to recruit new members.

Sahara, epitome of what Lawson called "world-mindedness," opens in Midwestern cities a few weeks after the conference ends, reaching New York in mid-November. Directed by a Hungarian-born British subject, adapted by Lawson from a 1937 Soviet movie, and starring Humphrey Bogart (Gary Cooper's only peer as an action-star draw), on loan from Warners, *Sahara* enjoyed the support of both the OWI and the army (which allowed Lawson to inspect its desert training facilities). Over the course of the movie, Bogart's beleaguered little unit takes in six allies—four Brits, a South African, and a Frenchman—as well as a Sudanese corporal and a captured Italian, to make a last stand defending their desert waterhole. The *New York Times* declares Bogart "truly inspiring. . . . His toughness, his trenchant laconism and genius for using a poker-face mark him as probably the best screen notion of the American soldier to date."

Samuel Goldwyn's super-production *The North Star* is already playing two Broadway theaters. This spectacular recounting of the Nazi attack on a Soviet village is itself attacked by the Hearst dailies as ludicrous propaganda—"the peasants are super-intellectual" and their breakfast table is "generously-laden," the *Journal-American* notes, while the *Daily Mirror* observes that the village hospital is so well equipped, it rivals "the swankiest endowed institution in Mr. Goldwyn's Beverly Hills." But other reviewers, notably those writing for Luce publications, are less offended by the spectacle of Russian villagers modeling in the glittering robe of entertainment. Punning on the director's name, *Time* declares *The North Star* a "cinemilestone," presenting the "heroic defense by the Russian people of their homes."

The Hollywood Canteen—renowned, the *Los Angeles Times* reminds its readers, as the fantasyland where "Joe Dogface can dance with Hedy Lamarr"—celebrates its first birthday. John Garfield dedicates the party to "the 6,254 guys from the motion-picture industry who are out there fighting for us." One of them, Captain Ronald Reagan—there among the stars—will soon be appointed captain of the Army Air Forces First Motion Picture Unit's basketball squad. The mission continues: on assignment in Hollywood, David Platt reports that, contrary to a recent story in *People's World* complaining that Warner Bros. and other studios have watered down their war pictures, many significant productions are on the assembly line and that, with the possible exception of Paramount (perpetrators of the openly fascist *For Whom the Bell Tolls*), the major studios remain appropriately "war-minded."

November 16, six thousand rally at the Shrine Auditorium to celebrate the tenth anniversary of U.S.-Soviet relations, complete with a speech by Olivia de Havilland; the presence of Walter Huston, *Mission to Moscow*'s ambassador and *The North Star*'s heroic doctor; *Casablanca*'s piano player, Dooley Wilson; activist-actor J. Edward Bromberg; and fellow lefty Albert Dekker. The next day, John Wayne learns that the Selective Service board has extended his 3-A deferment. Hot dog! The star celebrates Thanksgiving Day by carving turkeys at the

Canteen, even as Roosevelt, Churchill, and Stalin meet in Tehran to plan the U.S. invasion of Europe; the FBI bugs Mikhail Kalatozov's rented house up near Griffith Observatory; and MGM's *The Cross of Lorraine*, written by Comrade Ring Lardner Jr., opens in New York. The *Daily Worker* is excited—French villagers "turn upon the Nazis and wipe them out. It is great stuff!"

The Red Army is poised to cross into Poland, and Comrade Trumbo has written two huge Christmas movies, *A Guy Named Joe* and *Tender Comrades*—with another, *Destination Tokyo*, set to open New Year's Eve. In his first column of 1944, David Platt declares the previous year the greatest in Hollywood history: "The ostrich age is over as far as the silver screen is concerned. The year 1943 will go down as the year of the great awakening." Platt's top six movies, in order of preference, are *Mission to Moscow*, *Watch on the Rhine*, *Hangmen Also Die*, *Action in the North Atlantic*, *The Battle of Russia*, and *Sahara*. (Half are from Warner Bros., "the most progressive studio in the country"; all are written by comrades or fellow travelers.) *The North Star*, which *Life* declared the movie of the year, ranks thirteenth.

Are the Reds winning? That is the question. January 10, 1944: General Secretary Earl Browder informs a Madison Square Garden rally that the Party has been reinvented as the Communist Political Association. Fundamental differences between the United States and Soviet Union no longer exist, comrades—the Party bursts for joy!

Meanwhile, MGM screenwriter James K. McGuinness is hosting a series of informal meetings toward creating an organization to combat Commie infiltration. Russian troops are pushing westward toward the Baltic nations as seventy-five producers, writers, and actors gather in the Grand Ballroom of the Beverly Wilshire on the evening of February 4 to found the Motion Picture Alliance for the Preservation of American Ideals. The Motion Picture Alliance also has a mission. Newly elected president Sam Wood, director of the Red-smeared *For Whom the Bell Tolls*, explains that "highly indoctrinated shock units of the totalitarian wrecking crew" have persuaded the public that Hollywood is "a battleground over which Communism is locked in death grip with Fascism"—an erroneous impression that the MPA intends to correct, beginning with a full-page two-color statement of principles that will run as an ad in the next morning's *Hollywood Reporter*.

Walt Disney is named Wood's vice president. McGuinness is the chairman of the executive committee, which includes screenwriters Borden Chase, Frank Gruber, Howard Hughes's uncle Rupert Hughes (like McGuinness, a longtime foe of the Screen Writers Guild), Morrie Ryskind, and Casey Robinson, as well as directors Victor Fleming and King Vidor. Two other leading directors, FBI informant Cecil B. DeMille and FBI subject John Ford, are also in the house. So too a number of stars, including USAF Colonel Clark Gable, USN Lieutenant Robert Montgomery, Gary Cooper, Ginger Rogers, Barbara Stanwyck, Pat O'Brien, Irene Dunne, Ward Bond, and Robert Taylor, whose vehicle *Song of Russia* opens in Los Angeles on February 17, on the eve of the Big Week bombing campaign against German cities.

Taylor is not the only embarrassed MPA supporter; currently in production, RKO's contribution to the Soviet whitewash *Days of Glory* is a project written and produced by MPA board member (and *This Is the Army* adapter) Casey Robinson. RKO, which will attempt to negotiate a distribution deal with Kalatozov, is considered a particular hotbed of Communist activity, while MGM is the MPA's greatest source of strength. According to a March 22 FBI report based on information furnished by the MPA's executive secretary, George Bruce, 200 of the organization's estimated 225 members are MGM employees.

The FBI has also taken notice of the campaign organized against the MPA by John Howard Lawson (who, like Kalatozov, is under "technical surveillance") and his comrades Rossen and Trumbo. McGuinness has been complaining to his FBI contact that David O. Selznick and others are accusing the MPA of anti-Semitism—even his boss Louis B. Mayer is concerned. The MPA doesn't help its cause by sending a letter, signed only "A Group of Your Friends in Hollywood," to North Carolina's isolationist senator Robert Rice Reynolds, praising him as "the Nostradamus of the twentieth century," or by publicly welcoming the team of investigators from HUAC that arrives in Hollywood on April 21.

For David Platt, 1944 is a continuation of 1943. "Hollywood has been turning out at least one good war film every ten days," he writes exultantly, citing *Destination Tokyo*, *Three Russian Girls*, *Song of Russia*, *Passage to Marseille* (which "combines bold antifascist politics with thrilling drama"), *The Purple Heart*, and *None Shall Escape*. Platt is incensed when a *Daily Worker* colleague slams *Tender Comrade* as sentimental: "I saw it the other day and thought it was an excellent contribution to the war effort." The *Washington Times-Herald* prints a rumor that Stalin has asked the U.S. government for permission to confer decorations on Jack Warner, Samuel Goldwyn, and Manart Kippen (the actor who played him in *Mission to Moscow*). Kalatozov hosts a dinner party for Hollywood directors, including Michael Curtiz, Lewis Milestone, Robert Rossen, King Vidor, and Orson Welles.

The European war reaches a turning point. Barely twenty-four hours after Rome falls to the Allies, 155,000 troops land in Normandy: D-Day! John Wayne is reclassified 1-A! Comrades Trumbo and Cole's brainchild, the newly created Emergency Council of Hollywood Guilds and Unions, rallies against the MPA at the Woman's Club of Hollywood! Orson Welles telegrams support and Dore Schary sends a letter. "FILM AXIS STUNNED," *People's World* reports. July 11, President Roosevelt announces his intention to run for a fourth term.

At that moment, *Wilson* opens. A crowd of six thousand attends the New York premiere at the Roxy. The most expensive Hollywood movie since *Gone with the Wind*, with half a million dollars spent on exact replicas of rooms in the Capitol and in the White House, it may have originated in Zanuck's desire to see Wendell Willkie, Fox board member and 1940 Republican nominee for president, run again, but it opens as a de facto endorsement of FDR. The *Daily Worker* begins its favorable review by noting the "happy coincidence that, on the very day the tragic biography of Woodrow Wilson reached the screen," the State Department announced the U.S.-British-Soviet Conference on Security Organization for Peace in the Postwar World.

Even as the *Los Angeles Times* reports that someone has been leaving Commie pamphlets on a table at the Hollywood Canteen, FBI operatives break into the Los Angeles office of the Communist Political Association. The Allies liberate Paris on August 25. Two weeks later, Comrade Lawson's third wartime screenplay—*Counter-Attack*—goes into production at Columbia. The first V-2 rocket hits London, American troops enter Germany, and, just before Hitler calls up all German males ages sixteen to sixty, Comrade Biberman's *The Master Race*—which, despite its title (conceived before the movie even had a treatment), is more sanctimonious than sensational in addressing the problem of postwar de-Nazification—has its world premiere.[5]

Three days after the FBI learns that Boris Morros has entered into a business arrangement with the wealthy Communist Alfred Stern, who is married to Soviet spy Martha Dodd, J. Edgar Hoover briefs the attorney general on Communist infiltration in Hollywood. (Meanwhile, the NKGB's New York station cables Moscow regarding Comrade Julius Rosenberg's proposal to recruit his brother-in-law, Technician Fifth Class David Greenglass, stationed since August at the top-secret base in Los Alamos, New Mexico. The request will be

---

5. The FBI's Los Angeles special agent in charge (SAC), R.B. Hood, compiled a dossier on *The Master Race*—noting the portrayal of a sympathetic Russian officer and the various red participants in the production—and sent it to J. Edgar Hoover in case the FBI director was called upon to detail Communist propaganda in the movies. Hoover disagreed with Hood with the reasonable objection that an FBI agent had no particular expertise in content analysis and no way of knowing what effect, if any, such propaganda might have on an audience.

granted in early October. The NKGB has already been hearing for some weeks from another agent at Los Alamos—the brilliant nineteen-year-old atomic physicist Theodore Hall.)

Cecil B. DeMille orchestrates a spectacular rally for the Republican presidential candidate, New York governor Thomas E. Dewey, at the Los Angeles Coliseum, complete with elephants and brass bands, sweater girls and cowboys (and Indians). David Platt compares the event to *Triumph of the Will*. The industry is almost wholly united behind the Hollywood for Roosevelt Committee, headed by Jack Warner, Samuel Goldwyn, and Katharine Hepburn. As the United States and Japan enjoin the war's largest naval engagement in Leyte Gulf, RKO prepares to celebrate an earlier phase of the Philippine theater. Two Communists are put together with an MPA-friendly star: the studio has commissioned Ben Barzman to write *Back to Bataan*, which Edward Dmytryk will direct with the war's hottest new star, John Wayne, on loan from Republic.

Wayne, on whom Special Service Contact Cecil B. DeMille has also been filing reports, will recall confronting his director and demanding to know if he is a Commie. Dmytryk responds by saying, more or less, "If the masses of the American people want Communism, I think it'd be good for our country." (*Masses!?* Wayne sees red.) Others remember Wayne baiting Barzman on the set, identifying Stalin as the true threat; when the writer earnestly replies that it's precisely that sort of talk that causes wars and that, after the war, "the Russians will be our friends," Wayne crushingly replies, "They'll be *your* friends."

Norman Corwin's election-eve broadcast features James Cagney, Groucho Marx, and Keenan Wynn singing, "The Old Red Scare, It Ain't What It Used to Be." November 7, FDR defeats New York governor Thomas Dewey to win his fourth term—with California giving Roosevelt his greatest number of votes.

The final push toward victory: MGM premieres *Thirty Seconds over Tokyo*, directed by Mervyn LeRoy from Dalton Trumbo's script. It is, for David Platt, "one of the most rewarding films of 1944." Ten days into the movie's release, the U.S. Army rains bombs on Tokyo for the first time in the two and a half years since the Doolittle raid depicted in the film. Trumbo himself is a target. Thanks to constant complaints made by Ginger Rogers's mother, Lela, a founding member of the Motion Picture Alliance, to the FBI and DeMille, the Bureau is investigating the studio that perpetrated the writer's last hit, *Tender Comrade*.

In early December, Ruth Greenglass, former president of her neighborhood Young Communist League, travels to Albuquerque to rendezvous with her husband and comrade YCL-er David, given a weekend pass from Los Alamos; she's carrying a message from Julius. (Among other things, the couple see John Wayne's *Tall in the Saddle* at the Ki-Mo, "America's Foremost Indian Theater.") Bosley Crowther finds Warner Bros.'s star-spangled homage to the Hollywood Canteen "a most distasteful show of Hollywood's sense of its importance and what its people are doing for 'the boys.'" But, as 1944 ends, David Platt (who reveals that he once lived across the street from the Canteen and can vouch for the authenticity of Warner's tribute) again praises the movie industry: "Never before in the history of the screen have there been so many forward-looking people in positions of responsibility as in Hollywood."

Never in history! Just after New Year's 1945, the FBI again breaks into the Communist Political Association's Los Angeles office. During the first week of February, Roosevelt and Churchill fly to the Crimean resort town Yalta to meet with Stalin. Whither the postwar world? The firebombing of Dresden begins February 13, two days after the conference ends; Germany responds with the heaviest V-2 attacks on London ("A screaming comes across the sky . . ."). Down in Key Biscayne, John Ford is shooting his tribute to U.S. PT boats, *They Were Expendable.* As Tokyo is subjected to massive air raids, U.S. Marines invade the island of Iwo Jima, raising the American flag atop Mount Suribachi on February 23. Ruth Greenglass relocates to Albuquerque as the FBI once more burglarizes the Communist Political Association's Los Angeles headquarters.

Victory is in sight when Hollywood's wartime unity cracks: as part of an obscure jurisdictional dispute with the entrenched, formerly gangster-ridden IATSE, the progressive Conference of Studio Unions (CSU) walks out—in violation of the wartime no-strike pledge supported by the Communists, among others. The studios throw in with IATSE. Production is paralyzed at Warner Bros., Fox, RKO, and Universal; MGM and Paramount are on reduced schedules. Iwo Jima is finally secured after a monthlong battle, the day after Leo McCarey's *Going My Way* wins the Oscar for Best Picture—with striking set designers, illustrators, and decorators picketing the ceremonies at Grauman's Chinese. (The FBI will later complain about the Communist presence at the ceremony, despite the fact that RKO was virtually shut out of the awards.)

U.S., Canadian, and British troops cross the Rhine the following week; their advance is sufficiently leisurely to allow the Red Army to take Berlin. As the strike drags on into April, IATSE complains about the CSU's goon tactics at RKO and Paramount; the CSU maintains that Warners and IATSE have brought in scabs. The Screen Actors Guild (SAG) and Screen Writers Guild (SWG) both vote to cross CSU picket lines; not even the Reds support the CSU (yet). April 10, the Allies liberate the Buchenwald concentration camp. Two days later, FDR dies. CBS Radio drafts Orson Welles to broadcast a eulogy that night as new president Harry Truman learns about the Manhattan Project.

World aflame: The firebombing of Tokyo has been on going for weeks. By April's end, Hitler commits suicide; the morning after May Day, the Red Army enters Berlin. May 7, Germany surrenders. (Two days later, Corporal Samuel Fuller uses a 16 mm camera, sent to him by his mother, to document the Falkenau concentration camp in Czechoslovakia.)

May 24, the *Daily Worker* publishes a shocking letter from French Communist leader Jacques Duclos attacking Earl Browder's revisionist reformation of the American CP and naive faith in postwar peaceful coexistence between the bourgeois democracies and the Soviet Union. Hollywood Reds are blindsided! Abe Polonsky hosts a mass meeting at his Beverly Glen home: "There must have been one hundred people in my living room," he later recalls. "And of course, the FBI was outside, writing down license-plate numbers." June 3, spy courier Harry Gold shows up on Ruth and David Greenglass's doorstep (they're now living in Albuquerque) and is given schematic drawings of the high-explosive lens mold on which David has been working. June 25, one day before the United Nations Charter is signed in San Francisco, *Back to Bataan* has its world premiere in Honolulu. As intended by RKO, the movie is released as victory approaches. Five days later, General MacArthur declares the Philippines secure.

The Actors Lab is enjoying its greatest success with an anticapitalist sixteenth-century comedy. Up since late March, Morris Carnovsky's production of *Volpone*—starring Group Theatre comrades J. Edward Bromberg, Phoebe Brand, and Ruth Nelson—gets a three-page spread in *Life* that begins with the observation, "Some of the most skillful acting in the U.S. today is being done in Hollywood by some part-time refugees from the movies," citing as an example this "quirkish, complicated travesty on greed." Like a Hollywood producer, Volpone "likes to watch men debase themselves for money."

Saturday afternoon, July 7, as noted by the FBI, Albert and Margaret Maltz are hosting another meeting at their Fairfax home to discuss the Duclos article. Present this time: Browder supporter John Howard Lawson. July 16, the Manhattan Project comes to fruition with the successful detonation of the so-called Gadget at the Alamogordo test site. Truman gets the news the next day in Potsdam, just outside Berlin, while meeting victorious allies Churchill and Stalin. (Does the Everyman President drop a hint?) That month, the Communist Political Association is re-formed as the Communist Party USA. Browder is ousted and replaced by hard-liner William Z. Foster. The screenwriter Leonardo Bercovici is appalled by the rapidity with which branch members Trumbo and Lardner have turned on Browder; Richard Collins is amazed to see Lawson, initially deposed along with Browder, pirouette back from the dustbin of history. Others are simply pleased. Dining with his comrades Ben and Norma Barzman, Lester Cole hoists a glass and jokes, "Now we can toast the revolution again!"

At least seventy thousand people die when Hiroshima is incinerated on August 6. Nagasaki is obliterated three days later, with a minimum of forty thousand deaths. Japan surrenders; L.A. goes crazy. Moments after the news breaks (late afternoon, August 15), singing, snake-dancing revelers cram Hollywood Boulevard from Western Avenue to La Brea—"like a mob scene in a movie," per the *Los Angeles Times*. The Canteen is besieged. The crowd celebrates until dawn. Trolleys are jerked from their wires; patriotic bunting is turned to confetti; street signs are torn down. Hospital emergency rooms are packed; eight people die in traffic accidents. Their missionary task accomplished, the studios close for the rest of the week—although the race is already on to herald the Bomb.

I.

ALIENS AMONG US:
HOLLYWOOD, 1946–47

War ends, the universe shudders, it's a brand-new world. Europe lies in ruins, half-occupied by Red barbarians; the British Empire has imploded. America, having exploded the ultimate weapon, stands alone. Enemy spies are everywhere, and even creatures from other planets are fascinated by the Vital Secret of the Great Whatzit. National Insecurity reigns. Science fiction is real.

A new age dawned and on its very first morning, Carter T. Barron—Eastern division manager of Loews Inc.—hastened to register an atomic bomb title on behalf of MGM. Forty-eight hours later, the day after Nagasaki was destroyed, Barron telephoned the War Department's press office.

Twentieth Century-Fox had already managed to slip a topical, if anachronistic, reference to something called Process 97 ("the secret ingredient of the atomic bomb") into their spy film *The House on 92nd Street* before it wrapped in late August. Fox was also mulling a movie on the Manhattan Project, as was Paramount producer Hal Wallis.[1]

"The atomic bomb proved to be the war's biggest surprise," wrote science reporter Daniel Lang in the *New Yorker*. But the Great Whatzit was not the only revelation. America had defeated the Axis with a top-secret super-weapon and, it was now revealed, a top-secret spy agency, the Office of Strategic Services (OSS), headed by General William "Wild Bill" Donovan. Another race began. And another: September 12, FBI director J. Edgar Hoover told President Harry

---

1. Everyone was scooped by the Poverty Row studio PRC, which inserted newsreel footage of the atomic bomb into the final moments of Lew Landers's *Shadow of Terror*—converting a routine, if effective, espionage thriller in which a research chemist battles a mad gangsterish rival, as well as temporary amnesia, to deliver his formula for the world's most powerful explosive to the U.S. government, into an alternative myth of the Manhattan Project, set mainly in the same southwestern desert. The movie opened in Los Angeles scarcely a month after Hiroshima.

Truman that a week ago a defector named Igor Gouzenko, previously attached to the Soviet embassy in Ottawa, had informed the Royal Mounted Police of a Canada-based spy ring, its tentacles extending even into the U.S. State Department!

September 27, two days after President Truman's executive order eliminated a Hoover rival by disbanding the OSS, Fox announced *Diplomatic Courier*, eventually released as *13 Rue Madeleine*. Paramount and Warner Bros. (which, grossly misjudging the postwar mood, had rereleased their madly philo-Soviet *Mission to Moscow*) trailed in publicizing their respective plans for *OSS* and *Cloak and Dagger*.

The latter, based on a forthcoming book by two OSS officers, would be the first independent production for Harry Warner's son-in-law Captain Milton Sperling, newly returned from the marines, for whom he had supervised two documentaries. The OSS had entered Hollywood's phantom zone; although the outfit no longer existed, each project received Donovan's blessing and engaged one of his operatives as a special consultant.

Although the weeks following V-J Day saw thousands of workers laid off from Southern California's shipyards and aircraft plants, the war—or rather, its absence—really came home to Hollywood that season in the form of the intensified labor dispute between the CSU and the IATSE.

Ongoing since March, the CSU's strike was revitalized by victory overseas and strengthened by a shift in the now openly supportive Communist Party. The war's sudden end heartened the CSU and (or so the union assumed) put additional pressure on management. The bombs that fell on Hiroshima and Nagasaki "produced just as radical a change of heart in the producers as it did in the Japs," boasted the CSU's new strike daily, provocatively named the *Hollywood Atom*.

As CSU supporters began picketing Los Angeles movie theaters, union head Herbert Sorrell decided to tighten the screws on Hollywood's most New Deal–identified studio. Thursday, October 4, the CSU threw a picket line around Warner Bros.'s Burbank facility. That next day, Warners announced *Cloak and Dagger*. "The amazing, heretofore untold story of the Office of Strategic Services" would mutate from spy drama to something more topically apocalyptic once producer Sperling engaged the director who, in his Weimar youth, created cinema's original paranoid epic, greatest science fiction spectacular, and first space odyssey: Fritz Lang.

But if Lang would herald the new age with the first post-atomic espionage thriller, the action outside the studio lot on Barham Boulevard was a flashback to the class warfare of the late 1930s (or to *Metropolis*) as Warners attacked the CSU picket line Friday with tear gas, high-pressure water hoses, and truncheon-wielding goons. The battle was rejoined after the weekend. Picketers were greeted by rifle-toting L.A. police, helmeted L.A. County deputy sheriffs, and baton-wielding studio cops who, cued by the raising of the American flag, stormed the line.

Production shut down. "FASCISM RUNS WILD," Tuesday's *Atom* reported: "A rocket flare from the studio special effects department was shot off—a ghastly parody on the words of the national anthem which was being sung by the picketers. . . . Thugs rushed, whirling their chains and flinging their broken bottles, and swinging their clubs. The wave broke against the picket line where 400 honest union men proved more than a match for the Warners' 200 gangsters. Then, the uniformed police, with their clubs and gas masks in readiness, attacked from the rear . . ." Bloody Burbank! Commie chaos in the Dream Factory! The following Thursday, the action moved on. Strikers showed up at the gates of Universal and Republic (both of which temporarily suspended production), RKO, Columbia, Technicolor, and Paramount, where renewed violence broke out on Van Ness Avenue at the side entrance to the studio lot.

For the next two weeks, the picket lines were strengthened by union machinists from Lockheed Aircraft—"WAR WORKERS ANSWER WARNER TERROR," per the *Daily Worker*—and the celebrity militants of the Hollywood left. Comrades John Howard Lawson, Robert Rossen, Lee J. Cobb, and Larry Parks were all observed picketing, along with fellow travelers John Cromwell and Howard Koch. Incensed to discover that enthusiastic young observers from the Actors Laboratory Theater had flung themselves into a new role, eschewing the sidelines to join the pickets, Jack Warner reclaimed the props and sets the studio had lent the Actors Lab for its current production *A Bell for Adano*, directed by Warner Bros. employee Vincent Sherman.

It was in the aftermath of the strike that the Lab—which screened two spirit-lifting antifascist classics, *The North Star* and *The Seventh Cross*, during the October tumult—became publicly identified as a source of subversive agitation.

In late October, the AFL intervened to temporarily settle the strike. Fritz Lang took charge of *Cloak and Dagger*, bringing in Comrade Ring Lardner Jr. to rewrite a script already labored over by three writers; soon after, Milton Sperling hired Comrade Albert Maltz, who had turned down an earlier offer to work on the movie. Although deep into an antifascist adaptation of Lloyd C. Douglas's wartime biblical novel *The Robe*, Maltz was persuaded by Sperling's offer of $5,000 per week, ten times his usual rate. The two Communists worked separately, with Maltz assigned to improve *Cloak and Dagger*'s last third.

Over at MGM, the studio's not-yet-sanctioned atomic bomb title received a boost from another sort of activist—fresh-faced actress Donna Reed, soon to be seen in John Ford's *They Were Expendable* and Frank Capra's *It's a Wonderful Life*. Just as might have happened in an MGM movie, Reed discovered that Dr. Edward Tompkins, her handsome young high school science teacher back in Iowa, had spent the war working at the top-secret government facility in Oak Ridge, Tennessee. Reed wrote Tompkins, and he—a fervent member of the Federation of Atomic Scientists, newly founded by concerned participants in the Manhattan Project—responded to his glamorous former student, wondering why a movie hadn't been made on the subject of the atomic bomb.

Reed passed Tompkins's letter on to her husband, agent Tony Owen, who contacted MGM executive Sam Marx, producer of *Lassie Come Home* and its sequel *Son of Lassie*. A few weeks later, having secured clearance from Major General Leslie Groves, the Manhattan Project's chief officer (and the White House's current adviser on atomic energy), MGM dispatched Marx on a fact-finding mission to the still-classified facility. "We are very happy you are here," Tompkins said, welcoming the producer. "We hope you can soon tell the world the meaning of this bomb, because we are scared to death!"

As the U.S. Senate debated the peacetime use of atomic energy, J. Edgar Hoover provided Truman with FBI reports on scientists (and others) who, like the FAS, advocated civilian control of the Bomb. The FBI had identified Robert Oppenheimer as a potential subversive in 1941. The scientist abandoned his left-wing politics when he became the Manhattan Project's scientific director in 1942; still, Hoover tapped Oppenheimer's phone and repeatedly warned of Communist affiliations that included his wife, Kitty, whose first husband had died fighting for the Spanish loyalists. Oppenheimer himself alienated Truman when he told the president he felt there was blood on his hands. ("The blood is on my hands," Truman is said to have snapped. "Let me worry about that!")

The upbeat Hollywood producer made a better impression; a fifteen-minute presidential audience expanded into an hour. Truman gave MGM his blessing as well as the movie's title. "Make a good picture," he told Marx. "One that will tell the people that the decision is theirs to make. . . . This is the beginning or the end!"

MGM's Manhattan Project: *The Beginning or the End?*

December 10, MGM and Paramount announce their Atomic Age projects. Working from a story by journalist Bob Considine (who had provided the basis for MGM's *Thirty Seconds over Tokyo*), the paralyzed former navy test pilot Frank "Spig" Wead is writing *The Beginning or the End*. Wead, whose most recent script was *They Were Expendable*, finishes a draft just after Christmas.

Hal Wallis has meanwhile commissioned anti-Communist visionary Ayn Rand to work on *Top Secret*; Rand presents him with a confidential four-thousand-word-plus position paper, "An Analysis of the Proper Approach to a Picture on the Atomic Bomb," designed to make the point (italicized for emphasis) that *"The whole history of the atomic bomb is an eloquent example of, argument for and tribute to free enterprise"*—and against "statism." Wallis agrees to agree. Rand spends the first few weeks of 1946 interviewing Mr. and Mrs. Oppenheimer, General Groves, and the Manhattan Project's district engineer Colonel K.D. Nichols. Her script concerns a brilliant but confused young scientist who finds his destiny working with Oppenheimer on the Whatzit, realizing, in the movie's final line, that "man can harness the universe—but nobody can harness man."

February 5, 1946, two days before Paramount puts *OSS* into production and nearly a month into a steelworkers strike that will be the largest in history, *Washington Post* columnist Drew Pearson—acting on information furnished by J. Edgar Hoover—breaks the story of the Ottawa spy ring. Four days later, as if on cue, Stalin declares that war between Communism and capitalism is inevitable. Within a month, Winston Churchill makes his "Iron Curtain" speech in St. Louis.[2]

Then, just as the *Cloak and Dagger* shoot opens, the atomic race ends. Hal Wallis has pulled the plug on *Top Secret*. The *New York Times* reports an "unusual agreement" in which Wallis turned over his story material to MGM and

---

2. Soon after completing his chores on *Cloak and Dagger*, Maltz engaged in an infamous literary contretemps. Published in the February 12, 1946, issue of the *New Masses*, his essay "What Shall We Ask of Writers?" argued that the notion of "art as a weapon" is a straitjacket. Artistic value is not a factor of political use-value or even individual politics—see, for example, Marx on Balzac. No sooner did Maltz articulate this position than it was rabidly attacked by a host of Communist notables, including novelists Mike Gold and Howard Fast and Party chairman William Z. Foster. The *Daily Worker* ran a six-part rebuttal and John Howard Lawson served as de facto prosecutor when Maltz was called to account at a special meeting held in the basement of Morris Carnovsky's Beverly Glen home—a prelude to the recantation Maltz published simultaneously in the *Worker* and the *New Masses*, timed to his public apology at a Communist-sponsored Hollywood meeting humiliatingly called "Art: Weapon of the People."

Wallis acquired an interest in his former rival's production: a new Cold War alliance. While some have hinted there may be more behind Wallis's withdrawal,
the *Times* assures its readers that there was no conspiracy—beyond a form of
unfair competition—and "the truth seems to be that studio executives did not
want duplication."

In any case, MGM's technical advisers are not pleased. One physicist has
written to Sam Marx expressing concern that MGM has been seduced by army
propaganda. Really! For his part, Marx is annoyed that some "younger, less important scientists" are agitating for the movie as "a big, long speech for world
government." (Like the FBI, MGM is already making secret recordings of the
activists' telephone complaints.) A few advisers withdraw from *The Beginning
or the End*, expecting senior scientists and military men to do the same. But
MGM has already paid permission fees; Groves, used to operating outside the
chain of command, pocketed $10,000 in return for vetting the script.

MGM secures army approval, contingent on fictionalizing certain details of
the Trinity test. Oppenheimer is unhappy, but his objections are largely
aesthetic—the characters appear "stilted, lifeless and without purpose or insight." Marx promises the touchy genius that his character at least will be "an
extremely pleasant one with a love of mankind, humility, and a fair knack of
cooking." (Rand, taken off the project, returns to her novel *Atlas Shrugged*,
which now includes its ultimate villain, "Dr. Robert Stadler"—a brilliant scientist corrupted by his alliance with government funders and destroyed by the
very sound-wave weapon of mass destruction based on his theories.)

Marx further assures Oppenheimer that *The Beginning or the End* will emphasize that he was in charge at Alamogordo: "We have changed all the lines at
the New Mexico test so that General Groves is merely a guest and you give all
the orders." Thus mollified, Oppenheimer grudgingly signs his release in May,
with the $2 million project already in production—directed by Norman Tau-
rog, a founding member of the Motion Picture Alliance, whose previous credits
include the highly successful 1940 science project *Young Tom Edison*.

After considering contract stars Clark Gable and Spencer Tracy for the role
of Groves, MGM chooses a lesser personality, versatile veteran Brian Donlevy,
with MGM contract player Robert Walker in the role of Groves's invented adjutant Colonel Jeff Nixon and Tom Drake as the fictional young scientist Matt
Cochran. The real star is to be the dramatized destruction of Hiroshima that
Marx promises will be the most terrifying thing ever shown on the screen—
"even greater than the earthquake scenes in *San Francisco*."

Hume Cronyn is approved to play Oppenheimer, but Lionel Barrymore, who has a juicy cameo as FDR, is compelled to withdraw after Eleanor Roosevelt objects. (Barrymore had publicly supported Dewey and privately disparaged the president during the 1944 election.) So many egos to pamper and details to consider: by June, MGM's Manhattan Project project is known around the studio as "the Headache."

The Beginning or the End was in production when Operation Crossroads—the first postwar nuclear test, jointly administered by the army and navy—was staged in the vast South Pacific on Bikini Atoll.

Anxiety was endemic. "One man feared gravity would be destroyed and everything would fall up," *Newsweek* reported.

> Another prophesied that when the atomic bomb went off at Bikini, all the water in all the oceans would be turned to gas, automatically dropping ships to the bottom. Another thought the Operation Crossroads bomb would blow a hole in the bottom of the Bikini lagoon and let all the water in the sea run out.
>
> Earthquakes and tidal waves were commonly expected, and in Portland, Ore., a taxi driver was stoically awaiting a painful fate from huge radioactive waves which would "peel his skin like a banana."

"Many," the newsweekly added, "could feel a secret tug of sympathy for the uneasy inhabitants of the low flat plain fronting the Pacific at the foot of the Sierra Nevada. Los Angeles knew that most scientists had ridiculed the possibility of a tidal wave. Nevertheless thousands of Angelenos had already made their plans. On Sunday, June 30, when a small mass of plutonium is scheduled to explode 4,000 miles away across the international date line, they will be picnicking up in the mountains—just in case."

The world's fourth atomic device had a more direct Hollywood connection. The "Thing," as *Time* called it, was nicknamed "Gilda" after Rita Hayworth's current movie (although not, as is sometimes reported, adorned with a foot-high image of the bombshell herself). Days after the first test, a French designer dubbed his new skimpy two-piece bathing suit *le bikini*.

As the glamorous Hayworth was drafted into America's postwar arsenal, her then—albeit estranged—husband Orson Welles focused on the war's aftermath. In his newspaper columns and speeches, the thirty-one-year-old polymath had warned of a Nazi resurgence. *The Stranger*, which Welles directed for independent producer Sam Spiegel, enabled him to play a German war criminal—the very architect of Hitler's Final Solution—hiding in a small New England college town under the name "Rankin" (Welles's little joke, blatantly referencing a bona fide domestic fascist, the Hollywood-baiting Mississippi congressman John E. Rankin). The monster has even managed to marry an innocent maid, the daughter of a U.S. Supreme Court justice no less (tremulous Loretta Young), before he is tracked down and exposed by an American delegate to the Allied War Crimes Commission (Edward G. Robinson, who played a similar role in Warner Bros.'s 1939 film *Confessions of a Nazi Spy*).

Opening in July and eventually grossing some $2 million, *The Stranger* would be Welles's lone Hollywood hit. It was also the first Hollywood feature to refer to the Nazi death camps, incorporating clips from the newsreels of liberated Buchenwald and Dachau that had shocked American audiences when they were first shown in May 1945. (Ronald Reagan was so impressed with this footage that, nearly forty years later, he told Israeli prime minister Yitzhak Shamir and Nazi hunter Simon Wiesenthal that he had shot the material himself, saving a personal copy against the day that people might no longer believe these atrocities actually occurred.) The *New York Times* nevertheless deemed *The Stranger* "a bloodless, manufactured show," noting that a newsreel on the bill showing Operation Crossroads was "immeasurably more frightening."

The first anniversary of the bombs that fell on Hiroshima and Nagasaki was marked by the "March of Time" documentary *Atomic Power*. The movie was filled with reenactments: Albert Einstein pretended to dictate a letter to President Roosevelt; Robert Oppenheimer and I.I. Rabi exchanged well wishes before the first atomic test; and, with a dirt-filled Boston warehouse standing in for Los Alamos, James Conant and Vannevar Bush demonstrated how they had sprawled in the New Mexico sand. The *New Yorker* devoted its entire August 31 issue to John Hersey's "Hiroshima"—with its devastatingly matter-of-fact account of six survivors—and, in Hollywood, Fritz Lang previewed his statement on the Atomic Age.

Cloak and Dagger was predicated on the exciting notion of a nuclear-scientist spy, played by Hollywood's reigning action star, Gary Cooper. Lang and his scriptwriters advanced the notion of a two-fisted undercover all-American Oppenheimer, lured from his ivory tower to fight the fascists on their home ground, alongside Lili Palmer's winsome Italian partisan. Once the OSS gleans that the Nazis are trying to manufacture Something Big, an operative casually drops by his old friend's lab: "How's work in nuclear physics these days?" Making clear his knowledge of the Manhattan Project, the operative wonders whether Cooper thinks the Germans might also be developing nuclear weapons.

Cooper is bitter about the militarization of science. ("For the time, thousands of Allied scientists are working together—to make what? A bomb! But who was willing to finance science before the war to wipe out tuberculosis?") Nevertheless, he goes to Switzerland to meet an anti-Nazi Hungarian scientist who tells him that even the Italians are working on an atomic bomb; Cooper (now required to impersonate not simply a scientist, but an American whose assignment demands he impersonate a German) heads to Italy, where he is aided by the underground in liberating Mussolini's leading nuclear physicist.

This fantastic narrative does not lack for ambition. *Cloak and Dagger* was at once antifascist tract and pro-Communist partisan drama, espionage thriller and nuclear warning, a merging of World War II and Cold War concerns. Lang capped the movie with a spectacular super-climax: the Italian scientist dies on the escape plane and Cooper accepts a final mission to infiltrate and destroy the Germans' secret Whatzit lab. As Lang described the scene to Peter Bogdanovich twenty years later, Cooper and the OSS commandos parachute into Bavaria to find a camouflaged highway and an electrified barbed-wire fence. The power has been cut off and the pillboxes are deserted. The machines are gone. "A sergeant comes to report that sixty thousand slave workers have been found dead underneath the cave." The original press notes explain, "They have come too late. The factory has been thoroughly stripped by the Germans, its equipment probably moved to Spain or Argentina, where the Nazis had a foothold." One commando realizes that "our ultra, hush-hush absolutely exclusive top-secret" plans can no longer be contained: "Peace? There's no peace! It's year one of the Atomic Age and God have mercy on us all!" The last words belong to Cooper's character: "God have mercy on us if we ever thought we could really keep science a secret—or even wanted to! God have mercy on us if we think we can wage other wars without destroying ourselves, and God have mercy on us if we haven't the sense to keep the world at peace."

It is the cri de coeur of the postwar world. *Cloak and Dagger* was trade-screened in early September without the final reel. The irate Lang complained in vain to the *Hollywood Reporter* that Sperling had destroyed his "plea for peace."

Secretary of Commerce Henry Wallace would soon echo Gary Cooper's words (written by Albert Maltz, if not Fritz Lang). On the evening of September 12, in between the truncated *Cloak and Dagger*'s Los Angeles trade-show screening and the movie's Atlantic City premiere, Wallace warned a political rally at Madison Square Garden, "We cannot rest in the assurance that we invented the atom bomb—and therefore that this agent of destruction will work best for us.

He who trusts in the atom bomb will sooner or later perish by the atom bomb—or something worse." Wallace went on to argue that the United States should not join Great Britain in a de facto alliance against Soviet Russia and that "only the United Nations should have atomic bombs." President Truman had approved Wallace's speech but the ensuing firestorm caused him to ask for the secretary's resignation.

Progressives demanded peace, but Hollywood was still preoccupied with labor problems. In the aftermath of the 1945 strike, an American Federation of Labor arbitration team awarded the job of set construction to the IATSE grips rather than the CSU carpenters; in August, the team reversed itself. In late September, the CSU carpenters were locked out by the major studios. Picket lines returned. Tempers flared. Ronald Reagan, the newly elected third vice president of the Screen Actors Guild, verbally bested secret Communist Party member Sterling Hayden at a SAG meeting; soon after, as Hayden would later tell HUAC, he "broke once and for all with the Communist thing" and SAG voted overwhelmingly to cross the CSU picket lines. Reagan himself took to packing the .32 Smith & Wesson he would maintain had been issued by Warners security.

There was a near riot at MGM on September 25, as five hundred CSU picketers challenged scabs entering the studio, and an actual riot five days later, complete with bottles, stones, and fists thrown by CSU members, many of whom were picketing in their World War II uniforms. Despite the disturbances outside, *The Beginning or the End* neared completion. In mid-October, Sam Marx wrote Robert Oppenheimer to promise that "if we can know you are pleased we can cancel all orders for aspirin and feel that the 'big headache' is finally over with." He had spoken too soon.

Before the month ended, *The Beginning or the End* was previewed at the Navy Building in Washington, DC, for an audience of government officials, scientists, and other notables. Among them was political commentator Walter Lippmann, who was shocked by the scene in which General Groves—improbably "transformed into a dashing, romantic cavalier"—informs President Truman that the Japanese are prepared to meet an American invasion with their own atomic weapons. (The even more fanciful original script had a fictional German physicist deliver the recipe for the Great Whatzit to a Japanese laboratory in Hiroshima.)

This exchange, concluding with Truman's snap decision to use the Bomb, was an "outright fabrication" and "libel," the angry columnist told John J. McCloy, the former assistant secretary of war—it would disgrace Truman and America. The president had already approved the script, however (MGM had eliminated an earlier sequence wherein Truman, then chairman of the Senate's

Committee to Investigate the National Defense Program, was refused admission to Oak Ridge). White House secretary Charles Ross tactfully informed the studio that although *The Beginning or the End* was "a thrilling picture," something would have to be done about Truman's scene. Now the studio dispatched its most political producer, Motion Picture Alliance founder James K. McGuinness, to Washington to handle this delicate task by meeting with Ross, who was acutely aware that the president's popularity had plummeted, down from an 80 percent approval rating in late 1945 to its current dismal 32 percent.

November 11, less than a week after the Republicans recaptured Congress for the first time since 1932, McGuinness informed Lippman that the changes had been made. The offending scene was cut and replaced: Truman was now shown at the "Little White House" in Potsdam during the July 1945 conference, revealing the existence of the Bomb to none other than . . . an actor playing Charles Ross. With his back to the camera as he pages through a top secret file replete with mushroom cloud photo, Truman muses that "in peacetime atomic energy could be used to bring forth a Golden Age."

The presidential voice is calm, steady, and almost stentorian—in no way resembling the actual Truman's flat, nasal delivery. Ross is overcome with emotion: "Thank God we've got the Bomb and not the Japanese. If they had, they'd surely use it on us." The president notes that that wasn't the deciding argument and Ross sympathizes: "You must have spent many sleepless nights over it." His boss doesn't deny it. The Bomb, Truman points out, will shorten the war by a year. He's also given some thought to the Japanese targets. "We're going to shower all these places for ten days with leaflets telling them what's coming— and we hope these warnings will save lives." Then he reiterates that the Bomb will save half a million Americans (as well as Britons and Russians and even Japanese). "As president of the United States, sir, you could make no other decision," Ross exclaims.[3]

This new scene also featured a new Truman. Roman Bohnen, who had originally impersonated the president, was replaced by Art Baker, most recently seen as Rabbi Jacob Samuels in the 1946 remake of *Abie's Irish Rose*. The reason for the change, according to Samuel Marx, was that Ross and Truman's appointment secretary Matt Connelly found Bohnen lacking in gravitas: his "bearing was not sufficiently erect and military to duplicate the president's." Nor did Bohnen's politics duplicate those of the president.

---

3. Stressing speedy victory and saved lives, the movie repeats Truman's public statement of August 9, 1945; the claim that Japanese targets were showered with leaflets is original.

While the *New York Times* deemed the switch incidental to a request for a revision of the Truman sequence, Bohnen thought otherwise. A former member of the Group Theatre and a founder of the Actors Laboratory, Bohnen wrote Truman after being ousted, imagining "the emotional torture" the president must have experienced "in giving that fateful order" and afterward: "Posterity is quite apt to be a little rough [on you] for not having ordered that very first atomic bomb to be dropped *outside* Hiroshima." Bohnen further suggested that Truman play himself. Ignoring the actor's sarcasm, Truman replied with thanks, confessing that he lacked the talent to be a movie star and reiterating that, contrary to the movie, he had no qualms about using the Bomb.[4]

The rest of the cast was clean—although a half-dozen years later Robert Walker played a Communist spy in *My Son John*, and if not the security threat that the real J. Robert Oppenheimer was ultimately deemed to be, Hume Cronyn did espouse an outspokenly liberal position at a December 19 mass meeting of the Screen Actors Guild, where, along with Katharine Hepburn, he vigorously disputed SAG vice president Reagan's defense of the producers in the CSU strike.

February 15, 1947: The *Washington Post* announces that members of the "nation's atomic elite" will "see 'themselves' on screen" in "the most distinguished event of its kind in Washington's theatrical history."

All hail MGM! Recognizing its "duty to mankind," acting with "remarkable dispatch" and a "unique attention to authenticity," America's greatest movie studio has—in the words of its publicists—"assumed the greatest responsibility and undertook the most complex task in the history of picture-making." Not since *Mission to Moscow* has Hollywood so urgently addressed recent history. But this time, the filmmakers have taken the long view. Hedging its bets, *The Beginning or the End* opens with a blatantly misleading fake newsreel showing a group of atomic scientists burying their records—and this very movie, along with a 16 mm projector—in a time capsule meant for "the people of the twenty-fifth century."

The Beginning or the End is an artifact and presents itself as such. The audience

---

4. In February 1948, Bohnen was subpoenaed by the California Senate Fact-Finding Committee on Un-American Activities. According to the committee's report, he "followed the same pattern set by [actress] Rose Hobart and evaded or refused to answer most questions. . . . He refused to state when he had joined the Communist Party, or whether he had been or was presently, a member of the Communist Party." In 1951, Bohnen was posthumously named by Lloyd Bridges (a former student at the Actors Lab) as having recruited him into the CP.

must imagine being addressed by the shade of a long-dead man who was once the nation's "most famous atomic scientist": "How do you do . . . whoever you are. My name is J. Robert Oppenheimer. I'm an American scientist working in the year of Our Lord nineteen hundred and forty-six. I'm addressing you people of the twenty-fifth century in English, now, and I hope in your time, one of the leading languages of the world. . . . The people of my era unleashed the power which for all we know will destroy human life on this earth. . . . We know the beginning. Only you of tomorrow, if there is a tomorrow, can know the end." In addition to an ersatz voice from beyond the grave, *The Beginning or the End* introduces a new iconography of mushroom clouds, megabombers, radiation burns, and, heralded by appropriately weird music, uranium 235—not to mention a super-secret project so enormous as to "make the building of the pyramids seem like child's play."

MGM's Manhattan Project is a movie of leaden levity and strained human interest—as stilted as the Socialist Realist "publicist films" already being produced in the Soviet Union. The science fiction elements are eclipsed by a large, loquacious cast of scientists, politicians, and military men. Precisely because *The Beginning or the End* is close to unwatchable, *Variety*'s boosterish enthusiasm seems a patriotic obligation—to Hollywood if not the United States. Praising Cronyn's expert impersonation, Taurog's expert direction, and Wead and Considine's expert script, the showbiz bible declares MGM's Manhattan Project "a credit of new proportions to the motion picture industry," as well as "tip-top cinematic entertainment."

Hollywood has addressed a need to explicate the Bomb. The New York *Daily News* finds *The Beginning or the End* "far more thrilling and suspenseful" than the average movie and is adamant in recommending it to "every man and woman in the United States, as well as every child who has reached the age of reason." On the other side of the ideological spectrum, the liberal tabloid *PM* considers *The Beginning or the End* "an extremely clear, thoughtful and dramatic presentation," "informative," "extremely engrossing," and, most crucially, "reassuring." Jack Moffitt uses the same term in *Esquire* in what could be the movie's most enthusiastic notice, praising "a great film" that "stresses moral values rather than military triumphs."

The Luce publications are openly derisive. "The picture seldom rises above cheery imbecility," *Time* notes, while *Life* mocks the documentary preamble and the garish laboratory "equipped with enough phony instruments to outfit a laboratory for Dr. Frankenstein." (The Bomb itself resembles a "nickel-plated prop from a Flash Gordon serial.") James Agee, who writes the anonymous

Time review, is even more critical in the *Nation*: "You learn less about atomic fission from this film than I would assume is taught by now in the more progressive nursery schools; you learn even less than that about the problems of atomic control; and you learn least of all about morals." *The Beginning or the End* provides "a horrifying example" of a future, state-controlled American cinema.

The *New York Times* is less apt to blame the government than the system: MGM "seems to confuse the humbleness of its achievement with the magnitude of atomic power. It would seem that the [filmmakers] actually think that they have made history." Or at least made it up: Harrison Brown, the Manhattan Project geochemist who reviews MGM's version for the *Bulletin of the Atomic Scientists*, decries the overglamorized scientific equipment but is more concerned by the historical falsifications. In addition to ascribing more agony to Truman than the president evidently experienced and crediting him with warning the inhabitants of Hiroshima and Nagasaki to evacuate their cities, *The Beginning or the End* shows the *Enola Gay* braving historically nonexistent heavy flak to drop its payload on Hiroshima.

The young lab assistant Matt Cochrane (perhaps derived from Ayn Rand's abandoned script), serves as the audience's ethical compass. Nothing would happen without his good common sense. Ever practical, he regularly reminds the senior scientists of certain realities—such as the need to plug in the cyclotron. It's Matt who explains a chain reaction to Albert Einstein (Ludwig Stössel, last seen as a nasty Nazi in *Cloak and Dagger*) and persuades the dear codger to write President Roosevelt about the urgent need for atomic research (and then helps draft the letter).

Even more importantly, Matt is on hand to express personal misgivings regarding the morality of building the Bomb, even as he invokes the seriousness of the task to excuse his domestic absences. (He's a newlywed.) Responding to the movie's cuteness in kind, the *Daily Worker*'s review suggested that HUAC investigate the young scientist "to find out what foreign government paid him to make such 'un-American' statements as: 'What we discover should belong to the world,' 'I sometimes wonder whether we should go ahead with it,' [and] 'Most scientists do not want to make the Bomb.'"

Matt is an innocent! Even as he leaves for the Marianas to prime the Whatzit, he's expressing doubts; his wife, meanwhile, has her own secret. She's pregnant but he will never know. The night before Hiroshima is obliterated, Matt saves the entire project by sticking his hand into the Bomb mechanism to prevent a premature explosion. Dying of radiation burns, he wonders if "maybe this is what I get for helping build the Thing." Matt is the necessary human sacrifice. There's a solemn prayer ceremony, the plane takes off, and, without any suspense beyond Colonel Nixon's ability to assume Matt's role and assemble the deadly mechanism, it drops the Bomb. There are no visible victims, just aerial shots of the conflagration.

In the final scene, Nixon takes Matt's wife to the Lincoln Memorial to give her the news and a letter, testimony from beyond the grave, complete with a utopian vision of the post-Hiroshima future: "God has not shown us a way to destroy ourselves . . . atomic energy is the hand he has extended." Indeed, atomic energy is proof that "human beings are made in the image of God." Then it's back to the twenty-fifth century. Quoth *Life*: "On this depressing note the movie ends."

When HUAC Came to Hollywood . . .

For Hollywood, the terror began in 1947. Two weeks into the New Year, the naked corpse of Elizabeth Short was found dumped—or rather, arranged—in a South Central lot. The twenty-two-year-old aspiring actress had been surgically dismembered—her blood drained, body pieces strewn, face carved into a jack-o'-lantern grin. The details were suppressed but the victim, nicknamed the Black Dahlia by the press for her dark hair and matching wardrobe, entered local mythology as Hollywood's ultimate lost soul, the personification of film noir.

The industry had nowhere to go but down. Scarcely a month into 1947, trade publications (as well as the *Wall Street Journal*) were noting the box-office decline. The eight-page special supplement "Hollywood—The True Story," published in the January 24 edition of *Daily People's World*, ended by bemoaning the past year's movies in comparison to those of the war years, which, whatever their weaknesses, were characterized by their "warm humanity." Now "it seems that the men who control the destinies of Hollywood have ordered a retreat from reality."[5]

The 1946 strikes continued to reverberate. By February, the CSU newsletter

---

5. The *Daily People's World* (or perhaps Dalton Trumbo, said to have written the entire uncredited supplement) went on to single out the "trend toward unmotivated violence," citing such 1946 releases as *The Big Sleep*, *The Blue Dahlia*, *The Killers*, and *The Postman Always Rings Twice*—all examples of what would be called film noir. "After you have seen several such pictures, you wonder whether there is any conscious intent behind this glorification of brutality, and perhaps you then remember that the preoccupation with violence for its own sake and the cynicism of direct action is a Fascist concept." Hollywood's mission had already been co-opted!

Picket Line reported that over a third of studio personnel had been laid off without regard for seniority, and work speed-ups had been instituted in all crafts. Costs rose, production fell. Since the strikes, MGM had averaged but one new movie per month. "People are scared," *Picket Line* noted. In Washington as in Hollywood: the *New Republic*, now edited by Henry Wallace, was fretting that Argentina, Nazi-loving land of *Gilda* and Juan Perón, was two years from developing a nuclear device, while the *Bulletin of Atomic Scientists* reported Edward Teller anticipating an American "super bomb, one thousand times as powerful as the Model T dropped on Hiroshima."

Even as *The Beginning or the End* opened in theaters around the country—lobbies furnished with informational literature provided by the National Committee for Atomic Information, an organization closely associated with the Federation of American Scientists—congressional Republicans were fighting to block former Tennessee Valley Authority head David Lilienthal's appointment as chairman of the Atomic Energy Commission. Senator Kenneth McKellar of Tennessee wondered why General Leslie Groves (in his mind, the Man Who Split the Atom) should be replaced by a civilian who had previously presided over a Communist "hotbed," and Senator Robert Taft of Ohio chimed in with an accusation that would soon become a Republican catchphrase: Lilienthal was "soft" on Communism.

Both the Lilienthal hearings and the *Beginning or the End* premiere coincided with the publication of the official Hiroshima narrative. *Harper's* February 1947 issue featured "The Decision to Use the Atomic Bomb" by former secretary of war Henry Stimson. As detailed as Stimson's account was, it passed over certain issues that had greatly concerned American policy makers in the months before Hiroshima—namely, the Bomb's impact on postwar dealings with the Soviet Union. Now American-Soviet relations were paramount.

Republicans accused Truman of appeasing Communist aggression in Europe while ignoring Communist subversion in his own government. Newly elected California congressman Richard M. Nixon castigated those high officials who, unwittingly or otherwise, were fronting for "un-American elements." In mid-March, the president went before Congress to request military aid to Greece. His language was apocalyptic. Less than two years after World War II ended, Truman conjured a new conflict on the horizon. The anxiety regarding atomic weapons was redirected: America was threatened not with annihilation but by Communism.

The following week, the president issued Executive Order 9835, establishing the elaborate Federal Employees Loyalty and Security Program. Years later, presidential adviser Clark Clifford would admit that the program had more to do with the 1948 election than an actual threat: "We did not believe there was a real problem. A problem was being manufactured."

March 27, five days after Truman's executive order, J. Edgar Hoover appeared before HUAC to testify on proposed measures to outlaw the Communist Party. Thus Hollywood entered the equation.

Some believed that Louis B. Mayer had paid off HUAC's former chairman, Georgia representative John S. Wood, to stall a previously announced investigation of the movie industry.[6] But now the Republicans were in charge. Unable to appear, Cecil B. DeMille wired the committee's new chairman, J. Parnell Thomas of New Jersey, in support of legislation banning Communists from employment in "nationally vital industries, especially [those] that mold public thought." And, among other things, Hoover noted Communists had successfully infiltrated Hollywood to employ motion pictures in their propaganda.[7]

The next day, the committee heard testimony from the president of the Motion Picture Association of America, Eric Johnston. In response to Hoover, Johnston testified that, rather than propagandizing from within Hollywood, international Communism targeted its products with "bitter, organized attacks. . . . The Communists hate and fear American motion pictures. It is their number-one hate." Johnston maintained that Mississippi congressman John E. Rankin's DeMillean suggestion that the studios summarily fire all suspected Communists was unnecessary: whenever the Communists attempted to influence actual movie content, they suffered "overwhelming defeat."

Still, challenged by Representative Karl Mundt of South Dakota on the most notorious pro-Soviet movie of all, Johnston went on the defensive. Allowing that he had actually never seen *Mission to Moscow*, the MPAA president pointed out that its protagonist, Ambassador Joseph E. Davies, was a capitalist; to Mundt's observation that "the Communists in this country are supported by some

---

6. Drew Pearson published the allegations regarding Mayer and Wood in a June 1950 *Washington Post* column dutifully clipped and filed by the FBI.

7. Shortly after Hoover's testimony, a trio of FBI agents paid an unannounced home visit to an old source—and the newly installed president of the Screen Actors Guild—Ronald Reagan; noting Reagan's previous associations with two alleged Communist front organizations, HICCASP and the American Veterans Committee, they enlisted the actor and his wife, actress Jane Wyman, as informants within SAG.

capitalists," Johnston countered with a stout non sequitur, maintaining that no Hollywood studio had been "more desirous of presenting America in its true light abroad than Warner Bros."

Johnston had already gone on record declaring that the movie industry's true mission was to produce "good pictures of American life—and show an unhappy world how democracy works." The MPAA was even now creating two new entities that would correct objectionable sequences to ensure that American movies were acceptable abroad. Not that he expected Hollywood movies ever to be suitable for Communist Russia: "The old tale about the breakdown of capitalism in America becomes pretty flimsy stuff after people have had a chance to see our pictures."

Hearst columnist Hedda Hopper was not impressed: "Since when has it become a sin to sell Americanism?" she tartly wondered. And anyway, the problem was that the Reds were bringing their propaganda here. She had information that the late president's high-living son Elliott Roosevelt was planning to go into business distributing Russian films in America with no less a partner than Charles Chaplin. The world's most famous film personality was Hopper's bête noire. She scolded Chaplin for "fostering an ideology offensive to most Americans" and, a few days before his new movie *Monsieur Verdoux* was to have its world premiere, wrote to J. Edgar Hoover, begging for an opportunity to attack: "You give me the material and I'll blast."

Hoover already had a hefty file on Chaplin. A recent FBI report associated the star with a range of radical émigrés, notably Hanns Eisler and prominent Hollywood Communists Paul Jarrico, Herbert Biberman, and Dalton Trumbo, as well as the labor leader Harry Bridges. But *Monsieur Verdoux* brought its own disaster. For his first movie since *The Great Dictator* (1940), Chaplin had abandoned the Little Tramp to play a comic version of the French serial killer Henri Landru—a bluebeard who murdered at least eighteen people during World War I, mainly widows he'd married for their money.

Adding insult to injury, Chaplin placed his antihero's crimes in a particular explanatory context. An honest bank clerk, his Henri Verdoux is driven to murder by the 1929 stock market crash—shown in newsreels along with documentary footage of the Spanish Civil War—as well as Nazi and fascist militarism. Brought to trial at the movie's end, Verdoux declares his crimes paltry compared to those of Western civilization: "As for being a mass killer—does not the world encourage it? Is it not building weapons of destruction for the sole purpose of mass killing? Has it not blown up unsuspecting women and little children to pieces, and done it very scientifically? As a mass killer, I'm an amateur by comparison."

To introduce his movie, Chaplin insisted on a series of press conferences and, on the eve of *Monsieur Verdoux*'s premiere, entertained largely friendly questions from foreign journalists. But the screening at the Broadway Theater, a legitimate house refitted for movie projection, was less cordial. Viewers greeted the movie with audible hissing, and taken aback, Chaplin fled the theater. The following morning, when American reporters packed the Grand Ballroom of the Gotham Hotel to overflowing, he encountered even greater animosity. Chaplin tried to reinforce Verdoux's defense, calling the atomic bomb "the most horrible invention of mankind . . . creating so much horror and fear that we are going to grow up a bunch of neurotics," yet half the questions concerned his loyalty to the United States. He was asked in particular about his friendship with Eisler—shortly to be announced as the prime subject in HUAC's upcoming probe into Communism in Hollywood.[8]

In the *New York Times*, Bosley Crowther characterized *Monsieur Verdoux* as "basically serious and bitter" and warned that "those who go expecting to laugh at it may find themselves remaining to weep." James Agee, one of the few journalists at the Gotham to defend Chaplin, wrote a three-part defense in the *Nation*. Still, attacked by the American Legion and local censors, *Monsieur Verdoux* lasted less than a month at the Broadway. Soon after the Independent Theatre Owners of Ohio called for a national ban, United Artists withdrew the movie from release. It was as if *Daily Worker* critic David Platt had anticipated this hostility when he concluded his near rave review with the words "hats off to a brilliant comedy whose deep message will stir the hearts and minds of liberty-loving peoples all over the world."[9]

Monsieur Verdoux was a shot fired across Hollywood's bow from the left. Chaplin was not entirely alone; Dore Schary, who had become RKO's production chief back in January (on the same day that President Truman appointed General George Marshall secretary of state), had several progressive pictures in production, notably the anti-anti-Semitic *Crossfire*, produced by Comrade Adrian Scott and directed by Comrade Edward Dmytryk (although Dmytryk would later claim to have been suspended from the Party two years earlier by Commissar Lawson), and the socially conscious gangster film *They Live by Night*, produced by liberal John Houseman and directed by leftist Nicholas Ray.

---

8. Friendship with Hanns Eisler was double guilt by association: the composer's brother Gerhart had been named the "number one Communist in America" by former *Daily Worker* managing editor turned informer Louis Budenz.

9. The FBI took particular notice of this, as well as a positive review in the Communist journal *Mainstream*; an August 6 memo characterizes *Monsieur Verdoux* as "Soviet propaganda."

Scott was also developing the antiwar fantasy that, written by Comrades Ben Barzman and Alfred Lewis Levitt, would eventually be directed by Comrade Joseph Losey and released by RKO as *The Boy with Green Hair*. Schary's own name was on the newly opened New Deal–ish romantic comedy *The Farmer's Daughter*, a project he had brought with him to RKO and a source of mild political controversy.[10]

The industry, however, was more responsive to pressure from the right. Not even a week after defending Chaplin, the *Daily Worker* warned readers that when Eric Johnston paid HUAC a friendly visit, the committee ordered him to get busy producing movies on the evils of Communism, like those that had exposed totalitarian fascism during the war, and "Johnston bowed low and said he would talk it over with his pals in the industry." Now, as the headline put it, there were "TWO ANTI-SOVIET FILMS IN PREPARATION IN HOLLYWOOD": MGM's *The Red Danube* and Twentieth Century-Fox's *The Iron Curtain*.

In early April, within a week of Hoover's testimony, Fox portentously announced that, "in keeping with the motion picture industry's time honored mission to inform as well as entertain," the studio was preparing a film on "the dramatic story behind the efforts of foreign agents to steal the secrets of America's Atom Bomb." This picture was to be called *The Iron Curtain*. A hysterical Jack Warner, soon to break with his fellow moguls and capitulate to HUAC by calling for an "all out fight on Commies," claimed to have registered the title on January 7, 1946, almost two months before Winston Churchill's speech.

---

10. Played by thirty-four-year-old Loretta Young, the movie's eponymous heroine is a super-wholesome, strongly accented Swedish American farm lass who, thanks to her plainspoken idealism, is picked to run for the House of Representatives. Originally to be called *Katie for Congress*, this genial variation on *Mr. Smith Goes to Washington* (adapted, from a Finnish play, by Schary's friend Allen Rivkin in collaboration with Rivkin's wife, Laura Kerr) is the Hollywood equivalent of *The Shining Path*, a 1940 Stalinist musical about the political maturing of an unformed country girl. David Platt was particularly approving, hailing *The Farmer's Daughter* for its "healthy political slant" while hailing Katie herself as "a wide awake and courageous young woman." More surprisingly, or perhaps strategically, *The Farmer's Daughter* was effusively praised by Jack Moffitt in *Esquire* as "an honestly liberal movie . . . thoroughly democratic and thoroughly entertaining." Moffitt even suggested that Katie's upright father had a marked resemblance to Henry Wallace. A sometime and still-aspiring screenwriter, as well as a founding member of the Motion Picture Alliance, Moffitt went out of his way to credit and congratulate RKO production chief Dore Schary. On the other hand, *The Farmer's Daughter* was attacked in the Catholic journal *Tidings*, the official publication of the Los Angeles Archdiocese, as "Katie for Communism." For critic William Mooring, Katie's bland progressive politics were less significant than her opponent's negative qualities—he was not only a political hack but a closet fascist. The movie was a modest hit, finishing twenty-sixth for the year, and went on to garner a surprise Oscar for Young.

Fox production head Darryl Zanuck had little more than the title but imag- ined that he also had an inside track with Hoover. In a four-page confidential memo sent to producer Sol Siegel, screenwriter Martin Berkeley, Fox's Wash- ington representative, the studio publicist, and retired general Edward Munson (wartime head of the Army Motion Picture Service and now a Fox executive), Zanuck explained that he had reason to expect that the Bureau would help *The Iron Curtain* by providing "the lowdown on three or four cases that the govern- ment, or the FBI, has already solved . . . or the lowdown on a case now existent— which they are about ready to break."

Once the FBI made these files available, Zanuck assured his team, there would be ample material for a topical "semi-documentary screenplay." But this assistance was not forthcoming and so the studio boss switched focus to the Gouzenko affair, a story already red-hot. Independent producer Andrew Stone had registered the title *Soviet Spies* and proffered an offer to Canada's deputy minister of justice, the official responsible for managing Igor Gouzenko. As former Communist and future informer Berkeley developed a treatment based on the official report and an article published in the February issue of *Cosmo- politan*, Zanuck maneuvered to buy Gouzenko's story.

Stone would maintain that his offer had been accepted and he had secured a distribution deal with United Artists, when a New York literary agent, Gertrude Algase, with inside information, induced Gouzenko's representative to betray Stone. After two days of meetings and maneuvers, involving even former OSS chief Wild Bill Donovan, Stone's deal collapsed. Gouzenko signed with Fox. Berkeley worked on the *Iron Curtain* script through mid-May, at which point he was replaced by Milton Krims, who had written the sensation of 1939, *Confes- sions of a Nazi Spy*.[11]

Amid these maneuvers, HUAC member Richard Nixon announced that the long-anticipated investigation into Hollywood was scheduled to begin May 8. Chairman Thomas would visit Hollywood to scrutinize presumed target Hanns Eisler, with the full committee to follow during the summer to gather informa- tion on Communist infiltration of the film unions and hold public hearings.

---

11. Whether or not Berkeley—whose previous credits were slim—received (or lost) this assign- ment by dint of his experience is a matter of conjecture. According to his FBI files, the then thirty-three-year-old writer joined the Communist Party in 1937. Indeed, he would later testify that the Party's Hollywood section was organized at a June 1937 meeting in his Beverly Glen home. Berkeley remained in the CP at least through the summer of 1943 and, according to FBI information, was aligned with the pro-Communist faction in the Screen Writers Guild for some years after.

Nixon noted that, despite Eric Johnston's claims to the contrary, some of his colleagues remained convinced that Communists had inserted their propaganda into American films.

Thursday, May 8, Parnell Thomas, Representative John McDowell (Republican of Pennsylvania), chief investigator Robert Stripling, and former FBI man Louis J. Russell set up shop at the Biltmore Hotel in downtown Los Angeles.

Thomas has the benefit of some FBI intelligence. Agents have already debriefed longtime informant Ronald Reagan, along with his wife, Jane Wyman. No need for them to show, the couple is assured. The next morning, MGM producer James K. McGuinness and screenwriter turned *Esquire* film critic Jack C. Moffitt, both of the Motion Picture Alliance for the Preservation of American Ideals, arrive at the Biltmore to officially welcome the committee.

Although held in executive session, the hearings are leaked daily to the press. Thus it is reported that McGuinness praised the committee's war against propaganda, while calling for a return to movies as "pure entertainment." Moffitt himself tells reporters that the committee told him "quite a few things" he didn't know. (True or not, he will return to the Biltmore twice more.) Thomas informs reporters that Hanns Eisler has been subpoenaed to testify on Monday and notes that a hundred people have already volunteered information; after Eisler proves an "evasive" witness, Thomas promises to haul him up to Washington for a full committee hearing. Roy Brewer testifies on behalf of IATSE, complaining that, in thwarting his union, the National Labor Relations Board has acted as an accessory to the Communist Party.

After the committee spends all Tuesday huddling with Moffitt, the stars arrive: Richard Arlen, Robert Taylor, and Ginger Rogers's mother. Lela Rogers is still irate over *Tender Comrade*, naming its writer Dalton Trumbo as a Communist. Taylor, however, creates the greater stir by testifying that in 1943 a government agent—later identified as Lowell Mellett, coordinator of motion pictures for the Office of War Information—refused to allow him to enlist in the navy until he first starred in *Song of Russia*!

Thursday, Adolphe Menjou crosses a picket line set up by the Los Angeles chapter of American Youth for Democracy to inform the committee that Hollywood is "one of the main centers of Communist activity in America" and that the "masters of Moscow" have targeted Hollywood as a place to instigate overthrow of the U.S. government; hardly underdogs, "Communists in the film industry are so powerful that many little people in the industry—innocent people—are afraid to move or speak out against them." Menjou identifies a few

Reds, after which the committee hears a panicky Jack Warner offer up the names of any writers he believes to have been politically active, describing them as Communists and assuring the committee that he has fired them all.[12]

Other witnesses include a very successful director, Leo McCarey, and a pair of underemployed screenwriters, Howard Emmett Rogers and Rupert Hughes, both longtime foes of the Screen Writers Guild. It's Hughes who afterward tells newsmen that the SWG is "lousy with Communists, some of them making $3,000 to $5,000 weekly." A surprise final witness, Soviet defector Victor Kravchenko, promotes his book *I Chose Freedom*—which Rogers happens to be adapting for the movies.

In his last press conference, Thomas reports that both Menjou and Warner named industry Communists, with Hughes even supplying the numbers of their Party cards: "The committee was amazed at the revelations made by the witnesses who came before us over the past ten days." Thomas further reveals that the studios had been pressured to make pro-Soviet movies: "We were also amazed at the influence of the federal government in the part it played in the Communist conspiracy. I don't only refer to the Robert Taylor incident." Moreover, Thomas asserts, the SWG is "under the complete domination of the Communist Party." The day after the hearings end, the *Los Angeles Times* editorializes that "the Hollywood Communists who swarmed in 1942 are still holding the hive. They don't make any more *Songs of Russia* or *Missions to Moscow*, but they are where they can get a lick at the unwary, always in wait for the target of opportunity. They are proving that the pen is mighty They work among the Hollywood writers. They can't write a whole picture, but every now and then they can throw in a line or two for the Party. Sometimes they can kill a script that is not sympathetic." But *Variety* reports a certain skepticism ("'RED HERRING' JUST ANOTHER FISH STORY, MAJOR H'WOOD OPINION FEELS OF BAITING") and *Newsweek* is nonplussed: "No one could say whether Rep. J. Parnell Thomas was producing an epic or a turkey. The chairman of the House Committee on Un-American Activities was shooting without a script last week, turning his camera first on this star, then on that one." The second half of the double feature is set to open in Washington, possibly as soon as June 16.

The Monday after the committee's hearings end, some 28,000 Hollywood progressives rally for Henry Wallace. Denied use of the Hollywood Bowl, they

---

12. These included Alvah Bessie, Guy Endore, Julius and Philip Epstein, Sheridan Gibney, Gordon Kahn, Howard Koch, Ring Lardner Jr., Emmett Lavery, John Howard Lawson, Albert Maltz, Clifford Odets, Robert Rossen, Dalton Trumbo, Irwin Shaw, and John Wexley.

pack Gilmore Stadium, setting the house record for the Fairfax district home of professional football and midget car racing. The crowd includes stars Charles Chaplin, Edward G. Robinson, John Garfield, Hedy Lamarr, and Paul Henreid, as well as producer Cornelius Vanderbilt Jr., director Frank Tuttle, and writer Budd Schulberg (all of whom donate to Wallace's presidential campaign).

While positioning himself as Truman's adversary and attacking the president's "undeclared emergency," Wallace takes time to lambaste the Thomas committee as a "kangaroo court" and defend Lowell Mellett ("the gentlest, sweetest, kindest liberal that I know") against Robert Taylor's charges. The rally raises thousands of dollars, but the show is stolen by Katharine Hepburn, delivering a keynote speech ghostwritten by Hollywood's best-paid scribe, Dalton Trumbo.

Resplendent in a sweeping scarlet gown, the glamorous star reviews the attacks on various writers, actors, scientists, educators, and especially filmmakers. "J. Parnell Thomas is engaged in a personally conducted smear campaign of the motion picture industry. He is aided and abetted in his efforts by a group of super-patriots who call themselves the Motion Picture Alliance for the Preservation of American Ideals. For myself, I want no part of their ideals or those of Mr. Thomas. . . . The artist, since the beginning of time, has always expressed the aspirations and dreams of his people. Silence the artist and you have silenced the most articulate voice the people have." After the speech, Leo McCarey informs *Variety* that he has decided against casting the fiery actress in his next picture.

In late May, the *Los Angeles Times* reports that HUAC is planning to serve thirty subpoenas to those screenwriters, directors, and producers responsible for movies that glorified Communism while "degrading our own system of government and institutions." Chairman Thomas adds that the National Labor Relations Board has enabled these subversive elements to control Hollywood and that the industry's Communists "have succeeded in preventing certain good American pictures, which sought to glorify America and the American system."

Having failed to head off a public hearing, Eric Johnston meets with Thomas to assure him of MPAA cooperation and tells *Variety* that "producers are just as anxious as any member of the committee to expose any threat to the screen." Addressing an MPAA conclave on June 2, Johnston outlines his three-point program. First, producers must publicly "insist" upon an open investigation by the committee. Second, producers should not employ "proven Communists" in any job that might allow them to influence film content. And third, the MPAA should hire a powerful Washington insider like former secretary of state James Byrnes as their representative.

The producers agree to the first and third proposals but resist the second. Eddie Mannix, MGM's tough-guy general manager (and a onetime amusement park bouncer), tells Johnston that, so long as he is able to protect his movies from subversive content, he is "not about to join in any 'witch-hunt.'" Opening a second front, Johnston meets with two hundred members of the Screen Writers Guild, warning them that the tides of fashion are turning against the Reds and recommending ridicule: "I want to see it become a joke to be a Communist in America."

A joke in America, implacable abroad: red governments consolidate power in Poland and Hungary and Secretary of State Marshall urges the adoption of the European Recovery Plan. HUAC pushes its Washington hearing back to September—announcing that Charlie Chaplin, Edward G. Robinson, and Dorothy Parker will all receive subpoenas.

June 12, two days after Gerhart Eisler is found in contempt of Congress, congressmen Thomas and Rankin complain of death threats; Rankin ups the ante by calling for Chaplin's deportation. The following week, someone rubs out the heavily indebted Hollywood glamour gangster turned Las Vegas hotelier Bugsy Siegel, firing nine shots through the window of his mistress Virginia Hill's Beverly Hills home. June 23, Orson Welles, again cast as a murderer, begins shooting *Macbeth,* and the Republican Congress passes the Taft-Hartley Act, which—among other things curtailing rights to organize, bargain, and strike—requires that every officer of every American labor union file an affidavit attesting to a lack of Communist affiliation. The next day, Idaho businessman Kenneth Arnold has a vision.

Arnold is piloting his small plane over the Cascade Mountains when he sees a formation of "very bright" objects approaching at a speed he estimates to be 1,200 miles per hour. Arnold's account of these "saucer-like" airships is featured the next day on the front page of the *Pendleton East Oregonian* and sent out on the Associated Press wire—the first of some 850 such unidentified flying whatzit stories reported in the news media by midsummer. Implacable aliens occupying our skies! Back on terra firma, an estimated four thousand motorcycle enthusiasts converge on Hollister, California, a small city south of San Jose, for a July 4 weekend convention turned Main Street bacchanal. According to *Life*'s account, the cyclists race through town, running traffic lights and ramming restaurants: "Police arrested many for drunkenness and indecent exposure but could not restore order." The same issue notes the rash of flying saucer stories reported in the ten days since Arnold's sighting. It's bedlam!

July 7, New Mexico rancher W.W. "Mac" Brazel informs the local sheriff that he has discovered debris from a "flying disc." The sheriff contacts the army air-field at Roswell, home to the Strategic Air Command's Eighth Force; the base commander dispatches intelligence officers to Brazel's ranch. Simultaneously, General Nathan Twining, commanding officer of the intelligence-gathering Air Materiel Command, arrives at nearby Alamogordo Field. The metallic debris, oddly flexible and curiously marked with bizarre hieroglyphics, is retrieved; the following day the army air force issues a press release claiming recovery of the flying disc.

Brought to air force headquarters in Fort Worth, the debris is recognized as fragments from a device used by the highly classified Project Mogul, an Alamogordo-based program employing high-altitude microphones to detect such sound waves as might be generated by Soviet nuclear detonations. A cover story is put out, identifying the mysterious wreckage as the remnant of a "weather balloon." But that only seems to prove that the air force found some-thing to conceal: a genuine flying saucer, perhaps even with living alien pilots, has crashed! For decades hence, Roswell will be the code name for ongoing air force disinformation. Meanwhile, freelance flyboy Steve Canyon, the epony-mous hero of the hottest new comic strip of 1947, has just signed on to help protect foreign assets belonging to Happy Easter, an old cavalry trooper turned oil millionaire. And, up in an obscure Martian landscape of red buttes and me-sas, 125 dusty miles from the railroad in Flagstaff and about 350 miles north-west of Roswell, John Ford is shooting a new sort of cavalry Western: *Fort Apache*.

Monument Valley is located within the Navajo Indian reservation that straddles the Arizona-Utah border. Conditions are primitive. There are no phones; when need be, director Ford contacts his Hollywood office via short-wave radio. Actors, stuntmen, extras, and film crew are bivouacked in tents. Ford runs his set as a boot camp, replete with mandatory military drills. Why not? Produced by Argosy, the company Ford founded in January 1946 in part-nership with Merian C. Cooper and a dozen OSS comrades, including Wild Bill Donovan, *Fort Apache* will be as much war movie as Western.

The tale of an embittered, arrogant major who willfully leads his men into a disaster and becomes a martyred hero as result, Ford's new picture was adapted by former *New York Times* critic Frank Nugent from James Warner Bellah's short story "Massacre," first published in the *Saturday Evening Post* and pur-chased by Argosy in March 1947, a time when General Marshall's appointment to succeed James Byrnes as secretary of state occasioned talk of a military take-over. There was little precedent for a professional soldier serving in the nation's highest foreign-policy post; *Time* reported that "the world noted with some concern the emergence of top US military and naval officers as the top dispensers of US foreign policy."

These men in uniform included General Douglas MacArthur (who had grown up on a southwestern cavalry fort), ruling over occupied Japan, as well as General Mark Clark and Lieutenant General Lucius D. Clay, who administered the U.S. zones in Austria and Germany. A major general served as assistant secretary of state for occupied areas; another general headed up the U.S. embassy in Moscow. General Dwight D. Eisenhower was already being bruited as a replacement for President Truman (even, according to some, by Truman himself), although the Hearst press had been promoting another general. As the *Daily Worker* would fret in a July 27 headline: "IS GEN. MACARTHUR THE MAN ON HORSEBACK?"[13]

Ford had told Nugent that he'd been thinking about life at a cavalry post— "remote, people with their own personal problems, over everything the threat of Indians, of death." The situation in *Fort Apache* is nearly existential. The industry too is under siege. Attendance and box-office receipts continue their free fall as HUAC operatives prowl the studios.

Jack Moffitt's current *Esquire* column, titled "The Muse Discards Her Mask," begins with an amusing survey of the situation.

> These words are written from a Hollywood in turmoil. Magazine correspondents are alighting from every train to probe allegedly Communistic activities in the movie capital. The Federal Bureau of Investigation is said to have so many agents planted in the Actors' Laboratory that audiences aren't quite sure whether they're applauding J. Edgar Hoover or [named Communist] J. Edward Bromberg. *People's Daily World* has announced Metro's forthcoming production of *The Red Danube* and has proceeded to pan the script that has not been written yet. Warner Brothers, Columbia and Twentieth Century-Fox are locked in mortal combat. All three studios claim exclusive right to the title *The Iron Curtain*. . . . At the moment, even Communists are writing anti-Communist pictures.

---

13. James Warner Bellah was also a military man who claimed descent from a Confederate cavalry officer and, having joined the Royal Canadian Flying Corps during World War I, considered himself a defender of the British Empire. Described by his son as "a fascist, a racist, and a world-class bigot," the writer understood America's post–World War II mission as essentially imperial. (Soon after assuming the presidency, Ronald Reagan would recommend Bellah to the West Point Class of 1981 as "our Rudyard Kipling.")

(Was Moffitt thinking of Martin Berkeley when he added that "one highly touted exposé is being penned by a writer who has a Party Membership card in his pocket"?)

Moffitt assures his readers that "the day of the concealed 'message' is over" and that the movie industry will have its house in order in time for the congressional hearings. Indeed, producers are being warned of unpleasant consequences should they fail to cooperate with the committee. Zeroing in on the Hollywood tough guy who wouldn't join a "witch hunt," HUAC operative H.A. Smith threatens to subpoena Eddie Mannix if Mannix does not immediately fire Communist screenwriter Lester Cole, currently in Mexico researching a proposed biopic on the Mexican revolutionary Emiliano Zapata.

Widely regarded as a prime target, Charlie Chaplin had sent an open telegram to J. Parnell Thomas:

> You have been quoted as saying you wish to ask me if I am a Communist. You sojourned for ten days in Hollywood not long ago, and could have asked me the question at that time, effecting something of an economy, or you could telephone me now—collect. In order that you may be completely up-to-date on my thinking I suggest you view carefully my latest production, *Monsieur Verdoux*. It is against war and futile slaughter of our youth. While you are preparing your engraved subpoena I will give you a hint on where I stand. I am not a Communist. I am a peacemonger.

For his part, Orson Welles, suspect as the man who changed the name of the subversive Hollywood Democratic Committee to the more august-sounding Hollywood Independent Citizens Committee of the Arts, Sciences, and Professions (HICCASP), attempted to clear his reputation by submitting to an interview with Hedda Hopper: "I'm sick of being called a Communist. It's true that I've worked for some of the things the Communist Party has advocated. But that was merely coincidental. I'm opposed to political dictatorship [and] organized ignorance."[14]

In another response to HUAC, the Progressive Citizens of America convened the Conference on Thought Control in USA at the Beverly Hills Hotel. The same

---

14. The 1948 Tenney committee report associates Welles with fourteen "Communist front associations," including HICCASP, which had presented *The American Caravan*, a production—with Welles in the cast—that supported the United Nations Charter. Referred to as one of the "faithfuls," Welles was placed among Hollywood's "outstanding Communist Party liners and sympathizers."

day rancher Mac Brazel was placed in protective custody, John Howard Lawson delivered the conference's keynote address, something the FBI could hardly fail to note. Lawson assumed the burden of providing a historical setting. His paper invoked the seventeenth-century witch trials, the Alien and Sedition laws, slavery, the Civil War, American intervention in the Philippines, the Palmer raids, Sacco and Vanzetti, and Pearl Harbor to explicate the present moment:

> Today the old propaganda machine is again grounding out its lies. The imbecilities of the Illuminati campaign are repeated in our press and on the radio. The Klan rides again. I.F. Stone reports in *PM* that Washington is "living under the shadow of terror." Medieval superstition degrades our colleges. Professors are urged to take thought that the plague of non-conformity is a communicable disease . . .
>
> Those of us who retain our intellectual equilibrium are not impressed by tales of witches. We know that Karl Marx was a social philosopher, not a sorcerer. We are aware that Communists believe in the socialist organization of society, and that they have the inalienable right to express their views, which can be debated without danger that evil spirits will speak from our lips and convulse our limbs.

Much of the July 12 session on movies and acting was devoted to the baleful influence of the Motion Picture Alliance and its collusion with HUAC. Actually, the MPA's influence was far more pervasive than known or feared. That same month, the FBI had adopted the criteria developed by Ayn Rand for the MPA and later published as *Screen Guide for Americans*, internalizing the twelve "common devices used to turn non-political pictures into carriers of political propaganda."[15]

Mind control or mass suckerology? Untouched as it was by war, America in the Summer of the Flying Saucers reminded I.F. Stone of "those idle, dissatisfied

---

15. Rand's *Screen Guide*'s somewhat redundant commandments were: Don't Take Politics Lightly, Don't Smear the Free Enterprise System, Don't Smear Industrialists, Don't Smear Wealth, Don't Smear Success, Don't Glorify Failure, Don't Glorify Depravity, Don't Deify "The Common Man," Don't Glorify the Collective, Don't Smear an Independent Man, Don't Use Current Events Carelessly, and Don't Smear American Political Institutions. The lengthy FBI report "Communist Infiltration into the Motion Picture Industry," summarizing information filed on July 23, explained the use of associative montage in Communist propaganda: "One method used according to [redacted] and [redacted] was to photograph in close-up a very disgusting or revolting scene and suddenly shift the scene to include a close-up of the intended victim or its emblem such as a crest depicting England, or a rosary of the Catholic Church so that the viewer would get the idea that these latter things were connected with the ideas desired to be created by the Communists."

rich women with no babies to mind and no dishes to wash and lots of time to nurture neuroses." Space aliens, propaganda, and Charlie Chaplin were not the only threats. Official Washington was abuzz with the concepts advanced by "The Sources of Soviet Conduct," published anonymously in the July issue of *Foreign Affairs*: The "main element" of U.S. policy toward the Soviet Union must be a long-term "vigilant containment" of Soviet expansion.

Was war inevitable? July 25, General George Schulgen, chief of the Army Air Force Intelligence Requirements Division, convened a meeting at the Pentagon that decided to investigate reports of "flying discs." The next day, the president signed the National Security Act, establishing the air force as a separate military service, unified with the army and navy under the Department of Defense, as well as setting up the National Security Council and authorizing the Central Intelligence Agency. (By then, as air force investigator Captain Edward J. Ruppelt recalled in his 1956 book *The Report on Unidentified Flying Objects*, "the UFO security lid was down tight.")

A month later, as Milton Krim finished his *Iron Curtain* screenplay, *Newsweek* provided coming attractions for the "Red Scenario" set to premiere in Washington on September 24. Hanns Eisler was the scheduled opener; other headline acts would include Chaplin, Jack Warner, and Eleanor Roosevelt. The script (uncredited) had been furnished by the FBI, from a story (also uncredited) by the Motion Picture Alliance, with additional dialogue (again uncredited) by Ayn Rand.

The investigation, produced by HUAC and directed by its chairman J. Parnell Thomas, would focus on openly pro-Soviet movies as well as movies in which subversive material had been subtly inserted. *Newsweek* reveals:

> Since last May, experts retained by the committee have been studying scores of scenarios in a hunt for un-American propaganda. The persistent portrayal of congressmen as crooks and bankers as stony-hearted villains, to cite two examples, is considered evidence of "concerted efforts to deride everything American. To maintain the surprise element, the committee has hugged close to its bosom the names of the mined scripts which produced pay ore. One of these, however, is known to be the Academy Award winner, *The Best Years of Our Lives*, written by the playwright and New Deal Presidential ghostwriter Robert E. Sherwood.

Launching his own PR blitz, Chaplin scheduled *Monsieur Verdoux*'s Washington opening to coincide with the hearings and invited HUAC to the premiere. The forty-three bright pink subpoenas were served September 23, but

Chaplin's name was not on one. The same day, General Twining sent a classified memo on the saucer question to General Schulgen: "The phenomenon is something real and not visionary or fictitious."

Showtime ("Hooray for Robert Taylor!")

Communist Party chairman William Z. Foster had visited Los Angeles in early September, meeting with local leaders and prominent Party members at Dalton Trumbo's house on Rodeo Drive. According to one well-connected FBI informer, Foster praised Samuel Goldwyn's Oscar-winning returned-vet drama *The Best Years of Our Lives* as the "real stuff" and favorably cited two other RKO releases, *The Farmer's Daughter* and the anti-anti-Semitic *Crossfire*: "They are standing them on their ears." The anonymous FBI informers who doubled as movie critics were also impressed by *Crossfire*, as well as another summer release, the independently produced, United Artists–distributed *Body and Soul*, directed by Comrade Robert Rossen from a script by Comrade Abraham Polonsky.[16]

Body and Soul was excitedly previewed by the *Daily Worker* months ahead of its New York opening, but *Crossfire* became something of a cause. Not since *Mission to Moscow* had the *Worker* been so invested in a Hollywood film. In addition to David Platt's two highly favorable reviews—the second one devoted half the review to quoting the movie's most didactic scene, an analysis of prejudice delivered by Robert Young's police detective—the Communist daily published no less than four follow-up reports during *Crossfire*'s first month in release.

An oddly sanctimonious film noir, adapted from Richard Brooks's sensational 1945 novel *The Brick Foxhole*, *Crossfire* begins with a murder and proceeds through a fog of moral confusion and a thicket of false flashbacks. As the identity of the killer is soon known, the issue is not solving the crime so much as demonstrating that it is a manifestation of murderous prejudice. The novel's victim was a homosexual; after the MPAA's Breen Office declared this premise "completely unacceptable" and inalterably taboo, producer Adrian Scott and screenwriter John Paxton converted him to apparently heterosexual Judaism.

Their new script centered on a fearsome paradox—in the afterglow of America's antifascist triumph, a newly returned GI kills a Jewish fellow American out

---

16. *Body and Soul* may be the reddest movie Hollywood ever produced. CP members or associates include producer Bob Roberts and actors Anne Revere, Lloyd Goff (Gough), Canada Lee, and Art Smith; star John Garfield would be subpoenaed by HUAC.

of pure anti-Semitic malice. Breen demanded further script changes that would stress the villain's atypicality and ordered that the speeches on bigotry given by the movie's wearily heroic police detective invoke all forms of racial and religious intolerance, so as to avoid any charge of special pleading on behalf of Jews.

Dore Schary had made *Crossfire* a personal project, pushing it through with a frugal $500,000 budget on a twenty-two-day shooting schedule. He appointed himself executive producer and appeared in the movie's trailer, coyly invoking its unspecified major theme while linking *Crossfire* to the tradition of *I Am a Fugitive from a Chain Gang* and *The Grapes of Wrath*. For his part, Scott would add *Confessions of a Nazi Spy* and *Mission to Moscow*: "This is a story of personal fascism as opposed to organized fascism." Whether individual or social, the pathology was the same, however—murderous anti-Semitism is an expression of armed extremism. Demobilized soldiers swarm through the streets of Washington, and still wearing his uniform, the killer appears as something like a native-born brownshirt, waiting for a corn-fed führer to channel his rage.

After one of the many previews RKO held in early July, the FBI's anonymous informant predicted that the army would resent the depiction of a soldier "showing hatred." Moreover, *Crossfire* took "a subtle thrust at our police by showing the soldier murderer as a former cop and by the police captain saying nobody likes cops." The movie was "near treasonable in its implications and seeming effects [*sic*] to arouse race and religious hatred."

Crossfire suggested that the nation faced an internal fascist threat—and proposed itself as a panacea. Scott told the Conference on Thought Control that the enthusiastic response at *Crossfire* previews exorcized "that tired dreary ghost who has been haunting our halls, clanking his chains and moaning, 'The people only want entertainment.'" Writing that August in the *Los Angeles Daily News*, John Paxton argued that films like *Crossfire* were produced so that "audiences, conditioned by the reality of war, would rise up against the old glittering fairy tales." Like the FBI reviewer, anti-Communists considered the film deliberately inflammatory. A few years later, Myron C. Fagan would write in *Red Treason in Hollywood* that "Hollywood Reds" used *Crossfire*—as well as the Oscar-winning anti-anti-Semitic *Gentleman's Agreement* and the 1949 cycle of Negro problem pictures *Home of the Brave*, *Pinky*, and *Lost Boundaries*—to create "racial antagonisms" and inflame "minorities' grievances."

Body and Soul transgressed another sort of racial taboo. The FBI informant considered *Body and Soul*'s portrayal of the fight promoter as corrupt and murderous to be an example of putting "the rich and successful man in a bad light." This criticism was amplified by making the film's "finest character" the black prizefighter played by Canada Lee. While the promoter appeared as "unscrupulous, dishonest, and heartless," Lee (only recently named by Congressman Karl Mundt as a frequent supporter of Communist front organizations) played a character that was "noble and sympathetic."

Other current movies cited as Communist propaganda were William Wyler's Goldwyn production *The Best Years of Our Lives* (utilizing "a trick taught to all young writers in the Communist indoctrination schools": to associate criticism of Russia with "anti-Semitism, Jim Crowism [and] Ku Klux Klanism"), Frank Capra's *It's a Wonderful Life* ("demeaning" portrayals of bankers), Jules Dassin's *Brute Force* ("determined to arouse opposition to constituted authority"), and *The Farmer's Daughter* (aims "to throw mud at the political factions known to oppose Communism"). Schary too was interviewed that summer. SAC Hood's report notes the producer's proud self-identification as a New Deal Democrat and assertion that he did and would continue to employ Communists "until such time as Congress sees fit to pass a law against these people." Schary informed Hood that he was an "intimate acquaintance" of assistant FBI director L.B. Nichols and that Nichols had assured him that "we know all about you . . . and we are not going to investigate you."

The subpoenas arrived in late September. Rossen got one. So did Scott and Dmytryk, both served while sitting in Dore Schary's RKO office. ("Since I was no longer a party man, I took little notice of it," Dmytryk later claimed.) Schary was also invited to testify, as were Jack Warner, Louis B. Mayer, and Sam Goldwyn, the producers, respectively, of *Mission to Moscow, Song of Russia*, and *The North Star*.

Ring Lardner's subpoena arrived while he was revising a script on the Fox lot. Lester Cole was getting his hair cut at the MGM studio barbershop when a laughing Eddie Mannix called to alert him there was a U.S. Marshal with a subpoena in his outside office. Cole immediately called John Howard Lawson at home and discovered that Lawson had just been served. Alvah Bessie, who received his subpoena while staying at a Beverly Hills apartment that belonged to Dmytryk, remembers a feeling of relief and camaraderie: "Everybody was wondering who had received them and was calling everybody else on the phone to inquire. People who had been served were proud of the distinction; others were disappointed until their pink papers arrived."

Cole remembers Herbert Biberman organized the first meeting of the subpoenaed, along with several lawyers, at the home of Lewis Milestone. ("His

summons was a shock to most of us," Dmytryk recalled, "since he had been politically inactive for years." Of course Milestone *had* directed *The North Star*.)
Most were screenwriters (Bessie, Biberman, Bertolt Brecht, Cole, Richard Collins, Gordon Kahn, Howard Koch, Lardner, Lawson, Maltz, Samuel Ornitz,
Waldo Salt, and Trumbo). There were also four directors (Dmytryk, Rosson,
Milestone, and Irving Pichel) and one producer (Scott). Larry Parks, the lone
actor, successfully argued that every position the group would take had to be
unanimous—and, for a time, the town did seem to close ranks.

Within the week, the nineteen witnesses whom the committee considered
"unfriendly" (as opposed to the friendlies who had testified behind closed doors
in May) met again at Edward G. Robinson's place. He wasn't there, nor had he
been served, but liberal Hollywood was mobilized. A large meeting of Democrats was held at Ira Gershwin's house. William Wyler, writer Philip Dunne,
and director John Huston had formed a support group, Hollywood Fights Back,
later renamed the Committee for the First Amendment. Ads were taken out in
the trades.[17]

Cole maintained that he was sent to invite SAG president Ronald Reagan to
a First Amendment meeting.

> It was early evening when I arrived and Jane Wyman, then his wife, came to the
> door. I introduced myself, asked to see him, and she became uneasy. Wyman
> told me Reagan was lying down, not feeling well, but she'd talk to him. She was
> back in moments, I thought seemingly embarrassed, asked me to tell Hum-

---

17. Signatories included Lucille Ball, Richard Brooks, Louise Beavers, Eddie Cantor, Kirk
Douglas, Deanna Durbin, Melvyn Douglas, Jules Dassin, Melvyn Frank, Daniel Fuchs, Henry
Fonda, John Garfield, Ava Gardner, Judy Garland, Henry Hathaway, Van Heflin, Harold Hecht,
Fritz Lang, Burt Lancaster, Audie Murphy, Daniel Mainwaring, Burgess Meredith, Groucho
Marx, Vincent Minnelli, Gregory Peck, Vincent Price, John Paxton, Robert Ryan, Edward G.
Robinson, Donna Reed, Nicholas Ray, George Seaton, Robert Siodmak, Milton Sperling, Frank
Sinatra, Sylvia Sidney, Leo Townsend, Claire Trevor, Franchot Tone, Bernard Vorhaus, Walter
Wanger, Keenan Wynn, William Wyler, Orson Welles, Jane Wyatt, Billy Wilder, Jerry Wald,
Robert Young, and four U.S. senators—Harley Kilgore of West Virginia, Claude Pepper of
Florida, Elbert Thomas of Utah, and Glen Taylor of Idaho.
  Another petition organized (most likely by lawyer Bartley Crum) in the name of the Re-
publican and Democratic Joint Committee of Hollywood (For the Preservation of Civil Liber-
ties and the Defense of the People of the Motion Picture Industry) was signed by Lionel
Barrymore, Charles Brackett, Frank Capra, Bette Davis, Douglas Fairbanks, John Huston,
Walter Huston, Gregory Peck, David O. Selznick, George Stevens, Walter Wanger, William
Wyler, Darryl F. Zanuck, and Minnesota governor Harold E. Stassen, listed as chairman of the
Committee to Defend the Motion Picture Industry Against Unjust Attacks. Four days into the
hearings, Wyler received a letter from Selznick asking "Johnny and Willie" if they would strike
his name, along with Stassen's.

phrey Bogart and Willie Wyler that he was not well, but was thinking seriously about joining them. He would let them know the next day.

He didn't.

The night before the nineteen leave for Washington, where the hearings are to begin on October 20, the Committee for the First Amendment gives them a triumphant send-off at the Shrine Auditorium in downtown Los Angeles. "You would have thought we had the House Committee licked to a standstill before we ever got into the ring," Alvah Bessie will recall.

The mood in Washington is scarcely less festive. Everyone converges on the Shoreham Hotel; although Bessie assumes the rooms are bugged, he is naively awed by the copious amounts of free food and liquor delivered "almost every hour on the hour." Even more heartening is Eric Johnston's reassurance, as reported to the nineteen by their lawyers: "Tell the boys not to worry. There'll never be a blacklist. We're not going to go totalitarian to please this committee." Meanwhile, the committee is preparing to go Hollywood. Earlier that weekend, in the capacious, drafty Caucus Room of the Old House Office Building, the largest available theater for public hearings, J. Parnell Thomas had his screen test—his height bolstered by a silken pillow and the District of Columbia telephone directory.

The show opens Monday morning with all the electricity of a gala premiere. The Caucus Room's three overhead chandeliers are stocked with high-intensity bulbs and used to anchor six baby spotlights. Gordon Kahn will recall the hyperilluminated marble hall as "shadowless as an operating theater"—or, as others describe it, a movie set. Anticipation is high. There are ninety-four journalists in attendance, as well as four radio networks and a battery of newsreel cameras. The front row, per I.F. Stone, is reserved for "the most affluent group of alleged reds in modern history" with "a million dollars in movie names" scattered throughout the audience. Hundreds queue outside for a glimpse of the stars, as they will for the duration of the hearings.

First-called Jack Warner assures the committee that, having suffered through last autumn's Battle of Burbank, he shall make no further movies glorifying "the little man"—no doubt meaning "the common man," a term identified by Ayn Rand as one of the Communists' most egregious. Citing the plague of alien "ideological termites" tunneled into American society, Warner proclaims that he and his brothers will happily and generously subscribe to a pest-removal fund. Then, repeating his performance of the previous May, he offers the committee a dozen names while taking care to disclaim any personal knowledge. "When I say these people are Communists, as I said before, it is from hearsay." He had read it in the *Hollywood Reporter*.

Warner (who so appalls Eric Johnston that the MPAA president calls him a "stupid ass") is followed by Louis B. Mayer. The MGM executive recounts his studio's various contributions to the war effort—notably *Joe Smith, American* and *Mrs. Miniver*—before being directed to the crime that is *Song of Russia*. Like Warner, Mayer assures the committee that MGM has an anti-Communist movie in production. Expert witness (and FBI informant) Ayn Rand gives further testimony on *Song of Russia* at such length that she never gets to dissect her other bête noire, *The Best Years of Our Lives*.

Sam Wood, founding member and current president of the Motion Picture Alliance, is pleased to name names—including Pichel, Cromwell, and Milestone. (That none of these men are Communists suggests that the MPA has contributed as much information to HUAC as the FBI.) Wood also cites Katharine Hepburn's speech at the Wallace rally—a moment that, back in Hollywood, the actress is reliving on the set of Frank Capra's aptly titled *State of the Union*.

Some eighteen months in advance of the 1948 presidential election, shortly before HUAC arrived in Hollywood, Capra acquired the rights to Howard Lindsay and Russell Crouse's 1945 political satire, a play that ran for 765 performances on Broadway and won a Pulitzer Prize. Now, and not without trepidation, he was shooting it.

Principal photography began the week the subpoenas went out, and although Capra was not a recipient, he had cause for concern. HUAC was surely aware of the FBI's August report on *It's a Wonderful Life* suggesting that the movie was practically a Soviet production—credits did not list the various "non-registered Communists" who contributed to the movie, but official screenwriters "FRANCES GOODRICK and ALBERT HACKETT were very close to known Communists" and, while working on a picture at MGM, were observed to take their meals at the commissary's left-wing tables, "eating lunch daily with such Communists as LESTER COLE."

Moreover, the report asserted that Capra was "known to have associated with Left-wing groups." *Mr. Smith Goes to Washington* was "decidedly Socialist in nature" and *It's a Wonderful Life* was even worse, "an obvious attempt to discredit bankers" and "magnify the problems of the so-called 'common man' in society." Claiming that the script lifts a situation from the Soviet movie released in the United States in the early 1930s as *The Letter*, the informant asserts that the movie "deliberately maligned the upper class [by showing] that people who had money were mean and despicable."

That would not be a problem with *State of the Union*, the story of wealthy businessman Grant Matthews—loosely modeled on defeated 1940 presidential candidate Wendell Willkie—who reconciles with his estranged wife in the course of running for president as a moderate-to-liberal Republican. Spencer Tracy was cast as the candidate who, beholden to his press-baron mistress (Angela Lansbury, rehearsing the role she'd play fifteen years later in *The Manchurian Candidate*) and smarmy party boss (Adolphe Menjou), suspends his campaign to protect his integrity. Claudette Colbert was to play Tracy's strong-willed, outspoken spouse until, quarreling with Capra over her salary, she quit three days before she was scheduled to report. Tracy arranged to have Colbert replaced with his paramour, Katharine Hepburn, who had not worked since her speech in May.

The film was in production (and under frequent revision) during the Washington hearings with two players in that drama cast as antagonists on-screen—friendly witness and informant Menjou versus Hepburn, a prominent member of the Committee for the First Amendment and notorious Henry Wallace supporter. Menjou, Hepburn would recall, "was trying to cut my throat at the time we made *State of the Union*. But we were frightfully civilized on the set toward each other. I would pull his leg. I would just torture Menjou. Menjou was *ridiculous*." Or so she thought.

According to Capra's biographer Joseph McBride, the director was so concerned the press might observe Menjou and Hepburn arguing that he attempted to close the set. Still, the *Los Angeles Examiner* did manage to report Menjou's "explosive assaults on producers, directors, writers, and actors who have reputedly become involved in subversive activities." Flying from Hollywood to take the stand Tuesday morning, Menjou testified in praise of the MPA, suggesting to the committee that in addressing the Wallace rally last May, Hepburn had been rallying a stadium full of Communists.

Midweek, the hearings turned even more glamorous: Robert Taylor, Gary Cooper, Robert Montgomery, George Murphy, and Ronald Reagan each took the stand. Photographers pushed to the fore and klieg lights blazed as each enacted the ritual swearing-in. "All heavily sun-tanned, impeccably tailored, glibly rehearsed, it's hard to tell one day's stars from the next," the *New Republic* joked. "They act so much alike. Their testimony is all so inconsequential, carefully according to script. . . . The movie boys are so accustomed to exercising their faces—mugging, laughing, winking, grinning boyishly—that their performances on the witness stand are macabre masterpieces of flirtation. They are flirting with these old, susceptible committeemen and also, according to training, with the banks of cameramen . . ."

Not to mention the crowd. "More than 1,000 shoving, sighing women today mobbed the House caucus room to see film star Robert Taylor," the next morning's *Daily News* reported. "A 65-year-old woman, scrambling on a radiator for a better look at the film star, fell and struck her head. The clothes of others were torn in the mad scramble to the door. "Applause punctuated Taylor's testimony, during which he asked Congress to outlaw the Communist Party ("If I had my way they'd all be sent back to Russia"). After twenty-five minutes on the stand, the star made his departure accompanied by an ovation and, according to the *New York Times*, "shouts of 'Hurray for Robert Taylor' from a middle-aged woman wearing a red hat."

That weekend, the Progressive Citizens of America holds the Conference on Cultural Freedom and Civil Liberties at the Hotel Commodore in New York. Robert Kenny attacks the committee hearings, and Ring Lardner Jr. warns that, if J. Parnell Thomas "is given the right of script approval, any resemblance to American life or democratic notion will be strictly an oversight."

The conference hears a frantic Henry Wallace radiogram from Haifa: "Has America really gone crazy? Is the Un-American Activities Committee evidence that America is traveling the road to fascism?" Meanwhile, a plane furnished by Howard Hughes is en route from Hollywood to Washington, carrying a Committee for the First Amendment delegation led by Humphrey Bogart. Among the other members are Bogart's wife Lauren Bacall, Danny Kaye, Gene Kelly, John Huston, June Havoc, and Marsha Hunt; they will be joined in Washington by a Broadway contingent that includes John Garfield and Elia Kazan.

Even as the CFA stars are in the air, the ABC network broadcasts *Hollywood Fights Back*, cowritten by Norman Corwin. The show is HICCASP's last gasp. Myrna Loy delivers the keynote and Judy Garland furnishes the summation. In between are Lucille Ball, Charles Boyer, Joseph Cotten, Melvyn Douglas, John Garfield, June Havoc, Sterling Hayden, Rita Hayworth, Van Heflin, William Holden, Danny Kaye, Gene Kelly, Burt Lancaster, Peter Lorre, Fredric March, Groucho Marx, Gregory Peck, Vincent Price, Edward G. Robinson, Margaret Sullivan, Walter Wanger, William Wyler, Keenan Wynn, and Robert Young. Are they whistling in the dark? "Is democracy so feeble it can be subverted by merely a look or a line, an inflection or a gesture?" a prerecorded Bogie rasps before Judy Garland's tremulous sign-off: "When they put words in concentration camps, how long will it be before they put men there too?" ("I haven't seen the town so panicky since the banks closed," Frank Capra tells a reporter in L.A.)

When the hearings reconvene on Monday, Congressman Thomas sandbags the CFA. Rather than calling MPAA president Eric Johnston as scheduled, the chairman puts John Howard Lawson on the stand. For a week, Lawson has been repeatedly named as a Communist. Now he gets the chance to act the part. Hitching his pants over what I.F. Stone calls "a rather capitalistic paunch," Lawson is sworn in. Immediately, he attempts to commandeer the hearings with a demand to read his prepared statement labeling Thomas a servant of "forces trying to introduce fascism in this country" and characterizing the committee's "so-called evidence" as provided by "a parade of stool pigeons, neurotics, publicity-seeking clowns, Gestapo agents, paid informers, and a few ignorant and frightened Hollywood artists."

Thomas scans the document and rejects Lawson's request. But the pugnacious writer will not to be denied. Like Eugene Dennis the previous spring, he wags his finger at the committee and declares himself an American: "I am not at all easy to intimidate, and don't think I am." Seizing his historical moment by the collar, Hollywood's most public Communist proceeds to jawbone the committee for nearly half an hour, shouting over Thomas's gavel—which actually breaks under the strain of the chairman's pounding—and boos from the gallery. Finally, after four times refusing to answer questions regarding his Party membership, Lawson is forcibly ejected, still denouncing the committee. Thomas then calls HUAC investigator Louis J. Russell, who documents Lawson's affiliations, complete with CP membership card.

Lawson's strategy—attacking the committee as fascist or worse—is repeated by the next batch of unfriendly witnesses. Tuesday morning, the press table is laden with dossiers on Lawson and the other unfriendlies, thick with clippings from the Communist press. Dalton Trumbo, who approaches the witness stand with an armful of his wartime scripts, warns that "for those who remember German history in the autumn of 1932 there is the smell of smoke in this very room," and Albert Maltz follows with a ringing declaration that he "would rather die than be a shabby American, groveling before men whose names are Thomas and Rankin, but who now carry out activities in America like those carried out in Germany by Goebbels and Himmler." Alvah Bessie concludes the day's hearing by asserting that the committee's "true purpose" is "to provide the atmosphere and to act as the spearhead for the really un-American forces preparing a fascist America."

Wednesday's testimony begins on a similar note, as unfriendly witness Sam

Ornitz accuses Congressman Rankin of emulating Hitler. He is followed by
Herbert Biberman, who opens with the pompous declaration that he "was born
within a stone's throw of Independence Hall in Philadelphia on the day when
Mr. McKinley was inaugurated as president of the United States." According to
Lardner, it was only at the last moment that Biberman was dissuaded from ap-
proaching the witness stand singing "My Country, 'Tis of Thee." Even so, the
writer so maddens Thomas by his persistence in reading his statement that the
chairman directs the guards to take him away. In the confusion, no one seems
to know who is next. Edward Dmytryk is present but Adrian Scott is ill, and
Thomas had planned to interrogate the director and producer consecutively.
Thus SWG president Emmet Lavery finds himself on the stand; Lavery is no
doubt remembering his manhandling by the Tenney committee the previous
year when he is asked by Chairman Thomas if he didn't think "the gentlemen
who appeared before this committee have dramatized Communism to some
degree by the exhibition they put on." He does not, in any case, disagree.

That afternoon, the committee calls Dmytryk, Scott, and Dore Schary. In
his account of the hearings, Gordon Kahn will assert that Scott and Dmytryk
were subpoenaed because they produced and directed *Crossfire;* although neither man is asked about the movie, both attempt to foster that impression.
Dmytryk's statement, which he is not permitted to read, declares that over the
last few years, through pictures such as *Crossfire*, he has devoted himself to the
struggle against racial prejudice. Scott's statement goes further, noting that, in
an attempt to open up a dialogue, he and Dmytryk had encouraged the committee to see *Crossfire*. Sadly, but predictably, "our invitations were ignored. . . .
We expected them to refuse to discuss measures by which the practice of anti-
Semitism could be abolished. To do this would be incompatible with the committee's bigoted record and bigoted support." Scott goes on to cite "the cold
war" that the committee is currently waging against minorities, maintaining
that "the next phase—total war against minorities—needs no elaboration. History has recorded what happened in Nazi Germany." Not surprisingly, Thomas
refuses to allow Scott to read his analysis, remarking, "This may not be the
worst statement we have received, but it is almost the worst."

As with Dmytryk, Russell is recalled to detail Scott's CP membership, after
which Schary is questioned—not about *Crossfire*, but about his associations
with the dread Hanns Eisler, who in the past four years has scored no less than
five movies for RKO. Explaining that he arrived at the studio only last January,
Schary refuses to take responsibility. Only then does the committee remind
him that his employees Scott and Dmytryk have just been revealed as Commu-

nists. Schary denies that their movies had any subversive elements and asserts that he would not fire them or any other Communists unless it was proven that they were foreign agents.

Meanwhile, in New York, Samuel Goldwyn, subpoenaed by the committee but not called to testify, sits and stews in his Sherry-Netherland suite, ten floors above Central Park. The hearings are "a flop" and "a disgraceful performance," the irate mogul tells a *New York Times* reporter. "What do they want us to do, make anti-Communist pictures? Is that the way to bring about peace?" The last unfriendlies—Lardner, Cole, and Bertolt Brecht—appear on Thursday, followed by the mystery witness who turns out to be none other than Louis J. Russell, this time making a convoluted attempt to connect alleged Comintern agents with Hollywood screenwriters Lawson and Biberman in a plot to wrest the Secret of the Whatzit from Robert Oppenheimer.

Poor reviews in the *New York Times*, the *New York Herald Tribune*, and the *Washington Post* have prompted Thomas to bring down the curtain. Hollywood leftists, liberals, and progressives imagine themselves victorious. The Sunday *Worker* splashes a photo of the CFA delegation across page one—Bogart and Bacall front and center and the Capitol dome in the background. Sunday night brings the second installment of *Hollywood Fights Back* with Groucho Marx as a shouting Parnell Thomas, bellowing "no" fourteen times, and Keenan Wynn playing the "friendly" chairman. The tone is generally serious: Thomas Mann questions the "alleged state of emergency"; Dana Andrews, packing to leave to go on location for *The Iron Curtain*, reads a statement from Sam Goldwyn; Hollywood's own congresswoman Helen Gahagan Douglas concludes the evening by calling the hearings a "tragic farce."

The Communists are confident. For a moment, Hollywood appears to have stood its ground. The five unfriendly witnesses with studio contracts return to work; their five freelance colleagues set about looking for work; and Brecht, who testified with a transatlantic ticket in his pocket, departs for Soviet-occupied Berlin. And yet, within two weeks, liberal support will all but vanish.

Back home in New Jersey, Thomas reiterates that his committee's work on Hollywood has only begun, setting the next hearing for December 1. The same day, former assistant attorney general O. John Rogge warns that the Justice Department is planning a "dramatic round up of dozens of Communist leaders and alleged fellow-travelers" to coincide with the special session of Congress that the president has called for November 17. (In fact, Truman wants to ask Congress for the authority to impose price and wage controls.)

The studio heads are confused. Do the American people think that the movie industry condoned and defended the Communists in their midst? Were all witnesses linked in the public mind? Was Hollywood a suspected sinkhole of depravity?

Decision at the Waldorf: The Big Mop-up

As the *Iron Curtain* shoot opened in Ottawa, Canada, the Progressive Citizens of America held a mass meeting at Gilmore Stadium, with seventeen of the original nineteen unfriendlies occupying places of honor. John Howard Lawson accused HUAC of attempting "to secure control of motion pictures through a blacklist and police censorship," claiming that "the attack on the motion picture industry marks an entirely new phase of the drive toward thought control in the United States."

The next day, the committee unanimously approved contempt citations for the ten unfriendly witnesses. RKO announced a new policy against hiring "known Communists" and the Screen Actors Guild resolved that all officers would be required to sign affidavits that they were not Communists. Citing the deluge of Communist "fakery," Eric Johnston moved to distance the Motion Picture Association of America from the newly designated Hollywood Ten. November 22, the *New York Times* reported that, following an action taken the previous day by Twentieth Century-Fox, the MPAA would implement a policy of nonemployment for known Communists.

Thus began Hollywood's purge. The unfriendly witnesses had underestimated the force of HUAC's antipathy and overestimated the studios' resolve. Dore Schary, Samuel Goldwyn, Columbia boss Harry Cohn, and even Louis B. Mayer searched for an alternative to firing the Hollywood Ten. But the New York–based studio executives took a hard line, and despite his previous assurances, Johnston supported their position. Awaiting the House vote, fifty members of the MPAA, along with their lawyers, gathered in New York for a closed-door meeting at the Waldorf-Astoria Hotel, where, among other things, Johnston frightened the producers with the story of a North Carolina audience stoning a screen showing a trailer for a Katharine Hepburn movie (most likely and understandably the Robert and Clara Schumann biopic *Song of Love*). Now only Goldwyn opposed a blacklist.

In Washington, Representative Nixon explained that there were two issues, "whether the Committee had the right to ask the questions—yes—and whether the defendants had refused to answer the questions—yes." The Hollywood Ten were cited for contempt of Congress on November 24. The next day, Johnston issued a statement that, although Hollywood had produced nothing "subversive or un-American," the studios had decided to discharge the Ten and that, although the industry was "not going to be swayed by hysteria or intimidation," the executives in attendance had voted unanimously to refuse employment to all Communists.

A day later, as Schary flew back to Los Angeles to explain the MPAA position to the Screen Writers Guild, his employees Scott and Dmytryk jointly received their dismissals. The next day, Fox terminated Lardner. The Screen Directors Guild met on December 1 and Dmytryk was there, noting, "Interest was great; the hall was crowded." As the SDG's second vice president, Dmytryk made his way through the jostling crowd toward the table for members of the board and executives. "To my great surprise, I saw C.B. DeMille ensconced in an honorary seat." DeMille was neither a board member nor an officer; in fact, he hadn't attended an SDG meeting since his dispute some years earlier with the American Federation of Television and Radio Artists over a $1 contribution. "He did not belong on the dais, but there he was."

Sensing entrapment in "another losing battle," Dmytryk retreated to the rear of the hall to watch the nightmare unfold.

> After the meeting was called to order, one of the directors moved that the evening's vote be cast by secret ballot. The chairman called for the motion to be approved by a show of hands. But as the hands came up, Michael Curtiz [director of the much-maligned *Mission to Moscow*] jumped to his feet, and pointing accusingly in all directions, shouted, "Take their names! Take their names!" . . . In the midst of the hubbub that ensued, DeMille also rose to his feet and screamed at the startled crowd, "This is war! This is war!"[18]

The mop-up operation included disciplining the Committee for the First Amendment. December 6, Hearst columnist George Sokolsky published evidence of Humphrey Bogart's chastisement in the New York *Daily Mirror*. Bogie had sent him a prose poem, "I am not a Communist":

I am not a Communist sympathizer.

I detest Communism just as any other decent American does.

I have never in my life been identified with any group which was even sympathetic to Communism.

---

18. In his recollection of the evening, Dmytryk neglects to mention the speech made in his defense by Robert Rossen.

My name will not be found on any Communist front organization nor as a
sponsor of anything Communistic.

I went to Washington because I thought fellow Americans were being deprived
of their Constitutional Rights, and for that that reason alone.

That the trip was ill-advised, even foolish, I am very ready to admit. At the
time it seemed the thing to do.

I have absolutely no use for Communism nor for anyone who who serves that
philosophy.

I am an American.

And very likely, like a good many of the rest of you, sometimes a foolish and
impetuous American.

The firing of Scott and Dmytryk was, the *Daily Worker* wrote, a victory for
anti-Semitism, but progressives were not giving up yet. *Crossfire*—now Exhibit
A in the Progressive Citizens of America's campaign to "Free the Movies"—was
garnering prizes. Embarrassingly for Hollywood, the movie received *Ebony*'s
annual award for improving interracial understanding and was honored by a
Jewish philanthropic organization in Philadelphia. Schary, the lone Jewish member of the *Crossfire* team, was afraid to attend the banquet, so Johnston accepted
the award on his behalf, giving a brief talk about tolerance in Hollywood.

On December 15, the SWG voted to oppose the blacklist by any legal means
necessary. The same night, Senator Glen Taylor, Democrat of Idaho (and himself a former entertainer), was the principal speaker at a Progressive Citizens of
America "Free the Movies" rally in New York. Taylor attacked HUAC and further opposed outlawing the Communist Party. And suddenly: Henry Wallace!

Joseph Starobin, then the *Daily Worker*'s foreign editor, recalled that Wallace's "leverage in American politics was at its height" when he announced his
independent candidacy. Some thought he'd attract five million votes; others
thought ten. Desperately opposed to Truman, liberals and unionists were fever-
ishly searching for an alternative. At the same time, according to Starobin, "the
Communist Party achieved its largest postwar membership, its greatest battle
readiness and its largest number of connections with other real movements . . .
so important that even opponents were unwilling to ostracize it. Nothing seemed
more favorable to the Party than the fact that a dynamic movement headed by
a prestigious figure, a former vice president, was willing to defend its right to
participate in American political life."

The New Deal coalition might ride again! There was, however, another narrative. The day after Christmas, Republic introduced New York to *The Fabulous*

Texan, a Western about "a free people who throw over a dictatorship" that, already playing the hinterlands, was named by the *Daily Mirror* as "Movie of the Week."

Relatively deluxe for low-budget Republic, *The Fabulous Texan* was produced by Edmund Grainger, who had, seventeen years before, helped invent John Wayne; it was directed by another Wayne associate, Russian-born Edward Ludwig, whose previous credits included the star's 1944 vehicle *The Fighting Seabees*.

Shot during the summer that HUAC came to Hollywood and premiered the week after the Washington hearings ended, *The Fabulous Texan* was, in effect, a low-budget, right-wing riposte to *The Best Years of Our Lives*—albeit conceived well before William Wyler's Oscar-winning drama of returning veterans opened. Having loyally served the Confederacy, Jim (Republic star William Elliott) and Wes (John Carroll) come home to Texas to discover that the land of their birth has become . . . "Siberia"! Under the power-mad regime of the state adjunct general (Albert Dekker), the state police have supplanted the (not yet founded) Texas Rangers.[19]

These storm troopers are confiscating private weapons and censoring newspapers, as well as disrupting a sermon delivered by Wes's father proclaiming that "rebellion to tyranny is obedience to God." The situation is worse than in Eastern Europe; the rebellious reverend is murdered by the state police, and, after his vengeful son shoots the top cop, Texas comes under martial law. Wes turns freedom fighter, heading a guerrilla army, but Jim prefers to seek the legal route as a U.S. Marshal. Yet the federal government declines to act, even when the state police burn down the town: "If the people of Texas want action— they'll take action, if I know the people of Texas," muses President Grant. Is the president anticipating or echoing Adolphe Menjou's ringing declaration before HUAC, "If Communism ever came to the United States, I would move to Texas. I think the Texans would kill them on sight."[20]

---

19. Dekker had represented Hollywood for a single term (1944–46) in the California State assembly. A supporter of the Citizens Committee for the Motion Picture Strikers and the Progressive Citizens of America, Dekker figures prominently in the 1948 Tenney report as a "pro-Communist" member of the legislature. Horace McCoy, author of *They Shoot Horses, Don't They*, who was given a writing credit on *The Fabulous Texan*, is cited in the same report for a screenwriting class taught at the League of American Writers' School in 1943. His key association, however, is with a group of Parisians he never met: around this time Sartre and de Beauvoir (or their acolytes) pronounced him the "first American existentialist."
20. The introduction to *The Fabulous Texan* might have been written for HUAC's benefit: "This story was inspired by the heroic deeds of a war-weary but liberty-loving people over the strangling yoke of political treachery and dictatorship which would enslave free men today."

First submitted to the MPAA's Breen Office in September 1946, the screenplay—originally based on the life of outlaw Sam Bass—required a year to secure approval. Unacceptable aspects included the "glorification" of the Bass character, who, although he endeavored to correct a wrong, nevertheless relied on criminal activities; the rabble-rousing preacher; and the excessive violence ("little less than wanton slaughter"). The delay proved to be a blessing. Everything seemed perfectly justifiable in the aftermath of the committee hearings. Those fabulous Texans were . . . on a mission! The *Hollywood Reporter* was particularly enthusiastic: "At a time when Hollywood films have become a football for Congressional investigations and those in quest of lurking isms, here is a picture with one kind of ism—Americanism."

II.

FIGHTING FOR THE MINISTRY OF TRUTH, JUSTICE, AND THE AMERICAN WAY, 1948–50

Anxiety grows acute. Paranoia becomes normal. The newly named Cold War and the events of 1947 have imbued the industry with a sense of crisis. Hollywood is again mobilized, yet divided against itself. What is American and what is un-? Meanwhile, having declared the National Security State, America's accidental Everyman President struggles to maintain his position.

Visiting Hollywood in early 1948, soon after the Motion Picture Association of America's unexpected capitulation to HUAC, *New Yorker* writer Lillian Ross detects a widespread introspection. The industry is massively preoccupied with its public image.

Friendly witness Rupert Hughes has used *Variety*'s year-end annual to salute Hollywood in language at once exalted and postapocalyptic, wondering if three centuries hence Los Angeles will be filled with "shrines of the graves and birthplaces of moving picture writers, actors and directors." And, more to the point, "What will people three hundred years from now say of us who lived next door to the great geniuses who have created and perfected the world-shaking art of the cinema?"

A Gallup poll has revealed 71 percent of American moviegoers are cognizant of the October hearings. Particularly worrisome: over half of these saw the congressional investigation in a positive light, with 3 percent of them believing Hollywood overrun with Communists. The studio heads, Ross learns, are preparing a campaign that will convince this single-digit percentage of their audience that the movies are Communist-free.

How? Soon after the hearings, Ross discovers, many Hollywood influentials received copies of the Motion Picture Alliance booklet *Screen Guide for Americans*. This codification of Ayn Rand's criteria had already been made available to the FBI; now everyone in the industry had the opportunity to be on the same page. The implication was that the MPA *Screen Guide* would provide a political supplement to the MPAA production code. Citing a particular liberal bugaboo, one studio executive confessed that where he formerly read scripts through the eyes of his boss, he did so now through the eyes of the Daughters of the American Revolution.

William Wyler, one of the three leaders of the Committee for the First Amendment, tells Ross that, in the present climate, he would not have been able to make *The Best Years of Our Lives*—a movie that especially aroused Rand's ire. (Among other things, she singled out the scene wherein a banker denies a veteran a loan as an "all-time low in irresponsible demagoguery on the screen.") Wyler feels there will be no more films like *The Grapes of Wrath* or *Crossfire*, and yet a few progressive movies are in production—the antiwar and pro-tolerance *The Boy with Green Hair* is moving forward at RKO, albeit without its original producer Adrian Scott, and, although financially strapped, John Garfield's independent production company Enterprise is proceeding with its anticapitalist gangster film *Force of Evil*. On the other hand, Warner Bros. has revived its dormant adaptation of Rand's 1943 novel, *The Fountainhead*—a virtual illustration of *Screen Guide for Americans*.

Or perhaps *The Grapes of Wrath* of 1948 is *The Iron Curtain*. Darryl Zanuck's topical venture into "living history" and Soviet espionage has scooped the industry. The production is the talk of Hollywood—not least because of the well-publicized secrecy surrounding its production. One journalist compares the level of security to that around Hollywood's wartime indoctrination and training shorts. Ross hears that another local reporter attempted to breach *The Iron Curtain*'s iron curtain and found himself under investigation, if only by a man from Twentieth Century-Fox.

The Iron Curtain's Ottawa shoot coincided with not only the Waldorf Statement but the espionage trial of McGill professor Raymond Boyer. Igor Gouzenko, who provided characteristically alarming testimony, was again in the news, and the presence of a Hollywood movie on the subject was not universally welcome.

Fox spokesmen reassured Canadians that Gouzenko had no official connection to the production, and after a veterans' group protested against *The Iron Curtain* on Parliament Hill, the government rescinded permission to shoot inside the House of Commons. Both the *Ottawa Journal* and the *Ottawa Citizen* approved. "Canadians," the latter editorialized, "look with no favor on a propaganda stunt calculated to blacken Canada's good name and worsen international relations. Moreover, they do not overlook the fact that tolerance of political views is apparently no longer allowed in Hollywood."

Before the filmmakers left town in early December, the Ottawa Peoples Forum organized another demonstration on the steps of the Peace Tower. A mass rally was promised, although only twenty people showed up to unfurl their banners: "We Want No Iron Curtain Here" and "Hollywood Has Its Own Iron Curtain." A quarter of a century later, director William Wellman would claim that local Commies "ran a car into one of my assistant cameramen. He broke his leg. They didn't get me, but they damn near did." Nothing in the Ottawa or Toronto press substantiates this incident. A month before *The Iron Curtain* wrapped, however, Twentieth Century-Fox and the MPAA both received letters of protest from the Reverend William Howard Melish, the Brooklyn-based Episcopal minister who was the chairman of the National Council of American-Soviet Friendship.

For much of the spring, Melish would orchestrate a drive against the movie (even as his parishioners organized a drive against him). The campaign was on. The day *The Iron Curtain* finished shooting, the *New York Times* helpfully reported the movie was under attack in *Pravda*. Early March brought a surrogate war. The Polish Communist daily *Wolnosc* (Freedom) suggested that *The Iron Curtain* was underwritten by the Canadian government: the Canadian foreign minister and minister of justice were associate producers, the government labor exchange had provided cheap child actors, and Wellman himself had acknowledged the "friendly attitude of higher government circles"! Meanwhile, a copy of the movie's screenplay circulated throughout the Communist world; in an exasperated memo to his staff, Zanuck railed that he wished it were possible for the FBI or somebody to find out how they got it.

The Iron Curtain Parts and the Campaign Begins

The actual iron curtain was rippling that spring. Even as William Wellman concluded shooting, one nation passed into the Soviet sphere and another hung in the balance.

For the past year, the United States had worked to purge the Italian Communist Party (PCI) from that nation's governing coalition. Now there was concern that a Communist-Socialist alliance could win Italy's first postwar election—scheduled for April 18—and, as *Time* put it, bring Europe to the "brink of catastrophe." A classified State Department directive recommended an information program to combat red propaganda; the new Office of Policy Coordination enabled the CIA to embark on a covert political campaign in Italy. Then, in late February, a Communist coup in Czechoslovakia brought down Europe's only other coalition government.

The 1948 Czech crisis inevitably recalled the 1938 Czech crisis that preceded World War II. President Truman privately told his daughter that the situations were analogous and publicly called for the restoration of the draft. Washington buzzed with rumors. With the loss of Czechoslovakia, the former Axis powers— Italy, Germany, and Austria—were now freedom's front line. March 10, a day after General Douglas MacArthur let it be known that he was open to accepting the Republican presidential nomination, General George Marshall warned that the world situation was "very, very serious." On his own initiative, Lieutenant General Curtis LeMay, commander of the U.S. Air Force in Europe, was working up contingency plans for a war with the Soviets.

It was during those urgent days that the writer George Sumner Albee had lunch with a friend. As later recounted by Dore Schary, the pair "got to chatting about the state of the world, particularly man's misuse of certain scientific miracles." Albee, who had spent the war assisting Secretary of the Treasury Henry Morgenthau and was currently authoring commercials for the *DuPont Cavalcade* radio program, wondered what might happen if the next voice to commandeer the troubled airwaves was not Harry Truman or Douglas MacArthur but God. (He quickly fleshed out this premise and, although his literary agent refused to submit it, successfully pitched the idea to the fiction editor at Hearst's *Cosmopolitan*.)

The question of authority was in the air: Americans would soon elect a president, and for the first time since 1932, Franklin D. Roosevelt was not a candidate. A void had opened. Gallup's late-December preference poll, mixing Democratic, Republican, and independent possibilities, had General Dwight D. Eisenhower first (with 18 percent), just ahead of President Truman (17 percent). Behind them were the 1944 candidate Governor Thomas E. Dewey of New York (13 percent); Governor Harold Stassen of Minnesota, Secretary of State George Marshall, and former vice president Henry Wallace tied for fourth (10 percent each); General MacArthur (8 percent); and three more Republicans, Senator Arthur Vandenberg of Michigan, Governor Earl Warren of California (4 percent each), and, ranked last, Senator Robert Taft of Ohio (3 percent).

As 1947 ended, Wallace had announced that he would run as a "new party" candidate, and Marshall was named *Time*'s Man of the Year. There were those who encouraged Truman to take Marshall as his running mate but even more who thought that the unelected everyman should step aside in favor of General Eisenhower. Even after Eisenhower removed himself from consideration, he remained the Democrats' favorite candidate, openly endorsed by FDR's three sons. As war clouds massed over Berlin, many imagined a campaign between two military men. The *New York Times* was not alone in predicting that General MacArthur would win the Wisconsin primary, but MacArthur's refusal to campaign, together with an effective smear operation waged on the boyish Stassen's behalf by the state's junior senator, Joseph McCarthy, resulted in the Minnesotan's resounding victory.

A few days later, the First Family attended the world premiere of *State of the Union* at the Loews Capitol in Washington, DC. Frank Capra's alternately lugubrious and hectoring comedy, in which Spencer Tracy's independent businessman runs for president and reconciles with estranged wife Katharine Hepburn, achieved a certain topicality with its invocation of actual names (Taft, Eisenhower, Truman). Moreover, Capra attempted to address potential campaign issues, defending public housing and health care and envisioning the newly created Marshall Plan as American kids sending surplus bubblegum to their European counterparts.

A would-be master of triangulation, Tracy's candidate attacks labor bosses for leading wildcat strikes and rails against Wall Street for putting profit before the national good. No less than Mr. Smith, he sets himself against the political professionals. He's thwarted, however, by backroom deals struck with assorted sleazebags, as well as the machinations of Angela Lansbury, the right-wing newspaper publisher who is his mistress. Tracy's own campaign manager, Adolphe Menjou, walks out on him when, citing a need to control atomic weapons, the candidate endorses world government ("with or without Russia"). Most reviewers identified Tracy as a version of Wendell Willkie, although the *Daily Worker*, which dismissed his "boy scout platitudes" and requisite Red-baiting, was reminded of Tracy lookalike Harold Stassen. President Truman, however, saw something else.

In the climactic prime-time radio address, Tracy stages a triumphant tactical retreat, hijacking his own campaign ("I'm paying for this broadcast") to reiterate his independence. "I withdraw as a candidate for any office—not because I'm honest, but because I'm dishonest," he announces. "I want to apologize to all the good, sincere people who put their faith in me. . . ." According to Charles Alldredge, a Truman campaign aide who later described this event in *Variety*, the president nearly levitated in his seat. While *State of the Union* "may not have given the President any new ideas," Alldredge believed that the movie "confirmed [Truman's] determination not to quit" the race. The next morning, the White House requested the print for use on the presidential yacht and later asked to screen the movie again at 1600 Pennsylvania Avenue. *State of the Union* "is a scream," Truman would write his sister. "It gives the Republicans hell and, believe it or not, is favorable to your brother."[1]

Back in Beverly Hills, however, Hollywood Democrats had embarked on a new effort to draft Eisenhower. A mid-April announcement of the Hollywood Eisenhower for President committee would be followed by demonstrations and full-page ads in the trade press. This PR campaign was directed by two prominent liberals, RKO's soon-to-resign production head Dore Schary and independent writer-producer Milton Sperling. The campaign collapsed, but both men were named in the April 12 tirade delivered by anti-Communist agitator Myron C. Fagan from the stage of the El Patio Theater in Hollywood. It was the gala reopening night of Fagan's *Thieves' Paradise*, a play about Communism in Bulgaria, and Fagan's mind was racing as he addressed the subject of his own blacklist: "After the Thomas investigation fizzled out, and the 'friendly witnesses' returned from Washington, a strict but secret order had grapevined through all the agents' offices that anybody, *no matter how big a personality*, who would dare to talk about Communism in the motion picture industry would be blacklisted out of Hollywood!"

In other words, Hollywood was still crawling with Commies, protected by the studio bosses. As his first example, Fagan named Katharine Hepburn, whose scarlet reputation had been hastily whitewashed by MGM in advance of *State of the Union*. The star had recanted her infamous speech of May 1947 (and then recanted her recantation). Fagan continued, brandishing a list of one hundred "outright Reds," "members of red front organizations," "fellow travelers," and "poor fools who seek to ingratiate themselves with the Comrades."[2]

Not that the comrades were feeling so swell. The day of Fagan's speech, John Howard Lawson went on trial for contempt of Congress. Judge Edward M.

---

1. Thanks to Alldredge's revelation that *State of the Union* was perhaps "the most important film of 1948," *Variety* headlined his story "Film That Changed History?" Some eight presidential elections later, *State of the Union* intervened in American history once more. During the 1980 New Hampshire primary, candidate Ronald Reagan cast himself as Spencer Tracy by employing the actor's forceful protest—slightly modified to "I'm paying for this microphone!"—to prevent a supporter of rival George H.W. Bush from cutting him off in a televised debate. So decisive was this grasp of Hollywood logic that political commentator Sidney Blumenthal felt that with a single one-liner Reagan had "seized the moment and the [Republican] nomination."
2. These included directors Delmer Daves, John Huston, Robert Siodmak, Orson Welles, Billy Wilder, and William Wyler; actors William Holden, Peter Lorre, Burt Lancaster, Vincent Price, and Keenan Wynn; and producer Walter Wanger. Most had been associated with the Committee for the First Amendment; if some were being watched by the FBI, none had received a HUAC subpoena or been named during the October hearings.

Curran refused to admit the movies Lawson had written into evidence. Nor would he allow Dore Schary, still playing both sides, to appear as a character witness. Lawson was found guilty in scarcely more time than it would have taken the jury to screen *Action in the North Atlantic*.[3]

That evening, Cecil B. DeMille addressed the Economic Club of Detroit on the danger of Communist-controlled unions. Hypercognizant of the world-historical situation, DeMille titled his speech "While Rome Burns"—but, in fact, Rome held firm. Compounding the Lawson verdict, the Communists suffered a crushing defeat in the Italian election, an outcome MGM had influenced through the strategic release of the studio's 1939 anti-Communist satire *Ninotchka*. The movie was widely shown in working-class districts, where the Communists made determined efforts to block screenings; after the election, a PCI organizer reportedly complained, in vintage American, that *Ninotchka* "licked us."

And then there was *The Iron Curtain*, scheduled to open May 12, despite alleged threats on Zanuck's life, in five hundred theaters nationwide. Abandoning the original tagline "THE PICTURE THE GOVERNMENT DID NOT WANT THE PRODUCERS TO RELEASE," Fox promoted *The Iron Curtain* as "THE MOST AMAZING PLOT IN 3300 YEARS OF RECORDED ESPIONAGE!!"

With anti-Communism, per *Variety*, the "hottest" topic to "hit the screen this year," *The Iron Curtain* had been extensively previewed for prominent opinion-makers in New York, including top Hearst executives and Time-Life publisher Henry Luce.

Life anointed Zanuck's production "Movie of the Week," hailing it as the first to stand firmly against Soviet aggression ("The fanaticism, suspicion and amorality which characterize the Communist mind become more graphic and hideous in this one film than in a hundred editorials"), while stablemate *Time* praised the movie as not just "an above average spine-chiller" but "topnotch anti-Communist propaganda." Both magazines included information on the Communist campaign against *The Iron Curtain*, with *Time* opining that the Stalinists and their fellow travelers "recognized and feared" the movie's impact.

Its title dramatically stamped on the screen by a colossal fist, *The Iron Curtain* opens mid–World War II, at the height of Soviet prestige, as three uniformed honchos arrive in Ottawa, along with the humble code clerk Igor Gouzenko

---

3. Another member of the Hollywood Ten, Dalton Trumbo, lost his case in early May, although *Variety*'s front-page headline—"US VERDICT SHOCKS FILM BIZ"—referred to another legal landmark, namely the Supreme Court's decision ordering Paramount to divest itself of its theater chain.

(Dana Andrews). Andrews, who had previously appeared as a heroic Russian bomber pilot in *The North Star* and a sympathetic American veteran in *The Best Years of Our Lives*, here synthesized those roles. His colleagues are chain-smoking NKVD trolls (several played by actors who had specialized in villainous Nazis); they scout for potential spies among Ottawa's bureaucrats and flatter scientists with appeals to their idealism, drunkenly posturing beneath ubiquitous portraits of Stalin and blasting music to obscure their treacherous conversations with supercilious local Commies. Gouzenko—sarcastically described by one colleague as a "simple Russian"—is, by contrast, a straight arrow. He successfully resists the charms of a slinky blond comrade (CFA signatory June Havoc) and pines for his wife (Gene Tierney). When she arrives and they are reunited, she is amazed by his modest apartment: "We have a flat?!"

Although at one point the couple is confused by the sound of a hymn wafting from a neighborhood church, *The Iron Curtain* largely follows the *Ninotchka* scenario in posing Western consumer comfort against Soviet totalitarianism. Mrs. Gouzenko is pregnant and interrupts her husband's critique of democracy to ask if he wants a boy or a girl. (As if cued by a prearranged signal or hidden listening device, a neighbor butts in at that moment to offer them a piece of apple pie.) The simple Russian is decoding new words—"isotope," "neutron," "fission," "plutonium"—when his wife gives birth. The war ends but there's no question of returning to the Soviet fatherland. The clerk's decision to defect is clinched by the innocent babe. "It would be a pity for him to grow up thinking the world is his enemy," he muses. "Someday I'll have to answer to him." The family consults a minister and then goes to the newspapers. Meanwhile the spymaster is instructing a Canadian MP under Communist control to whip up the fronts and fellow travelers: "Start them howling about witch hunts [and] violations of democratic rights."

The Iron Curtain ends happily with a montage of spies being sentenced, as the Gouzenko family enjoys a new life on a bucolic farm. Although they must live in hiding, under constant protection, "they have not lost faith in the future." It was not the *Daily Worker* but the *New Yorker* that pointed out *The Iron Curtain* was "not opposed to treason per se, since the hero is a traitor."

"The documentary screen technique reaches the heights of timeliness," *Variety* announced enthusiastically, predicting healthy grosses. Had so dull a movie ever generated so much excitement? In New York, Fox scheduled a special preview for Tuesday night, May 11, at 10:30 P.M. The show was canceled by the

Roxy management but not in time to head off a bloody fracas. Or was it all a setup?

The evening was unseasonably hot. For some, it was red-hot. *Daily Worker* film critic David Platt arrived on the scene at 10:15 to find the Roxy lobby filled with "20th Century Fox executives, plainclothesmen, cops, FBI agents, and Catholic War Veterans [CWV], all waiting to 'greet' the expected picket-line." The bars on nearby Broadway were packed with CWV types, he thought, and the mood seemed festively pre-pogrom. Meanwhile, only a few blocks west of the Roxy, nineteen thousand Henry Wallace supporters had gathered in Madison Square Garden.

It was that night that Wallace announced his "Open Letter to Stalin," calling on the American and Russian people to take immediate action to end the Cold War. (A few days later, Stalin made a positive response.) When the rally ended around eleven, thousands of progressives flooded Fiftieth Street, most heading for the subway but many—as suggested by one of the speakers—making for the Roxy. Some were prepared, with signs and leaflets, to join the handful of National Council of American-Soviet Friendship demonstrators already there, chanting, "*Iron Curtain* is a gentleman's agreement for war." Others felt as if they were pushed into a cul-de-sac, hemmed in by mounted police and effectively ambushed by irate, drunken reactionaries.

Opinions of the flashpoint vary. *Time*'s reporter saw an anti–*Iron Curtain* picketer clobber a veteran with her pocketbook, while Platt reported "a couple of non-picketing vets with *Journal-Americans* in their pockets" grabbing an anti–*Iron Curtain* banner: "As if by a prearranged signal, the police went into action." Nightstick-wielding patrolmen began to disperse the demonstration, while mounted police charged the crowd, and, as *Time* joked, "for the next half-hour the Roxy's sidewalk was busier than Union Square on an old-time May Day." The police cordoned off and cleared a four-blocks-square area, with demonstrators and onlookers knocked to the pavement amid the splintered picket signs and scattered leaflets. "Not in years has New York witnessed such force and violence against a peaceful demonstration," Platt exclaimed. "The streets neighboring the Roxy soon resembled Nazi Germany." Four young Wallace-ites and two bystanders were arrested for disorderly conduct. The police were "vicious" in clearing the street, one would recall, maintaining he had been stunned into momentary unconsciousness, thrown into the police wagon, and roughed up en route to the precinct house.

Henry Wallace was not in New York to absorb his rally's aftermath. The candidate was en route to Los Angeles, where, among other things, he would dine at the Beverly Wilshire Hotel with four hundred "motion picture notables," meet Charlie Chaplin and Fritz Lang at an "informational" gathering cum discussion of the Stalin letter hosted by William Wyler at his Benedict Canyon home, and address 25,000 supporters at Gilmore Stadium. There, the candidate called on the United States to stand by the newborn state of Israel and condemned the "British-sponsored" Arab Legion. He also noted "the sad truth that freedom of speech already has been partially lost" in Hollywood.

The Iron Curtain opened the following day with uniformed police stationed outside the Roxy and plainclothesmen patrolling within. A bomb scare notwithstanding, the Committee Against War Propaganda picketing and the CWV counterpicketing were orderly. As Arab armies attacked Israel, pickets remained at the Roxy at least through May 25. Fox, which had successfully placed *The Iron Curtain* on the front page of several New York dailies, maintained a "round-the-clock press bureau."

Indeed, *The Iron Curtain* likely received more press coverage than any Hollywood movie released in 1948. It was not only reviewed but subject to political endorsements (Representative John Rankin plugged the picture during House debate on a bill to outlaw the Communist Party) and un-endorsements (Canada's prime minister William Mackenzie King felt obligated to communicate distance from the project). As demonstrations greeted the film throughout America and later the world, Fox presented the controversy as a First Amendment issue.[4]

The reliably liberal *New York Times* critic Bosley Crowther's characterization of *The Iron Curtain* as "an out-and-out anti-Soviet picture," as well as his humorous description of the Russian villains as "granite-faced super-gangster types who, curiously, speak with heavy accents, while Mr. Andrews does not," necessitated publication of Darryl Zanuck's extensive rejoinder: "Granting Mr. Crowther's charge that *The Iron Curtain* contains propaganda, has the screen less right to freedom of expression than books or newspapers?" (Jack Warner might have defended *Mission to Moscow* in the same terms, had he thought of

---

4. No sooner had the movie opened than Hollywood gossip columnist Louella Parsons reported that the American government had rushed prints to Sweden, Norway, Denmark, and "other countries threatened with Soviet domination." Be that as it may, *The Iron Curtain* would be protested in Stockholm, Brussels (which saw two pitched street battles around its premiere), Caracas, and Havana; held up for several months in Argentina; and banned in Siam, Holland, and France. More than an exposé of Communist espionage, *The Iron Curtain* proved useful sucker bait, helping the State Department identify local friends and enemies. Looking for evidence of international conspiracy in the protests, the State Department instructed embassies to monitor local responses to the film.

it.) "But," Zanuck continued, "the picture apparently has more than this in it, or it would not be playing to such crowds."

Perhaps: *The Iron Curtain* was May's second top-grossing movie, then faltered behind *State of the Union*, which, although tepidly received, eventually grossed a healthy $3.5 million to finish fourteenth on *Variety*'s list of the year's box-office attractions. *The Iron Curtain* made $2 million—disappointing but hardly the failure that *Izvestia* gloatingly reported.

Fort Apache, Our Home

C.B. DeMille was more powerful, Frank Capra was closer to a household word, and, thanks to the one-two punch of *Going My Way* and *The Bells of St. Mary's*, Leo McCarey was better paid, but Hollywood's preeminent director was fifty-three-year-old John Ford. No filmmaker had Ford's stature. He was a genuine people's artist, D.W. Griffith's heir as chronicler of the American past.

A filmmaker since 1917, Ford had directed over a hundred movies, including a succession of highly regarded and successful features, largely for RKO and Twentieth Century-Fox, during the 1930s and early '40s. These included *The Informer* (1935), for which he won his first Oscar; *Stagecoach* (1939), for which he was nominated; *Young Mr. Lincoln* (1939); *The Grapes of Wrath* (1940), which gave him his second Oscar; and the Best Picture–winning *How Green Was My Valley* (1941), which garnered Ford an unprecedented third Academy Award for best director.

Ford had also been regarded as a pillar of the Popular Front. In 1936, the left-wing journal *New Theater* celebrated him as an Irish "fighter," a Screen Directors Guild activist, and a "clear-eyed craftsman" who told his interlocutor that "there's a new kind of public that wants more honest pictures. . . . We're fighting the censors and the so-called financial wizards at every point." According to his biographer Joseph McBride, Ford then considered himself "a definite socialistic democrat—*always* left." He was an active supporter of the Spanish Republic and a member of the Hollywood Anti-Nazi League; he campaigned for FDR and, with *The Grapes of Wrath*, ascended to the acme of Hollywood social consciousness.[5]

---

5. Dating from the late 1930s, the FBI's file on Ford details his SDG organizing and support for groups considered Communist fronts, as well as accusations of fellow-traveling and even CP membership. Ford's sense of a new political situation and defensive shift rightward may be gauged by his presence at the February 1944 founding meeting of the Motion Picture Alliance for the Preservation of American Ideals.

During World War II, Ford organized a volunteer unit, the Navy Field Photographic Reserve, which came under the command of Wild Bill Donovan's Office of Strategic Services. Ford's unit was involved in both intelligence and propaganda; he made two Oscar-winning documentaries, *The Battle of Midway* (1942) and *December 7th* (1943); received a Purple Heart for an injury suffered filming in the Pacific; and left the navy as a rear admiral. Ford regarded his four years as an OSS operative, a naval officer, and a documentary filmmaker as the high point of his career. His first movie upon returning to Hollywood was *They Were Expendable*, celebrating PT-boat commander Lieutenant John Bulkeley in the person of actor/war hero Robert Montgomery.

They Were Expendable was followed by two films with Henry Fonda, the star of *Young Mr. Lincoln* and *The Grapes of Wrath*. First, Fonda played Wyatt Earp in the Western *My Darling Clementine*. In *The Fugitive*, based on Graham Greene's *The Power and the Glory* and shot in Mexico, the Popular Front icon was reconfigured as a priest hunted as a traitor by a totalitarian state that has banned the Catholic Church in the service of a better world. Ford's first feature for his new production company Argosy, *The Fugitive* was not just a political statement but Ford's most transparently ambitious movie since *The Informer*, and he would never make another like it. Bathed in holy light and suffused with choral music, this massively arty, self-described "timeless" anti-Communist allegory might have worked as a silent movie. As a talkie, it was insufferable and, despite respectful reviews, a flop.

Argosy's second project, *Fort Apache*, was conceived in early 1947, before HUAC came to Hollywood or *The Fugitive* opened. It materialized in a season of crisis—for the nation as well as Ford's company. The mid-April 1948 world premiere was a veterans' benefit that broke the house record at Chicago's Palace Theater. Rolling out that spring, Ford's cavalry Western opened in New York on June 25—one day after the Soviet blockade of Berlin created a beleaguered Western fort in the midst of hostile Red territory.

All spring, the Soviets were agitated by the prospect of a West German state; in early June, four-power talks on the German question broke down. The situation worsened as the Republican Convention opened in Philadelphia on June 22; the same day New York governor Thomas A. Dewey received his second presidential nomination, the Soviets effectively sealed off Berlin's western sectors. It was during *Fort Apache*'s Broadway run that Jimmy Roosevelt made a last-ditch attempt to draft General Eisenhower as the Democratic candidate, the Democrats split over a civil rights platform, and the Berlin crisis blossomed into the year's second full-blown war scare.

Here was a military Western with a distinctly postwar ambience and intimations of crisis. The anticipatory print ad that ran in the *New York Times* promised "ACTION on 1870 America's explosive Western rim!" employing an image suggestive of the most celebrated military defeat in American history before Pearl Harbor, the Battle of the Little Big Horn, popularly known as Custer's Last Stand. Placing the most notorious encounter of the three-hundred-year-long Indian Wars in the context of the long, costly Apache campaign that began in the early 1860s and continued for another twenty-five years, Ford's first cavalry Western replayed Custer's Last Stand as an incident in an ongoing military struggle.

Fort Apache merged the nineteenth-century war against the Indians with the World War II combat film. Manifesting a new fascination with the post-atomic southwestern landscape, it was set in a mobilized world and dominated by the personalities of rival military leaders. Henry Fonda played the Europeanized martinet Owen Thursday, cast against type in contrast to John Wayne's more relaxed and enlightened Indian-fighter, Kirby York. Fonda was top-billed but Wayne—who would appear in Ford's next two movies—occupied the film's moral center, his attempts at reconciliation with the Apache foe thwarted by Thursday's proud death-wish stupidity.

Unhappily returning home from a European posting, Fort Apache's new commander and eventual "Custer," Thursday, feels shunted aside by an ungrateful war department and was even downgraded from general to lieutenant colonel. *Newsweek*'s reviewer made the connection explicit: "It seems that after the Civil War, just as after the last one, the Army had too many generals on its payroll. Some of them had to be demoted. . . . Thursday is the kind of officer whom second-world-war GI's would have branded as 'chicken.'"

Fort Apache is very much concerned with the making of the American fighting man. The anachronistic twentieth-century anthem "You're in the Army Now" echoes throughout and barely two minutes into the film, Thursday, who is accompanied by his teenage daughter Philadelphia (Shirley Temple), is disrespectfully referred to as "soldier boy." It's as if that insult seals his fate. No sooner has Thursday arrived at the remote outpost, interrupting the annual Washington's Birthday celebration, than he sets about reforming the men now under his command. Their uniform, he snaps, is "not a subject for individual whimsical expression." Thursday does know something about military discipline. Yet he misunderstands the nature of the enemy and hence the war.[6]

For a war movie, *Fort Apache* is exceedingly peaceable. At several key junctures, mutual respect between adversaries has greater valence than military force, and the movie mainly advocates a form of benign containment, restricting the Apache to their reservation. Thursday's second-in-command, the experienced Indian-fighter Kirby York, is not only reasonable but actually accommodating in his dealings with the Apache. Thursday considers the Apache subhuman, degenerate "digger Indians," at least as compared to the noble Sioux. "Your word to a breech-clad savage!" he says with contempt when York defends the diplomatic settlement he negotiated with the Apache leader Cochise. *Fort Apache* advances the notion that there are good Indians and bad ones—and York is admirably able to distinguish between the two.[7]

In some respects, Ford remained a liberal. *Fort Apache* not only established a template for its own genre but also revised the Western with notions of racial tolerance. ("The sin of racial pride still represents the most basic challenge to the American conscience," Arthur Schlesinger would maintain in *The Vital Center*, the bible of Cold War liberalism, completed while *Fort Apache* was in release.) In that sense, *Fort Apache* was fellow traveler to the anti-anti-Semitism of the previous year's *Crossfire* and *Gentleman's Agreement*, anticipated the following year's racial melodramas *Pinky* (which Ford was originally set to direct), *Lost Boundaries*, and *Home of the Brave*, and even provided an analogue of sorts to what was then happening at the Democratic convention, where southern segregation was under attack.

---

6. Is Thursday Ford's version of MacArthur? Historian Richard Slotkin notes that, having served under MacArthur's command, Ford was familiar with the general's foibles: Thursday shares MacArthur's "aristocratic pretensions" and "inordinate vanity," as well as his "deserved reputation as a student of war" and for courage under fire. MacArthur too committed soldiers to a last stand (at Bataan), and if he was not as culpable as Thursday, he nevertheless made questionable tactical decisions. However, unlike Thursday, MacArthur did not make a stand with his men; he was ordered to abandon the Philippines and regroup in Australia. This damaged MacArthur's reputation and, Slotkin writes, required considerable public relations rehabilitation. "Perhaps more damaging, to a knowledgeable insider like Ford, were instances in which MacArthur's troops fought and died unnecessarily to make good erroneous press releases."
7. Thursday's insulting speech to the elderly Cochise is drawn almost verbatim from the basis for *Fort Apache*'s screenplay, James Warner Bellah's "Massacre," a story that proudly invokes the concept of the white man's burden and evinces a visceral loathing for what he elsewhere termed the "red beast in the night." Frank Nugent's script modifies Bellah's story. In the movie, the Apache are not villains but rather the victims of government-sanctioned criminal exploitation. Nor is the redskin menace monolithic. The reasonable Cochise, a "veteran" like York, is opposed to the young and irresponsible war leader Geronimo—introducing a dichotomy that would continue to characterize the cavalry Western.

Tolerant of Indians, *Fort Apache* further shows America defended by two out-groups—alienated ex-Confederates and déclassé Irish Catholic immigrants—both key elements of the New Deal coalition, both stoically doing society's dirty work. That Custer's martyrdom helped transform these minorities into the gallant heroes of the Seventh Cavalry is essential to the *Fort Apache* scenario. Thursday's contempt for Philadelphia's suitor, Michael O'Rourke (John Agar, Temple's actual husband), extends his class snobbery to the Irish. Life at the fort is characterized by constant socializing. Identified with tender domesticity, the soldiers of the Seventh Cavalry spend as much time dancing as they do fighting. Despite the harshly alien landscape and general absence of settlers, the abundance of women on the base makes *Fort Apache* as much a town Western as a combat film. Even Ford's version of Custer is a family man who fondly promises Philadelphia that she's going to make "a proper soldier's wife."

And yet, as nineteenth-century as it is, Ford's heroic daguerreotype puts postwar American life in an apocalyptic light. James Warner Bellah's tales of the U.S. cavalry appeared in the *Saturday Evening Post* along with Robert Heinlein's science fiction stories—each writer, in his way, offering an imaginative gloss on the magazine's Cold War reports and analyses. But *Fort Apache* might be set on one of the desert settlements of another science fiction writer, Ray Bradbury. Like the melancholy tales of interplanetary pioneers eventually collected as *The Martian Chronicles* that Bradbury began publishing in the late 1940s, the *Fort Apache* scenario merges the home front with the perimeter.

Fort Apache is a vision of total mobilization with an appropriate emphasis on order and eternal vigilance: militarized suburbia. The bombing of civilian populations in World War II suggested that the next war might have no front—or, rather, that the front might be in America's living room.

Expanding from Chicago, *Fort Apache* racked up "bang-up" grosses and made "big wampum" throughout May as it played Pittsburgh, Cleveland (where it upset *The Iron Curtain* as the week's "real smash"), and Los Angeles to finish fourth for the month. June was even better. New York was "loaded with Westerns," according to *Variety*, yet *Fort Apache* enjoyed five weeks at the Capitol, a theater without air-conditioning.[8]

Fort Apache saved Argosy, but the reviews were mixed. *Variety* deemed the movie blatantly commercial; if *Newsweek* was tolerant (veteran actors "succeed

---

8. The movie finished third for June and seventh for July. *Variety* estimated its 1948 grosses as $3 million, tied for twenty-first place with RKO's other hit, the supernatural fantasy *The Bishop's Wife*.

in bringing back the time-honored business of making redskins bite the dust as first-rate entertainment"), *Time* was less enthusiastic. James Agee called *Fort Apache* "an unabashed potboiler" with "many protracted and unrewarding views of domestic life around the post," not to mention "some of the bleakest Irish comedy and sentimentality since the death of vaudeville."

Others found the movie inert. Ironically saluting the "Oscar bait" photography, the *New Republic* saw *Fort Apache* as evidence that Hollywood had lost the knack for "the Custer's Last Stand sort of thing." Apparently harking back seven years to the glorious martyrdom of *They Died with Their Boots On*, Robert Hatch pronounced the climax "as dull a massacre as ever you've seen" while, in an odd complaint for a liberal journal, "the Indians are presented not as heathen devils but as a minority group with a grievance." Ford looked at postwar America and saw Fort Apache.

Reflecting in a 1955 essay upon the development of the Western, the French critic André Bazin would point out that World War II had effectively removed the genre from Hollywood's repertoire in favor of movies dealing explicitly with military combat. When the war ended, the Western reappeared—but with a difference. History, which had previously been merely the Western's material, was now its subject. (And Bazin noted that this was particularly true of *Fort Apache*, the movie that initiated the Indian's "political rehabilitation.")

Bazin was put off by the postwar development he termed the *surwestern*—a Western "ashamed to be just itself" and shouldering a burden of sociological, moral, or political content. In a turn of the dialectic personified by John Wayne, the innocent cowboy film assimilated the combat film to become the Cold War's preeminent ideological genre. Thus, *Fort Apache* ends with a flurry of political symbol making. Ford demystifies Custer's Last Stand only to remythologize it. The process begins even as Thursday leads the regiment out to battle. As the troops march to their doom singing "The Girl I Left Behind Me," one veteran officer's transfer back east comes through. His gallant wife refuses to embarrass him by conveying the news: "I can't see him," she explains. "All I can see is the flags." He's already legend.

Virtually unnoted by contemporary reviewers, *Fort Apache*'s now-notorious postscript meditates on the value of propaganda. The alchemy that transformed the Battle of the Little Big Horn into the myth of Custer's Last Stand was performed by American journalists. In *Fort Apache*, a passel of credulous reporters serve the same function, allowing the audience to understand that the conflict between Thursday and York has resulted in the successful repackaging of Thursday's position. Military idiocy and know-nothing chauvinism may have their value after all!

York, now the fort's commander, stands before a painting of Thursday's Charge (which represents the Apache as crypto-Sioux) and stubbornly refuses to debunk Thursday's battlefield glory: "No man died more gallantly." What's more, the soldiers led by Thursday to an apparently meaningless death will keep on living as long as the regiment lives. The movie's final shot shows York leading the regiment out of the fort. He has not only inherited Thursday's command but also adopted his Frenchified kepi headgear. There are no more liberals and conservatives, only blue coats and redskins.

Asked about *Fort Apache*'s ending, Ford would explain, "We've had a lot of people who were supposed to be great heroes, and you know damn well they weren't. But it's good for the country to have heroes to look up to." By showing Custer as a martinet and then allowing John Wayne to endorse the mythologizing of his defeat, *Fort Apache* has it both ways—a movie that is at once a demystification and an argument in favor of rewriting history as patriotic propaganda. The Battle of Little Big Horn was not only a necessary defeat—Custer's Last Stand was a necessary falsification.[9]

A former OSS man, Ford undoubtedly knew something about the strategic use of fiction. (It was while *Fort Apache* was in release that the U.S. National Security Council established the Office of Special Projects to administer "deniable" operations.) Whether or not Thursday is Ford's portrait of General Douglas MacArthur, York expresses the wisdom of Ford's wartime commanding officer (and current business partner) Wild Bill Donovan.

Implicit in America's Cold War role is the promise of a permanent garrison state, and implicit in the permanent garrison state is the necessity for a new martial religion.

---

9. On the eve of the 1980 election, Henry Fonda and John Wayne were opposed once more in the Dream Life. Fonda moderated President Jimmy Carter's final appeal to the voters, while in the half-hour all-network spot his campaign purchased, challenger Ronald Reagan evoked Wayne: "Last year I lost a friend who was more than a symbol of the Hollywood dream industry. To millions he was a symbol of our country itself. Duke Wayne did not believe our country was ready for the dustbin of history. Just before his death he said in his own blunt way, 'Just give the American people a good cause, and there's nothing they can't lick.'" Meanwhile, *Fort Apache* itself had become emblematic of American malaise. Released a few weeks after Reagan's inauguration, *Fort Apache, the Bronx* dramatized a South Bronx precinct house as a beleaguered bastion of civil order in a chaotic, violent, and derelict urban landscape.

Trumping the Czech coup and the Italian election, the Berlin Airlift is the year's preeminent spectacle—a costly but successful demonstration of the Truman Doctrine and the Marshall Plan in action. This long-running drama mobilizes American public opinion. As the Germans are recast as victims, the erstwhile Russian ally is assigned the role of aggressor, besieging a lonely outpost on freedom's frontier.[10]

Democrats project a Fort Apache under attack from without; Republicans imagine the fort subverted from within. July 20, only two days before the new Progressive Party will meet in Philadelphia to nominate Henry Wallace, a federal grand jury indicts twelve Communist Party leaders for violating the Smith Act in conspiring to "teach and advocate the overthrow and destruction" of the American government through "force and violence." The day the Progressive convention opens, *Daily Worker* film reviewer turned Hearst anti-Communist Howard Rushmore—a friendly witness at the past October's hearings—publishes a piece asking when the Truman administration plans to arrest the "more than 150 former and present New Deal employees" who, for over a decade, have operated a "Russian espionage ring in Washington."

Rushmore's next story begins by asserting that "a 'very high official' of the New Deal Administration passed along to the Soviet Union key ingredients in the early experiments on the atomic bomb." Is the official in Rushmore's scenario the Progressive Party nominee? That is scarcely the only question before the American people. "Could the Reds Seize Detroit?" *Look* wonders. *Cosmopolitan* publishes "The Next Voice You Hear" (soon MGM's new production head Dore Schary will buy the rights), but the summer's most resonant parlance belongs to *Time* writer and editor Whittaker Chambers.

Testifying before HUAC, Chambers maintains that, while a courier for Soviet intelligence in the late 1930s, he knew the former State Department official

---

10. April 12, 1949, even as the United States and Soviet Union engaged in prolonged back-channel negotiations regarding Berlin, Twentieth Century-Fox announced a movie on the Cold War's first great military victory. Writer-director George Seaton had already spent two months in the new Fort Apache, meeting with air force brass and soaking up atmosphere. Production began even before the script was finished, as soon as the blockade was lifted in mid-May. Soviet and East German attacks on the nonexistent shooting script began then as well.

Filmed in all four Berlin sectors, *The Big Lift* was the Cold War's most "official" production. The air force airlifted the production's equipment to Berlin, and save for stars Montgomery Clift and Paul Douglas, all U.S. military personnel were played by actual U.S. military personnel. Seaton assured the Air Force Public Affairs Office that filming the airlift "would be of even more dramatic value than the lift itself." (For its part, the State Department reportedly cautioned the filmmakers against excessively vilifying the Russians.) Once more, Zanuck had created an exercise in living history—a sequel to *The Iron Curtain*.

and Wallace protégé Alger Hiss as part of a Washington, DC, group of red New Dealers. The next day, at his own request, coolly patrician Hiss confronts plump, shifty-looking Chambers and convincingly denies his allegations. Someone has to be lying, and the committee's smartest member, Richard Nixon, decides to let a grand jury figure out whether or not the liar is Hiss.

Wallace charges HUAC with "political gangsterism and tyranny," accusing its members of scaring the American public by manufacturing crises on behalf of "international capitalists and munitions makers." Soon after, Representative Rankin demands Wallace be subpoenaed to explain how Communists like Hiss came to be placed in key government positions while FBI informant Louis Budenz (who, along with Elizabeth Bentley, had named a number of Wallace supporters as Soviet spies) publishes an article in *Collier's* claiming that Wallace himself was recruited as Stalin's designated candidate during a wartime trip to Siberia.

As HUAC takes the lead in attacking the Truman administration as soft on Communism, the campaign unfolds amid inquisitions and spy scares. "The next major step in the Thomas Committee investigation of Communist espionage in the United States will deal with the theft of the atomic bomb," the *New York Sun* had promised in mid-August, revealing that "evidence in committee hands points to the fact that the atom bomb secret was handed over to the Reds." In early September, HUAC issues a twenty-thousand-word report, *Soviet Espionage Activities in Connection with the Atom Bomb*, accusing the administration of inexcusable laxity in apprehending atom spies.

A portion of HUAC's election-year special is even telecast from Capitol Hill to Washington's ten thousand TV receivers. Timed to open as the hearings closed, Columbia's single minded procedural *Walk a Crooked Mile* provides a sort of sequel. This dark and moody thriller, directed by Gordon Douglas from George Bruce's script, focuses on a Communist spy ring operating in the fictitious Lakeview Laboratory of Nuclear Physics, an Oak Ridge–style top secret residential research facility located outside Los Angeles and guarded by the FBI.

Communists have thoroughly infiltrated an atomic Fort Apache. Early on, an FBI informer is gunned down phoning the Bureau with a "red-hot" tip. Effete and vaguely foreign, the Communists seem to have constructed their operation as a metaphor for Hollywood. They embed stolen secrets in oil paintings and hold cell meetings in the Lakeview Art Shop. Teaming up with Scotland Yard in an Anglo-American alliance, the FBI discovers that the traitor is a nuclear scientist. Indeed, the scientist turns out to be an upper-class WASP of impeccable ancestry; captured when the FBI storms a Communist safe house, he plays the Hollywood Communist to the hilt, arrogantly refusing to submit to the Bureau's "Gestapo practices," loudly insisting on his loyalty and constitutional rights until the disgusted FBI agent forces open the scientist's fist to reveal a secret formula scrawled on his palm.

Punched across by a *March of Time*–style voice-over and replete with didactic demonstrations of FBI laboratory and surveillance techniques, this fictional semidocumentary exposé is excitedly received by the trade press—although the *New York Times*'s Crowther finds it odd the FBI would lend its name to a movie as "specious and irresponsible as this little job."[11]

Negotiations over Berlin stalled, and the presidential campaign began amid rumors that, as Harry Truman noted in his diary after a mid-September military briefing, "We are very close to war." September 19 in Dexter, Iowa, Truman boarded the Presidential Special and began his "give 'em hell" whistle-stop tour; four days later, he arrived in Los Angeles to address fifteen thousand supporters at Gilmore Stadium.

The rally was coordinated by Warner Bros. producer Bryan Foy and involved much of liberal Hollywood. The welcoming committee included Melvyn Douglas (husband of Representative Helen Gahagan Douglas), John Garfield, and Robert Ryan. Lucille Ball and Desi Arnaz entertained the crowd, and Humphrey Bogart and Lauren Bacall were on the rostrum, as was Ronald Reagan—Hollywood's most prominent Americans for Democratic Action organizer—who stood at attention beside the president during the national anthem.

The next night, his arrival in California heralded by sky-sweeping searchlights, presumptive winner Governor Thomas E. Dewey addressed a crowd estimated by the *Los Angeles Times* as twenty thousand at the Hollywood Bowl. According to *Time*, the Republican candidate had picked Los Angeles as the appropriate setting for his "all-out attack on Communism." Dewey repeated the HUAC charge that the Truman administration was coddling the Commies.

Then, after chorus girls danced in formation and stars filed to the microphone, the candidate proposed to defeat the Soviet threat with a "mighty," "worldwide" "counteroffensive of hope" created by Hollywood. "Let's put Americans who know how to do this job in charge on it and let's tell our magnificent story of freedom as it can be told. . . . I am happy to have the opportunity to

---

11. *Walk a Crooked Mile* was filmed in the late spring of 1948, some months before Chambers accused Hiss of espionage. The apparent target was physicist Edward U. Condon, who had resigned after ten weeks as J. Robert Oppenheimer's deputy after clashing over security issues with General Leslie Groves.

make that proposal here at the world capital of the motion picture industry. Your industry is proof of the miracles that come to pass under our free system of productive enterprise." Without using the word "propaganda," Dewey called for movies that were not only entertaining but would also celebrate "the wonders of freedom and production under an enterprise system and the Bill of Rights." Dewey's industry supporters included three members of the Motion Picture Alliance: George Murphy, chairman of the Hollywood Republican Committee; Ginger Rogers; and Gary Cooper, who had recently completed his work on *The Fountainhead*.

Henry Wallace showed up the following week, addressing 22,000 partisans at Gilmore Stadium, where he was introduced by Robert Kenney, former state attorney general and lawyer for the Hollywood Ten. Unlike candidate Dewey, Wallace took a dim view of recent Hollywood product—and propaganda. He made a point of criticizing the industry (or, at least, Darryl Zanuck) for making "fatuous unrepresentative films under intellectual standards dictated by the House Un-American Activities Committee." Where the Progressive Citizens of America had once enjoyed a high industry profile, there were very few public Wallace supporters in Hollywood. These included Gene Kelly, Frank Sinatra, Edward G. Robinson (all of whom would come under pressure), and the actor Gary Merrill, who was among the narrators of *Strange Victory*, a feature-length independent documentary—produced by future publisher Barney Rosset and directed by Leo Hurwitz from Saul Levitt's screenplay—that might have been made for Wallace's campaign.

Given its extremely limited release, *Strange Victory* might also function as a metaphor for the Wallace campaign, as well as its assumptions. Fort Apache was *not* under attack. And yet, as the narration put it, "a fear runs through the country. . . . We feel haunted in broad daylight." Americans won the war against Hitler, but somehow "the native custom of race hatred was back," embodied in lynchings, right-wing demagogues, and HUAC. (The film's motto could have been taken from William Blake: "They became what they beheld.")

Strange Victory's press releases attempted to associate the movie with *Gentleman's Agreement* and *Crossfire*—and in one scene anti-Semitic placards were even juxtaposed with a poster for the latter film. *Variety*'s review noted that *Strange Victory* lacked even a single mention of "the Red question . . . just as if there were no problem at all," and one Hollywood insider for whom Rosset screened the movie warned him that criticizing HUAC was impolitic. Amazingly, only the *Daily News* review characterized *Strange Victory* as Communist.

The most popular movies that fall included the Warner Bros. melodrama *Johnny Belinda*, which would win an Oscar for Ronald Reagan's then-wife Jane Wyman; Leo McCarey's *Good Sam*, an allegorical comedy with Gary Cooper as the eponymous Good Samaritan; and Howard Hawks's epic Western *Red River*, en route to finishing as the year's third-highest-grossing picture and establishing John Wayne as America's reigning male star. Meanwhile, Harry Truman was putting on a remarkable performance.

As H.L. Mencken wrote, "the Missouri Wonder was roving and ravaging the land, pouring out hope and promise in a wholesale manner. . . . What had Dewey to offer against all this pie in the sky?" Dewey, per Mencken, was "a good trial lawyer, but an incompetent rabble-rouser" who addressed the "great multitudes as if they were gangs of drowsing judges." Truman, by contrast, appealed directly to their self-interest: "While Dewey was intoning essays sounding like the worst bombast of university professors, Truman was on the ground, clowning with the circumambient morons. He made votes every time he gave a show. . . . If he did not come out for spiritualism, chiropractic, psychotherapy and extra sensory perception it was only because no one demanded that he do so."

By mid-October, even *Time* noted Truman's "growing entertainment value." Noting the "pleased but oddly silly smiles" of the crowds who, perhaps out of curiosity, flocked to see the president in eastern Pennsylvania, the newsweekly felt that "for all their friendliness, [Truman's] listeners acted more like a vaudeville audience than a political crowd." The same issue noted, with some amusement, another show business first—the sixteen-page campaign comic book *Harry S. Truman, Farm Boy, Soldier, Statesman, President*, drawn by former *PM* cartoonist Jack Sparling.

The spectacular airlift was working as well. Still, nearly every reporter, newspaper, and polling operation predicted an overwhelming Dewey victory. Bookies had Truman a 15–1 underdog. The Democratic National Committee made no plans for a victory party. Both *Time* and *Life* confidently prepared their postelection editions in advance of the actual voting. The morning after the election, the *Chicago Tribune* made newspaper history with the headline "DEWEY DEFEATS TRUMAN."

In fact, Truman—the personification of the common man—beat Dewey by nearly the same margin of victory that the Gallup poll had projected for Dewey: 49.6 percent to 45.1 percent. Wallace received 2.37 percent of the vote, virtually all of it in New York City and California. (Dixiecrat Strom Thurmond got slightly more—2.41 percent—as well as thirty-nine electoral votes.) The New Deal coalition held on to beat the Republicans one last time.[12]

Strange Victory integrated newsreel footage with newly shot material in and around New York, employing a moody modernist score to enhance the overall anxiety. This downbeat paranoia anticipated the tone of Abraham Polonsky's *Force of Evil*, which, having wrapped at the height of the August HUAC hearings, opened in New York on Christmas Day 1948.

Adapted by Polonsky and the Pulitzer Prize–winning reporter Ira Wolfert from Wolfert's 1943 novel *Tucker's People*, *Force of Evil* was the greatest of Hollywood's red movies—as well as the industry's most radical view of Fort Apache. The threat in this openly anticapitalist gangster film is the system itself. *Force of Evil* was produced by John Garfield's Enterprise; no less than its resident star, the outfit had something of a Group Theatre mystique. Many of the creative personnel were openly left-wing. Some—including Polonsky, Robert Rossen, and John Berry—were Communists.

Rossen's *Body and Soul* (1947) had been tremendously successful, and Polonsky was seen as a hot writer, wooed, he would recall, by no less a star than Ginger Rogers: "She wore a fur bikini outfit, and she took me down to her cellar and made me a black-and-white ice cream soda. She was very affable and nice." But other Enterprise productions fared less well. *Arch of Triumph*, adapted from Erich Remarque's novel of political refugees and displaced riffraff trapped in Paris on the eve of World War II, was an expensive fiasco. *Time* put the budget at a hefty $5 million; *Variety* reported grosses of $1.7 million. Directed by Lewis Milestone, one of the original Hollywood Nineteen, the movie had its premiere the day of the Czech coup; its reception suggested that, three years after the war's end, the antifascist thriller was a hopeless anachronism.

Polonsky began work on the *Force of Evil* screenplay in early 1948, soon after the HUAC hearings and shortly before *Arch of Triumph* opened and effectively ruined its production company. Joe Morse (John Garfield), a street kid grown into an ambitious lawyer, implements a fix that will allow his boss, the numbers kingpin Ben Tucker (Roy Roberts), to consolidate his racket by driving the

---

12. Truman had run against the Republican-controlled Eightieth Congress. The Democrats would now run the Eighty-first Congress. Minneapolis mayor Hubert Humphrey, the Democratic convention's civil rights firebrand, was elected to the Senate—as was the future vice crusader and presidential aspirant Estes Kefauver of Tennessee. But, with Dewey's second defeat, conservatives took control of the Republican party.

small number banks out of business. One of these banks is run by Morse's delusional older brother, Leo (Thomas Gomez). A victim of Joe's attempt to manipulate the system, he is set up and killed.

An obvious art film, made with a surplus of shadows and a surfeit of colorful characters, *Force of Evil* is completely straightforward in its insistence on capitalism as crime. ("Waddaya mean gangsters—it's business," one enforcer whines, nearly a quarter-century before *The Godfather*.) Everything is money. The opening line, "This is Wall Street," hangs over the dealings. Much of the action is overshadowed by the skyscrapers of New York's financial district, and Leo's neighborhood bank suggests nothing so much as a Ma and Pa candy store or a struggling little dress factory.

In a telephone call made to Wolfert on March 20, 1948, during the aftermath of the Czech coup and the time of the burgeoning Berlin war scare, Polonsky described a studio executive's reaction to his script: "What are you trying to do—overturn the system?" The term "system" is ambiguous. Polonsky and Wolfert's initial script was rejected by the Breen Office and then Columbia, to which producer Bob Roberts had first brought the project. *Force of Evil* then reverted to Enterprise, itself acquired by MGM.

Polonsky revised the script throughout April and May in advance of a June start. The movie wrapped in early August, its production coinciding with the disaster of *Arch of Triumph* and Enterprise's collapse. Polonsky had told Wolfert that he was planning to set his revised story during the Depression to provide motivations for the honest characters involved in the racket and also to confound the movie's presumed censors: "We take their minds off the real point of the story." Most likely to placate the Breen Office, Polonsky concocted a framing narrative: the story would unfold in flashback, with Joe Morse giving testimony in a state rackets probe.[13]

Unavoidably recalling the HUAC hearings of the past year (and eerily anticipating the star's own fate), the device was dropped in favor of Garfield's voice-over explanation. Polonsky was still shooting retakes in late November, barely a month before MGM released the movie, cut by twenty minutes. Evidently the MPAA office, if not Dore Schary, compelled the filmmaker to make it

---

13. In Hollywood, as in *Force of Evil*'s New York, the authorities are understood to be passive and cynical—they are most present through their extensive telephone surveillance, the source of one of the movie's most elaborate scenes. This plot device takes on particular resonance in that Polonsky's own line was being monitored and he knew it. When he declined to tell Wolfert which studio was interested in the film, Wolfert asked if the phone was tapped. "Yep," Polonsky replies. "By the FBI—not by the studio." Both men laugh then—if not last.

clear that Joe had learned his lesson and, now a positive informer, was prepared to testify against Tucker.

Hollywood Alert: From *Red Menace* to *Storm Warning*

Harry Truman won a legendary victory in 1948; John Wayne entered the Dream Life. Thanks to *Red River* and *Fort Apache*, Wayne was named the year's fourth-biggest box-office attraction—cracking the top ten for the first time to edge past Gary Cooper as America's ranking action star.

Before 1948 ended, Wayne acted in two more movies for John Ford—*Three Godfathers* and the cavalry Western *She Wore a Yellow Ribbon*—and, like the president, he became the protagonist of his own comic book, *John Wayne Adventure Comics*. On March 29, 1949, Wayne followed Truman into politics, succeeding Robert Taylor as president of the Motion Picture Alliance for the Preservation of American Ideals.[14]

America was fighting back. That past weekend in New York, a thousand anti-Communist picketers ringed the Waldorf-Astoria, where the Cultural and Scientific Conference for World Peace had convened in the midst of the longest criminal trial in American history (ten subway stops downtown, eleven CP leaders were charged with sedition). Speaking at a panel on mass communications, John Howard Lawson assured fellow participants that "the fight for the conscience, for the soul, of the American film is not ended. The struggle centers around the Hollywood Ten," who were honored "to be chosen as leading defenders of the art we love." The day the conference ended, nine Communists who refused to answer the questions of a federal grand jury in Los Angeles were thrown in jail.[15]

Even as Wayne's friends in the Motion Picture Alliance prevailed on him to take the job and his MPA colleague Sam Wood called for an end to "the mania for inserting messages and social significance in films" and a return to "the simplicity, the warmth and human quality that fall under the heading of hokum," *Fortune* announced that the alliance itself had prevailed: "Not an alleged

---

14. Members of the new executive committee included actors Ward Bond, Gary Cooper, Clark Gable, Adolphe Menjou, Pat O'Brien, and Robert Taylor, as well as screenwriters Borden Chase and James K. McGuinness and directors John Ford and Leo McCarey.

15. In addition to Lawson and four other members of the Hollywood Ten, peace conference sponsors included Charles Chaplin, Thomas Mann, Albert Einstein, Henry Wallace, Norman Mailer, Arthur Miller, Marlon Brando, Brando's *Streetcar Named Desire* co-star Kim Hunter, Joseph Losey, and Jules Dassin.

Communist is visible [in Hollywood], except for the featured 'Unfriendly Ten.' The others, defeated in union and guild, are reported underground." The real "red menace," *Fortune* revealed, was red ink. The magazine's lengthy analysis of Hollywood began by asserting, "After a year of confusion the major representatives of the motion-picture industry have concluded that there is no crisis in the movies and there never was one. No crisis. Only this: Hollywood is in the red as a result of rising costs and falling revenues. . . . Domestic box office is off. The industry knows it the way the early American Indians knew when it was winter, without a calendar. It appears that a lot of Americans just do not like the movies as much as they used to."

Fortune noted that, because the typical gestation period for a motion picture was at least a year, expensive productions were failing to recoup their money in a smaller marketplace. But the lag also meant that the first movies put in production in the wake of the late-1947 HUAC hearings and the MPAA blacklist were now being readied for release just as the Cold War's key fictional text appeared.

George Orwell's *1984* was published in the United States and Britain in June and went on to sell over four hundred thousand copies during its first year. Orwell's fiercely unfunny satire projected a shabby, terrorized dystopia wherein a cynical elite ruled over a dilapidated domain of slogan-spouting clerks and mindless proles. Dominated by the Party—whose three slogans are "War is peace," "Freedom is slavery," and "Ignorance is strength"—and its official representation, Big Brother, Oceania is a mobilized society in a state of perpetual war, that being the most economical form of social control.

Winston Smith, the novel's luckless protagonist, is a middle-level employee of the Ministry of Truth, a bureaucracy devoted to updating or obliterating the past according to the political needs of the present—a task not altogether unlike Hollywood's. Most dramatically, the ministry consigns unpersons to the Memory Hole in support of the Party's central truth: "Reality exists in the human mind and nowhere else. . . . Whatever happens in all minds, truly happens." Smith is inspired by an affair with a fellow Party member to briefly rebel against the totalitarian order. He fails utterly and, cruelly tortured, truly learns to love Big Brother.

No one before Orwell had so vividly imagined how a Stalinoid terror state might actually feel—albeit transposed to postwar London with a two-way surveillance tele-screen in every miserable flat. *Time*'s unusually long review bracketed Orwell's novel with another Book-of-the-Month Club selection, John Gunther's report on the new Eastern Europe, *Behind the Curtain*. No less than the Gunther exposé, *1984* could hardly be seen as anything other than a comment on the events of late 1947 and 1948—the Communist consolidation of Poland and Hungary, the fall of Czechoslovakia, the siege of Berlin, the ongoing American security crisis.

As part of its horrifyingly concrete vision, *1984* introduced such useful concepts as the bureaucratic jargon called *newspeak,* the capacity for delusion or denial known as *doublethink*, and the organized, mandatory political demonstrations of Hate Week. The novel's human types included the invisible—save through his representations—maximum leader Big Brother and the Party's omnipotent Thought Police. The term "thought control" was already in circulation and, indeed, frequently used by leftists to characterize HUAC. The nightmare was collective.[16]

As the Supreme Court ordered Warners, Fox, and MGM to divest themselves of their theater chains and John Wayne prepared to make *Sands of Iwo Jima* (the movie that would fix his image in the heavens for all eternity), Wayne's low-budget home studio, Republic Pictures, took "unusual pride" in releasing *The Red Menace.*

"Personally supervised" by Republic's owner, Herbert J. Yates, and sprinting into theaters ahead of RKO's troubled *I Married a Communist, The Red Menace* was the first feature to focus on American Communists—written and directed by veteran Republic cowhands, with a talkative cast largely corralled from radio actors. A generic film noir, the movie opens with a terrified young couple driving across the southwestern desert. Their car is a nest of shadows; the atmosphere is viscous with paranoia. "What are they running from?" the disembodied voice of Los Angeles councilman Lloyd G. Davies sonorously inquires.

Basically, *The Red Menace* tells the tale of Bill Jones, a disgruntled ex-GI led by his libido into the worldwide Marxist racket. Just as the Tenney committee had warned, sex, not ideology, is the selling point; the Commies operate a secret bar, Club Domino, conveniently located across the alley from the downtown offices of their newspaper the *Daily Toiler,* that's stocked with eager Venus flytraps. Bill, who has been picked up by the CP steerer who observes him registering a

---

16. Although producer Charles K. Feldman optioned the rights soon after publication, *1984* was not ready for the movies. The project continued to be discussed even while CBS's *Studio One* broadcast an hourlong adaptation in September 1953 and, over a year later, the BBC televised a two-hour version. A British-American co-production, set in a post-atomic future and starring Edmond O'Brien, was released in 1956.

noisy complaint at the Veterans Administration office, is immediately seduced by red barfly Mollie O'Flaherty. He really falls hard, however, for the film's designated nice girl, Nina Petrovka—a Russian red-diaper baby and "real swell looker," in the words of the Texas sheriff who wanders onto the set for the surreal denouement.

Nina is in charge of Marxist instruction. At first, having guided Bill—a potentially valuable Party property—away from a demonstration turned violent and onto a nearby Ferris wheel, she makes his head spin. But soon, like her near-namesake Ninotchka, the comely Communist jettisons foreign-inculcated class consciousness for American-style love. Of course, romance cannot triumph before *The Red Menace* has treated the viewer to a guided tour of red Los Angeles. In addition to Club Domino and party girl Mollie's posh apartment (where Bill seems astonished to find actual books—for reading!), there is Nina's basement classroom and the *Toiler*'s entropic newsroom.

The Red Menace spends a surprising amount of screen time explicating Marxist dogma. Indeed, in exposing the Party leadership as cynical and manipulative, *The Red Menace* intimates that the Communists are betraying their own high ideals. Several true believers—Molly and her Negro comrade Sam Wright—have disapproving parents operating under the spell of more acceptable religious leaders. In one tumultuous scene, the cell's resident Jewish poet, Henry Solomon, is attacked for denying an immaculate-conception view of Communism: "We contend that Marx had no basis in Hegel!" the requisite fat, sweaty Party secretary sneers. Stung by this criticism, sensitive Henry tears up his Party card, denouncing his erstwhile comrades as a pack of "trained red seals" and "psychopathic misfits." The next morning the news of his expulsion from the Party is emblazoned across the *Toiler*'s front page; he reads it, rushes to the newspaper to tell his comrades, and takes a swan dive out the newspaper office window.

Contradicting the Party emphasis on free love, the most villainously crazed Communist is Yvonne Kraus, a sexually frustrated German refugee. Kraus also has eyes for Bill and works to purge both of the red cuties for whom he's fallen. Ultimately exposed as an illegal alien with phony papers, she flips into a breakdown of screaming hysteria, hallucinating the drumbeat of revolution, calling the police "fools," and ranting that she is actually someone named "Commissar Bloch." (As filmmaker Jack Smith wrote of the lead actor in the 1936 exploitation film *Reefer Madness*, actress Betty Lou Gerson—identified in the trade press as "Queen of the Soap Operas"—is "given every opportunity to disintegrate to the point of gilded splendor.")

That the CP is a haven for nymphos and neurotics has already been made clear one confused evening when, in a paranoid paroxysm of mutual surveillance, half the group goes skulking around the *Toiler* office's neighborhood. Not only do the Reds spend most of their time spying on each other, they liquidate their dissidents and ineptly try to pass off the murder as an anti-Communist hate crime. Indeed, the cell seems so self-destructive that it is difficult to ascertain the nature of the menace for anyone other than the Reds themselves. As the sheriff tells Bill and Nina in the happy denouement, "You folks have been running away from yourselves."

True to Hollywood tradition, *The Red Menace* invented a threat in order to dispel it and the *Hollywood Reporter* welcomed the movie with fervent gratitude: "Experimental and pioneering," a work of "vast courage and firm convictions," it "rates the wholehearted commendation of the film industry and the public." The *Los Angeles Times* hopefully predicted that *The Red Menace* would "do more to arouse the public to the dangers of communism than any other picture ever made." Yates arranged a special Sacramento preview for the California state legislature and was personally commended by the chairman of the California Senate Fact-Finding Committee on Un-American Activities, Jack Tenney.

RKO previewed *I Married a Communist* during the first week of *The Red Menace*'s Los Angeles run. The sensational title had been registered by Eagle-Lion in early 1948; the script, by George Slavin and his frequent writing partner, George W. George, was revised through June. The project was acquired by RKO that summer, shortly after Howard Hughes assumed control of the studio. Indeed, *I Married a Communist* was generally understood as the signifier of the new RKO, following Dore Schary's resignation as production chief.

Important as the project was, the original plan was to have a topical prologue provided by the tabloids' "Red Spy Queen," HUAC witness Elizabeth Bentley; newsreel clips of HUAC investigations; and an ending wherein the eponymous ex-Communist would testify before the committee in Washington. A new, possibly left-leaning writer, Art Cohn, was assigned to the script, along with John Wayne's buddy James Edward Grant. In December, they were succeeded by Herman Mankiewicz, who had written *Citizen Kane* for RKO nine years before.

Hughes used the project as a litmus test, initially offering it to RKO's known leftist directors and writers. The first was Schary protégé Joseph Losey; he passed on the assignment and soon departed the studio. (It was Losey who, in an extended interview nearly twenty years later, identified *I Married a Communist* as Hughes's device to determine a filmmaker's politics, maintaining that thirteen directors turned it down.) John Cromwell, a prominent British-born liberal named as a Communist by Sam Wood during the 1947 HUAC hearings, was next. Cromwell withdrew from the picture, scheduled to start shooting in November 1948. Despite what he termed this "nerve-wracking" offer, Cromwell directed two further films for RKO; leftist writer Daniel Mainwaring, however, had his option dropped when he refused to work on the project. Nicholas Ray, a former Communist who eluded HUAC attention, was then attached for six weeks, with his then-wife Gloria Grahame named as star; he quit in January 1949 and was replaced by Robert Stevenson, also British-born and later Walt Disney's house director.[17]

Meanwhile several new screenwriters entered the picture, which had finally begun rehearsing in April 1949. One of the writers, Robert Hardy Andrews, caused a stir when he changed the name of the Communist leader to "Nixon" (that Andrews was listed twice in the Tenney committee's 1948 compendium, *Report on Communist Front Organizations*, suggests that the joke may have been intentional). Three months before *I Married a Communist* finally opened, the *Christian Science Monitor* reported that writing credits—ultimately shared by Andrews and Charles Grayson—were still in flux.

Although *I Married a Communist* was presumed to be Hughes's pet project, his only extant memo regarding the film is a simple request for more passion in the kissing scenes between a red femme fatale and her naive prey; even more than *The Red Menace*, *I Married a Communist* is a movie about sex. Once upon a time, before the war and back east in New Jersey, Brad (Robert Ryan, a known liberal) and Christine (Janis Carter) were hot young Commies in love. But then Brad, a waterfront organizer relocated to San Francisco, left the Party and, having married the boss's daughter Nan (Laraine Day), changed teams to become a shipping executive. As the newly minted capitalist finds himself compelled to negotiate a contract with his former union, Christine, now a journalist but still red and carrying a torch, tries to lure him back.

As in *The Red Menace*, disgruntled or former Communists are controlled by the threat of blackmail from the Party. Unlike Elizabeth Bentley or Whittaker

17. Hughes's anti-Communism was characteristically eccentric and autocratic. He excised composer Hanns Eisler's name from *The Spanish Main* when the 1945 feature was rereleased in the early 1950s, fought a battle with the Screen Writers Guild to have unfriendly witness Paul Jarrico's credit removed from *The Las Vegas Story*, and in 1952 shut down RKO to "clean house," as he told Hearst columnist Howard Rushmore: "During the next two months we are going to set up a screening system as thorough as we can make it. . . . It is my determination to make RKO one studio where the work of Communist sympathizers will be impossible."

Chambers, however, Brad is precluded from turning informer because his erstwhile comrades have proof that he killed a shop steward back in the day. "The Party decides who's out and when," taunts the squat, bug-eyed commissar Vanning (Thomas Gomez) as he presents Brad with an updated membership card, shown in tight close-up and—thanks to Louis J. Russell, the FBI agent turned HUAC investigator—a facsimile of the genuine article. More effective than the hapless Commies of *The Red Menace*, those of *I Married Communist* suggest a ruthless crime syndicate. Early on, they fit an informer with concrete shoes and toss him into the San Francisco Bay. Vanning, many contemporary reviewers noted, is an iconographical gangster (and virtual twin of the troll apparatchik in *The Red Menace*), as well as a grotesque stand-in for labor leader Harry Bridges.[18]

In the course of vamping Brad's confused brother-in-law Don (John Agar), Christine genuinely falls for Don, something the leering Vanning refuses to believe. "An emotion is not something you're built to understand or appreciate," she haughtily tells him. Christine talks too much; she gets her young beau run over and herself "suicided." The Communists commit three brazen murders and, having abducted Nan, are about to execute a fourth when Brad storms Party headquarters and successfully shoots it out with Vanning and his henchmen before dying in Nan's arms.

More intense in its melodrama than *The Red Menace* (in part because of superior performances, in part because the narrative energy is heightened by a compact running time), *I Married a Communist* is passable film noir and *Variety* treated it as such: "It makes no contribution towards combating the Commie menace but shapes up as okay entertainment nonetheless." The screenplay, however, is not devoid of argumentation. Historian Daniel Leab, who studied its multifarious revisions, reports that each version includes a social gathering where characters take turns holding forth on the evils of foreign and domestic Communists. In addition, all versions spoke to the existence of Communist fronts, with thinly disguised references to organizations like the American Committee for the Protection of the Foreign Born and the Committee for the

---

18. Head of the International Longshoremen's and Warehousemen's Union (ILWU), Bridges was the most powerful labor leader on the West Coast—as well as a left-wing cause célèbre, threatened with deportation to Australia throughout the 1940s. According to the Tenney committee, the Harry Bridges Defense Committee included Orson Welles and screenwriter Dudley Nichols—along with Paul Jarrico, Dalton Trumbo, and John Howard Lawson (who celebrated the ILWU in his *Action in the North Atlantic* script). While *I Married a Communist* was in production, Bridges was prosecuted for denying his CP membership and sentenced to five years' imprisonment.

First Amendment. The Cohn and Grant draft even included a guided tour of these fronts (or "patsies," as the contemptuous Commie boss calls them).

For the finished movie, actual organizations were subsumed into a fictional entity with the Orwellian name Mankind Incorporated. This version was to be prefaced with newsreel footage of HUAC in action and J. Edgar Hoover declaring his hatred of Communism as "the enemy of all liberty, all religion, all humanity." But, as with *The Iron Curtain*, Hoover declined to personally associate either the FBI or himself with the movie, evidently to Hughes's displeasure.

I Married a Communist was released in Los Angeles only days after the season's scariest anti-Communist scenario was performed live at a picnic ground just outside the Hudson River town of Peekskill, New York. Mobs yelling racist and anti-Semitic epithets assaulted the audience gathered for a Paul Robeson concert to benefit the Harlem Civil Rights Congress.[19]

That summer, in between the openings of *The Red Menace* and *I Married a Communist* (as well as a second, violent Robeson concert defiantly held a week after the first, on a golf course outside Peekskill), Warner Bros. released a more extravagant, eccentric, and oblique attack on collectivist ideology: King Vidor's film of Ayn Rand's bestselling 754-page novel of ideas, *The Fountainhead*.

Although the word "Communist" is never used, *The Fountainhead* projected an ideal type in direct opposition to the heroic team player or crusading social activist. A radical individualist, Rand's hero Howard Roark is a modern architect even more confident of his genius than uncompromising in his purity. Rand began writing the novel in 1938, and her worshipful attitude toward Roark's proud extremism is complemented by a markedly anti–New Deal contempt for the "common man." Warner Bros. had purchased *The Fountainhead* in late 1943; Rand began work on the screenplay and completed it by June 1944.[20]

The Fountainhead was scheduled for production but, according to its pro-

---

19. Part of the legend of *I Married a Communist* is that the movie was never actually released under that title. In fact, it was released in both Los Angeles and San Francisco, where it performed so poorly that, as the *Daily Worker* exulted, Hughes was obliged to withdraw it from circulation. The movie was retitled (but otherwise unchanged) and, in June 1950, opened in New York (and reopened in Los Angeles) as *The Woman on Pier 13*. The *New York Times* deemed it "a right smart sampling of melodrama, fast paced and attractively padded with action and violence."

20. Rand wrote a note thanking Jack Warner and the studio for allowing her to preserve *The Fountainhead*'s "theme and spirit, without being asked to make bad taste concessions, such as a lesser studio would have demanded." (Apparently unperturbed by Warner's *Mission to Moscow*, she effusively praised the studio as Hollywood's most courageous.)

spective director Mervyn LeRoy, was scratched by the War Production Board. If, as some have suggested, Rand's anti-Russian politics were a factor, her much-publicized HUAC performance three years later undoubtedly contributed to the studio's revived interest in the project, now under the director King Vidor (a founding, if largely inactive, member of the Motion Picture Alliance) and budgeted at a generous $2.5 million.

Given his choice of Warner's leading men (even Ronald Reagan campaigned for the role), Vidor would have chosen Bogart. The studio, however, imported another featured performer at the 1947 HUAC hearings—natural nobleman Gary Cooper. Cooper's announced co-star was Mrs. Bogart, Lauren Bacall, but her prominent association with the Committee for the First Amendment made her anathema to Red-hunters; after the studio was inundated with letters of protest, she was replaced with the relatively unknown Patricia Neal.

As directed by Vidor, *The Fountainhead* is unusually expressionist, outrageously schematic, and, given Rand's empurpled hyperdramatic dialogue, relentlessly on message. As the embodiment of suffering integrity, Cooper has obvious difficulty with his chewier lines. Other allegorical figures include Roark's careerist classmate Peter Keating (Kent Smith); the newspaper publisher who first opposes, then befriends, and ultimately betrays Roark, Gail Wynand (Raymond Massey, after Rand vetoed liberal Melvyn Douglas); and the effete critic Elsworth Toohey (Robert Douglas), who, as vile as his name sounds, is both an impotent power freak and, in his attempt to dominate the mindless masses, the movie's crypto-Communist mouthpiece.

The Fountainhead is, in part, a criticism of the movie industry: throughout, people demand Roark give in and capitulate to the dictates of popular taste. Specifically, he is told simply to follow Hollywood's supreme mandate and "give the public what it wants." But, for Roark as Rand, nothing could be more ignominious. The stubborn genius gets no commissions and is reduced to working in a stone quarry, where, laboring without a shirt, he attracts the attention of the movie's sole female character: Dominique (Neal). Outwardly cold, she is secretly thrilled by the force with which he applies his drill to the rock wall and later inveigles him up to her boudoir so that he might rape her.

Worshipped by Dominique, whom he refuses to pursue, and blacklisted by jealous collectivists, Roark becomes an aesthetic vigilante—so uncompromising that he dynamites a housing project because his designs have been altered. The ensuing trial is highly ideological. "Does any man have the right to exist if he refuses to serve society?" the prosecutor asks; Roark defends himself by exalting the rights of the individual over the group. This conflict was played out in the production. Rand's script was inviolable and Neal remembered that she often visited the set "to protect her screenplay." Discovering the director's plan to abridge the lengthy trial scene, Rand appealed to Jack Warner, who compelled Vidor to shoot it in its entirety.[21]

Warners evidently had high hopes for their high-minded experiment. Two banks of bleachers were erected on Hollywood Boulevard to accommodate fans expected to mob *The Fountainhead*'s gala premiere at the Warners Hollywood. That the evening may have been stormy is suggested by the *Los Angeles Times*'s discreet observation that the audience "strongly responded to the unusual elements in the production." The twenty-three-year-old Neal recalled her first industry premiere as a public humiliation. The movie was received with complete silence, with spectators averting their eyes as she left the Warners' Deco-Moorish-Italianate flagship. Local response was nonplussed. *The Fountainhead* was not "orthodox entertainment," the *Hollywood Reporter* opined. "Its characters are downright weird and there is no feeling of self-identification." The *Los Angeles Times* had a similar response: "It will NOT be a film to catch the interest of what is known as the average movie audience—whoever they may be nowadays." (Hollywood had not produced so confrontational a social critique, didactic movie of ideas, or bizarre personal statement since the equally outrageous *Monsieur Verdoux*.) The *Daily Worker* naturally termed *The Fountainhead* "an openly fascist movie," but even *Variety* found it tendentious, "cold, unemotional, loquacious [and] completely devoted to hammering home the theme that man's personal integrity stands above all law."

While *Time* saw *The Fountainhead* as a symptom of the movie industry's current malaise, the *New Yorker* pronounced it "asinine and inept." *Cue* called *The Fountainhead* "shoddy, bombastic nonsense," but it was Crowther in the *New York Times* who had the most memorable squelch: Rand's "long-winded, complicated preachment on the rights of the individual in society [was] a picture which you don't have to see to disbelieve." *The Fountainhead* wound up grossing $2.1 million—some $400,000 less than its production budget.

MGM attempted to take the high road with its anti-Communist effort *The Red Danube*, adapted from Catholic novelist Bruce Marshall's 1947 bestseller *Vespers in Vienna*; it had its world premiere in San Francisco in late September, three weeks after *I Married a Communist* made its feeble debut.

---

21. Although *The Fountainhead* rejects any notion of the greater good, the public isn't entirely misled as the jury finds Roark not guilty. Indeed, Roark confounds the Production Code as well by committing a crime without suffering the consequence.

When questioned by HUAC about MGM's wartime *Song of Russia*, Louis B. Mayer had reminded the committee of his studio's prewar anti-Communist comedies *Ninotchka* and *Comrade X* and assured them that MGM would soon again be making "anti-Communist films." (According to reporter I.F. Stone, HUAC chairman J. Parnell Thomas leaned forward, grinning, to ask, "These hearings haven't anything to do with the promptness, have they?") Mayer cited an upcoming adaptation of *Vespers in Vienna*, which, per the publisher's request, was required to retain that title. Buffeted by geopolitical events and roiled by studio politics, however, the movie took nearly two years to reach the screen— and then as *The Red Danube*.

"MGM was ridden with conflict, envy, and rivalry," Dore Schary wrote in his memoirs. "It was peopled with employees who had been there for years— spoiled and wasteful, and yet many of them talented but hobbled by the old College of Cardinals system inaugurated by Mayer." According to Schary, Mayer and Nicholas Schenck, president of MGM's parent company Loews Inc., had, at Schary's request, disbanded MGM's long-standing basis in quasi- autonomous production units. This prompted the resignation of several key producers—including Motion Picture Alliance founder James K. McGuinness. For many, Schary was to blame. Some thought that he had maliciously fired McGuinness.

Despite his role in inaugurating and implementing the blacklist, MGM's new production chief was regarded as a Communist sympathizer and frequently denounced as such to the FBI. One lengthy memo, drawing on information furnished by the irrepressible Myron C. Fagan, concerns *The Red Danube*. The project was announced and had been assigned to producer Al Lichtman. Then, in July 1948, Schary arrived at MGM.

> Schary learned about the story and about Lichtman—knew that the picture would emerge as a truly anti-communist document. Through direct interven- tion by Dore Schary the script was reviewed and the title changed to *Storm Over Vienna*. The story was changed—the villains were now fascists who were trying to enslave the hapless Viennese and the noble communists were desperately fighting to rescue them. The cast was changed and the leading parts were as- signed to tried and true lovers of Stalin. . . . Al Lichtman and other MGM exec- utives protested Schary's action but the latter, with Louis Mayer's connivance, squelched the rebellion and Lichtman was requested to resign.

These developments, the FBI informant explains, were leaked to Hedda Hopper, and once she hinted at the truth in her column, "an avalanche of letters and telephone calls from exhibitors and movie-goers descended upon MGM." The studio then "dusted off the original shooting script of *Red Danube,* reassembled the original cast of loyal Americans and gave the direction to George Sidney, who at least was not 'a pinko suspect.'" Thus, MGM produced a top-notch anti-Communist film for which, the informant complained, Schary deviously took credit.

A talky scenario, set in postwar Vienna and thus a faint shadow of *The Third Man,* which had premiered the previous spring, *The Red Danube* focused on the relationship between two British officers—the one-armed colonel nicknamed Hooky (Walter Pidgeon) and his young adjutant Twingo (Peter Lawford)—and a sad, winsome ballerina (Janet Leigh) resisting repatriation to the Soviet Union. All are billeted at a convent presided over by a voluble mother superior (Ethel Barrymore); while the two young MGM contractees bat their eyes, agnostic Hooky debates religion with the wimpled grand dame who is their hostess. (At one point this odd couple flies together to Rome for an audience with Pope Pius.) The Brits fail to prevent the dancer's repatriation and she ultimately kills herself.

Still, not everyone was impressed. *Variety* called *The Red Danube* "overtalky and unwieldy." *Cue* found the movie an uneven "mess of religious-philosophical chatter." *People's World* was reliably outraged: "*Red Danube* hits a new low in slander," although *Daily Worker* critic Jose Yglesias took a more ironic attitude, noting that the movie was framed by Hooky and Twingo's cheery rendition of "Row, Row, Row Your Boat" and was itself nothing but a dream. Was it the American Dream? The season of anti-Communist movies coincided with a trio of movies dealing with the subject that Hollywood's Communists had most wanted to see treated on-screen—American racism—if not in the manner in which Communists wished to see it.

Producer's films all, these racial dramas included *Pinky,* Darryl Zanuck's follow-up to *Gentleman's Agreement,* and two independent projects, Stanley Kramer's *Home of the Brave,* adapted by Carl Foreman from Arthur Laurents's play, and Louis de Rochemont's *Lost Boundaries,* based on a true story published in *Reader's Digest.* The unheralded Kramer film arrived first, opening in New York in mid-May, where its account of a shell-shocked black soldier, driven half-mad by his buddies' wartime racism, was hailed by Bosley Crowther as "a drama of force and consequence."

The introduction of Negro roles and themes had been an important part of the Hollywood CP's program, and while criticizing the filmmakers for some "dangerous confusion" in downplaying the soldier's autonomy, Jose Yglesias saw *Home of the Brave* as a fundamentally healthy development—even "an important event in American movie making." A week later, a reader wrote in to set him straight, pointing out that "in a changing set of circumstances, Wall Street's Hollywood finds that the Uncle-Tom-clown stereotype as a weapon for the disruption of Negro-white unity is beginning to dull—and so a search for a more effective weapon is made. . . . This subtle technique—the use of the 'dignified' Negro who prefers submission to struggle—is being inaugurated in order to trap the increasing consciousness of the American people on the Negro question and channel it into a soft, humanitarian—and, at its core, contemptuous—attitude toward the Negro people."

Lost Boundaries followed six weeks later. A story of a light-skinned doctor and his wife (played by white actors) who are outed when they pass for white, it was praised by Crowther as a movie of "extraordinary courage, understanding and dramatic power" and dismissed by Yglesias as "sentimental," "shallow," and "patronizing."As noted by Manny Farber, *Home of the Brave* and *Lost Boundaries* argued that "the Negro will be accepted if he lives according to the rules of the stuffiest white gentility." Yglesias amended this: Negroes will be accepted if they actually are white. This was even truer for *Pinky*, which also addressed the condition of passing for white (and employed a white actress to dramatize it). The slickest and most hyped of the three, arriving at the end of September, it was received by Crowther with equal enthusiasm as "a picture that is vivid, revealing, and emotionally intense." Yglesias, who found the movie scarcely less reactionary than *Lost Boundaries*, did note a few laudable touches by director Elia Kazan ("whose progressive views are well known").

All three movies were box-office hits. *Pinky* finished second for the year; *Home of the Brave* and *Lost Boundaries* were notably successful independent productions, each grossing over $2 million. At the same time red termites were weakening the foundations of American life, perfectly lovely white people like Pinky were being persecuted for being "black."[22]

---

22. The Negro problem cycle, which also included MGM's less widely seen *Intruder in the Dust*, adapted by Comrade Ben Maddow from William Faulkner's novel, coincided with a crisis within the CPUSA—as Joseph Starobin italicized in his firsthand account, "*In the name of defying the witch-hunt against them, the American Communists complemented it by engaging in a witch-hunt of their own.*" While the international movement was embroiled in rooting out the Titoist heresy, their American comrades were catalyzed by *Political Affairs*'s June 1949 special issue on the "struggle against white chauvinism." Over the next four years, Party members were accused of racism, leaders were demoted, language was policed, and scores were settled. The basis of the conflict anticipated the Sino-Soviet schism as well as a basic New Left tenet: were African Americans an indigenous national liberation movement and, as such, were they, rather than the (white) working class, a revolutionary vanguard? The campaign against "white chauvinism" underlines Jose Yglesias's reviews as well as a lecture delivered by V.J. Jerome at

Other post-HUAC movies verged on allegory in their representation of fascism and political paranoia. Shot during the summer of 1948, Walter Wanger's *Reign of Terror* (subsequently known as *The Black Book*) opened some fourteen months later on October 15; Robert Rossen's long-germinating adaptation of Robert Penn Warren's Pulitzer Prize–winning *All the King's Men* premiered in early November, even as Jerry Wald's troubled *Storm Warning* went into production at Warner Bros.

Each in his way, Wald, Rossen, and Wanger had been affected by the hearings. Wald had produced movies written or co-written by four of the Hollywood Ten and publicly supported the Committee for the First Amendment; Rossen was a former Communist and one of the original nineteen subpoenaed unfriendlies; and Wanger, by contrast, was an unhappy accomplice to the blacklist. A New Deal liberal, the fifty-five-year-old Wanger had produced the antifascist *Blockade* (1938) from a script by John Howard Lawson. During the war, Wanger was active in the Hollywood Democratic Committee (Rossen and Wald were also both members), HICCASP, and the Hollywood Free World Association; during the October 1947 hearings, friendly witnesses Sam Wood and Howard Rushmore both cited his Communist associations.

Wanger was critical of HUAC and, after Schary's less-than-friendly testimony, cabled his support to the then–RKO studio head. Still, he followed Schary's lead; along with MGM producer Eddie Mannix, Wanger provided support for Schary at the tumultuous November 1947 meeting of the Screen Writers Guild at which Schary apologized for the Waldorf statement. In the post-HUAC climate, Wanger tacked with the wind. Following the line advanced by Republican candidate Thomas E. Dewey in his Hollywood address, the producer conceived a series of features to be distributed through the small Eagle-Lion studio that would showcase American industry and free enterprise.

In regard to his 1949 film *Tulsa*—the only one of these to be made—Wanger maintained "Hollywood has the medium which can do more in a cold war than anything else. . . . Just a picture of well-dressed people walking down Fifth

---

the Hotel Capitol in New York in February 1950 and considered sufficiently important to be published some months later as a booklet, *The Negro in Hollywood Films*. Jerome analyzes *Home of the Brave* et al. as a " 'new' brand" of Hollywood movies "designed to beguile the people of the Marshallized countries [and] mollify the colonial peoples, who feel a sense of fraternity with the American Negro in the common anti-imperialist struggle," evidence of a dangerously subtle means "through which the racist ruling class of our country is today re-asserting its strategic ideology of 'white supremacy' on the Hollywood screen." Further evidence that the Party has given up on Hollywood, Jerome ends with the utopian exhortation to build "Negro people's independent film producing companies."

Avenue would show what Americanism can do." The tale of oil industrialist Cherokee Lansing, played by fiery Susan Hayward, *Tulsa* was designed to help "spread the good news of what this wonderful country has and what it is willing to do to assist other countries to build up their industries." *Reign of Terror* (originally known as *The Bastille*) got its start at Eagle-Lion in early 1948, around the time the studio was developing *I Married a Communist*. The movie was designed as a spectacular that would recycle the sets from Wanger's 1948 film *Joan of Arc*; its melodramatic account of the French Revolution became increasingly political as its budget was reduced. Aeneas MacKenzie, a specialist in historical films, was first engaged to write the original screenplay; Wanger subsequently turned the job over to Philip Yordan, a roguish figure who later operated as a front for a number of blacklisted screenwriters and whose additions included the plot element of Robespierre's "black book" of political enemies.

Having already directed three highly atmospheric crime films for Eagle-Lion, Anthony Mann imbued *Reign of Terror* with a comparable mood of urban anxiety. An urgent, almost Wellesian film of endless treachery and perpetual night, *Reign of Terror* opens with a flaming montage and a hysterical voice-over decrying "the weapons of dictatorship." Here the Jacobin revolution is godless and ruthless, and although Richard Basehart's Robespierre makes a weak Stalin, *Reign of Terror* is a far better political gangster movie than either *The Red Menace* or *I Married a Communist*.

Still known as *The Bastille*, the movie was languishing on the shelf in March 1949 when Wanger happened to read an account of the Cultural and Scientific Conference for World Peace that claimed unnamed, Communist-influenced culture critics had used "an intellectual reign of terror" to coerce writers and musicians into supporting the peace conference. Always topically minded, the producer seized on the phrase. "The best way to make a lot of dough with this," he wrote associate Max Youngstein, "would be to go all out and maybe have some of the ads warn the public that we will be going through a REIGN OF TERROR in this country if we don't watch out and that there is a REIGN OF TERROR all over the world."

The model, Wanger thought, was *Hitler's Children*—the wildly successful 1943 cheapster that had established Edward Dmytryk's reputation. "Let this be hailed as the Motion Picture Industry's effort to stop all kinds of totalitarianism," he wrote. All kinds? While the French Communist critic Georges Sadoul associated *Reign of Terror* with "the worst kind of pseudo-historical melodramas," in the American context, the Jacobin terror unavoidably suggests HUAC; the movie is ultimately a struggle for the list of names in Robespierre's "black book." The bloodthirsty mob is identified with the audience, which proved to have little interest in the movie. *Reign of Terror* barely broke even, although it was the only profitable picture Wanger produced in the immediate postwar period.

All the King's Men was something else. In 1947, Robert Rossen rivaled Edward Dmytryk and Dalton Trumbo as Hollywood's most successful Communist. A party member since 1937, Rossen was proud to have been subpoenaed by HUAC and even felt angry at being denied a chance to testify. Soon after, he stood up at the first post-Waldorf Directors Guild meeting and urged his colleagues to protest Dmytryk's firing. (Not only was Rossen booed but the DGA passed a motion requiring all DGA officers—Dmytryk was then second vice president—to sign the Taft-Hartley "non-Communist" affidavit.)

Rossen's *Body and Soul* would eventually gross $3.25 million, finishing as distributor United Artists' top moneymaker for 1947. (The movie would be nominated for three Oscars—including Best Actor, John Garfield, and Best Original Screenplay, Abraham Polonsky—and win one, for film editing.) Before *Body and Soul* opened, Rossen was already working on the script for his next project: an adaptation of Robert Penn Warren's novel *All the King's Men*.

The rise and fall of a southern politician whose career inevitably evoked that of Louisiana governor and senator Huey Long, Penn Warren's novel had won a Pulitzer Prize in May 1947. Columbia paid $200,000 for the rights and negotiated a deal whereby Rossen would write, produce, and direct the adaptation. That summer, Walter Bernstein, then a young staff writer for the *New Yorker* (and a new member of the CP's New York section), landed a job through his agent Harold Hecht (a former Red) as Rossen's assistant. Initially, Bernstein worked on developing a Chekhov story but soon was put on *All the King's Men*, listening to Rossen's ideas and serving as his "left-wing barometer." Their politics were no secret. Bernstein recalls Columbia boss Harry Cohn dropping by and asking if Bernstein was one of Rossen's "Commie writers from New York." Nevertheless, Bernstein's actual impact was minimal. "We would discuss some leftist point to be made in a scene and then [Rossen] would go upstairs and present the scene to Cohn. He would return with the radicalism either deleted or softened to an acceptable liberalism. Sometimes that helped the scene, sometimes it didn't. None of it did anything to dilute Rossen's verbal militancy." New to Hollywood, Bernstein was unimpressed with Rossen's as-yet-unreleased *Body and Soul* and, although FBI investigators were evident and HUAC subpoenas thought imminent, does not remember being aware of any particular tension among movie industry leftists.

That would change. At some point in 1948, according to testimony given three years later to HUAC, Rossen sent Cohn a secret letter assuring him that he had left the Communist Party. (Even so, Rossen remained identified with the left; in November 1949, only weeks before *All the King's Men* opened, he signed an appeal to the Supreme Court for the reversal of Lawson's and Trumbo's convictions.) The production, budgeted at $1.75 million, went forward. Originally, Cohn wanted Spencer Tracy for the role of the demagogue Willie Stark. Then another star's name surfaced. In October, agent Charlie Feldman sent the script to John Wayne. According to Wayne's biographers, the star was scandalized; by the time he finished reading the script, "he was throwing ashtrays and knocking over furniture."

Wayne wrote Feldman a furious missive, informing him that he found Rossen's script despicable: populated by "drunken mothers; conniving fathers; double-crossing sweethearts; bad, bad rich people; and bad, bad poor people, if they want to get ahead," *All the King's Men* "smears the machinery of government for no purpose of humor or enlightenment," "degrades all relationships," and defames "the American way of life." Making sure that Feldman would not miss his point, Wayne ended by inviting him to "take this script and shove it up Robert Rossen's derriere." The part went to another, less glamorous specialist in Western roles, Broderick Crawford.

Shot in Stockton, California, under the influence of Italian neorealism, *All the King's Men* makes no specific references to Louisiana or the South, even as it presents a vision of a totally corrupt small town. Crawford's Stark is a baffling character—a self-absorbed, narcissistic idealist, fueled by resentment and ambition. Once he realizes that he's been set up to lose the election, he reinvents himself as an "angry hick" and enjoys a startling reversal of fortune—transformed into a two-fisted, corn-fed Mussolini who, once elected governor, makes himself virtual dictator of the state.

The combination of rough populist politics, orchestrated hoopla, and a hypnotized electorate comes close to imagining a fascist America. "Willie Stark, Messiah or Dictator?" a newsreel asks. "You can't make an omelet without cracking eggs," explains Stark's newsman apologist (John Ireland) by way of justifying Stark's strong-arm tactics—echoing the very phrase used by *New York Times* reporter Walter Duranty in his 1932 article "Red Square: Russia's Pulsing Heart." Power corrupts very quickly, and to make it obvious, the initially teetotaling Willie is always half-crocked. This monster autocrat looks back at Citizen Kane and forward a decade to Lonesome Rhodes, the cracker-barrel demagogue of Elia Kazan and Budd Schulberg's *A Face in the Crowd*. Wayne's distaste notwithstanding, *All the King's Men* would have been a far scarier movie had he taken the role of Willie Stark. (Fittingly, he would be beaten for the Oscar that year by the man who did.)

The political response scarcely ended with Wayne. After *All the King's Men* opened, according to Dmytryk, Rossen was called to account by Commissar Lawson. "*Censure* is too flabby a word. Rossen's *excoriation* took place during a meeting of the Ten held at [Albert] Maltz's home. Thoroughly bewildered, [Rossen] was, for the better part of the evening, pilloried by Lawson and those two acid-tongued specialists in the Party's disciplinary procedures, [Herbert] Biberman and [Alvah] Bessie, three men who, lumped together, had not one-tenth of Bob's talent. I was dumbfounded . . ." *All the King's Men*, like *1984*, dramatized Lord Acton's observation that power corrupts and absolute power corrupts absolutely. This was a phrase that, according to Dmytryk, "we [Communists] often used to denigrate conservatives in general and HUAC in particular. Yet Bob's comrades were now giving him hell for dramatizing it. The reason behind the attack was never verbally expressed, and it took me some time to recognize it: Rossen was really getting hell for exposing the evils of dictatorship, the rock on which the Communist Party was founded." Rossen "did his best to fight back," Dmytryk recalled, "but he was outnumbered, and there was no meeting ground." Per Dmytryk, the fed-up director paraphrased John Wayne—if not the Jewish poet in *The Red Menace*—in advising his erstwhile comrades to "stick the whole Party up your ass!" and walked out. Dmytryk assumed that Rossen also walked out of the Party, although if Rossen's secret letter to Cohn was correct, he had left the CP over a year before.

All the King's Men and its star were named best picture and best actor by the New York Film Critics Circle. Still, Rossen had to plead with Cohn to get the movie an Oscar-qualifying run in Los Angeles and personally paid for the trade-paper ads. Nominated for six Oscars, *All the King's Men* was named best picture—with Crawford and Mercedes McCambridge (in her screen debut) winning for actor and supporting actress. According to *Variety*, the movie grossed $2.4 million and was Columbia's top moneymaker for 1950.

As *All the King's Men* moved slowly into theaters, another, far more troubled political film was in production. Like *All the King's Men*, Jerry Wald's *Storm Warning* was set in the South—albeit shot "semi-documentary style" in Corono, California. Here the fascist regime was embodied by the Ku Klux Klan. Their reign of terror has nothing to do with race—the Klansmen fear that the IRS will audit their books, and their lynching victim is a nosy northern reporter.

Ambitious, crude, and aggressive (the supposed model for the antihero of Budd Schulberg's *What Makes Sammy Run?*), the thirty-eight-year-old Wald went to work for Warner in the early 1930s, vaulting from writer to producer during World War II, when he oversaw many of the studio's Popular Front combat movies, including *Action in the North Atlantic* (written by Lawson), *Objective, Burma* (co-written by Bessie and Cole), and *Destination Tokyo* and *Pride of the Marines* (both written by Maltz).[23]

Warner Bros. announced the project during the summer of 1948. A year later Wald hired novelist Daniel Fuchs to work on the script, in which a poised New York model visits her newlywed kid sister in a small southern town and discovers that her charismatic brute of a brother-in-law is a secret member of the local Ku Klux Klan. As the scenario has echoes of the Broadway sensation of 1948 *A Streetcar Named Desire*, so Wald angled to get Marlon Brando for the part and, failing that, instructed director Stuart Heisler to note Brando's *Streetcar* "outfits."

Wald cast Steven Cochran instead, with Doris Day playing his adoring wife and Ronald Reagan as the nominal hero, a straitlaced DA. (The role was Reagan's most political, though he had narrated one of the Writers Mobilization radio plays broadcast in September 1946 in opposition to the KKK.) Lauren Bacall, the original star, was suspended when, in an argument with the studio, she failed to report in late October and was replaced with Ginger Rogers. Two days later, the movie began shooting at a secret location with its script still in flux.

The first movie to focus on an unwilling informer, *Storm Center* was Wald's comment on post-HUAC Hollywood. Writing to *Chicago Sun-Times* columnist Irv Kupcinet, the producer paraphrased one of DA Reagan's lines in explaining that "the point we are trying to make is, 'Who is more guilty—the people who belong to the Klan, or the people who just turn their backs and say, 'It's none of my business'?" In the long nocturnal opening, Rogers arrives in the bus terminal of a sinister small town filled with hostile locals. Is this America? "Hey, what's going on around here anyway?" she asks and, trying to find her sister, walks straight into the answer, as the local KKK commits murder right on Main Street. Reagan investigates—"You want to start naming names?" he asks one

---

23. Bessie first came to Hollywood in 1943 to work with Wald on a script about corruption on the Brooklyn waterfront; he was amazed to hear the producer explain that the "rotten, reactionary union there" was nothing like "the honest union we got out here run by Harry Bridges." According to Bessie, Wald liked to say that he wanted to make pictures that were "topical—but not typical."

intimidated witness—but no one wants to testify against the Klan. There's no talk of the FBI; the DA wants the town to clean up its own mess.

Although the town has a sprinkling of black citizens—or rather extras—race is not an issue. The assistant DA confesses that he joined the Klan the way an idealistic Hollywood actor might have joined the CP. He had wanted to help people, then quit when he found it was "a lot of bunk." Of course, even at its height, the Hollywood CP could scarcely boast, as the head Klansman does, that "we're the law here—we're the judges and the jury." To prove his point, he personally whips the half-dressed Ginger Rogers beneath the fiery cross—cue for Reagan's last-minute rescue and the mad confusion in which Cochran is exposed and shoots Day, who dies in Rogers's arms.

Rewritten, revised, reshot, retitled, and re-retitled, *Storm Warning* would not be released until January 1951. By then Wald had left Warners, and HUAC was poised to return to Hollywood.[24]

"The Saucers Are Real!" (And *Guilty of Treason*)

Friday morning, September 23, 1949, one day after *The Red Danube* opened in San Francisco, President Harry S. Truman dropped a bomb: America's nuclear monopoly was over. The Soviet Union had detonated an atomic device.

The following Sunday, a hitherto-unknown thirty-one-year-old Baptist evangelist named Billy Graham opened his tent revival in Los Angeles. Earlier evangelical preachers had only metaphorical fire and brimstone, while Graham had the benefit of a doomsday scenario that had terrified the public since World War II ended four summers back. If the people are "afraid of war, afraid of atomic bombs, fearful as they go to bed at night," it is with good reason, he maintained.

---

24. *Storm Warning* was the evil twin to a low-budget movie that went into production as 1949 ended and similarly dealt with mob violence, albeit in a Northern California town. An eighteen-day wonder directed by Joseph Losey from a script by Geoffrey Homes (sometime pseudonym for Daniel Mainwaring), *The Lawless* harked back to the socially conscious Warners films of the 1930s and early '40s—the first Hollywood movie to acknowledge the rabid xenophobia of the wartime zoot suit riots. The battleground is the press: cynical, sensationalizing reporters fan lynch-mob hysteria against a Mexican boy falsely charged with attempted rape; when an honest editor attempts to defend the boy, the townspeople turn on his newspaper and trash it. Writing on *The Lawless* in the *New York Times*, Mainwaring (as Homes) linked it to Hollywood's recent anti-anti-Semitic and anti-prejudice films; reviewing it in the *Daily Worker*, Jose Yglesias echoed V.J. Jerome's lecture "The Negro in Hollywood Films," pointing out a failure to "challenge the class structure that produces this violence and economic oppression.... *The Lawless* courageously does give us as villains the corrupt press, the bigoted youth and lynch mobs. But the real villains, the capitalists and their police, are on the side of the angels."

Los Angeles was the third enemy target after New York and Chicago, and Communists were more rampant in L.A. than in any other American city: "If Sodom and Gomorrah could not get away with sin, if Pompeii and Rome could not escape, neither can Los Angeles! Judgment is coming just as sure as I'm standing here!" The world was divided into two camps: there was Communism and there was God. "This may be God's last great call," Graham warned. "Unless the western world has an old-fashioned revival, we cannot last!"

Perhaps only the low-budget indie *Project X*, which played New York and Los Angeles that fall, captured the full degeneracy of the Communist scenario. A young nuclear physicist and onetime Young Communist is blackmailed by a former comrade into supplying crucial information that will reveal the secret of the atomic bomb and thus ensure peace. The physicist goes to the FBI and is recruited to infiltrate a New York nightclub known as the Paradise, where a Communist kingpin is hiding—disguised, it turns out, as Gigi the Cigarette Girl! (Kit Russell, a local drag performer, played the role.) No one but the trades and the *Daily Worker* bothered to review the movie: "Piling lie upon lie in the finest tradition of the builders of Buchenwald and Auschwitz," David Platt fumed. "The only thing missing from this piece of gutter sewage is a dedication to Ilse Koch—art lover and butcher."

Days after Truman's announcement, another awful portent: the world's largest nation fell to the Communists. October 1, Mao Tse-tung proclaimed the People's Republic of China. Meanwhile, William Randolph Hearst mobilized his newsreels, magazines, and newspapers to promote Reverend Graham. ("I am convinced that God uses the press in our work," Graham would tell the readers of *McCall's*.) *Life* magazine featured the young preacher in its November 21 issue, just before the crusade closed with eight great "sin-smashing" weeks. Attendance totaled 350,000. Perhaps to publicize the imminent opening of his biblical spectacular *Samson and Delilah*, Cecil B. De Mille offered Graham a screen test.

Hell on Earth: *Samson and Delilah* aside, the great successes of late 1949 were three World War II movies.

Back in January, *Variety* imagined Truman's surprise victory—as well as the defeat of several HUAC members—might revive interest in "pictures smacking of 'social significance,' " citing as evidence the fabulous price Twentieth Century-Fox paid for a story about the travails of a young black doctor in a white-dominated world. But, reporting in the *Nation* on Hollywood a year after the election, Carey McWilliams noted that social-problem movies were still anathema: "Racial tolerance is apparently the one controversial theme that may be presented from the liberal or progressive point of view," while war movies filled the need for "occasional pix with a bit more in them than pure entertainment."

Released in November and December, MGM's *Battleground*, Republic's *Sands of Iwo Jima*, and Fox's *Twelve O'Clock High* would finish among *Variety*'s top ten grosses for 1950. *Battleground* was MGM's biggest moneymaker for the year; *Sands of Iwo Jima* was the greatest success in Republic history. Both programmatically celebrated the ordinary soldier and each was a personal triumph.

Battleground, which depicted the Siege of Bastogne during the Battle of the Bulge, was Dore Schary's pet project—and had been even at RKO. Screenwriter Bob Pirosh's first draft was submitted in mid-January 1948; by early spring, Schary had begun casting the main roles. He resigned from RKO that summer, after the project was terminated by the studio's new owner, Howard Hughes, and brought *Battleground* with him to MGM. Louis B. Mayer could not imagine that Americans wanted to be entertained by the Battle of the Bulge but supported Schary for his own reasons, telling Nicholas Schenk that the film's flop would teach the new boy a lesson.

Supervising every aspect of the project known in-house as "Schary's folly," MGM's new vice president in charge of production was a man with a mission. *Battleground*, Schary told the *New York Herald Tribune*, had to be made. As the prospect of a new war against Communism loomed, Schary wanted to reiterate the ideals of the last war. His interviews paraphrased the movie's dialogue. "As the years go by, a lot of people are going to forget, but you won't," an army chaplain tells the beleaguered troops. "Don't let anybody tell you that you were a sucker to fight in a war against fascism." Still, as the movie begins and ends on the field of battle, there is a sense that the war is not yet over.

Battleground's battleground was, quite literally, a soundstage—or, rather, two soundstages. Schary removed a wall to create an enormous controlled environment populated by numerous war movie veterans. If the studio was ambivalent, the military proved highly supportive. Pirosh's script was vetted by the man who had commanded the 101st Airborne Division during the siege of Bastogne, and one of his officers was present during the shooting. The army furnished tanks, trained director William Wellman's actors, and provided extras (listed in the credits as "the original 'Screaming Eagles' of the 101st Airborne Division, who play themselves").

Telecast live on NBC, the premiere was an occasion for much fanfare. Two military bands played outside the Astor Theatre; New York's mayor William O'Dwyer was present, along with assorted army and navy brass; and Schary was decorated for his contribution to morale. Already hailed in *Variety* as Hollywood's "first great [World War II] picture," *Battleground* confounded studio expectations by becoming both a tremendous critical and commercial success. "The Intimate Story of a Bunch of Fellows from Anybody's Home Town," the movie received six Oscar nominations and won four, including James Whitmore's for supporting actor.

As *Battleground* vindicated the liberal antifascist Schary, *Sands of Iwo Jima* served to canonize his ideological other, John Wayne. Wayne's career was already approaching the stratosphere. His biographers note that during a single week in mid-November, close to the release of *She Wore a Yellow Ribbon*, there were nine Wayne vehicles playing in Los Angeles, and all were doing outstanding business.

The second installment of John Ford's cavalry trilogy, again adapted by Frank Nugent from a story by James Warner Bellah, *She Wore a Yellow Ribbon* was elegiac, pictorial, and shot in Technicolor. The action goes around and around through Monument Valley, the cast striking poses appropriate to the weather. Still shooting throughout the 1948 campaign and in postproduction during the winter of 1949, the movie opens with the ominous announcement that Custer is dead and a hyperbolic warning that "one more such defeat" will ensure that a century shall pass "before another wagon train dare[s] to cross the plains."

John Wayne plays Nathan Brittles, an older officer six days from retirement, yet "fated to wield the sword of destiny." Like *Fort Apache*, *She Wore a Yellow Ribbon* advocates a peaceful settlement with the Indians. But problems have arisen. The redskin leadership is more bellicose, and the federal government has emboldened them with its tendency toward appeasement. The young officers—John Agar and Harry Carey Jr.—are distracted by their romantic rivalry for Joanne Dru's favors, and Wayne's character is obliged to save a dangerous situation by countermanding orders and acting on his own.

As the movie began with the articulation of a crisis, it ends with voice-over intimations of eternal vigilance: "So here they are, the dog-faced soldiers, the regulars, the fifty-cents-a-day professionals, riding the outposts of a nation. From Fort Reno to Fort Apache, from Sheriden to Stark, they were all the same. Men in dirty-shirt blue, and only a cold page in the history books to mark their passing. But wherever they rode, and whatever they fought for, that place became the United States." Did that now include Europe?

Ford received respectful reviews. *Newsweek* found *She Wore a Yellow Ribbon* "forceful" if "excessively sentimental." The *New York Herald Tribune* deemed Ford "in fine form." Others, including the *Daily Worker*, saw the movie as continued evidence of Ford's decline. The *Worker's* review specifically objected to the movie's representation of the Indian wars as "a glorious page in our history." Adding insult to injury, *She Wore a Yellow Ribbon* seemed "terribly solicitous about the Confederacy" (for which several officers had fought), thus doing "its best to put the stamp of reaction on an already obscured and distorted era."

Variety predicted good box office, and indeed, the movie grossed a hefty $5.2 million. Wayne's *Sands of Iwo Jima* followed a month later. Armed with the knowledge that *Battleground* and *Twelve O'Clock High* were in production, Republic producer Edmund Grainger ripped his title from a newspaper headline and his finale from the famous news photo of the American flag raised on Mount Suribachi, dashed off a treatment, and commissioned Harry Brown, who had written the novel on which the 1946 war film *A Walk in the Sun* was based, to knock out a script. Brown mixed elements of *Bataan*, *Wake Island*, and *Guadalcanal Diary*, leaving plenty of space for interpolated combat footage. The marine corps, as historian Lawrence H. Suid has noted, was the service branch that most successfully publicized itself, often with motion pictures. *Sands of Iwo Jima* was the quintessential marine corps movie—dedicated to the corps, emblazoned with the *Semper Fidelis* insignia, and playing the marine corps hymn under the opening credits, serving as a recruiting poster well into the 1960s.

Budgeted at $1 million (the most expensive movie Republic ever made), *Sands of Iwo Jima* was the most successful movie in the studio's history, grossing nearly $4 million and finishing eighth on *Variety's* list of 1950 releases, and was nominated for four Oscars, including Best Actor. It was on the basis of *Sands of Iwo Jima* and *Rio Grande*, released in late 1950, that Wayne would displace Bob Hope as Hollywood's top box-office attraction. The role of a tough marine sergeant with a massive chip on his shoulder and a battlefield martyr elevated Wayne to myth—America's Cowboy Warrior.

A day after Wayne's Sergeant Stryker burst on the scene, Fox's *Twelve O'Clock High* opened in Los Angeles. *Twelve O'Clock High* recounted the Britain-based daylight bombing missions that pounded Germany throughout 1942—with devastating results for the often poorly equipped fliers as well as their targets. Even more than *Sands of Iwo Jima*, this movie concerned the psychological cost of war and the burden of leadership. Just as Sergeant Stryker overcomes difficult personalities to whip his marines into combat shape, so Gregory Peck's equally tough General Savage molds the character and fighting attitude of his air force division.

Despite his name, Savage is a more evolved soldier than Stryker. He is sensitive as well as patriotic, and he realizes the cost as well as the benefits of the brutal discipline that he demands of his demoralized men. (And, of course, himself: the burden of his responsibilities results in a temporary nervous breakdown.) But where *Battleground* advanced a rationale for war, *Twelve O'Clock High* accepts war as an existential condition. Savage neither preaches the benefits of democracy nor warns against the triumph of fascism. Rather, he tells his men that they can expect to die—and that the meaning of their mission is to inflict maximum destruction upon the enemy before they do.[25]

In his attempt to secure air force support for the movie, Darryl Zanuck wrote directly to air force chief of staff Hoyt Vandenberg. It was mid-September 1948, two months into the Berlin airlift, and war tension was high—indeed, Vandenberg was already involved in contingency plans to use atomic weapons against the Soviets. Noting that, like his Oscar-winning *Gentleman's Agreement*, *Twelve O'Clock High* was unconventional entertainment and hence a financial risk, Zanuck assured Vandenberg that this "powerful, sincere, and dramatic story" served as "tremendous propaganda" for the air force. Zanuck told Vandenberg that he was ready to assign William Wellman to direct the movie, but he first had to know if the air force wanted this film made and was prepared to provide assistance. He consequently received the promise of an air force field, a minimum of eight obsolete B-17 bombers, and the use of actual combat footage; in return, the Pentagon requested script approval. (Among other things, the air force wanted less consumption of alcohol, at least by the officers.)

More air force glory: some fifteen months after it was first announced, Howard Hughes's long-announced *Jet Pilot* had, as *Variety* put it, finally taxied to a takeoff with no less than John Wayne in the title role. Janet Leigh was cast as his Russian counterpart—no ballerina this time but a Soviet sex bomb who worships the state, even as she rejects teamwork. Seduced by this "silly Siberian cupcake," Wayne defects, although true love ensures that the couple will ultimately redefect to the USA. One of the least likely productions of the era, *Jet Pilot* was actually a variation of *Ninotchka*, directed (initially) by Josef von

---

25. In his 1953 book *Film in the Battle of Ideas*, John Howard Lawson would criticize *Twelve O'Clock High* as "an important step in Hollywood's development of the Nazi theory that training for war, enforced by the will of a 'superior' class and accepted without question by 'inferiors,' is the highest aim to which we can aspire." According to Lawrence H. Suid, the movie has enjoyed a long afterlife in leadership-training seminars, illustrating the problems of decision making in business and education as well as war.

Sternberg, who may or may not have been responsible for the movie's aerial double-entendres, with the rival pilots buzzing each other's planes.

December 27, a month before President Truman will announce development of a "super-bomb" five hundred times more powerful than those dropped on Hiroshima and Nagasaki, the air force concludes a two-year investigation by denying that the country is being probed and spied on by alien spaceships from outer space.

Too late: *True* magazine has just published former marine corps pilot Major Donald E. Keyhoe's sensational assertion that the government is lying and "the flying saucers are real." Chief of information for the Commerce Department during the Hoover administration, Keyhoe had numerous government contacts and, angered by the absence of official information, decided that the air force must be concealing something important—namely that "for the past 175 years, the earth has been under systematic close-range examination by living, intelligent observers from another planet" and that this examination had "increased markedly during the past two years."

The opposite point is argued in *The Flying Saucer*, a cheapster written, produced, and directed by thirty-year-old actor Mikel Conrad that wobbles into theaters during the first week of the New Year. Conrad, most recently seen as a police officer in *Abbott and Costello Meet the Killer*, cast himself as a playboy recruited by the U.S. government to go to Alaska, in the company of a female agent, to investigate reports of a flying saucer. Battling a gang of Soviet spies who are also seeking the saucer, Conrad discovers that the device has actually been developed by a reclusive American inventor. A providential avalanche dispatches the spies and the saucer is blown up—its secret is safe.

Variety terms Conrad's directorial effort "feeble," but the neophyte filmmaker is at least able to hoax Louella Parsons when he engages an actor to impersonate an FBI agent and confiscate a print of *The Flying Saucer* in the name of national security. The credulous Parsons reports this in her column as a straight news item. But who can really blame her? The spies are real and the U.S. Air Force may not be the only government agency involved in a cover-up.

January 21, 1950, former State Department official Alger Hiss is found guilty of perjury, having testified before HUAC that he never turned over classified papers to former Communist Whittaker Chambers. Five days later, California congressman Richard M. Nixon—an announced candidate for the Senate—stands before the House of Representatives to review his own part in the Hiss investigation and account for a conspiracy "so effective, so well entrenched, and so well defended by apologists in high places that it was not discovered and ap-prehended until it was too late to prosecute."

February 5, the British government reveals that their German-born atomic physicist Karl Fuchs is a confessed Soviet spy. Four days after that, in Wheeling, West Virginia, Senator Joseph McCarthy of Wisconsin informs the Ohio County Women's Republican Club that he has the names of 205 Soviet agents "known to the Secretary of State as being members of the Communist Party and [never-theless] still working and shaping the policy of the State Department." Senator McCarthy projects himself as the nation's Patriot Roughneck, predicting all-out war between Christianity and atheistic Communism. By mid-February, Soviet dictator Joseph Stalin has signed the Treaty of Friendship and Alliance and Mu-tual Help with China's victorious leader Mao Tse-tung. February 20, McCarthy repeats his charges on the floor of the Senate, as screenwriter Emmet Lavery clears himself once more with the dark and grim *Guilty of Treason*—an Eagle-Lion cheapster opening that day in Los Angeles.

As president of the Screen Writers Guild, Lavery had been subpoenaed to testify at the 1947 HUAC hearings. His major screen credits were two luridly exploitative examples of wartime propaganda, both directed by Edward Dmy-tryk: the phenomenally successful *Hitler's Children* and its atrocity-rich, anti-Japanese follow-up, *Behind the Rising Sun*. Although frequently assumed to be Red, Lavery was a moderate liberal, as well as a practicing Catholic, albeit with a New Deal background and numerous Popular Front associations. He had served as director of the Federal Theater's Play Bureau and, once in Hollywood, was active in the Hollywood Writers Mobilization, the Hollywood Democratic Committee, and HICCASP. Before he was elected president of the SWG, he was considering a run for Congress.

Having already tangled with HUAC when the committee investigated the Federal Theater in 1938, Lavery was subpoenaed by the Tenney committee in late 1946: "While probably not enrolled as a bona fide member of the Commu-nist Party," the committee concluded, Lavery "has proved himself a faithful fellow-traveler and has gone along at all times with the Communists in the Screen Writers Guild. [His] record, both in the Screen Writers Guild and in the Hollywood Writers Mobilization, indicates either a deep sympathy for the Communist movement or an amazing stupidity which is hardly compatible with his background and education."

A few months later, Jack Warner informed HUAC investigators that Lavery was one of the twelve supposed Communists Warner had identified and fired from his studio; in Washington that October, Warner repeated the charge with another friendly witness, Rupert Hughes, suggesting that Lavery was a Communist masquerading as a Catholic. Lavery himself testified a few days later—understandably more interested in clearing his name than questioning HUAC's right to investigate his political associations. Once back in Hollywood, he supported the implementation of an SWG loyalty oath.

Guilty of Treason, which evolved out of an earlier anti-Communist movie that Lavery had worked on, represented another attempt to establish his bona fides, presenting the case for Jozef Cardinal Mindszenty, primate of Hungary. The day after Christmas 1948, Mindszenty and thirteen others had been arrested for black-marketeering and conspiracy to overthrow Hungary's Communist government; he was jailed for thirty-eight days, tried, and sentenced to life imprisonment. Showing the influence of *1984*, as well as October 1947, *Guilty of Treason* opens with newsreels of marching Communists and Mindszenty's warning that "the enemy will appear as one who wishes to save us." A low-budget affair in which everyone hangs around the same informer-ridden Budapest café, the movie was shot Hollywood "documentary" style, with actors impersonating such real-life Hungarian heavies as Mátyás Rákosi and Gabor Peter, as well as Cardinal Mindzenty (veteran tough guy Charles Bickford).

Human interest is provided by a chain of unrequited love: the avuncular American journalist Tom Kelly (Paul Kelly) mopes after Hungarian cutie Stephanie Varna (Bonita Granville, playing a version of her role in *Hitler's Children*), but Stephanie is engaged to a Russian colonel (Richard Derr) who believes the Party infallible. She, however, has ties to Mindszenty; when the prelate is arrested and medicated to change his personality in preparation for his show trial, the brainwashed Soviet true believer gives up his shocked fiancée to the authorities without a qualm. As in *Hitler's Children*, Granville receives a salacious whipping.

If the actual Mindszenty, an unreconstructed monarchist, implacable foe of land reform, and passive accomplice with the Nazi deportation of Hungarian Jews, believes that a third world war is imminent, he isn't alone.

In Washington, DC, Secretary of State Dean Acheson and Paul H. Nitze, the new director of the State Department Policy Planning staff, are preparing National Security Council 68, a secret document outlining a rapid buildup of political, economic, and military strength toward a conflict between the Eurasian monolith and the Free World. The risks are unprecedented, the expense seems outrageous, the tone is beyond apocalyptic: "With the development of increasingly terrifying weapons of mass destruction, every individual faces the ever-present possibility of annihilation."

The situation cannot be pondered at leisure. Debate must be sacrificed. The Soviet Union "is animated by a new fanatic faith [that] seeks to impose its absolute authority over the rest of the world." To defend freedom, it will be necessary to reinforce and expand the security state. The struggle is total and while victory can never be complete, defeat will be absolute. "The issues that face us are momentous, involving the fulfillment or destruction not only of this Republic but of civilization itself."

Moreover, Soviet political propaganda—which is to say their Ministry of Truth—is deemed no less dangerous than actual military aggression. Any loss of credibility is as dangerous as an actual defeat. Perceived intimidation might force a change in the international balance of power. American security depends on not only arms but also public opinion. I.F. Stone notes "the panic which is sweeping over the American people," as the Patriot Roughneck McCarthy zeroes in on Owen Lattimore, the erstwhile State Department employee whom he has declared America's most dangerous Soviet spy—like Cardinal Mindszenty, he is *guilty of treason*!

The Next Voice You Hear goes into production, wrapping four days before Pope Pius XXII issues his encyclical letter "Anni Sacri." Like Senator McCarthy and the National Security Council, the pope has declared 1950 a Holy Year. On March 12, under the headline "POPE URGES FIGHT AGAINST GODLESS," the *New York Times* reports that "Anni Sacri" enunciates a program to counteract atheistic propaganda throughout the world and particularly in the Soviet Union: "What seems to us to be not only the gravest evil, but also the root of all evil is this: That often truth is replaced by lies, which are used as instruments of dispute."

Vast populations hypnotized by the flux of modern information, baffled into paralysis by a surfeit of data—each in its way, MGM, the NSC, and the papacy are responding to the world of *1984* or the panicked search for coherence that will be described in Jacques Ellul's *Propaganda*: people yearn for "simple thoughts, elementary explanations, a 'key' that will permit them to take a position, and even ready-made opinions. . . . The majority prefers expressing stupidities to not expressing any opinion."

Sunset / Panic / In a Lonely Place

The scenarios proliferate. March 23, 1950: Secretary of Defense Louis Johnson receives a draft of NSC 68 the day before *The Next Voice* has a sneak preview and even as the *New York Times Magazine* prepares to run an article, signed by mogul

Samuel Goldwyn, on the challenge of television. (Among the platitudes: the new medium's "effect on Hollywood is already clear. Hollywood is starting to make fewer pictures—and, I believe, better ones.")

Mid-April, the movie industry's nightmare self-portrait materializes. Initially conceived as a grotesque comedy about a silent film star who attempts to revive her career, Billy Wilder's *Sunset Boulevard*, co-written with Charles Brackett, has mutated into something far darker: Norma Desmond, a deranged movie queen played by actual silent star Gloria Swanson, takes a young and unsuccessful screenwriter as her lover cum script doctor and winds up killing him in a jealous rage. Indeed, the dead man narrates the film floating facedown in Desmond's swimming pool.

Shooting throughout the spring of 1949, its production shrouded in secrecy, *Sunset Boulevard* began previewing months before its scheduled opening to select audiences of Hollywood influentials. According to the legend, after one such screening on the Paramount lot, enraged MGM potentate Louis B. Mayer confronted Wilder, screaming that the Vienna-born filmmaker had disgraced the industry that made and fed him and should be tarred and feathered and run out of Hollywood. (To which the unintimidated Wilder supposedly replied, "Fuck you.") Never mentioning the specter of television, *Sunset Boulevard* displaces Hollywood's current crisis to the technological crisis of twenty years earlier—the coming of sound. "I'm still big," Norma protests, "it's the pictures that got small."

"Movies are dreamlike and fantastic," Parker Tyler wrote in his preface to *Magic and Myth of the Movies*, first published in spring 1947, along with Siegfried Kracauer's *From Caligari to Hitler*, a moment when Hollywood was distracted by the visiting HUAC. "Camera trickery really is camera magic. Cinema illusion creates a throwback in the mood of the spectator to [ancient] beliefs in ghosts, secret forces, telepathy, etc."

Populated by capricious producers, hungry writers, and indifferent agents, *Sunset Boulevard* trades on an insider's view of Hollywood. But even as it works to dispel the notion that motion pictures are made in heaven ("audiences don't know somebody sits down and writes the picture, they think the actors make it up as the picture goes along"), *Sunset Boulevard* evokes their uncanny aura— satirizing as it attests to the power of motion pictures to reanimate the past and restore the dead to life.

The dream factory is Nathanael West's dream dump, haunted by a pathetic, obsolete, murderous star. "The whole place seemed to have been stricken with a kind of creeping paralysis," muses the screenwriter Joe Gillis (William Holden). Fleeing repo men about to seize his car, he has turned in to a handy driveway to discover the moldering mansion where sacred monster Norma Desmond lives in seclusion, save for her director-turned-chauffeur (played by director-turned-actor Erich von Stroheim) and the rats who scamper in the empty swimming pool. When they first meet, Norma mistakes Gillis for the undertaker, come to bury her dead pet monkey.

With *Sunset Boulevard*, the movies recognize themselves as history. But while the silent era, as James Agee would write in *Sight and Sound*, is "granted a kind of barbarous grandeur and intensity," present-day Hollywood is a ruin. The cubicle in which Gillis and another writer work on their script turns out to be a fragment of Norma's once-palatial dressing room on the Paramount lot. ("Hollywood's like Egypt. Full of crumbling pyramids," producer David O. Selznick is said to have told writer Ben Hecht as they wandered the studio one dawn that spring. "It'll never come back. It'll just keep crumbling until finally the wind blows the last studio prop across the sands.")

Swanson and Stroheim are supported by other silent "waxworks," including Buster Keaton, Anna Q. Nilsson, H.B. Warner (who played Christ in Cecil B. DeMille's silent *King of Kings*), and even Swanson's young self, shown in *Queen Kelly* (which had been directed by Stroheim). It's over; they are all ghosts. *Sunset Boulevard* is narrated from beyond the grave—Wilder had actually shot an opening scene, discarded after a disastrous preview, with the dead protagonist perched on a slab in the morgue, recounting his tale to an audience of fellow corpses. It's as if the movie colony was, as Diana Trilling called the world shown by Orwell's *1984*, "a perpetual nightmare of living death."[26]

That nightmare is dramatized in *D.O.A.*, which opens in late April. The protagonist of this most existential of films noir marches into a police station to report a murder—his own. Inexplicably, someone has spiked his drink with some sort of radioactive radium poison. Under sentence of death, this crass everyman lurches via flashback through a gaudy labyrinth of liars, crooks, and killers. Crazed hepcats party like there's no tomorrow; ranting psychopaths are ever eager to shoot up the joint (the latter include the highly decorated World War II

26. *Sunset Boulevard* was understood as an event. *Newsweek* put Swanson on its cover six weeks before the movie premiered on August 10, 1950, at Radio City in New York. *Sunset Boulevard* was critically well received and set an opening-day record at Radio City, but its success was relatively modest—grossing $2.35 million to finish twenty-ninth for the year, per *Variety*. Nominated for eleven Oscars, the movie took home only three: for best story and screenplay and two minor ones.

vet Neville Brand, making his debut). Reality disintegrates. The normal world seems contaminated. The doomed antihero runs through downtown San Francisco past a mocking newsstand rack of *Life* magazines. Dead on arrival but still talking, he looks right into the camera and states, "All I did was notarize a bill of sale." His case is consigned to the files. Had the combination of nuclear jitters, divestment blues, ascendant TV, and political paranoia inspired the industry's more sensitive souls to see themselves as Left Bank philosophers, beset with dread?

Meanwhile, another tale of animated corpses is nearly complete. In later interviews, Elia Kazan will fondly describe *Panic in the Streets* as his first real movie: "I got my confidence, finally!" The much-lauded forty-one-year-old director is at the peak of his success: his production of Tennessee Williams's sensational *A Streetcar Named Desire*, introducing Marlon Brando as Stanley Kowalski, opened in December 1947; a few months later, he received an Oscar for his direction of *Gentleman's Agreement*; February 1949 brought his production of Arthur Miller's Pulitzer Prize–winning *Death of a Salesman*.

Shot on location in New Orleans with many nonactors, *Panic in the Streets* was for him an experiment in neorealism and fluid camerawork. It was also, Kazan would recall, something of a vacation—although the premise, derived from two stories published in *Dime Detective* by the team of Edward and Edna Anhalt, suggested an urgent social crisis. Rather than an individual, there's poison in the body politic. Plague comes to America, and for much of the movie, only Dr. Clinton Reed (Richard Widmark) is willing to admit it.

Reed first appears as a dad, the father of an eight-year-old boy, and later introduces himself as "Dr. Reed of the U.S. Public Health Service." Sharing a surname with Walter Reed, the nineteenth-century public health hero who instituted quarantines against yellow fever and cholera, he is army doctor as government activist: "One of the jobs of my department is to keep the plague out of this country," he asserts. On the other hand, he's also something of a loner—an Ibsenesque "enemy of the people," a self-described alarmist who orchestrates a manhunt for the criminals unwittingly carrying the plague but whose actions turn out to be entirely justified.

Mainly, he's a certain kind of professional who has to join forces with another professional—Paul Douglas's tough cop. The cop hates doctors and has an irrational dislike of civil servants. Nevertheless, after some initial sparring, they bond in battling dithering politicians and nosy reporters for control of the situation. In particular, the two government professionals agree on controlling the press through preventive detention. Kazan saw this professional alliance as a left-right coalition. "The doc was a New Dealer and the policeman a Republican," he explained to French critic Michel Ciment. "That was the way we thought, the remnants of my former political training: everybody representing some social political position." What then was the epidemic threatening the city? Acutely aware that *Panic in the Streets* went into production only a few years after the appearance of Albert Camus's novel *The Plague*, Ciment asked Kazan if the plague interested him as a symbol. "I should be able to say yes, but no," was Kazan's response. "I minimized it."[27]

As in Camus's allegory, Kazan's hero struggles against apathetic authorities as well as social catastrophe—but Camus's protagonist is also in revolt against absurdity. *The Plague* evokes the mood of the isolated town ("each of us had to be content to live only for the day, alone under the vast indifference of the sky") whose citizens realize that "they [have] been sentenced, for an unknown crime, to an indeterminate period of punishment." The people of New Orleans are granted no such consciousness. Camus evokes a particular sense of solidarity: "once the town gates were shut, every one of us realized that all [were] in the same boat. . . . No longer were there individual destinies; only a collective destiny." Kazan raises the possibility of a total—possibly worldwide—emergency but without solidarity and as a problem for the experts.

Diseased illegal aliens and their gangster cohorts emerge from teeming waterfront dives, threatening to pollute the nation! *Panic in the Streets* ends in a spectacle of mindless contagion. Scrambling, climbing, fighting, running from the police, the infected gangster Blackie (Jack Palance) demonstrates a will to escape—and thus contaminate—so powerful as to suggest a force of nature. In April 1950, Attorney General J. Howard McGrath went McCarthy one better, noting that Communists "are everywhere—in factories, offices, butcher stores, on street corners, in private businesses. And each carries in himself the germ of death for society."

The fear is not foreign occupation, as in *The Plague*, but foreign subversion; quarantine is not a condition but a weapon. The danger is such that Dr. Reed is justified in taking the law into his own hands. "If there's a plague here," Mrs. Reed (Barbara Bel Geddes) tells him, "you're the most important man in town."

---

27. *The Plague* was published in the United States during the summer of 1948 and was subsequently acquired by MGM as a vehicle for Spencer Tracy. Embarrassed by the prospect of a Hollywood movie, Camus canceled the deal in early 1949. Richard Brooks, who was adapting the novel, incorporated his material into another MGM property, *Basra*; the movie was released in July 1950 as *Crisis*. Cary Grant starred as an American doctor compelled to operate on the dictator of an unnamed Latin American country. In the parallel universe that is the movies, *Panic in the Streets* appeared in place of the never-made but similarly scheduled *The Plague*.

Dr. Reed's suggestion of martial law, his aggressive questioning, and his demand for press management in fighting contamination is an unavoidable but powerful metaphor. As J. Edgar Hoover told HUAC in the spring of 1947, anticipating the U.S. publication of Camus's novel by some eighteen months, Communism "is a way of life—an evil and malignant way of life. It reveals a condition akin to disease that spreads like an epidemic; a quarantine is necessary to keep it from infecting the nation."

What was on Kazan's mind? It's striking that he changed the ethnicity of the original carrier and his cousin to Armenian and emphasized that the restaurant owners who cover for them were, like Kazan, Greek. Among other things, the Internal Security Act of 1950 prohibited entry or settlement of immigrants who— again like Kazan—were or had been Communists. Kazan was a CP member for a little over a year during the mid-1930s, while he was with the Group Theatre— although it was not until May 1943, when he attempted to enlist in the OSS, that the FBI was alerted to his "close Communist affiliations." Four years later, after making two Hollywood movies, Kazan was categorized by a Los Angeles informant as one of the "weird and radical people" Walter Wanger had imported from New York; he was named as a Communist by Jack Warner during his May 1947 HUAC interrogation. The next issue of the anti-Communist magazine *Plain Talk* ironically proposed Kazan for "the Order of Lenin."

Nevertheless, Kazan was not subpoenaed, and whatever the autumn of 1947 might have been for other Hollywood Reds (ex and otherwise), he was monumentally distracted—back in New York City, rehearsing his production of *A Streetcar Named Desire*. The play that launched Marlon Brando and was arguably the greatest stage success of Kazan's career had opened on Broadway in early December, only a few weeks before the New York Film Critics Circle named his *Gentleman's Agreement* the best picture of the year. At first, Kazan seemed to imagine that he was immune. As his anti-anti-Semitic problem film went on to be the eighth-highest grosser of 1948 and win the Oscar for best picture, the director continued to play fellow traveler. He served on the East Coast "Freedom from Fear" committee and participated in a testimonial dinner in support of the Hollywood Ten.[28]

Allegations kept piling up. Kazan landed on the American Legion's "undesirable" list, and his FBI file fattened even as he scored his second great career

---

28. Shortly after the academy anointed him best director, Kazan began negotiating a fifteen-year, six-picture, million-dollar deal with Fox. The tenacity with which he fought (in vain) to eliminate the studio's boilerplate morals clause—used to blacklist the Hollywood Ten—suggests anxiety that his red past might someday catch up with him.

triumph. The month after *Death of a Salesman* opened on Broadway, the director saved his patron Zanuck considerable embarrassment by taking over *Pinky*, after its first director, brusque John Ford, alienated the movie's sensitive co-star Ethel Waters. In a message to the Peace Conference, Soviet director Sergei Gerasimov had singled out Kazan for praise as an "honest artist" who, along with Trumbo, Dmytryk, Lawson, and Chaplin, was using the film medium "to promote mutual understanding among nations." In June, Kazan's name was attached to a telegram protesting the prison sentences given CP functionaries John Gates, Harry Winston, and Gus Hall after they were convicted of conspiring against the government in 1949.

This pattern will continue through the summer that *Panic in the Streets* is released to excellent reviews—albeit not from the *Daily Worker*, which deems the director's "neo-realist" use of locations and actors to be ersatz and his movie's premise a "mighty cheap" gimmick. The reviewer doesn't elaborate; perhaps confused by Kazan's politics, he doesn't characterize the doctor as a G-man or criticize a situation where professional anti-disease fighters prevail.

Elia Kazan would not be the lone ex-Communist to have a movie released that season. Nor was *Sunset Boulevard* the only production to manifest the darkening mood that accompanied the implementation of the blacklist after the 1947 HUAC hearings. There was *In a Lonely Place*, a movie by Kazan's old associate and sometime protégé Nicholas Ray, which began shooting in late 1949 and was released in Los Angeles in mid-May, a few months ahead of *Sunset Boulevard*. *In a Lonely Place* similarly represents the movie industry as a crime scene.

Two years younger than Kazan, Ray had joined the Party in late 1934, while a member of the Theatre of Action in New York; holding several WPA jobs during the late 1930s, he had an FBI file going back to June 1941, when a neighbor reported his suspicious quantity of "Communist Party literature." Involved as he was with the Federal Theater and the Almanac Singers, Ray scarcely lacked for left-wing associations. The FBI kept tabs on him throughout World War II, when he worked with John Houseman on the Voice of America under William Donovan's Foreign Information Service. (Perhaps collecting Communists with ties to Donovan, J. Edgar Hoover requested a "custodial detention card" for Ray.)

Meanwhile, agents checked material in HUAC files to see if Ray had been discharged from the Works Progress Administration for political radicalism. But after he left the OWI and went to Hollywood to work with Kazan on *A Tree Grows in Brooklyn*, the FBI lost interest—filing only desultory reports on Ray's activities as part of the Hollywood Writers Mobilization, including the 1946 radio adaptation of the Federation of American Scientists' bestseller *One World or None.*

Unlike Kazan or Houseman or even Billy Wilder (all of whom supported the Committee for the First Amendment), Ray is nowhere cited in the Tenney committee reports; perhaps his burgeoning movie career had curtailed his political activity. Houseman, now in Hollywood, interested RKO's new head, Dore Schary, in an adaptation of the proletarian novel *Thieves Like Us,* and Ray became the director and adapter. Eventually titled *They Live by Night,* this mixture of late-1930s Popular Front sentimentality and late-1940s romantic fatalism was in production during the summer of 1947; it would subsequently become a haunting allegory of Hollywood's lost innocence, in part because the doomed, painfully naive lovers were played by two key young actors. Farley Granger first appeared as the teenage partisan in *The North Star,* blinded in defense of the motherland, while Cathy O'Donnell plucked the nation's heartstrings in her debut as the handless war veteran's faithful sweetheart in *The Best Years of Our Lives.*

In early 1948, Ray made *A Woman's Secret* for RKO, and the following summer he directed Humphrey Bogart in the Columbia release *Knock on Any Door.* Some months later, a confidential source told the FBI that Ray (an associate of "persons strongly suspected of Communist connections") would be assigned to *I Married a Communist.* Ray actually took the job and then quit. Despite this, he would maintain, Howard Hughes protected him. Ray's source was Robert Mitchum, an RKO contract star busted for marijuana possession in 1948 and sentenced to a two-month stretch in an honor farm. "A guy out of the DA's office had told [Mitchum] in a drunken moment that my office, my house, my car, my everything had been bugged to the teeth, and that Howard Hughes had learned about it, and had called his executive producer, Sid Rogell, and said he wanted all the bugs and harassment taken off Nick Ray: 'I don't want that boy hurt.' And he asked nothing in return."

Still, Ray didn't get another assignment from Hughes for over a year, until May 1949, when he was assigned to the Joan Fontaine melodrama eventually released as *Born to Be Bad* for RKO. A few months later, he was loaned to Columbia to direct *In a Lonely Place,* again with Bogart. Working from and substantially changing Dorothy B. Hughes's crime novel, Ray emphasized the Hollywood atmosphere and used the movie as a means to critique the star's tough-guy persona.

Bogart had been bruised in the press for his prominent role in the Committee for the First Amendment. Perhaps still smarting from his embarrassing volte-face, including an admission that he had been a Communist dupe, Bogart plays an embittered writer whose career has foundered not as a result of his left-wing politics, but because of his heavy drinking, bad attitude, and terrible temper. Building in intensity, *In a Lonely Place* is the story of a writer who tries to change his (if not *the*) world and is ultimately betrayed by his own nature. For Ray, Bogart was "much more than an actor." He was a symbol, "the very image of our condition [whose] face was a living reproach."

The opening scene—set in a fashionable Beverly Hills boîte modeled after Bogie's lunchtime clubhouse, Romanoff's—allows Hollywood's then-best-paid actor to mock his agent, insult a successful director ("You're a popcorn salesman"), and physically assault the son of a studio head ("You give nepotism a bad name"). Rather than read the inane bestseller he's been given to adapt, he inveigles the simpleminded hat-check girl—the embodiment of Hollywood's imagined audience—to just tell him the story.

If the hero's character suggests a measure of existential alienation, the film itself verges on psychodrama. Ray used his first Hollywood apartment as the tormented writer's lair and cast his estranged second wife Gloria Grahame in a role that might naturally have gone to Lauren Bacall. (More complex than Bacall, Grahame gives the impression of having been wounded in ways Bogart cannot even begin to fathom—if he even cared to try.)[29]

As the title suggests, the movie colony is an environment of smashed careers and free-floating paranoia. Mistrust is endemic. Noting in the script's margin that their relationship "must be *warm*—endure everything—friend to the death," Ray put special emphasis on the Bogart character's unusual relationship with his agent (Art Smith). A former member of the Group Theatre, Smith would be blacklisted after being named by his erstwhile comrade Elia Kazan.

Countdown

This is where we came in. . . .

The century declared by *Time* to be America's approaches its midpoint amid dreams of disaster, memories of cosmic cataclysm, the suggestion of vast conspiracies, visions of extraterrestrial visitation, a sense of impending jihad, and intimations of Judgment Day.

---

29. Ray and Grahame later seemed to reconcile, but their marriage ended in June 1951, after Ray returned to his Malibu beach house to discover Grahame in bed with Tony, his thirteen-year-old son by his previous wife. This notorious incident has been seen as the trauma that ultimately produced Ray's most enduring movie, the 1955 juvenile delinquency film *Rebel Without a Cause*. In 1960, Grahame married Tony Ray.

May 26, 1950: *Rocketship X-M* opens in New York, scripted by uncredited Dalton Trumbo. The movie has been made to beat the much-publicized *Destination Moon* and warn the nations of the world. Trumbo's scenario—attributed to director Kurt Neumann—blasts a rocket into space in order to establish an unassailable lunar base and thus control world peace. But the ship is knocked off course by a perhaps divinely directed meteor shower and, instead of the moon, lands on Mars.

Prophecy or déjà vu? This "familiar-looking rocky wasteland which one uninhibited soul in the Criterion balcony yesterday recognized as Arizona," per the *New York Times* review (and was in fact Death Valley), could just as well have been the testing grounds at White Sands from where the rocket ship was launched. The Geiger counter goes wild. The future merges with the past. *Rocketship X-M* has a circular logic. This postapocalyptic, radioactive planet is replete with ruined cities and cave people more devolved than the digger Indians for whom Henry Fonda expressed such contempt in *Fort Apache*. "You must get back to Earth," the dying mission commander tells his surviving crewmembers. "Tell them what we have found. . . ."

June 6: Richard Nixon, the two-term congressman who spearheaded the exposure of Communist traitor Alger Hiss, wins the primary to be the Republican candidate for U.S. senator as General Curtis LeMay directs Sunday Punch, a simulated first-strike attack on the Soviet Union, involving more than a hundred planes dropping unarmed nuclear-type bombs over airbases across the country. Three days later, Trumbo and fellow Communist screenwriter John Howard Lawson are handcuffed and shackled to an upper berth on a Kentucky-bound train, en route to the Ashland Federal Prison, where they will occupy adjoining cots in a dormitory with 119 other prisoners. The following week in New York City, an obscure twenty-eight-year-old machinist (and erstwhile Young Communist) named David Greenglass is arrested by the FBI at his Lower East Side hovel and charged with giving the Russians the Vital Secret of the Great Whatzit.

All hands on deck. American Business Consultants Inc., publisher of *Counterattack: The Newsletter of Facts to Combat Communism*, has just put out the first edition of *Red Channels: The Report of Communist Influence in Radio and Television*, listing several hundred prominent performers and producers along with their alleged Communist front affiliations. *Counterattack* promotes their guide to broadcasting subversion as follows:

IN AN EMERGENCY (at any given time)
IT WOULD REQUIRE ONLY THREE PERSONS (subversives)—

One engineer in master control at a radio network
One director in a radio station
One voice before a microphone
TO REACH 90 MILLION PEOPLE WITH A MESSAGE!

Simultaneously!

Threatened by the new power of broadcasting, movies plan to be bigger than ever. *Time*'s current issue features "Hollywood on the Tiber," a report on the $6 million super-production just undertaken by America's preeminent motion picture studio, Metro-Goldwyn-Mayer. *Quo Vadis*, for which a mammoth model of Nero's Rome has been constructed by three thousand Italian workmen in the 148-acre studio Cinecittà, will employ the Biggest Budget in Movie History to create nothing less than the Most Colossal Film Spectacle of All Time.

Not just imperial but planetary drama: For the fourth consecutive week, the *New York Times* bestseller list is topped by Immanuel Velikovsky's *Worlds in Collision*—an account of "wars in the celestial sphere" marshaling archeological evidence, ancient astronomical inscriptions, and stories from the Old Testament to argue that our Earth was struck by a comet with epoch-ending results twice within historical times. And then, on June 25, 1950, Seoul radio informs the universe that the Korean People's Army has crossed the Thirty-eighth Parallel and invaded the Republic of Korea.

Can this really be It? Reading the initial cables, General Matthew Ridgway envisions "armageddon, the last great battle between East and West." What will the ruthless Soviet dictator, now armed with the atomic bomb, do next? President Truman notes in his diary that "it looks like World War III is here." Three days later, the North Korean army captures Seoul. In between, the sober pseudo-documentary "view into the future" *Destination Moon* appears. Even more than *Rocketship X-M*, *Destination Moon*—directed for Eagle-Lion by Hollywood Nineteen survivor Irving Pichel—is obsessed with the notion of a lunar base. "There is no way to stop a missile launched from outer space," one space visionary explains. "That is the most important military fact of this century!"[30]

---

30. Where *Rocketship X-M* repeatedly contemplates Earth—our one world—through the rocket's portals, *Destination Moon* prefers images of the moon; Earth is described as "vulnerable . . . exposed." *Rocketship*'s progressive agenda mocks nationalism, mainly in the person of the team's comic relief—a ridiculously bragging Texas chauvinist. (*Destination Moon* also has a Texan, but he's an industrialist and not an idiot.) Less successfully, Trumbo's screenplay attempts to show the pilot (future friendly witness Lloyd Bridges) as an overbearing male chauvinist with regard to the female crew member (Osa Massen), who is the most humane and intelligent member of the expedition.

The day after Seoul falls, five Hollywood screenwriters (Alvah Bessie, Lester Cole, Ring Lardner Jr., Albert Maltz, and Samuel Ornitz), two directors (Herbert Biberman and Edward Dmytryk), and one producer (Adrian Scott) are found in contempt of Congress for refusing to answer questions regarding their membership in the Communist Party put to them by HUAC back in October 1947. Six are sent to prison—joining the already-jailed members of the so-called Hollywood Ten.

By week's end, President Truman has ordered American air and naval units to Korea (although his public statement characterizes the U.S. deployment as a mere "police action"), and as heralded by a six-page spread in *Look* magazine, another sort of hallucinated documentary joins *Destination Moon*, opening at New York's Radio City Music Hall along with a special July 4 stage show.

Like the cover of the *Bulletin of the Atomic Scientists*, the newspaper ads feature a clock, here superimposed over the globe with words that promise "the story of what happened at 8:30 PM all over the world." After a five-year lull, America is back at war, and thanks to MGM, *The Next Voice You Hear* is . . . God's.

A month before, under the rubric "Schary, the Messenger," *Newsweek* hailed MGM's forty-five-year-old head of production as "Hollywood's strong man." Some thought that Schary, a former writer, had been altogether too cozy with the Reds during the war and even afterward, when he was production chief at RKO. Others, most now blacklisted, felt that Schary epitomized the movie industry's spineless capitulation to HUAC and the witch-hunters. But Schary believed in the future—bravely optimistic, so *Newsweek* reported, in the face of "lowered box-office receipts, lost foreign markets, [and the] vanishing box-office pull of established (and aging) stars," not to mention scandals, congressional investigations, and the menace of television.

Movies were also smaller than ever. Arriving at MGM during the summer of 1948, Schary cut production costs by 27 percent. And with his second personal production, he performed what *Newsweek* and the *New York Herald Tribune* both deem to be a Hollywood "miracle." Shot in fourteen days for less than $500,000, this movie—displacing the nation's current box-office champ *Father of the Bride* to have its world premiere at Radio City Music Hall—is the antithesis of *Quo Vadis*, the least costly, most quickly made major production released by MGM since the dawn of the sound era. Thus, *The Next Voice You Hear* is both a Hollywood miracle and Hollywood's representation of miraculous divine intervention into human affairs. Will audiences take it for mass suckerology or once again believe in movie magic? (And would that make Schary heir to Orson Welles?)

By the movie's end, Joe is made to believe. The media, however, is generally unimpressed. The Catholic weekly *Commonweal* labels *The Next Voice* "pretentious corn" and excoriates MGM's self-congratulatory self-importance. The *New Yorker* deems the movie "a meandering, maudlin affair," gratuitously adding that "it's reassuring to know that God is still a better producer than Mr. Schary, but I rather pitied the actors who had to help demonstrate that fact." *Time*'s review is straight down the middle: *The Next Voice You Hear* is "an inspirational fable, shrewdly manipulated to warm moviegoers' hearts. Almost sure to receive both cheers and sneers, the picture fully merits neither. Simpleminded, ploddingly earnest, sometimes awkward and dull, it is less intriguing than its idea. Yet it is also more wary of the subject's pitfalls than might be expected . . ."

Only *New Republic* critic Robert Hatch seems to recognize that *The Next Voice You Hear* was something of a manifesto, a declaration not so much of faith in God as belief in the movies, the gospel according to Hollywood: "Mr. and Mrs. Average Smith, in whose California bungalow home we watch the divine family counselor at work, eat and talk and dream middle-class clichés." And where did those clichés arise? Actors Whitmore and Davis are "facsimiles of facsimiles," Hatch notes, and in commenting on "the manners and morals of present-day America," *The Next Voice You Hear* "resembles nothing so much as a mirror held up to a mirror."[31]

World War III has broken out, and MGM offers a new covenant. Big Brother in Hollywood, *The Next Voice You Hear* is the opposite of *1984*: no television, no Communists, no worries. The moral, however, is the same: *Reality exists in the human mind and nowhere else. . . . Whatever happens in all minds truly happens.* "Now and in the foreseeable future," Schary predicts in *Case History of a Movie*, a far from psychoanalytical but nevertheless revealing account of the making of *The Next Voice You Hear*, published to coincide with the film's release, "images on film are going to be a principal influence on our hearts and emotions and minds."

A principal influence and also a necessary one: "More than any other form of art or entertainment, movies are of the people, by the people and for the

---

31. Hatch was also the only critic who commented on the similarity between Ronald Reagan's divorced wife and his future spouse: "Whitmore's resemblance to Spencer Tracy is exceeded only by Miss Davis's likeness to Jane Wyman."

people. 'Of' in the sense of being about people, real people, whom audiences recognize as true; 'for' in the sense that the picture truly exists only when it is being viewed by the people of the audience; and 'by' in the sense that any one picture is a sum total of the minds and muscles of a great many contributors." Of the people, by the people, for the people: even in the apocalyptic, cathode-ray light of 1950, the regime of the movies shall not perish from the face of the earth.

III.

REDSKIN MENACE FROM OUTER SPACE:
AMERICA AT WAR, 1950–52

The Voice has spoken: war at last and the battlefield is everywhere! North Koreans in South Korea and Commies on the airwaves. Apaches threaten Los Alamos. Aliens buzz the pole. Washington, DC, is targeted by robots and infested with spies. Who then can lead us?

Five uneasy years of peace, a new enemy sneak attack, and American boys were again heading west (or was it east?), leaving Fort Apache to fight the Red Menace at Freedom's Frontier. It was familiar yet strange.

"No more glint of sunlight on the saber, the sweet music of saddle harness, the champ of bits," rhapsodized *New York Times* military correspondent Hanson Baldwin in an article published on July 2, 1950, scarcely a week into the Korean police action. "The sound of Boots and Saddles sings no more across the Great Plains; the horse has retired from the field of battle. The 'yellowlegs' who won the West with carbine and colt; the 'Garry Ovens' of the famous Seventh who died with Custer at the Little Big Horn ride no longer, for the cavalry has gone forever . . ." But, despite this odd non sequitur, the cavalry had hardly vanished. Rather, thanks to the success of John Ford's *Fort Apache* and *She Wore a Yellow Ribbon*, the Garry Ovens of the famous Seventh had found a new place to dwell. Ford was even then in Moab, Utah, shooting his third cavalry Western, *Rio Grande*.

The source, once more, was a James Warner Bellah story—"Mission with No Record," published in the *Saturday Evening Post* in September 1947. This time, however, the screenwriter was James K. McGuinness, who had recently departed his longtime base, MGM—forced out by devious fellow traveler Dore Schary, or so McGuinness's friends were convinced, in retaliation for his anti-Communist activism. And, rather than RKO, Ford's latest cavalry Western was to be released by star John Wayne's home studio, Republic—it was as though the director had embedded himself in the organization McGuinness co-founded, the Motion Picture Alliance for the Preservation of American Values.

The filmmaking had an almost defensive frugality (*Rio Grande* was modestly budgeted at under $1.3 million, too tight for Ford to use his beloved Monument Valley as a location) and, at least as compared to *Fort Apache*, zero tolerance for tolerance. The Apache were now seen through Bellah's eyes (or those of Henry Fonda's Colonel Thursday) as subhuman savages without a noble Cochise to articulate their grievances. *Fort Apache*'s real villain was the exploitative Indian agent; *Rio Grande* extends this contempt to the concept of civilian government as a whole, despite the presumption that General Ulysses S. Grant is the current president. The Civil War figures in the narrative with a strong undercurrent of sympathy for the defeated Confederacy. Even more striking is the anger directed against Washington for its insistence that, in pursuing marauding Apache guerrillas, the cavalry respect the Mexican border—and, more generally, for asserting that civilians, not soldiers, make policy.

Rio Grande is itself a right-wing attack on the status quo. There's a Wagnerian solemnity to the opening scene, as John Wayne rides through the fort gate. Sporting a George Custer–style mustache and goatee, the second-term president of the Motion Picture Alliance seems a sterner version of the character he played in *Fort Apache*. He answers to the same name, Kirby Yorke (albeit dignified with a final "e") and, promoted to colonel, now has a family past. *Rio Grande*'s nameless garrison is even more suburban than Fort Apache—the landscape seems more settled and the militarized social order more naturalized. The base is populated by school-age kids, who rush from their classroom to greet returning warriors as if heading to a personal appearance by TV cowboy Hopalong Cassidy.[1]

The narrative operates on two tracks—foreign and domestic. Yorke is introduced returning from a mission against the marauding Apache bands that op-

---

1. Silent star William Boyd received the opportunity of a lifetime when Paramount cast him as Hopalong Cassidy, the lead in a low-budget Western. Between 1935 and 1944, Boyd made fifty-three sequels; after Paramount dropped the series, he acquired the rights and produced a dozen more. In 1948, Boyd turned to the new medium of TV and, as described in *Life*'s June 12, 1950, cover story, became "the cowboy Pied Piper of America's children." More than any figure, the affable, silver-haired Boyd personified the early TV juggernaut: "American youth is more aware of Hoppy than earlier generations ever were of Buffalo Bill, Lindberg, Babe Ruth." Hoppy appeared on 57 television stations, and his half-hour radio drama was heard over 517 outlets; carried by seventy-two daily and forty Sunday papers, the *Hopalong Cassidy* comic strip reached 11.2 million readers. No wonder President Truman would invite Boyd to ride beside him in the presidential limo on "I Am an American Day" in 1950.

erate from safe havens across the Mexican border. He angrily complains that State Department meddling has compelled him to halt on the American side of the river. Another boundary is breached when the colonel's own long-lost son Trooper Jefferson (named for Thomas or Davis?) Yorke (Claude Jarman Jr.) is assigned to the fort, followed by his mother, the colonel's long-estranged wife Kathleen (Maureen O'Hara in the first of five films opposite Wayne). The feisty belle, who is seeking to purchase the boy's discharge, is an unreconstructed southerner who cracks wise on the subject of "Yankee justice," as well she might: her family plantation was burned during the Civil War by Yorke's faithful subaltern Sergeant Major Tim Quincannon (Victor McLaglen), acting on Yorke's orders. Thus the War Between the States is imagined as a family squabble.

The fort's commander (J. Carrol Naish), named Sheridan after the general who famously remarked that "the only good Indian is a dead Indian," complains of insufficient support from the pusillanimous politicians back in Washington. Cue the Apache surprise attack, replete with uncanny coyote calls—torching the fort, stampeding the horses, and kidnapping a group of children. Retaliation must be unhampered by diplomatic niceties and absolute.[2]

Sheridan orders Yorke to pursue the Apache across the Rio Grande. To ensure plausible deniability, these orders are necessarily unwritten—although Yorke is assured that, in the unlikely event he should face court-martial for exceeding his authority, Sheridan will personally ensure that the jury is stocked with fellow veterans of the Shenandoah campaign. In any case, the mission resolves all. Although the cavalry rides into an Apache ambush, the children are saved. Adding to the family drama, Yorke is struck by an arrow during the assault and everything grinds to a halt as he asks his son to pull it out. "Our boy did well," he informs Kathleen back at the fort. To complete Kathleen's triumph, *Rio Grande* ends with the regiment marching off to "Dixie" as she sways and smiles encouragement, twirling her parasol in coquettish satisfaction.

McGuinness wrote and revised his script throughout the post-Hiss-conviction spring of 1950—when the "fighting marine" Senator Joseph McCarthy charged the chicken-livered traitors in Truman's State Department with the loss of China. Shooting began in mid-June and continued through July, the North Koreans advancing south and the newly appointed United Nations supreme commander General Douglas MacArthur warning the Joint Chiefs of Staff that

2. Rescuing captives is, as historian Richard Slotkin notes, "the strongest of mythical imperatives, a self-evident 'higher law' that supersedes government regulations."

the situation was critical. Ford worked fast, needing only 665 takes for 646 individual camera setups; according to his son Pat Ford, the project was nearly free-
associational. Scenes were rewritten and rehearsed the night before they were
shot—"it was kind of an impromptu thing."

July 7, two days after U.S. troops join the ground fighting in Korea, FBI director
J. Edgar Hoover furnishes President Truman with a list of twelve thousand subversives to be immediately apprehended as protection against treason, espionage, and sabotage. The following week, David Platt (most likely on, if not soon
added to, Hoover's security index) arrives in Karlovy Vary, Czechoslovakia, as a
delegate to the fifth edition of the Communist world's preeminent international
film festival.

Platt has a message. The *Daily Worker*'s film critic (and film editor) opens
his address with the observation that "unlike the film industries of the Soviet
Union, Republic of China and the People's Democracies, which serve peace and
the advancement of humanity," his own country's does not. Sadly, Hollywood
"is controlled by the same gang that owns the munitions industry": American
movies are "an instrument for war and the destruction of humanity."

> Yes, the engineers of the war in Korea who dream of world empire have brought
> about the complete degradation of film art in America. Gangster films, police
> films, imperialist war and racist film make up the majority of Hollywood films
> today. . . .
>
> The aim is to force the acceptance of the view that man is instinctively, nat-
> urally a killer. Human beings in Hollywood films are depicted as irrational and
> insane, homicidal and sex crazed. They seek to mold, to condition the people
> and the youth especially for imperialist war.

With the exception of the last assertion, any of Platt's complaints might have
been and were made by the MPAA's Breen Office, not to mention various American religious leaders and organizations, among them the Legion of Decency.
But the critic inoculates himself against religious intolerance in implicating the
Catholic organization: Platt notes that the Legion of Decency actually deemed
two "warmongering films," *The Red Menace* and *Guilty of Treason*, suitable for
children: "This is how reactionary groups in my country contribute to juvenile
delinquency."

Aliens among us: while Platt is away in Karlovy Vary, FBI agents in New
York arrest Lower East Side machine-shop owner Julius Rosenberg, implicated
by his brother-in-law David Greenglass in stealing the Secret of the Whatzit,

and NBC's *We the People* broadcasts an interview with Matt Cvetic, longtime double agent within the Communist Party's Pittsburgh chapter, telling a tale of treason and subversion that is currently serialized in the *Saturday Evening Post* and will soon be acquired by Warner Bros.

Rio Grande has nearly wrapped on July 19 when President Truman makes his first nationally televised speech. Speaking live from the White House motion-picture room, Truman denounces the raw aggression of North Korea's Communist-controlled hordes, explaining that any appeasement will only encourage further such aggression and warning that, despite General MacArthur's optimistic assessment that the enemy "has had his great chance but failed to exploit it," tough times lie ahead.

The next morning brings what will prove the season's hit Western, a movie that, among other things, stresses war's terrible cruelty, the ultra-appeasin' *Broken Arrow*. Directed by Delmer Daves, *Broken Arrow* is another descendant of *Fort Apache*, which, in similarly pitting the reasonable Apache chief Cochise against his younger rival, the irresponsible warmongering Geronimo, introduced notions of racial tolerance into the genre. *Time* identifies *Broken Arrow* as a "merger of the old Western and the new problem film"; the movie not only dramatizes but also serves as an example of integration and intermarriage.

Both *Broken Arrow* and its makers skew left. Julian Blaustein, a young independent producer already planning the coexistence-ist science fiction *The Day the Earth Stood Still*, had circumvented the blacklist. The secret author of this progressive manifesto is Albert Maltz, who has just begun serving his ten-month sentence at the Mill Point Prison Camp in West Virginia. Maltz's credit is tactfully suppressed by Twentieth Century-Fox; the writer prevailed on a longtime comrade, Michael Blankfort, to act as his (eventually Oscar-nominated) front.

Shot during the summer of 1949, *Broken Arrow* had been brainstormed a year earlier, in the midst of the Berlin Blockade and the presidential campaign. Blaustein, an active supporter of Henry Wallace, acquired the rights to Elliott Arnold's 1947 quasihistorical novel *Blood Brother* in September 1948. Nothing could be further from James Bellah's worldview. Arnold's glorification of the Chiricahua Apache had been criticized by its *New York Times* reviewer as a politically suspect apology: "The story of Apache atrocities is sickening, yet *Blood Brother* makes them a persecuted people."

A man who believes that "it is good to understand the ways of others," *Broken*

Arrow's hero Tom Jeffords (James Stewart) is a Civil War veteran who saves the life of an injured Apache boy. Fox's head of production, Darryl Zanuck, deemed Jeffords unnaturally high-minded and made him a gold prospector. Even so, Jeffords is defined almost entirely by his ideals, walking the audience step-by-step through a lesson in peaceful coexistence: "Funny, it never struck me that an Apache woman would cry over her son like any other woman or that Apache men had a sense of fair play."

Jeffords masters the Apache language and makes a pilgrimage to Cochise (Brooklyn-born Jeff Chandler) to explore the possibility that their respective peoples can live in peace like brothers. Cochise is amazed to hear such strange talk coming from a white man. Although, in another Zanuck improvement, Jeffords is nearly lynched by white racists for his integrationist views, he helps negotiate a treaty between Apaches and Americans founded on equality and mutual respect. (His ally is a one-armed Union officer known as the Christian General.) Meanwhile, the Apaches hold their own "peace conference," where Cochise is criticized by the hothead Geronimo (Jay Silverheels, soon to gain a lifelong sinecure as the Lone Ranger's braided sidekick, Tonto).

During the course of a ninety-day armistice, Cochise allows the stagecoach to carry the mail through Apache territory and is consequently required to save various whites attacked by Geronimo; he also dispenses summary justice to the fanatical Geronimo-ite who tries to knife Jeffords. The ultimate instance of racial harmony arises, however, when Jeffords woos the Apache maid Sonseeahray (demure Debra Paget). *Broken Arrow* treats this taboo romance with the utmost propriety while failing to solve the problem of exactly where the couple will live. Integration into white America seems impossible, although the best Indians in the movie are white and the most eloquent exponents of civilized values are Indian: not only do Paget and Chandler, Oscar-nominated for supporting actor, perform in redface, the latter's character becomes a stronger advocate of peace than even Stewart's.

Ultimately, Cochise's well-behaved Apaches are led into an ambush contrived by intractable white racists. Sonseeahray is killed and Jeffords wounded but Cochise escapes . . . to teach Jeffords and the world that peace must be preserved. Jeffords's white friends (led by the soon-to-be blacklisted Will Geer) attend the funeral of his red wife. Nonetheless, the tragic prospector—a true American hero—turns his back on civilization and rides off into the mountains alone. "An honorable endeavor," per the *New York Times*, albeit more notable for "nobleness of purpose" than filmmaking.

Across *Rio Grande* . . . into Manchuria?

Hot summer 1950: disturbances began breaking out in Los Angeles in mid-July, prompted by the circulation of peace petitions and "Communist handbills."

A few days after two women were jailed for ringing doorbells for peace in San Pedro, police arrested a pair of signature-seeking teenagers in Long Beach and three women leafleting outside the Lockheed Aircraft factory in Burbank; in early August, two men and a boy were busted for passing out handbills in Pershing Square; workers brawled with "'peace' advocates" at the Douglas plant in Santa Monica and a Park La Brea building site; the next weekend, an eighteen-year-old national guardsman was charged with roughing up three women circulating a petition in an East L.A. market, and two more Commies were booked for disturbing the peace in Ocean Park.

In New York City, Ethel Rosenberg was arrested and, like her husband, charged with the Crime of the Century: furnishing the Soviet Union with the means to produce the atomic bomb. Hearst columnist Westbrook Pegler agitated to make membership in the Communist Party a capital offense. Steve Canyon got his hair trimmed and went back on active duty in the air force, where he would remain for the duration of the strip. Secretary of the Navy Francis P. Matthews called for preventive nuclear strikes. A secret shelter was already under construction beneath the White House, and General MacArthur publicly challenged Truman's war policy, urging the administration to unleash Chinese nationalist Chiang Kai-shek in an all-out war to retake the Chinese mainland.

Despite the presence of U.S. and UN troops, the South Korean army had been driven nearly into the sea, clinging tenaciously to the refugee-swollen port of Pusan and preparing for a last stand. A few weeks before the Strategic Air Command began bombing North Korea (and half a century before the story broke that in late July retreating U.S. troops had machine-gunned hundreds of civilians beneath a railroad bridge south of Seoul), *Time*'s August 21 issue termed the U.S.-UN police action "an especially terrible war . . . sickening [and] ugly."

Enormously popular, *Broken Arrow* would gross $3,550,000 (the year's ninth best) and win a Golden Globe for "Promoting International Understanding." Maltz's internationalist perspective was likely responsible for an additional utopian spin: red men and white share common economic interests. Back from Karlovy Vary (where the Crystal Globe had gone to the Soviet super-production *The Fall of Berlin*) and catching the movie relatively late in its run, David Platt was not unduly impressed, however. *Broken Arrow*, he wrote, was "a good film up to the point where the Indians stop fighting the whites and begin fighting each other."

For the *Daily Worker* critic, *Broken Arrow* was compromised by its liberalism—extolling the moderate Cochise while vilifying the resistance fighter Geronimo, who Platt boldly bracketed with immortals like Nat Turner and John Brown, if not North Korea's revolutionary leader Kim Il Sung. Platt vastly preferred *Devil's Doorway*, directed by Anthony Mann from a screenplay by Guy Trosper, an FBI-designated CP-liner, which MGM had begun rolling out in the spring and released in New York that fall. Platt argued that *Devil's Doorway* stood up for the Indians, unlike *Broken Arrow*, where the theme was "back to the reservation—peace at the white man's price. The new film has as its hero the villain of *Broken Arrow* . . . a Geronimo-type hero who knows only that he must keep on fighting for what he is convinced is a just cause despite the odds against his survival."

The MPA's president emeritus had been tricked again into fronting a Communist movie: Robert Taylor in a role tailor-made for John Garfield! First seen as a cavalryman, Lance Poole is a Shoshone Indian who returns home to Wyoming a decorated veteran of the Civil War to become a successful cattle rancher. Though an idealistic integrationist ("No man, red or white, will ever be turned away from our door"), Lance encounters only prejudice and exploitation, as embodied by the cigar-smoking shyster (Louis Calhern) who attempts to appropriate his land and repopulate it with sheep farmers from back east. Innately progressive, Lance enlists a female lawyer (Paula Raymond) and turns out to be, in fact, her first client. Their relationship is chastely honorable. A sort of New Deal liberal, she tries—and fails—to negotiate a just settlement. But the government fails to protect Lance. He is not permitted to homestead because he is not a citizen.

As the situation escalates, Lance turns increasingly redskin, waging a hopeless war against his colonialist oppressors. In the final scene, Platt noted, the now-long-haired Shoshone brave—who had donned his old cavalry jacket and pinned his Congressional Medal of Honor to his chest "to remind the destroyers of his people of their shame"—stands alone, doubly wounded. "He salutes his former army officer who is waiting with his men to drag him off to a concentration camp, then drops dead at his feet, a victim of the same kind of war now being waged by the white supremacists against the dark-skinned peoples of Korea." Unlike *Broken Arrow*, *Devil's Doorway* was a box-office failure.

How anachronistic was *Broken Arrow*? Something had changed. Engaging in a form of semiotic analysis at Karlovy Vary, David Platt had proposed a list of recent titles to illustrate "the degeneracy of the American movie under Truman. *Annie Get Your Gun, Singing Guns, Colt 45, Winchester '73, Six Gun Mesa, The Gunslingers, Gunmen of Abilene, Gun Crazy, Under the Gun, The Gunfighter, Smiler with a Gun,* and just plain, ordinary *The Gun.* Who can say that tomorrow the Hollywood studios will not bring out such titles as *Singing Atom Bombs* or *Smiler with an H-Bomb*?" Two-thirds of the cited titles were Westerns (although that genre went unmentioned in Platt's speech). For now, more than ever, the Western was the American movie industry's quintessential product— every fourth feature-length movie coming off the Hollywood assembly line, per the *New York Times Magazine,* and the percentage was only increasing.

Censors, the *Times Magazine* maintained, viewed Westerns with "delighted approval—a fact which has undoubtedly sustained the popularity of the genre with the producers. 'Crime on the prairies' never seems to worry the women's clubs or PTAs." But, as Robert Warshow would theorize some years later, the Western was a genre where violence was crucial. Soon after the *Times* piece, *Daily Variety* reported that the Monogram studio had shelved plans for *Hiawatha* because the title character was known for his "constant striving for peace among the warring Northeast Indians" and this "might be construed now as Communistic."[3]

Although conventionally set in the twenty years following the Civil War, the Western could not help but address Cold War concerns, including the impact of advanced weapon technology (the Gatling gun, cannon, and repeater rifle), mobilization, instrumentalized violence, and war against a racial enemy. Two of the upcoming movies cited by the *Times* were cavalry Westerns: *Rio Grande* and *Two Flags West,* a Twentieth Century-Fox production directed by Robert Wise from a script by producer Casey Robinson (a founding member of the Motion Picture Alliance).

Nor were these the only examples in the works. If the Western was Hollywood's quintessential genre, those Westerns involved with fighting Indians on the Southwest frontier—the cavalry Western, as reintroduced by *Fort Apache*— would, for the next few years, be the genre's quintessential mode. As Warner Bros.'s *Only the Valiant* wrapped in early September in Gallup, New Mexico, Paramount began shooting *The Last Outpost* in Tucson, Arizona, with Screen

---

3. When the movie finally appeared, over two years later, on Christmas Day 1952, the *New York Times* review began by suggesting that "anyone who would criticize" this "Cinecolored holiday package deserves to suffer the slings and arrows of every moviegoer from the age of 4 to 14." As befitted a movie with a "pacifist hero," the reviewer added, *Hiawatha* had not even a single gunshot.

Actors Guild president Ronald Reagan working on his new action image in the role of a prankish Confederate cavalry officer.

Rio Grande, Two Flags West, and *The Last Outpost* represented another trend—namely, the rehabilitation of the Confederacy. Frank Nugent, co-credited with the original story for *Two Flags West,* based his treatment on previous research; while working on *She Wore a Yellow Ribbon,* he learned of an amnesty for Confederate prisoners of war who volunteered to serve the Union on the Western frontier. Thus, *Two Flags West* pits a bitter northern major (Jeff Chandler) against the proud and chivalrous Southern colonel (Joseph Cotten) assigned to his fort; just as the southern officer and his followers are poised to escape to the freedom of Confederate Texas, the major wantonly kills the son of a Kiowa chief, precipitating a massive Indian attack. The gallant southerners return to save the fort. As Bosley Crowther put it, "the two flags and the two loyalties are joined in the drive west."

That point was reinforced a few weeks later with the opening of Warner Bros.'s *Rocky Mountain,* starring Errol Flynn as a Confederate captain distracted from his secret mission to overthrow the Union in California—the Crime of the Nineteenth Century!—by the necessity of rescuing a beautiful girl from redskin savages. The *Daily Worker* nearly exploded with rage: *Rocky Mountain* desecrates "a ravishingly beautiful locale to panhandle sympathy for the Southern cause. In the end, Flynn and his brave band, carrying aloft the Stars and Bars, are killed by the Indians after drawing them away so the girl can escape. In honor of this breathtaking exhibition of southern gallantry, the Yankee lieutenant raises the Confederate flag on top of Rocky Mountain, saluting it while Max Steiner's music score swells with 'Dixie.'" In conclusion, reviewer R.C. invited readers to imagine a future movie in which the ubiquitous Stars and Bars flew in the breeze beside Old Glory atop UN headquarters in Korea.

A month later, an anonymous autoworker wrote the *Worker* from Flint, Michigan, to improve upon R.C.'s analysis. As he saw it, *Rocky Mountain's* real point was that "any differences between whites must be secondary in view of their common bond against the non-white Indians. In view of the attempt of the bourgeoisie to condition our people to accept fascism and the inevitable war theory, the increase in national chauvinism in general, and white chauvinism in particular, are weapons to achieve these ends. This picture's main ideological message taken in the present world context is to condition all Americans to accept the brutal slaughter of thousands of Asians."

By the time *Two Flags West* (paired in New York with a two-reel short, *You*

Can Beat the A-Bomb), *Rocky Mountain*, and *Rio Grande* opened that fall, the Asian battlefield had changed. The North Koreans launched an all-out offensive on September 1. U.S. troops were ordered to "stand or die" on the Pusan perimeter. Midmonth, MacArthur orchestrated a surprise amphibious landing behind enemy lines at Inchon, 150 miles up Korea's west coast. Thanks in part to Kim Il Sung's obtuse overconfidence, MacArthur's bold plan worked.

Ten days later the North Koreans were in flight with UN forces in hot pursuit. By the end of September, the UN recaptured Seoul; October 1, the South Korean army crossed the Thirty-eighth Parallel. UN troops followed on October 7, and B-29 bombers staged a saturation raid on the North Korean side of the Yalu River, burning 90 percent of the city of Sinuiju and killing thousands of civilians. American F-80s strafed an airfield near Vladivostok two days later, even as the conquering hero MacArthur—newly authorized by the UN General Assembly to pursue the enemy—flew in from Tokyo and entered North Korea himself.

Heady days of Golden October! With V-K Day in sight, MacArthur met with Truman midmonth on Wake Island, the Pacific site of a previous U.S. victory, assuring the president that China posed no threat. Soon after, the First Cavalry marched into the North Korean capital of Pyongyang, unaware that the tens of thousands of Chinese "volunteers" that had been massing along the Manchurian banks of the Yalu were now in Korea. The supreme commander had chosen to ignore intelligence reports that thousands of Chinese were waiting in the mountains of North Korea to ambush his army. MacArthur intended to push to the Chinese border and a recent Gallup poll showed 64 percent of the American public marching behind him.

Opening in Los Angeles on November 1 and rolling out without the benefit of a major theater-chain affiliation, *Rio Grande* was a surprise hit. While *Time* saw the Republic production as evidence of Ford's continued descent "into his latter-day role as scourge of the redskin and glorifier of the US Cavalry," *Variety* considered the movie "outdoor action at its best" and predicted strong box office.

The historian Richard Slotkin later imagined *Rio Grande* complemented by newsreels with General MacArthur staring resolutely across the Thirty-eighth Parallel or gesturing toward the Yalu even as John Wayne glared at the Apache sanctuaries across the Mexican border that the cowards in Washington prevented him from attacking. In actuality, MacArthur was reprising Henry Fonda's doomed role in *Fort Apache*. "Like Custer at the Little Big Horn," his eventual successor General Matthew Ridgway would recall, MacArthur "had neither eyes nor ears for information that might deter him from the swift attainment of his objective."

MacArthur dreams of the conquest of Korea. November 6, he issues a communiqué declaring virtual victory. Miraculously, a virtual MacArthur materializes twenty-four hours later—Election Day 1950—when Fritz Lang's first Technicolor opus, *American Guerrilla in the Philippines*, has its New York premiere.

Although unimpressed with the movie, which was shot on location at no small expense, Bosley Crowther notes its prophetic topicality: the "tattered hordes of fleeing refugees, strung across strange and rugged landscapes," the "marauding Oriental troops," and the "bearded, unkempt American fighters" produce "a peculiar sense of the present," particularly as wrapped in the "magical aura of General Douglas MacArthur [who is] cleverly impersonated by Robert Barrat, with braided cap, dark glasses and all."

Similarly dismissive ("plenty of pretty scenery but very little action"), the *Daily Worker* nevertheless recognizes *American Guerrilla* as a Hollywood equivalent of socialist realism, perhaps even *The Fall of Berlin*, saying the movie "presents a new messiah whose threat to organized religion cannot be minimized. General MacArthur's deathless promise, 'I Will Return', is uttered over and over in the manner of a Gregorian chant. . . . The words, either spoken or appearing together with the general's signature on the back of a package of cigarettes in many scenes, cannot fail to impress and perhaps convert thousands of moviegoers." *An American Guerrilla in the Philippines* clicks with audiences upon its release, but, a week after the election, the nation's top-grossing motion picture is *Rio Grande*.[4]

This Is Korea?

How did Hollywood go to war? Six weeks into the U.S.-led UN action, *Newsweek* found the industry bizarrely hopeful and a bit blasé. "Bewitched, bothered, and bewildered by taxes, television, and the unalterable aging of its top stars," Hollywood saw Korea as a sequel of sorts, "something it had been through before and could survive again."

---

4. With eventual domestic grosses of $2,250,000, *Rio Grande* wound up Republic's second-biggest hit (behind *Sands of Iwo Jima*, at $3,900,000) of 1950, as well as the year's second-most popular Western (after *Broken Arrow*).

According to *Newsweek*, studio savants and members of the trade press imagined that this new war might actually help save movies from the real threat: television. Government mobilization of the electronics industry would slow down the production (and hence the sale) of new TV sets. A new war might even bring back the old wartime audience—swing-shift shows and all—craving a familiar diet of musicals, Westerns, and crime films, plus science fiction, which some thought the happening midcentury trend. Combat movies also got a boost, although that had more to do with the late-1949 success of *Battleground*, *Twelve O'Clock High*, and *Sands of Iwo Jima* than with whatever drama was unfolding in East Asia.

And so there was no mad rush to make films about Korea. In mid-August, Darryl Zanuck had told the president of the United States that within three weeks, his Twentieth Century-Fox would be ready with a short documentary, helpfully titled *Why Korea?* (He was off by nearly five months.) A few publicity-conscious producers registered titles; *Hiroshima USA* and *Pentagon* were the liveliest. David O. Selznick claimed *Crisis in Korea*, Samuel Goldwyn took *Dateline Korea*, and Hal Wallis reserved *Korea*, possibly to make sure that nobody else got them. None were ever used.

By late September, the *New York Times* noted a marked increase in service pictures, most produced with active Pentagon assistance. Republic had put *Wings Across the Pacific* and *Fighting United States Coast Guard* on its production schedule in late July; Warners was now shooting *Operation Pacific*; Columbia and RKO were prepping *The Flying Jeeps* and *Flying Leathernecks*, respectively. A few independents were more topical: Christian Productions claimed to be planning *First Battalion in Korea*, Jack Schwartz had something called *Korean Patrol*, "Jungle Sam" Katzman cooked up *Rookie from Korea*, and Lippert's in-house writer-director Samuel Fuller was working on a Korean script, drawing on his experiences as a World War II infantryman.

Not surprisingly, RKO was the lone major studio to seriously contemplate a movie about the current war. Airplane manufacturer and aviation buff Howard Hughes had personally contacted air force brass, dispatching producer Sam Bischoff and *Iron Curtain* screenwriter Milton Krims to Washington for further discussions. According to Bischoff, *Operation O*, as the project was known, would dramatize the current cooperation between air and ground forces.

That fall, the navy finally asked Admiral John Ford for a new documentary, but for many in the movie industry, the civil war in Hollywood was a lot more urgent than whatever was happening in Korea.

Back in May, the Motion Picture Alliance for the Preservation of American Ideals had called for a complete delousing of the movie industry: "Let us in Hollywood not be afraid to use the DDT on ourselves." The MPA warned that HUAC had compiled a list of one hundred Communist subversives in the industry and was prepared to reopen its investigation during the coming year. Praising the MPA statement, the *Los Angeles Times* deemed it "strange that many motion picture executives [had] no sympathy with this effort." Yet, well in advance of Korea, the nature of the product had changed.

David Platt didn't mention the blacklist when he revisited the state of Hollywood, some weeks into the war, at the Karlovy Vary Film Festival, but he did opine that in the current climate, the once-progressive directors of the Roosevelt era were now churning out the "trashiest" material of their careers. Anti-Nazis like Fritz Lang and William Dieterle had turned to crime stories; liberal populist Frank Capra was reduced to a racetrack comedy, *Riding High*; King Vidor had directed the "openly fascist" *The Fountainhead* while William Wellman made *The Iron Curtain*; Popular Front stalwart John Ford had taken refuge in films of a "reactionary, mystic-religious character" like *The Fugitive* and *Three Godfathers*.

Everyone was jumpy. Appearing in late June, the new broadcast-industry watchdog *Red Channels* listed a number of prominent Hollywood personalities as subversives, including John Garfield, Judy Holliday, Edward G. Robinson, and Orson Welles. Korea fed the anti-Communist frenzy. Harry Warner demanded that members of un-American organizations be stripped of their citizenship and shipped to Russia. Scores of former Communists—among them actor Sterling Hayden, screenwriters Richard Collins and Leo Townsend, and recently released Hollywood Ten-nik Edward Dmytryk—scrambled to cut deals with the FBI and HUAC.[5]

Liberals also panicked. Edward G. Robinson was frantic to clear his name, begging for help from James K. McGuinness, who advised him to voluntarily go before HUAC. (Robinson appeared twice, on October 27 and December 21, 1950). Walter Wanger headed up the Los Angeles branch of Crusade for Freedom, a privately funded anti-Communist group founded in 1949 to support Radio Free Europe and other forms of "spiritual airlift," including a ten-ton

---

5. Preparing to shoot *Rio Grande*, John Ford had been alarmed to discover that even he was under investigation. In 1948, an independent filmmaker who served under Ford in Field Photo was denied a contract with the Signal Corps because, as he discovered, he was deemed a security risk—along with his former commanding officer. In early October, Ford's brother-in-law, former lieutenant-colonel Wingate Smith, intervened with the Department of Defense to resolve the matter.

Freedom Bell to be installed at the Berlin Airport; when California state senator Jack Tenney resigned from the Crusade to protest Wanger's previous association with "subversive" groups as well as his criticism of the MPA (which, in welcoming the producer to the anti-Communist cause, demanded he recant his 1944 condemnation), Wanger published his mea culpa in the *Hollywood Reporter*.

Encouraged by Paramount vice president Y. Frank Freeman, FBI special agent Cecil B. DeMille maneuvered to make the Screen Directors Guild the first industry craft union to implement a loyalty oath—thus providing an example to other unions, and not just in Hollywood. Exploiting the temporary absence of SDG president Joseph Mankiewicz, vacationing in Europe, DeMille convened an emergency meeting of the guild's board to approve his proposed loyalty oath. Hedda Hopper said the oath should be extended to the entire industry, adding that "those who aren't loyal should be put in concentration camps before it's too late."[6]

But upon his return, the hitherto apolitical Mankiewicz unexpectedly opposed DeMille's plan (which, according to director Robert Parrish, also proposed a rule that, upon completing a film, directors file a report with the guild detailing the politics of everyone who'd been involved) and forced his faction to initiate recall proceedings against Mankiewicz. Mankiewicz's supporters countered with a petition for a general meeting. On the evening of October 22, the SDG convened at the Beverly Hills Hotel for a conclave that would last past two o'clock the next morning. Nearly three hundred members were present to hear Mankiewicz denounce the recall petition as "foreign to everything I have ever known or learned or thought as an American." DeMille, who had arranged to have his bald pate bathed in a flattering pink spotlight, embarked on a flowery speech that—once he accused Mankiewicz's supporters of "leftist or subversive" affiliations—ended amid a lusty chorus of boos. The lengthy meeting featured demands for DeMille's resignation from the board.[7]

---

6. By now DeMille had established his own agency, the Foundation for Americanism (administered by a former president of Republic Steel), to compile dossiers on all screen directors. The information was made available to the FBI, HUAC, and the Tenney committee.

7. DeMille's faction included board members Tay Garnett and Frank Capra (at least at first), as well as Gordon Douglas and Leo McCarey, both soon to direct anti-Communist films. Among those directors signing a petition opposing the recall were Richard Brooks, John Farrow, Felix Feist (who directed *Guilty of Treason*), Richard Fleischer, Michael Gordon, John Huston, Andrew Marton, Robert Parrish, Mark Robson, George Seaton, John Sturges, Robert Wise, Billy Wilder, William Wyler, and Fred Zinneman. Joseph Losey and Nicholas Ray objected to a handwritten insert added by the editor of *Daily Variety* that each signatory need also swear he was not a member of the Communist Party and thus did not sign. Neither did Jules Dassin and Elia Kazan, who both gave Mankiewicz verbal support.

Then, in a moment of high drama, the maker of the soon-to-be-released *Rio Grande* rose to speak, identifying himself as "a director of Westerns" (rather than as a founding member of the SDG). Hollywood's grand old man defended Mankiewicz, and after DeMille refused to retract his charges against the directors who had supported Mankiewicz, Ford again moved that the entire board resign.[8]

The show ended, and three days later, the SDG voted for new officers. Mankiewicz was reelected with Ford as his vice president. Mankiewicz then advised the membership to sign the loyalty oath as a voluntary act. What had all the fuss been about? October 27, his proposal was ratified.

Similar battle lines had been drawn over the 1950 election with two high-profile members of Congress battling for California's open Senate seat: one of Hollywood's own, the former actress and liberal representative Helen Gahagan Douglas, versus Representative Richard Nixon.

DeMille supported Nixon; Mankiewicz backed Douglas. Dore Schary campaigned for Douglas, organizing a rally on her behalf; Louis B. Mayer was for Nixon, along with a number of other prominent MGM employees, including the studio's chief attorney, Mendel Silberberg, and its new head of publicity, actor George Murphy (who had flirted with the idea of running for Douglas's seat and would be elected U.S. senator himself fourteen years later). Most studio bosses were for Nixon: Walt Disney, Howard Hughes, Herbert Yates, Harry Cohn, and Y. Frank Freeman. Twentieth Century-Fox volunteered the use of a staff photographer for official Nixon campaign photos and several studios collaborated on a pro-Nixon newsreel—written at MGM, shot at Republic by Columbia contractee Edward Buzzell, and distributed by the head of Fox's West Coast movie chain.

Douglas's chief Hollywood fund-raisers were the liberal screenwriters Allen Rivkin and Philip Dunne. Other supporters included agent Lew Wasserman; producers Walter Wanger, Hal Wallis, and Mervyn LeRoy; directors John Huston, Billy Wilder, George Cukor, Vincente Minnelli, Otto Preminger, and Fritz

---

8. Covering all bases, Ford wrote DeMille the next day to commend him on his behavior under fire. After DeMille's grateful response, Ford further elaborated his sense of the event: "That meeting Sunday night was a disgusting thing to see—not a wolf pack, but a mice pack attacking you. That was your greatest performance. I just wish you could have seen yourself—a magnificent figure so far above that goddam pack of rats. I have recommended men for courage in battle, but I have never seen courage such as you displayed Sunday night. God bless you, you're a great man."

Lang; screenwriters Albert Hackett, Sidney Sheldon, and Comrade Paul Jarrico (who succeeded the jailed John Howard Lawson as head of the Hollywood CP and had already written a speech for Douglas); and stars Edward G. Robinson, Bette Davis, James Cagney, Joan Crawford, July Garland, Myrna Loy, Eddie Cantor, Frank Sinatra, Groucho Marx, Gene Kelly, and Danny Kaye. In a sign of the times, Screen Actors Guild president Ronald Reagan began as a Douglas supporter but switched sides.[9]

Nixon's support drew heavily on the MPA leadership: John Wayne, Robert Montgomery, Ginger Rogers, Adolphe Menjou, Ward Bond, Leo McCarey, Cedric Gibbons, and Morrie Ryskind. James K. McGuinness wrote campaign material; Hedda Hopper lent her talents by narrating a radio play and producing a "Women for Nixon" telecast featuring Irene Dunne and Louise Beavers. Dick Powell narrated a radio dramatization of the Ralph de Toledano book *Seeds of Treason*, which described the Hiss case as "astutely plotted, incredibly acted, a terrifying criminal melodrama" featuring a "bizarre cast of characters" and an authentic hero in Richard Nixon, "the law-maker who doggedly moved through the persistent vapors of deceit."

Nixon prevailed, as did the Republicans, picking up twenty-eight seats in the House and five in the Senate. Among the Democratic losers was Senator McCarthy's nemesis, the chairman of the subcommittee delegated to investigate McCarthy's charges, Millard Tydings, four-term senator from Maryland.

A month earlier, the same October day General MacArthur triumphantly crossed the Thirty-eighth Parallel into North Korea, thirty-eight-year-old producer-director Samuel Fuller, a former crime reporter as well as a World War II veteran, had presented the MPAA's Breen Office with the script for his Korean War project for Warner Bros., *The Steel Helmet*.

There were a number of objections: Fuller's loudmouthed antihero Sergeant Zack used the words "gook" and "lousy" and made a profane reference to Omaha Beach. Applied to a Japanese American soldier, the nickname "Buddha-head" was a problem, and so was the bit of business where Buddha-head rubs manure on Baldy's pate to make his hair grow. There was also a questionable use of a Buddhist temple. The scene that would prove most inflammatory, described as

---

9. The wartime Reagan was regarded as so left-wing that Douglas's supporters discouraged him from taking part in her 1944 campaign. Some Democrats had hoped that Reagan, not Douglas, would run for Senate in 1950. Although Reagan moved steadily right after his 1952 marriage to actress Nancy Davis, it was likely his friend Dick Powell who facilitated his support for Nixon.

"Zack firing his machine gun three times into the Red's belly," was noted only as "excessively gruesome," although a few days later an office memo expressed concern that, in murdering a POW, Zack had violated the Geneva Convention.

Mid-October, around the time Truman and MacArthur met on Wake Island and Chinese "volunteers" began stealthily crossing the Yalu, Fuller sent the *Steel Helmet* script to the Pentagon, hoping to secure official cooperation. He failed. The Department of Defense's suggestions would have necessitated a total rewrite. Fuller's sense of battlefield humor was hardly acceptable—consider the scene in which a rules-conscious lieutenant orders a man to recover a dead GI's dog tag and the hapless soldier is blown to bits because the North Koreans have booby-trapped the corpse, prompting an officer-hating sergeant to split his gut, spraying the screen with a mouthful of casaba melon. At the time, the Public Information Office merely noted that "many opportunities are taken to show the service in a derogatory light, not always with any foundation in fact or reality." Later, the DoD would characterize Fuller's script as "absolutely awful [and] technically inaccurate," not to mention "vicious [and] full of perversions."

Jumping the gun on Breen approval, *The Steel Helmet* was already in production—seven days of rehearsal and ten days of shooting, including one day on location in Griffith Park. According to Gene Evans, the original lead was Robert Hutton as Private Bronte. "About the second day of shooting Bob cut his hand in an explosion—Sammy was always big for explosions on the set. So he couldn't work right away that day. . . . I had a hunch my part was about to get bigger." He was right. As played by Hutton, Fuller's original protagonist brought to mind the political trajectory of certain American Trotskyists—a World War II conscientious objector who refused to fight against Hitler but, for reasons no longer apparent in the finished movie, enlists to kill Commies in Korea. Now Evans's irascible, antiauthoritarian racist Sergeant Zack moved to center stage. The platoon was complete.

November 22, the Department of Defense Office of Public Information screens *The Steel Helmet* in rough cut. Sam Fuller is cleared to view and obtain Signal Corps stock footage, although the army declines his offer of an official credit line and denies his request for a military band at the movie's world premiere. The Breen Office remains unsure that *The Steel Helmet* has actually been approved; Fuller assuages their anxiety by spinning this limited Pentagon okay into a blanket endorsement.

Two days later, MacArthur announces his "end the war" offensive. American forces push their way into the frigid, inhospitable North Korean mountains and the arms of the waiting Chinese. Two days after that, the Reds attack in force. Within forty-eight hours, American forces suffer more than a thousand casualties. It's the prelude to *The Steel Helmet*'s opener, in which the bound Zack is the sole survivor of a massacred platoon.

The war, as historian J. Ronald Oakley will write, has turned nightmarish. The enemy is not only alien but implacable. Blowing bugles and shrill whistles, the "Chinese attacked at night as well as in the day, knifing American soldiers as they tried to sleep in their sleeping bags on the frozen ground, engaging them in terrifying hand-to-hand combat, fighting as if oblivious to subzero temperatures, blizzards, snow drifts. American soldiers were slaughtered in such numbers it became difficult to give them a decent burial—after one battle 117 bodies were hurriedly buried in a mass grave by fleeing comrades."

Lured into one trap, the Americans retreat into another—fired on by Chinese troops who, acting like Apache, control the heights above the rough, narrow roads. The six twisty miles from Kunuri to Sunchon are known as "the Gauntlet"; years later, a survivor will describe it for David Halberstam: "A vehicle would be hit, and it would block the road for others, and some brave soul would try to move it aside, and all the while the Chinese would be pouring fire down. . . . Bodies lay right in the middle of the road—some possibly still alive, for all anyone knew—and the driver of the next truck or jeep would have no choice in that narrow passage but to run right over them."

His mood swinging between wild optimism and alarmed pessimism, MacArthur blames the debacle on Truman and Acheson (who later calls it the greatest American defeat since the Battle of Bull Run). The vociferous Patriot Roughneck, Senator "Tail-Gunner Joe" McCarthy is issuing near daily denunciations of the State Department. Before the month ends, Truman lets it be known that using the Bomb in Korea is under active consideration. The president further compounds the panic by seeming to suggest that use of nuclear weapons would be at the discretion of the field commander—that is, MacArthur, who will soon make a secret request to drop atomic bombs on twenty-six targets.

On December 15, Truman goes on TV to declare a national emergency. The president calls for all-out military and economic mobilization, placing 3.5 million men under arms: "Our homes, our nation, all the things we believe in are in great danger." The mass media gets the message. CBS institutes loyalty oaths for its 2,500 regular employees. *Life* warns that "World War III moves ever closer" (as Time-Life considers relocating its offices out of midtown Manhattan, presumed ground zero for a Soviet attack), and, prompted by Breen

Office anxiety, the Department of Defense asks for a screening of Fuller's finished movie.

The day after Christmas, the newly appointed Eighth Army commander, General Matthew Ridgway, meets with MacArthur and is more convinced than ever that his superior is maneuvering for all-out war with red China. John Ford leaves for Korea to make his documentary, and *The Steel Helmet* has its Los Angeles trade preview. *Variety* notes that the movie's most shocking scene had been passed by the Breen Office on the basis of Department of Defense approval. Ford arrives in Korea in time for the New Year, spending six days in Pusan before he is summoned by MacArthur to Japan.

January 8, the same day Ford meets (and films) MacArthur in Tokyo, *The Steel Helmet* opens in downtown Los Angeles at the 2,100-seat United Artists (and a quartet of smaller first-run houses) on a double bill with the Western *Three Desperate Men* and, within forty-eight hours, explodes like a bazooka in the kisser. *Variety* reports that the Pentagon actually withheld full approval. Too late: the next morning, David Platt's *Daily Worker* column is gleefully headlined "WAR DEP'T OK'S SLAYING OF PRISONER OF WAR IN COMING FILM." The Communist daily is pleased to view *The Steel Helmet* as an official statement, "approved by the War Department in complete defiance of the Geneva convention."

As the Breen Office wonders how Fuller bamboozled them, *Variety* reports on the implications of Platt's piece: "Following widespread newspaper reports that the War Department had fully O.K.'d the film, the Department issued formal denial, particularly denouncing the killing of the POW episode." Again too late: Hearst columnist Victor Riesel has leaped on the story. The industry that could produce a movie like *The Steel Helmet* has no right to "squawk" about a congressional investigation into its Communist infiltration.[10]

---

10. Fuller would often maintain that the Commies loved *The Steel Helmet*. It would be more accurate to say they loved the controversy it provoked. David Platt's review is profoundly confused. On one hand, Platt calls *The Steel Helmet* "racist to the core." On the other, he endorses the analysis of American racism provided by the North Korean major. Platt complains that the movie desecrates a Buddhist temple but writes that it truthfully "shows that primarily Americans are fighting in Korea." With regard to Zack's famous one-liner—"If you die, I'll kill you"— screamed at the POW he has just shot, Platt notes that "the audience is provoked to laughter at this fascist-like act, which was precisely the intention of the makers of the film." Taking credit for exposing *The Steel Helmet*, Platt kept the story going well into February 1951, at one point disputing *Variety*'s headline "DAILY WORKER PLUGGING OF STEEL HELMET STIRS TEMPEST": "We didn't plug the film, we attacked it!" Long after its release, *The Steel Helmet* continued to figure in the *Daily Worker*'s Korean War narrative. In July 1952, Platt paid Fuller a left-handed compliment, writing that "the savage treatment of North Korean and Chinese prisoners of war was accurately forecast in the racist, warmongering Hollywood film *Steel Helmet*."

"SHOESTRING FILM JOLTS HOLLYWOOD," the *New York Herald Tribune* reports the Sunday before *The Steel Helmet* opens in a 3,450-seat Broadway theater, the first independent production to play the Loews State. *New York Times* critic Bosley Crowther notes, "Mr. Fuller has managed to work into his modest film a great many implications of ineffectualness in the Korean war," and for a few weeks, Fuller's movie *is* the war. *The Steel Helmet* has been picked up by the Loews chain for national release; in San Francisco, it plays the 5,000-seat Fox, then the biggest theater in California. *The Steel Helmet* is even booked for army and air force camps. Then the Department of Defense panics and sets up another special screening for twenty-five responsible officers and high-ranking civilians representing various military agencies.

"The Pentagon asked me to come to Washington to be questioned about the movie," Fuller would recall. "So I went. It turned out to be more like an inquisition. About twenty officers sat around a big conference table. There was a screen and a projector. They'd just watched *The Steel Helmet* before I walked in. 'Your film looks like communist indoctrination, Fuller,' said one general."

According to a Department of Defense memo, however, "the consensus of opinion was that if *The Steel Helmet* was subtle communist propaganda, it was too subtle for the ordinary person to see." (Indeed. Embodying the tension arising from Fuller's attempt to reuse the official mythology of World War II and his journalistic desire to expose the scandal of American racism is *Steel Helmet*'s heterogeneous platoon—a band of luckless dogfaces including an officer-hating World War II retread, a rehabilitated conchie, a black medic, a formerly interned Nisei, a neurotic mute, a chicken lieutenant, and a simpering war orphan—which might have filled a lifeboat off the *Pequod* about to be rammed by Moby-Dick.) By then atomic tests had been telecast live in Los Angeles, and in mid-February, the Pentagon announced that *The Steel Helmet* was appropriate for the nation's service theaters—if not for our boys overseas.

John Ford arrived in Korea at the war's lowest point, three days before the North Koreans recaptured Seoul; on February 10, three days after he left, UN forces would win two key victories—the Battle of Wonju and the Battle of Chipyong-ni—successfully containing a massive Chinese push down Korea's central corridor. Thus, Ford was not present to reap the fruits of General Ridgway's late-January offensive; nor would he be on hand to document the longest naval siege in U.S. history, accompanied by the greatest sustained bombardment of any city yet seen.

Although he reported for duty and spent several weeks aboard the USS

Philippine Sea, Ford missed by a week the forty-one-day blockade-bombardment of Wonsan. He even missed the grim celebration that opens *This Is Korea*: "It was Christmas in the year of grace 1950," the narrator reports, and the American forces were having their "first hot meal in two months," steaks the navy had flown in for the holiday. His soldiers are winter soldiers: "You remember Valley Forge? Well, look at it again."

Largely written by James Warner Bellah, with an assist from Frank Nugent, the laconic voice-over was provided by two actors (John Ireland and Ward Bond) and two directors (Allan Dwan and Irving Pichel), in both cases a liberal paired with a conservative. "This is Korea, chums—this is Korea," someone says by way of explicating Ford's lurid Trucolor assemblage in which bubble gum is distributed to Korean urchins as billowing orange fireballs are launched against the "ruthless red hand of Communism." Grimly paraphrasing General Oliver P. Smith's celebrated statement during the marines' withdrawal from Chosin, Ford's narrator declares that U.S. forces were "not retreating [but rather] advancing in a different direction." No less than *The Steel Helmet*, *This Is Korea* projects unending combat—another hill, another enemy position to take—the existential weariness underscored by geographic disorientation.[11]

"Well, what's it all about?" the narrator asks. "You tell us. Ask any of these guys what they're fighting for, and they can't put it into words. Maybe it's just pure cussedness and pride in the marine corps," he suggests before concluding on a somewhat more positive note that the marines are fighting for the kids and all of us, too. "Aren't you glad you gave that pint of blood last week? Or did you? But you will now, won't you?" By the time *This Is Korea* opened in early August 1951, Americans were engaged in what MacArthur contemptuously characterized as an "accordion war"—pushing the Chinese north and then retreating south—and, however appropriately downbeat, the movie proved a tough sell.

The accordion war wheezed on for several more years, but its greatest outpouring of emotion occurred when President Truman fired General MacArthur on April 11, 1951. "There were arguments in saloons, arguments in the club cars," reported *Time*. "Newspaper switchboards were jammed with calls denouncing the President, supporting the President, or simply expressing shock. Western Union offices were in turmoil. By the week's end, Congress had re-

---

11. As noted by Steve Fore, "Ford shows his usual disregard for all principles of screen direction, so that allied forces often appear through editing to be shooting each other" or "firing into apparently empty landscapes."

ceived 100,000 telegrams. Telegraph officers said they had never seen anything like it." *Time* saw madness and hysteria on the floor of the Senate, with William Jenner of Indiana bellowing, "Our only choice is to impeach President Truman and find out who is the secret invisible government which has so cleverly led our country down the road to destruction," as the galleries roared in approval.

Eight days later, the general—back in the continental United States for the first time since 1937—addressed a joint session of Congress. His speech was televised live, and in New York, Con Edison reported a spectacular jump in power consumption. Fifteen minutes after MacArthur assured the rapt assembly that "old soldiers never die," Darryl Zanuck had registered these four words as the title for his new hire Sam Fuller's next Korean War flick.

Newsweek's cover story on "the crisis" maintained that MacArthur had come to embody an international issue ("using the Chiang Kai-shek army now neutralized on Formosa to open a second front in China proper"), as well as a political possibility.

> Washington, which can't hear about a famine in India or a flood in Africa without wondering what the political effect in the United States will be, inevitably started reassessing the 1952 Presidential picture in the light of Gen. Douglas MacArthur's ouster.
>
> The Republicans, in rallying around MacArthur, were putting the party on record as the "Asia first" party. That would seem to increase the chances of Sen. Robert A. Taft of Ohio getting the GOP Presidential nomination, although the Eastern internationalists were still determined to make Gen. Dwight D. Eisenhower the candidate.
>
> On the other hand, it made Eisenhower more than ever a logical choice for a Democratic draft. Like the Democratic Party, Eisenhower was committed to a strategy of "Europe first."

"A General for President?" wondered *US News & World Report*. Of course, some Republicans were also talking about a MacArthur draft. Some deliriously overestimated the turnout for MacArthur's April 21 ticker-tape parade at 7.5 million people, though it was still the largest such celebration in New York City's history.

The most eloquent military film that spring was, naturally, a cavalry Western. Directed by Gordon Douglas from a 1943 novel by Charles Marquis Warren, Warner Bros.'s *Only the Valiant* was a singlemindedly grim and stringently brutal affair that, although shot during the summer of 1950, suggested a synthesis of *Rio Grande* and *The Steel Helmet*.

Gloomy, coarse, and largely nocturnal, *Only the Valiant* has a backbeat of horror—and even a bit of spurting blood. Like *The Steel Helmet*, the movie gives combat a distinctively lunar dimension and opens in the wake of defeat. Down in New Mexico, the Apache have overrun and torched Fort Invincible, the laughably named citadel specifically built near a mountain pass to contain the savage horde. A cavalry detachment led by Captain Richard Lance (Gregory Peck) captures the Apache leader Tucsos, but by bringing him to the undermanned Fort Winston, he makes the outpost an Apache target. Tucsos has to be shipped east, and Lance is blamed when the Apache massacre a cavalry detail charged with conveying the prisoner to a more secure fort. Seeking redemption, he leads a suicide mission through the ruins of Fort Invincible—a rearguard action to hold the pass against the Apache onslaught until reinforcements reach Fort Winston.

Lance's leadership issues are compounded not only by the requisite Union-Confederate tensions but by his deliberately picking for the mission those men he believes expendable. Most already hate him; those who don't turn ugly once he explains why they have been chosen. The well runs dry and the esprit de corps runs out. Lance is threatened by his men no less than the Apache. Still, the captain is counting on a secret weapon—dynamite—to block the pass. This "strong medicine" is one metaphor for the Great Whatzit. So is the Gatling gun. ("That new weapon of yours is going to revolutionize war!" someone says.) Neither ideology nor esprit de corps can defeat the Apache; only technological superiority has the power to cow the redskin horde.

If *Rio Grande* dramatized a blithe mixture of resentment and megalomania that characterized Korea's brief second act, *Only the Valiant*, which opened in New York two days into the post–MacArthur era, evoked the resigned yet paranoid mind-set necessary to wage the war's interminable act 3.

The Communist Was a Thing for the FBI!

And what of the home front? Heralding a new season of investigations and trials was the belated premiere of *Storm Warning*. Warner Bros.'s anti–Ku Klux Klan melodrama had opened in Los Angeles in late January 1951 to strong reviews from the trades. The *Hollywood Reporter* saw *Storm Warning* as not simply entertainment but an indictment of those "vicious and corrupt groups [that] dictate to and control whole communities. . . . Whether the picture is box-office or not, in these troubled times, remains to be seen but certainly the brothers Warner are to be commended for their courage."[12]

The darkling mood was expressed by the February release *The 13th Letter*, produced and directed by Otto Preminger from a screenplay by the man who wrote *Mission to Moscow*, Howard Koch. Although based on Henri-Georges Clouzot's 1943 thriller *Le Corbeau*, an allegory about occupied France, the spectacle of a small town driven mad by a series of anonymous accusations had particular local meaning. Not unlike Hollywood, the town is shrouded in a miasma of free-floating suspicion. As one character puts it, "everyone is beginning to look guilty—everyone and no one."

While *The 13th Letter* was in production, Edward G. Robinson had voluntarily presented himself before a group of HUAC investigators, requesting an opportunity to testify with reference to his participation in organizations classified as Communist fronts either by HUAC or the attorney general. Robinson provided detailed documents annotating his involvement, financial and otherwise, with a host of charitable and political organizations from 1939 through 1949. The actor further took the opportunity to declare his allegiance to the principles of Franklin Roosevelt and assert "directly and unequivocally" that he was not now nor had he ever been a fellow traveler or member of the Communist Party, and that he had never been approached to join the CP, had never attended a CP-sponsored meeting, and had no Communists among his friends or acquaintances. He also distanced himself from the Wallace campaign.

In late December, soon after FBI informant T-17 reported that Robinson's "past Communist activity" had rendered him unemployable, the actor was recalled for interviews with three committee members. Robinson's name did not appear on senior investigator (and former FBI agent) Louis J. Russell's list of Hollywood's known and suspected Communists; nor was his name on any of the Communist Party registration cards in Russell's possession. Nevertheless, Donald L. Jackson, the Republican congressman who represented Robinson's own district, objected to a committee report that appeared to clear the actor.

---

12. The equation between the KKK and the Communist Party would be extensively played out during the next round of hearings; unfriendly witnesses who took the Fifth Amendment when questioned about their membership in the CP were asked if they were now (or had ever been) members of the Klan. None took their constitutional privilege when it came to that question. "Is it degrading to say you have never been a member of the Communist Party, but not degrading to say you have never belonged to the Ku Klux Klan?" one congressman snapped at screenwriter Leonardo Bercovici.

Witnesses had to be called; the inquiry would be reopened and Robinson rein-
vestigated. Such was HUAC's hunger for star power.

The season's stellar legislator—and "Hottest Draw on the Gabfest Circuit," per
Variety—was forty-eight-year-old senator Estes Kefauver, Democrat of Tennessee, whose Special Committee to Investigate Crime in Interstate Commerce was
barnstorming the country, with a return Los Angeles performance scheduled
for February.

In early 1950, Kefauver saw organized crime as an issue upon which to
launch his career; a member of the Judiciary Committee, he called for a congressional probe into interstate gambling and racketeering, thus outmaneuver-
ing another ambitious freshman, Senator Joseph McCarthy, who, as a member of
the Special Investigations Committee, sought to initiate a similar project. (Thus
stymied, McCarthy seized on the issue of Communists in the State Department.)
By May, Kefauver was heading up a special committee authorized to employ all
governmental law-enforcing agencies, including the Treasury Department and
the FBI.

The first crime committee hearings had opened six months earlier in Washington on June 22, 1950. While largely focused on wire-service gambling, the
committee spent some time looking into teenage crime and comic books—
subjects to which Kefauver would later return. Initial hearings were staged in
Miami, with Kefauver accumulating ever more publicity as his show traveled
from city to city. Early in this national tour, Hearst reporter Lee Mortimer (who
viewed the first-term senator as a naive crusader, positioning himself for a presidential run) advised Kefauver that his scattershot hearings were "bad theatre."
Mortimer suggested Kefauver take McCarthy's approach as a model and develop a master narrative, in this case centered on the "Mafia" crime syndicate and
its use of legitimate business.

Arriving in Los Angeles in November, Kefauver subpoenaed Hollywood
hoodlum Mickey Cohen to testify and was himself invited to provide a prologue for Warner Bros.'s new crime film *The Enforcer*, produced by Milton Sperling. A "semi-documentary" treatment of the Brooklyn-based underworld
elimination service known as Murder Incorporated, *The Enforcer* featured
Humphrey Bogart as a two-fisted, gat-packing assistant DA while introducing
such key underworld argot as "hit," "finger," and "contract." A few weeks later in
New Orleans, Kefauver expanded his show-business career—and initiated a
shift in the political paradigm—by arranging for a local TV station to preempt
regular commercial programming in favor of a live telecast of the hearings.

The results were sensational. Kefauver had orchestrated a "living" newsreel that featured real criminals and could be seen by everyone at once. Although the telecast lasted only an hour, the show dominated popular discourse for days and put the senator on *Variety*'s front page. "Kefauver fever" spread first to Detroit, where the crime hearings were telecast in their entirety without commercial interruption and with an estimated 90 percent of the city's TV sets tuned in, and then St. Louis, where the local TV stations were compelled to extend their coverage.

The Enforcer opened in Los Angeles on February 24, three days before Kefauver's return. The telecast of these hearings included testimony on the 1947 shooting of Bugsy Siegel and a gangland plot to ambush the new L.A. police chief, William Parker. Independent producer Stanley Kramer, then preparing his adaptation of *Death of a Salesman*, wired station KECA to praise the crime commission telecasts as "the most intelligent coverage ever rendered in this community." Kefauver took a meeting with RKO's newest producer, Edmund Grainger, who wondered if the senator would be open to playing a dramatic role, based on himself, alongside Shelley Winters in an updated version of *The Racket*, a gangster flick that Howard Hughes had produced in 1928.

Meanwhile, HUAC had sent twenty-six subpoenas, mainly to actors—although not Robinson. The summoned included Larry Parks, José Ferrer, John Garfield, Sterling Hayden (but not, as threatened, his ex-wife Madeleine Carroll), Ann Revere, Gale Sondergaard (Mrs. Herbert Biberman), and Howard Da Silva, as well as writers Richard Collins, Collins's sometime partner Paul Jarrico (whom the CP had sent into temporary hiding), and Waldo Salt (chairman of the Committee to Free the Hollywood Ten and, along with Collins and Park, one of the original Hollywood Nineteen).

March 6, 1951: the trial of Julius and Ethel Rosenberg opens at the federal courthouse at Foley Square four days after *Storm Warning* blows into New York and two days before the second round of hearings into the Communist infiltration of the Hollywood motion picture industry begins in Washington with the public questioning of Communist cultural apparatchik V.J. Jerome. Setting a precedent for subsequent unfriendly witnesses, while creating an unfortunate parallel to the mobsters interrogated by the Kefauver committee, Jerome invokes the Fifth Amendment over one hundred times in the course of a two-hour hearing.

At the beginning of the trial's second week, Kefauver arrives in New York. The Rosenbergs are upstaged and then displaced. Initially booked into a tiny room on the courthouse's twenty-eighth floor, the crime committee hearings will, after three days, move to a more spacious accommodation—taking room 318 as well as the spotlight from the Crime of the Century. Kefauver succeeds in creating an alternative tale of subversion. Where J. Edgar Hoover has long denied the existence of organized crime in America, Kefauver introduces Americans to the concept of the criminal cabal known as the Mafia, whose members—as diplomat Spruille Braden, chairman of New York's newly created crime committee testifies—are "even more dangerous than the spies convicted of stealing our atomic and military secrets."

Kefauver frenzy: New Orleans, Detroit, St. Louis, and even Los Angeles were but out-of-town tryouts for the senator's New York debut. *Time* magazine has not only plastered the bespectacled visage of the "homely, rawboned, always eager to please" senator on its cover, alongside a masked octopus of sin, but is sponsoring his TV coverage. Telecast in their entirety in New York by the local DuMont affiliate and partially by five other stations, the hearings are relayed to twenty-one cities along the East Coast and throughout the Midwest, with kinescope highlights shown around the country.

The reviews are sensational. "The television viewer at home and the hundreds who crowded around sets in bars and radio stores saw yesterday probably the most remarkable, absorbing and instructive day of video ever presented on the screen," opines the *New York Times*. "The opening session of the Senate Crime Investigating Committee was nothing less than a Hollywood thriller truly brought to life.... At times it was almost difficult to believe that it was real." The central characters ("who could hardly have been cast to type more perfectly or 'played'") included the calm and courtly southern senator (Kefauver); the earnest, lisping young prosecutor (Rudolph Halley, who, born into a theatrical family, also served as the show's producer); and their first witnesses, notably the pomaded Broadway mobster Joe Adonis, "talking with the blunt toughness usually associated with a Humphrey Bogart movie."

The hearings are variously compared to a carnival sideshow, a medieval morality play, and a revival camp meeting; the *Times* reports that New York "has been under a hypnotic spell." (During the weekend break, Kefauver performs solo on the new CBS panel show *What's My Line?* The first question, "Are you in the entertainment business?" convulses the studio audience. Although the senator keeps his cool, the panel requires two minutes to guess his identity.) The second week is even better, as stevedore strikebreaker Anthony Anastasia, brassy gang moll Virginia Hill, and dapper gambler Frank Costello take the stand.

With his stage Italian accent, the burly Anastasia seems to be channeling Chico Marx, responding to questions with "I no remember, sir . . . I dunno, sir" and explaining that "some Communist accuse me." Hill delights reporters when she expresses her impossible-to-broadcast wish that "the fucking atom bomb falls on every one of you." Costello, however, inadvertently steals the show by insisting on his privacy. Forbidden to show the mobster's face and thus deprived of the conventional shot-reverse-shot, the cameraman focuses exclusively on interlocutor Rudolph Halley wincing at Costello's reasonable demurrals. ("It don't fit my recollection, but it's possible.") Then it occurs to someone to cut to the witness's hands. Telecast in screen-filling close-up, Costello's manicured fingers take on a life of their own, grasping a handkerchief or grabbing the water glass, picking at a hangnail and even nervously rolling a spitball—not since Chaplin's dance of the rolls in *The Gold Rush* has there been such manual eloquence.

Given this competition, the New York's movie houses are all but empty—although two enterprising theaters feature the broadcast, inviting the public to a free show. The morning TV audience increased twelvefold; afternoon set usage doubled. The demand for power is such that the city's electrical utility has to bring another generator online. The committee will receive as many as a quarter of a million fan letters and *Time* over a hundred thousand. A few days into the hearings, President Truman's poll ratings drop to an all-time low of 26 percent while Kefauver is openly bruited as a potential successor. The day after the hearings end, the senator has reportedly been offered a book deal that Hollywood studios already consider "one of the hottest properties in years." Two studios, in addition to Warner Bros., are showing a lively interest in Kefauver.[13]

Film Daily runs a full-page ad for Fox's upcoming newsreel feature *The Kefauver Crime Investigation*. The senator has graciously supplied an explanatory prologue and epilogue, but TV itself is the real star. *Life* recognizes the cosmic significance: "The week of March 12, 1951, will occupy a special place in history. . . . In the eerie half-light, looking at millions of small, frosty screens, people sat as if charmed. . . . Never before had the attention of the nation been riveted

---

13. For reasons not made clear, Warner Bros. abruptly excised Kefauver's preface to *The Enforcer*. Perhaps the senator himself was concerned that his staid introduction, invoking "an assault upon society by one of the worst criminal elements in history" while stressing that the criminals were apprehended and "completely destroyed" by legal means "without denying them any of the rights that American citizens are guaranteed," was undercut by the movie's excessive violence.

so completely on a single matter." Television has cashed the check written by *The Next Voice You Hear.*

HUAC reconvened in Washington the day that the Kefauver hearings ended in New York, this time with actors. The hearings were not the only local production. Three movies were shooting in Washington. The second unit for Fox's top secret science-fiction production *The Day the Earth Stood Still* was in town, as was Paramount's hush-hush spy drama *My Son John*; Warner Bros.'s nearly completed *I Was a Communist for the FBI* would film a last-minute scene in the committee's hearing room, the week after Larry Parks took the stand.

Parks had already been debriefed in a closed session, but, once under the lights, he tried to change the script. The actor freely admitted that from 1941 to 1945 he had been a card-carrying Communist—the first Hollywood witness to so confess!—but refused to name his erstwhile comrades, at least in public. Representative Francis E. Walter, Democrat of Pennsylvania, thought such informing was irrelevant: "How can it be material to the purpose of this inquiry to have the names of people when we already know them?" Others were more demanding. After more than two grueling, chain-smoking, often barely audible hours on the stand, Parks pleaded with the committee not to compel him to name names: "I don't think this is American justice to make me . . . crawl through the mud for no purpose, because you know who these people are."

Dismissed (until a second closed, executive session later that afternoon), Parks was followed by two other actors. Gale Sondergaard and Howard Da Silva—hard-core progressives both—took the stand and the Fifth. The next day the *Los Angeles Times* reported that Parks had identified more than a dozen Communists, including several big stars and even some whom the committee had not previously suspected.[14]

Newly embarked on his third term as president of the Motion Picture Alliance for the Preservation of American Ideals, John Wayne spoke for the industry when he declared, "We do not want to associate with traitors. . . . We hope that those who have changed their view will cooperate to the fullest extent. By that I mean names and places, so that they can come back to the fellowship of loyal Americans." By the time the Hollywood hearings reconvened in Washington,

---

14. This is hard to fathom. Parks named the actors in his cell (Carnovsky, Bromberg, Revere, Cobb, Sondergaard), none major stars and all known to the committee. The congressmen, on the other hand, went wildly fishing, asking if Parks knew James Cagney, Andy Devine, Edward G. Robinson, Gregory Peck, and Humphrey Bogart to be Communists. Six weeks later, Columbia announced that it had canceled Parks's contract.

the Rosenbergs and alleged accomplice Morton Sobell had been found guilty of espionage, and, after deliberating for more than a week, Judge Irving R. Kaufman had condemned the couple to death, telling them, "I consider your crime worse than murder." Sterling Hayden, another red actor star, took the stand.

Film and TV coverage were permitted—just this once—as Hayden recounted a story worthy of Hollywood. A New England lad, he quit school and shipped out to sea at fifteen, became a captain at twenty-one, met a movie producer "by accident," made a screen test, and got a contract at Paramount; lonely in Hollywood, "not really being an actor by inclination," he visited some fellow sea dogs in San Francisco and was there introduced to Pop Folkoff ("an old warrior in the class struggle"), joined the OSS, enlisted in the marines, went back to the OSS, spent the most of the war serving as a recon and supply man with the Yugoslav partisans, met Spanish Civil War vet Steve Nelson, returned to Hollywood, was recruited into the CP in June 1946 by his agent's secretary (the oft-named Bea Winters), attended meetings mainly at Abe Polonsky's place, was sent to organize the Screen Actors in support of the 1946 strike until he ran into Ronald Reagan ("a one-man battalion against this thing"), and then broke once and for all with the Communists in December 1946, which had something to do with his living on his boat in Santa Barbara.

Not all witnesses were so obliging. Folksy actor Will Geer declined to give the committee any information, while humorously suggesting that congressmen too were working in show business: "We all of us have to appear in a turkey once in a while." But two days after Hayden's saga, Richard Collins filled almost an entire day with a detailed, almost scholarly account of his Communist decade. Having joined the Party in 1938, Collins became one of the leaders of the Northwest Section; he told the committee that he logged some five thousand hours at political meetings, mainly during the war, until he felt like "a trained zombie."

Like Parks, Collins was one of the original Hollywood Nineteen, but after the 1947 hearings, he ceased to pay dues and moved to New York. The writer held the congressmen rapt as he explained the Maltz affair, the Duclos letter, and the struggle against *Tennessee Johnson*, MGM's 1942 biography of Lincoln's successor Andrew Johnson, a movie regarded by Communists as offensively pro-Confederate. Collins quoted Sartre ("thinking brings them in and thinking can take them out") and, while providing inside information on the Hollywood Writers Mobilization and the making of *Song of Russia*, attempted to school the committee on the nature of peace conferences and fronts ("people joined the peace conferences not because they were Communists, but because peace is very alive"). The witness also named a number of comrades, including five members of the Hollywood Ten—screenwriters Budd Schulberg, Gordon Kahn, Waldo Salt, and Collins's old writing partner Paul Jarrico—and three directors, Frank Tuttle, Abraham Polonsky, and Robert Rossen (in whom the committee suddenly seemed very interested).

The name that proved to be most significant was mentioned in passing. Collins remembered a prewar Communist group that "met at the house of a man called Martin Berkeley who was a screenwriter at the time and who I think subsequently left [the Party]." Berkeley had indeed left the Party and, as it turned out, had no FBI file until he wired the committee accusing Collins of perjury ("it is well documented that I have fought Communism consistently inside my guild and out"). For support, Berkeley recruited several prominent screenwriters as character witnesses. Then he disappeared for months, only to resurface with a list of names even longer than Collins's when HUAC came to Hollywood in September.[15]

At this point, the hearings were interrupted by another spectacle: MacArthur. Yet testimony continued sporadically for the rest of the month with unfriendly witnesses Salt, Jarrico, Polonsky, Carnovsky, Ann Revere (a descendant of the revolutionary patriot), and Edward Dmytryk, who, having served his six months in prison, turned friendly and named names. No testimony was more painful than John Garfield's, which took up the morning of April 24. The actor denied that he was a Communist and spent hours insisting that, despite his copious close personal associations, he had never knowingly met a Communist in his life.

Later, two members of the committee told the press that the actor's testimony had been submitted to the Justice Department for investigation of possible perjury. Not only was Garfield a product of the scarlet Group Theatre, but his wife, Roberta Seidman, had been a Party member, while his secretary, Helen Slote Levitt, served as membership secretary and financial director of the Party's celebrity-rich Northwest Section at the time when it was the largest section in the Los Angeles CP.

May Day 1951: two hundred warplanes fill the Moscow sky, and tens of thousands of troops march through rainy Red Square under the solemn gaze of Soviet

---

15. A few days after Collins's testimony and Berkeley's telegram, the current Broadway dramatization of Arthur Koestler's novel of the Soviet purge trials, *Darkness at Noon*, suddenly became a hot property. The *New York Times* reported three studios—Columbia, MGM, and Twentieth Century-Fox—all expressing interest. The movie was never made, although the play toured widely in late 1951, with Edward G. Robinson striving toward rehabilitation in the role of Rubashov, the old Bolshevik tried for treason.

premier and Communist Party general secretary Joseph Stalin, flanked by members of the Politburo atop Lenin's tomb. Later, an estimated two million Soviet citizens parade with floats and banners exhorting the world's people to fight for peace and caricaturing the "capitalist warmongers" Truman, Acheson, MacArthur, Eisenhower, and Winston Churchill.

Chairman Mao Tse-tung, rumored to have just returned from Moscow, makes his first public appearance in Beijing since late January, reviewing the six hundred thousand Chinese Communists massed in Tiananmen Square. The western press detects a certain disappointment; the Chinese had hoped to celebrate May Day by recapturing Seoul. In Tehran, thirty thousand members of Iran's outlawed Communist Party, the Tudeh, pack Parliament Square for three hours to denounce British imperialists, American aggressors, and Iran's new premier, Mohammed Mossadegh, who has just nationalized the Anglo-Iranian Oil Company.

In New York, twelve thousand Communists mass at Eighth Avenue and Thirty-ninth Street. Accompanied by a funereal drumbeat, pushing baby carriages, and carrying American flags (as well as banners demanding justice for Willie McGee, a Mississippi black man convicted of raping a white woman five years before whose execution is days away), the procession wends its way to Union Square. The *New York Times* reports "sporadic applause, salvos of eggs and obscenity and long stretches of apathetic silence." The Cold War reaches a climax of sorts the next day when two much-ballyhooed movies, RKO's *The Thing from Another World* and Warner Bros.'s *I Was a Communist for the FBI*—explicit warnings, both—have simultaneous premieres at Broadway theaters three blocks apart.

The Thing or the Communist: one can choose to experience alien invasion or alien subversion, enjoy the thrill of resourceful American soldiers battling a flying saucer at the North Pole or ponder the spectacle of a heroic informer working undercover to thwart a red plot to take over Pittsburgh. Contagion is contagious.

Warner Bros.'s belated sequel to their 1939 exercise in premature antifascism *Confessions of a Nazi Spy*, *I Was a Communist for the FBI* (or something like it) had been promised to HUAC back when Jack Warner testified in 1947; the movie, however, was not announced until the Korean summer of 1950 when freelance informant Matt Cvetic's memoir, "I Posed as a Communist for the FBI," was being serialized in the *Saturday Evening Post*.

As the *Daily Worker* monitored the various actors bruited for the production, Cvetic's story went through several scripts and writers. Beefing up a treatment

by Crane Wilbur, Motion Picture Alliance stalwart Borden Chase wrote a glo-
balized manifesto. His scenario opened in Korea ("This is Communism in
action . . . visible Communism!"), flashed back to Pittsburgh to show Cvetic in-
filtrating the local CP, and climaxed with Cvetic's star-making HUAC testimony before returning to Korea for a final warning: "Now, please God, America
is awake to the danger within our shores—awake to the danger of invisible
Communism."

In addition to Cvetic, the screenplay featured several actual people as
characters—Superior Court Judge Blair F. Gunther, an activist in the group
Americans Battling Communism, Gerhart Eisler, and the villain of the piece,
CP leader Steve Nelson. As rewritten by Crane Wilbur, who was reattached to
the project after Chase's stint, the story became more compact; by the time the
movie was released, Nelson had been lightly disguised as a sinister blond
brawler called Jim Blandon. Eisler, Blandon's desiccated, gnomish superior, appeared in the opening scene boarding a plane from New York to Pittsburgh and,
after promoting Cvetic to "chief Party organizer," disappeared.[16]

In early January, the script was still being written when *I Was a Communist*
went into production two days before Nelson's sedition trial opened in Pittsburgh. Soon, *Variety*'s front-page report "It's Tough to Produce Commie Pix
These Days" humorously detailed the production's travails: first, "no print shop
would turn out needed subversive handbills for fear outsiders, getting hold of
one and noting the union stamp, would point a finger at the shop." Then, a scene
of a Communist-inspired wildcat strike—replete with a factory-gate brawl surely
meant to evoke the Battle of Burbank—inspired an actual ruckus at Warner's
studio in which "a group of visitors set up clamor when they saw a truck towing
a large sign reading 'Free Coffee and Donuts Donated by Communist Party
USA.'" Finally, "the studio had to assign a prop man to lock up a large framed
photo of Stalin nightly after the day's shooting. Someone took the original home
as a souvenir."

Even as Richard Collins finished testifying in Washington, the Hollywood
press previewed the movie (from which the FBI had already begun quietly
dissociating itself). A lively audience response prompted the elimination of
some dialogue, notably the assertion that Soviet "state capitalism is a fascist
horror far worse than anything Hitler ever intended for the world. That great

---

16. Cvetic, a Communist since 1943, surfaced in February 1950, the same month as Senator
McCarthy's Wheeling speech, to name some 335 alleged Communists, thus precipitating an
extensive purge of western Pennsylvania and eastern Ohio factories and unions.

liar of all times spoke the truth when he warned that to the east there was an enemy far more dangerous than he!" A week later, only hours after General MacArthur addressed Congress, *I Was a Communist* had its world premiere in Pittsburgh.

In town to cover the Nelson trial, the *Daily Worker*'s senior labor reporter, Art Shields, filed a report on the city's celebration of Matt Cvetic Day. A testimonial luncheon in a downtown hotel was followed by a parade from the courthouse to the movie house. But "stool pigeons are not heroes to the great body of working people in this steel city. And the crowd on the street looked on coldly as the much advertised Matt Cvetic parade went down Fifth Avenue towards the theater . . . a thin, straggly line one block long." The show started late, according to Shields, and, despite the distribution of hundreds of free tickets, the theater wasn't full. Although the journalist found the picture both "vicious and dull," he was frightened nevertheless by its "constant incitements to violence," which he thought deliberately timed to prejudice Nelson's trial. Back home in Hollywood, however, the critical response was generally positive. The *Hollywood Reporter* deemed *I Was a Communist* "provocative, entertaining and valuable" and the *Los Angeles Times* deemed it "a crackling good melodrama," which it is—a tense, violent thriller.

From its percussive, portentous titles—each word filling the screen—to the sign-off dolly into a bust of Abraham Lincoln, *I Was a Communist for the FBI* projects ample conviction while blithely blending fact and fiction. Cvetic, played by Frank Lovejoy with a blank, sour expression, stoically endures considerable abuse, much of it from his son and his siblings, who seldom miss an opportunity to denounce him. No sooner has he shown up for his mother's birthday than he receives a phone call from the Party. "Get out of this house and don't come back, you slimy Red," one brother orders. When his mother dies, he is compelled to slink to the funeral under his brothers' withering glare and winds up getting slugged for his trouble.

Neighbors are furious when the Commie pariah takes time out from counterespionage to show a six-year-old the correct way to bunt ("Stay away from my kid. . . . Baseball's an American game!") and Cvetic's teenage son is picked on by the other kids. Not until the last scene can the undercover agent tell the boy who he really is: "Even when you hated me, I loved you for it," he declares as "The Battle Hymn of the Republic" rises on the soundtrack. Moreover, posing as the only idealist in a world of cynics and spies, Cvetic suffers the further indignity of hanging with the comrades as, mouths stuffed with caviar, they raise a champagne toast to Stalin or, apparently mistaking themselves for the Ku Klux Klan, repeatedly use the epithet "nigger."

Communist tactics are illustrated (like the FBI, they have everyone under constant surveillance) and Party strategy is explained. Anti-Semitism is deliberately inflamed and a fake fascist threat is used as a means to raise money. Party apparatchiks are forewarned and kept apprised of North Korea's impending invasion—their new job is to foment defeatism. Amid a Moscow-ordered campaign of ridicule against HUAC, Cvetic journeys to Washington to testify that the Communist Party is a "vast spy system founded in this country by the Soviet Union, and composed of American traitors whose only purpose is to deliver the people of the United States into the hands of Russia as a colony of slaves."

Subversion from within, attack from without: the summer of 1947 had brought the first sightings, but for Hollywood, 1951 was the year that the saucers landed and the extraterrestrials arrived.

The Thing, produced by Howard Hawks for RKO, was one of the most widely publicized movies of early 1951, albeit beaten to theaters by Edgar G. Ulmer's ultra-low-budget *The Man from Planet X*. Ulmer's expressionist *kindermärchen* was characterized by the *New York Times* as "one of the most excruciating bores ever to emerge from the pinpoint on this planet known as Hollywood . . . [with] a handful of sluggish actors—a doddering scientist, a conniving doctor, a pretty girl, an American journalist and a few villagers—milling around a couple of cardboard sets, blankly reciting dialogue that would insult a child."

Of course, Hawks's extraterrestrial project had its juvenile aspect as well. The *Saturday Review*'s notice began by acknowledging that "a couple of kids around the house have been whipped up for some time by announcements in the newspapers of a movie called *The Thing*." But its genius, as the reviewer noted, was in its stark visualization of adult fears. Congealed hysteria, *The Thing*'s preproduction coincided with the emergence of Senator McCarthy and the early stages of the Korean War.

Having negotiated a three-picture deal with RKO in early 1950, and thus reunited with his erstwhile employer Howard Hughes for the first time in the eighteen years since *Scarface*, Hawks was looking for a comparable contemporary shocker—not the threat of Italian gangsters but the specter of a saucer piloted by an implacable vampire vegetable from another world—and even hired *Scarface* screenwriter Ben Hecht to doctor Charles Lederer's script. (Manny Farber would make the connection, calling *The Thing* as "raw and ferocious" as *Scarface* in its battle of wits between the vegetal "screaming banshee" and an all-American "air-force crew that jabbers away as sharply and sporadically as Jimmy Cagney moves.")

Also in his capacity as producer, Hawks closely supervised his longtime editor Christian Nyby's neophyte direction (taking 90 percent of the budgeted directing fee for himself) and embargoed all publicity—or rather, put out the word that the set was closed and the project "top secret." Naturally, a journalist from the *Los Angeles Daily News* managed to "blow-torch" through the "iron curtain" that—appropriate to the tale of an arctic outpost under assault by the lone pilot of a flying saucer that has crash-landed nearby—the studio wrapped around Hawks's "Man-from-Mars-pseudo-scientific horror tale." (He reported back that the Thing, played by six-foot, seven-inch James Arness, was envisioned as "an Adonis with claws.") And the press somehow learned that co-producer Edward Lasker had submitted the script to both the army and the air force with a request for military cooperation and was told by the latter that, since the air force had devoted half a million dollars to proving that flying saucers didn't exist, it felt little obligation to help make a picture in which a saucer landed.

Typically for RKO, the production, which began shooting in late October and wrapped in early March, suffered delays and ran over budget. Hawks and company spent an inordinate amount of time in Cut Bank, Montana—a location chosen by Hughes for its proximity to an airfield that had once been used for B-29 reconnaissance flights. Hawks, however, was confounded by the snow that fell each night but blew away by day. After seven weeks, the cast and crew decamped to an arctic landscape created on the RKO ranch in Encino—another sort of ordeal with sweaty, parka-swaddled actors tramping over the artificial snow that had been created from rock salt, ground-up Masonite, and crystallized photographic solution. Other scenes were filmed in a Los Angeles ice house.

Hyped and released, *The Thing*'s "war of the worlds" inevitably conjured memories of Orson Welles's 1938 broadcast, in both its premise and urgent mode of delivery. (With its nonstop talking, overlapping dialogue, and wisecracking esprit de corps—what Farber described as "a flashy, interesting, erratic jumble reminiscent of disc jockey chatter"—the movie could almost be a radio play.) Everything was put in the service of a fantastically blunt metaphor. A typically Hawksian group of professionals circles the wagons against the alien invader. Their ongoing heroism is celebrated by the newshound Scotty, a World War II combat photographer who provides the celebrated final warning to "keep watching the skies"; their unity is threatened by an effete little Nobel Prize–winning scientist affecting a blazer, turtleneck, and goatee.

Time thought the scientist was costumed as a Russian; he actually seems more like a wannabe Russian, the sort of useful idiot who might be counted on to support the likes of a Steve Nelson. Thwarting the men of action whenever possible, this crypto-Commie (who values knowledge above all else) wants only to appease the Thing in the name of science. For him, the carnivorous carrot is an evolutionary advance with "no pain or pleasure as we know it—no heart, no feelings—our superior in every way."

Although the *New York Times* noted the topical jokes about Truman and the military, only the *Daily Worker* took the movie seriously. The sociologist Harold Cruse, whose brief, youthful stint as the paper's film critic raised both the level of analysis and the quality of writing, contextualized *The Thing* ("called what it is because it obviously had to be called something") in the world situation and addressed it as a symptom, "'invasion psychosis' from 'enemies' known and unknown." He also wittily characterized the movie as "anti-scientific fiction"—a bias for which Hawks himself took credit.

The Thing's antithesis was even then in production—and Twentieth Century-Fox thought that the box-office success of RKO's space invader film boded well for their own.[17]

Produced by Julius Blaustein, written by Edmund North, and directed by Robert Wise, *The Day the Earth Stood Still* was shooting second-unit work in Washington, DC, as Larry Parks gave his March 21 testimony to HUAC; the project moved to the Fox backlot just before Sterling Hayden took the stand in April and wrapped around the time unfriendly witness Leonardo Bercovici appeared before the committee in mid-May.

Apocalyptic yet sober in its demeanor, *The Day the Earth Stood Still* was almost rational. Whereas engine failure caused the mind-bending Man from Planet X to touch down in the Scottish highlands and the Thing had to crash-land at the North Pole, alien Klaatu (Michael Rennie) had a precise mission: the whole world is watching even before his saucer lands midday in a baseball field

---

17. *The Thing* was well received, with *Variety*'s sense that the movie lacked "genuine entertainment value" a minority opinion. The *New York Herald Tribune* thought it "well-written, horrific, and funny." The *New York Times* concurred: "Not since Dr. Frankenstein wrought his mechanical monster has the screen had such a good time dabbling in scientific-fiction." Thanks to skillful promotion and healthy runs in New York and Los Angeles, *The Thing* hovered among Hollywood's top early spring releases and, grossing nearly $2 million, was RKO's sixth-biggest earner for 1951—forty-seventh overall, just ahead of *The Day the Earth Stood Still*. Manny Farber, who included both movies in his "'Best Films' of 1951," praised *The Thing*'s lack of "progressive-minded gospel-reading about neighborliness in the atomic age."

near the Washington Monument and, in an instant cliché, the dapper extrater-restrial emerges. "One of those things is here again," Bosley Crowther would warn, allowing that this alien was "so well-mannered and peacefully inclined, that you'd hardly expect [him] to split an infinitive, let alone an atom or a human head. . . . [His] command of an earthly language must have been acquired from listening entirely to the BBC. . . . We've seen better monsters in theatre audi-ences on Forty-second Street."

Klaatu does not utter the words "take me to your leader" but his message is close enough: "We have come to visit you in peace and with goodwill. . . . I want to meet with representatives of all the nations on earth." The spaceman, it would seem, is an internationalist who incredibly fails to grasp the distinction be-tween America and Russia. (But was it chance that brought him to the Wash-ington Mall rather than Red Square?) Of course, the Americans don't recognize the difference between Klaatu and the Thing. Minutes after he emerges from his saucer, the visitor is shot—perhaps fatally—by a nervous soldier.

The violence activates Klaatu's robot associate Gort (played by a seven-foot-seven-inch doorman at Grauman's Chinese), who vaporizes all nearby earth-ling weapons as his master is rushed to the Walter Reed Army Medical Center. Miraculously recovered, Klaatu continues his peace mission incognito, seeking refuge in a Washington rooming house whose tenants include an attractive war widow (Patricia Neal) and her young son (Billy Gray, soon of the situation com-edy *Father Knows Best*). Eventually the alien will entrust the pair with his iden-tity as well as the code words to deactivate Gort: "*klaatu barada nikto*," carefully committed to memory by kids across America.

Klaatu also makes contact with Dr. Barnhardt, the smartest man on earth, played by wide-eyed, wild-haired Sam Jaffe as an obvious stand-in for Albert Einstein. This was not an innocent choice. America's most famous brain was a proponent of world government and an opponent of loyalty oaths, reviled as a Communist fellow traveler for co-sponsoring the 1949 Cultural and Scientific Conference for World Peace. Encouraged by Klaatu, Dr. Barnhardt organizes an international peace conference similar to the Waldorf conclave—a gathering repeatedly invoked during the recent HUAC hearings.

Although the movie's poster image—Gort carrying the comatose Helen—echoed *King Kong*, *The Day the Earth Stood Still* was far from a horror film. If anything, it was a more dynamic version (and critique) of *The Next Voice You Hear*. Obviously and unfashionably progressive, it unfolded in a looking-glass world where the brainy scientist is a good guy and Helen's fiancée, eager to drop a dime on Klaatu, is a villain (or at least a would-be friendly witness). As with

Blaustein's first film, *Broken Arrow,* which opened while *The Day the Earth Stood Still* was in preproduction, this one had a purpose. Blaustein told the press the film was an argument in favor of a strong United Nations. During the summer of 1950, however, it seemed doubtful that so pacifist a scenario would be made (and, "in an effort to avoid any unnecessary criticism being brought against the motion picture industry," the Breen Office would repeatedly request changes whenever "the space-man's words seem to be directed at the United States"). Still, Zanuck was enthusiastic and, at an August 10 story conference with Blaustein and North, stressed the need for rendering the fantastic in a believable fashion—a practical as well as an aesthetic consideration.

While director Robert Wise was also politically liberal (he later described himself as a left-wing sympathizer who hadn't joined enough front groups to come under government scrutiny), his main contributions were stylistic. Wise had directed two low-key atmospheric chillers for producer Val Lewton and before that had served as Orson Welles's editor. *The Day the Earth Stood Still* shows the influence of both Lewton and Welles. As the premise was Wellesian, so was the use of actual newsmen—including Elmer Davis, H.V. Kaltenborn, and Drew Pearson—and the references to mass hysteria. (Wise also recruited Welles's composer Bernard Herrmann to provide a moody, theremin-enriched score.)

Variety would praise the locations that gave *The Day the Earth Stood Still* "an almost documentary flavor," but Wise was documenting something more than Washington landmarks. Paranoia is palpable and the spectacle of the nation's capital under martial law seems all too probable. (Having read the script, the army refused to supply any jeeps and tanks; Fox managed to enlist the national guard instead.) While commending *The Day the Earth Stood Still* for its seriousness, the *Los Angeles Times* critic fretted that "certain subversive elements" might co-opt the movie's philosophy. The *Daily Worker* wasn't much impressed, however, noting that, while acknowledging the people's desire for peace, the movie hardly inspired its audience to work toward ending war: "That, it appears, is a job for men from other planets."[18]

Be that as it may, men from other nations were pleased to see *The Day the*

---

18. Recognizing the "sharply-pointed moral," *Variety* predicted "okay grosses." This child-friendly visitation proved a moderate hit, grossing $1.85 million in the United States. (The budget was put at $960,000, of which approximately 10 percent went toward the spaceship.) Thanks to the futuristic technology of television, *The Day the Earth Stood Still* would become the best-loved science-fiction film of the Cold War era—precursor to, if not inspiration for, Steven Spielberg's *Close Encounters of the Third Kind* and *E.T.: The Extra-Terrestrial.* John Carpenter, who remade *The Thing* in 1982, followed it two years later with *Starman* (1984), a crypto-remake of *The Day the Earth Stood Still.*

Earth Stood Still as a plea for cooperation. While it is possible to read the movie as a vision of American hegemony (albeit less unconscious than *The Next Voice You Hear*), Hollywood's foreign press awarded the movie a special Golden Globe for promoting international understanding. And in Paris, the young critics of *Cahiers du Cinéma* were also taken with the film, hailed by Pierre Kast as the most unlikely American production since Charles Chaplin's *Monsieur Verdoux*, a "secret cry of agony, the expression of a terrible vertigo . . . almost literally stunning." Kast praised the movie's moral relativism, citing the scene in which an aide to the American president explains to Klaatu that Earth is divided between the forces of good and evil and that "we are the forces of good," only to be brushed off by the alien's disdainful disinterest in such foolishness. Clearly, Kast noted, "this is a far cry from corn-fed physicians looking for the American way of life on the moon, one finger on the trigger of their secret weapon."[19]

Three Cases: Joseph L., Carl F., and Elia Kazan

The Day the Earth Stood Still appeared at the end of a strange, paranoid summer— a month after MGM fired Louis B. Mayer and one day into the first HUAC hearings on "Communist infiltration of the Hollywood motion picture industry," to be held in Los Angeles and televised for the world.

The subpoenas had begun going out in late spring. Hastening back from Mexico, where he'd recently made *The Brave Bulls* and to which he had unaccountably returned even as the movie had its Hollywood premiere, Robert Rossen spent June 25 on Capitol Hill grilled by the committee. While asserting that he was not now a member of the Communist Party, Rossen declined to say "never" and, when asked about his associates, took the Fifth. One comrade, *Brave Bulls* screenwriter John Bright, had also been named in the March hearings and remained south of the border.

---

19. *The Day the Earth Stood Still* does allow for a more hard-nosed reading, with Gort's capacity for mayhem embodying the doctrine of Mutually Assured Destruction. But most of the movie's fans have extrapolated an internationalist message—including at least one U.S. president. According to biographer Lou Cannon, Ronald Reagan was so stirred by the notion that extraterrestrial invasion would trump national differences that he floated the scenario upon meeting Mikhail Gorbachev at Geneva in 1985. This departure from script flummoxed Reagan's staff, not to mention the Soviet premier. Cannon writes that, well acquainted with what he called the president's interest in "little green men," national security adviser Colin Powell was convinced that the proposal had been inspired by *The Day the Earth Stood Still*. Reagan revisited the idea two years later in a speech at the UN: "I occasionally think how quickly our differences worldwide would vanish if we were facing an alien threat from outside this world."

Bright, who had been married to a Mexican activist, was part of a burgeoning expatriate screenwriters' colony. Albert Maltz and Gordon Kahn were already
living in Mexico. Other writers—including newly released Dalton Trumbo and
Ring Lardner, as well as the couple Hugo Butler and Jean Rouverol, and, briefly,
Bernard Gordon—would soon join them. (Julian Zimet arrived a bit later and
suffered the indignity of being taken for an informer.) Elia Kazan had hoped to
stop by, but because the Mexican government disapproved of John Steinbeck's
script for *Viva Zapata!*, he was shooting his revolutionary spectacle in South
Texas.

It was just as *Viva Zapata!* wrapped in July that Ronald Reagan declared victory. Filling in for vacationing labor reporter Victor Reisel, the Screen Actors
Guild president contributed a guest column to the *Hollywood Citizen News* that
explained how, acting under orders from Joseph Stalin in accordance with a doctrine that Reagan called *kinofiktatsiya* (and translated as "using entertainment
movies as propaganda"), the Communists had "concentrated their big guns on
Hollywood," only to be defeated by . . . Reagan's union! "They tried every trick
in the bag but the actors, led by the Board of Directors of Screen Actors Guild,
out-thought them and out-fought them. We fought them on the record and off
the record," Reagan wrote, paraphrasing Winston Churchill. "We found them
in meetings and behind the scenes."

> Our Red foes even went so far as to threaten to throw acid in the faces of myself
> and some other stars, so that we "never would appear on the screen again." I
> packed a gun for some time and policemen lived at my house to guard my kids.
>
> But that was more than five years ago and those days are gone forever, along
> with the deluded Red sympathizer and fellow travelers.

Then who were those picketers marching outside the Federal Building, thread-
ing their way around a fixed marine recruiting sign, shouting and brandishing
placards that quoted the post-Dmytryk Hollywood Nine as the hearings opened
on Monday morning, September 17?

The committee's first order of business was the reading of a letter signed by a
dozen industry organizations (including SAG, SDG, and SWG) specifically denouncing the picketers from the Hollywood Council of the Arts, Sciences, and
Professions. Next, onetime CP functionary turned friendly witness Harold J. Ashe
held forth, explicating the degree of Communist influence on the industry: "I
have seen many, many films out of Hollywood in which some part of the Communist line was injected by deliberate intent. It couldn't have been otherwise."

But could it still be going on? As the hearings continued that week and into the next, scores of alleged Communists would be newly named in public, among them screenwriter Carl Foreman and director Joseph Losey, both with connections to Hollywood's liberal hope, thirty-eight-year-old producer Stanley Kramer—a feisty independent who had recently struck a distribution deal with Columbia. Foreman and Kramer had met in the Army Signal Corps and joined forces after the war, even entering into a business partnership, with Foreman writing Kramer's first four productions, including *Home of the Brave*, as well as the current Gary Cooper Western *High Noon*. Losey, a former protégée of Dore Schary's at RKO, had been set to sign on as one of Kramer's house directors; after Kramer made his deal with Columbia, he offered Losey a three-picture agreement, including *High Noon*, as well as the topical exposé later released as *The Wild One*.

Early summer was Losey's time. A pair of his crime films, drenched in creepy expressionism and fraught with fascist menace, were in release, and the forty-two-year-old director was working on a third—the last movie he would make in Hollywood.

The Big Night had just gone into production when director Frank Tuttle named its screenwriter Hugo Butler among thirty-six former comrades. The next morning, May 25, *The Prowler*—directed by Losey from a script that Butler had fronted for Dalton Trumbo—opened in Los Angeles. Basically the story of a wealthy would-be actress trapped in a tawdry police state, *The Prowler* starred two active members of the Committee for the Defense of the First Amendment. The adulterous protagonist (Evelyn Keyes) plays the entire movie in a kind of trance—totally vulnerable, spied upon by and submitting to the predatory cop (Van Heflin) who kills her husband. Butler was already dodging a subpoena. According to his wife, Jean Rouverol, he and Losey had worked on the *Big Night* screenplay as though they were antifascist partisans or noir victims on the lam, carrying their portable typewriter and yellow pads from motel to motel throughout Central and Northern California. After Butler disappeared into Mexico, Ring Lardner Jr. finished the script and then left the country himself.

The *Big Night* cast included two people of interest, future blacklistees Howland Chamberlin and Dorothy Comingore, both in supporting roles. Best remembered for playing Susan Alexander in *Citizen Kane*, Comingore was working with a wig. Her ex-husband Richard Collins's friendly testimony in April had filled her with disgust: "I suddenly realized I was married to an informer," she told Losey. "I felt like a collaborator after the liberation, and so I went out and had my hair shaved off." (Comingore's next public performance would be on the picket line outside HUAC's Los Angeles hearings.) The movie's seventeen-year-old star, John Barrymore Jr., was a future FBI informant—at least according to Losey, who would recall that, after he had relocated to London, Barrymore unexpectedly showed up with plenty of time and money to spend, later confessing that he'd been assigned to contact and report back on his former director.

On June 11, soon after *The Big Night* wrapped, Losey's remake of Fritz Lang's *M*—an effectively unsettling transposition of Weimar paranoia and social chaos to contemporary Los Angeles—opened in New York. Two days into *M*'s run, HUAC agents attempted to serve Losey's subpoena—albeit at his old address, where friends of his then-in-laws were able to send the G-men on a wild-goose chase. Foreman was home working on the script for *High Noon* when he received his subpoena that same day. Losey had been prepared but not Foreman. "It came as a bit of a shock," he would recall.[20]

More shocking perhaps was Foreman's discovery that, after the subpoena became known, friends and acquaintances began avoiding him—even crossing the street as he approached. These incidents colored his screenplay, in which the honest Marshal Kane refuses to run from the outlaws who have returned to avenge themselves on him and, deserted by the townspeople he had served, takes on the outlaws alone: "I began to write it as a parable of what was happening in Hollywood." (Was no one safe? The next morning, the Senate's Patriot Roughneck attacked Secretary of Defense George Marshall as a Communist dupe, complicit in "conspiracy on a scale so immense as to dwarf any previous such venture in the history of man.")

Having managed to dodge his subpoena, Losey was editing *The Big Night* in mid-July when the liberal fixer Martin Gang informed him that he'd been named as a Communist by two prospective HUAC witnesses. ("They were persons I had gone to Marxist classes with. I hardly knew them," Losey later told the French critic Michel Ciment.) Gang invited Losey to clear himself and secure his agreement with Kramer by signing a loyalty oath and giving friendly testimony in executive session. Instead, Losey turned *The Big Night* over to the producer and skipped town. By July 17, he was in Paris.

---

20. Foreman maintained that he quit the Party in 1942 before entering the army and that, on his return to Hollywood, his activism was mainly a matter of teaching screenwriting at the People's Education Center through the summer of 1947. The writer Stanley Roberts's friendly testimony had Foreman leaving his branch in mid-1946 "due to the pressure of work," however—information Roberts presumably furnished the FBI. Foreman's FBI file also notes that he registered with the Progressive Party in April 1948 and appears to have subscribed to *People's World* as late as June 1951.

Foreman decided to stay. No one knew what he planned to do. In mid-August, the Hollywood Council held a meeting of subpoenaed witnesses in order to coordinate unfriendly testimony and strategize countermeasures to the hearings. Foreman had been a no-show, and the Party dispatched screenwriter Eddie Huebsch to sound out his position. After a lengthy lunch at Lucy's ("the fanciest restaurant in Hollywood," across from the Paramount studio on Melrose), Huebsch concluded that Foreman was preparing to inform . . . or something. "The main point," he told Victor Navasky years later, was that "Carl wouldn't tell the committee to go fuck themselves."

The *High Noon* shoot opened on September 5. In addition to Foreman and another partner in Kramer's company, publicist George Glass, three cast members had been served subpoenas: Lloyd Bridges, Marshal Kane's deputy; Howland Chamberlain, the supercilious hotel clerk who openly dislikes the marshal and looks forward to his comeuppance; and Virginia Farmer, the woman who talks about not being able to walk safely down the streets of Hadleyville before Kane cleaned up the town.

Glass had decided to name names while Foreman planned to take a "diminished Fifth" and discuss only his own Party membership. Kramer had no patience with this position; according to Foreman, he panicked, telling his partner, "They'll say, 'Do you know Stanley Kramer?' and you'll take the Fifth and then I'll be in trouble." Kramer would maintain that Foreman lied to him about his onetime Party membership and then threatened him with exposure; Foreman claimed that, pressured by Columbia (already spooked by the subpoena served to the studio's premier producer-director, Sidney Buchman), Kramer simply caved.[21]

Two weeks into the *High Noon* shoot, on the third morning of the HUAC hearings, Carl Foreman turns on the TV to hear himself named by Martin Berkeley:

---

21. Although a non-Communist, Kramer was susceptible to pressure. His FBI file includes favorable movie reviews clipped from the *People's World* and a June 1951 statement by a "confidential informant of known reliability" that he was a reputed CP sympathizer. Ten days before the hearings, a former Communist "voluntarily" came to the FBI's L.A. office, identifying the "Kramer outfit" as "Red from the top to the bottom." Chamberlain testified on September 18; accused of having been a Communist since 1938, he proved a most contentious witness—invoking his Mayflower heritage as he attacked the committee—and did not work again in Hollywood until 1976. Farmer, a co-founder of the Actors Lab, took the stand and the Fifth three days later. She was accused of being a leading Communist operative while an administrative supervisor with the Federal Theatre in the late 1930s. Glass and Bridges, who studied at the Actors Lab, gave friendly testimony after the movie wrapped, both in executive session.

"There is on the [Screen Writers Guild executive board] today only one man I know who was ever a Communist. This man has never to my knowledge disavowed his Communism. His name is Carl Foreman."

A self-described voluntary witness who, according to his lawyer, has been the subject of threatening phone calls warning him against appearing before the committee, Berkeley will testify for three hours, massively detailing his six years in Hollywood's Communist Party and naming 152 names, each carefully spelled out. Prompted by the committee's counsel, Berkeley singles out Foreman with a challenge that, as an SWG official, Foreman had an obligation to appear before HUAC and clear himself.

The following week, Foreman is in the hot seat. He tells the committee he's currently working on a Western starring Gary Cooper that concerns "a town that died because it lacked the moral fiber to withstand aggression." They don't get the hint. Foreman declares that he is no longer a Communist and voluntarily signed an SWG loyalty oath to that effect a year ago; when asked to supply the dates of his Party membership and the names of his comrades, however, he takes the Fifth Amendment.

Lectured by various members of the committee, Foreman loses his temper when Representative Francis E. Walter suggests that members of the Motion Picture Alliance were blacklisted after the 1947 hearings. Foreman reminds Walter that he is currently making a movie that stars an MPA member and friendly witness, adding that he has set up a project in which none other than Edward Dmytryk will direct another MPA friendly, Adolphe Menjou. Unimpressed, Representative Robert Jackson, Republican of California, calls Dmytryk's testimony "among the finest and most complete ever received by this committee" and wonders if Foreman thinks that "Mr. Dmytryk was doing the American thing, the right thing, in coming before this committee and giving us the benefit of his knowledge regarding Communism and Communist activities?" After conferring with counsel, Foreman replies that it isn't important what he thinks about Dmytryk—what's important is what Dmytryk thinks about Dmytryk.

The committee's final witness and prize catch is Columbia writer-producer Sidney Buchman, author of *Mr. Smith Goes to Washington*, former president of the SWG, member of the Hollywood Writers Mobilization and the Committee for the First Amendment, and the brains behind the wildly popular *Jolson Sings Again*. Buchman himself invokes the First Amendment in his testimony, admitting that he joined the Party in the late thirties and dropped out after the Duclos letter. He not only refuses to name names but attempts to clear several people named by Dmytryk and other friendlies.

Buchman could be charged with contempt of Congress, although, for reasons never made clear, he will not be. In effect, Foreman has stolen the show, emerging from the hearings as the object of particular animus. John Wayne and Hedda Hopper, two outspoken members of the MPA leadership, are demanding that Kramer cut him loose. Things are so bitter that the partners are no longer speaking by the time *High Noon* finishes shooting on October 6, with Foreman refusing even to put in an appearance at the wrap party. Kramer buys out Foreman's interest in their company; a few days later, Foreman surprises the industry with the announcement that he's forming a new company with producer Robert Lippert and superstar Gary Cooper. Hearing this, the Duke goes nuts.

Wayne demands a private meeting with Foreman, where he gives a performance that is HUAC redux. Wayne begins reasonably enough ("You're the kind of man we need—you can't turn your back on us") but, impatient with Foreman's explanation of his position, is soon on his feet pounding the wall with the largest fist the writer has ever seen and shouting, "Who do you think you are!?"[22]

There were demonstrations outside Hollywood movie houses in the wake of the hearings. Pickets denounced the "known Reds" in and behind Joseph Losey's *M* as well as *Saturday's Hero*, a college football exposé written by Sidney Buchman. Other targets included Kramer's production of *Death of a Salesman*, William Wyler's *Detective Story*, and Twentieth Century-Fox's biblical spectacular *David and Bathsheba* (written by liberal Philip Dunne and starring liberal Gregory Peck). Some of the picketers were individual crazies, like Donald G. Nelson, a twenty-three-year-old stock clerk soon to be fired by Weber Aircraft in Burbank and apparently the sole member of the Crusade for Freedom. Others belonged to a new group called the Wage Earners, against whom Kramer, and later Dore Schary, would retaliate with libel and damage suits.

Kramer attempted to steer a middle course. On one hand, he had Edward Dmytryk and Adolphe Menjou "reunited in a redbaiting friendship," per the incensed *Daily Worker*, which reported that the "ex-member of the Hollywood Ten who turned informer for the FBI, is now palsy walsy with his erstwhile

---

22. Cooper subsequently withdrew from Carl Foreman Productions; Foreman, realizing he had no future in Hollywood, left for London the following spring, later joined by Joseph Losey.

foe—the rabid witch-hunter and haberdasher's gentleman." (Dmytryk was directing Menjou in *The Sniper*, a project the *Worker* neglected to mention was originally to be produced by Foreman.) On the other hand, Kramer acquired Daniel Taradash's antiblacklist script *The Library*, inspired by the case of an Oklahoma librarian fired for refusing to cancel the subscriptions to certain subversive periodicals—the *Nation*, the *New Republic*, *Negro Digest*, and *Consumer Reports*. None other than America's onetime sweetheart Mary Pickford planned to emerge from an eighteen-year retirement to act in the movie because, as she explained, "this is a picture which stands for everything we Americans hold dear. It is the most important subject in the world today and the one nearest my heart."[23]

The Wage Earners regarded *David and Bathsheba* as "a Satanic Plot to Destroy Christianity and America," while in New York, Communists were demonstrating against another Fox production: *The Desert Fox*, starring the urbane British actor James Mason as the German general Erwin Rommel. Despite the script approval granted by the U.S. high commissioner in Germany, John J. McCloy, opposition had been expressed well in advance of the shoot, mainly by gossip columnist Walter Winchell. *The Desert Fox* opened in New York on November 18 and within days, ad hoc groups of veterans were out picketing. A few weeks after the premiere, the Warner theater chain canceled all bookings and terminated some runs.

Pickets and cancellations were reported throughout December—and not just in the *Daily Worker*, which was also supporting protests organized by the Anti-Defamation League and the American Jewish Congress against David Lean's *Oliver Twist*. Alec Guinness's grotesquely stereotyped Fagin put the kibosh on the British import, but despite its "glorification of a Nazi beast," *The Desert Fox* was successful enough to finish twenty-fifth for the year. It was at this moment of Hitlerite rehabilitation that Howard Hughes chose to release *The Whip Hand*, an anti-Communist tract that began life as an anti-Nazi warning titled *The Man He Found*.[24]

---

23. Ten months later, Pickford changed her mind, citing the project's lack of Technicolor. Taradash, who would attribute her withdrawal to Hedda Hopper's pressure, ultimately got the movie made at Columbia in 1955, under the title *Storm Center*, with Bette Davis as the librarian.

24. In late 1950, Hughes had discovered that *The Man He Found*, a just-finished thriller directed by William Cameron Menzies, concerned a Nazi cell based in a remote Minnesota town, sheltered by locals and led (it is revealed in the movie's final minutes) by a ranting, disfigured Adolf Hitler. Hughes demanded changes; producer-writer Stanley Rubin refused and was replaced. Hughes had new footage shot (and existing footage dubbed) so the Nazi agents became

In Hollywood, the year concluded on a note of triumph with the local premiere of MGM's *Quo Vadis*. A suitably Romanized movie palace on Wilshire Boulevard provided the setting for the conversion of Robert Taylor's patriotic warrior to the mysterious new "slave" religion of He who "died to make men free." All hail the Christian Soldier! Yet even more gratifyingly unexpected were the crowds that lined up outside two Los Angeles theaters for Paramount's sci-fi disaster spectacle *When Worlds Collide*. ("Evidently it takes a scientific thriller to prove that movies are still the favored entertainment of a large segment of the public," the *Los Angeles Times* opined.) Like *Quo Vadis*, *When Worlds Collide* was both a Hollywood spectacular and an American origin story. Rather than Americanize ancient Rome, however, George Pal's apocalyptic follow-up to his previous production *Destination Moon* presented a new band of interplanetary pilgrims escaping Earth on a rocket ship equivalent of the *Mayflower* to found a new civilization on the virgin world Zyra.

For some, America was already a disaster and 1951 a year to forget—the lone Hollywood movie on David Platt's annual ten-best list was *Saturday's Hero*. Just before Christmas, HUAC urged that all spies be put to death and sent Elia Kazan the subpoena he'd been dreading for the past eighteen months, if not longer.

Although only a bona fide Communist for nineteen months back in the long-ago 1930s, Kazan was associated with the left and conscious of his vulnerability. He prudently ducked out of the October 1950 Screen Directors Guild meeting, telling Joseph Mankiewicz that Cecil B. DeMille knew of Kazan's scarlet past and would use it against them; indeed, his FBI file had a number of recent reports that characterized him as a Communist or fellow traveler.[25]

Kazan appeared before a HUAC executive session on January 14, 1952, using a strategy resembling Carl Foreman's. He admitted his own Party membership but refused to implicate anyone else. Perhaps, like Foreman, he imagined that his next movie would speak for his current position; perhaps he even

---

Communists, Hitler was cut, and the movie was retitled *The Whip Hand*. *Daily Variety* called it "a near masterpiece of suspense . . . a little too close to contemporary history to be taken lightly."

25. A disgruntled actor complained that *Death of a Salesman*'s Broadway production was dominated by Reds; another informer linked Kazan to a 1950 radio defense of the Hollywood Ten. The director would tell HUAC that his name had been used without permission ("By that time I was disgusted by the silence of the Ten and by their contemptuous attitude"), and perhaps it was, but Kazan continued to identify with the left. Asked by the 1951 Film and Fine Arts World Festival of Belgium to list the ten best films of all time, he led with Sergei Eisenstein's *Battleship Potemkin* and recklessly ranked another Soviet film, Alexander Dovzhenko's *Frontier*, second!

imagined that its political line would help him avoid Foreman's fate. The timing was right. Kazan's most ambitious project to date, a biopic of the early-
twentieth-century Mexican revolutionary hero Emiliano Zapata, was made to
expose the Communist mind-set and scheduled to open in three and a half
weeks.

Years later Kazan maintained that *Viva Zapata!* was a personal project he'd
nourished since he first arrived in Hollywood: "The figure of Zapata was particularly attractive to me, because after he got all the power that comes with triumph,
he didn't know what to do with it or where to put it or where to exert it."

Kazan's ambitions (or neuroses) notwithstanding, however, Hollywood had
long entertained the idea of celebrating the Mexican revolutionary. Soon after
the succès d'estime of Warner Bros.'s *Juarez*, MGM purchased Edgecumb Pinchon's biography *Viva Zapata* as a vehicle for Robert Taylor. Having languished
during World War II, the potentially controversial project was revived in 1947
with Communist writer Lester Cole researching a screenplay for Louis B. Mayer's nephew, producer Jack Cummings. According to Cole, his unmistakably
red treatment was submitted to MGM general manager Eddie Mannix, who,
upon reading it, summoned Cole and Cummings to his office for a scolding.
However, once Mannix learned that the Mexican government had offered the
project a million dollars' worth of services, he changed his tune: "What the hell,
Jesus Christ was a revolutionary, too."

A few months later, Cole was blacklisted, but by the following summer,
another studio had become interested in Zapata. Twentieth Century-Fox un-
officially queried the Breen Office regarding the problems that might arise in
adapting Pinchon's biography. These, delivered in a numbered memo, were: first,
that many Mexicans, including the government, regarded Zapata as a national
hero; second, that the Catholic Church considered him an enemy; third, that Zapata was, if not a Communist, "an extreme agrarian radical"; fourth, that it would
be necessary to portray Mexico's bloody revolution; fifth, that the film could not
avoid controversy. Still, looking perhaps for a new *Grapes of Wrath*, Darryl F. Zanuck hired John Steinbeck to write an original Zapata screenplay, and before 1948
ended, MGM transferred its tainted property to Fox.[26]

---

26. MGM had scheduled *Zapata* for early 1949, still planning to cast their workhorse Robert
Taylor in the title role. Marguerite Roberts, another Communist (and future unfriendly witness), was hired to rework Cole's screenplay.

In January 1949, Fox announced that Kazan would direct Steinbeck's screenplay as a vehicle for the studio's leading male attraction, Tyrone Power. Steinbeck completed the finished script four months later, although Kazan, who was busy with the film version of *A Streetcar Named Desire* and *Panic in the Streets*, would not turn his attention to it for nearly a year. Conceived during the *Fort Apache* summer of 1948; written (and rewritten) throughout 1950, the year of McCarthyism at home and Korea abroad; and produced between the second and third installments of the HUAC Hollywood investigation, the *Viva Zapata!* scenario was effectively dictated by the Cold War.

Kazan hoped to shoot the movie on location in Mexico, but Mexican authorities did not favor Steinbeck's script as they had Cole's treatment, and the project was relocated to Texas. In May 1951, *Viva Zapata!* began shooting on the north side of the Rio Grande, with an angel blessing the project. Fox starlet Marilyn Monroe was on the set, continuing her affair with director Kazan and, once his family arrived in Texas, bestowing her favors on the movie's star, Marlon Brando.

Kazan and Steinbeck, two men of the thirties, both nurtured by the Popular Front, struggled to articulate an emancipatory mission that opposed both Stalinism on the left and neocolonialism on the right. What image might embody this struggle? Kazan prevailed upon Zanuck to drop the idea of Tyrone Power and have the freedom fighter played by the hipster who stunned Broadway as Stanley Kowalski, the brutish protagonist of *A Streetcar Named Desire*.

Kazan's initial conception of Zapata was as a social-climbing snob with a New Deal mentality; over the course of the project, the Mexican revolutionary evolved into an idealized working-class hero with an innate sense of injustice, a desire for self-improvement, and a perverse absence of ruthlessness. Might this, like Kowalski, have once been a role for John Garfield? Or did the impetuous Garfield lack Brando's ruminative quality? On his wedding night, the illiterate revolutionary demands his wife teach him to read, using the Bible as a text and enacting what Richard Slotkin sees as a progressive alliance between revolutionary peasant and "enlightened middle class." The movie dramatized this in another way as it was cast entirely with New York actors, including the village extras. (The exception was Jean Peters, as Zapata's wife. Kazan originally wanted Julie Harris in the role.)

Brando's Zapata was "a new type of bandit hero . . . a thoughtful rebel," the *New York Herald Tribune* would report; the filmmakers had created a "man of savage passion devoted to the poor," charismatic but not Communistic. Even as Steinbeck and Kazan presented their Zapata as a brooding, instinctually just, Actors Studio mestizo, they downplayed the most radical aspects of the actual Zapata's plan for the redistribution of land and wealth. The movie includes a scene of triumphant guerrilla warfare but declines to recall Zapata's endorsement of the Russian Revolution. Indeed, concerned that audiences might imagine *Viva Zapata!* supported armed overthrow of the state, Zanuck inserted a scene in which the Zapatistas speak with approving envy of American democracy.

To further establish their hero's centrist credentials, Kazan and Steinbeck had introduced the negative revolutionary Fernando (Joseph Wiseman). Fernando was a minor character in the screenplay of August 1950. During the cold Korea winter, this chilly abstraction grew into the movie's presiding villain—an opportunistic crypto-Communist intellectual whose abstract love of freedom inevitably promotes totalitarian terror. By the time *Viva Zapata!* was released, Kazan would describe it as a movie about how power corrupts. Demonstrating its own dominance over history, the scenario imagines Zapata as president. A peasant delegation arrives to complain (just as Zapata had himself, back in the days of Porfirio Díaz) about a petty local tyrant, in this case, his brother. The thoughtful rebel (and confirmed social democrat) returns to his people, advising them that "there are no leaders but yourselves." Disgusted by this weakness, authoritarian Fernando treacherously sets up Zapata for assassination; the hero thus becomes a Christlike martyr, symbolized, according to Zanuck's stipulation, by the riderless white horse that canters through the final scene as the embodiment of eternal hope.

Promoted as a supreme prestige production uniting the sensational talents of "MARLON BRANDO! . . . DARRYL F. ZANUCK! . . . ELIA KAZAN! . . . [and] JOHN STEINBECK!" *Viva Zapata!* opened in New York in February 1952 and, according to Bosley Crowther's *New York Times* review, provoked as "lively a swirl of agitation as has been stirred in quite a time." The tumult was not confined to the screen.

Before the premiere of *Viva Zapata!*, Fox's nervous president, Spyros Skouras, had requested that everyone connected with the movie put their political position in writing—furnishing affidavits that he turned over to the Communist-hunting newspaper columnist George Sokolsky. Then HUAC leaked the transcript of Kazan's unfriendly testimony to the *Hollywood Reporter*, which announced that, although the director admitted his own mid-1930s membership in the Communist Party, he declined to discuss "his old pals from the Group Theatre days"—including John Garfield, whom HUAC was still hoping to nail for perjury.

Crowther began his Sunday follow-up on *Viva Zapata!* by remarking that the movie broached a delicate subject: "It is bloody revolution, savage and unrestrained, aimed at established authority and at the holders of property." And, initially at least, leftist critics gave *Viva Zapata!* a mixed reception. *Film Sense* accorded it a surprisingly positive capsule review ("a superior film that makes an enigma of the great Mexican revolutionary hero, but does not undercut his greatness or the importance of the people who gave him strength") and elsewhere cited its progressive gender representation: "Women are seen fighting side by side with their husbands and sons" and "give their lives to dynamite a fort." Even the *Daily Worker* praised a number of individual episodes (mainly involving peasant heroism) while excoriating the movie for its historical falsifications ("it serves to take millions of people into never-never land where the US bankers and generals play no role in Mexico"). The villain held responsible for transforming the great Zapata into a "petty bourgeois revolutionary" was not Kazan, however, but the "anarchist- Trotzkyite [sic]" John Steinbeck. But this was before Kazan's public testimony.[27]

Movie critic for the generally liberal, devotedly middlebrow *Saturday Review* Hollis Alpert unexpectedly attacked *Zapata* from the left, citing Steinbeck's "bombastic and wooden script" and ahistorical approach: Where were the "foreign oil concessionaires, the grasping hand of the church?" What about the "proletarian ferment"? The "political and military machinations?" He answered himself: "It's in the history books, plainly written, but not here. Instead we have some of the usual platitudes about democracy and freedom. . . . Steinbeck has written [his screenplay] so that the meaning of events remains beautifully obscure and also free from the criticisms of those quick and eager to smell scarlet rats."

Three issues later, Laura Z. Hobson, author of the book that provided the basis for Kazan's Oscar-winning *Gentlemen's Agreement*, rose to defend *Zapata* as "sensitive, stirring, often noble." Hobson claimed to have been so upset by Alpert's review that she telephoned Steinbeck, who graciously accepted her call and, with regard to Alpert's criticism, explained, "Whenever a man disagrees with the ideas involved in a book, a play, or a movie, and cannot publicly admit his disagreement, he attacks on grounds of grammar or technique."

---

27. Despite a successful first week, *Viva Zapata!* was undermined by mixed reviews and tepid promotion—it grossed just under $2 million to finish fifty-third on *Variety*'s 1952 list.

Hobson stressed that she'd never met nor previously spoken to Steinbeck, without acknowledging her prior connection to Kazan, who, five issues later, favored the *Saturday Review* with a lengthy letter, at once clarifying his feelings about Zapata ("in the moment of victory, he turned his back on power") and shoring up the movie's anti-Communist credentials. Kazan explained that any possibility of making *Viva Zapata!* in Mexico had been sabotaged by local Reds. Humbly and in good faith, he and Steinbeck had shown the script to two prominent members of the Mexican film industry: "They came back with an attack that left us reeling." The Mexicans took issue with a few details in the script ("which we knew to be historically true"), but, mainly, "they attacked with sarcastic fury" the movie's central premise—Zapata's renunciation of the authority he had attained.

> We digested all this on the terrace of the Hotel Marik in Cuernavaca. Four feet away, on the other side of a low wall, the Indians went by in the street. Over the houses the mountains loomed and the air was soft. John said, "I smell the Party line."
>
> I smelled it too. Nearly two years later our guess was confirmed by a rabid attack on the picture in the *Daily Worker*, which parallels everything the two Mexicans argued.

And, Kazan did not have to make explicit, much that Alpert had written. The director also took it upon himself to explicate Fernando, a character whom Alpert professed to find a deliberately mystifying symbol of "the damage rigid adherence to doctrine can do to a sincere cause." There is, Kazan explained, a thing called the "Communist mentality" and Fernando embodies it—"men who use the just grievances of the people for their own ends, who shift and twist their course, betray any friend or principle or promise to get power and keep it." Kazan had known such people in the Party, he would write, and so, he assumed, had Steinbeck.[28]

---

28. Seven issues later, the radical journalist Carleton Beals—a witness to the Mexican revolution—wrote to defend Alpert's review ("more than generous to Steinbeck-Kazan's slicked-up interpretation of the great agrarian leader") and attack the movie's historical distortions, including the notion that Zapata had renounced power and the transformation of Zapata's revolutionary career into "a cream-puff of Gandhi hocus-pocus for school-boy platitudes about democracy." Beals also noted as "unworthy" Kazan's use of guilt by association, resorting to "the McCarthyite technique of branding critics as dupes of the Communist Party line." Given the last word, Kazan blamed any historical inaccuracies on Steinbeck while denying any intention of equating Alpert's review with that of the *Daily Worker*. Years later, Kazan all but reflexively outed his screenwriter, telling Jeff Young that "John and I were both ex-Communists." But despite the canonical status of *The Grapes of Wrath* for the Popular Front—as well as a fat FBI file dating back to his participation in the 1936 Western Writers Congress—Steinbeck was never a CP member, nor even a reliable fellow traveler.

Whatever its relationship to Kazan's political biography, *Viva Zapata!* introduced something new into Hollywood's political discourse. The year of the movie's release, French sociologist Alfred Sauvy characterized nations that took no side in the Cold War as a "Third World," a phrase soon synonymous with former European colonies. Pondering this arena in *The Vital Center*, Arthur Schlesinger had implied that, in order to thwart the Soviets, the United States was obliged to back—even foment—non-Communist national movements. In the spring of 1952, Supreme Court Justice William O. Douglas urged American support for "peasant revolutions" to stop the spread of Communism. Was the judge thinking of French Indochina or *Viva Zapata!*?

Steinbeck remained extraordinarily attached to *Viva Zapata!* In March 1963, he wrote Kazan, proposing that their movie be rereleased. Steinbeck felt that *Zapata* had failed eleven years before because the "studio was scared of it—at least unsure—and that communicated," while Communists kept it from being widely shown in Mexico or Latin America. Suggesting that the film be reworked to make a parallel to contemporary Cuba, Steinbeck proposed to seek State Department support and President Kennedy's backing. Was it a movie out of time? Sam Peckinpah included several visual allusions in *The Wild Bunch* (1969), and a decade later historian Paul J. Vanderwood would maintain that, in the late 1960s, *Viva Zapata!* became a cult movie for student and black audiences even as it found new popularity abroad. A man for all seasons, Kazan told Vanderwood that he felt vindicated in his movie's appeal to "disgruntled and rebellious people" throughout the world.

On April 10, the thirty-third anniversary of Zapata's murder, and two days after Leo McCarey's *My Son John*—the most artful of McCarthyite tracts and the most passionately personal of anti-Communist movies—had its New York premiere, Kazan returned to HUAC at his own request. This time, he named Clifford Odets as a Communist, as well as the seven Group actors who had been in his Party group: Lewis Leverett; the late J. Edward Bromberg, who had suffered a fatal heart attack soon after his unfriendly testimony a year before; Phoebe Brand and her husband Morris Carnovsky; his old roommate Tony Kraber, soon to lose his job at CBS; Paula Miller Strasberg; and Art Smith, the crotchety factory foreman in *The Next Voice You Hear*. "I have come to the conclusion that I did wrong to withhold these names before," he stated. "Secrecy serves the Communists and is exactly what they want. The American people need the facts, and all facts, about all aspects of Communism in order to deal with it wisely and effectively. It is my duty as a citizen to tell everything I know."

Going further than any previous friendly witness, Kazan supplemented his testimony with an annotated résumé explaining how virtually every play or movie he had ever directed was already anti-Communist. He further took out an ad in the *New York Times* that (projecting Korean War rhetoric back to 1936) condemned Communist thought control and seconded HUAC's assertion that the Party was a "dangerous and alien conspiracy."[29]

Thus blindsided, the *Daily Worker* could only moan in pain. "We have seen a lot of belly-crawling in this time of the toad," exclaimed Samuel Sillen. "But nothing has quite equaled last week's command-performance. . . . At least Larry Parks made a bow to decency. He claimed to be a bit uncomfortable when he turned fingerman on orders of the Un-American Committee."

Kazan's recollections of his Group Theatre days came in the midst of a highly praised, fifteenth-anniversary revival of Clifford Odets's *Golden Boy*, directed by the author himself. (Kazan was set to direct until he received his subpoena.) The production starred John Garfield, who had been promised and denied the role of the tragic boxer (as had Kazan) back in 1937. Three other Group Theatre veterans were in the cast: Lee J. Cobb, Art Smith, and Tony Kraber. Garfield and Cobb had appeared in the original production; Smith and Kraber had been named by Kazan, another member of the original cast, in his HUAC testimony. Odets would also name Kraber (as well as Kazan, among others) when, having been subpoenaed at the same time as Kazan, he appeared before HUAC, the month after *Golden Boy* completed its run.

Garfield had not worked in Hollywood since his June 1950 listing in *Red Channels*; having given unhelpful testimony to HUAC in 1951, he was also under FBI surveillance and the threat of being prosecuted for perjury. While appearing in *Golden Boy*, the actor was working on a mea culpa for *Look* magazine titled "I Was a Sucker for a Left Hook." On May 8, a month after Kazan's appearance, Garfield contacted the FBI, hoping to clear himself to work; evidently

---

29. By his own account, Kazan thrived on alternating secrecy and disclosure, rebellion and compliance. Born to subterfuge, he characterized his early relationship with his mother as conspiratorial, and he re-created that atmosphere throughout his life. Arthur Miller described rehearsing with Kazan as "a conspiracy not only against the existing theatre but society, capitalism—in fact, everybody who was not a part of the production." Throughout his memoirs, Kazan complains that he was perceived as a betrayer of trust but even more frequently cites his "gift of dissembling." Dissembling or acting? Kazan's HUAC testimony was unique for its emotional intensity. As noted by theater historian Mel Gordon, "Kazan actually hooked into the Method by re-living some sensational hidden memory." This dark trauma was the 1936 Party meeting at which, in his words, he felt expected to "grovel, make excuses" and, as before HUAC, "confess [his ideological] errors." Gordon points out that Kazan's testimony and subsequent statements are "right out of an Affective Memory exercise. All the other friendly witnesses had to be prompted to answer questions, only Kazan emotionally connected."

he was asked to give evidence against his wife, an active member of the Hollywood CP, and refused. The day before Garfield's FBI appointment, blacklisted actor Canada Lee, who had appeared with Garfield in *Body and Soul* and gave his last performance in Zoltan Korda's British adaptation of *Cry, the Beloved Country* (scripted by John Howard Lawson through a front), suffered a fatal heart attack at the age of forty-five. The night after Odets's testimony, the thirty-nine-year-old Garfield died of a massive coronary.

Only the week before, Kazan had given a lecture at Harvard in which he self-righteously decried the movie industry's cowardice: "Right now, Hollywood studios have gone overboard in their attitude of not trying to offend anyone. Actors are afraid to act, writers are afraid to write, and producers are afraid to produce anything amateur sleuths could possibly attack." Kazan was already preparing his penance film, aptly titled *Man on a Tightrope*, based on the true story of a Czech circus family that escaped to West Germany. After this requisite anti-Communist melodrama (which also served to "clear" the too-liberal Fredric March), Kazan would direct the six features on which his reputation rests: *On the Waterfront, East of Eden, Baby Doll, A Face in the Crowd, Wild River,* and *Splendor in the Grass.* All feature some form of betrayal.

Campaign '52: Take Us to Our Leader, Big Jim

As 1951 ended, three ambitious Korean War movies were in various stages of completion—all focused on the previous year's disasters.

Solicited by the air force in mid-September 1950, even as General MacArthur orchestrated the assault on Inchon, Howard Hughes began an RKO production to dramatize the cooperation between bomber planes and infantrymen. The project, eventually titled *One Minute to Zero*, was delayed after U.S. ground forces were compelled to retreat and the war lost popularity; meanwhile, Warner Bros. producer and ex-marine Milton Sperling obtained Pentagon approval to make a movie about the new situation in Korea, eventually called *Retreat, Hell!*

RKO reactivated *One Minute to Zero* once MacArthur addressed Congress in April 1951 and Darryl F. Zanuck announced his Korean War project, to be directed by Sam Fuller. Sperling's movie was delayed and production on *One Minute to Zero* would drag on to the end of the year. Thus, Fuller, who had been first in 1950 with *The Steel Helmet*, was again first with his second Korean War bummer, which opened at the Rivoli in New York on November 21, 1951, two days after Universal-International announced their (never-realized) plans to dramatize the past winter's seesaw battle over the Thirty-eighth Parallel.

Fixed Bayonets!, as the project was felicitously retitled, revisited the previous winter's rout: American soldiers in the "iron triangle" south of Pyongyang are forced to retreat under the Chinese onslaught, leaving a rearguard of forty-eight men to hold a mountain pass. Morale is low. "They told me this was going to be a police action," one grunt grouses. "So why didn't they send cops?" his buddy asks. Characterizing the Rivoli as being "as empty as the heads of those who made the film," *Daily Worker* reviewer M.V. credited this humorous exchange with inspiring "the only visible sign of audience reaction."

That *Fixed Bayonets!* concerns a crisis in authority is made apparent in the first shot, when an enemy shell scores a direct hit on an American general's jeep. The protagonist, Corporal Denno (Richard Basehart), has a psychological block, unable to fire on individual enemy combatants. Much to his horror, the platoon lieutenant is killed by a sniper; this death is followed by that of the two sergeants, leaving the corporal in command. Denno rises to the occasion, however, blowing up a Chinese tank to block the pass and allow his surviving men to rejoin the division. The movie's key sequence embodies Fuller's characteristically brutal irony. The fearful corporal risks his life by venturing into a minefield to save a wounded sergeant and carrying him back to safety, only to discover that the man is already dead.

Nation critic Manny Farber considered *Fixed Bayonets!* "funny, morbid; the best war film since *Bataan*," but his was a minority opinion. For lack of anything more positive, Fuller's grim spectacle premiered in New York as a benefit for wounded soldiers while the Armed Forces Radio Service arranged a live broadcast of the Los Angeles opening two weeks later at Grauman's Chinese. Contrary to M.V.'s impression, the movie enjoyed a solid opening but wound up with disappointing grosses—only a bit more than half the money made eleven months earlier by Fox's hit war movie *Halls of Montezuma*.[30]

The armed forces might be popular. Five of the twenty-five top-grossing films of 1951 were service pictures. According to *Variety*, the Dean Martin–Jerry Lewis comedy *At War with the Army* finished ninth for the year, followed by four

---

30. Directed by Lewis Milestone from a script by Michael Blankfort, *Halls of Montezuma* synthesized the 1949 hits *Sands of Iwo Jima* and *Twelve O'Clock High* into a marine corps movie with a troubled commanding officer (Richard Widmark). It was also the first World War II film to humanize the Japanese foe, or at least illuminate the nature of anti-Japanese racism, albeit not enough for Harold Cruse, who wrote in the *Daily Worker* that "the urge to inject realism and three dimensional characterization in war films is hampered by the insistent demand that war films be first of all warmongering films. Hence, considerations of any social realism in such films must always be subordinate to the use of battle experiences of World War II to propagandize for World War III."

World War II flicks: *Halls of Montezuma* (#15); two John Wayne vehicles, Nicholas Ray's aerial *Flying Leathernecks* (#16) and Warner Bros.'s submarine drama *Operation Pacific* (#23); and, despite the campaign waged against it, *Desert Fox* (#25).

Korea, however, was no longer anything that the American people wanted to see. His approval rating mired below 25 percent, President Truman secretly offered to bow out of the election and throw his support to General Dwight D. Eisenhower—but only if Eisenhower, topping public opinion polls for months, agreed to run for president as a Democrat. Eisenhower soon made it clear that he was a Republican, immediately picking up an early endorsement from the *New York Times*.

America was desperate for martial leadership. Someone had entered General MacArthur's name in the upcoming New Hampshire primary and "for the past several weeks," Bosley Crowther reported in February 1952, "Warner Brothers has been bombarding the critical front with a barrage of placards inscribed with famous American fighting words—'Don't give up the ship!' 'Damn the torpedoes!' 'Give me liberty or give me death!' and such as those—all the high and fine tradition of flag-waving history. Apparently the bombardment was intended to soften us up for that studio's new film." That picture was *Retreat, Hell!* which required military intervention to secure Breen Office clearance for its title, "the fightin'est words in the whole fightin' history of the U.S. Marines."

Retreat, Hell! provided the Korean War's first historical narrative, chronicling events from the initial invasion through the landing at Inchon and the liberation of Seoul to the Chinese counteroffensive and the battle at Chosin Reservoir where the First Marine Division was encircled. "Retreat? Hell! We're just attacking in another direction," General Oliver Smith is supposed to have exclaimed in leading his division's evacuation to the coast. Warner Bros. had proposed *Retreat, Hell!* even while the withdrawal was in progress; producer Milton Sperling promised the Defense Department that he would spin a tale of American victory. The marines provided full cooperation while the movie was shot—during the following summer's bloody stalemate—under the eye of General Smith, whose command had conveniently been transferred to Camp Pendleton, California.

Having discharged his duty in *I Was a Communist for the FBI*, Frank Lovejoy was assigned to play the tough marine commander who delivers the title line, with Richard Carlson (soon to be Lovejoy-as-Cvetic's TV equivalent as the star of *I Led Three Lives*) cast as an unwilling World War II retread. *Retreat,*

Hell! itself struck some critics as a retread—inspired less by Korea, per *Time*, than "countless Hollywood war movies of the past."

From both an audience and an official point of view, however, *Retreat, Hell!* was preferable to RKO's long-germinating *One Minute to Zero*, which would open in August, around the time of the first major marine ground action in western Korea, with the Pentagon having withdrawn its endorsement. Specifically, the Defense Department objected to a scene wherein the hero—Robert Mitchum's know-it-all roughneck colonel—shells a column of Korean refugees infiltrated by Communist agents.

Writing in the first issue of *Hollywood Review*, a newsletter published on behalf of the "American audience" by HICCASP's successor, the Southern California Council of Arts, Sciences, and Professions, blacklisted screenwriter Michael Wilson called *One Minute to Zero* "an apology for total war"—in fact, "the annihilation of half the world through atomic war"—further noting that "propaganda specialists who found the murder of one Communist in *The Steel Helmet* 'objectionable' in 1951 find nothing objectionable in *One Minute to Zero*'s mass murder in 1952." As usual, the agenda was Hughes's: having secured considerable air force cooperation in filming or otherwise obtaining elaborate aerial material, and satisfied that the Pentagon would not penalize him by terminating any agreements with Hughes Aircraft, RKO's owner ignored official protests and simply released *One Minute to Zero* without Defense Department sanction.

Adding to the madness of the key scene, Ann Blyth, the naive UN observer who is the overbearing Mitchum's romantic interest, becomes hysterical and has to be slapped into submission: "Get these civilians out of my sight," Mitchum growls. Later, Blyth sees a pile of GI corpses, hands bound by their Communist killers, and this actual atrocity footage convinces her that the colonel acted correctly. She goes to church to pray first for divine forgiveness and then ask for Mitchum's: "I want to be your wife." "You will," is his laconic reply, issued from the jeep that takes him back to the front.

As the hero of *One Minute to Zero* masterminds the first U.S. offensive of the Korean War, the movie might have packed more political punch had it been released early in the campaign—or had General MacArthur been actively running for president. But in the first months of 1952, MacArthur acted coy. While Truman was indecisive and Eisenhower remained in Europe, another leader filled the vacuum. In late January, Estes Kefauver, the racket-busting, TV-savvy junior senator from Tennessee, declared his intention to seek the Democratic nomination.[31]

It was while tromping through the New Hampshire snow that Kefauver—or rather the Kefauver committee—was awarded a special Emmy "for bringing the workings of our government into the homes of the American people." But running for president, Kefauver showed a more traditional approach. The senator revived the practiced folksiness of his 1948 campaign, complete with trademark coonskin cap—signifier of the original frontiersman politician Davy Crockett. On March 11, this newfangled old-fashioned Western hero defeated the everyman president 19,800 to 15,927 to become the Democratic front runner. His juggernaut moved on to the Midwest, skipping the Minnesota primary—where Senator Hubert Humphrey ran as a favorite son—to focus on Wisconsin.

Starting March 26, Kefauver addressed the American people from the silver screen: *The Captive City*, directed by Robert Wise, was a Kefauver crime film that was framed by statements from Kefauver himself—on the big screen at last! An exposé of what lay beneath the surface of what the voice-over narrator calls "any town," *The Captive City* was actually shot in Reno, Nevada, and has a generic resemblance to *The Red Menace*. The openings are the same: a frantic young couple (here John Forsythe and Joan Camden) drive through the night, fleeing some unseen enemy, to take refuge in a police station where they can tell their story. Forsythe plays a small-town journalist who discovers that his cozy little burg is a sinkhole of corruption. The cops are beholden to gamblers and the "combination" has moved in on the local bookie.

When an imported hit man disposes of a private investigator, the newspaperman turns crusader. The police harass him, chamber of commerce gladhanders suddenly turn sinister, and his wife, who had previously asked, "What is the Mafia?" is amazed to discover that their phone's been tapped. Anticipating the *High Noon* scenario by some months, *The Captive City* has its hero seek help in the local church. The reverend commiserates but explains that he can't oppose his own congregation. At last, the journalist reads about the Kefauver

---

31. Some had thought a Kefauver candidacy was inevitable back in November 1951, when Rudolph Halley—the crime committee's young attorney, even then hosting a TV show inspired by the crime hearings—was elected president of the New York city council, winning by 160,000 votes on the third-party Liberal line. The nation's first TV-produced star pol, Kefauver projected what media theorist Marshall McLuhan would characterize as a cool personality. But, unlike his eventual rival John F. Kennedy, Kefauver was not charismatic. His affect, as noted by the *Nation*, was "more reassuring than inspiring."

committee and decides to go to Washington to testify. On March 29, three days after *The Captive City* opened in New York, Truman announced he would not be a candidate for reelection.[32]

Virtually unopposed in the April 1 Wisconsin primary, Kefauver scored his second victory, while on the Republican side, Senator Robert Taft won a substantial plurality despite his inability to secure an endorsement from his colleague Senator Joseph McCarthy. (Pundits speculated that McCarthy's real preference was Douglas MacArthur and that he was positioning himself for the vice presidential nomination.) Now that Truman had taken himself out of the equation, the crime commission scenario seemed less compelling to audiences than the tale of spies, informers, and government agents. It was, after all, wartime as well as a presidential election year, and the Democrats, everyone knew, were the party of treason.

Senator Taft had long blamed the loss of China on a pro-Communist cabal within the State Department. This charge, first made two years before in January 1950, was greatly elaborated by Senator McCarthy, who, among many other allegations, identified the China scholar Owen Lattimore as a top Soviet agent in America, Alger Hiss's "boss" in the State Department espionage ring. Now the State Department was engaged in spying on itself—security men searched desks, opened letters, tapped phones, and recruited secretaries as informants—while Whittaker Chambers's autobiography *Witness* was being serialized in the *Saturday Evening Post*.

February 26, 1952, the same day the Republican Party's most popular young speaker, Senator Richard Nixon, accused the Truman administration of losing a hundred million people to Communism each year (whether by "questionable loyalty" or stupidity), Lattimore appeared before Democratic Nevada senator Pat McCarran's Senate Internal Security Subcommittee, which included McCarthy among its members. The combative Lattimore battled his interrogators for twelve grueling sessions. On March 21, he was dismissed—after having been lambasted by McCarran at length for slander and perjury. That was also the day Hiss began serving a five-year term at the federal penitentiary in Lewisburg, Pennsylvania. A version of his story was about to reach the screen.

---

32. Whether by luck or design, the Los Angeles opening was scheduled to coincide with Kefauver's visit to the city. Opening in March, *Hoodlum Empire* was another Kefauver film that fictionalized the previous year's hearings; here, the criminal mob resembled the CP in that it was run by foreigners and refused to let anyone leave.

My Son John had its New York premiere on April 8, the same day Taft won the Illinois primary. Writer-director Leo McCarey brought the Cold War back home by dramatizing the plight of an all-American family that has produced a traitor who is not only Communist but homosexual as well. (According to MPAA files, the Breen Office had no problem with McCarey's screenplay beyond questioning the rights to the patriotic doggerel song "Uncle Sammy.") Mc-Carey had sworn his cast to secrecy and, while declining to go into the details, told the *New York Times* that, although concerning a Communist in an average American family, his "secret movie plot" was not, as *Variety* had suggested, the Alger Hiss story. Rather, he said:

> It's about a mother and father who struggled and slaved. They had no education. They put all their money into higher education for their sons. But one of the kids gets too bright. It poses the problem—how bright can you get? . . .
>
> The mother knows only two books—her Bible and her cookbook. But who's brighter in the end—the mother or the son?

It's a question that might have equally occurred to Mrs. Hiss.

My Son John opens on a Sunday morning with Dan Jefferson (Dean Jagger) and his sons Chuck and Ben, who are set to leave for Korea, chucking the football before driving to Mass. Lucille Jefferson (Helen Hayes) is upset because the family's third and eldest son, John (Robert Walker), is too busy with his government work to come in from Washington, but a week later John unexpectedly shows up, entering the house through the back door. As supercilious and sarcastic as his brothers are plainspoken and straightforward, overeducated John has "more degrees than a thermometer"—something that disturbs Dan, not just a gung-ho member of the American Legion but a small-town schoolteacher who "thinks with his heart." This hostility is displaced. It's not John's brains that drives Dan crazy but his son's place in the family; Lucille worships her firstborn child. Thus, while his doting mom keeps thinking that John is somehow not himself, his dour dad is forever bringing up the subject of Commies. Infected with terminal irony, John has clearly gone wrong—but what sort of American family produces an Alger Hiss? Dan, who at one point thwacks his son with the Holy Bible, is a flag-waving crypto-fascist, while Lucille teeters on the verge of a nervous breakdown.

With its running gags and amusing secondary performances, *My Son John* aspires to the warmth of a domestic comedy while remaining tendentious to the core, relentlessly unfunny and starkly melodramatic—though unusually devoid of music, save for the climactic holy chorale, the eponymous nursery rhyme

chanted by Lucille, and the bombastic anthem with which Dan, more McCarthy fan than authentic avatar of the Patriot Roughneck, entertains his American Legion post: "If you don't like your Uncle Sammy, then go back to your
home o'er the sea."

A giggly priest notwithstanding, the Jefferson family is counseled by a solicitous FBI man (Van Heflin). As much of the movie is devoted to the management of Lucille's convulsive anxiety, the final third, once John carelessly leaves
some spy material in the torn pants his mother has offered to mend, involves
the FBI's attempt to turn a mother against her own son. "She's an angel from
heaven," someone says as the hysterical woman prays for John's soul. Lucille is
surrounded by men who venerate her as a precious object—a cross between a
porcelain icon of the Holy Virgin and a diminutive Kate Smith belting out "God
Bless America." John eventually sees the light: he decides against fleeing the
country and turns the speech he'd been invited to give into a confession that—
having substituted faith in man for faith in God—he has been a Communist spy
and traitor to his country.

Essentially reprising the glib, murderous character he played in Alfred Hitchcock's *Strangers on a Train*, Walker died—in an apparent allergic reaction to a
sedative administered in the midst of an emotional crisis—late in the production.
This shocking turn of events forced McCarey to kill off his character as well. Thus,
taking a taxi to deliver his speech, John is ambushed and apparently gunned down
by his Communist masters with the cab careening onto the steps of the Lincoln
Memorial—followed by Walker's dying close-up from the Hitchcock film. In an
odd echo of *The Beginning or the End*, in which Walker read the A-bomb martyr's
speech from beyond the grave, his final warning is delivered via tape, the recording machine bathed in a spotlight and set on an empty podium.[33]

While it was hardly surprising that David Platt would tell his readers it was
"no coincidence that the release of this anti-American film coincides with the
current frame-up trial of the 16 Communist leaders at Foley Square," *My Son
John*'s hectoring tone drove even liberals to distraction. The Catholic weekly
Commonweal (which termed the movie "a sickening spectacle") and the *New
York Times* were equally appalled, with Bosley Crowther comparing Jagger's
rendition of "Uncle Sammy" to "a Nazi singing the 'Horst Wessel song.'"

33. This alienated ending is a spooky echo of *The Next Voice You Hear*, another drama of
middle-class family pathology. A rich, if unpleasant, contribution to the texture of the times,
My Son John further presages the generational warfare of *Rebel Without a Cause*, which, released three and a half years later, also features a posthumous performance in the role of the
delinquent son.

The *New Yorker* summarized the movie's moral as a recommendation "that Americans ought to cut out thinking, obey their superiors blindly, regard all political suspects as guilty without trial, revel in joy through strength, and pay more attention to football," and the moderate Republican *New York Herald Tribune* was scarcely less incensed: future congressman Ogden Reid wrote, "McCarey's picture of how America ought to be is so frightening, so speciously argued, so full of warnings against an intelligent solution of the problem that it boomerangs upon its own cause." Robert Warshow, another responsible anti-Communist who often published in the *Partisan Review*, took it upon himself to warn the readers of the pro-McCarthy *American Mercury* that there was "a wrong way, a dangerous way, to be anti-Communist. Those who do not believe this may find it illuminating to see Leo McCarey's new film, *My Son John*, an attack on Communism and an affirmation of 'Americanism' that might legitimately alarm any thoughtful American, whether liberal or conservative." But at the ever-leftish *Nation*, Manny Farber adopted a bemused hipster attitude: "Plotwise," *My Son John* was a reversal of *Mr. Smith Goes to Washington*, worth seeing "if only to dig Hollywood's latest political orientation."

My Son John received a somewhat friendlier reception when it opened in Los Angeles two weeks later—ads emblazoned "I AM A LIVING LIE!"—as civic, church, and military leaders mingled with the stars at the Fine Arts on Wilshire Boulevard. A few days afterward, Paramount president Barney Balaban hosted a screening at the Motion Picture Association of America headquarters in Washington, DC, and McCarey came to New York to "rebuke" local critics. According to the *Motion Picture Herald*, "Mr. McCarey feels he has been slighted as a director, insulted as an artist, and more importantly, has been libeled as a human being. The implication that he is a 'bigot' hurt him most deeply." According to the *Paramount News*, "for the first time in its history the Catholic Institute of the Press unanimously has adopted a resolution commending a motion picture for the excellence of its production." On May 5, Senator Karl Mundt read his praise for *My Son John* into the *Congressional Record*, calling it "undoubtedly the greatest and most stirring pro-American motion picture of the past decade. . . . It should be seen by the people of every American home."[34]

The May issue of *American Legion Magazine* devoted its editorial page to

---

34. Nevertheless, *My Son John* did extremely poor business, failing to gross a million dollars or place among *Variety*'s 119 top-grossing films of 1952—although it did garner McCarey an Oscar nomination for best original screenplay.

praising *My Son John*. That month, the Legion presented the studios with its own list of three hundred subversives—including actors, writers, directors, and producers who variously signed the amicus curiae brief to the Supreme Court in connection with the Hollywood Ten, were associated with the 1949 World Peace Conference, or criticized HUAC. *Variety* considered the dossiers "remarkable in their detail," including "even obscure incidents and accusations relating to members of their families or persons of similar names." David Platt could barely contain himself:

> Anyone who thinks that the anti-Communist campaign threatens only Communists should note that in Hitler Germany in 1934, the film workers of UFA studios in Berlin were ordered to sign oaths stating they were not Communists, sympathizers or liberal dupes, as proof of their loyalty to Germany. The Nazis began by eliminating the "Communists" and ended by making lampshades out of the flesh of all opponents of their reign of terror.
>
> How will it end in Hollywood?

Would it ever?[35]

My Son John leads the spy and subversion parade: *Walk East on Beacon* through *The Atomic City* to *Red Planet Mars* with *Big Jim McLain*. Even Dore Schary has an anti-Communist movie in production, a documentary featurette called *The Hoaxters.*

Stimulated generally by the shooting war in Korea and the oft-reiterated warning that this might be the prelude to World War III, not to mention by the 1951 round of HUAC hearings, a third of all the anti-Communist movies produced between 1948 and 1954 will be released in the presidential election year 1952.

On April 29, Louis De Rochement's *Walk East on Beacon* has its world premiere in Boston, where this quasidocumentary "drama of real life" was filmed. A year before, soon after *Reader's Digest* featured J. Edgar Hoover's tale of atomic spies, "The Crime of the Century," De Rochement had announced Hoover's

---

35. Prompted by the American Legion, which had begun picketing selected subversive releases, Roy Brewer's Motion Picture Industry Council made another attempt to institute a loyalty board. This new form of clearance was rejected by the SWG membership, whose "confused thinking" was then excoriated by SAG president Reagan: "There seems to be a new breed around town, the anti-anti-Communists. These are non-Communists who denounce anyone out to get the Communists."

account would be the basis for his new film. Mata Hari was obsolete. As recent cases demonstrated and Columbia's press release explained, "The modern spy is the insignificant little man whom no one suspects. He receives no money, travels by bus, never frequents hotels, popular restaurants or bars. He is a dedicated Communist who never meets his superiors personally."

Unlike *I Was a Communist*, *Walk East on Beacon* can boast the FBI's full cooperation, even in terms of casting. The Bureau specifically requested George Murphy for the lead, in recognition of "his long and effective real-life fight in Hollywood against communism," and furnished the project with actual FBI personnel. Hoover himself can be briefly glimpsed in one of the opening scenes. Although the movie's unit publicist proudly hinted that twenty-seven instances of "classified, secret material" had been removed at the FBI's request, *Walk East on Beacon!* is filled with gadgets and largely fixated on the Bureau's surveillance, laboratory, and communication procedures. Murphy's self-effacing supervising agent briskly processes data and issues alerts as his team expertly confounds the Soviet espionage ring's attempt to purloin Project Falcon by picking the brain of the world's greatest scientist, an Einstein with craggy features and a well-coiffed mane of white hair (Finlay Currie, the Saint Peter of *Quo Vadis*).

The spies are shown as ruthless, efficient, fanatical true believers in the guise of ordinary Americans, albeit ruled through blackmail. Communists can never quit; "once you sign up, they've got you." While the capitalist press dutifully noted plot similarities to the Klaus Fuchs and Judith Coplon cases, Art Shields's *Daily Worker* review seizes on the grandiose nature of Project Falcon (Hoover put "a similar fantastic story of the theft of the Pentagon's interplanetary 'secrets' into the mouth of the FBI's witness, David Greenglass"), notes an "anti Semitic caricature," and complains, with wistful irrationality, that the FBI (meaning the movie) "never gives the slightest hint that the Communist Party is a working class movement that is fighting for democracy, Negro-and-white equality and PEACE and ultimate Socialism."

Bosley Crowther praises De Rochemont's seriousness but notes that *Walk East on Beacon* "suffers somewhat because of its late arrival [and] familiar format." Shields is pleased to report that he "didn't hear a laugh during the 98-minute show. The boys and girls who came for entertainment were frustrated and puzzled." Even the climax was a fizzle: "Just two persons clapped as the FBI finally caught the top bogy man, who was about to escape in a Russian submarine off Portsmouth, NH." Before declaring the movie a "crushing bore" with the "crawl of a Hawaiian travelogue," Manny Farber attempts to account for the alienated atmosphere, making the straight-faced observation that, although *Walk East on Beacon* is "against Communists," it nevertheless

> pays a lot of respect to the shrewd, tortoise-like craftsmanship of the spies. Besides being so dedicated to their jobs that they tap their fingers, or sit down to lunch with a mechanical and somewhat hypnotized air, they are seldom seen doing anything except their daily jobs as taxi-driver, florist, or photo finisher. The idea is that they are too clever to expose their devilish skills.

The enemy agents in *The Atomic City*, a low-budget sleeper directed by Jerry Hopper from Sidney Boehm's script that opens on May 1 to enthusiastic New York notices, are also kidnappers. Seeking to extort the Vital Secret of the Great Whatzit, they snatch the young son of Los Alamos–based nuclear physicist Dr. Addison (Gene Barry in preparation for a role he'd reprise a year later in *The War of the Worlds*). The boy already has articulated an ontological insecurity. After a new television set is delivered to the family home, little Tommy decides that he'd like to go into electronics—"if I grow up." Mom is shocked. Soon after, Tommy is snatched on a school trip to a Santa Fe fiesta. Again, the FBI is summoned. Like *Walk East on Beacon*, *The Atomic City* has its procedural aspects—the operatives use disguises and employ high-tech kinescope surveillance techniques.

Moreover, in discouraging the frantic Addison from making his own deal with the spies, the agents establish that Tommy's life cannot be weighed against the potential risk to millions of Americans. It's an angst-ridden situation, although perhaps less scary than the constant security checks, references to lethal radioactive contamination, and "routine morning test" that shakes the family's house every day. Los Alamos is another Fort Apache, a barren, gated, militarized suburb on the edge of existence; the spies even hole up in Indian ruins, the Puye cliff dwellings near Santa Fe.

Help is on the way: on June 4, General Eisenhower finally announces his candidacy in a live telecast from his hometown of Abilene, calmly ad-libbing through a violent electrical storm. Opening soon after is the movie that dares to ask the question "Is the Man from Nazareth the Man from Mars?"

It is *The Next Voice You Hear* redux—more martial, more Christian, and more entertaining. Despite ads promising "THE WORLD TORN ASUNDER BY A

THREAT FROM OUTER SPACE," the danger in Harry Horner's *Red Planet Mars* was neither an oncoming comet nor a fleet of flying saucers piloted by carnivorous carrots. Rather, it was a radio transmission—an interplanetary sermon. In its patriotic spirituality (as well as its image of a U.S. president), *Red Planet Mars* may be considered the first Eisenhower movie, as well as the most visionary of anti-Communist films.

Using plans for a "hydrogen tube" recovered from the rubble of Nazi Germany (the same threat Warner Bros. excised from Fritz Lang's *Cloak and Dagger*), two independent scientists, Chris and Linda Cronyn (Peter Graves, kid brother to James Arness, and Andrea King), are trying to establish radio contact with Mars. So too, it would seem, is the tube's bitter, ranting inventor—a German named Calder (Herbert Berghof), now in the service of the Communists.

Thanks to Calder's trick transmissions, bounced off Mars from his secret hideout—a hut high in the Andes mountains, beneath a giant statue of Jesus Christ—and picked up by the Cronyns, the world learns that Mars is far more technologically advanced than Earth. Knowledge of this super-civilization triggers global economic panic; the Kremlin is ecstatic while America's president is so concerned that he invokes national security to shut down the Cronyns' transmitter. But then, Radio Mars sends a new signal, quoting Jesus's Sermon on the Mount. Linda wants to broadcast this holy message to the world, as does the president: "Now we're following the star of Bethlehem."

In effect, God seems to be speaking from Mars, using the Voice of America to address the people of Earth—or, at least, some of them. (The montage of worldwide radio reception features only white listeners.) Naturally, the transmission has its greatest political impact on Soviet Russia; China is never mentioned. Now it is the Communists' turn to panic. The enormity of the crisis is indicated by mysterious stock footage of Russian peasants ripping portraits of Stalin off their walls and digging up vestments buried in 1917. As seen on the flatscreen TV on the wall of the Cronyns' laboratory, an Orthodox priest is placed on the once-Romanov Russian throne. In a further cataclysm, an avalanche sweeps away Calder's shack; he survives to visit the Cronyns and gleefully inform them of his cosmic prank. "What were you after?" they cry. His answer: "Shall I say . . . amusement?" Realizing that Calder is less a Communazi than a nihilistical Satanist, about to reveal his earth-shaking fraud, the couple contrive to blow up their lab, sacrificing themselves to destroy the Antichrist and preserve the "truth" of God's message. That this is done to secure the future of the baby boom children is implicit in Chris's declaration that their two young sons belong to a "blessed generation."[36]

Shot during the winter of 1951–52, this vision of divine intervention opened shortly before the prestigious CBS news program *See It Now* telecast a mock nuclear attack on New York City and a few weeks in advance of the world's first televised political convention, which gave the Patriot Roughneck a standing ovation and nominated General Dwight D. Eisenhower as the Republican presidential candidate on the first ballot, hailing him as "the spiritual leader of our times." Here, at last, is the Christian Soldier projected by *Quo Vadis*—indeed, the president in *Red Planet Mars* is a former military commander played by an actor, Willis Bouchey, with a strong resemblance to Ike. *Time* magazine has recently reported Eisenhower's credo: the American flag stands for a civilization built on religious beliefs "and now another type of civilization challenges it; a civilization built upon the godless theory that man himself has no value."

God, not Harry Truman, is with us now. Amid rumors of "guided missiles" and "super bombs" no one admitted having, Congress voted to allocate $52 billion toward a worldwide network of air bases, and the syndicated Sunday supplement *This Week* echoed *Red Planet Mars* with a yarn wherein a Martian flying saucer spooks the Communists into cranking up their Iron Curtain. And on the last two Saturday nights in July, routine air traffic was directed away from the Washington, DC, airport as F-94 jets blasted off to defend the nation's capital against an armada of mysterious radar blips.

The week between the two visitations, the media buzzed with weird static. The *New York Times* announced that "current intelligence reports reflect an increasing Russian capacity for air attack upon the United States." *Time* magazine ran an ad reading, "Faster than you can drink a cup of coffee, Lockheed Starfires can destroy an air invader—without even seeing it!" with a picture of three F-94s fanned out over the Washington Monument. American jets were reported to be holding "maneuvers" over China. A late edition of the *New York Daily Mirror* went with a "WAR ALERT IN NORTHWEST" headline.

The United States launched a massive air strike against North Korea's hydroelectric power grid. As saucer sightings filtered in from Central Park to

---

36. The 1954 W. Lee Wilder cheapster *Killers from Space* (1954), shot in one week without sets, also features Peter Graves as a nuclear scientist—here "taken over" by aliens with painted Ping-Pong-ball eyes. Like J. Robert Oppenheimer, the "alienated" scientist is an object of suspicion and subject to surveillance. The authorities question his wife—"Has he made any new friends lately, you know, people not in the usual group?"—and he is caught by a vigilant FBI man leaving a message for his controllers under a rock in an otherwise deserted canyon.

Indiana, New York and New Jersey signed a mutual defense pact in the event of atomic bombing, and the Democrats opened their convention in Chicago. Unexpectedly, the party nominated an intellectual who, like Alger Hiss and (My Son) John Jefferson, had worked in the State Department—the governor of Illinois and grandson of a vice president, fifty-two-year-old Adlai E. Stevenson.[37]

The campaign began as the July 26 Saturday night replay of *"F-94s Over the White House"* brought forth a tumult of hysterical headlines ("AIR FORCE ORDERS JETS TO SHOOT DOWN SAUCERS"), radio broadcasts directed at the aliens, and a buried admission from the Strategic Air Command that "simulated bombing raids" had been staged over ten large American cities. Soon after, the Pentagon reveals that, due to the threat of "all out war," every inch of American airspace would be placed under constant surveillance. A month later, opening amid a 1,403-sortie assault on Pyongyang in the largest single-day raid of the war, *Big Jim McClain* arrived in Los Angeles.

As opposed to the cool and professional FBI men of *My Son John*, *Walk East on Beacon*, and *The Atomic City*, the HUAC investigators in *Big Jim McClain*, played by John Wayne and James Arness (the Thing in *The Thing*), are true Patriot Roughnecks—a pair of proudly two-fisted McCarthyite brawlers. As explained on the posters, "Uncle Sam Said: 'Go-get-'em!' . . . and Big Jim was the man they sent!"

Duke had resolved to push the envelope. In mid-March, six weeks before the movie's shoot was to open on location in Hawaii, the head of Warner Bros.'s research, Carl Milliken Jr., had sent a confidential memo to studio lawyer Finlay McDermid noting the discrepancies between James Edward Grant's screenplay (announced as "a modern adventure yarn" about "a Texas cattle buyer who follows a trail of excitement to Hawaii") and its source material, the recent *Saturday Evening Post* article "We Almost Lost Hawaii to the Reds," on the 1949 strike by (and ensuing HUAC investigation of) the International Longshoremen's and Warehousemen's Union. The time frame had been advanced to the

---

37. An insurgent candidate, Estes Kefauver enjoyed a considerable lead in committed delegates, although not enough to win on a first ballot. He was followed in the delegate count by Senator Richard Russell, Averell Harriman, and President Truman's choice, noncandidate Stevenson, who entered the race following the withdrawal of Vice President Alben Barkley and was nominated on the third ballot. The 1952 Democratic Convention was the last of the proverbial "smoke-filled rooms." Kefauver's embittered partisans thought Truman and the party bosses had conspired to steal the nomination from their independent-minded candidate.

early Korean War, and the stories had no direct relationship: "The fiction seems to be fashioned from whole cloth," Milliken wrote.

Milliken was also concerned that HUAC investigators were shown cooperating with the Honolulu police to extract information by illegal means—including wiretaps, physical intimidation, and threats of deportation. He was also disturbed by their character, which seemed

> somewhat less than the superior type of individuals the Public is wont to consider FBI agents or representatives of a Congressional Committee. They are given to physical violence [while] . . . expressing more than once the wish that the protective mantle which American law throws about all individuals on trial be cast aside in the case of "these scum."

In short, Milliken feared that the studio would show HUAC investigations "done in illegal and offensive ways and by individuals of a rather low caliber." His fear was that the movie might backfire—"even to the possible extent of placing *us* in contempt of Congress."

Despite a revised screenplay and assurances it would be submitted to HUAC as well as the Breen Office, Milliken grew increasingly nervous. He noted J. Edgar Hoover's name was used without clearance and that Hoover and his second-in-command, Clyde Tolson, were cited as Big Jim's personal friends. Wiretaps were still mentioned, warrants still disparaged, threats of physical intimidation still made, and Alger Hiss was not just mentioned in the dialogue but shown as a manacled prisoner. Two weeks into the shoot, producer Robert Fellows assured a Warner Bros. lawyer that Milliken's complaints had been addressed. Hoover was out and "HUAC [was] cooperating with personal clearances," including those for "three HUAC investigators who were in Hawaii." Most importantly, "The business of BUGGING THE PREMISES and the ILLEGAL ENTRY—have been okayed by both the House Un-American Activities Committee who have urged us not to eliminate it; and by CAPTAIN ED LAYTON, who is the Chief Naval Intelligence Officer in the Pacific." Milliken, however, continued to express concerns regarding illegal procedures (one of which was cut after a preview), noting that the necessary personal clearances had not yet been received.[38]

---

38. Tenor of the times: Milliken was panicked by Fellows's jocular assurances to Warners legal staff: "I will be happy to get all of these clearances except I think Carl should get STALIN's." The day after the memo's receipt, Milliken sent one to veteran studio lawyer Roy Obringer, adding, "I hope—that in writing Mr. Fellows—you will object kiddingly on my behalf to his implication that I have a closer avenue of approach to Joe Stalin than he has. All is lost if the clearance depends upon me because I know neither Joe nor any of his cohorts."

Making at least one thing clear, *Big Jim McLain* opens with a stirring medley of "Yankee Doodle," "Dixie," and "Columbia, the Gem of the Ocean." A stormy landscape dissolves to Washington, DC, where the voice of nineteenth-century senator Daniel Webster is heard: "Neighbor, how stands the union?" Cut to the HUAC hearing room, where we learn of the great debt owed, as well as the campaign of slander waged against the committee. Watching in the gallery, HUAC investigator Jim McLain (Wayne) expresses his frustration as a Commie professor of economics gets off free and goes back to contaminate more kids—his buddy Mal Baxter (Arness) explains, Big Jim "hates these people [because] they shot at him in Korea."

The two investigators are dispatched to Hawaii—the nation's first line of defense after the Thirty-eighth Parallel—where they visit the shrine of the USS *Arizona* before implementing Operation Pineapple, exposing the Red plot to take over the islands. In addition to saving Hawaii, Big Jim figures he'll rescue the pretty receptionist (Stevenson supporter Nancy Olson) who innocently works for a CP psychiatrist, proposing marriage twenty minutes into the movie. (When she goes into a church to thank God, he comes along as a chaperone.) Amid much mutual bugging, Big Jim and Mal discover a reformed Communist doing penance at the Molokai leper colony and a harmless lunatic (Hans Conried) who babbles of meeting Stalin and inventing a super-secret weapon before exposing union subversion, sabotage, and homicide. (As usual, the Commies are mainly killing each other. Indeed, the Party's murderous leadership speaks for the Motion Picture Alliance in complaining that the "domesticated Party members" who believe themselves "dedicated Communists" make him sick.) One object of Communist prejudice is Big Jim himself, maligned by one local Red as an "East Texas cotton-chopping jerk [working] for white trash and niggers."

The movie ends with HUAC's arrival in Honolulu. Disgusted with the spectacle of Reds hiding behind the Fifth, Big Jim walks out to watch marines boarding an American battleship. "There stands the Union." End titles thank the committee for its cooperation.

The August 31 edition of the *Indianapolis Star* created a front page bracketing the week's two releases, *Big Jim McLain* and *High Noon*. It was the former that the ultraconservative *Star* (owned by the grandfather of future vice president Dan Quayle) would subsequently highlight. As *Big Jim McLain*

opened in Los Angeles last week, a California court of appeals was reversing the ruling of a local judge and permitting 14 convicted Commies—called the second most dangerous batch in the US—to roam the countryside on $20,000 bail. . . . With their own money at stake on the venture, the co-producers decided to take no chances on the New York critics' "circle" handing them the same sort of scathing whiplash that greeted Director Leo McCarey and his *My Son John* when it was premiered in New York a few months ago. McCarey hasn't quite recovered to this day from the ferocious lampooning his anti-Red movie received from the metropolitan paper reviewers and as a result, perhaps, the movie itself bogged down badly all over the country.

Fellows and Wayne saw to it that *Big Jim McLain* opened in every key city throughout the country before it went on to beard the typewriter lions of the big town.

High Noon in the Universe

In *Big Jim McLain*, John Wayne presented himself as the most intuitive Hollywood hero since Gary Cooper blazed his solitary path to glory in *The Fountainhead*. The movie was not so much a warning as a paean to direct action.[39]

Someone had to take charge. Although the 1952 election was ultimately a referendum on the Korean War, Americans enjoyed no consensus on what they wanted to do about it; they only knew Ike was the man to do it. His opponent, campaigning on the poignantly inappropriate slogan "Let's talk sense to the American people," was a minor-league alien, an egghead elitist sissy, or worse. Going Big Jim one better, Senator Joe McCarthy boasted, "If somebody would only smuggle me aboard the Democratic campaign special with a baseball bat in my hand, I'd teach patriotism to little Ad-lie."

As the 1952 election was the first to privilege a candidate's persona over his positions, so Dwight D. Eisenhower would be the first national leader sold as a product. The general was coached by actor Robert Montgomery, founding member of the Motion Picture Alliance, friendly witness, naval hero offscreen and on (in *They Were Expendable*), director of the subjective camera experiment *Lady in the Lake*, and host of a TV anthology series. Montgomery replaced Eisenhower's eyeglasses, powdered his forehead, and supervised the mise en

---

39. Vice chairman of the Hollywood Committee for Senator McCarthy, Wayne credited *Big Jim McLain*—by far the most commercial anti-Communist movie of 1952, grossing $2.6 million—with helping to reelect the Wisconsin senator. (The Hollywood Committee was chaired by Rupert Hughes, with Ward Bond and Morrie Ryskind also part of the leadership; members included Cecil B. DeMille, Harold Lloyd, Louis B. Mayer, Adolphe Menjou, Ray Milland, George Murphy, Leo McCarey, Pat O'Brien, Dick Powell, and Randolph Scott.)

scène of these twenty-second spots—all produced by the Madison Avenue advertising agency BBDO in a single day.

The United States of Television was blitzed with the image of a folksy, God-fearin' warrior; TV proved even more useful when the Republican campaign hit its only speed bump. Six weeks before Election Day, the *New York Post* broke the story that Ike's running mate, Richard Nixon, was the beneficiary of a political slush fund. On September 23, with Milton Berle's wildly popular *Texaco Star Theater* as his lead-in, the vice presidential candidate went on prime time with the most widely watched political message in history (thus far). Waging a successful defense, the uncoached Nixon projected himself as an honest everyman in part by showing his wife's "Republican" cloth coat and invoking his daughters' pet dog, Checkers. "Video-wise, it was a brilliant feat of political journalism," *Variety* wrote. "Translated into a commercial suds saga, it would have been a cinch to garner a renewal for at least another 52-week cycle."

As the election played out on a new political battleground, so the key movie of that summer would provide America's leadership scenario for the next half century. *High Noon* had opened in New York on July 24, the same day that the vacillating Adlai Stevenson became a presidential candidate. Even more than Gary Cooper's marshal, Eisenhower and Stevenson were initially unwilling to shoulder their respective burdens. But, reluctant or not, Eisenhower was far easier to imagine as the marshal who—pusillanimous allies notwithstanding—took on the outlaws and established the image for a post-televisual presidency.

While providing an Oscar-winning comeback vehicle for middle-aged action star Cooper as Marshal Kane and introducing future princess Grace Kelly in the role of his young bride, *High Noon* was almost an anti-spectacle—stingy on scenic splendor and stark as a woodcut, a laconic, aggressively economical eighty-five minutes shot in dour black and white with an abundance of close-ups. The mode is elemental, abstract, and urgent. Nothing exists outside the town of Hadleyville (defined as a bar, a jail, a church, a hotel, and the train station); urgency is made material. The movie opens with a flurry of activity under the credits: church bells ringing, the townspeople head for church as Frank Miller's gang rides in on Main Street, anticipating Miller's own arrival on the noon train. The judge is packing up his law books, even taking down the U.S. flag over his desk.

The sound of a ticking clock alternating with the movie's dolefully insistent theme, *High Noon* approximates real time. That was the gimmick: the viewer was temporally tied to the hero's situation. *High Noon* was a Western for Now, its handful of locations sufficient to map a moral landscape, while evoking the immediacy of live teledrama.

The story of a town marshal who eschews retirement and ignores demands that he just get lost in order to protect a cowardly, ungrateful constituency from a vengeful criminal, *High Noon* is a pessimistic film—at least in its view of human nature—expressing contempt both for bourgeoisie and salt of the earth alike, as the marshal does by tossing his badge in the dust after once more saving Hadleyville.

The town is supremely gutless. A church congregation's moral fortitude is limited to their singing "The Battle Hymn of the Republic." The few citizens who volunteer to help the marshal are reminded by the town's glad-handing mayor that, technically, he is no longer the marshal. Their pointless arguing suggests Hadleyville's ethical paralysis. The mayor's point that a shoot-out between Kane and the villains would be bad for business proves decisive—as in Hollywood, the economic imperative rules.

The marshal's mentor advises him to leave town ("Die, for what—a tin star?") and his young bride, a Quaker pacifist, threatens to leave him if he doesn't. *High Noon* thus also becomes an existential drama: the stubborn marshal defines himself by repeatedly insisting, without much elaboration, that he's *"got to stay."* Kane's solitary courage was itself projected back onto the movie. "At first, *High Noon* did not do very well at the box office," director Fred Zinnemann would recall in his 1992 autobiography. "It took a long time for [the movie] to take hold of the public's imagination. Interestingly, its popularity waxes and wanes; people become aware of it at times of decision, when a major national or political crisis is threatening."

High Noon has long been unfashionable among, as well as downgraded by, auteurist film critics. But, contra Zinnemann, the most celebrated Western that Hollywood ever produced and the genre's highest-ranked example in the American Film Institute canon did enjoy instant appreciation. *New York Times* critic Bosley Crowther declared *High Noon* a Western "to challenge *Stagecoach* for the all-time championship," and, edging out the Bob Hope comedy *Son of Paleface* as the top-grossing Western of 1952, *High Noon* would be the year's eighth-biggest box office attraction. *Mad*'s 1953 parody "Hah Noon!" hails the movie as "an all-time never-to-be-forgotten great classic that changed the course of western history . . . Hollywood western history that is."

With three versions of its plaintive ballad competing on the hit parade, *High Noon* initiated a trend for original theme songs; as a Western, it elaborated key genre motifs and introduced new ones, particularly the notion of the flawed, unworthy town and the vulnerable lawman. In his highly appreciative review,

Crowther called *High Noon* "a stunning comprehension of that thing we call courage in a man and the thorniness of being courageous in a world of bullies and poltroons," and, in a follow-up Sunday feature, he further noted in what appears to be an explicit comment on the blacklist that Cooper's character's courage could "give a fine lesson to the people in Hollywood today."

A few weeks after the movie opened, Foreman wrote to Crowther from London, detailing his situation during the film's writing and production. It was a narrative that Foreman would tell and retell for the rest of his life: the betrayal and persecution of an honest man. *High Noon* was always about something; it had its origins in a 1948 allegory that Foreman was asked to write about the United Nations. But the scenario took on another meaning after June 1951, when Foreman was subpoenaed by HUAC. *High Noon* became a movie about the failure to stand together against the blacklist.

This allegory, per Foreman, "was perfectly recognizable to people in Hollywood when they saw the picture because I was using dialogue that was in spirit the same thing that I was hearing—'Don't do that; the town has so much trouble; go away.'" According to Foreman, a number of scenes were directly taken from life: "The scene in the church is a distillation of meetings I had with partners, associates, and lawyers. And there's the scene with the man who offers to help and comes back with his gun and asks, where are the others? Cooper says there are no others."

Some would say Foreman chose the name Hadleyville because it suggested Hollywood; others equated Frank Miller and his gang with HUAC and the townspeople with the committee's friendly witnesses. Foreman himself maintained that he became the Gary Cooper character. So, in a sense, did Cooper— a founding member of the Motion Picture Alliance—who, although warned that there could be repercussions if he worked with Foreman, stuck with the project.

Producer Stanley Kramer, Foreman's friend and partner, was more fearful— not unlike the mayor of Hadleyville, who points out that Kane is no longer town marshal and therefore has no authority to organize against the Miller gang. Foreman told Crowther that, even before the hearings, Kramer attempted to bar him from the set—although a contractual technicality allowed Foreman to remain with the production through the end of shooting, thus branding *High Noon* with a scarlet "C." Even after the movie was released, with Foreman's producing credit stripped, animus continued in Hollywood—at least among some.

High Noon would be the first Western nominated for an Academy Award in the nine years since *The Ox-Bow Incident*; indeed, its seven nominations broke the genre record set by *Stagecoach* in 1939, and *Variety* predicted it would sweep the awards. Still, Hedda Hopper continued to criticize Cooper for promoting "Foreman's picture" and campaigned against it from early December until mid-March 1953, while Paramount executive Luigi Luraschi politicked behind the scenes. Luraschi would tell his CIA liaison that he'd been instrumental in denying *High Noon* the Oscar for best picture, although the movie did win four other Oscars, including Cooper's for best actor, in the first-ever televised ceremony (with Ronald Reagan as announcer).

Foreman's allegory aside, *High Noon* epitomized the new Western; it crystallized the moment when the meaning of the Western shifted. The genre had matured—not just wildly popular and recognized as quintessentially American, it asked to be taken seriously. This ambition stirred resentful ambivalence among intellectuals with fond boyhood associations with cowboys and Indians and the capacity to rationalize them.

In "The Myth of the Western Hero," published in late 1950 in the as-yet-unnamed "Beat Generation" literary magazine *Neurotica*, editor Jay Irving Landesman and novelist John Clellon Holmes, collaborating under the name Alfred Towne, satirized the notion of the so-called adult Western by proposing the cowboy as "America's number one candidate for the cultural analytical couch." The pleasures offered by the new Western were hardly innocent: "Escape from the subtle anxieties of to-day into a utopia populated entirely by outlaws, rustlers, dance hall girls, gamblers, weak-willed sheriffs, and ferocious Indians, is like a vacation from Sodom in Gomorrah." The Western was a masculine fantasy realm where sexual potency was "a material possession, made of metal and firing six shots without reloading" and the ferociously popular Hopalong Cassidy was a "father surrogate" for a whole new generation.

Had the piece been written two years later, genial, self-assured Hoppy might have been recognized as an Eisenhower avatar—but that would have been to take the Western at least as seriously as did the *Daily Worker*, where vulgar Marxist analyses of *Broken Arrow*, *The Devil's Doorway*, and assorted cavalry Westerns coincided with *Neurotica*'s publication of "The Myth of the Western Hero." More fun was the notion that, behind their simpleminded façade, Westerns teemed with antisocial impulses and mad desire. Indeed, soon after the *Neurotica* piece appeared, its parody was parodied by the more mainstream *Saturday Review*. Writing on two current releases, John Ford's *Rio Grande* and the Gary Cooper vehicle *Dallas*, Hollis Alpert noted that John Wayne played a father surrogate in the former and Cooper represented a blatant "potency symbol" in the latter. Alpert feigned danger: "It's a situation that clearly demands more than a cultural analytical couch—perhaps as much as a full-scale Congressional committee with the stated objective of cleaning up Hollywood's subconscious." (Perhaps that was why Billy Graham was even then making what he called "the first Christian Western." The protagonist of *Mr. Texas* is a happy-go-lucky hedonistic bronco-buster who comes to Christ after a bad spill and listening to a Billy Graham radiocast in the hospital.)

In early 1949, *Life* magazine declared the Western "an art form as formal as the ballet or the symphony" and "a changeless, stylized struggle between good and evil." What else was there today? Appropriating a Sartrean concept to write on the "inauthentic Western" in the *American Mercury* soon after *High Noon* opened, *New Leader* film critic Wallace Markfield took a more historical view than his sometime *Neurotica* colleagues. Simpleminded escapism was good. Markfield maintained that early Westerns—as exemplified by the silent vehicles for William S. Hart, Tom Mix, et al., and especially *The Virginian*, the movie that, released in 1929, when the author was three years old, made Cooper a star— were a form of pure cinema. By contrast, the inauthentic Western (like *The Virginian*'s crypto-remake *High Noon*) had "a pallid cast to its features, as though sick unto death." As cowboy Cooper had grown old, so the genre's purity was contaminated by present concerns. Inventing a B movie in which Randolph Scott quoted T.S. Eliot, Markfield declared that the inauthentic Western had been "pruned and crossbred to the point where it brings forth only monstrous, cinematic hippogriffs." The genre "has taken on all the colors and shapes of our modern anxiety, as contemporary as tomorrow's headline. If things keep up, it's likely that the next dust cloud you'll see on the prairie will turn out to be an atomic mist after all."

In an instance of unanticipated Cold War fallout, meaning had contaminated the Western. Markfield was mainly bugged by the social consciousness foisted on the Western by "men who have a basic contempt for the genre, who must disguise and distort it into a sickening parody that converts Custer's Last Stand into a lesson on race relations and makes a band of train robbers symbolize society's persecution of the unorthodox"—not just Freudian pollution but Marxist subversion. Markfield maintained that, in "upending the old formulas," the inauthentic Western addressed itself to a series of overwhelming questions:

What happens to the gunfighter when he's no longer fast on the draw? How about the Indian who believes in peace? And the cowboy when he's unemployed? Is it right for the cattle king to squeeze out the small rancher? Lurking in every frame is the cold, anesthetic hand of social constructiveness, stripping the Western of everything that was once true and pleasureful . . .

But was this, as Markfield thought, "a ritual sacrifice to the public good" or, perhaps, the desire for a new social mythology?

Hollis Alpert had deemed the hero of *Dallas* a sort of superman; Markfield was struck that this "moody, unrelenting" figure, who "opens his mouth only to rail at the horde of bankers, merchants, and manufacturers that razed his plantation, stripped his cotton fields and brought the Old South to its knees," existed mainly to teach a lesson in economic determinism. "What seems to be profoundly disturbing the Western lately is an overpowering sense of guilt that forces it into the weirdest gyrations in order to atone for some of the less pleasant aspects of American history."

As noted with somewhat different emphasis by David Platt in late 1950, the "uprooted southerner" and the "gallant redskin," each the representative of a lost cause, were the new Western clichés. Evoking *Broken Arrow* without mentioning it, Markfield voiced a "sneaking impression that [the Indian is] being groomed to take over the throne vacated by the deposed union leader and tenant farmer . . . a fantasy whose origin is only in the mind of Hollywood's new social workers."

For Markfield, *High Noon* was exhibit A, suffering from "the compulsion to sprinkle its action with pellet-like messages of high moral purpose." The movie was "a solemn plea for civic responsibility [and] to make sure that you don't miss a single point, a weird, pseudo-folk ballad is always in the background to provide a tom-tom-like commentary on what is unfolding." But weren't movies something to take seriously? Even *Life* had declared the Western in essence America's national "morality play."

Largely due to John Ford and his collaborators, the post–World War II Western had become the way America explained itself to itself: Who made the law and set the order? Where was the frontier? Which ones are the good guys? What is it that a man's gotta do—and how does he do it? By 1952, every Western, no matter how trite, was part presidential election, part baseball game, dramatizing and redramatizing the triumph of civilization, usually personified as the victory of the socially responsible individual over "savage" Indians or outlaws.[40]

---

40. Ford's cavalry trilogy introduced themes that naturalized America's Cold War role and became central to the Vietnam discourse of the sixties—mobilization, intervention, militarism, imperialism, racial conflict, genocide, truth to image versus truth to fact. Yet, even before Ford returned to the Western, Dore Schary and Sinclair Lewis had hatched their mad scheme to dramatize World War II in the never-produced cowboy epic *Storm in the West*.

Aspiring to the canonical when it appeared some eighteen months later in *Partisan Review*, Robert Warshow's essay "The Westerner" would be less apparently subjective and somewhat more thoughtful than Markfield's. Warshow too was partial to *The Virginian*, which opened when he was trembling on the brink of manhood, at age twelve, and serves as his template. But his discourse is consciously devoid of nostalgia—among other illusions. "Why does the Western movie especially have such a hold on our imagination?" he wondered, serving up the question before slamming it over the net. "Chiefly, I think because it offers a serious orientation to the problem of violence such as can be found almost nowhere else in our culture."

Warshow brought Freud and Marx together to ponder an apparently intractable fact of human nature, and perhaps a necessary one. A tough realist and Cold War liberal, writing for a formerly Trotskyist but not yet neoconservative journal, Warshow considered among the "well-known peculiarities of modern civilized opinion" a "refusal to acknowledge the value of violence." This conflict-averse, appeasing, even pacifistic position was, he maintained, quintessentially feminine and Eastern; the West, lacking the graces of civilization, is the place "where men are men."

The Virginian, like *High Noon*, was founded on the conflict between man who has to do what he has to do and woman who doesn't understand that. In *The Virginian*, the cowboy hero is compelled to choose between the civilized values embodied by his fiancée and the harsher dictates of his conscience—namely, that he hang his best friend for cattle rustling. Violence is necessary to enforce the law. And if intellectuals don't accept that, Warshow warns, "the celebration of acts of violence [will be] left more and more to the irresponsible"—hardened outlaws or immature boys, as in *High Noon*. It's fortunate for Marshal Kane that his Quaker bride realizes this truth and rises to the occasion, helping the marshal's cause by shooting one of the outlaws in the back. (It is thanks to her and this alliance that, despite his own apparent agnosticism, Kane can be a true Christian Soldier.)

Warshow doesn't dismiss *High Noon*, but neither does he care for it; echoing Markfield, he notes that "the falsity of the 'social drama' is less important than the fact that it does not belong in the movie to begin with." Warshow recognizes yet resents the political implications of Kane's dispute with his bride (as he ignores her ultimate conversion to Kane's cause). The question of violence may be crucial but not, evidently, as a subject. Indeed, Warshow removes the Western from the social realm altogether in declaring that the Westerner is "par excellence a man of leisure." (Does this natural aristocrat assume no role in class struggle?) "We know he is on the side of justice and order. . . . But such broad aims never correspond exactly to his real motives; they only offer him his opportunity." To do what?

According to Warshow, violence is justified as the presentation of an ideal masculinity and that which the Westerner ultimately defends is "the purity of his own image—in fact his honor. . . . The Westerner is the last gentleman, and the movies which over and over again tell his story are probably the last art form in which the concept of honor retains its strength." Warshow doesn't need to say that this is more than amply demonstrated in *High Noon*. Marshal Kane articulates no ideal. He is not a churchgoing man; on the contrary, when he approaches the town's better element, he interrupts the Sunday service. (He can do this because *High Noon* is itself the Sunday sermon.)

Cooper was also present in late 1952 as the star of *Springfield Rifle*, the last of the year's military Westerns—a movie with a brutal edge and a certain amount of realpolitik. Unlike *Warpath*, *Distant Drums*, *Bugles in the Afternoon*, or *Red Mountain*, however, *Springfield Rifle* had nothing to do with the redskin menace. Directed by André De Toth from a Charles Marquis Warren screenplay, the Warner Bros. production was set during the Civil War, taking its name from the secret weapon that the Union army planned to deploy in its "spring offensive" against the Confederacy.

Springfield Rifle was mainly shot on location in the Sierra Nevada, where production had to be halted one day when a mushroom cloud appeared on the horizon. (Across the state line, the army was testing tactical nuclear weapons.) Cooper appeared again as an inexplicable loner staggering under a solitary moral burden, as worn and worried looking as in *High Noon*. Early on, Cooper is court-martialed for cowardice—a ruse that allows him to go undercover. (His commanding officer might have been quoting *I Was a Communist for the FBI* when he muses, "I hope someday his family will appreciate what he's done for his country.") But, by the movie's end, Cooper has been reinstated with honors, recommended to head the government's new Department of Counter Intelligence.

Bosley Crowther recognized the topicality.

Three things are shown by *Springfield Rifle*. . . . The first is that counter-intelligence—or counter-espionage—was effectively employed on the western frontier by Union forces at the time of the Civil War. The second is that the Springfield rifle was a weapon of exceptional power. And the third is that the hard-pants-cavalry western is still a considerable movie stock in trade.

The third thing was a factor of the other two. In other words, *Springfield Rifle*—like *High Noon*—spoke directly to its historical moment, as did Cooper.[41]

Springfield Rifle was essentially a war movie, but thanks to Cooper's presence, it was something else. Warshow understood that war movies, like Westerns, featured "the uses of violence within a framework of possibility." But war was a cooperative venture, with impersonal violence and group heroism, and the hero was a pragmatic leader whose bravery was a form of denying the heroic—that is, understanding the need to stay alive and get the job done: "At its best the war movie may represent a more civilized point of view than the Western. But it cannot supply the values we seek in the Western. Those values are in the image of the single man who wears a gun on his thigh."

The fantasy mocked in the pages of *Neurotica* is complete. Warshow concludes with the declaration that, ultimately, "it is not violence at all which is the 'point' of the Western movie, but a certain image of man, a style, which expresses itself most clearly in violence. Watch a child with his toy guns and you will see: what most interests him is not (as we so much fear) the fantasy of hurting others, but to work out how a man might look when he shoots or is shot. A hero is one who looks like a hero." That is, the image of a hero.

Like the new Western, Warshow articulated (almost behind his back) the political economy of American heroism. No wonder that *Pravda* thought it appropriate that Cooper received an Oscar for *High Noon*, a film "in which the idea of the insignificance of the people and masses and the grandeur of the individual found its complete incarnation." As Leslie Fiedler had riffed in *Partisan Review*'s 1952 symposium "America and the Intellectuals": "A hundred years after the *Manifesto*, the specter that is haunting Europe is—Gary Cooper!"[42]

For John Wayne, the worst thing about *High Noon* was the spectacle of Coop begging his inferiors for help—or even having to justify his actions. In his view,

---

41. Two days after *Springfield Rifle* opened in New York on October 24, 1952, candidate Eisenhower addressed the nation on television. In his culminating campaign speech, the general termed Korea "the burial ground for twenty thousand American dead" and promised, if elected, to end the war: "I shall go to Korea." *Springfield Rifle* was not even two weeks in release when the U.S. Army successfully tested its first hydrogen bomb in the Marshall Islands—although the existence of this new "super-bomb" was not announced until twelve days after Eisenhower's landslide victory.

42. *High Noon* was also understood as a critique of conformity, a postwar issue that had been rehearsed in works of popular sociology like *The Lonely Crowd* and *The Organization Man*. Indeed, Warshow's essay on the Westerner appeared in the same issue as the exchange between Warshow and Howe over Howe's "This Age of Conformity," an attack on anti-Communist "conformity" among intellectuals.

Cooper's character was not antidemocratic but insufficiently fascist—a weary liberal rather than a Patriotic Roughneck.

Accepting the Oscar on Cooper's behalf, Wayne sublimated his hostility.

> I'm glad to see they're giving this to a man who has conducted himself through-out his years in this business in a manner that we can all be proud of him. And now I'm going to go back and find my business manager, agent, producer, and three name writers and find out why I didn't get *High Noon* instead of Cooper. Since I can't fire any of these very expensive fellas, I can at least run my 1930 Chevrolet into one of their big black new Cadillacs.

Nearly twenty years after *High Noon* opened, Wayne was still angry. *High Noon* was "the most un-American thing I've ever seen in my whole life," he told *Playboy*. "The last thing in the picture is ole Coop putting the United States mar-shal's badge under his foot and stepping on it. I'll never regret having helped run Foreman out of this country."

From Wayne's perspective, *High Noon* was unpatriotic. There is, however, another way of looking at the movie: *High Noon* is about America's lonely bur-den. "I see *High Noon* as having an urgent political message," the Swedish critic Harry Schein wrote in a mid-1950s essay called "The Olympian Cowboy." Schein noted that "the little community seems to be crippled with fear before the ap-proaching villains." Because Hadleyville was "timid, neutral, and half-hearted," like the United Nations in the face of Soviet–Red Chinese–North Korean ag-gression, while "moral courage is apparent only in the very American sheriff [*sic*]," *High Noon* struck Schein as the most artistically convincing and

> certainly the most honest explanation of American foreign policy. The marshal (America) had wanted peace after clearing up the town five years before (i.e. WW2), and reluctantly must buckle on his gun belt again in the face of new ag-gression (the Korean War), and eventually his pacifist wife (American isolation-ists) must see where her true duty lies and support him.

Just as Marshall Kane cleaned up Hadleyville, making it safe for women and children, so the Truman Doctrine had maintained that it was now Ameri-ca's obligation "to support free peoples who are resisting attempted subjuga-tion by armed minorities or by outside pressures." (And as Kane was deserted by the selfish townspeople, so congressional Republicans had attacked Truman as a "do-gooder.") America's postwar foreign policy was predicated not on self-interest but on the need to protect freedom in that "world of bullies and pol-troons" Bosley Crowther saw in *High Noon*.

Writing in *Sight and Sound* the year after *High Noon* was released, Herbert L. Jacobson went so far as to credit the Hollywood Western (in which "the horse galloped and the heroes fired not for land but for abstract concepts of Justice and Honor") with facilitating America's miraculous transformation into a supreme military power; American tenacity at the Battle of the Bulge or in Korea was at least partially derived from the Western axiom that "the good hero always wins if he holds out long enough," as was the new American mission. For "the cowboy, though violent once in action, is never the aggressor, and is moved to take up his guns only by injustice."

According to this formulation, righting a wrong rather than acting in vengeance or even out of national self-interest, the United States fought for an abstract ideal—call it "honor." Better than any movie before or since, *High Noon* made a case for the Western as America's civil religion and the expression of the nation's existential identity.

High Noon not only won Cooper an Oscar but also restored his position as Hollywood's premier box office star. Wayne, who reigned in 1950 and 1951, fell to third place.

President Dwight Eisenhower would screen *High Noon* three times in the White House. Present for one show early in Eisenhower's first term, a writer for *Collier's* magazine reported the president unusually engrossed. On the screen, Cooper's weary marshal stood alone; stalked through his empty town by four implacable killers, he took refuge in a barn, and now the bad guys had set the place aflame. Eisenhower "bent forward in genuine anxiety," the journalist noted. "As Cooper leaped onto the horse and headed out of the barn, the President of the United States could contain himself no longer. 'Run,' shouted Ike."

This sense of identification would prove to be prophetic. As a historical drama, *Fort Apache* might be transposed to Vietnam or Afghanistan, but the *High Noon* scenario was eternally present—it was meant to be lived! According to White House projectionist logs, *High Noon* ranks as the movie most requested by American presidents. This weary loner—with his courageous certainty in the face of public cowardice—is the American politician's ego ideal, if sometimes in the guise of his 1970s avatar Dirty Harry. *High Noon* looked forward to the period when political leaders would be defined by their image and a political stance would trump a political platform.

Perhaps none loved *High Noon* more than Bill Clinton, a six-year-old when the movie he called his favorite was released. Clinton had *High Noon* projected some twenty times during his White House residency. "It's a movie about courage in the face of fear and the guy doing what he thought was right in spite of the fact that it could cost him everything," the president told TV newsman Dan Rather in 1993. As he prepared for the high noon January 20, 2001, transfer of power, Clinton confided, again in Rather, that he would recommend the Gary Cooper Western to his successor, George W. Bush.[43]

---

43. Bush only screened *High Noon* once in the White House. Yet in late September 2001, not long after declaring that he wanted Osama bin Laden "dead or alive," the president presented a *High Noon* poster to Japanese prime minister Junichiro Koizumi, who told him that "Gary Cooper fought a lonely battle against a gang, but this time the whole world stands with the United States." (According to the *Kyodo News*, the two leaders had bonded over *High Noon* several months before, "comparing themselves to the lone, stoic and honor-bound marshal.") More forcefully than any American president since his fellow Texan Lyndon Johnson, Bush argued for the necessity of action to forestall the violence that his gut told him would occur.

IV.

THE PAXAMERICANARAMA:
EISENHOWER POWER, 1953–55

A Christian Soldier takes command, even as a Patriot Roughneck rules the Senate. War subsides. Despite invasion alerts, America learns to live with the H-bomb and like it. Not change but mutation: new cities, new highways. With movies bigger than ever, a blond goddess rises from the radioactive foam.

January 20, 1953, having won the greatest landslide victory since Franklin Roosevelt's 1936 reelection, General Dwight D. Eisenhower is president at last. "I think America wants new leadership," observed the supercilious hypnotist/ clairvoyant in the winter's bargain-basement scare-film triumph *Invasion USA*. "I suggest a wizard."

For five years, the American people yearned for this Christian Soldier. And now God sheds His grace: Ike's inauguration, per the *Washington Post*, is bathed in "the radiance of an unlooked-for sun." This is the most lavish such ceremony in U.S. history, nothing less than "the mightiest pageant ever to pass before a President," reports the *New York Times*. The parade is headed by a last-minute addition, the hastily assembled "God's Float," in which enlarged photographs of churches flank an ecumenical place of worship that will be described by the *Episcopal Church News* as resembling "an oversized model of a deformed molar."

Marching behind are sixty other floats (ten depict scenes from Eisenhower's life), thousands of servicemen (some returned from Korea for the occasion), three hundred horses, two elephants, several flag-waving turtles, and a block-long "atomic cannon." This is PaxAmericanArama: a thousand jets streak across the sky in a formation coordinated by the man who piloted the B-29 that dropped the atomic bomb on Hiroshima—Colonel Paul Tibbets, subject of MGM's just-opened docudrama *Above and Beyond*.

Eyes above and beyond: supreme commander of what, on the eve of D-Day, he termed the Great Crusade (a phrase also applied to his presidential campaign),

Eisenhower breaks tradition to preface his inaugural address with a three-paragraph personal prayer addressed to Almighty God. The man the Republican National Committee had declared the spiritual leader of our times thus inaugurates a new epoch of public religiosity: "Recognition of the Supreme Being is the first, the most basic expression of Americanism," Ike declares. Each cabinet meeting will open with a prayer, and it is during his first term that the motto "In God We Trust" is inscribed on the nation's currency and the phrase "One Nation Under God" inserted into the Pledge of Allegiance.

Eisenhower's parents were followers of the Watchtower Society, a sect that later took the name Jehovah's Witnesses. Adherents believe the biblical injunction against false idols includes human governments and thus regard pledging allegiance to a national flag as a sin. The new president had never attended services as an adult, but on the second Sunday after his inauguration, he is baptized (or rebaptized) at Washington's National Presbyterian Church. That night, former Taft man Cecil B. DeMille receives the first Screen Directors Guild D.W. Griffith Award. DeMille is the living personification of the motion picture industry, although not everyone is thrilled with the award's recipient. Hedda Hopper reports DeMille's standing ovation marred by the occupants of one particular table who sit on their hands; Hopper identifies this Ungrateful Ten as a party of one actor, two writers, and three directors, including Fred Zinnemann—Oscar nominated for *High Noon*, as is DeMille for *The Greatest Show on Earth*. Neither wins: the Oscar goes to John Ford—his fourth—for *The Quiet Man*. Still, *The Greatest Show on Earth* is named best picture, and three weeks later at Valley Forge, new vice president Richard Nixon presents DeMille with a Freedoms Foundation Award for exemplary citizenship. Ike's drama coach Robert Montgomery is similarly honored.

"No One on This Earth Can Help You": *Above and Beyond* and Fantasies of Invasion

The first president with a Hollywood image adviser is also the first fully armed with the thermonuclear thunderbolt. Nearly a thousand times more powerful than the device dropped on Hiroshima, the hydrogen bomb was successfully detonated three days before the 1952 election. Elugelab Island had become nothing but a crater two hundred feet beneath the South Pacific. The results were announced November 16, and MGM was ready.

Scarcely had news of Soviet atomic capability arrived in late 1949 than the

Truman administration began planning a "super bomb." The president announced his intention January 31, 1950; ten months later, around the time Polish mathematician Stanislaw Ulam advanced a new approach to the H-bomb that was soon endorsed by nuclear physicist Edward Teller, Ivy League bomber pilot turned Hollywood screenwriter Beirne Lay Jr. brought MGM a proposal for *Above and Beyond*, a movie about the development of nuclear weapons focused on the Hiroshima mission commander Colonel Paul Tibbets.

All hands on deck: the Atomic Energy Commission opened the new Nevada Proving Grounds, the just-established Federal Civil Defense Administration initiated a program of community bomb shelters, and MGM optioned the Tibbets story. As Lay wrestled with his treatment, the White House authorized the FCDA to fund nine short educational films, while a team of scientists in Los Alamos worked on hydrodynamic calculations, using a computer kiddingly nicknamed MANIAC (for Mathematical and Numerical Integrator and Computer). By early May, when a military-civilian joint task force on Eniwetok Atoll successfully created the first thermonuclear reaction, MGM production head Dore Schary grew increasingly involved in the Tibbets project, assigning the script to Melvin Frank and Norman Panama. MGM's emphasis shifted from Tibbets to his marriage; story conferences reworked the original concept to emphasize unhappy wife Lucey Tibbets.

The horror of the bomb was displaced onto splitting the nuclear family, but General Curtis LeMay (played in the movie by Jim Backus) was not displeased. This development, LeMay thought, would reflect the domestic tensions suffered by the men of the Strategic Air Command (SAC) and hence help boost morale as well as enhance public perception of SAC. Panama and Frank worked throughout the summer; physicist Marshall Holloway became leader of the H-bomb project. Teller left Los Alamos on the day the Soviets detonated their second atomic bomb. The White House announced the explosion on October 3, just before Holloway's Theoretical Megaton Group had its first meeting to discuss the design and construction of the first megaton-scale thermonuclear device.

Meanwhile, Panama and Frank's script was being vetted by the military. Admiral William Parsons, who, as a navy captain, designed the fuse for the Hiroshima bomb and briefed Tibbets's crew, complained the screenplay made Tibbets appear emotionally "all mixed up." The RAND Institute's newly initiated Project Sunshine, a top-secret study on the worldwide effects of nuclear weaponry, would not include a psychological component; nor should *Above and*

Beyond, Parsons argued. Tibbets had never expressed any doubt or remorse, yet the writers wanted to explore his presumed sense of guilt; as they explained to Parsons, they felt they could not show "an American airman killing 80,000 Asiatics in a flash, and expressing no feelings of conscience about this, without seriously playing into the propaganda hands of the Kremlin."

The first Federal Civil Defense Administration films—*Duck and Cover* and *Our Cities Must Fight*—had their world premieres in early January 1952, kicking off the Alert America Convoy, a tour that would crisscross the land for the next ten months promoting civil defense. While the animated *Duck and Cover*, featuring a lovable turtle, was made for schoolchildren, the noirish *Our Cities Must Fight* was overtly adult: two men discuss the proper response to the nuclear attack that "could come smashing out of the sky at any time." Evacuate or stand and fight? The movie ends by asking the viewer: "Have Americans got the guts? Have *you* got the guts?"

In mid-January, RKO released the sixteen-minute short *Operation A-Bomb*, which for the "FIRST TIME IN COLOR!" showed two test explosions at Yucca Flats as production began on Paramount's *The War of the Worlds*, concluding the trilogy of Cold War f/xtravaganzas George Pal began with *Destination Moon* (1950) and extended in *When Worlds Collide* (1951). A few weeks after that, *Above and Beyond* opened its top secret shoot at Davis-Monthan Air Force Base in Tucson, Arizona, with Robert Taylor—the Christian Soldier of *Quo Vadis*—as Paul Tibbets.

A licensed pilot, Taylor had served as a navy flying instructor during World War II; his performance may have been further aided by his recent divorce from his wife of twelve years, Barbara Stanwyck. Tibbets, who made repeated visits to the set per Taylor's request, suggested that he may have cooperated with the movie because SAC was experiencing a sky-high divorce rate and hence a "tremendous morale problem." (Tibbets characterized the movie as "reasonably accurate," though noted that his own marital tensions had been far worse.)

In May 1952, as Teller informed the FBI's Albuquerque special agent in charge that Robert Oppenheimer had been opposed to developing the H-bomb as far back as 1945 (and that were it not for Oppenheimer's resistance, the thing could have been developed by 1951), Panama and Frank brought a print of *Above and Beyond* to Washington, DC, to show Secretary of Defense Robert Lovett, Secretary of the Air Force Thomas K. Finletter, and General Hoyt Vandenberg, among others. Still, the air force did not grant official approval until just before the movie had its world premiere in Washington on December 30, with opening credits that thanked the Department of Defense and the air force

and declared that *Above and Beyond* "could not be made until the highly classified material upon which it is based was released."

Deeply alienated and no less unpleasant, *Above and Beyond* is narrated largely
by the hero's wife, Lucey (Eleanor Parker). Theirs is the opposite of the standard
World War II love story. Indeed, given an absence of period markers, the movie
could be set in 1952. The Tibbets children wear contemporary kid clothing; their
father might be a workaholic executive who, terminally testy and emotionally
withholding, plods through the movie with grim determination—a company
man utterly devoted to his mission.

Taylor's Tibbets exhibits none of the self-doubt that plagued the young scientist in *The Beginning or the End*. Indeed, most of the scientists appear margin-
alized, even confused; military men are responsible for telling government
officials what they need to know regarding the Vital Secret of the Great Whatzit.
The actual Tibbets had no input into where or when to drop the Bomb, but
Above and Beyond's crucial scene has the Leslie Grove stand-in hand Taylor a
gizmo and ask if he would kill a hundred thousand people by pressing a button,
if he knew it would end the war. Taylor thinks for a millisecond . . . then firmly
pushes down. The responsibility for that decision, he'll later be informed by his
commanding officer, belongs to "you and you alone—and no one on this earth
can help you."

In his way, Taylor's Tibbets is as agonized a loner as Gary Cooper in *High
Noon*, and yet as certain of himself as Robert Mitchum's colonel in *One Minute
to Zero*, both of whom appeared on-screen in the heightened-awareness summer of 1952. Tibbets's one moment of moral discomfort arises when Lucey tact-
lessly invokes the Japanese children who will die. Scientists may dither about
additional tests; Tibbets assumes the double burden of protecting and using the
Bomb. Lucey, of course, has little to do but complain, even when she is allowed
to take up residence under her husband's regime on the highly restricted Wendover Army Air Field. (Why should she appreciate it? This Utah military base
is a domestic prison—the world's worst Fort Apache. The Atomic City at least
had TV.)

Innocently informed by Lucey that his best friend sneaked off base to go
fishing, Tibbets has the man arrested. With this Lucey loses the last of her com-
posure and the security major (James Whitmore) who has always considered
her a risk swiftly hustles the little lady and her kids off the base. The dictates of
the Hollywood ending, if not the Production Code, allowed for a final reconciliation, necessarily repressing the actual Tibbetses' divorce. Months before the

movie's release, Hedda Hopper helpfully suggested that MGM change the title to *A Woman's Heart*.

Oppressive as it is, *Above and Beyond* encourages the viewer's desire that Tibbets get it over with and drop the damned thing (and thus end the movie). The real moral issue is military secrecy and national insecurity. The real Tibbets—assigned by the air force to accompany Robert Taylor on a promotional tour that included their being decorated by Curtis LeMay—precipitated a flurry of headline hysteria when, addressing a private screening at the Washington office of the Motion Picture Association of America two days before the world premiere, he revealed that foreign agents had attempted to penetrate his Wendover base but that these hitherto-unknown spies had been apprehended.

After a daylong spy hunt, the air force issued a statement that Manhattan Project records showed no such arrest; the *New York Times* dryly noted that "the freshest part of the cloak-and-dagger intrigue appeared to be a new movie opening here tomorrow."[1]

Throughout 1952, as the Alert America Convoy toured America and Edward R. Murrow's TV show *See It Now* dramatized a nuclear strike on New York City, Hollywood germinated fantasies of the nation under attack.

First to arrive was Albert Zugsmith's independently produced *Invasion USA*. Made (so Zugsmith would later maintain) for a mere $127,000 in one week, *Invasion USA* was essentially a feature-length version of an Alert America informational short. Indeed, the night of the movie's mid-December world premiere at the RKO Keith in Washington, DC, helmeted civil defense wardens staged a parade to the theater, where an official Federal Civil Defense Administration model of a bombed-out city was displayed in the lobby.

Set largely in a Radio City gin mill, *Invasion USA* framed a montage of World War II and nuclear test footage provided by unspecified "military sources" with a story in which six ordinary citizens face the apocalypse. A TV reporter, a cattle rancher, a tractor manufacturer, a congressman, and a "former model," as well as the blasé bartender, are punished for their indifference to imminent peril and petulant beefing about high taxes when a mysterious stranger named

---

1. *Above and Beyond* was positioned as a love story when it opened in Los Angeles; the featured short-subject was a Technicolor short, *The World's Most Beautiful Girls*. Reviews focused on the Tibbetses' relationship and MGM discovered women liked the picture better than men. Although the number one box-office attraction the week it opened, it wound up only a minor hit, finishing the year at number 29 on *Variety*'s list, with a $2.5 million gross.

Ohman (Dan O'Herlihy) hypnotically sloshes his brandy glass to induce a threadbare mass hallucination.

Ohman thus provides the movie: as the bons vivants learn from the TV, an unnamed enemy invades Alaska and bombs California. "Another day of infamy has come," the president glumly reports. Some of the movie's principals remain in the bar; others attempt to secure plane tickets home. The TV reporter and the ex-model fall in love even as enemy paratroopers machine-gun panic-stricken politicians under the Capitol rotunda, Bela Lugosi–like aliens establish a "People's Republic of America," and, in a newsreel atomic blast superimposed over a miniature set, Manhattan is reduced to smoldering rubble. The newsman is shot by the invaders; in order to avoid a fate worse than death, the model jumps out a window . . . and into Ohman's spinning brandy glass. No less than the young Orson Welles, who had terrified America with his 1938 radio adaptation of *The War of the Worlds*, Ohman is a practioner of mass suckerology, although his voodoo has a social-use value, having hypnotized the audience into vigilance. (The movie ends with a quote from George Washington: "To be prepared for war is one of the most effectual means of preserving peace.")

Meanwhile, a new *War of the Worlds* was itself in production. Aware of its historical context, this most elaborate invasion fantasy would begin by conjuring black-and-white memories of World Wars I and II, before switching to strident Technicolor for postatomic extraterrestrial combat. Producer George Pal added a religious dimension to H.G. Wells's anticlerical story—including a plug for Paramount's greatest hit, *Samson and Delilah*—but the movie has the feel of triumphalist Pop Art. A gaggle of mercenary rubes imagine the spacecraft crater as a tourist site, "like having a gold mine in our own backyard!" The middle of the picture is pure spectacle—comic-book chiaroscuro, flaming skies, multicolored mushroom clouds. At one point, Pal considered presenting the atomic blast and all subsequent scenes in 3-D.

Invaders from Mars, directed by production designer William Cameron Menzies, was conceived as a rival spectacular. (The original screenwriter, John Tucker Battle, had been involved with both the Mercury Theater and Welles's live magic show.) Although modestly budgeted, *Invaders from Mars* was the first science fiction film to present flying saucers and space aliens in color. (The "advancing" titles in the opening credits suggest that it may have been originally intended for 3-D; immediately after completing *Invaders from Mars*, Menzies contributed to one 3-D feature and directed another, *The Three-D Follies* and *The Maze*.) Stylized and almost avant-garde in its use of minimal forms, forced perspective, and bursts of color-field frames, *Invaders from Mars* suggests a Cold

War *Cabinet of Dr. Caligari*, complete with added dream "frame." (As with *Invasion USA*, history was a nightmare.)

Most effectively, the movie takes the point of view of a terrified child—product of a suburban neighborhood heavily involved with a hush-hush secret government project. The boy becomes aware that aliens have landed in his backyard, hiding their saucer under a mound of dirt, and are abducting humans, whom they control with a device surgically implanted in their brains. The movie's ad evoked this paranoia:

> From Out of Space . . . came hordes of green monsters!
> Capturing at will the humans they need for their sinister purposes!
> A General of the Army turned into a Saboteur! Parents turned into . . . rabid
> Killers! Trusted police become . . . Arsonists!
> Told in a panorama of fantastic, terrifying COLOR

The movie's first half is a child's nightmare that his parents have become Martian-ized; the second is a war film with the twelve-year-old hero right in the middle of the action. The movie is recapitulated in a lengthy flashback superimposed over the boy's face in the split second before the climactic explosion. When the saucer leaves, the mound blows up. The kid wakes up—was it all a dream or is it about to happen?[2]

Although released a few days before *Invaders from Mars* and several months ahead of *The War of the Worlds*, Universal-International's *It Came from Outer Space* was the only invasion film in preproduction after the Eisenhower landslide—it wrapped during the brief period when Ike's reign overlapped that of the Soviet Great Satan, Joseph Stalin.

U-I's $750,000 spectacle, directed by Jack Arnold from a story and script by Ray Bradbury, was shot in wide-screen (albeit black-and-white) 3-D. The most hyped special effect, however, was the barely glimpsed It. Cast and crew were required to sign a pledge of secrecy, and, according to the trades, the alien creature was created, filmed, and destroyed in a single day. The movie had its Los Angeles premiere in late May, a few weeks after Cecil B. DeMille informally joined the Eisenhower administration as chief motion picture consultant for the newly established U.S. Information Agency. The Pantages theater was

---

2. Some credit *Invaders from Mars* as the template for the alien abduction scenario recounted by Betty and Barney Hill in 1961. In 2005, Dr. Stephen A. Zerby published an article describing his use of the movie as a means of teaching child psychiatry residents at Cambridge Hospital the principles of child development, including clinical features of separation anxiety.

equipped with catapults that flanked the screen; tripped by Arnold during the avalanche scene, these hurled Styrofoam boulders at the audience. The stunt was never repeated, but *It Came from Outer Space* became one of the summer's biggest hits and, with a $1.6 million box office, U-I's seventh-highest-grossing movie for 1953.

Shot on location in and around the Mojave Desert, *It Came from Outer Space* was both U-I's first foray into science fiction and the first sci-fi film that used the desert to provide a cosmic sense of our home planet. "This is Sand Rock, Arizona," hero John Putnam (Richard Carlson) says in the introductory voice-over. "It's a nice town, knowing its past and sure of its future." Putnam, an amateur astronomer who has relocated to Sand Rock, is relaxing with his fiancée Ellen Fields (Barbara Rush) when a sudden flash illuminates the desert night, followed by strange mist. This event could hardly fail to recall an atomic test, and Putnam, who with his ubiquitous pipe and tweed jacket has the mien of a glamorous atomic scientist, characterizes it as "the biggest thing that's ever happened in our time. . . . It lit up the sky like the end of all creation."

Putnam concludes that the explosion and ensuing crater resulted from an extraterrestrial visitation and initiates his own investigation. Regarded as possessing a singular intellect, Putnam is also the object of suspicion. An older colleague characterizes him as "individual and lonely . . . a man who thinks for himself." The local sheriff, a rival for Ellen's affections, is less sympathetic. "This town doesn't understand geniuses," he tells Putnam. "Your poking around in the desert and squinting up at the stars frightens them and what frightens them they're against."

That fear—merging the never-articulated terror of the hydrogen bomb with the amply emphasized horror of difference—provides the film's subject. Putnam, of course, is correct, an egghead cousin to Hadleyville's Marshall Kane. The crater was caused by a crashing spaceship, and miraculously, the aliens have survived. In a recognizable Bradbury trope, these extraterrestrials have no interest in Earth; they simply want to repair their craft and move on. Attempting to hold the humans at bay, the aliens temporarily assume the form of local earthlings and attempt to act "normal"—not unlike the outsider Putnam. *It Came from Outer Space* thus introduces the idea of alien subversion. "They could be all around us and I wouldn't know it," the sheriff exclaims after Putnam finally has persuaded him that Sand Rock is the epicenter of a cosmic visitation.

Remarkably, these creatures mean no harm—and, while not plumbing the depths of alien psychology, *It Came from Outer Space* does include occasional shots from their enigmatic point of view. At one point Putnam, who comes to sympathize with the extraterrestrials and shield them from hostile vigilantes, confronts the alien version of himself. The battle in the liberal invasion vision does not pit earthlings against extraterrestrials but a rational liberal worldview against reflexively hysterical, ignorant paranoia. Incredibly, Putnam prevails and the final image has the people of Sand Rock gathered around him as he gazes into the sky to offer the comforting bromide that someday, when humanity has sufficiently evolved, the aliens will return.[3]

Praising the film's direction ("Arnold has made good use of the barren brooding desert expanses with their lonely, unreal look of another world") and acting (particularly Carlson's "mystically inclined astronomer"), *Time*'s anonymous reviewer was one of the few to note the film's politics, characterizing the film as "a crisp combination of shocker and sociological comment." Indeed, the filmmakers were not without social consciousness. Arnold, a New York actor and self-taught 16 mm filmmaker who had served as Robert Flaherty's camera operator in the Signal Corps, directed several documentaries for the International Ladies Garment Workers Union. He also appeared uncredited as a sinister Communist organizer in *With These Hands*, which opened theatrically in New York in 1950 and was later distributed overseas by the State Department's Information Service.

From the far future vantage of the Reagan era, Arnold would maintain that *It Came from Outer Space*'s "point was that we are prone—all of us—to fear something that's different than we are, whether it be in philosophy, the color of our skins, or even one block against another in a big city." The film addressed its moment, "the worst period this country has ever gone through," made "when we were running scared of everything and you didn't have to be a Communist to be suspect." Like the other invasion movies, *It* can be traced back to Orson Welles. Producer William Alland was an erstwhile associate of the Mercury Theater (he played the reporter in *Citizen Kane*) as well as a former member of the Communist Party. Echoing Arnold, Alland would tell an interviewer that *It Came from Outer Space* was his most political movie, an anti-McCarthyite tract warning audiences that fear of aliens might be even more dangerous than the aliens themselves.

As such, the movie anticipated a warning against such fears issued by President

---

3. This mystical optimism prefigures that of Steven Spielberg's *Close Encounters of the Third Kind* (1977) and *ET: The Extra-Terrestrial* (1982). Spielberg, who saw *It Came from Outer Space* as a child, has acknowledged its formative influence.

Eisenhower himself nearly a year later. That was too late for Alland. The producer was called before a HUAC subcommittee in November 1953, and, testifying in executive session, told the subcommittee that he joined the Communist Party in 1946 but that his section had banned him from meetings in 1948 after the leadership discovered he was seeing a psychiatrist: "I found psychotherapy very helpful. As a matter of fact 95 percent of the Party membership is emotionally disturbed." Alland named a number of former comrades, including Virginia Mullen (an actress with a small part in *It Came from Outer Space*) and his ex-wife Ruth Myerson.[4]

The Hammer, the Witch Trials, and *Pickup on South Street*

Reality exists in the human mind and nowhere else—so the Party maintained in *1984*, so *Invasion USA* purported to demonstrate, and so the spell cast by the epoch-defining demagogue Senator Joseph McCarthy was amplified by the 1952 Republican victory.

Four incumbent Democratic senators against whom McCarthy campaigned went down in defeat, while he himself was easily returned to office. The *New York Times* credited McCarthy with electing eight Republicans—some thought the number higher—and thus gaining the party's control of the Senate. The real story was General Eisenhower's personal popularity, but McCarthy held the power of illusion. Perceived as the Senate's dominant figure, he became so.

McCarthy's rise dramatized the reorganization of American politics according to precepts of public relations and the imperatives of advertising. And yet the Wisconsin senator played by his own rules. "He didn't want the world to think of him as respectable," McCarthy's biographer Richard Rovere would write. The senator was a rogue. He "encouraged photographers to take pictures of him sleeping, disheveled, on an office couch, like a bum on a park bench, coming out of a shower with a towel wrapped around his torso like Rocky Marciano, or sprawled on the floor in his shirt sleeves with a hooker of bourbon close at hand."

---

4. Around the same time as Alland's testimony, *It Came from Outer Space*'s liberal scientist Richard Carlson achieved iconic status as the FBI undercover informer in America's then-top-rated syndicated TV series, *I Led Three Lives*. Each show began with Carlson telling viewers they were watching "the fantastically true story of Herbert A. Philbrick, who for nine frightening years did lead three lives—average citizen, high-level member of the Communist Party, and counterspy for the FBI." Anticipating *Invasion of the Body Snatchers*, this no-frills anti-Communist noir exported Philbrick's wartime experiences as a member of the Boston CP to generic 1950s suburbia where Communists were potentially everywhere and anyone.

The forty-four-year-old ex-marine had cast himself as a barroom brawler and frontier bully, a one-man mob and yet the only honest Joe in a lawless town. Scarcely six weeks after McCarthy addressed the Republican women of Wheeling, West Virginia, in February 1950, *Washington Post* editorial cartoonist Herblock scrawled "McCarthyism" on a tar pot. McCarthy reveled in the epithet, which he redefined as "Americanism with its sleeves rolled up." The senator made no apologies for his tactics, telling the 1952 Republication convention that "a rough fight is the only fight Communists understand." McCarthy's acolyte, Senator Herman Welker of Idaho, described his hero as a "fighting Irish Marine [who] would give the shirt off his back to anyone who needs it—except a dirty, lying, stinking Communist. That guy, he'd kill."

Assuming the chairmanship of the Senate Committee on Government Operations in January 1953, McCarthy deputized a posse. He packed its Permanent Investigations Subcommittee with cronies who met at the chairman's discretion, often on less than a day's notice, with scant advance knowledge of what or whom he planned to expose. McCarthy thrived on improvisation. The element of surprise heightened the exaggerated threats and outrageous accusations. It was part of the act, like the senator's sepulchral tone, which—amplified by the committee room's marble mausoleum walls—reminded I.F. Stone of a radio soap opera's Voice of Doom.[5]

McCarthy was naturally drawn to show business (and was suspected of angling for his own TV program), but his show was politics. After casting about, the senator targeted the State Department and particularly the Voice of America, the agency charged with broadcasting the American point of view to Europe's captive nations. The VOA was something of a miniature Hollywood, filled with frustrated prima donnas and jealous tattletales eager to report each other's real or imagined political and moral shortcomings. None of this added up to much, but, as Rovere pointed out, "the magic of McCarthyism lay in its Luther Burbank touch with humble and unpromising materials. Working with nothing but a mass of trifling, unrelated, and mostly negative facts, it could produce whole fields of Shasta daisies."

Intermittently televised, the VOA hearings themselves were a media hall of mirrors. (Thomas Doherty has called them a "prematurely postmodern media

---

5. Others were struck by McCarthy's perverse professionalism: his cross-examination of witnesses contained "no rancor, no anger, not even personal animus," Robert Griffith wrote. "It was a performance played to a giant and invisible audience." Off mike and away from the cameras, the senator could be quite friendly toward his victims.

event" in which "a politician used television to propagandize against the propaganda arm of the government for insufficient zeal in propagandizing the government.") The *New York Times* dismissed the investigation as a TV carnival produced, staged, and directed by McCarthy. But, as noted by *Variety*, the carnival impressed the movie industry—and later that month, HUAC returned to Hollywood yet again.

March 23, the committee set up shop in the Federal Building, opening another inquiry into Communist infiltration of radio, movies, and TV—as well as the education, legal, and medical professions. The show was televised daily each morning over three local channels.

In one of the first sessions, producer and friendly witness Harold Hecht caused a stir when he testified that during the recess a former associate and agent (and onetime business manager for the *New Masses*), George Wilner, had accosted him in the hallway and called him "stool pigeon." Not to be outdone, screenwriter David A. Lang claimed the following day that, once word got out that he'd be a friendly witness, a Mrs. Bargeman phoned his wife to warn her she was married to a traitor: "In ten years they'll line him up against a wall and shoot him!" Lang then named seventy people, including actress Dorothy Comingore, the other woman in *Citizen Kane* and Richard Collins's former wife, humiliatingly busted on a morals rap five days before.

Comingore, forty years old and often described as "Titian haired," made no secret of her politics. She had picketed HUAC's previous Los Angeles appearances and was a resolutely unfriendly witness at hearings held in L.A. the month before the 1952 election, sarcastically calling the committee's counsel "cute" the fourth time he asked her if she was or had ever been a member of the CP. Three weeks later, the actress again refused to answer the question in California Superior Court where—accused of excessive drinking and allowing her children to frolic in a swimming pool belonging to "persons of doubtful loyalty"—she was losing a custody battle with her ex-husband, a major friendly witness during the spring 1951 hearings.

On March 19, Comingore was picked up by two guys in a West Hollywood café, driven to a nearby bar—at which, they claimed, she propositioned them—and then on to Plummer Park. There, she was passed a marked ten spot and placed under arrest. The political implications were obvious, at least to the *Daily Worker*: it was the climax of "a campaign by the FBI, sheriff's deputies and city police to roust and frame the actress that has been under way since her refusal in October to give stoolpigeon testimony to the un-Americans."[6]

Given the timing, Comingore's miserable fate could hardly seem anything other than a warning to unfriendly witnesses such as screenwriters Eddie Huebsch and Ben Maddow, or Simon M. Lazarus, a Los Angeles exhibitor identified in the *Los Angeles Times* as the head of a company producing an "allegedly Communistic motion picture" in Silver City, New Mexico, and hence a genuine threat. Lazarus, like the two writers, took the Fifth, refusing to name his partners, who included two members of the Hollywood Ten, Herbert Biberman and Adrian Scott; one of the Ten's attorneys, Charles Katz; and blacklisted screenwriter Paul Jarrico, current leader of the CP's Hollywood section. Their project, in production since early January and recently wrapped, was a dramatic account of the Empire Zinc strike of 1951, *Salt of the Earth.*

The story broke in early February that a group of "Hollywood Reds" were out in the desert shooting an "anti-American racial issue propaganda movie." An industry-savvy local schoolteacher tipped off Walter Pidgeon, Ronald Reagan's successor as Screen Actors Guild president; Pidgeon informed HUAC, the FBI, the CIO, and the State Department, as well as the *Hollywood Reporter*, which—confusing director Herbert Biberman with another one of the Hollywood Ten—revealed that *Salt of the Earth* was being produced under orders from the Kremlin funneled through John Howard Lawson.

Alerted by the Silver City chapter of the American Legion, columnist Victor Riesel explained that the movie was actually funded by the pro-Soviet Mine, Mill, and Smelter Workers and, as close as production was to Los Alamos, posed a grave threat to the nation's vital secrets as well as its vital zinc mines. Two

---

6. The *Worker* provided Comingore's side of the story: dining alone, she was joined at her table by two customers who offered to take her home, a few blocks away. Instead of dropping her off, they stuffed a bill in her pocket and drove downtown to the Los Angeles county jail, where she was charged with prostitution. According to the *Worker*'s account,

> The deputies said Miss Comingore had told them she was broke and needed $10 [although she] had more than $20 in her possession when she was booked. . . . Friends of the actress told how she has been subjected to a continuing campaign of harassment. They said her telephone had been tapped, and she had received lewd calls. "About three months ago," one friend said, "Dorothy was at Hollywood and Vine, and a couple of vice cops tried to pick her up. She ran from them and went to friends for protection. Another time she was walking along Hollywood Boulevard when a vice cop grabbed her arm and said, 'Let's go places, baby!' She ran from him too."
>
> The actress herself told how her apartment had been ransacked either by local cops and deputies, or by federal agents.

In May, Comingore was committed to Camarillo State Mental Hospital.

weeks later, HUAC member Donald Jackson took the House floor to warn of a motion picture being made with the express purpose of undermining the U.S. war effort in Korea. Soon after, the movie's lead actress, Rosaura Revueltas, was arrested by the Immigrant Service and deported to Mexico. Jackson's speech was repeatedly broadcast over Silver City radio; in early March, vigilantes attacked the Mine-Mill's international representative Clinton Jencks and a fellow union officer, warning the filmmakers to leave town or face the consequences. Demonstrations peaked on March 6 (the day Joe Stalin died), when local businesses shut down, aircraft strafed the ranch where *Salt of the Earth* was being shot, and the local movie theater devoted itself to continuous screenings of Dore Schary's anti-Communist documentary *The Hoaxters*.

As reported in the *Daily Worker*, *Salt of the Earth* was shot "despite three fires, two sluggings, bullet holes in a car, property damage, the illegal arrest and detention of a leading Mexican actress and other acts of violence against the members of the production company by vigilantes, inspired by false reports in the press and in the halls of Congress." It was expected to be released in June, the month of the scheduled Rosenberg execution, although that proved a bit optimistic.

The first stage of McCarthyism coincided with the great ongoing martyrdom of the self-described unassuming Jewish couple arrested during the first weeks of the Korean War, tried for atomic espionage the following March, found guilty, and sentenced to die in the electric chair. Two years later, Julius and Ethel Rosenberg remained on death row at Sing Sing, where they protested their innocence in the great cause célèbre of Cold War America.

It was Ethel who most horrified the public. If Julius seemed a bland little Commie nonentity, his wife—like Dorothy Comingore or Rosaura Revueltas—was a witch. Although the president was squeamish about sending a woman to the stake, he felt that the circumstances were mitigated by what he perceived as Ethel's uncanny power: "It is the woman who is the strong and recalcitrant character, the man is the weak one," Eisenhower wrote to his son. "She has obviously been the leader in everything they did in the spy ring."[7]

Anti-McCarthyism developed its own mythology: perhaps only the *Daily Worker* believed that McCarthy sought "to build a Nazi-style mass movement," but, as the Wisconsin senator solidified his status as the nation's Witchfinder

---

7. In fact, as declassified files reveal, Ethel was at most a passive accomplice in her husband's espionage activities; her death sentence was intended as a lever to extract Julius's confession.

General, so dissident writers drew on the historical precedent of the Salem witch trials. The opening session of HUAC's recent hearings ended with an unfriendly witness, former animator Philip D. Eastman, maintaining that his great-great-great-great-great-great-grandmother Mary Bradbury had been convicted of witchcraft in Massachusetts. Such accusations of an anti-Communist witch hunt were nothing new.

The summer of 1947 Thought Control Conference was rife with references. Published two summers later, Marion L. Starkey's history *The Devil in Massachusetts* ended by making a parallel between late-seventeenth-century Salem and contemporary America: "Our age too is beset by ideological 'heresies' in almost the medieval sense, and our scientists have [similarly forced] on us the contemplation of Doomsday." Arthur Miller's play *The Crucible*, which drew on the Starkey book and focused on the trial of an innocent couple, John and Elizabeth Proctor, who refuse to confess to witchcraft, opened on Broadway in late January 1953.

Miller's drama not only mirrored the Rosenberg case but ultimately merged with it. As reported by David Platt in the *Daily Worker*, in early June, "at least a dozen curtain calls" were capped when "a very clear voice rang out from the gallery saying:

> "Only two weeks are left to save the Rosenbergs from death. They are victims of the same kind of frame-up that you have just seen on this stage."
>
> A friend of mine who was in the audience that night said most of the people around him were very sympathetic to these words from the gallery. He saw "faces just shining with delight."

Two months into *The Crucible*'s run and the day after the latest installment of HUAC in Hollywood had closed with a sixty-eight-year-old grandmother and FBI informant furnishing a list of 128 Los Angeles Commies, the new CBS television series *You Are There*—in which historical events were dramatized as breaking news and narrated by network reporters—broadcast a show on the witch trials. Salem is hysterical, although a few cool heads see an underlying social cause behind the mass delusion and even wax psychological: "Are we destroying the Evil One or are we destroying each other?" The protagonist is Bridget Bishop, "the first of the Salem witches to go unconfessed to Gallows Hill," shown as young, courageous, and resolute in the face of rampant irrationality.

The Salem episode was written through a front by Arnold Manoff, who—along with fellow blacklistees Abraham Polonsky and Walter Bernstein—would furnish *You Are There* with shows on the trials of Joan of Arc and Galileo, the persecution of Socrates ("first master of the method of dialectics"), and the Dreyfus case, all telecast in the months before the Rosenberg execution. "The Final Hours of Joan of Arc" was particularly intense, with graylisted Kim Stanley's distraught, suffering Joan reviled both by her captors ("nothing but a witch and a traitor") and the mob ("I'd burn her myself"), dragged to the stake as she steadfastly refuses to recant or confess, or, as she says, tell a lie. It was her truth that prevailed, Cronkite solemnly states before the final commercial message, a witty spoof of Soviet scientific claims from America's electric light and power companies.

Blacklisted writers managed to suggest that Communists or suspected Communists were being treated like the great martyrs of history; from McCarthy's point of view, Joan, Galileo, and Socrates were Commies avant la lettre. In April, having discovered that one of the State Department's overseas information centers had a book on its shelves by the Communist novelist Howard Fast (interrogated by McCarthy's subcommittee back in February), the Grand Inquisitor turned his attention to these libraries.[8]

McCarthy's aides Roy Cohn and David Schine set off on a madcap grand tour. "Like some wounded prehistoric animal," as historian Robert Griffith put it in his account of McCarthy's career, the State Department "aroused itself first in puzzlement and then in panic." Even before Cohn and Schine arrived, the department began issuing a stream of policy directives and counterdirectives to the overseas libraries that were frantically purging their shelves of potentially incriminating volumes. Ultimately, President Eisenhower was obliged to recognize the ruckus. Addressing the graduating class at Dartmouth College in June 1953, he cautioned Americans against joining the "book burners."

Wizards and witches and things that bumped in the night: American social reality had altered and so had collective fantasy. Political rhetoric mutated genre convention. The hard-boiled detective was now the ultraviolent vigilante avenger. As McCarthy, per Rovere, valued above all "his reputation for toughness,

---

8. The blacklist went international that spring: Jules Dassin, named as a Red by Frank Tuttle (among others), went to France (ahead of a subpoena that never came) and was offered a job directing a comedy with Fernandel. A few days before the shoot was to open, Dassin would recall, "a man called Roy Brewer" contacted the French producer and informed him "that if this film was made with me it certainly would not be released in the States, nor would any film he ever made afterward. . . . After Roy Brewer got to the producer, he then went to [the star Zsa Zsa Gabor], threatened her and frightened her to death." Dassin was taken off the film.

ruthlessness, even brutality," so McCarthyism was anticipated by the fictional private eye Mike Hammer.

Hammer was the most sadistic shamus in crime fiction, and his creator Mickey Spillane was the most commercially successful American writer during the first phase of the Cold War. Between 1947 and 1952, when Spillane became a Jehovah's Witness (like the president's late parents) and temporarily retired, his novels, including *I, the Jury, My Gun Is Quick,* and *Vengeance Is Mine,* sold some 24 million copies. The writer imagined a new sort of savior who was detective, judge, jury, and executioner in one—a vigilante killer for whom the ends justify the means. A humble man in some ways, Hammer respected the FBI and the police (who in turn loved him). He—and he alone—understood that these professionals were constrained, their hands tied.

In his first appearance, Hammer explained to the chief of the homicide squad that while the cop was bound by all manner of rules and regulations and answerable to his departmental superior, he, Hammer, was not: "Someday, before long, I'm going to have a rod in my mitt and the killer in front of me. I'm going to watch the killer's face. I'm going to punk one right in his gut, and when he's dying on the floor I may kick his teeth out." Thus, Spillane offered his readers the essential Patriot Roughneck, God's Angry Man—an analogue to irate evangelists and a precursor to talk-radio personalities, as well as fictional characters like the Legal Vigilante, Dirty Harry. Some saw Hammer's exaggerated individualism as the unintended consequence of the paperback revolution meant to bring literature to the masses. In the spring of 1952, the editors of *Partisan Review* noted that the implacable growth of mass culture had created "a new obstacle: the artist and intellectual who wants to be a part of American life is faced with a mass culture which makes him feel that he is still outside looking in"—an alien in spite of himself. America promised cultural freedom yet produced something else. Mike Hammer was the nightmare personification of cultural democracy, just as Joe McCarthy would be the nightmare of political democracy.[9]

Squeamish, pusillanimous liberals were naturally horrified by Hammer, unable to grasp that only such a one as he could guarantee their freedom. Hammer mainly fought criminals. But in his first post-McCarthy adventure, 1951's *One Lonely Night,* he turned his attention to another evil. Hammer became politi-

---

9. After meeting Spillane in 1961, Ayn Rand wrote to tell him that that he was "the only modern writer with whom I do share the loyalty of my best readers—and I am proud of this." Rand was sympathetic to McCarthy as well, telling one young acolyte that were she not so busy writing *Atlas Shrugged*, she'd defend him as Zola defended Dreyfus.

cized. At the novel's end, he exults in having "killed more people tonight than I have fingers on my hands. I shot them in cold blood and enjoyed every minute of it. . . . They were Commies." These domestic Communists, Hammer explains, had "figured us all to be as soft as horse manure and as stupid." It is now that Hammer realizes why society tolerates and even nurtures his own rottenness. He recognizes his purpose: "I lived only to kill the scum and the lice . . . I lived to kill so that others could live . . . I was the evil that opposed other evil."

Big Jim McLain, in which John Wayne plays a two-fisted HUAC investigator who busts up a Communist plot to take over Hawaii, had been a straightforward glorification of the Hammer-McCarthyite worldview. Samuel Fuller's *Pickup on South Street*, rated B ("morally objectionable in part") by the Legion of Decency and released in June 1953 a few days after Eisenhower warned against book burning, was at once more nuanced and more extreme. Unafraid to push a situation to near-ridiculous limits, Fuller imagined that a pickpocket—which is to say a professional thief and the personification of laissez-faire capitalism—came into possession of the Vital Secret. What then?

Pickup on South Street had been conceived during the campaign season that brought *My Son John* and *Big Jim McLain*; it was written and shot during the summer and fall of 1952, in the midst of a presidential election dominated in large measure by McCarthy's accusations that the Democrats were responsible for twenty years of treason.[10]

The movie was Fuller's second effort for Fox studio boss Darryl F. Zanuck. Handed a courtroom drama about a female attorney who falls in love with a criminal, Fuller proposed altering first the milieu and then the premise: "I wanted to do a story set among the real criminal class. I like them." Populated by low-life—a pickpocket, a professional informer, and, as Fuller described her, "a half-assed hooker," with an irate cop for comic relief—*Pickup on South Street* takes place half in the subway or beneath the Brooklyn Bridge, the rest mostly unfolding in police stations, Bowery flophouses, and all-night Chinese noodle joints. According to Fuller, "Zanuck said, 'What kind of characters have you got here? You've gotta have a "nice" boy and girl subplot in this thing.' But I didn't change it." Rather, he added a topical hook.

"All the newspapers at that time in the United States were talking about

10. Although often assumed to be right-wing, Fuller was a Stevenson supporter who, during an interregnum on *Pickup*, hosted a fund-raising party for the Democratic candidate: "Everybody who was anybody in Hollywood, no matter what their politics, came to my shindig," he recounts in his memoirs.

Klaus Fuchs," Fuller would recall in his autobiography. "Richard Nixon had just been chosen as the Republican vice presidential candidate, having made a name with his phony Alger Hiss exposé. . . . I wanted to take a poke at the idiocy of the cold war climate of the fifties." Or perhaps Fuller wanted to participate in that idiocy and celebrate its vitalism. Fuller's Skip McCoy was a different sort of tough guy than Wayne's Jim McLain—although, in their ruthless pragmatism, both McCoy and McLain shared certain characteristics with Joe McCarthy.

Pickup on South Street opens in a packed and sweltering subway car, with a brilliant, wordless thirty-seven-shot montage of surveillance, theft, and sexual tension: watched by a pair of incredulous FBI agents, McCoy (Widmark) deftly grifts the wallet from the daydreaming, somewhat cheap-looking dame they have been tailing. Candy (Jean Peters) is not only Skip's mark but also, as recruited by her boyfriend Joey (Richard Kiley), the unwitting courier for a Communist spy ring.

Skip is subsequently fingered by the lovable stool pigeon Moe (Thelma Ritter), who sells his identity first to the FBI and then to Candy, dispatched by Joey to recover the stolen microfilm. Hauled in for questioning, Skip realizes what he possesses and begins playing off the principals to get his big score. *Pickup on South Street* has elements of anti-Communist films noir like *I Married Communist* and *I Was a Communist for the FBI*, but, unlike these, it does not simply equate Communism with organized crime. Instead, *Pickup* reduces capitalism to its lowest common denominator, blatant self-interest, and poses that as America's alternative to the collectivist enemy. The United States and Soviet Union are presented as rival economic entities. "This is big business," Joey explains to Candy (who, unaware of his Communist political agenda, naturally thinks him a criminal).

Fuller's view of informing is similarly complicated. Moe will sell Skip to anybody except a Communist: "Even in our crummy business you gotta draw the line somewhere." Candy is nearly killed, because, having fallen for Skip, she won't give the pickpocket's address to Joey. Where the role of the informer would be justified a year later in Elia Kazan's *On the Waterfront*—and declassified FBI files show that the Rosenbergs could have saved their lives by naming names—Fuller's characters are adamant in their refusal to talk. Irrationally loyal to Skip, Candy and ultimately Moe are the equivalent of unfriendly witnesses who refused to reveal their political associations to HUAC—even if they do hate Commies.

Thus *Pickup on South Street* pushes McCarthy-style anti-Communism through the looking glass to the far side of self-parody. America is protected by its outcasts—the very people who embody the plague in *Panic in the Streets*. Moreover, they act from a personal necessity that is pointedly apatriotic. "Are you waving the flag at me?" Skip snarls in response to an FBI agent's platitudinous speech and not-so-veiled threat that if he refuses to cooperate, he'll be a regular Rosenberg, "as guilty as the spies that gave Stalin the A-bomb."

Pickup on South Street acknowledges McCarthyism both as roughneck politics and as reflexive Americanism, rather than as a political position. As analyzed by Jacques Ellul, McCarthyism is the pure expression of a particularly Manichean worldview: alcoholism and homosexuality are associated with Communism because the Communist is a priori abnormal in his failure to accept the normal—that is, the American—way of life. And so it is for the principals of *Pickup on South Street*. Candy's feelings are genuinely hurt when Skip calls her a Commie. Moe's antipathy toward Communists is even more reflexive: "Commies, wadda I know about Commies?" she wails when confronted by Joey. "I only know I don't like 'em."

Moe has an equally automatic aversion to official authority: "Who's the creep?" she asks the police detective Tiger when she spots an FBI agent in his office. "He looks like a second-story cat thief." (Actually, as played by Willis Bouchey, the president in *Red Planet Mars*, he looks a bit like Ike.) But why should Moe like Commies? She's an independent entrepreneur, a seller of information. A police state would put her out of business. Thus, *Pickup on South Street* taps into another aspect of American ideology. One of the movie's recurring lines, heard in a variety of contexts, is "We're in business."

The business of America is business. Having come into the Vital Secret through his own professional skills and effort, Skip can and should sell it to the highest bidder, if he's a real American. Similarly, Moe's prices for information are, as she points out, pegged to the cost of living. Her greatest fear is that she will die a pauper and spend eternity in an anonymous grave. "If I was ever buried in Potter's Field it would kill me. . . . I have to go on living so I can die," she explains. Moe knows too much to romanticize free-market capitalism.

Submitted to the Breen Office in August 1952, Fuller's *Pickup on South Street* script had been immediately turned down as "unacceptable by reason of excessive brutality and sadistic beatings, both of men and women." In a subsequent letter, Breen further advised the studio to consult the FBI for "proper technical advice." Actually, Fuller had already done so. In the spring of 1952, the filmmaker requested a meeting with an FBI agent, explaining that he wished to accurately portray a G-man in his movie. According to Bureau records, Fuller wanted to know whether it would be credible to depict the FBI offering money to a pickpocket who unknowingly lifted some top secret microfilm. Fuller already had an active FBI file thanks to *The Steel Helmet*; a memo on the meeting was forwarded to J. Edgar Hoover, who informed the Los Angeles SAC that Fuller was to receive no further assistance.

In his memoirs, Fuller recalled a special screening arranged for Hoover and then a lunch meeting at Romanoff's.

> Hoover was sitting alone at a table in the back. His squad of bodyguards in black suits was at the next table. They never took their eyes off Darryl and me as we sat down across from Hoover and one of his top Los Angeles lieutenants. The FBI chief told me he didn't care for *The Steel Helmet* or *Fixed Bayonets*, but that *Pickup on South Street* had gone too far.

Hoover was upset that Fuller's hero would do business with both Communists and Americans. ("Hoover was also shocked at the way the G-man in the movie, working with a New York cop, bribes a stool pigeon to get information"— as well he might have been, having seen the memo reporting Fuller asking an FBI agent if this was possible and being told that it wasn't.) But mainly, Hoover hated Skip's contempt for the "flag-waving" agents who implore him to cooperate. According to Fuller, Hoover asked Zanuck to cut or reshoot the offending scenes and, remarkably, was politely refused: "Mr. Hoover, you don't know movies."

In no way a B picture, *Pickup on South Street* had its New York premiere at the Roxy—complete with floor show—on June 17, 1953, just two days before the electrocution of Julius and Ethel Rosenberg. On the eve of the execution, David Platt attempted to inspire readers by recalling the glory days, marking the tenth anniversary of *Mission to Moscow*: "Rarely, if ever, has a film won such high praise from Americans of all classes," so unlike "a saber-rattling film like *Invasion USA* which says that war is inevitable"—or, he had no need to add, *Pickup on South Street*.

The *Los Angeles Times* noted *Pickup*'s naturalism ("Hard-Boiled Film Stresses Realism") as well as its paperback antecedents: "*Pickup on South Street* follows the Mickey Spillane school in [its] exposition of sex and sadism." The *New York Times* was impressed mainly by the underworld milieu and "brutish," "sadistic" mayhem: "Violence bursts in every sequence, and the conversation is slangy and corrupt," per Bosley Crowther. "It looks very much as though someone is trying to out-bulldoze Mickey Spillane." The sexual violence with which

Skip saves Candy from her pansy Commie boyfriend as well as the choreographed mayhem of their cathartic fight (Joey tackled in a subway station and pulled down the stairs so his chin hits every step: "dat dat dat—it's musical," Fuller chuckled) did seem close to Hammer. But unlike Hoover, Crowther failed to notice that Skip espouses no patriotism and is hostile to all authority.[11]

Representing the United States at the Venice Film Festival, *Pickup on South Street* was awarded one of four Bronze Lions. It was also attacked as a McCarthyite tract, most vociferously by the French Communist critic George Sadoul. As the magic of dubbing transformed *Big Jim McClain* into a movie about heroin smuggling (at least in Italy), so French subtitles would render *Pickup on South Street* a more palatable thriller also about illicit narcotics, locally known as *Le Port de la Drogue*.

If demonstrating the movie's arbitrary premise, this transformation also deprives it of its urgency—not to mention Fuller's audacity in investing the familiar world of comic books and pulp fiction with the political anxiety of the mid-twentieth century. Then in production, his follow-up *Hell and High Water*—CinemaScope applied to a back-lot submarine engaged in a top secret mission to thwart an unspecified nation's scheme to drop an atomic bomb on Korea and blame the United States for the attack—would be the quintessential Cold War cartoon.

Lambasting the movie as "preposterous and irresponsible," Bosley Crowther was particularly annoyed that Fuller's "fantastic yarn" was

> introduced by a foreword, which gives the impression that what follows is literal truth. In the fall of last year, says a narrator, "the White House announced that an atomic bomb of foreign origin had been exploded somewhere outside the United States."
>
> "Shortly afterwards," the narrator continues, "the Atomic Energy Commission indicated that this atomic reaction had apparently originated in a remote

---

11. In this, Skip is actually close to McCarthy, who, as Richard Rovere notes, "never thought positively" of but "denounced the very institutions that are customarily thought of as the fortresses of American conformity: the Army, the Protestant clergy, the press, the two major parties, the civil service." McCarthy "never affected the pieties of a Dwight Eisenhower," Rovere wrote.

> He made little pretense to religiosity or to any species of moral rectitude. He sought to manipulate only the most barbaric symbols of "Americanism" . . . never motherhood or the love of a man for a cocker spaniel. . . . He was inner-directed. He was closer to the hipster than to the Organization Man.

area in North Pacific waters, somewhere between the northern tip of the Japanese Islands and the Arctic Circle. This is the story of that explosion."

In fact, Crowther was quoting a hastily changed introduction; the release print dropped references to the White House and AEC.

Hell and High Water was banned as anti-Communist in France, dismissed by David Platt as "brutally insulting to the People's Republic of China" (presumed to be the unnamed nation), excoriated in *Hollywood Review* as a "new low in fraudulent war propaganda," and attacked by former FBI agent and current SAC employee William Parker, who, obviously lacking a sense of humor, cited it as an example of the continuing "Communist ability to influence what the public sees on the screen."[12]

After *Quo Vadis*: Onward Christian Soldier, Watch Out for *The Wild One*

The dawn of a new epoch inspires dreams of mythological origins, triggers visions of antiquity, and prompts collective fantasies of an imagined past. So it is with the movies, still in search of their lost audience.

Visions of disaster are incorporated in brash demonstrations of Hollywood might. Opening the same month *Collier's* magazine devoted its entire issue to World War III, *Quo Vadis* offered apocalypse entertainment: Rome burns! Panic in the Colusseum and the streets! Flaming death from the sky!!! Color runs riot and every set is overdressed. The cinema was once again a fairground attraction. On the last evening of September 1952, the new super-wide-screen technology known as Cinerama had its world premiere before an invited audience at New York's Broadway Theatre. In a front-page *New York Times* story, Bosley Crowther reported that, "with due account for the novelty of the system, it was evident that the distinguished gathering was as excited and thrilled by the spectacle presented as if it were seeing motion pictures for the first time." (They were also hearing something new, the huge semicircular screen complemented by the newfangled audio system known as stereophonic sound.)

This Is Cinerama was a glorified travelogue with attractions including a roller coaster ride, a helicopter tour of Niagara Falls, a bullfight, and the finale

---

12. According to *Variety*, Parker maintained that the movie's original, Pentagon-approved script used Soviet leader Georgi Malenkov as the villain, but Fox "hired a producer who was a member of several communist fronts to make the film. Said producer rejected the script because it cast Chiang Kai-shek in too favorable a light and because Siberia was used as a locale."

of *Aida*. While the first half had a global perspective, the film ended with a pro-longed patriotic celebration. Running for two years in New York, *This Is Cinerama* would eventually gross $20 million. Cinerama's general manager Merian C. Cooper announced that his longtime associate John Ford would be directing a Civil War epic in the new format. Ousted from MGM, Louis B. Mayer signed on as Cinerama's chairman and eventually became its largest single stock-holder. But cash flow was a problem, and Cinerama would not release its second feature until 1955.

Less than two months after *This Is Cinerama* wowed Broadway, the stereo-scopic color feature *Bwana Devil* had its premiere at two L.A. theaters, jump-starting a 3-D craze that would take hold in 1953 and continue through 1954. In early 1953, Twentieth Century-Fox announced that, beginning with its New Testament spectacular *The Robe*, all of the studio's features would be exclusively produced in their patented (and more practical) new wide-screen process Cin-emaScope.

Ancient world and Stone Age motion-picture industry reborn through the miracle of high technology—military might merges with Christianity and show business. The spectacle of power is the power to command excess, to create gi-gantic public displays of singing and dancing crowds. Even as *Quo Vadis* sides with the downtrodden Christians, the movie celebrates the imperial power that brought it into existence. God appears as pure radiance ("I am the way, the truth, and the light"), but Emperor Nero speaks for the studios when he main-tains that the people demand orgiastic parties, triumphal processions, and cruel sports—and declares that "the burning of Rome must be colossal."

A trend story *Time* published in late June 1953 declared that the megahits *Samson and Delilah*, *David and Bathsheba*, and *Quo Vadis* proved beyond doubt that biblical movies pay. For one thing, the "cast-of-thousands picture" is ideal for the wide screen; for another, it is thought to appeal to older moviegoers who might otherwise be inclined to stay home and watch TV. Such movies not only represented the world-historical, they were themselves events. *Quo Vadis* would be the third-highest-grossing picture in Hollywood history, behind *Gone with the Wind* and *The Birth of a Nation*. *David and Bathsheba* had only half the box office of *Samson and Delilah*, but that was enough to make it the top-grossing movie of 1951 and Fox's greatest hit.

By the summer of 1953, a dozen or more biblicals were reported to be in production: Cecil B. DeMille's remake of *The Ten Commandments*; a sequel to *The Robe*; *Pilate's Wife*, written by Clare Booth Luce before her appointment as U.S. ambassador to Italy; *The Galileans*; *The Holy Grail*; *Joseph and His Brethren*;

The Prodigal; The Story of Mary Magdalene; Queen of Sheba; Slaves of Babylon; and, Hollywood being Hollywood, three movies about Jezebel. *Salome,* directed by William Dieterle from a treatment Jesse Lasky Jr. supposedly knocked out over a weekend, was already in theaters, having opened in March 1953, during the week of the televised HUAC hearings. The story Norma Desmond imagined as her comeback featured Columbia's most valuable property, Rita Hayworth, in the title role.[13]

In the beginning was DeMille's *Samson and Delilah,* which he is filming during the making of *Sunset Boulevard,* when Norma visits him on the Paramount lot. DeMille cast Victor Mature and Hedy Lamarr in the title roles because, as he put it, "they embody in the public mind the essence of maleness and femininity." *Samson and Delilah* itself embodied the essence of ballyhoo. The movie revived the old-time religion of spectacle, stars, and sex (mixed with piety) perfected by DeMille in the silent era.

Variety hailed *Samson and Delilah* as a fabulous anachronism, "a fantastic picture for this era in its size, in its lavishness, in the corniness of the story-telling and in its old-fashioned technique." In an unmistakably contemporary touch, however, DeMille prefaced the movie with a speech in which he endorsed freedom and concluded the movie by reiterating Samson's "bold dream—liberty for his nation." Opening for Christmas 1949, *Samson and Delilah* too was a bold dream as well as a long struggle. DeMille conceived the project in the late 1930s and for a decade had himself ranched peacocks, gathering their molted feathers for Delilah's costume.

DeMille boasted that he was a stickler for accuracy, telling the *New York Times Magazine* that Paramount's property department had provided him with a genuine jawbone of an ass, which, he discovered, was a formidable weapon: "The double pronged mandible, he explained, waving his arm in vigorous illustration, could easily dispose of three men at a clip." A perfectionist, the filmmaker

---

13. The biblicals were imagined as censor-proof, surefire Sin-a-Rama. Although the hero of *David and Bathsheba* is guilty of adultery and murder and punished for neither, the Production Code could hardly object to the story. (Still, when the screenplay was first submitted to the Breen Office during the apocalyptic summer of 1950, it was initially rejected as "too lurid" in detailing the adultery, and David's "cynicism and irreligion" were deemed "highly offensive.") Hoping to assuage the Legion of Decency's concerns regarding a striptease (or "lascivious dance in a picture dealing with John the Baptist and Christ"), Columbia carefully consulted the Breen Office in the matter of Hayworth's outfit. The Legion of Decency nevertheless rated *Salome* "B" while the Los Angeles city council banned as indecent a billboard showing Hayworth mid-pirouette.

maintained that he had the temple toppled no less than three times until he got what he wanted. *Samson and Delilah* cost $3.2 million but returned $12 million—the number one box-office attraction of 1950 and the greatest success in Paramount's history, as well as one of the most heavily promoted. (The *New York Times* noted the ubiquitous posters that "brightly display a sleek siren embracing a bronzed and bulging athlete while fingering a knife behind her back.")

Well in advance of *Samson and Delilah*'s appearance, MGM had resuscitated a long-standing plan to remake Nobel Prize laureate Henryk Sienkiewicz's novel of imperial Rome, *Quo Vadis*. John Huston, who had left Warners for MGM and received the assignment to direct in early 1949, imagined Nero as a proto-Hitler and suggested that the persecution of the Christians was analogous to the Nazi persecution of Jews. Louis B. Mayer loathed the idea, but Dore Schary loved it, and Nicholas Schenck had his back.

Shooting was scheduled to start on July 1, 1949, in Rome with Gregory Peck as the Roman centurion Marcus Vinicius; Elizabeth Taylor as Lygia, the enslaved barbarian princess who converts him to Christianity; and Peter Ustinov as Nero. This would be the first Technicolor feature made in Italy—shot at the vast Cinecittà studio built by Mussolini, using $4 million worth of frozen lire plus another million dollars in blocked sterling (rental revenues that had to be spent abroad) to pay the requisite British actors. Huston and producer Arthur Hornblow had already spent $2 million when Peck came down with an eye infection and the project was shelved.

As 1949 ended, both Huston and Hornblow quit *Quo Vadis*, worn out by difficulties with the cast and the studio, and, in a decision made public the same day that MGM announced *The Next Voice You Hear*, Mayer took control, replacing Peck with Robert Taylor (who was to have played Nero's courtier Petronius in the 1939 version), hiring Motion Picture Alliance activist John Lee Mahin to patch together a new script, and bringing in the faithful warhorse Mervyn LeRoy to direct. LeRoy recognized his awesome responsibility. "As I was about to leave for Rome I called DeMille," he recalled. "'Master,' I said, using the form of address most of us reserved for him . . .'"

DeMille was not LeRoy's only spiritual guide. The Catholic Church assigned a Jesuit priest to the production as technical adviser. It was nearly midway through the Holy Year that had been declared by Pope Pius XII, and Rome was filled with pilgrims. The first day of shooting, May 22, 1950, Robert Taylor, Deborah Kerr (who had replaced Taylor as Lygia), and twelve others from the *Quo Vadis* production were given a private twenty-minute audience with the pope, who recalled his own visit to Hollywood in 1936. LeRoy, in fact, was enjoying his second audience with the pope, who had previously blessed his copy of the script. The *New Yorker*'s European correspondent blithely wrote of *Quo Vadis* as "a gigantic sunshine, celluloid, and Technicolor event that for months has been involving lions, bulls, Christian martyrs, pagan slaves, Max Baer's giant brother Buddy, Robert Taylor in a gold breastplate, ten thousand costumes, and a replica of the Circus Maximus."

The burning of Rome required twenty-four nights to film—twenty-one more than the wartime firebombing of Dresden. *Quo Vadis* was often reported to be the most expensive movie ever made and routinely conceptualized as a military operation; Ustinov, who deemed LeRoy's "vocational addiction to shouting the right of any Army commander," characterized it as such. *Quo Vadis* was a logistical tour de force requiring "enough costumes to outfit a small army," per *Time*. The *New York Herald Tribune* reported on the production as a Cold War adventure—"a transportation officer maneuvered a fleet of 22 passenger vehicles and up to 29 trucks as though he were flying the boys home from Berlin"—complete with cloak-and-dagger intrigue. Five of the sixty-three lions "had to be smuggled past Iron Curtain authorities in Vienna"—anticipating the plot of Elia Kazan's *Man on a Tightrope*.

The Korean War broke out in another theater during the fourteen months Commander LeRoy spent in Rome directing thirty thousand extras in what *Life* called "the most genuinely colossal movie you are likely to see for the rest of your lives." The war was slogging on when *Quo Vadis* had its world premiere on November 8, 1951, at the same Broadway theater that had showcased the 1912 version.

Quo Vadis begins where *Fort Apache* ends, with a file of marching soldiers. The same admiration for the military is tempered by a similar sense of postwar malaise: after three years of fighting against the Britons, Marcus returns to Rome. Falling for the beauteous Lygia, he finds himself embroiled in an "immortal conflict" between imperial Rome, where "the individual is at the mercy of the state," and Jesus Christ, the "rebel against the state" who "died to make men free." Rome is ruled by the mad dictator Nero, capable of purging his wife and mother, a neurotic crybaby with pronounced Hitlerian qualities. "People will believe any lie if it is fantastic enough," he boasts, and he is sufficiently megalomaniacal to present his campaign to scapegoat the Christians as a promise to "exterminate" them. The public feeding of Christians to the lions is a spectacular Auschwitz with women, children, and old people going to their deaths. Nero has aesthetic pretensions (referring to himself as the Artist Who Creates with Fire) and, like the Austrian carpet-biter, winds up ranting in the *führerbunker*.

The Christians do not hate Rome, just Nero, and even look forward to the marriage of church and state. Paul recognizes the importance of converting the super-patriotic Marcus to Christ: "If we could teach [him], we could teach the world." Indeed, *Quo Vadis* concludes, per MGM publicity, with the triumph of "Marcus and Lygia's faith" and the birth of the "Christian world." In the last scene, Marcus and his comrade Flavius watch Galba's army arrive. A general will be the new emperor. The decadent Nero is replaced by a military hero whose task is "to rebuild Roman and bring back Rome justice."

"Babylon, Egypt, Greece, Rome . . . what follows?" Flavius asks.

"A more permanent world, I hope, or a more permanent faith," replies Marcus. "One is not possible without the other."

Dwight Eisenhower could not have put it more succinctly.

The *New York Times* proclaimed *Quo Vadis* an instant anachronism: "the last of a cinematic species, the *super* super-colossal film." *Time* concurred. *Holiday* wrote, "All signs point to this picture being the last of the truly great spectacles"—a mode "due to become as obsolete as the Roman Empire whose antics it so lovingly commemorates." *Variety*, however, offered a more realistic (and optimistic) assessment.

> *Quo Vadis* is a b.o. blockbuster. No two ways about its economic horizons. It's right up there with *Birth of a Nation* and *Gone with the Wind*. . . . This is a super-spectacle in all its meaning. At a time when the industry was perhaps asking itself with the same self-examination as the title—"whither goest thou?"—Metro shows the way.

Forward into the past.

Variety reported Church of Christ parishioners demonstrating outside the Los Angeles theater showing *David and Bathsheba*, protesting the representation of biblical figures as well as the involvement of "known Reds" Gregory Peck, who played David, and screenwriter Philip Dunne. Meanwhile, some Communists were pondering the ancient world. Novelist Howard Fast's self-published *Spartacus* had sold 48,000 copies in just three months—an ancient freedom fighter reentering history, just in time for the 1952 American presidential election.

Progress was where you found it. David Platt saw something in *Quo Vadis* that he felt had been completely overlooked by the New York reviewers—a "timely story" in which an "arrogant and ruthless" ruling class persecuted a "subversive movement." Quoting at length from Engels's introduction to *The Class Wars in*

France, the *Daily Worker* critic concluded that "there is so much food for thought" in *Quo Vadis*, he was "tempted to suggest" leafleting Broadway with his analysis, "noting the parallel between witch-hunting a thousand years ago and today." The *New York Post* reported that *Salome*'s Hollywood premiere audience was convulsed when a "be-bop kid" greeted the sight of John's head on a platter by yelling, "Dig that crazy dessert!" But, echoing Platt's thoughts on *Quo Vadis*, published over a year earlier, and reflecting on the current "thought-control trials at Foley Square," the *Daily Worker* spotted substance amid the nonsense. "Interesting parallels can be found between the persecution of the Christians shown in the film and the political jailings in the United States today. . . . John the Baptist is accused of sedition and inciting the people to violence. If he were speaking out today he probably would be tried under the Smith Act." And Jesus might have been sent to the electric chair.

Empire brought imperial responsibilities. The Cold War began with America taking charge of Greece and securing Italy. Now the faraway land once known as Persia required attention. "If the Communists grab Iran," *Time* had warned in early 1951, "they will get an asset far more valuable than Korea."

Another ancient world epic unfolding: Iran's pro-American leader, General Ali Razmara, was shot dead on March 7, 1951, by a fanatical twenty-six-year-old Crusader of Islam as he attended a funeral at a mosque in Tehran's Bazaar Quarter. "Why do you give the country to foreigners so that I must do this deed?" the killer shouted. Persian nationalists had embarked on a struggle against the British for control of the kingdom's buried riches—the so-called "blood of the eagles." This, the *New York Times* declared, was "The Land Where Anything Can Happen." That spring the Majlis—the legislative body that the *Times* described as a chamber of "shrieking neurotics and table-thumping demagogues"—voted to nationalize the oil industry. Then someone assassinated the shah's prime minister. In his place, the Majlis elected the venerable Muhammad Mossadegh, a wealthy landowner who had served in the Majlis since 1915.

Nationalization went into effect on May Day 1951. *Time* described a demonstration in Majlis Square with 35,000 people cheering the "heroic nations of the USSR." Some months later, *Time* named Mossadegh its 1951 Man of the Year, although the Iranian prime minister's name was not revealed on the magazine cover, only in the explanation that it was he who "oiled the wheels of chaos." Inside, Mossadegh was described as a "dizzy old wizard," given to spells of "weeping [and] fainting."

Both the Iranians and the British appealed to America for help. Mossadegh, who had taken to wearing the aba, or "robe of spiritual leadership," journeyed to faraway Washington and debated the British at the International Court of Justice at the Hague. In July 1952, he resigned but, after street riots rocked Tehran, was reappointed. In October, Mossadegh broke diplomatic relations with Great Britain; throughout 1952, the old wizard was routinely characterized in *Time* and the *New York Times* as a dictator. Was he a prophet or buffoon, a geriatric Herod or would-be Nero?

Anxiety mounted. In March 1953, *Newsweek* anticipated what would be called the Domino Theory in proposing Iran as the first domino:

> If Iran goes, then Pakistan—where the Reds have done a remarkable job of infiltration—would probably be next. This would isolate India, probably topple the rest of the Middle East within months, and would mean that the West would have to make the terrible decision whether to begin a fighting war or accept the loss of the cold war.

Who would break the spell? Some rallied around the handsome young monarch His Imperial Majesty, the King of Kings, Mohammad Reza Shah Pahlavi, Light of the Aryans, whom the British had placed on the throne as a twenty-one-year-old boy when Iran was occupied in 1941. Others supported the grim old mullah Ayatollah Sayed Abolghassem Kashani, speaker of the Majlis. On the last day of February 1953, bazaars shut down and a screaming mob filled the streets. According to the *New York Times*, "a notorious Kashani follower known as 'The Brainless One'" drove a jeep into Mossadegh's residence as the premier fled out the back in his pajamas. Yet days later Mossadegh was back, agitating for a republic.

July 21, 1953: a hundred thousand Iranian Communists stage the largest popular demonstration in the nation's history. August 16, the shah attempts to dismiss Prime Minister Mossadegh with a midnight coup. Mossadegh refuses to go; the shah panics and flees the country. The next day, mobs topple his statues and those of his father.

By the time the shah has arrived in Rome, Communist rioters have invaded the bazaar, battling the police with metal-tipped wooden spears. American diplomats accuse Mossadegh of losing control and threaten to abandon Tehran unless order is restored. But no sooner has Mossadegh quieted the city than another mob takes to the streets. August 19, a rumor spreads that Mossadegh had been replaced by the shah's choice, General Fazollah Zahedi. The army mutinies, the old wizard collapses, and his foreign minister is reportedly "torn to pieces" by the mob. August 22, the King of Kings returns in triumph to celebrate the fall of his "evil" adversary. The new prime minister is the onetime Nazi sympathizer General Zahedi. Who is the hero of this scenario?

Only weeks after the armistice is implemented in Korea, the Eisenhower administration has scored a second foreign policy coup as if by magic. ("In a manner fitting in well with the Christmas spirit, Iran and Britain have now formally resumed diplomatic relations," the *New York Times* editorializes on December 25.) There are no fingerprints, although, even as the coup was in progress, *Pravda* published a bitter denunciation of its presumed backstage organizer, New Jersey police official Norman Schwarzkopf, onetime trainer of the Iranian gendarmerie and father of the future Desert Storm hero. Some fifteen months later, the *Saturday Evening Post* will publish a piece on the restoration of the shah titled "The Mysterious Doings of CIA [*sic*]." Largely unremarked upon at the time, the piece was planted by the Central Intelligence Agency itself.

The hits keep coming. *Quo Vadis* is now the third-biggest grosser in movie history, but, by the end of 1953, it will be surpassed by *The Robe*, Twentieth Century-Fox's adaptation of Lloyd Douglas's 1942 bestseller. In her wisdom, Norma Desmond declared that it was "the pictures that got small." So the weapons in the anti-television jihad include sex, religion, and screen size. Ancient-world spectaculars are rarely less than three hours long, and such extravagant time wasting is complemented by vast space expansion. *The Robe*, which has been in the works since the mid-1940s, is the first movie to be shot in Cinema-Scope. (Two months later, *Quo Vadis* will be rereleased in a widescreen format.)[14]

---

14. Like *Quo Vadis*, *The Robe* is rooted in the antifascist struggle of World War II, pitting Christian "peace and brotherhood" against Roman "aggression and slavery," as personified by the mad tyrant Caligula. Soon after the novel's publication, producer Frank Ross paid $100,000 for the screen rights, entering into a financing and distribution deal with RKO. The picture was budgeted at $4 million. Mervyn LeRoy was set to direct; Albert Maltz, who'd written the Ross-produced Popular Front short *The House I Live In*, went to work on the adaptation during the summer of 1945. Production was delayed by wartime shortages and postwar strikes, and then there were other problems after the October 1947 HUAC hearings. The following spring, RKO's new owner Howard Hughes canceled the project altogether and demanded Ross repay the studio a million dollars. Ross battled Hughes until May 1952, when Darryl F. Zanuck purchased the rights for Twentieth Century-Fox. For Zanuck, *The Robe* was a logical follow-up to Fox's *David and Bathsheba* (as well as MGM's *Quo Vadis*), and Philip Dunne, who'd written *David and Bathsheba*, was hired to rework the Maltz script. Dunne did not know that Maltz had written the script because Fox made their interest in *Quo Vadis* conditional on his name being removed. According to Maltz, Frank Ross visited him in Cuernavaca, Mexico, where he'd moved after his release from prison, to ask that he waive screen credit. Dunne regarded *The Robe* as an anti-totalitarian allegory; attempting to interest Zanuck in an adaptation of *1984*, he wrote the studio boss in June 1953, "We could make another *The Robe*, set in the future instead of the past."

As reported on the *New York Times*'s front page, *The Robe* has its world premiere on September 16, 1953, at the Roxy before 6,500 invited guests. Nearly as many jam the intersection of Seventh Avenue and Fiftieth Street. Klieg lights sweep the sky, and just before the show begins, Broadway movie houses flash their marquee lights in navy code for "good luck." The drapery parts, and then, in the opening image, another red velvet curtain slowly opens to reveal a spectacular panorama of ancient Rome. *Variety* thought that the Roxy's sixty-five-by-twenty-five foot curved screen seemed to "meet the audience. The slave market, the freeing of the Greek slave from the torture rack, the Christians in the catacombs, the dusty plains of Galilee, the Roman court splendor, and that finale 'chase' (with the four charging white steeds head-on into the camera creating a most effective 3-D illusion) are standouts."

So too are the electric-blue marble floors and characters clad in flaming orange cloaks, the indoor swimming pools and off-center compositions that flaunt a surplus of empty space. Wax museum of imperial clutter: "Rome—Master of the Earth!" Small wonder that the military tribune Marcellus Gallio (Richard Burton) is miffed upon being transferred, thanks to the machinations of his erotic rival Caligula (Jay Robinson), to a garrison on the Palestinian frontier: "Where's Jerusalem?" he asks his father, Senator Gallio. The senator, who is trying to reinstate the Republic, warns him that the inhabitants are "a stiff-necked, riotous people always on the verge of rebellion."

The PaxAmericanArama amplified the audience's sense of living in cosmic times. In the midst of *The Robe*, the emperor Tiberius muses on the tale of an obscure Galilean carpenter who has been crucified and declares that, when the end of the empire comes, "this is how it will start. . . . Man's desire to be free [is] the greatest madness of all." Then he orders Marcellus to infiltrate the underground meetings held by the carpenter's followers: "I want names, Tribune, names of all the disciples, of every man and woman who subscribes to this treason." Marcellus passes Jesus entering Jerusalem even as his servant Demetrius (Victor Mature) bumps into Judas in the aftermath of betrayal. Assigned to crucifixion detail, Marcellus is simply inscribed into the Passion, gambling beneath the cross for Christ's robe.

History unfolds, and You Are There. Writing on the Douglas novel, Edmund Wilson had observed the continuity established by treating antiquity as familiar. Both *Quo Vadis* and *The Robe* focus on Roman soldiers returned from the battlefield and readjusting to imperial life; in *David and Bathesheba*, the Hebrew king similarly suffers from the stress of his old battles. There is also the sense of a "stalemated war" (albeit in Rabbah rather than Korea).

Reviewing *Quo Vadis*, the *New York Post* had commented on the oddness of Robert Taylor's American speech among all the British performers, but that was the point. Hollywood epics naturally superimpose the situation of the American Revolution upon the ancient world, refracted through the lens of the new Cold War imperium. The effete rulers use the King's English; the oppressed are not only God's chosen but, as the *Saturday Review* wrote of Taylor, "defiantly Midwestern in manner and accent." Rita Hayworth's blond Salome is a good girl who does her Dance of the Seven Veils to *save* John the Baptist. The movie ends with this wholesome child and her crypto-Christian Roman boyfriend attending the Sermon on the Mount. They share the desire, as Christ's disciple Miriam declares in *The Robe*, to build a "new world."

In *The Robe*, as in *Quo Vadis*, the Christians—or, as Caligula describes them, a "secret party of seditionists who call themselves Christian"—are persecuted. At one story conference during the summer of 1952, Zanuck proposed having Caligula appoint Gallio to head a Senate Committee on Un-Roman Activities, where he would be placed in the position of investigating his own son. This subplot never appeared in the script, although, once the Christians are put on trial, Caligula offers to spare Marcellus if he will recant. Instead, Marcellus denounces the emperor and seals his fate. Although not herself a Christian, Diana (Jean Simmons) rejects Caligula and elects to die with her beloved Marcellus. Like the Rosenbergs, the couple march proudly to eternity. Caligula's shrieks are drowned by a sudden chorus of "hallelujah"s and Rome dissolves into clouds and sky.

A week after the New York world premiere, *The Robe* opens in Chicago and Los Angeles, where the Hollywood Chamber of Commerce has declared a four-day festival. In order to secure the picture's only Southern California run, Grauman's Chinese has refurbished not only its equipment but its seats and lobby. By the end of 1953 A.D., *The Robe* has grossed $16.5 million, despite the fact that barely a quarter of American theaters are equipped for CinemaScope, and liberal producer Stanley Kramer issues an urgent bulletin: *The Wild One*. The movie stars the most modern actor in Hollywood, Marlon Brando. As the ads warn, "That 'Streetcar' Man Has a New Desire."

Brando, whom *Time* would term "the supreme portrayer of morose juvenility," was an even more blatant construction than the year's other blossoming star, Marilyn Monroe, playing *The Wild One*'s eponymous bad boy in the full panoply of butch character armor—studded leather jacket, greasy T-shirt, blue jeans, engineer boots, visor cap, aviator shades, and, when visible, sullen glare.

The barbarians were at the gates. (Even then, Douglas Sirk was shooting *Sign of the Pagan* with Jack Palance as a bizarrely neurotic Attila the Hun.) Directed from John Paxton's screenplay by Laslo Benedek, *The Wild One* dramatized the terrifying night when a marauding motorcycle gang of disaffected youths took over a small Northern California town. Columbia's advertising campaign positioned the movie as part of an ongoing struggle against juvenile delinquency—which, as the Korean War lost its urgency, had begun to rival Communism as a national obsession.

But unlike the scarifying drug-addled *Teenage Menace*, released outside the MPAA Production Code earlier in the year (and banned in New York State), *The Wild One* was not an exploitation film. It was made by serious men: Kramer and Benedek previously collaborated in adapting Arthur Miller's *Death of a Salesman* for the screen. (Benedek, forty-six, had studied psychiatry in Vienna and worked at UFA before going into exile; he was familiar not only with the Nazis, who haunt *The Wild One* in various guises, but likely with the angel-of-death motorcyclists of Jean Cocteau's 1950 film *Orphée*.) *The Wild One* was a scoop—albeit one somewhat delayed in reaching the screen. Inspiration came from the 1947 incident in which three thousand cyclists converged on Hollister, California, for a July 4 road rally and wound up staging a bacchanal on Main Street. Many of the bikers were restless World War II veterans, newly demobilized and looking for action. Nationally reported, the Hollister incident was used as the basis for Frank Rooney's antifascist allegory "The Cyclists' Raid," published in the January 1951 *Harper's.*

Attuned to Rooney's message, Hollywood lefties were the first to see its movie potential. According to screenwriter Jean Rouverol, the idea came up in early 1951 when she and her husband Hugo Butler were visiting the jailed Dalton Trumbo's wife Cleo at the Trumbo family's Tehachapi Mountain ranch. Butler had fronted two movies for Trumbo, *The Prowler* and *He Ran All the Way*.[15]

---

15. Released some two and a half years before *The Wild One* roared onto the scene, *He Ran All the Way* marked the disintegration of Hollywood's old left even as it prophesied the antiheroic youth cinema to come. John Garfield plays a confused, impulsive punk who kills a cop in a botched robbery, picks up a naive young woman (Shelley Winters), and holes up in her family's apartment, holding them hostage for several days before dying miserably in the gutter. The movie was produced by Garfield and made by a quartet of Hollywood Reds: the director, John Berry—like Hugo Butler—left the country ahead of a subpoena and the movie's spring 1951 opening, ten months after it was shot during the apocalyptic summer of 1950. The other credited writer, Guy Endore, was blacklisted. The movie was released six weeks after Garfield's HUAC testimony; just before it went into production, Garfield had been named in *Red Channels*. Suffering with frightening intensity, the actor makes no attempt to woo the audience. If his torment barely seems like acting, the paranoia he projects on-screen was totally justified.

"While we were there," Rouverol recalled, Cleo brought their attention to "a wonderful story" in *Harper's*.

> I read it, and I almost died of excitement, it was so good. Hugo got [Trumbo's agent] Ingo Preminger to take an option on it, and Ingo gave it to Carl Foreman, who took it to Stanley Kramer, who said, "Yes, we'll do it as soon as Hugo is free." But when things got hot, Ingo notified us that what Kramer really wanted to do was to buy Hugo out for three thousand dollars. Would he sign a quit claim? Foreman rode over on his bicycle with a check for three thousand dollars. This became *The Wild One*.

Foreman had just been served by HUAC. Butler, who was dodging an earlier HUAC subpoena, took the money and left for Mexico. The original script, titled *The Cyclists' Raid*, emphasized the antihero's class envy and alienation; after Kramer broke with Foreman in October 1951, the script was developed by Ben Maddow, who had worked for Kramer on the *High Noon* screenplay. In early 1953, Maddow too was subpoenaed and, proving an unfriendly witness, left Kramer's employ.[16]

Although Kramer announced *The Cyclists' Raid* in January 1952, with Benedek attached as director, and approached Brando the following September, it was not until December that a script was submitted to the Breen Office. The MPAA deemed the script unacceptable, requiring Kramer and his new screenwriter John Paxton, best known for his credit on *Crossfire*, to meet with the MPAA staff through the end of 1952. In February 1953, while the movie was in production, Louella Parsons reported that Kramer would not be able to export his film, now called *The Wild One*, presumably because it was too un-American. On the domestic front, Johnson Motors—the Pasadena-based distributor of Triumph motorcycles—filed a complaint with Eric Johnston.

The motorcycle nightmare movie was now known as *Hot Blood* but reverted to *The Wild One* before its world premiere, December 30, 1953, at New York's Palace along with eight acts of vaudeville.

The Wild One's problems with the Breen Office are implicit in the movie's opening disclaimer: "This is a shocking story. . . . It is a public challenge." Adult perspective is amply inscribed—and defied—throughout. The members of the

---

16. Maddow appeared before HUAC on March 28, 1953, and took the Fifth Amendment. He was subsequently blacklisted but continued to write scripts with Philip Yordan as his front. (One of these may or may not have been *Johnny Guitar*.)

Black Rebels motorcycle gang are, from the onset, constructed as bad children; the first scene, in which they disrupt an innocent road rally, pushes them into the viewer's face and asks the audience, what are you going to do about it?

These kids need discipline. (When challenged by a cop to move on, they tauntingly chant, "We want to watch the thrilling races, Daddy.") Run out of one town, the Black Rebels descend upon another, where they're soon brawling on Main Street and, by nightfall, making a mockery of law and order. The Black Rebels precipitate a crisis in authority. "You let something like this go and anything goes," an old man says, criticizing the cop. *The Wild One*'s premise resembles that of *High Noon*, complete with rhyming high-angle shot of Main Street. For *Life*, *The Wild One* suggested a global situation, teaching the familiar lessons that "chaos ensues when law and order waver even for an instant in the face of organized hooliganism." Is the threat from fascists, Reds, or craven conformists? Like gutless Hadleyville, this unnamed town is the realm of cowardly cops, greedy businessmen, and sadistic bullies. Only here there is no Gary Cooper. Once the gang takes over, the local vigilantes get ready to reassert control.[17]

Time described the Black Rebels as "a bop-sent, trouble-hungry 'sickle club' of teenage boys." Neither Brando nor his wilder, more degenerate rival, played by Lee Marvin, are teenagers—both actors were pushing thirty—but there's no mistaking their adolescent protest. Whatever age, they embody a generational revolt. The town has few young people, other than the pretty waitress played by Mary Murphy, who works at the town diner, and a somewhat bolder girl who asks Brando just what he's rebelling against. ("Whaddaya got?" is the celebrated answer.)

Brando is at once tougher and more sensitive than his followers. Employing a form of verbal bebop, this eerily soft-spoken hoodlum communicates in odd phrases and fragmented sentences. The key to Brando's mystery, Molly Haskell would point out years later, is his inarticulate eloquence. Brando improvised much of his dialogue and often speaks with vaguely African American cadences. "Man, you're too square. I have to straighten you out," he tells Murphy when she naively asks if the Black Rebels go to picnics. "You don't go to any one special place. . . . You just go. The idea is to wail, to make some jive." *Mad*'s parody of Brando echoes each instance of his character's punctuating "I mean" with a nerdy background character repeatedly asking, "Whadz he mean?"

---

17. Scenes of vigilante violence suggest that in an earlier incarnation *The Wild One* might have been intended as an attack on mob violence similar to Joseph Losey's *The Lawless* or another 1950 release by a soon-blacklisted director, Cy Endfield's *The Sound of Fury*. Endfield's movie is more radical than Losey's in that the men who are lynched are criminals rather than persecuted innocents.

The ineffectual cop (Robert Keith), who is also Murphy's father, is weak because he attempts to find a rational solution. He wants to "talk it over" with the
Wild One, who simply refuses to talk. Murphy had already equated the Brando
character with her father, insisting that both were fakes—pretending to be
something they're not. Yet there is nothing fake about the Brando character's
hostility toward the police. Brando's attitude seems to deform reality even as the
jagged rhythms of his line readings noticeably disconcert the other actors. No
less than his character, Brando is the star of his own personal movie, creating a
new scenario apart from the actual script.

Throughout *The Wild One*, people wonder just what the Black Rebels are
trying to prove. In a sense, the gang signifies the arbitrary nature of everyday
social intercourse. The bikers put a new spin on common words like "chick,"
"kicks," and "crazy;" they don't confine their secret handshakes to the Elks Lodge
and refuse to recognize normal rules of conduct (like saying "thank you").
Many of their crimes are sign crimes. Quasi-police uniforms have been drafted
to serve disorder by men who dress like proles but eschew the work ethic. The
sound of revved-up motorcycle engines, heard well before the Black Rebels are
seen on-screen, heralds the opening of the movie and amplifies the ongoing semiotic noise throughout.

The normals are confounded. This is a free country, and the bikers have
money—so where do you draw the line between the Black Rebels' mad impulse
behavior ("Oh man, we just gonna go!") and the town's desire for law and order?
What's appeasement and what's fascism? Can you lock someone up for looking
weird or is it like, live and let live? And what *are* Brando and his gang, anyway?
At the moment of *The Wild One*'s appearance, there was no vocabulary to describe such creatures, although the *New York Times* made the attempt:

> Given to jive or be-bop lingo and the grotesque costumes and attitudes of the
> "crazy" cognoscenti, these "wild ones" resent discipline and show an aggressive
> contempt for common decency and the police. Reckless and vandalistic, they
> live for sensations, nothing more—save perhaps the supreme sensation of defy-
> ing the normal world.

A French review was even more explicit, analyzing the movie under the rubric
"The Martians Have Landed." More would follow.[18]

---

18. As *The Wild One* intimated a counterculture to come, the CIA unwittingly provided a potential sacrament. It was while *The Wild One* was in production that the agency initiated a two-
year-long series of experiments involving the hallucinogenic drug LSD-25. The drug seemed a
possible weapon in what the new CIA director Allen Dulles termed "the battle for men's

Marilyn Ascends, Joe Goes Down

When the force called McCarthyism and the institution known as TV first collided in late summer 1953, it was the latter that prevailed. Sunday night, September 6, gossip columnist Walter Winchell revealed the sensational news that two days earlier, in a closed HUAC session, the biggest star on TV had been confronted with evidence of a flaming past. The redhead was a Red!

There could be no doubt that the performer to whom Winchell referred was Lucille Ball. In the two years since her situation comedy *I Love Lucy* ascended to the show business stratosphere, the forty-two-year-old erstwhile glamour girl had become, in effect, television personified. Nearly 70 percent of America's TV sets were tuned to *I Love Lucy* for the show in which the character Lucy gave birth—which aired the very day that the actress also became a mother—and all but upstaged Dwight D. Eisenhower's inauguration. A few months later, Lucille (or was it Lucy?) and her baby graced the first issue of *TV Guide*.

With a similarly blurred identity, Ball appeared before HUAC in the guise of zany scatterbrain Lucy Ricardo. Unlike Rosaura Revueltas or Dorothy Comingore or Ethel Rosenberg, this lady was not for burning. She named no names— except for that of her grandfather, an equally wacky character for whose sake, she explained, she had registered as a Communist back in 1936. The press frenzy lasted a week. Lucy's ratings held, her sponsor remained true, and so did CBS, not to mention the Spiritual Leader of our Times.[19]

On November 23, Lucy and husband Desi Arnaz (a.k.a. Ricky Ricardo) gave a command performance at the White House. The next day, Senator McCarthy suggested, for the first time, that the Eisenhower administration was soft on Communism.

The war in Korea ends, the Red Tide recedes, and America turns inward, combing the beach for new icons. The president grants permission for his portrayal as

---

minds," three days before authorizing the clandestine program known as MK-ULTRA. CIA operatives dosed federal prisoners as well as unwitting colleagues with LSD, precipitating the breakdown and eventual suicide of army scientist Frank Olson in late 1953, and carried out tests on unknowing civilians in San Francisco throughout 1955. By the early 1960s, some 1,500 members of the armed forces had served as experimental subjects.

19. Ball's actual associations are vague. In 1943, aspiring screenwriter Rena M. Vale told the Tenney committee that six years earlier she attended a Communist "new members class" in a house in West Hollywood. There, "an elderly man informed us we were guests of the screen actress Lucille Ball, and showed us various pictures, books, and other objects to establish that fact, and stated she was glad to loan her home." Ball herself was not present.

a young West Point cadet in John Ford's upcoming Columbia production *The Long Gray Line*.[20]

Among the war's other greatest beneficiaries is a Twentieth Century-Fox starlet—pinup queen Marilyn Monroe, who, having established her incandescent platinum hair, moistly parted lips, rounded bottom, thirty-nine-inch bust, and artfully dazed innocence as the defining attributes of an American love goddess, elects to visit those remaining GIs who man the parapets of the Free World.

HUAC inadvertently helped blur the distinction between the actual Lucille Ball and the television character Lucy Ricardo. During that same 1953–54 season, the actress Marilyn Monroe becomes indistinguishable from her public image—so much so that whatever she might do, she will never seem out of character. Monroe's bombshell performance in Henry Hathaway's *Niagara*, followed by the back-to-back release of the comedies *Gentlemen Prefer Blondes* and *How to Marry a Millionaire*, directed by Howard Hawks and Jean Negulesco respectively, makes her the nation's number-one female box-office attraction for 1953.

At the year's end, the twenty-seven-year-old actress graces the cover of *Playboy*'s maiden issue, while Willem de Kooning is action-painting his own abstract expressionist *Marilyn*. It is the deadly siren of *Niagara*—a force of nature, per the movie's title—that will provide Andy Warhol with the basis for his multiple Marilyns, whereas the proto–pop art of *Blondes* and *Millionaire* presented Marilyn in the cartoon role of "Marilyn Monroe." Yet there is no particular movie that can be considered the definitive Monroe vehicle. As the first movie star to project herself directly onto the screen of life—what will come to be called the media—Marilyn anticipates the further transformation of American politics that already has been intuited by Washington's master of revels, Joseph McCarthy. She is, however, far more benign.

Monroe is one embodiment of Pax Americana and her death in 1962 will herald the onset of a new era. Although she lives her life in the show-business stratosphere, she seems as though she could be available to any man. "Sex might be difficult and dangerous with others, but ice cream with her," Norman Mailer will write. Marilyn is milk and honey, the representative of a sweet, carnal democracy, a vision of abundance for the average Joe. To one auto-industry observer, Chrysler's newly elongated, blatantly forward-thrusting, gaudily two-toned design is so exciting yet accessible that it suggested "Marilyn Monroe as a housewife."

---

20. The young Eisenhower is played by Ford regular Harry Carey Jr., with Elbert Steele (with his back to the camera) as the president to whom the tale of Sgt. Marty Maher's half-century career as the academy's athletic director is recounted. This epic celebration of U.S. military traditions, which opened in New York on February 10, 1955, was Ford's first CinemaScope production.

Only weeks after *Playboy*'s glorification, Marilyn commandeers every tabloid front page in America by marrying the greatest of baseball players, Yankee center fielder Joe DiMaggio. (Appropriately, DiMaggio fell in love with Monroe after seeing her photo in a newspaper.) *Life* proclaims it the Merger of Two Worlds: "Two huge fan clubs found their differing interests focused, for the moment, on the same event." The stars had shrouded their plans "with the secrecy of an atomic test, [slipping] into San Francisco's city hall unnoticed." Still, an eyewitness account is broadcast over a national radio hookup—the judge who pronounced the couple man and wife is first shoved aside by crazed reporters and then mobbed by them.

Marilyn and Joe plan to honeymoon in Japan. Even as their plane approaches Tokyo, an American general aboard invites them to entertain the American forces in Korea. DiMaggio is unenthusiastic, but, according to C. Roberts Jennings, then a reporter for *Pacific Stars and Stripes*, "The announcement of [Monroe's] visit spread like wild grass fire across the tense neutral zone. . . . Some [GIs] actually wept. Others froze in a sort of yearning silence." Marilyn will later tell Jennings that she owed her success to the war: "When I first started in I had several little parts at Fox. Then the letters began pouring in from Korea and my studio was so impressed they began to give me wonderful parts." Thanks to the soldiers, her fan mail "jumped from 50 letters to 5,000 letters a week."

February 16, 1954: Marilyn arrives in Korea. Her entrance is magnificent. She asks the helicopter pilot to swoop down over the troops in the field so she can wave to them. Lying on the helicopter floor, Marilyn extends her upper torso fully outside the bay (a pair of hefty enlisted men holding her legs) as the chopper repeatedly strafes the front with glamour. The star, who has never before played to a live audience, pulls together an act out of numbers from *Gentlemen Prefer Blondes* and *How to Marry a Millionaire*. Monroe's posthumous memoir, *My Story*, would describe her experience waiting in the wings before the first performance. As the roar of the crowd drowns out the music, an agitated officer rushes her out onstage, afraid that the audience will riot; at the last of Monroe's ten performances (during which she entertains an estimated hundred thousand troops), the men *do* riot. Forced to wait for hours in subzero cold, some six thousand members of the Forty-fifth Division stomp down the barriers and throw rocks to clear the stage for Marilyn. The next morning she returns to wish them good-bye, but instead uses *eleewah*, Korean for "come here," thus precipitating another mad stampede.

Marilyn leaves Korea with a mild case of pneumonia and the sense that it was the best thing that ever happened to her—she tells DiMaggio that until then she had never felt like a movie star. Back in Hollywood, Marilyn confides in gossip columnist Sidney Skolsky that "for the first time in my life I had the feeling that the people seeing me were accepting me and liking me." The image of Monroe performing for ecstatic troops is transmitted around the globe as the inspector general of the Armed Forces Far East launches a full-scale investigation into the chaotic behavior that greeted her Korean serenade.

New York Times military correspondent Hanson W. Baldwin irately juxtaposes Marilyn's tour with Senator McCarthy's investigation: while the senator "demeaned his position by bullying and browbeating officers of the Army . . . the weaknesses in service morale [were] epitomized by the visit of Miss Monroe to Korea. On two occasions during the visit of the motion picture actress, troops rioted mildly and behaved like bobby-soxers in Times Square." It seems surprising McCarthy didn't pick up on this: such unruly conduct surely "must have delighted the Communists and all who hope for signs of degradation and decline in the United States."[21]

Throughout the summer of 1953, Senator McCarthy had restlessly gone from one abortive investigation to the next. He announced that he would subpoena

---

21. Monroe disturbed the peace again when *The Seven Year Itch* started shooting in New York City later that year, in September. Illuminated by a blaze of publicity, she posed, legs akimbo, above a subway grating so that the rush of air billowed her skirt nearly to the level of her stolidly haltered breasts, thus expressing a paradoxical mixture of childlike naïveté and ecstatic sexual display. There were fifteen takes, shot at two A.M. on the corner of Fifty-first Street and Lexington Avenue for a crowd of a hundred photographers and reporters, several thousand cheering onlookers, and one irate husband. (October 4, it was announced that the Monroe-DiMaggio marriage was over.)

The climax of Marilyn's career as a "studio-manufactured" celebrity, *The Seven Year Itch* was essentially the pretext for the publicity photograph—or photographs. Scores of images were generated during the display, which the Catholic weekly *America* labeled "New York's Disgrace." They rippled out along the wire services, circulating throughout the world for nearly a year before coalescing the following June in the form of a four-story cardboard Marilyn clutching her skirts above Times Square: Venus rising from the foam of Mechanical Reproduction.

"Even the *Daily Worker* doesn't publish sexy pictures which help erode the moral basis of American democracy," *America* complained. But, if the *Worker* was the one place where you would be guaranteed not to see Marilyn, David Platt *had* praised Marilyn's progressive consciousness. (Did he know of her youthful association with the Actors Lab?) In July 1953, the Worker critic noted that the star "jolted the press with a moving plea for peace in Korea.

It happened a day or two before the truce was signed when the actress stopped over in Seattle on her way to Canada to make a movie. At a press conference, a reporter facetiously asked her if she had a message for the people of Seattle.

She replied gravely: "I was given a very nice reception here and I appreciate it. If I have a message for the people of Seattle, I guess it would be that the war in Korea will end so that the men there can come home. More than anything that is what we should be thinking about. Thank you for asking me if I had a message."

Thank *you*, Comrade Marilyn!

former president Harry Truman and force him to reveal a classified list of suspected spies. He held a one-day hearing on a supposed conspiracy to assassinate . . . himself. At various times, McCarthy proposed to probe the Atomic Energy Commission, the Central Intelligence Agency, and the Pentagon— strenuously demanding that the army turn over to him its "confidential files on loyalty and security." As the year waned, the senator investigated allegations of "subversion and espionage" in various defense plants; it was while probing the Monmouth Signal Corps (where, he maintained, a wartime spy ring organized by the late Julius Rosenberg might yet be in operation) that he happened on the case of Major Irving Peress. Who, McCarthy demanded, had given this Communist dentist a promotion?

When attorney general Herbert Brownell accused Truman of ignoring an incriminating FBI report in nominating Harry Dexter White, a former New Dealer identified as a spy by professional informer Elizabeth Bentley, to head the International Monetary Fund, Truman took advantage of a television interview to charge the Eisenhower administration with "McCarthyism." Seizing the moment, McCarthy happily interjected himself into the debate, demanding— and receiving—free network airtime to answer Truman. The night of November 24, 1953, when the senator appeared live on all three networks, might be considered the height of his power. Previously, only a president had enjoyed such treatment, and some thought that, three years before the next election, McCarthy was indeed running for president. Rather than respond to Truman, the senator attacked Eisenhower for failing to fire the foreign service China specialist John Paton Davies (a familiar McCarthy target) and permitting American allies to trade with China.

The January 1954 Gallup poll gave McCarthy a 50 percent favorable rating (against 29 percent unfavorable and 21 percent indifferent). By early February, Senate Democrats were calling on the army to issue a report on an instance of favoritism originating with McCarthy's. McCarthy meanwhile went on demanding that General Ralph W. Zwicker give him the names of all officers who signed off on Peress's promotion, attacking Zwicker as "not fit to wear [his] uniform." On March 9, Edward R. Murrow's *See It Now* telecast its critical "Report on Senator Joseph R. McCarthy."

Two days after CBS fired this shot across the senator's bow, the Department of the Army released documents chronicling the attempts made by McCarthy's aide Roy Cohn to obtain special treatment for the newly drafted Private G. David Schine, the subcommittee's erstwhile "chief consultant." McCarthy responded with charges that the army had attempted to forestall further investigation by inducting Schine into the service and, in effect, taking him hostage. The Senate authorized televised hearings to begin on April 22. McCarthy ceded his position on the subcommittee, the better to sit in judgment and act as prosecutor in his own case. By constantly insisting on various "points of order," he will successively disrupt and effectively direct the hearings.

By now, Eisenhower had broken with the Wisconsin senator. At a mid-March press conference, the president had mused on the current situation. "You know, the world is suffering from a multiplicity of fears. We fear the men in the Kremlin. . . . We are fearing what unwise investigators will do to us here at home as they try to combat subversion or bribery or deceit within." A few weeks later, Eisenhower materialized in prime time, sitting on the edge of a desk, arms manfully folded and smiling gently, to address these anxieties.

Allowing that he was addressing a "very big subject," the president encouraged viewers to draw upon their spiritual strength as they confronted the H-bomb, Communist penetration, and the fear of intemperate means to combat that penetration—a "great threat imposed upon us by aggressive Communism, the atheistic doctrine that believes in statism." Ike asked Americans to have faith in the FBI and Divine Providence.

> I don't mean to say, and no one can say to you, that there are no dangers. Of course there are risks, if we are not vigilant. But we do not have to be hysterical. We can be vigilant. We can be Americans. We can stand up and hold up our heads and say: America is the greatest force that God has ever allowed to exist on His footstool.

New York Times television columnist Jack Gould considered this "information chat" to be Eisenhower's most successful TV appearance, crediting Robert Montgomery for finding a format that brought out the president's warmth and charm. Thanks to the use of cue cards, rather than a teleprompter, the president was able to make eye contact with the camera: "The viewer had a sense of being spoken to directly." Eisenhower projected a comforting confidence. Media historian Thomas Doherty has described his speech as "a presidential therapy session."

Ike was not the only national therapist in action. In a televised sermon given the Sunday before the presidential address, the positive-thinking Reverend Dr. Norman Vincent Peale blamed "suppression of the need for religion" for widespread "tension and frustration"; prayer and psychiatry were "team-mates" capable of mending human lives. New York psychiatrist Fredric Wertham saw another threat and offered his own diagnosis. In his bestseller *Seduction of the*

Innocent, published two weeks after the president's address, Wertham diagnosed the cause of juvenile delinquency: comic books!

On April 21, Dr. Wertham testifies in New York at the Senate Subcommittee to Investigate Juvenile Delinquency hearings. The next morning, however, the comic book investigation is upstaged by the opening of the Army-McCarthy hearings.[22]

Although the Army-McCarthy show will run for nearly two months and build a mass audience, initial interest is not a given. CBS has passed on the telecast; NBC drops out after two days. The full hearings are carried by the dying DuMont and new ABC networks, the latter so weak it has no daytime schedule to preempt; the hearings account for over 40 percent of its programming. This pragmatic gambit proves brilliantly prescient. Public response is enormous, particularly on the East Coast. (Even in Los Angeles, where the hearings are carried with live sound only—wire-service photos providing a form of illustration—the program is still, per *Variety*, "a smash hit.")

Not since Kefauver has the government served up such an appealing spectacle. In June, as the hearings churn toward their climax, the Gallup poll reports that an astounding 89 percent of adult Americans are following the show; CBS and NBC affiliates have dumped their afternoon soap operas to pick up the ABC feed; and some afternoons, the audience is estimated at 20 million. McCarthy, as the *New Republic*'s Michael Straight would write in his 1954 account, was a showman who "understood that the investigation was not a court proceeding, where order would reign and rules of evidence would prevail, but a vast, disorderly drama whose plot would be shaped and whose end would be written by the actors possessing enough power to take command of the stage." As in *A Midsummer Night's Dream*, the narrative motor was a struggle for possession of an abducted princeling. Schine was the scion of a wealthy hotel family.

Confusion is rife. Who is investigating whom? Generals, cabinet officers, senators, even lawyers are placed under oath. Senator Karl Mundt becomes the

---

22. The comic book hearing has its own McCarthyite moment. EC publisher William Gaines—responsible for the most creatively horrifying horror comics, Harvey Kurtzman's antiwar war comics, and the meta–comic book *Mad*—created an in-house ad with the headline "ARE YOU A RED DUPE?" and, citing the *Daily Worker*'s antipathy for comics, the wise-guy assertion that "the group most anxious to destroy comics are the Communists!" As a joke, Gaines sent the ad to the committee, which took it as a ridiculous smear. (Wertham actually was a progressive who, among other things, had testified on behalf of Ethel Rosenberg and before the Supreme Court on the psychological damage inflicted in segregation in *Brown v. Board of Education*.)

subcommittee's temporary chairman so that McCarthy might have the unpre-cedented right of cross-examination. The chaos produces a series of one-on-one confrontations, predicated less on rational discourse than on volume, quips, and personality. The inquiry meanders from Schine to alleged Communist (and homosexual) infiltration of the armed forces, the question of McCarthy's sources, and finally, in a stunning non sequitur, the political associations of a young lawyer who is not part of the hearings but a junior partner in the firm of the army counsel Joseph N. Welch.

McCarthy is playing to something larger than the committee or even the Senate. The television audience, he says more than once, is "the jury in this case." That the spectacle is being produced for the camera is underscored by the vari-ous debates on the quality of color-coded charts and photographic evidence. The crudeness of the TV image only serves to render the antagonists more iconic. But, although appreciated by his fans as a sort of Roughneck Mr. Smith gone to Washington to purge the Commies, McCarthy's sepulchral urgency and mirth-less laugh prove perversely untelegenic (so too his five o'clock shadow, despite the "cream-colored make-up" noted by Straight).

The Roughneck bombs! It is the prim and puckish Joseph Welch, a skilled trial lawyer (as well as a lifelong Republican), who blossoms under the lights. The army counsel also badgers witnesses, even alluding to Cohn's rumored homo-sexuality. But where McCarthy specialized in menace, Welch proved a master of deflationary humor. Although the frustrated senator attacked his nemesis as an actor who "plays for laughs," the army counsel could also seize the high moral ground.

The hearings climax on June 9 when, exasperated by Welch's cross-examination of Cohn (and over Cohn's silently mouthed objections), McCarthy exposes Welch's partner Fred Fisher as a former member of the left-wing Law-yers Guild. This gratuitous guilt by association exposes McCarthy himself to Welch's withering scorn: "Have you no sense of decency, sir? At long last, have you left no sense of decency?" Welch exclaims to a round of spontaneous ap-plause. Well before the hearings end a week later, McCarthy has become the butt of TV comedians. Steve Allen and Milton Berle mimic his interruptions and shouted points of order—in another first, McCarthy's fate demonstrates the image-breaking power of sustained tele-ridicule. The subsequent subcommittee report would be ambiguous, but the spell had been broken.

McCarthy's approval ratings fall to 34 percent after the hearings, with 45 percent of those polled holding an unfavorable opinion. *Variety* meanwhile hails Welch as "one of the great performers ever to appear on the small screen," and the ever-alert Otto Preminger later casts him as the presiding judge in his 1959 movie *Anatomy of a Murder*.

The massive distraction of the Army-McCarthy hearings diverted attention from other momentous events. On May 7, the French were defeated at Dien Bien Phu by the Communist Viet Minh and effectively driven from Indochina (to be replaced by the Americans). Ten days later, the Supreme Court ruled on *Brown v. Board of Education*, declaring school segregation unconstitutional. Seventy-two hours after that, *Salt of the Earth* opened at last in Los Angeles at the Marcal Theater, a 964-seat house on the eastern end of Hollywood Boulevard (the location for the 1949 noir *Destination Murder*). And, just as the hearings ended, the CIA scored a second great success, toppling Jacobo Arbenz to overthrow an elected progressive government in Guatemala.[23]

The tactics used to deny the will of the Guatemalan people were not unlike those employed against *Salt of the Earth*—guilt by association, Red-baiting accusations of Moscow gold, rampant disinformation, physical intimidation, and terror. As the U.S. government acted to protect United Fruit in Guatemala, so it protected Hollywood's interests against the spectacle of what producer Paul Jarrico and director Herbert Biberman (known on the set as "El Biberman") describe as a movie "drawn from the living experience of people long ignored by Hollywood—the working men and women of America." Not just living but fighting for their right to live! Against all odds and despite government terrorism, *Salt of the Earth* has been willed into existence and laboriously assembled, with Sol Kaplan's score (full of minor-key fanfares), Rosaura Revueltas's voice-over, and somebody's editing papering over the gaps created by her absence.

Writing in a recent issue of *Film Sense*, Jay Starr was convinced that *Salt of the Earth* had revived the social ethos of the New Deal period ("there is no hokum here; no easy solutions") and, cast almost entirely with nonprofessionals, gone beyond Italian neorealism. He's so excited by the script, which had been published in 1953 as a special issue of the *California Quarterly*, that he's "willing

---

23. All had been foretold: only a few months before, *Salt of the Earth* screenwriter Michael Wilson had written a piece in *Hollywood Review* on an au courant Hollywood protagonist, the "free-booter hero who brazenly interferes in the affairs of another nation—usually a colonial country." Wilson had not seen *Secret of the Incas*, which opened in late May, but this scenic soldier-of-fortune saga left an impression on George Lucas and/or Steven Spielberg, with Charlton Heston providing the prototype for their 1980s freebooter, Indiana Jones.

to wager, sight unseen, that *Salt of the Earth* is one of the greatest films ever produced in America."

Unlike the Arbenz government, *Salt of the Earth* prevailed. The movie had already enjoyed a nine-week run in New York at the Grande, a small neighborhood house on East Eighty-sixth Street, heralded by twenty-eight separate stories and items in the *Daily Worker*—more coverage than even *Mission to Moscow* received, including a second front-page review by former *New Masses* editor Joseph North that declared *Salt of the Earth* "surpassing in significance the advent of sound with the *Jazz Singer.*" Although the Los Angeles press and broadcast media refused to take paid ads, and the American Legion picketed the Marcal, waving signs reading "Welcome Comrade" and "Back to the Salt Mines with *Salt of the Earth*," a substantial crowd turned out for the Hollywood premiere, complete with searchlights, personal appearances, and a telegram from El Biberman declaring a victory in the struggle to "haul down the pirate flag of blacklist, boycott, and conformity in Hollywood."

It was during the Army-McCarthy hearings as well that Hollywood released its first Red Scare critique, albeit in the form of a luridly operatic Western starring Joan Crawford and called *Johnny Guitar.* Nicholas Ray's allegorical *film maudit* mixed Freudian sexual pathology with a political subtext that undoubtedly owed something to the project having been packaged by super-agent Lew Wasserman, whose clients included Ray, novelist Roy Chanslor, and screenwriter Philip Yordan, as well as that most dogged of stars, who was making her first Western since 1928. Crawford demanded the man's role, essentially switching parts with the movie's nominal hero, Sterling Hayden. ("Feminism has gone too far," began the *New York Herald Tribune*'s review.)

Although saturated in Cold War atmospherics, *Johnny Guitar* is less allegory than distillation; its plot turns on vigilante justice, xenophobia, and guilt by association. Ray was a former Communist. So was Hayden, already regretting the "friendly" testimony that saved his career. Yordan fronted for blacklisted writers, including Ben Maddow. Ward Bond, a leader of the Motion Picture Alliance for the Preservation of American Ideals, played a wealthy rancher who heads a lynch mob, joining forces with Mercedes McCambridge as the resident demagogue to burn Crawford's witch.

Nutty as it was, *Johnny Guitar* was Republic's biggest hit. Thanks to the Pax Americana, the Cold War might be played for entertainment, if not camp. Twentieth Century-Fox followed the fun and games of Samuel Fuller's *Hell and High Water* with another preposterous military escapade, the espionage thriller *Night*

People, written and directed by Nunnally Johnson (who characterized the movie as "Dick Tracy in Berlin"). Despite the presence of Gregory Peck, *Night People* made less money for Fox than *Hell and High Water*, but Bosley Crowther was amused by the spectacle of a self-assured American intelligence officer hoodwinking his Russian counterparts, calling *Night People* "first-rate commercial melodrama—big, noisy, colorful and good. . . . It may be the sheerest piece of fiction, and a reckless piece at that, but it is fun."

The summer of 1954, the first without war since 1949, had a celebratory aspect. One of the season's great hits, Alfred Hitchcock's *Rear Window*, playfully used the notion of total surveillance as the basis for a brilliantly self-reflexive murder mystery; another, Douglas Sirk's posh melodrama *Magnificent Obsession*, seemed the domestic version of *Quo Vadis*, projecting the notion of Divine Providence at work in the imperial splendor of America's upper (upper) middle class.

The Army-McCarthy hearings were themselves a form of Cold War entertainment, as was the summer's greatest success (and the year's top-grossing movie behind *White Christmas*), *The Caine Mutiny*. Stanley Kramer's triumph, as well as reformed Communist Edward Dmytryk's ultimate statement, the movie opened a week after the hearings closed, June 24—although Columbia had held special previews for official Washington (reportedly saluted by navy brass with a standing ovation) earlier in the month, and the committee's temporary chairman, Karl Mundt, obligingly shilled for the movie on television. (Senator McCarthy mentioned it as well, albeit in a typically anarchic fashion, with an ambiguous pun on the "Cohn Mutiny.")

Herman Wouk's novel was a presold property—a two-year bestseller, winner of the 1952 Pulitzer Prize—that packed a powerful ideological punch. Implicit in the book's "runaway success," Stephen Whitfield would note, was the ease with which "popular taste could accommodate an authoritarian ideology, justifying submission to a demented superior." The movie is less subtle and more personal, rife with ex-Communists and chastened liberals. Dmytryk, of course, had defected from the Hollywood Ten. The screenwriters Stanley Roberts and Michael Blankfort were both former Communists who had given friendly testimony in April 1952. José Ferrer, charged with articulating the movie's moral, was a fellow traveler who had been humiliated by HUAC in 1951, just as the movie's star, Humphrey Bogart, was publicly chastened in the aftermath of the 1947 hearings.

Kramer, who had proved his anti-Communist bona fides by breaking with

Carl Foreman, was proud that the screenplay received a near-instant "delighted okay" from Rear Admiral Lewis Parks. The production wears its allegiance like a medal ("The Dedication of this Film is Simple—the US Navy"), pledging loyalty to cherished notions of presumed democracy and unquestioning patriotism and defining treason as the questioning of military authority. The villain is supercilious intellectual and would-be writer Keefer (Fred MacMurray), who goads the honest naïf first mate Maryk (Van Johnson) into wresting command from the incompetent and unstable Captain Queeg (Bogart) in the midst of a storm.

Taking charge of the USS *Caine* in November 1943 (the very height of Communist prestige), Queeg has long since alienated his men with his terrible personality—as paranoid, rigid, and insecure as Henry Fonda in *Fort Apache,* not to mention craven, stupid, inept, and given to speaking in ludicrous clichés. Thanks to Bogart's performance, Queeg is less an object of fear than pity, obviously traumatized and weirdly evocative of future president Richard Nixon in his awkward attempt to convey "friendliness."

Queeg's pathos is heightened by the speech (written for the movie) he makes to his officers. The captain all but begs for their support—thus setting them up to betray him when, egged on by Keefer, Maryk assumes command. Something is wrong, but, as a pitiful victim, Queeg cannot command respect or even much sympathy. The movie's spokesperson only arrives in the final act as the mutineers' court-appointed defense lawyer Greenwald (Ferrer). Although he discharges his duty and effectively destroys Queeg's reputation to free his clients, Greenwald barely conceals his revulsion with the assignment, the mutiny, and, particularly, its wise-guy theorist, Keefer. As the filmmakers likely feel themselves most closely represented by Maryk, the working-class dupe led astray by the pretentious phony Keefer, so the movie's cathartic moment of victory is not the mutineers' exoneration but the ensuing victory celebration where Greenwald contemptuously flings his drink in Keefer's face—and, realizing he had it coming, the coward takes it.

Dramatizing the rage of the unwitting fellow travelers betrayed by glib Commies—and set up to be browbeaten by anti-Communist politicians—the brilliant lawyer unmasks the smugly arrogant crypto-Communist, liquidating his fancy notions and phony airs (although, having ruined Maryk's career with the mutiny, Keefer will presumably get a novel from it).

Edward Dmytryk's self-defense was followed a month later by Elia Kazan's. Working from a prizewinning piece of journalistic muckraking and the 1952

New York State Crime Commission hearings, Budd Schulberg, another ex-Communist who cooperated with HUAC and replaced Kazan's erstwhile scenarist Arthur Miller, came up with the best screenplay that Clifford Odets never wrote.

On the Waterfront, which begins with longshoreman Terry Malloy (Marlon Brando) fingering a courageous informant and ends with Terry himself testifying against the gangster Johnny Friendly (Lee J. Cobb), who controls his labor union, is also the first movie that Kazan directed after appearing as a friendly witness to ritually identify his former Communist Party comrades (and then make his own requisite anti-Communist film, *Man on a Tightrope*). Never mind that Terry's heroic testimony against the gangster Friendly has little resemblance to Kazan's opportunistic (and friendly) naming of names— *On the Waterfront* unavoidably evokes the director's potent mixture of guilt and self-justification.

"Terry Malloy felt as I did," Kazan told Michel Ciment in a 1973 interview. "He felt ashamed and proud of himself at the same time." Kazan would elaborate in his memoirs, referring to the scene where Brando yells at Cobb, "I'm glad what I done—you hear me?"

> That was me saying, with identical heat, that I was glad I'd testified as I had. I'd been snubbed by friends each and every day for many months. . . . The scene in the film where Brando goes back to the waterfront to "shape up" again for employment and is rejected by men with whom he'd worked day after day—that too was my story, now told to all the world. So when my critics say that I put my story and my feelings on the screen, to justify my informing, they are right.

Kazan had applied the Method to his friendly testimony; now he triumphantly adapted the Method to directing! At the same time, *On the Waterfront* is deeply evocative of Kazan's aesthetic heritage—the left-wing theater of the 1930s. The look is less faux neorealism than the bittersweet naturalism of the Workers Film and Photo League. It takes no great familiarity with Pop Front rhetoric to appreciate Karl Malden's waterfront priest as a crypto-Communist labor organizer or at least a two-fisted improvement on the antifascist priest in Rossellini's *Open City*—or to imagine Depression-era slum goddess Sylvia Sidney in the role played by Eva Marie Saint. According to Schulberg, the part of Terry was conceived for lefty street kid John Garfield, who (having had his own screen apotheosis in an earlier, no less primal, tale of brother-against-brother corruption in the urban jungle, Abraham Polonsky's *Force of Evil*) died before the movie was made.[24]

But it is thanks to Brando that this posthumous Popular Front classic is a heart-clutcher from beginning to end. The greatest and most influential actor of postwar Hollywood, Brando would here redefine movie stardom with the eloquence of his strangled inarticulation ("one glorious meathead," per *Time*). The scene of scenes, in which Terry reproaches his smarter brother (Rod Steiger) for selling him out, is the most triumphant expression of failure in American movies.

Always on the verge of unshed tears, his face a smooth mask of tragedy, Brando's Terry is as soulfully stupid as he is beautiful—a male Marilyn Monroe. No other actor ever made more poignant use of what, with regard to John Steinbeck's *Of Mice and Men*, might be called the Lenny factor. Terry is a sort of brute yet vulnerable animal trembling on the brink of consciousness. In class terms, he embodies what culture critic Harold Rosenberg termed "the pathos of the proletariat." *On the Waterfront* reaches its climax not with the outrageous grandstanding of Terry's beating (a scene criticized as "fascist" by future director Lindsay Anderson) but rather with his breakthrough declaration: "I'm just gonna go down there and get my rights."

On the Waterfront would be one of the supreme success stories of 1950s Hollywood. (On its fiftieth anniversary, it ranked eighth on the AFI poll of the "greatest American movies," ahead of *Schindler's List* but behind *The Graduate*.) And like many cult films, it is also less than the sum of its parts. To whom does this triumph belong? Kazan's Oscar-winning direction? Brando's career performance? The three Stanislavskians who support him, Lee J. Cobb, Karl Malden, and Rod Steiger? Schulberg's pungent dialogue and didactic speechifying? Producer Sam Spiegel's willingness to bankroll a project turned down, per Schulberg, by "every studio in town"? Leonard Bernstein's moody clarion-call score? The polished grit of Boris Kaufman's open-air Hoboken cinematography?

Or was it the historical moment that was the summer of 1954? In karmic terms, *On the Waterfront* had the enormous good fortune to premiere only

---

24. Garfield's connection to *On the Waterfront* actually pre-dated that of Schulberg and Kazan; entertainment journalist Sam Shaw maintains that in early 1952 he approached Garfield as the possible star in an independently produced feature based on the 1949 Pulitzer Prize–winning series "Crime on the Waterfront," opposite Marilyn Monroe (who showed Shaw's script to Kazan). That this pairing was to be directed by still-blacklisted Robert Rossen raises less the possibility of an alternate film than an entire alternative universe.

weeks after America's One-Man Mob dispersed and its reigning demagogue went down for the count. Eight days before the movie opened, Senator Ralph Flanders, Republican of Vermont, introduced a resolution that would censure Senator McCarthy.[25]

In late 1954, the *Saturday Review* published the poet Christopher La Farge's essay comparing Mike Hammer to Senator Joseph McCarthy as a "privileged savior." Hammer's antagonists—Communists and members of the Mafia—are, of course, all Very Bad, La Farge observed, not to mention "soft, homosexual, stupid, gullible, childish or easily tricked." At the same time, they represent "the Most Dangerous Thing in the United States" and "any means which will, with Hammer, lead to their extirpation and in particular their death by his hand are Good." Similarly, he noted,

> With Senator McCarthy, any means that will expose Communists, including the derogation of all Public Servants, the telling of lies, the irreparable damaging of the innocent, the sensational and unfounded charge, is justified so long as he thinks it is the right thing to do. Each, then, reflects the other, though McCarthyism kills but careers where Hammerism (perhaps in the end more mercifully) kills life itself.

This analogy seems also to have occurred to Robert Aldrich, who was already working on an adaptation of *Kiss Me Deadly* around the time the *Saturday Review* article appeared. Or perhaps Aldrich and fellow fellow-traveler A.I. Bezzerides, whom he hired to adapt the novel, simply made use of it. As written by Bezzerides, directed by Aldrich, and played by Ralph Meeker, the Hammer of *Kiss Me Deadly* would be the stupidest and most brutal private eye in Hollywood history.

---

25. *Hollywood Review's* November–December issue was largely devoted to John Howard Lawson's vitriolic critique ("Union Leaders Are Gangsters, Workers are Helpless"), yet for some, *On the Waterfront* just felt like a left-wing movie. Keeping the FBI director current on the Compic front, the Bureau's Los Angeles SAC informed him that on August 3, 1954, even as *Salt of the Earth* won the Crystal Globe at Karlovy Vary International Film Festival, a redacted "prominent motion picture executive" had reported *On the Waterfront* as "the type of picture which could be shown in foreign countries by the Communists to the detriment of the American way of life." The memo further noted that the source explained this danger to Hedda Hopper, who, overly impressed with Marlon Brando's performance, initially missed the movie's "anti-American propaganda potentialities." (A month later, *On the Waterfront* won the second-prize Silver Lion at Venice.)

Sh-Boom *Them!* (DeMillennium Approaching . . .)

America finds itself in that great southwest desert to which all of Southern California had once belonged: Death Valley, the Mojave, the Great Basin, the Colorado Plateau, the Great Salt Lake, the Moab, White Sands.

This territory is both distant past and onrushing future—the landscape where, as presaged by *Rocketship X-M*, the prehistoric merges with the postapocalyptic. Land of lunar canyons, Martian mesas, and isolated military bases—Fort Apache, Los Alamos, Roswell, Tombstone, Glitter Gulch, Yucca Flats—this is the alien place that newsweeklies call the Most A-Bombed Area on Earth and Walt Disney has anthropomorphized in his highly successful Thanksgiving 1953 release and first feature-length True-Life Adventure, *The Living Desert*.

When the fire ship lands it will be here where saucers crash and mutant insects spawn, where John Wayne's cavalry charges across the Rio Grande and his Mongol horde routs the Tartars. We are not the Roman Empire but ancient Egypt. Civilization is doomed, or perhaps destined for reconstruction as Hollywood's new satellite city, the mirage metropolis Las Vegas. *Time* hailed the $40 million capital investment in the seven pleasure domes of the Las Vegas Strip— the Desert Inn, the Flamingo, the Last Frontier, El Rancho Vegas, the Sands, the Sahara, and the Thunderbird—noting their use of Hollywood stars, "gold-horned Judas goats who lure the herds of tourists to the gaming tables" of this "unspiritual Mecca."

In August 1953, *Newsweek* declared Nevada's electric oasis the nation's new entertainment capital; a few months later Marlene Dietrich, reportedly receiving $30,000 a week to appear at the Sahara, thought Las Vegas "the most fabulous place in the world." But *Harper's* reported that some "big West Coast dailies call Las Vegas a desert Babylon, and warn that it is built on sand. . . . It's only a matter of time until some prophet comes out of the Nevada wastelands and curses the whole glittering shebang as a modern Gomorrah destined for destruction."

Did we all not live with the threat of destruction? Some had feared that tourists might be scared off once the Atomic Energy Commission initiated the Nevada Proving Grounds at Yucca Flats, sixty-five miles northwest of Las Vegas. "On numerous occasions," Daniel Lang told the readers of the *New Yorker*, "a piercing flash of light, many times the intensity of the sun's, has burst over the proving ground in the very early morning, momentarily transforming a gloomy Nevada dawn to a dazzling noon." Mushroom clouds turned the sky iridescent mauve; shock waves shattered display windows on the Strip. But instead of fleeing, according to the *New York Times*, even more tourists swarmed to "the palpitating sea of electric illumination" that the newspaper called "Klondike in the Desert." Were they hoping to collect glowing relics of Pompeii before Vesuvius?

A year and a half after the first one-kiloton bomb was tested on January 27, 1951, Lang reported, the Desert Inn's glass-enclosed Sky Room cocktail lounge was a popular spot to greet the dawn. "It was a wonderful place for what the customers wanted," one waitress informed Lang. "They could sit around and listen to our piano player and look out the big windows and see the pretty hotel fountain and the guests swimming in the pool and the traffic speeding by on Highway 91, and then, just when they were starting to get tired, the A-bomb."

The Chords' uptempo doo-wop novelty "Sh-Boom" was a monster hit early that summer, peaking at number 2 on the R & B chart. (A cover version by the Crew Cuts reached number 5 on the Hit Parade.) By some accounts, the song—which prefaced its sonic explosion with the proposition that "life could be a dream"—was inspired by last March's Bikini Atoll H-bomb test: "Wouldn't that awesome sound of a big bomb exploding make a wonderful song title?" is how a surviving member of the Bronx-based quartet remembers the moment. Urban legend has it that a mushroom cloud emblazoned the original 45 jacket.

Silver City, New Mexico, celebrated "Americans for Americanism Day" on July 3, 1954. The following week, Robert Aldrich's suspiciously un-American *Apache*, once a Joseph Losey project, with Burt Lancaster as the last unreconciled member of Geronimo's warrior band, opened in New York en route to becoming the top-grossing Western of 1954; among other things, it dramatized the natural Man of the Desert's incredulous, disorienting experience of white civilization. (Cut from the movie, however, was the original ending in which a U.S. cavalryman shoots the Apache hero in the back.) Desert Man down, another Desert Man triumphant: Dick Powell was in Utah's Escalante Valley directing *The Conqueror*, a six-million-dollar epic, RKO's most expensive and first CinemaScope production, as well as Howard Hughes's last spectacular, with John Wayne playing the young Genghis Khan.

The part had actually been written for Marlon Brando, but Fox (which was then hoping to feature the enigmatic actor in the studio's own desert-world extravaganza, *The Egyptian*) refused to loan him out, instead furnishing Susan Hayward. Wayne got wind of the script and—looking for a role that might afford him a stretch—asked to do the film, a highfalutin visionary Western in which he played both cowboy and Indian (and looked, *Time* could not resist noting, like a "Mongolian idiot.")

Full of blustery, swaggering bonhomie, despite his wispy "Oriental" mustache and Gobi-style coonskin sombrero, Wayne's Temujin gallops across a landscape of stony canyons and sagebrush mesas, defying the character he calls "My Mother" (a frothing Agnes Moorehead, a mere seven years older than Wayne) to ride with his "blood brother" Jamuga (Mexican star Pedro Armendáriz) in search of the auburn-tressed spitfire Bortai (Hayward at her most petulantly scowling). Temujin must tame the haughty "Tartar woman"; when he is captured and flayed like Jesus, she realizes he is a world-historic figure who will dominate the Gobi and the earth as Genghis Khan.

The Conqueror's opening credits conclude with a written preface:

> This story, though fiction, is based on fact. In the twelfth century the Gobi Desert seethed with unrest. Mongols, Merkits, Tartars, and Karkaits struggled for survival in a harsh and arid land. Petty chieftains pursued their small ambitions with cunning and wanton cruelty. Plunder and rapine were a way of life and no man trusted his brother.

How like Hollywood—as the anthropologist Hortense Powdermaker might say!

Taken as documentary, *The Conqueror* is richly absurd and unavoidably tragic. The day after the shoot opened, *The Motorola Television Hour* broadcast the drama "Atomic Attack," focusing on a suburban family coping with the effects of an H-bomb dropped on New York City. Sh-boom! So too, *mutatis mutandis*, was the cast of *The Conqueror*. These colorfully garbed characters are dying before our eyes. Eleven nuclear devices had been tested in Yucca Flats in 1953 and, thanks to the prevailing winds, covered the Escalante Valley, 150 miles east, with radioactive ash. Snow Canyon, where many of *The Conqueror*'s most spectacular scenes were staged, was a veritable fallout magnet. The levels of strontium 90 and cesium 137 set the Geiger counters gyrating as furiously as the near-naked harem dancers in the palace of the wily Wang Khan (Thomas Gomez).

According to Wayne's biographers Randy Roberts and James S. Olson, *The Conqueror*'s cast and crew were bathed in ash: "Crew members were covered in dust by the end of each day's shooting, and cast members had to be frequently blown clean of dust with compressed air and given time to rinse the dirt out of their mouths and eyes." Moreover, in order to ensure that the studio scenes matched the location shots, director Powell shipped sixty tons of Snow Canyon dirt back to Culver City. "For another two months the cast and crew wallowed in the radioactive mix."

The cast and crew numbered 220; an actuarially remarkable 91 of them would eventually be diagnosed with cancer. A quarter of a century later, over 40 had died of the disease, including the movie's director, Powell, and four of its stars: Wayne, Hayward, Moorehead, and Armendáriz. These statistics were not parsed until 1980 when Jeanne Gerson, who played Bortai's slave woman, filed a class-action suit against the American government. Instead, the great radioactivity story the summer of 1954 was Warner Bros.'s *Them!*, set in and around the Alamogordo test site.[26]

Weeks before *Them!* had its mid-June openings in New York and Los Angeles, the trades were reporting the unusually fast playoff that Warners had planned. A studio record of six hundred prints were made. Saturation booking of two thousand engagements would be accompanied by the most extensive and elaborate TV and radio advertising campaign in motion picture history. So far as promotion is concerned, the first great insect fear movie anticipated *Jaws* by two decades—and, as with *Jaws*, the monster struck America where it is most vulnerable. The Thing has landed (or perhaps erupted) in Fort Apache.

Them! gets its title from the single word uttered by a traumatized child who survived the surprise attack of . . . gigantic ants! The Them's first victims are an FBI agent and his family. (Is it a surprise that the Bureau has an office right on the test site?) G-men may resent the remote, hyper-rational scientists, but it's the nuclear physicist Dr. Medford (Edmund Gwenn) who, like the modern Isaiah that *Harper's* predicted, suggests that "we may be witness to a biblical prophecy come true . . . and there shall be destruction and darkness come over creation, and the beasts shall reign over the earth." Of course, it's also pointed

---

26. In 1957, *US News & World Report* investigated the towns around Yucca Flats to discover the quality of life. Despite a few isolated cases of baldness or cancer, the newsweekly could discern no "general alarm or any convincing evidence that things are much different than before tests began." The piece is a veritable parody of life in Jacques Ellul's propagandized society. Those quoted include a local politician, a young doctor (who blames baldness on anxiety), a cowboy, a waitress, a mathematics instructor at a local college ("our big problem here is finding a physics teacher"), an elderly woman who is no longer opposed to the tests, and a dairyman who refuses to worry: "I think the guys who are doing it are competent. If they weren't, they wouldn't be doing it." The report ends with a tractor driver's analysis: "It might be dangerous—this fall-out and all—but I'd rather have us find out all about this atomic business so the Russians won't be the only ones."

out that, from a research perspective, the plague of giant ants is "a scientist's dream come true."

The story was conceived during the spooked-out summer of 1952 and initially pitched to George Pal at Paramount. Pal, however, had his own soldier-ant movie in the works and by September, Warner Bros.—which was enjoying considerable success with its monster movie *The Beast from 20,000 Fathoms*—paid $25,000 for the story. Although Warners was anxious to get their giant ant film out before Pal's swarm fest *The Naked Jungle* (as well as Jack Arnold's *Tarantula*, already shooting in Honduras), production did not get under way until fall 1953.

Time had recently noted there was "no sense of doom in Las Vegas even when mushroom clouds are rising beyond the horizon," but Warners was nervous. Only days before shooting began, the studio decided against color and 3-D (as well as a scene that would have been shot in the New York City subway), albeit reassuring director Gordon Douglas that, "We all know this will not be a 'class production' but it has all the ingredients of being a successful box office attraction."

Like *The Thing* (or the H-bomb), *Them!* was at once "super secret" and hyper-publicized. The *Los Angeles Herald* soon learned that the movie would show the FBI attempting to exterminate giant robot ants "with eyes as big as skillets." *Variety* revealed that Warners had developed a new type of sound truck, fashioned from a converted army weapons carrier. The production, which was filming mainly in the Mojave Desert with scenes in the Los Angeles storm drains, had, per the *Brooklyn Eagle,* "assumed the aspects of a full-scale military operation."

> Jeeps, bulldozers on land, a plane and helicopter overhead and a 14-unit radio hookup were used. Like a general, Director Gordon Douglas coordinated his action on the ground, in the air, and underground by constant communication over his radio networks. Members of the studio greenery department came from Hollywood to rearrange the topography of the desert to suit the director . . .

The studio was pleased, reopening the shoot so that Douglas could add more scenes.

Korea now a memory, Hollywood was free to imagine total war on the home front. Nature attacks. Howling sandstorm winds confuse the senses. The radio crackles with news of "European defense," the "political situation," and a "closely guarded secret." Information is controlled by the military in accordance with "national security." The FBI, the army, and the state troopers are mobilized. A montage of L.A. civil defense preparations shows the citizenry in frozen postures, receiving instructions from the radio and TV.

This is the Living Desert with a vengeance. *Them!* certainly articulates a fear of atomic radiation, particularly its effects on children, but mainly, the movie offers a fantastic metaphor for the Communist menace. "Ants are the only creatures on earth, besides man, who make war," Dr. Medford explains. Them are "ruthless and courageous fighters . . . chronic aggressors, they make slaves of those they can't kill. . . . They have a talent for industry, social organization, and savagery." On the one hand, the Red Chinese anthill; on the other, the subversive Fifth Column. Them infiltrate the Los Angeles drainage system, there multiplying unseen and preparing to attack.

The *New York Times* called *Them!* an "ominous view of a terrifyingly new world," "awesome," "fascinating," "tense, absorbing and, surprisingly enough, somewhat convincing." Not since Orson Welles scared the nation with his Halloween 1938 *War of the Worlds* broadcast had anything been quite so persuasive: "Perhaps it is the film's unadorned and seemingly factual approach which is its top attribute." Warner's summer hit would gross $2.2 million in rentals while filling the nation's drive-ins with its progeny—the outsized wasps, grasshoppers, mantises, and scorpions who swarmed through the mid-1950s.[27]

Late August brought yet another desert spectacular and far bigger box-office bonanza. *The Egyptian*, directed by Michael Curtiz from a script by Philip Dunne and Casey Robinson (liberal and conservative united by Twentieth Century-Fox), might as well have been set on a dying planet—inert, underpopulated, lugubriously death obsessed, and bizarrely uninterested in Egyptian splendor.[28]

The protagonist Sinuhe (Edmund Purdom) is an illustrious brain surgeon, court physician to the namby-pamby pharaoh Akhnaton (Michael Wilding), who, as Bosley Crowther put it, is a "premature monotheist." His religious reforms and pacifist beliefs are opposed by his malicious sister (Gene Tierney) as well as her eventual consort Horemheb (Victor Mature), the captain of the palace guards and Sinuhe's childhood friend. The palace intrigue, which unfolds within an extraordinarily convoluted narrative, suggests Joseph Stalin's para-

---

27. *Them!*'s Japanese equivalent, *Gojira*, opened in November 1954, reaching the United States in April 1956 as *Godzilla: King of the Monsters!*

28. Despite his studio contract, Marlon Brando refused the lead role—fleeing Hollywood for New York because, he claimed, he needed to see his psychiatrist.

noia fulfilled: the entire court is conspiring to persuade the pharaoh's doctor to poison his patient.

By the time Horemheb initiates a pogrom against Akhnaton's followers, the doctor has gone crypto-Christian; as the movie ends, he's a proto-American who opposes Egypt's race-based caste system, maintaining that "a man cannot be judged by the color of his skin" and paraphrasing the Declaration of Independence ("all men are created equal"). Sinuhe's prescience is also manifest in his recognition that iron is the A-bomb of the twelfth century B.C.: "I think this new metal of the Hittites might change the world." As the end title marvels, "These things happened 13 centuries before *the birth of the Christ*."

The Egyptian was the year's fourth-highest-grossing movie, although, as a vision of the past superimposed on the present, it would be topped by Warner Bros.'s rival *Land of the Pharaohs*, directed by Howard Hawks from a script by Nobel laureate William Faulkner (after Hawks failed to interest Robert Graves) and already in production for a summer 1955 release. Again the story is narrated by an intellectual, in this case the royal scribe Senta (Dewey Martin). Unlike *The Egyptian*, however, *Land of the Pharaohs* is essentially triumphalist, opening with a military parade among the pyramids and the assertion that "Egypt has taken its place among the greatest of all nations in the world." The pharaoh Khufu (British journeyman actor Jack Hawkins) is a living god, his enemies are generic nobodies, war is waged for "treasure" because "riches are power and power is to be desired"—which makes sense only if one understands that power is the state of being desired, as when an audience desires to see a particular star or movie.

Egypt is transformed through Khufu's megalomania. "Why can't we do away with the desert, Haman?" he asks his high priest. Faulkner supposedly conceptualized *Land of the Pharaohs* as the tale of an obsessed Kentucky colonel and his scheming young bride, living in doomed plantation splendor, but the scenario necessarily projects a totalitarian regime. (The art director Alexandre Trauner recalled that Hawks thought of the pharaoh as a Hollywood tycoon, while Harold Jack Bloom, a young writer on the project, believed Hawks totally identified with Khufu: "He was like a pharaoh himself.")

While the ruling elite is obsessed with "life in the future," the mobilized common people—scarcely more differentiated than ants—undertake a collective "holy labor," building the tyrant's pyramid. "Never in the history of the world has so great a task been performed. Their faith gave them strength and their joy gave them song." But the work drags on and transforms into slave labor. The masses are whipped and beaten. "The pyramids will be cemented with blood and tears," the master builder predicts. As for the brutalized people, "they stopped singing years ago."

So what if they did? Finished on schedule but massively over budget, *Land of the Pharaohs* was itself a grand tautology—a great movie because it rebuilt the pyramids. Beginning with the Warners logo written in gold and carved in stone, this visually splendiferous fascist folk opera ends with a last look back at a solitary white pyramid, a monument to the American dollar bill.

A new age demands new monuments. The sky above, the earth below: from the Strategic Air Defense to interstate highways. In the two years since the Christian Soldier took command, the U.S. nuclear stockpile has increased by a factor of forty: nearly two hundred thousand Hiroshimas are at the ready.

No demobilization follows the Korean armistice, but under the policy known as Massive Retaliation, an increasing chunk of American military spending is devoted to the navy's submarine-launched Polaris missile and the air force's strategic bombers. Paramount is laboring over its celebration of America's nuclear power, reshooting sequences of *Strategic Air Command*, a movie made at the behest of General Curtis LeMay with the full cooperation of the Pentagon and the SAC and input from the CIA.[29]

Strategic Air Command is intended to introduce America to the new B-47 bomber (to be heralded in the finished film with an organ peal of religious grandiosity) and, as Paramount's second feature to be shot in VistaVision, further the studio's campaign against the new industry standard, Fox's CinemaScope. Emphasizing the image's height rather than its width, VistaVision is perfectly suited for the stunts and formations that SAC pilots are pleased to execute at director Anthony Mann's request—including a dramatic midair refueling that will be parodied a decade later in Stanley Kubrick's *Dr. Strangelove*.

The spectacle is pure PaxAmericanArama, with human interest supplied by Jimmy Stewart, who served as an air force colonel during World War II, as the St. Louis Cardinals' star third-baseman who, like real-life Boston Red Sox slugger Ted Williams, is recalled to duty in Korea—and then sticks with SAC after an injury ends his baseball career. Stewart is reunited with wholesome June

---

29. Soon after Paramount contracted with screenwriter Beirne Lay Jr. for the movie that would be *Strategic Air Command*, studio executive Luigi Luraschi sought guidance from his CIA contact. Specifically, Luraschi wanted a critique of Lay's script for the just-released *Above and Beyond*; his concern was to keep a celebration of SAC from seeming overly bellicose: "We don't want this project to develop into a picture which the enemy can use to show that we are a lot of trigger-happy, war-mongering people."

Allyson, his spouse in *The Stratton Story* and *The Glenn Miller Story*, and goaded by Frank Lovejoy, who has been promoted to the LeMay role.[30]

Meanwhile, the Eisenhower administration is poised to undertake a forty-thousand-mile freeway system at a cost of $26 billion—the greatest public works project America has ever seen and the most colossal plan for building roads since (what else?) the Roman Empire. "A Great Event Repeats Itself," *Life* reports in its seven-page spread on *Land of the Pharaohs*, photos emphasizing the near-naked Third World masses toiling in the Sahara. Excavating half-forgotten tombs and repopulating the desert, "Hollywood [has] brought to life the colossal pageantry and ruthlessness of a long-dead past"—its own.

Scarcely has *Land of the Pharaohs* decamped for Cinecittà than another, even greater Great Event is scheduled to repeat. Cecil B. DeMille arrives in Egypt to begin shooting a remake of his 1923 biblical spectacular. *The Ten Commandments* will open with DeMille himself announcing its world-historical importance.

> The theme of this picture is whether men ought to be ruled by God's laws or whether they are to be ruled by the whims of a dictator like Rameses. Are men the property of the state or are they free souls under God? This same battle continues throughout the world today. Our intention was not to create a story but to be worthy of the divinely inspired story created three thousand years ago: the five books of Moses.

Even the Paramount logo has been tinted red and recast to resemble Mount Sinai while the creator's on-screen credit is enlarged to assert, "Those who see this motion picture Produced and Directed by Cecil B. DeMille will make a pilgrimage over the very ground that Moses trod more than 3,000 years ago." The last shot has Moses (Charlton Heston) ascending a mountain alone. He raises his arm as if to mimic the Statue of Liberty and delivers a last mighty commandment: "Go! Proclaim liberty throughout all the lands."

Just outside Cairo, DeMille's crew has spent six months near the excavation site of Beni Youseff, reconstructing the mythical desert city of Per-Rameses on a budget that Paramount's surviving founder Adolph Zukor deemed unlim-

---

30. Senators and generals were in attendance at the movie's April 1955 world premiere in New York, where Paramount was awarded the Air Force Association's annual Citation of Honor. "One soaring, supercolossal recruiting poster," per *Time*, *Strategic Air Command* struck Bosley Crowther as "far and away the most elaborate and impressive pictorial show of the beauty and organized power of the United States air arm that has yet been put on the screen." In Los Angeles, a five-minute promo film was televised in place of a canceled atomic test.

ited. The modern ruins are stupefying: gates a hundred feet high and a quarter-mile long are flanked by two thirty-five-foot statues of DeMille's chosen pharaoh, Yul Brynner. An avenue a quarter of a mile long is lined with brand-new sphinxes and white, unweathered pyramids. Other locations include Luxor, Kharga, Abu Rawash, and Aswan—near the site of the hydroelectric dam that Egypt hopes to build with American aid.

Even as Hollywood projects Egyptian splendor, wondrous new pleasure domes are under construction. The Nevada desert has already been transformed into an air-conditioned mirage of Babylonian hanging gardens and Roman bathtubs, while in the sleepy town of Anaheim, Walt Disney is building a $17 million wonderland, ballyhooed by *Life* as the "most lavish amusement park on earth." The mobster Meyer Lansky and his associates, including Cuban dictator Fulgencio Batista, are developing an offshore luxury gambling center in Havana, and regular note is taken of the palatial luxury hotels rising along a South Florida sand bar. The *New York Times* declares the new Miami Beach skyline "more awesome than the Acropolis."

Opening for Christmas 1954, the $15 million Fontainebleau is the largest and most lavish of Miami palaces, a curvilinear frozen symphony of rosewood, marble, crystal, porphyry, and bronze. The staff of 850 equals the number of potential guests. There are nine governor's suites, nine presidential suites, and one royal suite—plus a lobby terrarium with live alligators. Among the innovations introduced by architect Morris Lapidus is the grand stairway to nowhere. "Hotel-keeping down there has become almost indistinguishable from show business," Lapidus explains. "Your building's a stage set, and your actors and your audience are one and the same."

Indeed, the Mesopo-Moderne Fontainebleau might be a location for *The Silver Chalice*, which opens on December 28, or *The Prodigal*, which MGM is preparing for a spring release. "The Mightiest Story of Tyranny and Temptation Ever Written—Ever Lived—Ever Produced" (by Victor Saville in between two Mike Hammer flicks, one in 3-D), *The Silver Chalice* features sets by Boris Leven, so stylishly spare and functional they project ancient Rome into a science-fiction future. *The Prodigal*, by contrast, is pure PaxAmericanArama. Generic movie star Lana Turner, a blond in the land of Canaan, plays the high priestess of Astarte. No color scheme is too outlandish—blood-orange walls rendered nearly three-dimensional by electric-blue divans and huge decorative vases. No costume—leopard-skin togas and pointy metallic brassieres—is too outré. Most of the cast members are dressed as guests, running around in bikinis and swimming trunks.

Wasteful, expensive, and yet the expression of a delirious democracy: describing the dream that is Las Vegas—"Olympic swimming pools . . . waitresses
beautiful as movie stars . . . bars a block long . . . royal buffets [with] obsequious
waiters offering free drinks"—*The Nation* notes that "the illusion is created that
we are all rich, that money means nothing." Such is the techno-progress of
America's exploding consumer utopia that, as *Life* crows, "anyone with the price
of a cup of coffee can see the costliest nightclub shows in the US." Are the exotic
dances in *The Conqueror* (showgirls in pasties and pink chiffon harem pants, a
"Woman of Samarkand" dressed only in stripes) or *Land of the Pharaohs* (painted
Africans capering to the beat of a tom-tom chorus masked as pigs) inspired by
Las Vegas floor shows or is it vice versa?[31]

More than a movie, *The Ten Commandments* was an awesome responsibility, a
cosmic undertaking, nothing less than a second bringing of the Law. Before
each of his big scenes, DeMille recalled, Charlton Heston went off by himself for
a half hour, costumed as Moses: "When he came back to the set and walked
through the crowd of Arab extra players, their eyes followed him and they mur-
mured reverently, 'Moussa! Moussa!'" But if Heston was Moses, what did that
make DeMille?

"For more than twenty years, and increasingly in the years since World War
II," the Master explained in his autobiography, "people had been writing to me
from all over the world, urging that I make *The Ten Commandments* again."

> The world needs a reminder, they said, of the Law of God; and it was evident in
> at least some of the letters that the world's awful experience of totalitarianism,
> fascist and communist, had made many thoughtful people realize anew that the
> Law of God is the essential bedrock of human freedom.

After flirting with the idea of a movie about the world's most beautiful woman,
Helen of Troy, DeMille announced his plans for a *Ten Commandments* remake
in the summer of 1952. This, *Variety* reported, was to be the "biggest picture of
his career." DeMille was anxious to shoot in Egypt, which had entered a period
of critical unrest. Riots in Cairo set off a chain of events that would culminate in

---

31. Not just pagan debauchery but Western civilization is also available. The Eden Roc, another Lapidus production under construction next door to the Fontainebleau, included the
Café Pompeii nightclub, the Villa d'Este coffee shop, and the Mona Lisa Pavilion dining room,
adorned with facsimiles of famous paintings by great European artists. Sitting amid these masterpieces "glaring down at the borscht," as Horace Sutton would waggishly note, was like being
"in the Louvre with a waiter at the elbow."

July with a military coup d'état, led by Major-General Muhammad Naguib and a group of junior officers, and the abdication of King Farouk. Egypt's monarchy ended a month before the United States orchestrated the restoration of the shah in Iran.

DeMille identified the making of his movie with the modernization of the Middle East. "There was a revolution in Egypt shortly after we decided to go there on location, to film the scenes of the Exodus and the giving of the Law," he would recall. "Since the co-operation of the Egyptian government was essential, I immediately communicated with President Naguib, cabling him the very day the Republic was proclaimed." Naguib promised to furnish Egyptian cavalry officers to serve as extras; in return, DeMille would produce a color promotional documentary, *Ancient Egypt and Modern Egypt.* (Nor was DeMille Hollywood's only emissary to the region; in mid-October 1953, President Eisenhower appointed Eric Johnston his special ambassador to the Near East.)

A few weeks into 1953, Egypt's revolutionary leadership staged the massive Liberation Rally. Addressing the crowd gathered in the square before the former royal palace, Naguib called for a national revival, promising massive industrialization and great hydroelectric projects. But the following month, just as DeMille's production manager Don Robb arrived with his team to coordinate set construction and line up the eighty-two assistant directors who would manage the thousands of extras that would be required for the exodus and other crowd scenes, a smoldering power struggle erupted between Naguib and his young supporter Colonel Gamal Abdel Nasser.

Nasser forced Naguib's resignation as prime minister and president and, backed by the Revolutionary Command Council, proclaimed a state of emergency. The thirty-six-year-old colonel became prime minister, although his reign lasted only a few stormy days before street protests returned Naguib to power. For the next few weeks Cairo was the scene of riots, shootings, and explosions. Anglo-Egyptian talks on the disposition of the Suez Canal broke down. The army was on the verge of revolt, and fearing chaos, the king of Saudi Arabia attempted to mediate between Nasser and Naguib. Finally, on April 18, Nasser took back the title of prime minster, leaving Naguib the largely ceremonial post of president. The unrest was blamed on a Communist plot. "It's amazing how much our story parallels the world situation today," DeMille would tell the *Los Angeles Times* that summer.

As the *Ten Commandments* scenario impressed DeMille with its prescience, others would note the parallels between DeMille's ancient Egypt and the contemporary United States. Moses returns from a successful war to a burgeoning

economy characterized by an extraordinary construction boom. How to succeed in business: Egypt, as cultural historian Alan Nadel observed, is "less like
a nation than a corporation that builds pyramids, with Pharaoh as chief executive officer"; ambitious Moses "proves his management potential through his
ability to direct and fill the screen with Sethi's city." Or his capacity to make a
blockbuster, special-effects extravaganza at a Hollywood studio.

The Ten Commandments was a mission, at once civilizing and, created as it
was under the most arduous conditions, decivilizing. According to DeMille,
"Every day we shipped back to Cairo the precious film, packed in ice to keep the
desert heat from damaging it, and from Cairo it was flown daily to Hollywood
to be developed and then flown back to Cairo for us to project." Signs and portents: soon after DeMille's arrival, Prime Minister Nasser finally removed President Naguib altogether. For his part, DeMille took the opportunity provided by
a state reception, two days before shooting was to start on October 13, to confer
with Egypt's new maximum leader.[32]

As a Christian soldier, as well as an American, DeMille was particularly
pleased with his support from the Islamic world.

> One of the strongest voices urging me to make The Ten Commandments had
> been that of the distinguished Moslem Prime Minister of Pakistan, Mohammed
> Ali, who saw in the story of Moses, the prophet honored equally by Moslems,
> Jews, and Christians, a means of welding together adherents of all three faiths
> against the common enemy of all faiths, atheistic communism.

The path was arduous. Nasser survived an assassination attempt, blamed on
Islamic radicals, during an Alexandria rally, and DeMille, after climbing a 107-
foot ladder to the top of the Per-Rameses set, suffered a heart attack. Fortunately,
his old friend Dr. Max Jacobson, the Park Avenue physician famous among his
celebrity patients for dispensing amphetamine cocktails, was on the set, and the
Master was back at work the next morning. DeMille returned home December
3, six days before the execution of the Muslim Brotherhood leadership. Back in
Hollywood, he attended a luncheon at Paramount for the shah of Iran. Soon

---

32. Among other things, DeMille learned that his 1935 production The Crusades had profoundly impressed Egypt's future prime minister. Nasser's comrade General Abdel Hakim
Amer told DeMille and actor Henry Wilcoxon, The Crusade's Richard the Lionhearted, the
movie was so popular in Egypt it ran for three years in the same theater: "When Colonel Nasser
and I were first in military academy, we saw The Crusades perhaps as many as twenty times. It
was our favorite picture." Amer said that Nasser was so voluble in his obsession with the Lionheart that other cadets called him "Henry Wilcoxon."

afterward, his granddaughter Cecilia Harper married Abbas El Boughdadly, the Egyptian officer who played the pharaoh's charioteer.

The Ten Commandments planted the American flag on the shifting sands of the Middle East. Six months after DeMille's return to Hollywood, however, Egypt nationalized all foreign companies and joint ventures.[33]

---

33. Promoting his movie as well as God's word, DeMille joined forces with the Fraternal Order of Eagles to place several thousand granite replicas of the Ten Commandments in towns and cities across America, sometimes with the movie's stars present for the dedication ceremonies. Half a century later, one of these monuments, planted on the grounds of the Texas state capitol building in Austin, would be validated by a U.S. Supreme Court ruling on the separation of church and state.

V.

SEARCHIN':
AMERICA ON THE ROAD, 1955–56

Pax Americana is celebrated in CinemaScope epics and vouchsafed by the divine power of the almighty H-bomb. Its characteristic landscape is the desert, where ancient civilizations, nuclear tests, and newly built pleasure domes leave fabulous footprints on the sands of time. Graffiti scrawled on these irradiated monuments belies a rebellious desire for some other America—if only one knew where to find it.

June 1955: Walt Disney's *Davy Crockett, King of the Wild Frontier* is playing in nearly one thousand movie theaters, and CBS-TV has refused to accept advertising for Robert Aldrich's new Mickey Spillane flick, *Kiss Me Deadly*—already condemned by the Legion of Decency and deemed by the network's Los Angeles censor to have "no purpose except to incite sadism and bestiality in human beings." Once-mighty Walter Wanger wonders if Orson Welles will lend his voice to Wanger's latest low-budget production, eventually released as *Invasion of the Body Snatchers*. Nicholas Ray is editing the movie that will be his most enduring, *Rebel Without a Cause*; John Ford takes his new Western, *The Searchers*, on location in Monument Valley; Budd Schulberg begins writing the screenplay for Elia Kazan's resilient telephobic warning, *A Face in the Crowd*; the Democrats have regained control of the Senate; and the Subcommittee to Investigate Juvenile Delinquency, chaired once more by Senator Estes Kefauver, arrives in Los Angeles to turn its spotlight on Hollywood.

Or is it vice versa? Kefauver, assumed to be planning another presidential campaign, has identified the next great internal threat. Commies are passé, the Mafia is old news—JDs are the new Martians! Youth crime, according to the fifty-two-year-old Tennessee senator, has been mounting at a disgraceful, perhaps implacable, rate—especially since Dwight Eisenhower was elected president.

In his introduction to the pop-sociological study *Teen-Age Gangs*, published shortly before *The Wild One* roared into theaters in late 1953, Kefauver warned that, at the rate juvenile delinquency was increasing, "a million and a half children will be picked up by police in 1960." The teenage crime wave was rehearsed in books, magazines, and congressional hearings throughout 1954. America had detonated the hydrogen bomb, and President Eisenhower contemplated its use to stave off French defeat in Indochina; McCarthy was investigating the army, and Capitol Hill was invaded by gun-wielding Puerto Rican nationalists. Why the furor over juvenile gangs?

Was it a displacement—reading back into the presumably manageable nuclear family all the terrors of a lawless, uncontrollable world? Were these kids symptomatic of a weakening social fabric? How did youthful misfits threaten the Pax Americana? Not as producers but as consumers: the previous April, the JD Subcommittee had investigated the relationship between delinquency and comic books. The hearings had resulted in a new comic book code of ethics and effectively suppressed the hugely popular horror comics that had been adopted by a nascent youth culture.

Now, per the *Los Angeles Times*, Hollywood is again on tenterhooks. *Variety* reports that the celebrated crime-buster is studying studio press books to learn the art of thought control—the techniques by which movies appeal to the delinquent mind. MGM's current hit *Blackboard Jungle* ("A Drama of Teen-Age Terror!") is a rumored subject of interest, as is Warner Bros.'s not-yet-finished *Rebel Without a Cause*. Just ahead of Kefauver's arrival, MPAA president Eric Johnston strategically predicts "the abatement of pictures of violence, which frequently have been cited for contributing to juvenile delinquency."

The day Kefauver's investigation commences, writer-director Harry Essex's independent cheapster *Mad at the World*—in which a teenage "wolf pack" terrorizes first a young family and then much of Chicago—materializes at eight Los Angeles theaters and five drive-ins. The senator's image is prominently emblazoned on the newspaper ad ("a motion picture that strikes close to the heart of a problem that is the tragic concern of a special committee upon which I serve!"), and, indeed, Kefauver is present in the movie, for which he provides a typically earnest introduction. "Long, windy, sermonizing and depressing" was the *New York Herald Tribune*'s summary when the picture opened a month earlier on Broadway, adding that, as *Mad at the World* "plays its subject for sensationalism rather than presenting a sober, straightforward account of the problem, the senator's approval of the production seems misplaced."[1]

So too Kefauver's showmanship: more than four years have passed since the Crime Commission spectacle. *Los Angeles Times* columnist Bill Henry dismisses the upcoming hearing as "a second-run performance," joking that the homespun senator has lost even his trademark raccoon-tailed cap to Walt Disney's TV (and now motion picture) kiddie sensation: "If the Senator puts one on nowadays he's likely to be greeted by kids hooting, 'you're not Davy Crockett.'"[2]

He is not. Even as the Teenager reawakened with a vengeance after twenty-five years in Depression- and war-induced suspended animation, Walt Disney resurrected the figure of the Frontiersman, uniquely American protagonist of the three-hundred-year-long Indian Wars. Thus, a nineteenth-century frontier bon vivant rematerializes out of the musty past as the idol of the nation's six-year-olds.

A few days after the Los Angeles hearings wrap, the *New York Times* will report that, having been misidentified by a visiting schoolchild, a statue of mid-nineteenth-century explorer Dr. Marcus Whitman in Congress's statuary hall has been drafted to stand in for Crockett. America had a new founding father! Just the week before, the former HUAC chairman Martin Dies of Texas advised colleagues to reform Congress by adopting Davy's motto: "Be sure you're right and then go ahead." Fess Parker—the lanky young actor first spotted by Walt Disney as a victim of *Them!*, who played Davy—has already visited Washington, DC, meeting not only Kefauver but also his Texas descendants, Senator Lyndon Johnson and Speaker of the House Sam Rayburn.

But in Los Angeles, Kefauver is less coonskin kid than Lone Ranger—the sole member of the subcommittee to make the trek. The hearing is largely a one-man show. Setting up in room 518 of the Federal Building, the senator is positioned before a huge American flag across from a witness stand flanked with lurid posters chosen to demonstrate the supercharged sex he believes is being used to promote the movies. "Purple prose is keyed to feverish tempo to cele-

---

1. On the eve of the committee hearings, producer Bert Friedlob invited Kefauver to use his current production, directed by Fritz Lang—eventually released as *While the City Sleeps*—as "a weapon in the growing battle against the corrupting force of comic books." The film's youthful serial killer (John Barrymore Jr.) not only reads crime comics but dresses like the Wild One. Before the hearings end, John Wayne's Batjac Productions announced its own anti-JD Little League drama, *Cappy*.

2. Signifier of his Tennessee frontier independence, Kefauver's coonskin headgear was a trademark and a rich source of photo-op publicity during his insurgent 1948 senatorial campaign and again four years later when he challenged President Truman and the Democratic Party.

brate the naturalness of seduction, the condonability of adultery and the spontaneity of adolescent relations," Kefauver gravely explains as the hearings open on the morning of Thursday, June 15.

First witness is William Mooring, the motion picture and television editor for *Tidings*, weekly newspaper of the Los Angeles Archdiocese. Mooring is a veteran foot soldier in the Hollywood wars. In 1947, he attacked *The Farmer's Daughter* as pro-Communist. *The Steel Helmet* was another movie serving the "crooked purposes of the Soviet Union," while *High Noon* constituted a Communist attack on religion. Most recently, Mooring declared that in their challenges to the MPAA production code, various cinematic "scummies" were playing into Red hands—not Communist perhaps, but certainly Communist-helpful.

Mooring informs Kefauver that "criminal violence, human brutality, sadism, and other psychopathic disorders" are rife in the movies and have been increasing over the past two years. Such fare is dangerous: "As sure as marijuana leads to heroin, morally vicious pictures create a desire for pornography." As proof that movies and television promote imitative behavior, Mooring cites the "millions of youngsters [who] now clamor for Davy Crockett hats."

Coonskin Kids, or the Martians *Have* Landed

"Davy Crockett: Indian Fighter" had materialized on the evening of December 15, 1954—a presentation of Walt Disney's new television show *Disneyland*, itself designed in part to promote and pay for his work in progress.

A second episode, "Davy Crockett Goes to Congress," was televised five weeks later; the trilogy was completed on February 23, 1955, with "Davy Crockett at the Alamo." The memorable fade-out shows the hero fighting on alone, ammunition gone, swinging his musket like a baseball bat against the Mexican horde swarming like the Korean War's worst nightmare over the mission wall. By then America was in the throes of a full-blown mania. It had taken months of televised Westerns to trigger the Hopalong Cassidy craze of 1950. No less than Lucy's baby, the Army-McCarthy show, or the original Kefauver crime hearings, Crockett madness demonstrated the medium's capacity to mobilize an audience around a specific event—all but instantly.

Davy Crockett was the zeitgeist made material. Every child in America with access to a television set was watching the same exact thing at (more or less) the exact same time: as he had twenty-five years before with the first talking cartoon character, Mickey Mouse, Walt Disney harnessed the power of a new medium to

create a ubiquitous icon. Indeed, Disney created a new embodiment and emblem of what, increasingly in the two years since *Partisan Review*'s symposium
"America and the Intellectuals," was called mass culture; as Jacques Ellul would
observe, it is precisely the exaltation of such a hero (not just "model and father"
but "mythical realization of all that the individual cannot be") that provides
one's participation in that culture. And there was money to be made!

Not only a demographic statement, Davy was a marketing bonanza, TV's
first true festival. The merchandizing blitz sold over ten million coonskin caps
(along with fringed jackets and frontier pajamas, comic books and trading cards,
inflatable wading pools and vinyl tepees, kid-sized chuck stools and rocking
chairs, bear cub dolls and fake grizzly-pelt rugs, saddlebags for every little trike
with molded plastic powder horns to dangle off the handlebars, beaded-moccasin
slippers and soap bubble peace pipes, T-shirts and toy guitars). The new national
anthem was "The Ballad of Davy Crockett," which, after its release in March 1955,
sold more copies in less time than any recording in history.

Were these uniformed children mimicking their conformist parents or was
it something else? Were they junior Wild Ones, born to the Wild Frontier? The
nation's soundtrack was in upheaval. *Blackboard Jungle* had reintroduced the
raucous Bill Haley jump song "Rock Around the Clock" as a generational anthem to rival "The Ballad of Davy Crockett." In April, *Life* ran an article on teenage rock 'n' roll nuttiness. The kids born during the war and those of the postwar
baby boom each formed a market—frightening in the avidly mindless group-
think of their zombie consumer desire. Each craze promoted certain types of
group behavior. Brandishing their muskets and shouting the "Ballad," children
playacted the passion of Davy, according to Disney. Their older siblings were
observed dancing in the aisles during *Blackboard Jungle*'s credits and then, in a
few cases, trashing the movie theater.[3]

---

3. Far stranger things were happening that spring in the South and Southwest. A twenty-year-
old Memphis truck driver had become a honky-tonk sensation. "This cat came out in red pants
and a green coat and a pink shirt and socks, and he had this sneer on his face," country singer
Bob Luman would recall.

> He stood behind the mike for five minutes, I'll bet, before he made a move. Then he hit
> his guitar a lick, and he broke two strings. I'd been playing ten years, and I hadn't bro-
> ken a total of two strings. So there he was, these two strings dangling, and he hadn't
> done anything yet, and these high school girls were screaming and fainting and run-
> ning to the stage. Then he started to move his hips, like he had this thing for his guitar.
> That was Elvis Presley playing Kilgore, Texas. He made chills run up my back, man!

By summer, when "Rock Around the Clock" became the number-one song in America, even
the most bizarre spacemen would snag a share of the spotlight. Onetime GM assembly-line

And so 1955 was the year of the JD and Davy Crockett, and there were those who believed that the two were not dissimilar. *Harper's* included a diatribe by the magazine's editor, John Fischer:

> Infant brainwashees have been bedazzled into worshipping a Crockett who never was—a myth as phony as the Russian legend about Kind Papa Stalin. The historic truth is that Davy Crockett was a juvenile delinquent who ran away from home at the age of thirteen, to dodge a well-deserved licking by his father.

Crockett, fumed Fischer, was an "unenthusiastic soldier," a "backwoods justice of the peace who boasted about his ignorance of the law," and worst, "a hack writer, heavily dependent on some unidentified ghost"—ersatz hero for an increasingly ersatz time.

From where did this conformism and fakery arise? "It would be easy to say this is a passing craze, but do we know that; are we sure?" Mooring darkly warned Kefauver. "Are we sure that these ideas which take root in the young mind do not bear fruit later?" Witness the behavior that occurs in parked cars at drive-ins showing pictures "calculated to provide emotional excitement" for the youthful audience. In his testimony, Mooring cited several current movies including *The Seven Year Itch* (a "generally bad influence") and *Kiss Me Deadly* ("the usual mixture of Mickey Spillane trash and crime and—I think they call them 'dames'"). But he was particularly disturbed by a small Stanley Kramer production that had its brief run eighteen months earlier: *The Wild One.*

Mooring noted that, despite its incendiary content—dramatizing the terrifying night when a marauding motorcycle gang of disaffected youths took over a California town—*The Wild One* was booked for numerous children's matinees and consequently attracted large numbers of impressionable young people. Did Mooring remember that, at the height of *The Wild One*'s disorders during the bacchanal on Main Street, one Black Rebel can be spotted wearing a coonskin cap and buckskin jacket? Was it the cult of personality developing around the movie's star that most disturbed him?

> I saw young men at several of these shows dressed like Brando in leather jackets. It was clear they identified themselves with the arrogant character he played in

---

worker Chuck Berry had a hit with his high-powered car ballad "Maybellene," while the more garishly demented Little Richard recorded his supremely manic "Tutti Frutti," an untranscribable blast of yipping, screaming wild-man gibberish that the singer would claim to have conceived while washing dishes at a diner in Macon, Georgia's Greyhound bus terminal.

the film. And they put on his swagger, and some of them went off recklessly on their motorcycles, just like the gang in the picture.

I wouldn't suggest that this impression was a deep or permanent one. I do say it was not a good one. It to some extent immediately undermined them with respect to the authority, at least to the management of the theater.

A movie and a charismatic actor challenged authority—or, at the very least, challenged the audience to do so.

Behavior was even worse at screenings of *Blackboard Jungle*. A contemporary drama set in North Manual High, an all-boys, inner-city trade school where alienated teens run roughshod over their beaten-down teachers, the movie prompted *Variety* to predict "explosive exploitation box office" when it was previewed back in February. Kefauver admits to never having seen *Blackboard Jungle*, but he understands what it is about. Despite the solemn disclaimer preceding the movie ("public awareness is a first step towards the remedy for any problem"), *Blackboard Jungle* offended both left and right, denounced by the CP's Labor Youth League and the American Legion, which declared it the movie that most hurt the U.S. image abroad in 1955.

It had, however, delighted kids. *Blackboard Jungle* is replete with nightmarish intimations of social breakdown and martial law; the threat to America is crazy, mixed-up nihilism. Manual High is at once totally chaotic and explicitly compared to a prison or a war zone: "The last time I felt like this is when I hit the beach at Salermo," one new teacher says. The protagonist Richard Dadier (Glenn Ford), mockingly nicknamed "Daddy-o" by his students, is also a recent veteran.

There is a suggestion, made by a tough cop, that juvenile delinquency is the product of wartime trauma. In any case, Artie, the most vicious delinquent (Vic Morrow), is blatantly unpatriotic, a draft dodger avant la lettre who taunts Daddy-o by telling him that he would rather serve a six-month stretch in reform school than a two-year army tour of duty. This key exchange allows the twenty-six-year-old Morrow (who, although making his screen debut, had already played Stanley Kowalski in summer stock) to confound an adult square by holding forth in full twitch, stutter, bebop Brando mode.

Artie turns out to be a genuinely evil sociopath; left unchecked, adolescent group behavior naturally tilts toward the demonic. Dadier's students, several of whom ambush him in a back alley after he saves a fellow teacher from rape, are never less than a potential mob. Still, there is a sense the generational divide might be bridged and a mature missionary could pacify the "blackboard jungle." Entertainment works. Dadier successfully uses a 16mm "Jack and the Beanstalk" cartoon to stimulate class discussion. ("Hey, teach, maybe I'll turn out to be a critic of movies," one appreciative pupil riffs. Later, an exhilarated Dadier tells a colleague that, at the very least, his lesson served to "get their minds out of comic books.") *Blackboard Jungle* also takes a positive view of school integration. Like MGM production head Dore Schary's long-ago triumph *Crossfire* (also based on a novel by Richard Brooks), *Blackboard Jungle* is unafraid to deploy racial epithets to illuminate prejudice and promote brotherhood. Indeed, Dadier ultimately prevails over Artie by enlisting the support of the alienated African American student Miller (Sidney Poitier), whom he recognizes as a "natural-born leader."

MGM promoted *Blackboard Jungle* as a serious social-problem film, but, like *The Wild One*, it was seen to have exacerbated (and exploited) the problem through dramatization. With young people mimicking Brando in *The Wild One*, Mooring believed that "youths already involved with crime and violence will immediately identify themselves with the ringleaders in *Blackboard Jungle*." For them, cool and crazy Artie is the real hero. Juvenile criminals will "derive satisfaction, support, and sanction from having made society sit up and take notice of them." Mooring pointed out that theater owners were reporting "unusually loud, noisy, belligerent behavior and some disturbances" in the streets outside. This counted as a successful embrace, and the movie that the *New York Times* had called "a vicious and terrifying tale of rampant hoodlumism and criminality" was en route to a $5.2 million gross—the twelfth-highest for 1955 and MGM's biggest hit of the year.

At the hearings, Mooring's critique of *Blackboard Jungle* was followed by a witness for the defense: Ronald Reagan. Although representing the Screen Actors Guild, Reagan seemed to be defending MGM. (He took care to plug his most recent movie, *Prisoner of War*, which had also been made at the studio.) Following two experts—a criminologist and a psychiatrist, both from Beverly Hills and neither inclined to blame juvenile crime on the movies—the next voice belonged to MGM's vice president in charge of production, Dore Schary. Asked about *Blackboard Jungle*, Schary took the long view: "We believe deeply and honestly that when the picture is reviewed a couple of years from now, it will be found that it did an awful lot of good, because it brought the subject into public view." (What's more, the movie improved on the novel, ending with Dadier addressing Manual High's institutional failures as well as subduing the school's out-of-control delinquents.)

Rebutting gloomy Mooring, Schary argued there was no evidence that movies prompted bad behavior. Au contraire: there was every reason to believe that the medium would have a benign effect on youthful opinion and conduct. As demonstrated by Daddy-o, movies are inherently positive! Schary, who had by now publicly criticized the blacklist and recently released a movie, *Bad Day at Black Rock*, that—taking *High Noon* as its model—acknowledged Hollywood's recent cowardice, could no longer be intimidated. He suggested that, not unlike the more than sixty anti-Communist pictures produced by Hollywood since 1948, *Blackboard Jungle* had a specific social function: the industry made a movie that identified a particular menace, articulated public revulsion, and proposed a specific solution. Rather than prompting criminal behavior, *Blackboard Jungle* would educate the young people in the audience.[4]

Not a month after the hearings, MGM announced that, given *Blackboard Jungle*'s box office, the studio was contemplating another film about "juvenile terrorists." Based on "The Red Car," a story to be published in the *Saturday Evening Post*, it would concern a vacationing family threatened by a group of teens in a souped-up hot rod.

On the Brink of the Wild Frontier: *Kiss Me Deadly*, *Rebel Without a Cause*

Should the late spring and summer of 1955, memorialized as a static pop culture utopia thirty years later in *Back to the Future*, be remembered as the beginning of the great thaw?

On one hand, there was the sense of an achieved utopia: "The incredible postwar American electro-pastel surge into the suburbs!" as Tom Wolfe hyperbolized it.

> Out here at night, free, with the motor running and the adrenaline flowing, cruising in the neon glories of the new American night—it was very Heaven to be the first wave of the most extraordinary kids in the history of the world. . . .

---

4. Other studio executives were even more shamelessly self-serving than Schary. Paramount vice president Y. Frank Freeman touted *The Ten Commandments*, enabling Jack Warner to mention his studio's upcoming *Land of the Pharaohs* ("a great educational film [that] shows the building of the pyramids"). Basking in the spotlight, Warner bragged about another project—*Rebel Without a Cause*—a social-problem movie that would show the "juvenile delinquency of parents." Kefauver seized this opening: "We have had some calls saying this is not a good picture, from the point of influence on young people." Warner was aghast. "They must be working from radar," he told the senator. "Because I myself haven't seen it put together." When Kefauver countered that his informants appeared to know what they were talking about ("one or two of them seemed right reliable"), Warner suggested they were most likely jealous competitors.

One's parents remembering the sloughing common order, War & Depression—
but Superkids knew only the emotional surge of the great payoff, when nothing
was common any longer—The Life!

On the other hand, the media absorbed by these kids had developed a critical component. Newly evolved from a 10¢ comic book to a 25¢ magazine, *Mad*
opened a parody of the popular television show *This Is Your Life* with a full-page
Will Elder portrait of the studio audience that might have been titled "This
Is Our Life"—a collection of movie stars, TV personalities, brand logos, world
leaders, and American politicians, including an owlish Senator Kefauver so engrossed in a horror comic that he is oblivious to the goddess Marilyn sitting
next to him. *Mad*'s next issue celebrated "Blackboard Jumble" with Wally Wood's
hilariously frantic two-page spread—violent as the horde that overran the Alamo and busy as a Pollock abstraction, a mob of screaming teenage punks pul-
verize their school.

Thanks in part to *Blackboard Jungle*, "Rock Around the Clock" ruled America's airwaves. July 18, the day after Disneyland's grand opening was shown in a
live telecast (Ronald Reagan officiating a ceremony that, the *New York Times*
thought, delivered the "gloss of a commercial travel brochure" with the gravitas
due the "dedication of a national shrine"), the United States, Great Britain, and
the Soviet Union convened the first Great Powers summit meeting in the decade since Potsdam. The new spirit of Geneva wafted across the planet. HUAC
returned to Foley Square in August, investigating Communist infiltration of
the Broadway theater; after four farcical days, the committee was essentially
laughed out of town.

Communists? Another form of dialectical materialism transfixed people in
New York and across the country. Tuesday nights were given over to television's
newest spectacle, *The $64,000 Question*. Average-seeming people won bushels
of money by demonstrating surprising knowledge of arcane topics. *The $64,000
Question* was based on the old radio quiz shows of the 1940s, but TV amplified
the jackpot a thousandfold. (Even the losers received a consolation Cadillac.) By
August, the show had a weekly audience of 47 million—not as many as watched
Disneyland's opening day, but nearly one-third of the total population.

If Disneyland was America scaled down and represented as an earthly paradise for kids, *The $64,000 Question* was TV as cornucopia for adults. As the
United States scaled the peak of post–World War II prosperity (a record eight
million new cars sold in 1955, an unprecedented million and a half new housing
starts), the show materialized like a collective thought balloon ready to ponder

this astonishing abundance—as well as demonstrate upward mobility, illustrate the dogma of self-improvement, and testify to the hidden potential of the ordinary American. (Anything seemed possible: this was the year the hard-luck Brooklyn Dodgers would finally defeat the mighty New York Yankees in the World Series.)

Time magazine's May 30 issue exulted that

> spring was full-blown in the US, and the nation's prevailing mood seemed to be as bright as its blossoms. The people of the US had never been so prosperous. Never before had the breadwinner taken home so much money. . . . Not since the first delirious, mistaken weeks after V-J day had there been so much expectancy—with caution, this time—for peace. . . . The people were spending. . . . There was a waiting list for Cadillacs in New Orleans. . . . Although parents were worried about growing juvenile delinquency, it was the best spring ever for millions of young Americans.

The newsweekly called it "Davy's Time."

The season was bracketed by two startling movies, at once lurid and visionary, mythic and topical, summarizing and prophetic, redolent of affluence and spooked by obliteration. Each featured a protagonist who seemed a bit of a Wild One, heedlessly driving fast toward the edge of some psychic frontier. Both were directed by men who had extensive leftist associations and yet were miraculously untouched by the purges of 1948 and 1951—although the films themselves had figured in the recent Kefauver hearings.

The titles were fabulous and almost interchangeable. Robert Aldrich's *Kiss Me Deadly* opened in June and Nicholas Ray's *Rebel Without a Cause* in October—and in between came *Time*'s new hero and America's latest greatest son, ideal dad, and reigning pop icon. Just in time for summer vacation, Davy Crockett's three television adventures were cobbled together as a theatrical feature.

Davy Crockett, King of the Wild Frontier sanitized the hero's life in bright Technicolor. Fess Parker's Davy embodied fair play. The amiable Indian fighter tries to talk peace with bellicose Seminole chief Red Stick but must best him in a tomahawk duel to teach the lesson "Thou shalt not kill." Later, Davy helps defend a dispossessed Native American family before hastening to Washington to defeat his former commander President Andrew Jackson's Indian Bill and protect the redskins under the umbrella of democracy.

Davy anticipated baby boomer consciousness: he naturally opposed officious military types, long-winded politicians, and crooked lawyers but was generous to the childlike wild Indians he single-handedly defeated. This frontier hero was also, at least metaphorically, the greatest World War II dad of them all. Davy wanted only to clean up the neighborhood for his suburban family. Thanks to his combat exploits, he is drafted to march on the Capitol in full buckskin regalia, a costumed Ike or Mr. Smith gone to Washington who serves a term in Congress before volunteering to fight for independent Texas—a place, he declares, with "room for every dream I ever had."

A few historically minded Democrats recognized Crockett as a Democrat turned Whig. Perhaps afraid this new role model might be appropriated by the Republicans, the United Auto Workers education director attacked Crockett during the course of a radio address as an "ordinary backwoodsman, who probably spat on the sidewalk [and was] not an admirable character." *New York Post* labor reporter Murray Kempton went even farther with his four-part series debunking Crockett as a political hack "purchasable for no more than a drink." Agitated kids demonstrated outside the *Post* carrying signs that dared Kempton to expose Santa Claus next. In the waning days of the craze, the *New York Times Magazine* proposed "Dan'l, Dan'l Boone" as an alternative, although noting that the independent loner Boone was clearly less appropriate to the current "other-directed" cultural climate than the congenial, conforming, civic-minded Crockett.

But the *Daily Worker* knew enough to defend the myth. "It is all in the American democratic tradition, and who said tradition must be founded on 100 per cent verified fact?" TV critic Ben Levine asked, praising "the way Davy puts snobs in their place." Perhaps for the only time, William F. Buckley (whose new journal, the *National Review*, published its maiden issue toward the end of the Crockett craze) made common cause with the Communists, blaming anti-Crockettism on "resentment by liberal publicists of Davy's neurosis-free approach to life."[5]

This contemporary Crockett had been conceived for Disneyland, and like the theme park, he seemed to range at will throughout American history. "With

---

5. During the spring and summer of 1955, the *Daily Worker* expressed a giddy enthusiasm for Davy. In addition to Ben Levine's piece on the "excellent" TV show (and a movie review that went out of its way to compliment "The Ballad of Davy Crockett"), the *Worker* reported, without comment, on a *Wall Street Journal* story that Davy had been a boon to business, generating $100 million in retail sales. In July, the paper published a lengthy Sunday supplement essay, "Davy Crockett, the Man and the Legend," hailing the King of the Wild Frontier as a people's hero.

a rifle like this, a man could put a rifle ball on the moon," the Disney writers had him presciently muse upon first meeting his trusty musket Old Betsy. Indeed, the Crockett scenario was not without a measure of realpolitik. Somewhat ominously, *Davy Crockett, King of the Wild Frontier* begins and ends with war, first against the Indians and later the Mexicans. America was beset by enemies within and without, and perhaps always would be. (The memory of a mushroom cloud darkens the sky. . . .) What's more, Davy's slogan "Be sure you're right, then go ahead" provided a model for sociopathic positive thinking.

In its Spirit of Geneva headiness, the *Daily Worker* praised Phil Karlson's *The Phenix City Story*, one of the last of the Kefauver committee films, dramatizing the cleansing of an Alabama vice town. The *Worker* even had a few kind words for Samuel Fuller's *House of Bamboo*, decrying its violence while praising the cinematography and the dignified treatment of Japanese characters, as well as the frank appreciation for "the contempt [they] feel for the corruptions of their conquerors."

The *Daily Worker* thought that *House of Bamboo* might have been titled "Mickey Spillane in Tokyo." *Kiss Me Deadly*, directed by Robert Aldrich from an A.I. Bezzerides script, was more like Mickey Spillane on Mars—a hard-boiled film noir veering into apocalyptic sci-fi. Rather than a scientist, the protagonist was a mercenary private detective, playing the system in search of the big score. (His repeated mantra: "What's in it for me?") The social problem here is unrecuperated. As embodied by Ralph Meeker, this lowlife tough guy exhibits a surplus of macho behavior that, aggravated by sexual repression and crass self-interest, ultimately becomes a criticism of itself.[6]

Kiss Me Deadly's ads, like those for *Blackboard Jungle*, had been displayed during the juvenile delinquency hearings, with Senator Kefauver interrogating the director of the MPAA's Advertising Code Administration, Gordon S. White. Pointing to a poster for "Mickey Spillane's Latest H-Bomb," Kefauver lectured White.

---

6. Born in 1918, Aldrich was the scion of a prominent Rhode Island family. His grandfather Nelson Aldrich served as a U.S. senator; his uncle was ambassador to Great Britain during the period *Kiss Me Deadly* was made; his aunt married John D. Rockefeller Jr.; and his first cousin was Nelson Aldrich Rockefeller. Aldrich broke with his family in 1941 when he went to work at RKO. During the 1940s, he served a distinguished apprenticeship as an assistant director for Jean Renoir (*The Southerner*), Lewis Milestone (*Arch of Triumph*), William Wellman (*The Story of GI Joe*), Joseph Losey (*The Prowler* and *M*), and Charles Chaplin (*Monsieur Verdoux*). Most crucially, Aldrich worked with Abraham Polonsky, Robert Rossen, and John Garfield on *Body and Soul* and *Force of Evil*. Given these associations, it is striking that Aldrich seems to have no FBI file. Perhaps he was too unimportant or, conversely, too well connected.

These producers have told us that in all of the pictures, horror and crime and sex pictures, there is some moral they are trying to prove. I just wonder if you get the moral in this advertising up here. There is a *"Kiss Me Deadly.* White Hot Thrills. Blood Red Kisses." That is all it says about it. What is the moral?

"I don't like that any more than you do, Senator," White maintained without answering the question—should the ad, more patriotically, have promised Blood Red Kisses, White Hot Thrills, *and* Baby Blue Bruises?—even though *Kiss Me Deadly* was a movie with a good deal to say about greed, vigilante justice, and the apocalypse.

Geoffrey Shurlock, Joseph Breen's successor as Production Code director, told Kefauver there was never any discussion of withholding approval from *Kiss Me Deadly*. In fact, there had been a good deal of back-and-forth between the filmmakers and the MPAA. After reading the script submitted in September 1954, Shurlock informed Aldrich that his story was unacceptable for its treatment of narcotics as well as the hero's cold-blooded and never entirely justified vigilante killings—both violations of the code—not to mention "numerous items of brutality and sexual suggestiveness." The script was resubmitted in early November sans narcotics and with atomic spies substituted for gangsters. What remained was the mercenary antihero.

Screenwriter A.I. Bezzerides had made substantial changes to the novel—shifting the location from New York to Los Angeles, eliminating the first-person narration, and downgrading Hammer from private eye to divorce dick. Rather than an adoring fiancée who "could whip off a shoe and crack a skull before you could bat an eye," Hammer's secretary Velda is a devotedly amoral mistress who serves as sexual bait to entrap the husbands of Hammer's female clients. It's a not-unprofitable line of work. The detective drives a Jaguar, has a futuristic telephone answering machine built into his bachelor pad's wall, and (a bag of golf clubs glimpsed in the corner) lives a version of what was not yet called the *Playboy* philosophy.

On one hand, Hammer is a hustler who, as one cop grudgingly allows, "can sniff out information like nobody I ever saw." "Sniff" is an understatement—once Hammer deduces that a murdered woman who stumbles into his life is connected with Something Big, his quest turns outrageously mercenary. On the other, he's a voyeuristic, adolescent creep who takes sadistic pleasure in violence: the movie stops in its tracks to focus on his excited grin as he snaps a collector's priceless 78 record, a crime also committed by the punks of *Blackboard Jungle*, or slams a desk drawer shut on another potential informer's fingers—or when, with a mix of pity and contempt, a police detective gives him the clue "Manhattan Project" as though addressing a dumb animal. In this radioactive climate, the Roughneck mutates into the Wild One.

Navigating a nocturnal, inexplicably violent labyrinth toward a white-hot vision of cosmic annihilation, the sleaziest private investigator in American movies pursues and is pursued by a shadowy cabal—"the nameless ones who kill people for the Great Whatzit," as the material product of the Vital Secret is called in the film's key exchange. From the perversely backward title crawl (outrageously accompanied by a woman's orgasmic heavy breathing) through the climactic explosion, the film eschews straight exposition for a jarring succession of bizarre images, bravura sound matching, and encoded riddles.

A nineteenth-century poem furnishes the movie's major clue. Like one of *Mad*'s parodies, *Kiss Me Deadly* unfolds in a deranged Cubistic space amid the debris of Western civilization—shards of opera, deserted museums, molls who paraphrase Shakespeare, mad references to Greek mythology and the New Testament. ("Do you believe that a democratic society necessarily leads from a leveling of culture, to a mass culture which will overrun intellectual and aesthetic values traditional to Western civilization?" *Partisan Review*'s editors had asked.)

The faux Calder mobile and checkerboard floor pattern of Hammer's overdecorated pad add to the crazy, clashing expressionism and the free-floating paranoia. Everyone is under surveillance, everything is a secret; the protagonist, who is described as returning from the grave, is a walking corpse. Fear of a nuclear holocaust fuses with terror of a femme fatale. Hammer plays with fire and, like a number of characters, gets burned—literally—by the Whatzit.

This great movie was never reviewed in the *New York Times* and was banned in Britain. In France, *Kiss Me Deadly* was mainly admired by the young critics at *Cahiers du Cinéma* and Aldrich, dubbed "Le Gros Bob," was hailed as "the first director of the atomic age." *Kiss Me Deadly*, Claude Chabrol wrote in his passionate review,

> has chosen to create itself out of the worst material to be found, the most deplorable, the most nauseous product of a genre in a state of putrefaction: a Mickey Spillane story.
>
> [Aldrich and Bezzerides] have taken this threadbare and lackluster fabric and splendidly rewoven it into rich patterns of the most enigmatic arabesques.

Artie, the worst kid in *Blackboard Jungle*, had been characterized by Bosley Crowther as a "sinister replica of a Marlon Brando roughneck." The same might have been said of *Kiss Me Deadly*'s antihero, played by the very actor who had replaced Brando in the Broadway production of *A Streetcar Named Desire*. The specter of the Wild One also haunted *Rebel Without a Cause*—and not only because its star too was a Brando disciple.

Pondering "mass culture," the "crazy, mixed up kid," and the "glamour of delinquency" in the year of *Rebel Without a Cause* and *Blackboard Jungle*, free-lance film critic Pauline Kael mocked America's "prosperous, empty, uninspiring uniformity" and noted its antithesis: "For the first time in American history we have a widespread nihilistic movement, so nihilistic it doesn't even have a program, and, ironically, its only leader is a movie star: Marlon Brando."

Like *The Wild One* and *Blackboard Jungle*, *Rebel Without a Cause* was a social-problem film that posited a crisis in authority through the violent, if deliberately inarticulate, expression of an apparently pointless youthful rebellion. Nothing in the adult world seemed worthy of emulation. Revolt in *Blackboard Jungle* was ultimately tied to class—the point inadvertently made when Mr. Dadier compares North Manual High to a normal institution in suburban Los Angeles. *Rebel*, however, centered on delinquency in that suburban school—the Electro-Pastel Brave New World of mad mobility and overprivileged super-kids. Riding in a police squad car, a frazzled mother directly addresses the camera: "You never think it could happen to your son." *Rebel Without a Cause*: the enemy comes from within.

Nicholas Ray's movie took its title (if little else) from a 1944 case study by psychologist Robert Lindner. Subtitled *The Story of a Criminal Psychopath*, *Rebel Without a Cause* recounted a story of successful rehabilitation—a juvenile delinquent whom Lindner considered a nascent Nazi storm trooper. Warners purchased the rights in early 1946, and the first treatment was by political cartoonist Theodor Seuss Geisel (later Dr. Seuss). Broadway sensation Brando tested for the lead in 1947. Still, the project lay fallow until September 1954, when Ray told his agent, Lew Wasserman, that, after *They Live by Night* and *Knock on Any Door*, he wanted to make another movie about crime-prone kids—a hot subject that season.[7]

Soon after the new year, months before the rest of the movie would be cast and well ahead of the script's completion, Warner Bros. announced that James Dean, not yet twenty-four, would star. Brando had already established the precedent for Dean's use of antipublicity. The studios were more than ready for an

---

7. *Newsweek*'s "Our Vicious Young Hoodlums: Is There Any Hope?" and *US News and World Report*'s "Why Teenagers Go Wrong" both ran that month.

arty punk who dressed like a bum, spat on a photograph of a reigning star, and then charmed Louella Parsons with his outrageous manners. (For his part, Ray had been intrigued to learn that, while shooting *East of Eden* with Elia Kazan, Dean lived on the Warners lot, just as Ray had while making *In a Lonely Place*—although, unlike Dean, Ray hadn't slept with a loaded .45 beneath his pillow.)

The new Brando had studied (briefly) at the Actors Studio, rode a motorcycle, read Camus (or claimed to), and let his cigarette dangle in the French style. He was typecast by TV as a crazy mixed-up kid and, in December 1954, a year after *The Wild One* opened, appeared on *General Electric Theater* as a "hepcat" killer who wakes a country doctor at night and, at gunpoint, forces him to help his wounded companion. (After the companion dies, the doctor—played by series host Ronald Reagan—overpowers the hepcat and disarms him.)

Ray wanted Dean, and perhaps inspired by Kazan's "neorealistic" use of actual dockworkers in *On the Waterfront*, he wanted real teens on the set to interact with his professional cast. The kids were actual kids: Natalie Wood and Sal Mineo were both sixteen, and Dean's rival, Corey Allen, was still twenty when shooting began. The adult characters, by contrast, were cartoons (the ineffectual father was even played by Jim Backus, voice of the nearsighted animated cartoon character Mr. Magoo, as well as *Above and Beyond*'s embodiment of General Curtis LeMay). Dean was something else—David Thomson has called *Rebel* "a movie about a 23-year-old genius packed off to school with peanut butter sandwiches." This super-duper kid was a permanent hipster; his classmates describe his character as "a new disease." (Adolescent audiences wondered how to catch it.)

If Brando was the most eloquent exponent of a failure to communicate, Dean embodied the charismatic outcast. In take after take, nineteen-year-old Dennis Hopper, a minor member of Allen's gang, can be glimpsed studying Dean's performance. Mineo's character functions in the movie as the first James Dean fan, explicating Dean's personality for the second Dean disciple, Natalie Wood: "He's sincere." To which she gravely answers, "That's the main thing."

Going into production on March 25, 1955, the day *Blackboard Jungle* opened in Los Angeles, *Rebel Without a Cause* was originally to have been shot in black and white; the studio raised the hyperbole level by switching to color after shooting began. Such cinematic bravado was more important than the script's primitive sociology or pop psychologizing, although the MPAA was nervous about the Mineo character's latent homosexuality and the Wood character's implied promiscuity. It had no pop music, but Nicholas Ray's wide-screen paean to American youth was visual rock 'n' roll—a movie of poetic flourishes, cosmic reference points, and free-floating delirium.

Rebel introduced a mad, new, highly ritualized mythology of teenage violence, based on the hot rod and the switchblade and located in suburbia. Some found it too much. Writing in the *Nation*, Robert Hatch complained that "it would seem that the juvenile gangs of the West Coast have been organized by [Jean] Cocteau. Rich kids playing dreamy games of suicide, floating hand in hand through ruined mansions, doomed children reading to one another through mists of alcohol, comic books and police car sirens." And that didn't even mention such romantic conceits as the end of the universe, the edge of the earth, and the world turned upside down—all visualized in the film—or even the influence of existentialism. Before the "fatal chickie run," Dean asks Allen, "Why do we do this?" and Allen answers, "You gotta do something." The hot-rod race toward the cliff and into the void reads as an outrageous evocation of Cold War brinksmanship; indeed, the night the scene was shot, the sky was illuminated by a twenty-eight-kiloton bomb detonated on the Yucca Flats testing site.[8]

Pauline Kael had observed that "alienation, the central theme of modern literature, has, like everything else, entered mass culture." (A dozen years later, she would make a similar point regarding Arthur Penn's *Bonnie and Clyde*, the *Rebel Without a Cause* of 1967.) Perhaps she should have added that alienation was now a product. And, in any case, Dean was also Dionysian, representing a force Hollywood worshipped and feared. Like the shopkeepers in *The Wild One*, the burghers of Beverly Hills were trapped between a lust for profit and a love of order, a desire to attract the new youth audience and a fear that such youth films would open them to charges of inciting juvenile delinquency. One solution was to articulate youthful alienation while denying any rational reasons for revolt. In *Rebel*, as in *The Wild One*, the hero's problems were individual rather than social.

Seeking to appeal to the widest possible audience and convert everyone into a potential consumer, Hollywood intuitively looked for ways to bring crazy, mixed-up kids into the fold. Thus *Rebel Without a Cause* picks up where *The Wild One* left off—in the police station. Authority is not entirely absent, as made clear in the opening scene, where three troubled teens (Dean, Wood, and Mineo) are addressed by the town's juvenile officer. He's as tough as the übercop who restores

---

8. Known as Operation Teapot, this round of tests had earlier triggered an all-California alert.

order in *The Wild One* but far more understanding—a kind of two-fisted social worker named Ray, after the movie's director.[9]

A diligent Method actor, Dean did his own research and, according to an interview given at the time, discovered that teenagers modeled themselves on the movies. The circuit was complete! Biographer David Dalton would report that Dean "felt a moral obligation to present an alternative to the kids who didn't have a positive image on which to model themselves." The actor too was acting as a social worker. "The thing that interested me in *Rebel*," he told a movie magazine,

> was doing something that would counteract *The Wild One*. I went out and hung around with kids in Los Angeles before making the movie. Some of them even call themselves "wild ones." They wear leather jackets, go out looking for somebody to rough up a little. These aren't poor kids, you know. Lots of them have money, grow up and become pillars of the community!

"They scared me!" Dean was quoted as saying. He stressed that *Rebel* was "a constructive movie" that would give "some of these kids, the ones who aren't out to be tough guys, something to identify with."

Whether or not these claims reflect Dean's actual thoughts, they are implicit in the movie's narrative trajectory. *Rebel* has a rock 'n' roll soul and a New Deal heart. (Ray even called upon Clifford Odets to help doctor the script.) Society and its institutions are privileged over the family. Dean's father is a walking sign crime, given to wearing an apron and saying things like "Hi, Jimbo—you thought I was Mom?" (Dean, meanwhile, is always asking this ridiculous figure what he has to do to be a man. Dad is too stupid to quote Davy Crockett's "Be sure you're right, then go ahead.")

Dean has problems because his father is too weak, Wood suffers because her father is too strong, and Mineo is mixed up because his parents are absent, thus covering every bet. Ray subscribes to the adolescent view that parents shouldn't exist—but he also hints at things that the state simply cannot regulate. *Rebel* is awash with teenage desire. There's a Reichian subtext of frustrated adolescent sexuality—or, rather, of adolescent sexuality being an adult concern. "I don't

---

9. Adrian Scott's lengthy article on the blacklist and conformity in the September 1955 issue of the *Hollywood Review* singled out *The Wild One* and *Blackboard Jungle* as evidence of liberal despair: in both of these would-be social-problem films "the cruelty of the youths was rendered vigorously and dramatically," albeit "directed against protagonists who were either totally impotent or incapable of answering the challenge with effective humanist counter-measures." The fault lay in the state ideological apparatus!

know what to do," Woods's father complains. "All of a sudden, she's a problem!" Late in the movie, Dean, Wood, and Mineo construct a communal, substitute family and Dean has a flash of insight regarding Mineo: "I guess he just wanted us to be like . . ." Then he trails off, unable to say the dread word.

The Wild One presented a subculture; *Rebel Without a Cause* has intimations of a counterculture. Alternately aggressive and needy, these teenagers are groping toward a new society; the *New York Times* would characterize them as "lonely creatures in their own strange, cultist world." This was replicated on the set. Dean smoked marijuana and ran head trips on the cast. As in the movie, Mineo and Wood were both under his spell and Hopper imagined that Ray was as well: "In my opinion James Dean directed *Rebel Without a Cause*, from blocking all the scenes, setting the camera, starting the scene and saying 'cut.' Nicholas Ray intelligently allowed him to do this." Hopper and Ray were romantic rivals during the shoot: Wood was carrying on simultaneous affairs with fellow teen Hopper as well as their forty-three-year-old director.

Rebel ends with the formation of a new couple (unlike *The Wild One*, where Brando simply resumes his endless road trip). Wood, who initially announces that she can "never get close to anybody," is now in love with Dean—having assumed responsibility, he's figured out what it is to be a man. (Corey Allen is the real Wild One—he even dies because the sleeve of his Brandoesque black leather jacket catches in the car door handle, preventing him from bailing from his hot rod during the fatal chickie run.)

The film establishes a new hegemony without the two real delinquents, the hot-rod racer Allen and the neurotic puppy-killer Mineo. The cops appear at the beginning of the movie to identify the crisis and are present at the end to preside over its bloody resolution. There's a definite sense of closure. The only one left on the outside is Mineo's black caretaker—the discordant final image shows her standing alone. But then, the movie's real ending was provided by the audience.

Rebel Without a Cause has its first preview September 1. Soon after, the venerable radio star George Jessel will petition Jack Warner and begin a campaign to have the movie banned.

MGM has already withdrawn *Blackboard Jungle* from the Venice Film Festival after Clare Boothe Luce, the American ambassador to Italy, complained that it portrayed the United States in an unfavorable light and threatened to boycott the festival. In response to Dore Schary's charge that her intervention amounted to "flagrant political censorship," *Time* magazine (which gave *Blackboard Jungle* a relatively favorable notice but was also published by the ambassador's husband, Henry Luce) chose to attack Hollywood:

> Probably the deepest trouble of the contemporary US is its inability to produce a reasonably accurate image of itself. In plays, movies, novels, it cruelly caricatures its life, parades its vices, mutes its excellences. This tendency, far more than Communist propaganda, is responsible for the repulsive picture of US life in the minds of many Europeans and Asians.

As if to prove the point, when *Blackboard Jungle* opens in London, branded with an X rating, conservative critics are irate but the reviewer for London's Communist daily will praise it as "an honest, clean, courageous film"—deficient in its analysis but nevertheless stressing the struggle of "decency and social responsibility [against] the amorality and thuggery born of decaying society."[10]

Where *are* the authorities? Could nothing restrain the Wild One? Did Davy have to die at the Alamo? Is there a power vacuum on Main Street? Two weeks after John Wayne himself introduces the first episode of *Gunsmoke*, a new prime-time Western that will be the longest-running dramatic series in TV history, the Leader of the Free World lies incapacitated. On September 24 in Denver, President Eisenhower suffers a coronary thrombosis.

Our Christian Soldier is old, but like the punk poet run over by death angel motorcyclists in the first scene of Cocteau's *Orpheus*, James Dean will be forever young! September 30, less than a month before *Rebel Without a Cause* is scheduled for release, the twenty-four-year-old star drives his racing Porsche through an intersection on California's Highway 101 and is killed in a head-on collision.

A few days later, Jack Kerouac hitchhikes past this now-sacred spot en route to visit his friend Allen Ginsberg in San Francisco. Only that June, Kerouac had finally landed a publisher for his novel *On the Road*—naturally imagining Marlon Brando, two years his junior, as the star of a movie version. By the night of October 13, Kerouac has made it to San Francisco; he's collecting money for jugs of cheap Napa burgundy when Ginsberg galvanizes a few score shaggy bohos at the Six Gallery in North Beach giving his first public recitation of a poem with an opener nearly as attention-grabbing as Little Richard's *a-wop-bop-a-loo-bop-a-bim-bam-boom*: "I saw the best minds of my generation destroyed by madness, starving hysterical naked, dragging themselves through the negro streets at

---

10. The *Daily Worker* also supported the movie, at least in theory. Speaking for his comrades, David Platt wrote that "we believe along with the Teachers Union and others that the film falsifies the facts about our schools but we're for opening up debate on the film, not suppressing discussion, which is what Mrs. Luce is aiming at."

dawn . . ." (Compare this to William Mooring's testifying prose poem: "I saw young men at several of these shows dressed like Brando in leather jackets . . .")

Ike is still hospitalized when *Rebel Without a Cause* has its premiere, October 27, at the Astor Theater in New York and Bosley Crowther expresses guarded concern at the possible social effect of the movie and the "restless, mumbling misfit" who is its hero.

> The insistence with which the scriptwriter and director address sympathy to the youngsters at the expense of their parents and others who represent authority . . . renders this picture's likely influence upon real youngsters with emotional disturbance questionable.
>
> We certainly would not want to argue for the prohibition of such films, but we continue to insist that producers be more careful and responsible in what they say. To paraphrase an old axiom, little egos have big eyes.

Wild![11]

Better Red Than Dead: Body-Snatched Prisoners of Comanche Mind Control

Existential rebel in his black leather jacket or soulless conformist of the gray flannel suit? Split Hadleyville or defend Fort Apache? As Norman Mailer will write sixteen months hence in "The White Negro," "One is a frontiersman in the Wild West of American night life or else a Square cell, trapped in the totalitarian tissues of America."

---

11. Dean's adolescent angst transcended gender, class, and nationality. In 1956, twenty-year-old François Truffaut wrote that

> in James Dean, today's youth discovers itself. Less for the reasons usually advanced: violence, sadism, hysteria, pessimism, cruelty, and filth, than for others infinitely more simple and commonplace: modesty of feeling, continual fantasy life, moral purity without relation to everyday morality but all the more rigorous, eternal adolescent love of tests and trials, intoxication, pride, and regret at feeling and, finally, acceptance—or refusal—of the world as it is.

Three years later, Truffaut made his own version of *Rebel Without a Cause*, *The 400 Blows*. Meanwhile, West Germany and Poland produced their native Deans, Horst Buchholz and Zbigniew Cybulski. There was also *The James Dean Story* (1957), directed by Robert Altman. In an interview with Truman Capote, Brando revealed that he'd been asked to do the narration:

> This glorifying of Dean is all wrong. That's why I believe the documentary could be important. To show he wasn't a hero—just a lost boy trying to find himself. That ought to be done, and I'd like to do it—maybe as a kind of expiation for some of my own sins. Like making *The Wild One*.

President Eisenhower had barely been released from Walter Reed hospital in November 1955 when, addressing the American Booksellers Convention, independent producer Walter Wanger characterizes his new, still-unreleased, and luridly titled picture as a warning on the menace of conformity. *Invasion of the Body Snatchers* shows "how easy it is for people to be taken over and to lose their souls if they are not alert and determined in their character to be free." The celebrated famous B-movie allegory of the 1950s, *Invasion of the Body Snatchers* gave the scenario of extraterrestrial conquest an additionally topical twist. Drifting down from the sky, seedpods from outer space replicate human beings. As they sleep, people are replaced with perfect, emotion-free, vegetable doubles—Earth successfully colonized by the robotic asexual other-directed drones of a harmoniously single-minded mass society!

After a near-decade of cold war, Americans were used to the subversion scenario and familiar with its science fiction analogues. *Invaders from Mars* had opened in New York only three weeks before the Rosenbergs were executed—both it and *Invasion* a demonstration of what the Communists like to call thought control. Indeed, beginning in February 1952 and continuing intermittently through March 1953, the North Koreans released a series of recorded confessions by captured U.S. servicemen. Several air force lieutenants, a colonel, and even a general admitted to using germ warfare against the Korean people and turned their ire against the capitalist system. These statements were assumed to have been forced (many were in fact scripted by the British Communist reporter Alan Winnington and his Australian associate Wilfred Burchett). But the war's end brought a shocking development: twenty-one American soldiers refused repatriation.

The aliens were no longer among us. Suddenly, the aliens were us—mass identity crisis! What, save the presence of a coercive Big Brother, distinguished Davy Crockett's youthful fans from the uniformed Young Pioneers of the Soviet Union? Perhaps the most insulting aspect of John Fischer's attack on the Crockett craze was his suggestion that America's coonskin-capped kids had been brainwashed—the exact term coined two years into the Korean War to account for the mystifying behavior of the American prisoners who confessed to imaginary war crimes and praised the Communist system.

Mid-November 1953, around the time a CIA prankster spiked the cocktails served at a three-day work retreat with LSD-25, MGM production head Dore Schary dispatched old friend and veteran screenwriter Allen Rivkin to interview the first returning POWs and work up a script. By December, a few weeks before *The Wild One* opened, Andrew Marton was shooting what was hyped as the most quickly developed project in MGM history.

Prisoner of War was quickly released, disowned by the Pentagon, in the middle of the Army-McCarthy hearings, a day after the French defeat at Dien Bien Phu and a day before the *New York Times Magazine* published Dutch psychiatrist Joost Meerloo's article on behavioral modification. Not altogether helpfully, "Pavlov's Dog and Communist Brainwashers" warned that "intervention into free thinking and free mental development does not occur only on the other side of the Iron Curtain."

Given his most serious role since he played a crusading DA in *Storm Warning*, Ronald Reagan starred as an army intelligence officer airlifted behind enemy lines to join a forced march of captured American soldiers. His assignment, as an undercover POW, was to document Communist violations of the Geneva Convention. *Prisoner of War* presented itself as a scoop—although that's not how it was received. The *New York Times* thought the movie "only rings faintly of the horrible truth . . . uninspired fare, whose shocks appear superficial and hastily contrived." The *Daily Worker*, not quite as dismissive, called upon "patriotic Americans and particularly the parents of Army-age sons" to "demand that Congress investigate why MGM released this fraudulent, war-whooping film which is an affront to the nation and even outraged the Pentagon."

Indeed, *Prisoner of War* almost seemed a demented rehash of Hollywood's internal struggle. (Hadn't the star himself found brainwashing in the industry? "Lots of people in our community don't realize that their thinking is dictated, in that it was implanted by the Communists a few years ago. Their minds need reconditioning," Reagan told the press in 1952.) The POW camp is a Stalinist nightmare, administered by a hammy comic-opera Russian (Oskar Homolka, the lovable Maxim Litvinov of *Mission to Moscow*), wagging his eyebrows and puffing evilly on a cigarette holder as his prisoners maintain their spirits with a doggerel chant that might have been written by the father in *My Son John*, proclaiming Uncle Sam's superiority to Uncle Joe.

All confessions are filmed—when Reagan's is shown, the POWs riot and trash the 16 mm projector. In the end, the worst "collaborators" turn out to be actors fooling the Reds, while, despite the emphasis on physical torture, the Communists (like the filmmakers) understand that the most effective atrocity is the liquidation of a POW's pet dog.

In popular culture, brainwashing was the post–Korean War Korean War scenario. The notion of the brainwashed American prisoner tapped into the most deep-rooted of national myths, expressed in the late seventeenth- and early eighteenth-century New England "captivity narratives" wherein white settlers— usually women—were abducted by Indians and even went native.

The conclusion of Alan LeMay's novella "The Avenging Texans," published in the December 4, 1954, issue of the *Saturday Evening Post*, conjoined the brainwashing and captivity scenarios. Rescued years after her abduction by Comanche raiders, a white girl accuses her saviors of misleading her.

> "You lie," she answered . . . "All white men lie. Always."
>
> Charlie looked at him. "Is she——? Have they——?" He didn't know how to put it. "Mart, has she been with the bucks?"
>
> Mart said, "Charlie, I don't know. I don't think so. It's more like—like they've done something to her mind."
>
> "You mean she's crazy?"
>
> "No, that isn't it, rightly. Only, she takes their part now. Like as if they took out her brain and put in an Indian brain instead."
>
> "Doesn't want to leave 'em, huh?"
>
> "Almost seems like she's an Indian herself now. Inside."
>
> "I see something now," Mart said. "I see why the Comanches murder our women when they raid—brain our babies even—what ones they don't pick to steal. It's so we won't breed. They want us off the earth. I understand that, because that's what I want for them. I want them cleaned off the face of the world."

A parallel account of genocidal war appeared simultaneously, serialized in *Collier's* magazine: former adman Jack Finney's "The Body Snatchers."

Although science fiction, Finney's story was a period piece and, in a sense, a secret history. The writer would deny that "The Body Snatchers" was a Cold War allegory but it was specifically set during the summer of 1953, immediately following the Korean armistice and soon after the Rosenberg execution capped a six-year hunt for Communist traitors. The war had not quite been a victory, and the American press was preoccupied with stories of GIs subjected to Communist brainwashing.

Finney imagines the collectivized pods as naturally apathetic. The town they infiltrate falls into a state of seedy decline—stores are as empty of produce as those in a drab Eastern European city. ("You can hardly even buy a Coke in most places," a traveling salesman complains to Miles. "Lately, this place has been out of coffee altogether, for no reason at all, and today when they have it, it's lousy, terrible.") Going into battle, hero Dr. Miles Bennell invokes Winston Churchill: "We shall fight them in the fields, and in the streets, we shall fight in the hills; we shall never surrender."

The story has a happy ending: the FBI successfully beats back the invasion. The movie, however, will exude "the stench of fear" that Norman Mailer has detected rising from "every pore in American life."

"The Body Snatchers" was acquired by producer Walter Wanger, now associated with Allied Artists, while it was still being serialized. Wanger had emerged from a brief stretch in prison—having shot and wounded Jennings Lang, the agent representing his then-wife Joan Bennett—to produce the reformist *Riot in Cell Block 11* (1954). This comeback was directed by Don Siegel from a screenplay written by ex-Communist HUAC informer Richard Collins, and Wanger hoped to assemble the same team.

Collins, however, was unavailable. Scarcely had *Collier's* finished running Finney's serial in early 1955 than the author met to discuss the movie version with Wanger, Siegel, and screenwriter Daniel Mainwaring. Siegel, who had directed his 1949 debut, *The Big Steal*, from a Mainwaring script, saw the writer as similar in background to Collins—jokingly characterizing him as a "member (nonpaying) of the older Communist League."[12]

Siegel and Mainwaring changed Finney's story so that all major characters, except the heroic doctor Miles Bennell (Kevin McCarthy), ultimately become pods; their ending was also more pessimistic. A lone rebel railing against the encroaching mass society of the pods, Miles was left shouting an unheard warning amid the heedless freeway traffic. Completed in mid-February, Mainwaring's draft was then reworked by Collins, who suggested the pod invasion as an epidemic of mindless conformity. Collins drafted Miles's speech on the changes in American society: "In my practice I see how people have allowed their humanity to drain away . . . only it happens slowly rather than all at once. They didn't seem to mind." Collins, who had told HUAC four years earlier that his

---

12. Siegel has described himself as a liberal, though his oeuvre is more suggestive of an antiauthoritarian libertarian belief in rugged individualism. Mainwaring, never apparently a Communist, produced socially conscious journalism and pulp fiction during the Depression; his previous scripts, some written under the name Geoffrey Homes, include two exposés, Joseph Losey's *The Lawless* (1950) and Phil Karlson's *The Phenix City Story* (1955), that, like *Invasion of the Body Snatchers*, suggest that American normality is a Hadleyville façade. During the Korean War, Mainwaring wrote two topical cavalry Westerns: *The Last Outpost* (1951), from a story by David Lang, was a key film in the construction of the "new" action-oriented, guntoting Ronald Reagan; *Bugles in the Afternoon* (1952) similarly stressed the importance of white antagonists uniting to fight a common Indian enemy. In 1955, his anti-Communist crime drama *A Bullet for Joey*, a relentlessly perfunctory tale of atomic chicanery, served to "clear" graylisted co-screenwriter A.I. Bezzerides and beleaguered liberal Edward G. Robinson. An anti–*Pickup on South Street*, the movie has Robinson's Royal Mountie inspector turn around the American gangster (George Raft) hired by a foreign power to kidnap a Canadian nuclear scientist.

thousands of hours of work for the Communist Party during World War II turned him into a "trained zombie," also wrote the podified psychiatrist's admonition to Miles and Becky: "Love. Desire. Ambition. Faith. Without them life's so simple, believe me."

Body Snatchers went into production in late March 1955, its twenty-three-day shooting schedule coinciding with rampant pod behavior: the height of the Davy Crockett craze, growing rock 'n' roll fever. Exteriors were filmed in Sierra Madre, a self-contained town east of Los Angeles with some aspects of *The Wild One*'s rural nowhere and others resembling the suburban bedroom community of *Rebel Without a Cause*. The final chase was shot overlooking Hollywood on Mulholland Drive. Although working on a budget of less than $400,000, Wanger considered *Body Snatchers* an important, even daring, production—a science-fiction movie for adults. The MPAA Code Administration objected four times to having the romantic leads Miles and Becky (Dana Wynter) both divorced; like *Kiss Me Deadly*, the movie would eventually receive a "B" rating from the Legion of Decency. With the movie's release set for September 1955, the filmmakers embarked on a lengthy postproduction debate on how best to position its unusual narrative. The script originally ended with a tight close-up of the distraught, now-solitary pod fighter Miles screaming at the audience that there was no escape and no time to waste: "Look, you fools, you're in danger! Can't you see! They're after you. They're after all of us—our wives, our children. They're here already. You're next! *You're next!*" Wanger thought to preface the movie with a recent quote from Winston Churchill and, as he had in his wartime thriller *Foreign Correspondent*, add a didactic final warning.[13]

The necessity for a framing story, set up by an on-screen narrator, seemed increasingly urgent after a series of previews during the summer of 1955. Siegel would recall that "when the lights came up everyone looked nervously at his immediate neighbor at either side of him and wondered uneasily if he were surrounded by pods"; after one Encino preview, art director Ted Haworth wrote Wanger that, when the movie ended, he

> heard "Jesus" over and over and over. Also, "Mother, Mother, I'm scared," and a hundred other varieties of great reactions. . . . I have never worked on a suspense film that generated an audience fever like this. They were scared, and they resented it because they were shamed by their own obvious cowardice. . . .

---

13. Wanger's first choice for narrator was Orson Welles, who would establish an obvious link to *The War of the Worlds*.

At a subsequent preview, however, Wanger was himself panicked by inappropriate laughs and walkouts. Mainwaring drafted a framing story shot—sans celebrity narrator—in late September, ending the movie on a marginally more optimistic note.

The title also presented a problem. As *The Body Snatchers* was too similar to Val Lewton's 1945 *The Body Snatcher*, Allied Artists proposed the generic *They Came from Another World*. Siegel strongly objected, offering instead *Sleep No More* and *Better Off Dead*—titles suggesting the familiar Cold War metaphor of sleep versus wakefulness and the Cold War mantra "Better dead than red." It was not until late November that the threat of "invasion" was finally affixed to that of "body snatchers." The debate over the title and framing story pushed back the movie release while adding $30,000 to the negative cost.

Invasion of the Body Snatchers finally opened on a limited basis, double-billed with *The Atomic Man*, in March 1956. Few future classics were ever so disreputable or obscure; the *New York Times* never bothered to review it. Two months later, Wanger wrote Bosley Crowther begging the critic to only look at his movie: "I tried to make it a plea against conformity, and apparently the exhibitor didn't think it was right to have an idea in a picture of this sort, and instead of a Broadway showing, it opened in Brooklyn."

Communism had long been visualized as a disease, a germ, a form of alien mind control; it was not, however, generally conceived as a tranquilizer. By the time *Invasion of the Body Snatchers* appeared, however, the nation had embraced the soothing presence of President Eisenhower; moreover, the specter of conformity was now associated with submission to McCarthyism, even by McCarthy's acolytes.[14]

Bestsellerdom pondered the question. Who were the real Hidden Persuaders? Was the Organization Man an analogue to the Master of Deceit? Like *High Noon*, *Invasion of the Body Snatchers* lent itself to both right- and left-wing readings—either a drama of Communist subversion or a parable of suburban conformity, unfolding in a hilariously bland atmosphere of extreme hypervigilance. *High Noon* attacked Hollywood cowardice while providing a scenario that could justify America's Cold War foreign policies; *Invasion of*

---

14. By 1954, the problem of "conformism" was a commonplace subject of college commencement speeches and liberal sermons. *McCarthy and His Enemies* (1954) by William F. Buckley and L. Brent Bozell devotes a full chapter to debunking "the new conformity" imposed by McCarthy's so-called reign of terror, pointing out that the only conformity on which McCarthyism insists is conformity in opposition to Communism.

the Body Snatchers proposed another sort of Hadleyville, an all-purpose metaphor for the nation's domestic life. Wanger was committed to the movie's liberal interpretation. But, just as European commentators were quick to recognize *High Noon*'s foreign-policy implications, so the Italian critic Ernesto G. Laura was apparently the first, writing in 1957, to link *Invasion of the Body Snatchers* to the anti-Communist rhetoric of J. Edgar Hoover and *Reader's Digest*. The transformation of ordinary Americans into soullessly Sovietized Babbitts was a pop *1984*, complete with the notion of sexual love as a subversive crime.

So familiar has the Body Snatchers metaphor become—and so common had the alien invasion scenario been in the years immediately preceding its release—it's notable that *Variety*'s 1956 notice found the movie "difficult to follow due to the strangeness of its scientific premise." But if the reviewer is being willfully obtuse, his refusal to recognize the movie's premise mirrors its story. *Invasion of the Body Snatchers* offers a near-textbook illustration of the rare condition known as Capgras syndrome—the delusional belief that close relatives or associates, sometimes including one's pets or oneself, have been replaced by sinister doubles.[15]

Capgras syndrome has been variously analyzed as either a form of projection (if a familiar person no longer elicits the same affective response, the person must have changed, rather than the subject's feelings) or a form of denial (rationalizing negative traits in one with whom the subject has strong emotional ties). As Capgras syndrome suggests the idealization of a particular individual, it follows that *Invasion of the Body Snatchers* would appear soon after the 1948–54 period of maximum mobilization—once it was safe to dramatize the recent hysteria. More than any other Cold War fantasy, *Invasion of the Body Snatchers* showed America alienated from itself: the "good" motherland experienced as a nearly identical "bad" one.

Invasion of the Body Snatchers is all the more enjoyable for the podlike quality of its impassive performances and cheap, open-air noir naturalism. Nor is that the only source of deadpan humor. An innocuous small town is the fount of contagion; the cops have become criminal and love terror ("I never knew what fear was really like until I kissed Becky"); tranquilizers are prescribed by creatures from another planet; adjustment is made synonymous with conform-

---

15. *Invaders from Mars* and the British *I Married a Monster from Outer Space* (1958) are related examples of Capgrasoid sci-fi. The latter's title echoes the similarly premised *I Married a Communist*, and a study of the syndrome's case histories shows that imagined Communist conspiracies were scarcely unknown during the heightened suspicion of the Cold War.

ist coercion; the family is infiltrated by inhuman enemies; the telephone is transformed into an instrument of surveillance. Normality was rendered sinister; overwhelming anxiety fed a powerful desire for security, a longing to merge with the group, whether in suburbs or Party cells, even as this urge was experienced as a threat to the individual. *Invasion of the Body Snatchers* provided an imaginative visualization of the national security state and reckoned its psychic cost to America's self-image.

Looking back on the Cold War from the post-McCarthy period, Siegel and company not only naturalized the Red Scare but imbued it with Darwinian angst—the fear that, as the Reds themselves were pleased to suggest, Communism, having resolved all manner of social conflicts and individual anxieties, was actually a higher stage on the evolutionary ladder. At the same time, another movie advanced the oddly appealing notion that Americans might be more primitive than they assumed. *Invasion of the Body Snatchers* was a movie with a mission; *The Searchers* projected one.

Texas, 1868: A demobilized soldier returns to his family after a long absence. The following day, they are massacred by Indians, save for his young niece. The man spends the next five years in pursuit of the guilty Comanche band, seeking revenge and the abducted child; when he realizes that little Debbie has grown into an Indian woman, however, his goal shifts from rescue to murder. In the end he finds the girl—and also that he is unable to kill her. This, briefly, is the plot of *The Searchers*, the greatest and—in its return to the genre's root issues—the most radical Western that John Ford ever made.

Did the mid-1950s thaw prompt Ford's introspection? His politics remained solidly right-wing: he maintained his association with the Motion Picture Alliance and consulted on Militant Liberty, the National Security Council's secret program to promote the concept of "freedom" in American movies. But something was on Ford's mind. Before he began filming in June 1955, America's preeminent director announced that his new Western would be "a kind of psychological epic."

Dealing with race hatred and psychosexual obsession, *The Searchers* is nothing if not a movie about pathology—not just Ford's but America's. Framed by a song that asks a question it declines to answer directly (namely, why there can be no peace of mind for its protagonist), this most troubling of Westerns dramatizes a seemingly familiar story. Yet, filled with things unspoken and unseen, *The Searchers* leaves much to the viewer's imagination (or, better, unconscious), lending itself most fruitfully to what the Surrealists called "irrational enlargement." With the nation at peace, the Western declared war on itself. At once hero and villain, the deeply disturbed and savagely single-minded protagonist Ethan Edwards was played by the nation's reigning male star and (now that Tail-Gunner Joe had crashed) its most outspoken anti-Communist, John Wayne.

Kiss Me Deadly, *Rebel Without a Cause*, and *Invasion of the Body Snatchers* came from or appealed to the margins; *The Searchers* was projected from the heart of the establishment. In 1954, Cornelius Vanderbilt "Sonny" Whitney—a fifty-five-year-old sportsman and industrialist, co-founder of Pan American Airways, creator of Florida's Marineland, backer of David O. Selznick's *Gone with the Wind*, and former member of the Truman administration—reentered the movie business, helping Ford's longtime partner Merian Cooper finance *This Is Cinerama* and thereafter forming his own company. Whitney admired Ford's cavalry trilogy and proposed to produce another series of Wayne vehicles, based on James Warner Bellah's Civil War stories. Cooper, however, imagined a less epic project, optioning "The Avenging Texans"; still, Whitney saw *The Searchers* as the opening shot in "an American series" intended "to show our own people their country and also to make certain that the rest of the world learns more about us."

The Searchers fulfilled Whitney's mandate with a vengeance. Was it not the three-century Indian war that constructed America's national identity, in part by providing white settlers with a ready-made Other as well as a uniquely American protagonist, the Frontiersman? (In his search for a viable youth hero, Walt Disney was even then domesticating that very character as Davy Crockett.) The historical prototype for the King of the Wild Frontier was Daniel Boone, the solitary hunter most at home in the primeval forest; Boone was first fictionalized as the protagonist of James Fenimore Cooper's Leatherstocking Tales, a figure D.H. Lawrence described in his *Studies in Classic American Literature* as "a man who keeps his moral integrity hard and intact. An isolate, almost selfless, stoic, enduring man, who lives by death, by killing." Who else could this be but our Cowboy Warrior, John Wayne?

Lawrence called Leatherstocking "pure white," but Lawrence's American disciple Leslie Fiedler understood that the backwoodsman was actually a sort of cultural mulatto: the White Indian, the settler gone native or even wild. The original inhabitants of America's unspoiled Eden may have been originally conceived as noble savages or uncanny demons; by the nineteenth century, however, these so-called Indians were an obstruction to progress, an inferior race destined to disappear through either assimilation or extermination. "The Avenging

Texans" articulated the war against the Comanche in suitably cosmic genocidal terms, complete with sexual component.[16]

"The Avenging Texans" may have been inspired by the case of a settler woman who, kidnapped at age nine by Comanche, married a Comanche chief; subsequently recaptured by whites, she starved herself to death. The underlying story is much older. Cooper based *The Last of the Mohicans* (1826) on Boone's rescue of three white girls, including his own daughter, from the Cherokees. This tale was retold by Cooper's followers, spectacularly staged a decade later, in Robert Bird's *Nick of the Woods*—the most successful American melodrama of the first half of the nineteenth century. Having suffered the loss of his family and bride in an Indian massacre, Bird's hero devotes his life to vengeance. Quaker (!) by day, killer by night, schizoid Nick declares war on all Indians; he is determined to murder as many as he can, taking care to carve a cross on each corpse.

Nick could hardly be characterized as Christian. In fact, he's dangerously close to being a redskin savage himself. Twenty years into *Nick*'s marathon run, Herman Melville addressed this notion in *The Confidence-Man*, which includes a chapter on the "metaphysics" of Indian hating. Melville's narrator takes pains to establish that, because the backwoodsman's life is "a life which, as related to humanity, is related mainly to Indians," he is in constant danger of himself becoming an Indian. What prevents this is the elevation of Indian hating to a universal principle—usually in response to "some signal outrage." Having fled white civilization, the frontiersman projects his unconscious desires onto the Indian from whom he must protect the white civilization (and its embodiment, the white woman) if he is to remain white at all. It is from this premise that *The Searchers* begins.

In January 1955, Ford and his son-in-law Frank Nugent began work on a script that would enrich the *Nick* scenario (as well as LeMay's original story) with new characters and more extreme situations. Among other things, they complicated the racial equation by making Ethan Edwards's sidekick—and Debbie's adopted older brother—the part-Indian orphan Martin Pawley. The white man and his red companion have their traditional roles reversed. Ethan is the savage and Martin the Christian, but the half-breed is the most rooted character

---

16. In *Regeneration Through Violence*, Richard Slotkin notes that although the post–Civil War anti-Indian campaigns were often provoked to justify expropriation of Indian land by railroads and associated interests, "the essentially economic basis of the conflict was concealed behind a rhetoric which emphasized the need to rescue white captives, particularly women, from the brutal rapists of the plains."

and the white hero the most alienated—although the title unites them under the rubric of the terminally restless.

The first shot of *The Searchers* has Martha Edwards open her cabin door onto the bright world outside and see her returning brother-in-law, Ethan, riding alone over the prairie. Theirs is a fateful reunion.

The atmosphere is thick with sexual metaphor and displacement: What is the significance of husband Aaron's limp? The basis for Martha's barely concealed hysteria or Ethan's rage? Ethan's character is quickly developed in largely negative terms. He is a loner, an unreconstructed Confederate rebel, an Indian-hater, and presumably an outlaw. There is the unmistakable suggestion that he has committed a crime to get the money that he throws on his brother's table—and a more subtle suggestion of another crime whose unspoken effect hovers over this scene and the next. Is it possible that Ethan and Martha were lovers, and if so, that seven-year-old Debbie may in fact be Ethan's daughter?[17]

Ethan has returned home with some purpose in mind. Was his wandering a self-imposed penance now served or broken? Is it his fantasy, in an affront to every ideal of Christian civilization, to purchase his brother's wife? As noted by Michael Wilmington and Joseph McBride in their 1974 monograph *John Ford*, Ethan heralds the destruction of his brother's family. In carrying out the massacre that occurs the very day after Ethan's arrival, the Comanche chief called Scar seems to fulfill—or rather, overfulfill—the prodigal's agenda.

The Searchers's first twenty minutes establish the psychological necessity for all that must follow. Ethan appears as a sexual threat to settler civilization. Scar's crimes enact a terrible desire that cannot be represented and must be repressed. The guilty hero is compelled by his inflamed Indian-hatred to rescue civilization, in the person of his abducted niece—and reestablish his own whiteness. In the course of this quest, the taboo fantasy of possessing his brother's wife is superseded by the horror of miscegenation. In order to save the despoiled and brainwashed Debbie (grown into Natalie Wood, who had just been "kid-

---

17. This Freudian slip has been made in more than one description of the film, including Wayne's. During the course of a 1974 interview with Wayne, Brian Huberman ventured to say that the star had "a great part" as *The Searchers*'s "villain." The irate Wayne replied that his character "was no villain. He was a man living in his times. The Indians fucked his wife. What would you have done?" Recounting this exchange, Joseph McBride wonders whether Wayne was thinking of Martha or Debbie or both.

napped" by James Dean in *Rebel Without a Cause*), Ethan has to destroy her. For him, Debbie is better dead than red.

In December 1955, Warners publicist Walter MacEwen wrote Jack Warner that *The Searchers* had previewed in San Francisco to an enthusiastic audience. Allowing that, given its scene of two crazed white girl captives, display of white scalps, and the star's attempt to shoot a young girl in cold blood, *The Searchers* was "brutal in spots to the point of being daring," the response was terrific. "The house was packed for REBEL WITHOUT A CAUSE, and I don't believe we lost more than 2 or 3 people who probably just had to go . . ."[18]

As predicted, and as massively advertised ("THE BIGGEST, ROUGHEST TOUGHEST . . . AND MOST BEAUTIFUL PICTURE EVER MADE!"), *The Searchers* was a hit. It ruled the national box office for weeks in late June to finish first for the month en route to a $4.45 million gross and tied *Rebel Without a Cause* (whose title it might almost have appropriated) as the eleventh-highest-grossing movie of 1956.

Fifteen years later, the critic Andrew Sarris would write that *The Searchers* had been "generally misunderstood" by contemporary reviewers. Misunderstood perhaps (as Ethan's quest passes from vengeance through nihilism into absurdity) but hardly misappreciated: *Variety* called the movie "a Western in the grand scale." The *New York Herald Tribune* deemed *The Searchers* "distinguished." *Newsweek* called it "remarkable." *Look* hailed this new "Homeric odyssey." *Cue* praised its "astonishing wealth of minute detail and honest, strikingly natural characterizations." The *New York Times*, which found *The Searchers* "a rip-shorting Western, as brashly entertaining as they come," praised Wayne as "uncommonly commanding." (The *Los Angeles Times* took note of Duke's favorable reviews in the East Coast press in its own review.) *Life*'s preview juxtaposed *The Searchers* with the long-delayed *The Conqueror*—"East and West Meet in Wayne"—complete with complementary photos of the star on horseback, in battle, and carrying the girl.

---

18. MPAA code-enforcer Geoffrey Shurlock had objected to an earlier instance of Ethan scalping a dead Indian, so Ford eliminated any verbal reference to the act in the script; the audience sees Ethan emerging from Scar's tent with a bloody hank of hair and, as with much in *The Searchers*, can draw its own conclusions. Ford handled Shurlock's only other objection—that the "gun-carrying leader of a quasi-military group" played by Ward Bond was a minister—in a similar fashion. Shurlock suggested that Bond be changed from a minister to a judge; Ford presents him as both.

Audiences saw *The Searchers*, enjoyed the movie, and repressed it. For the *Daily Worker*, it was business as usual: "John Ford uses his directorial skill to glorify the slaughter of Indians of any age or sex." Only intellectuals were disturbed. The *Nation*'s Robert Hatch called attention to *The Searchers*'s pathology, characterizing the movie as "a picnic for sadists" and describing Ethan as "a psychotic with homicidal tendencies which he is given almost unlimited opportunities to indulge"; other Ford fans and Western buffs were made uneasy by the rambling narrative and Ford's representation of his hitherto beloved cavalry as alternately ridiculous or genocidal.[19]

Writing in *Sight and Sound*, future director Lindsay Anderson objected to Ethan as "an unmistakable neurotic, devoured by an irrational hatred of Indians." The role of Captain Ahab's Texas cousin was something Humphrey Bogart might have played, if one could imagine him chasing Comanche in a Stetson hat, but never a straight shooter like Gary Cooper. Only the Cowboy Warrior would have had the swaggering confidence to play an obsessed white supremacist as a true American. (And what was the white outlaw if not the successor to the savage Indian, an alien id-monster who must be tamed if law and order are to prevail?)

In *The Confidence Man*, Melville describes the frontiersman in familiar Leatherstocking terms as "self-willed," "self-reliant," and "instinctual," "not merely content to be alone but anxious to be so," and then makes explicit what can only be hinted at in Cooper or Bird: "Though held to be a sort of barbarian, the backwoodsman would seem to America what Alexander was to Asia— captain in the vanguard of a conquering civilization." Midway through *The Searchers*, Ford makes this point with a near match cut, deleting six months, and perhaps six hundred miles, to show Ethan and Martin halted in falling snow at the moment Debbie's trail is coldest. Ethan is about to swear eternal vengeance; before he does, he explains to Martin the source of his confidence that he will fulfill it: the Indians, he says, cannot conceive of "a critter that'll just keep coming on." It is not the Reds who are implacable, it is us.

Ethan's connection to the civilization he both rejects and represents is inescapable. He is national destiny made manifest. Ethan takes America's sins— racism, cruelty, violence, intolerance—onto himself. He is not just the Necessary Evil, frontier precursor to the Patriot Roughneck, but an utterly unapologetic,

---

19. Even the French were tepid. Jean-Luc Godard was notable for regarding *The Searchers* as a masterpiece. In a 1959 *Cahiers du Cinéma* essay on Westerns, Godard echoed *Newsweek* by comparing *The Searchers*'s ending to "Ulysses being reunited with Telemachus"; four years later he ranked it as the fourth-greatest American sound film.

self-reliant, pod-fighting force of nature—the rootless Wild One given a cause, perhaps even made a saint in his essentially selfless quest to liberate an innocent child from the Redskin Menace.[20]

In a sense, *The Searchers* is a movie of the late 1960s. Perhaps it required the madness of Sam Peckinpah's *Major Dundee* or *The Wild Bunch* to be fully appreciated—or recognizing Ethan as an unapologetic segregationist in a nation apparently filled with them, or living through America's Indochinese adventure, or the presence of a counterculture that valorized ramblin' around and identified not with the comrades but the Comanche, feeding acid to teenage runaways.

By the end of Richard Nixon's first term, when Westerns were routinely founded on violent social schisms, set in morally depraved towns, and populated by murderous crazies, Joseph McBride and Michael Wilmington published a near canonical appreciation in *Sight and Sound* that ended by calling *The Searchers* nothing less than "the story of America." That same year, Andrew Sarris dug it as an existential road movie: "*The Searchers* is concerned as much with a peculiarly American madness and wanderlust as with anything else."

If *The Searchers* was the precursor to *Easy Rider*, however, its sequel was the fantastic media pageant that was the abduction of heiress Patty Hearst and her transformation into the counterculture's last heroine, the bank-robbing revolutionary Tania. Writing in *New York* magazine, three years after Hearst's recovery, film journalist Stuart Byron agreed that *The Searchers* exposed the psychosexual economy of imperialism, riffing that it might have been retitled, after Norman Mailer, *Why We Are in Vietnam*. But the reason why *The Searchers* had been fetishized by an influential group of young American directors was the narrative: an obsessed man's search for someone possessed by aliens who, when found, refuses, at least initially, to be rescued.[21]

---

20. As Ford would say of *Fort Apache*'s conclusion: "We've had a lot of people who were supposed to be great heroes, and you know damn well they weren't. But it's good for the country to have heroes to look up to. . . ." But Wayne had no such ambivalence, saying of the character, "I loved him and I loved playing him." He looked up to himself. *The Searchers* was not only Wayne's favorite film—he named his next son Ethan.

21. Characterizing *The Searchers* as "the Super-Cult Movie of the New Hollywood," Byron paraphrased Hemingway on *Huckleberry Finn* to make the hyperbolic claim that "all recent American cinema" derived from Ford's masterpiece. As evidence, he cited movies by a number of young filmmakers: Paul Schrader (*Hardcore*), John Milius (*Dillinger, Big Wednesday, The Wind and the Lion*), Martin Scorsese (*Mean Streets, Taxi Driver*), Steven Spielberg (*Close Encounters of the Third Kind*), George Lucas (*Star Wars*), and Michael Cimino (*The Deer Hunter*). Nine years later, Schrader would make the most explicit of captivity stories, *Patty Hearst*.

But is it the brainwashed captive or the fanatical frontiersman who refuses white civilization? Almost simultaneously with Byron's piece, film scholar Brian Henderson's 1980 essay "*The Searchers*: An American Dilemma" analyzed the movie as both time capsule and myth, a response to the racial issues of the mid-1950s. Henderson pointed out that the essential conflict concerned the nature of kinship; employing precepts of structural anthropology, he went on to identify the binary oppositions that Ford attempted to resolve.

Specifically, *The Searchers* was preoccupied with the question of Indianness. Was Martin an Indian? Had Debbie become one? What about Ethan? Half-breeds were ubiquitous: the secondary character Mose Harper is a settler who behaves as bizarrely as any Comanche, but whose longing for a home is stronger than any other white person's in the film; the villainous Scar (played by a blue-eyed German actor specializing in exotic roles) sought revenge on the whites for the savage murder of his sons. Perhaps the question should be turned around: Who is an American?

As a narrative function, Henderson writes, Martin was alternately part red or pure white, depending on the situation. In the dream life, however, he is understood as pure red. Martin is introduced bursting into Aaron and Martha's cabin as the family sits down for the dinner that will be their last. The question that the narrative poses—will he be chastised for his late arrival?—conceals a deeper issue, at least for Ethan. Does this red man have a place at the white family table? Similarly, what's at stake when the Comanche attack the pursuit party is less Martin's baptism under fire than his willingness to use violence on his racial brethren. That Martin passes these tests hardly mitigates his running debate with Ethan on the nature of family ties: does consanguineal kinship trump adoption?

Henderson argues that the issue was acutely relevant because of *The Searchers*'s historical moment. The movie was conceived, produced, and released in the wake of the Supreme Court's landmark decision making segregation unconstitutional in American public schools—a time when tremendous, often hysterical, opposition to this ruling in a number of states was, at least on the level of rhetoric, fueled by fear of race mixing. This was precisely the subject of *The Searchers*, which further addressed two issues arising from the Supreme Court decision. The first involved the renegotiation of American race relations, and the second was the South's refusal to comply with the new law of the land. Ethan and Martin's ongoing discussion concerns the first; Ethan's reconciliation and capacity to rejoin society is an implicit response to the latter.

In *The Searchers*'s final shot, a near-rhyme of the first, Debbie and Martin are reintegrated into white civilization, reentering a frontier cabin—Debbie still in Comanche buckskin and beads. Even a brainwashed white girl gone temporarily native, Communist, or out of her mind for Elvis might be returned to the fold. So might a racial Other as loyal, civilized, and given to Christian understanding as Martin Pawley. Ethan, however, remains outside.

The frontier closes—or at least the door. Has Ethan accepted the Supreme Court's new order or will he remain an unreconstructed white-supremacist supporter of the old one, condemned as he condemned the dead Indians he mutilated to "wander forever between the winds"? Had the Cowboy Warrior consigned himself, his desires and his ideas, to the shining void? *The Searchers* made it possible to think so.

"That'll Be the Day!" The Spirit of '56

America changed in 1956—and so did America's sense of America. "America you don't really want to go to war," Allen Ginsberg suggested in a poem dated that January. To explain, the poet adopted the broken English of a Hollywood Indian. "America it's them bad Russians . . . Her wants our auto plants in Siberia." The notion of a Soviet America was absurd. ("Ugh. Him make Indians learn read.")

The chronicler, the de Tocqueville or maybe even the Tom Paine of this new New World, was a thirty-one-year-old Swiss-born photographer named Robert Frank. From June 1955 into the following summer, Frank crossed and recrossed the continent in a used 1950 Ford. "I am photographing how Americans live, have fun, eat, drive cars, work, etc.," he wrote to his parents back in Europe. Frank's first road trip took him from New York through the industrial cities of western Pennsylvania and Ohio to Detroit; his second went from New York to Savannah. Supported by a Guggenheim fellowship, Frank drove south once more in late 1955, this time to Miami, and then headed for California, taking a circuitous route through the old Confederacy—and the Southwest, driving Route 66 to Las Vegas and then on to Los Angeles. Frank spent the winter in California, before heading back east to New York by way of Reno, Salt Lake, Butte, the Great Plains, and Chicago—to which he returned in mid-August for the Democratic Convention that again nominated Adlai Stevenson.

Over the course of his travels, Frank exposed nearly eight hundred rolls of film. His subjects included Detroit autoworkers, Hoboken politicians, New York City drag queens, the workday crowd on New Orleans's Canal Street, and radio preacher Oral Roberts, as well as folks attending rodeos, picnics, funerals, and political rallies. But mainly, Frank was the first photographer to document that ubiquitous-yet-ignored, nowhere-but-everywhere realm of billboards, drive-ins, and gas stations later called the Strip. For centuries, America's "natural paradise" had been a source of transcendent value: "Is not the landscape, every glimpse of which hath a grandeur, a face of Him?" Emerson asked. Thanks to Frank, what had been familiar was now made strange.

Intimating the loneliness inherent in the American notion of freedom, his photographs revealed America to itself—a Capgras Nation of empty two-lane blacktop, seedy bus depots, empty casinos, solitary lunch counters, and all-night diners with incandescent jukeboxes inhabited by a restless tribe of waitresses, truckers, and midnight cowboys. *The Americans* appeared first in France in 1958, to little attention, and then in the United States a bit more than a year later. Despite some positive reviews, the book was characterized as "sick," "warped," "joyless," "dishonest," "sad," "neurotic," "marred by spite, bitterness and narrow prejudice." It was as if Frank turned the natural paradise inside out to reveal an everyday America many chose to ignore or repress.

Working ahead of the curve, Frank completed his road trip before Congress authorized a forty-thousand-mile interstate highway system and *Time* enthused that such highways were "really *the* American art." His yearlong trip had its literary analogues. Shortly before he set out, the *Paris Review* published a chunk of Jack Kerouac's *On the Road*; around the time Frank split California, Allen Ginsberg gave the first public reading of "Howl." Like the Beats, Frank presented a chaotic countryside at once concrete and allegorical, vital and death haunted. His photographs of an L.A. street evangelist hawking *Awake!*, the sign "Remember Your Loved Ones 69¢" posted above a row of Styrofoam crosses, the "Christ Died For Our Sins" card taped to a Chevy, and the stone St. Francis presiding over skid row could serve as the subject of a Ginsberg poem or Kerouac riff.

Taken as a narrative, *The Americans* suggested a pilgrim's progress through a hardscrabble land, subjugated by images and ruled by machines, where unexpected beauty sprouts like weeds in a vacant lot. With their iconic use of U.S. flags and TV sets, Frank's photographs heralded the coming of pop art. The same season Walt Disney opened his theme park, Robert Frank found another. *The Americans* anticipated the stranger-in-a-strange-land iconography and attitudes of movies that would not be made for another dozen years—the Hollywood new wave of Arthur Penn, Dennis Hopper, and Robert Altman. Understood as prophecy, *The Americans* pointed toward an alternate America of subculture and counterculture, the realm in which the Wild One and Black Rebels dwelt.[22]

And also perhaps the figure that Norman Mailer the following year termed the White Negro—a new American type, a psychic frontiersman, a hipster, a white man who, like the narrator of Kerouac's *On the Road* (finally published in 1957), walks through Denver's "colored section," wishing that he were a Negro because "the best the white world had offered was not enough ecstasy for me, not enough life, joy, kicks, darkness, music, not enough night." The source of hip is the Negro, Mailer would argue, even as he returned to the original subject of Robert Lindner's *Rebel Without a Cause* to posit the "criminal psychopath" as the man of the future.

Bleak as it seemed, *The Americans* had intimations of reconciliation. By comparison to previous photo-travelogues, Frank's paid striking attention to the "colored section"—Black America, separate and unequal.[23]

It was while Frank was on the road that, less than two years after the Supreme Court ruled school segregation unconstitutional, the Montgomery bus boycott led by a twenty-six-year-old pastor, the Reverend Martin Luther King Jr., initiated organized resistance against American apartheid. *Time* first reported the boycott in mid-January 1956. There were segregationist riots in nearby Tuscaloosa—where Autherine Lucy, the first Negro student to enroll at the University of Alabama, had been banned from campus for her own safety. King's home was bombed twice in February. By the end of the month, he and ninety other civil rights leaders were arrested for violating the state's anti-boycott law. By now, Montgomery was an ongoing national news story and King's conviction front-page headlines.

Even network television covered the boycott and arrests. For the first time

---

22. The members of the Black Rebels motorcycle club had all been white—but the name alone could send a shiver through the American soul. As if to explicate this, *The Americans* includes a photograph of a Negro biker in Brando regalia straddling a Harley-Davidson, a solemn young woman perched behind him—the two looking down with such disdainful concentration that the segregated earth might have split at their feet. Another image of a black Black Rebel looking angrily back at the camera graced the cover of the winter 1957 issue of *Evergreen Review*—also notable for containing work by Ginsberg, Kerouac, and Lawrence Ferlinghetti.

23. As the son of a German Jew, Frank was horrified by the state-sanctioned segregation of public facilities he found, and as a shabby-looking, camera-toting foreigner driving a car with New York plates through the Deep South, he encountered his share of hostility. Frank was arrested in McGehee, Arkansas, a small town a hundred miles southeast of Little Rock near the Mississippi border, on November 7, 1955, because he seemed as though he might have a "Communist affiliation."

(as would later be said), the whole world was watching. The context was global. ABC commentator Edward P. Morgan compared the protests in Alabama to those led by Gandhi against the British in India. King himself made the point more forcefully, implicitly linking the civil rights movement to the previous year's Bandung conference, when he told a mass meeting that the Montgomery boycott was part of a great moment in history, bigger than Montgomery, and that the protesters belonged to a global movement: "The vast majority of the people of the world are colored [and] up until four or five years ago [most] were exploited by the empires of the West."[24]

Meanwhile, behind the Iron Curtain, an earthquake: shock waves were spreading from Moscow. The twentieth Communist Party Congress opened mid-February with Nikita Khrushchev's criticism of the Stalinist personality cult. Eleven days later, this attack was greatly elaborated in Khrushchev's so-called secret speech enumerating Stalin's crimes. Even before the *Daily Worker* opened the floodgates as the world's lone Communist daily to publish the complete speech, the newspaper editorialized against Soviet anti-Semitism and, for the first time in memory, let a thousand flowers bloom (or at least a nosegay). Following up on a column by its managing editor Alan Max, the newspaper frankly acknowledged the tumult convulsing world Communism, giving space to both Stalin's attackers and his defenders, as well as those seeking a middle position.

Beginning with a spirited debate on the merits of the French thriller *Diabolique*, the same newspaper's culture pages found a host of new enthusiasms. The *Worker* extolled Jackie Gleason ("perhaps the most important figure on television . . . an artist of exceptional qualities") and the new ABC TV series *Broken Arrow* ("Finally . . . A Dignified Approach to Indians"), endorsed the sci-fi fantasy *Forbidden Planet* ("ingenious, comic, ludicrous, and utterly absorbing"), praised Marilyn Monroe's "superb acting" in *Bus Stop,* mourned the loss of James Dean after seeing him in *Giant* ("angry, brilliant, raucous, and hard-hitting"), championed Robert Aldrich's *Attack* ("a Hollywood war film with guts"), and pondered the merits of rock 'n' roll.

---

24. During the spring of the Davy Crockett craze, representatives of twenty-nine Asian and African states met in Bandung, Indonesia—the "first international conference of colored peoples in the history of mankind," per their host Sukarno. Notables included Nehru, Nasser, Tito, and Chou En-lai. There were even representatives of colonized people within developed nations. Representative Adam Clayton Powell of Harlem attended; so did novelist Richard Wright, a former Communist, who thought gathering the "underdogs of the human race . . . smacked of something new, something beyond Left and Right."

In the midst of the thaw, T-men padlocked the *Worker* office, located in a shabby building on East Twelfth Street, presenting the Commies with a lien of $46,000 for unpaid income tax. The raid made headlines across the country—"REDS IN THE RED!"—and was condemned by some as an attack on the freedom of the press. Meanwhile, as noted in *Hollywood Review*, the anti-Communist picture had vanished from the studio production plans. "My research has failed to turn up a single 1956 release in which an attack on Communism, foreign or domestic, is basic to the theme," Michael Wilson reported. "This is a curious phenomenon, particularly in view of the fact that anti-Communist melodramas are still a staple commodity on TV."

The Old Left was dead, the New Left not yet born. The All-American was contested; the Un-American was fading. In late June, playwright Arthur Miller went before HUAC and refused to name names. Miller defied the committee to lift his passport; his fiancée, Marilyn Monroe, defied her studio to stand by him. July 1, 1956, the pair were married in a Jewish ceremony. (Imagine John Wayne standing outside the cabin, unable to enter.) The *Daily Worker* treated both Miller's testimony and the Miller-Monroe marriage as front-page news.

In early March, with *Invasion of the Body Snatchers*'s nightmare conformist vision finally in theaters, Allen Ginsberg began running off mimeographed copies of "Howl," the barbaric yawp with which he had stunned North Beach several months earlier. It was a moment for manifestos. The same day Ginsberg's countercultural samizdat appeared, the rockabilly declaration "Blue Suede Shoes" became the first single to top the pop, country and western, *and* R & B charts.

As self-assertive in its way as "Howl," Carl Perkins's hit was a new, if necessarily evanescent, national anthem. Years later, rock journalist Stanley Booth would declare it

> one of the most important steps in the evolution of American consciousness
> since the Emancipation Proclamation. . . . The success of "Blue Suede Shoes"
> among Afro-Americans represented an actually grass-roots acknowledgment
> of a common heritage, a mutual overcoming of poverty and lack of style, an act
> of forgiveness, of redemption.

And, all the while, Elvis Presley—variously known as the Hillbilly Cat, the King of Western Bop, and the Atomic-Powered Singer—was enjoying what was then the most meteoric rise in the history of American showbiz.

Time's May 14 issue (Marilyn on the cover, celebrating her post–Actors Studio comeback) covered the story of the "Teeners' Hero": "Heartbreak Hotel" had gone to number one and "all through the South and West, [Elvis was] packing theaters, fighting off shrieking admirers, disturbing parents, puckering the brows of psychologists, and filling letters-to-the-editor columns with cries of alarm." Along with Marilyn and Lucy, Ike and Duke, Steve Canyon and the newly invented Marlboro Man, Mickey Mantle and Davy Crockett, young Elvis became a character in the national folk culture—combining white country music and black blues, the tough image of the urban delinquent and the sweet soul of a backwoods hick.

The first and greatest of White Negroes reaches a national audience just as *The Searchers* is articulating America's racial dilemma in Western terms.[25]

Throughout the summer of '56, implacable Elvis is attacked by newspapers, preachers, teachers, cops, politicians—the entire state ideological apparatus. There are demands he be banned, curbed, run out of town, castrated. *Life*'s August 27 issue features pictures of fundamentalist congregations praying for Elvis's soul and fans prostrating themselves on his front lawn. Of course, Elvis the Pelvis has no need to minister to teen spiritual angst; at the very moment of his apotheosis, a less corporeal idol hovers over America, the subject of a parallel and equally hysterical craze.

In late summer, *Time* reports "a weird new phenomenon is loose in the land; a teenage craze for a boyish Hollywood actor who has been dead for 11 months." When James Dean crashed out, he had but one film in release; only after *Rebel Without a Cause*, released in October 1955 and rereleased early the following year, did Dean become a star, *the* Star. Not since the death of Rudolph Valentino, thirty years before, has so fervent a movie cult coalesced. The Dean craze, like Elvis madness, is a spontaneous demonstration of the power of the teenage market. Ezra Goodman's article in the September 24 *Life* reveals that Dean receives more fan mail than any Hollywood star—some eight thousand letters a month, mainly from young devotees who refuse to accept that their god is dead.

Desperate for new Dean material, Goodman reports, fan magazines are interviewing anyone who ever knew him, from his grandmother in Indiana to the waiters at his favored Hollywood eatery, the Villa Capri, applying "an exhaustiveness worthy of research on the Dead Sea scrolls." Warner Bros. is doing SRO

---

25. Ethan Edwards had his own rebel appeal. A twenty-year-old Texas rocker, Buddy Holly, took Ethan's pet phrase "that'll be the day" as the basis for a boastful anthem of sexual domination that would be a national hit for Holly and his band, the Crickets, during the summer of 1957.

business with limited engagements pairing *East of Eden* and *Rebel Without a Cause*. Teenagers made *Rebel Without a Cause*, but *Rebel Without a Cause* also defined teenagers. Years later, Martin Sheen, who'll have a crucial early film role as a Dean-like delinquent in Terrence Malick's 1973 *Badlands*, will maintain that if Brando changed the way people acted, Dean changed the way people lived—and also the way that Hollywood saw its audience.

According to Nicholas Ray (who, according to *Life*, was writing one of three prospective books on Dean), Elvis too idolizes this disembodied spirit of adolescent rebellion. Ray will recall being approached by Presley in the MGM commissary. "He knew I was a friend of Jimmy's and had directed *Rebel*, so he got down on his knees before me and began to recite whole passages of dialogue from the script. Elvis must have seen *Rebel* a dozen times by then and remembered every one of Jimmy's lines."

When Elvis first arrived in Hollywood in 1956, he sought out Dean's crowd—hanging with Nick Adams, Dennis Hopper, Sal Mineo, and Natalie Wood. Meanwhile, the industry imagined Elvis as the new Dean. He was touted for the lead in *The James Dean Story* and cast as a sensitive outsider in *Love Me Tender*, *Jailhouse Rock*, and *King Creole*.[26]

Elvis's Teen Devil embodies teenage energy; Dean's Teen Angel immortalizes adolescent angst. Their appeal transcends gender, class, and nationality. By the year's end, Gerald Weales will write a piece in The *Reporter* on the new movie hero as an overgrown adolescent, a Crazy Mixed-up Kid—the title of another 1956 rockabilly hit and precisely the phrase a Twentieth Century-Fox publicist used to characterize Marilyn Monroe's first serious role as unstable babysitter in *Don't Bother to Knock* (1952).

Meanwhile, an enormous, block-long billboard has appeared in Times Square showing a nubile blonde in a flimsy nightgown, sucking her thumb and lying in a crib! Crazier than crazy, more Marilyn than Monroe, Elia Kazan's latest mixed-up creation . . . *Baby Doll*! The *New York Times* estimates her height at 60 feet and reports her sprawl at 135 feet "from toes to loose-flung red-blond locks." Written by Tennessee Williams, the movie concerns a child bride (Carroll

---

26. Originally conceived for Marlon Brando and inarguably the best movie of Elvis's dismal career, Don Siegel's *Flaming Star* (1960) features the White Negro as a tragic mulatto. The tag line, addressed to Elvis's character, was "CHOOSE! Between your white father and your Kiowa mother!" His identity crisis precipitated by the outbreak of Indian war on the Texas frontier, he chooses his mother. Nearly matching *Invasion of the Body Snatchers* in its allegorical intensity, *Flaming Star* was banned in South Africa and, among other things, provided the publicity image used by Andy Warhol in his Elvis paintings.

Baker) who refuses to allow her frustrated husband, a Mississippi cotton gin proprietor (Karl Malden), to touch her—further revenging herself by engaging in a prolonged flirtation with his hated ultra-ethnic rival (Eli Wallach), much to the amusement of a Negro chorus on hand to laugh at the white folks' antics.[27]

The tumult reaches its climax in November. *Time* reports that TV has "joined the weird posthumous cult of James Dean" by rebroadcasting three undistinguished teledramas in which Dean played minor parts. "He's hotter than anybody alive," one unnamed executive declares. Well, almost anyone. President Eisenhower is overwhelmingly reelected in his rematch with Adlai Stevenson and the opening of *Love Me Tender*, the routine Western into which Elvis was hastily inserted, is returning its investment so quickly, industry savants are reminded of *The Jazz Singer*. Like James Dean, Elvis's character dies at the end, so the star sings his last song posthumously. What wasn't possible? And what was Baby Doll—iconic heroine of "a droll tale in the manner of Balzac," per *Nation* critic Robert Hatch—if not an American version of the French liberty goddess Marianne?[28]

Another myth is domesticated that month: the Saturday before the election, CBS makes TV history and immeasurably adds to the stockpile of American kid-culture with a prime-time telecast of MGM's 1939 film *The Wizard of Oz*, a television premiere for which the studio is paid a cool $500,000. "Watching such a film in glorious color in one's own home, with the entire family sharing in the laughter without paying a box-office admission, made one realize that this form of programming could be an important part of television's future," writes *New York Times* TV critic Jack Gould, who also notes that the movie afforded "two heavenly hours away from the anxieties of the weekend."

For early November had brought the Soviet invasion of Hungary and the end of the hopes inspired by the twentieth Communist Party Congress, hastening the CPUSA's devolution from a small political party into an even smaller and less consequential sect lost in the neon glories of the new American night.

The Voice of America encouraged the Hungarians to revolt, but America itself paid only lip service. Still, *Time*'s Man of the Year is a long-haired kid with

---

27. Among other things, *Baby Doll* was the first Hollywood movie to feature a black R & B song, Smiley Lewis's 1952 single "Shame, Shame, Shame."

28. Despite its MPAA seal, *Baby Doll* was condemned by the Legion of Decency. Two days before it opened, New York's Francis Cardinal Spellman made his first pulpit appearance in the seven years since he had condemned the jailers of Cardinal Mindszenty to inform his flock that seeing *Baby Doll* was in itself a sin. The movie was "evil in concept . . . certain to exert an immoral and corrupting influence." Joseph Kennedy refused to have it shown in his theater chain.

a gun, perfect sublimation for the juvenile delinquency that succeeded Communism as America's great internal threat. A turn of the dialectic and the ideological apparatus has turned cheerleader, reimagining the crazy mixed-up Wild One as Freedom Fighter—as though there weren't another freedom struggle closer to home.[29]

As 1956 waned, the Supreme Court rejected Montgomery's last appeal, and the bus boycott ended, triumphant. Black militancy was asserted on behalf of the entire Third World, a brazen counterculture had announced its presence, America's vernacular landscape was recognized, a youthful demographic sang out, found itself, and ran wild. Everything was in place for the convulsive cultural revolution that would reach its climax a dozen years later, at least in the Dream Life.

---

29. Mailer concludes "The White Negro" with this observation:

> The organic growth of Hip depends on whether the Negro emerges as a dominating force in American life. Since the Negro knows more about the ugliness and danger of life than the white, it is probable that if the Negro can win his equality, he will possess a potential superiority, a superiority so feared that the fear itself has become the underground drama of domestic politics.

EPILOGUE:
THE FACE OF THE CROWD

Throughout the epochal year of 1956, Elia Kazan and Budd Schulberg were at work on a warning—not about internal subversion or alien invaders or the threat of nuclear weapons. Their concern was the next Next Voice You Hear, the power of the American mass media and the fate of American democracy. Unlike Dore Schary, Kazan and Schulberg did not speak for a studio or an industry or on behalf of the ruler of the universe. Their movie sought to give the *Next Voice* a human face—the face of the crowd.

Directed by Kazan and adapted by Schulberg from his own 1953 story "Your Arkansas Traveler," *A Face in the Crowd* followed the Davy Crockett craze and the rise of Elvis Presley; its creation was contemporaneous with Robert Frank's *The Americans*, the triumph of the TV quiz shows, Vance Packard's bestselling exposé of market research and advertising *The Hidden Persuaders,* and Norman Mailer's essay "The White Negro." Mass communication was not America's superego but its id, a mouthpiece for the Wild One. Thus *A Face in the Crowd* introduced a new menace—not unrelated to the danger of juvenile delinquency that had obsessed congressional committees and the popular press since the end of the Korean War. This peril was the tele-demagogue, vulgarity personified as itinerant guitar picker Larry "Lonesome" Rhodes.

A priori criminal Lonesome Rhodes (Andy Griffith) is introduced as a prisoner, locked up for vagrancy in an Arkansas county jail; a star is born when he's discovered there by local radio reporter Marcia Jeffries (Patricia Neal). Having amusingly decided to broadcast her morning "Face in the Crowd" sequence from the local drunk tank, the well-bred Sarah Lawrence girl is captivated, if not thrilled, by Lonesome's expansive, perhaps dangerous, personality. After he wows her with a spontaneous rendition of "Free Man in the Morning," she manages to make him a regular on her uncle's radio station; thus enabled, Lonesome immediately demonstrates the influence of the broadcast medium on the suggestible. He addresses his housewife listeners directly and mischievously intervenes in the political life of their small Arkansas town.

Intuitively understanding how to transform his audience into a virtual community, Rhodes soon graduates from local radio to TV variety shows, first in Memphis and then New York, and from mocking his sponsor's commercials to refurbishing the images of national candidates—just as Robert Montgomery had coached Dwight Eisenhower. At once performer, tribune, and member of the audience, ingenious enough to invent a "reaction machine" that approximates the effect of canned laughter, Lonesome is a focus group of one—as well as the essence of TV. (Kazan had at one point considered the most gifted of telecomics, Jackie Gleason, for the role.) Lonesome though he may be, Rhodes can instrumentalize mass culture because he personifies it. Before the movie ends, he is also a major threat to American democracy. "The ruthless unity in the culture industry is evidence of what will happen in politics," Adorno and Horkheimer had predicted. A new program, *Lonesome Rhodes's Cracker Barrel*, becomes a forum for manufacturing public opinion with Lonesome himself bruited as a potential cabinet officer, secretary for national morale.[1]

As a true American, Lonesome is always singing about freedom—all the more stridently as he comes to stand for something else. Was *this* what Hegel meant when he described the history of the world as the progress of human consciousness toward the Land of the Free?

A Face in the Crowd's resident intellectual, writer Mel Miller (Walter Matthau), labels the picture of Rhodes that he and his colleagues use for impotent target practice with the title of Erich Fromm's then-popular analysis of the mass mind, *Escape from Freedom*. Later, Miller begins writing an exposé, to be called *Demagogue in Denim*.

As a megalomaniacal, power-mad opportunist, Lonesome has a family resemblance to Schulberg's most famous creation, the ferocious Hollywood careerist Sammy Glick, as well as to the charismatic, self-described "hick" politician Willie Stark in Robert Penn Warren's *All the King's Men*. In *Forerunners of American Fascism*, Raymond Gram Swing had described Louisiana governor and senator Huey Long, Penn Warren's model for Stark, as "the hillbilly come into

1. This position looks back to the 1934 New Deal musical *Stand Up and Cheer*, in which President Roosevelt appoints Warner Baxter to be secretary of amusement, and ahead to Ronald Reagan, who more or less served as his own secretary of national morale.

power, with the crudity of the hillbilly and his native shrewdness multiplied tenfold." The description fits Lonesome Rhodes, but it's another specter that haunts *A Face in the Crowd*. Like its kindred showbiz allegories, José Ferrer's *The Great Man* (which opened less than six months before *A Face in the Crowd*) and Alexander Mackendrick's *Sweet Smell of Success* (which followed a month later), *A Face in the Crowd* is an example of crypto-anti-McCarthyism that, appearing some three years after the demagogue's fall, reeks of self-disgust.[2]

The Patriot Roughneck had been toppled—by television, some thought. Now television had brought something else, a singing roughneck, the Wild One as entertainer. The spirit of 1956 coalesced in the figure of the TV-spawned hillbilly demagogue up from Memphis. Schulberg would plead with a reporter for the *New Yorker* not to bracket Lonesome Rhodes with Elvis Presley, leaving it to *Life* to do precisely that. Who else could this raucous hayseed be?

As American pundits were obsessed with the new "communicable disease" that was rock 'n' roll, Elvis had enjoyed the most meteoric rise in the history of American showbiz. Competing television variety shows used this bizarre new creature to boost their ratings; Elvis would make twelve appearances on network TV in 1956. He brought rock 'n' roll but was produced by television—not simply a voice but an image, an icon, *the* icon. Already in 1956, a prescient New York artist, Ray Johnson, was fashioning collages from his publicity photos.[3]

Lonesome Rhodes is something less than Elvis but also more—an insanely ambitious force of nature played by Griffith with a rabid ferocity the nominally amiable thirty-one-year-old stand-up comic turned actor would never again reveal. (It is he who is ultimately the film's Implacable Alien Other.) "I *became* Lonesome Rhodes," Griffith told an interviewer. "It was something bigger than I was. . . . You play an egomaniac and paranoiac all day and it's hard to turn it off by bedtime. [My wife and I] went through a nightmare—a real genuine nightmare both of us." "Nightmare" is the operative word.

A Face in the Crowd is essentially a political horror film—not funny enough to work as satire, a bit doggedly literal-minded for allegory, yet too hyperbolic to convince as drama. Lonesome seems on the verge of running for office himself when his jilted Marcia destroys his career by opening a mike so that the American people can hear the true nature of the monster they've embraced. The Next

2. The liberal Ferrer had been a fearful HUAC witness; so had Kazan's Group Theatre associate Clifford Odets, who co-wrote *Sweet Smell*, and Harold Hecht, the movie's co-producer.
3. The Presley vehicle *Jailhouse Rock*, a more benign version of *A Face in the Crowd*, was released in November 1957.

Voice You Hear exposed! Drunk with power, as well as liquor, and now pure id, Rhodes commits a gaffe of historic proportions, referring to his fans as "morons" and describing the public as "a cage full of guinea pigs.... Good night, you stupid idiots, good night, you miserable slobs. They're a lot of trained seals—I toss them a dead fish and they'll flap their flippers."

Of course, the audience flips its flapper: a montage of incredulous listeners, seeming scarcely more intelligent when motivated by outrage rather than approval, phone the station in aroused revulsion. It's a spectacular crack-up. Lonesome is through on TV before his elevator reaches the lobby (although, just to make sure the audience gets the point, the filmmakers have him gratuitously insult the Negro waiters in an empty banquet hall). In the script, Schulberg had Rhodes commit suicide, but Kazan opted for something more uplifting. The last word belongs to Miller, who unconvincingly suggests that people ultimately "get wise" to demagogues: we—or rather They—the People![4]

Kazan and Schulberg's spiritual sequel to *On the Waterfront*, *A Face in the Crowd* was made, like *Baby Doll*, by Newtown Films, the independent production company enabled by *On the Waterfront*'s success, and it would be the company's last. While the sensational *Baby Doll* was seen as part of the mass-culture problem, *A Face in the Crowd* was framed as a contribution toward a solution.

Kazan and Schulberg began discussing the project during the spring of 1955. That summer, characterized by the huge popularity of *The $64,000 Question*, the two men would venture down from Connecticut to hang out at Madison Avenue ad agencies and soak up their ambiance. Schulberg started work on the script in the fall, while Kazan was shooting *Baby Doll* on location in Benoit, Mississippi. After *Baby Doll* wrapped in early 1956, the pair traveled to Washington, DC, where they interviewed several senators, including Stuart Symington of Missouri and Lyndon Johnson of Texas (both Democrats with presidential ambitions). Johnson, Kazan remembered, seemed particularly impressed that Hollywood people were talking to him.

The *Face in the Crowd* shoot opened August 13 in the Ozark town of Piggott, Arkansas. During the ten days that the filmmakers were on location (Kazan gave the Piggott treasury $8,700 to complete a swimming pool begun twenty-one years before by the Works Progress Administration), the Democrats and

---

4. But just what is the meaning of that blinking Coca-Cola centered on the screen under "The End"? Is it the 1957 equivalent of the American flag? An ironic salute to Madison Avenue? A reminder that advertising rules?

the Republicans held their national conventions. "Politics has entered a new stage, the television stage," the veteran operative General Haynesworth declares in *A Face in the Crowd*. "Instead of long-winded public debates, the people want capsule slogans: 'Time for a change!' 'The mess in Washington!' 'More bang for a buck!' Punch lines and glamour." It might have been the sell line for the two conventions, for which TV viewership was projected at 120 million (the "largest mass audience in the history of man," per one TV columnist).

A new totality was made visible as politics, advertising, and show business merged. Los Angeles appliance stores advertised "convention specials" on new television sets. Walt Disney dispatched a pair of teenage Mouseketeers on behalf of *The Mickey Mouse Club*. The *Los Angeles Times* ran stories explaining how Republican women were expected to dress for the TV cameras and why the exigencies of a national broadcast and the realities of prime time caused the San Francisco sessions to be scheduled for midafternoon; the paper also noted that, in nominating the absent Dwight D. Eisenhower, Representative Charles Halleck addressed the president directly, explaining that Ike was watching the convention on television. *Time*, meanwhile, covered the conventions in terms of their TV coverage, complete with negative reviews.

All had been anticipated. Former adman John G. Schneider's comic novel *The Golden Kazoo*, published in January 1956, imagined the 1960 presidential campaign as completely dominated by advertising agencies, with the candidates as products sold to TV viewers on the basis of their looks and one-liners. The *New York Times* praised the book as "a way station on the road to George Orwell's 1984." Adlai Stevenson, who had been criticized by his rivals as lacking a presidential image, incorporated Schneider's critique into his acceptance speech:

> The men who run the Eisenhower administration evidently believe that the minds of Americans can be manipulated by shows, slogans, and the arts of advertising. This idea that you can merchandise candidates for high office like breakfast cereal—than you can gather votes like box tops—is I think the ultimate indignity to the democratic process . . .

In *The Hidden Persuaders*, Vance Packard described the 1956 Republican convention at the Cow Palace in San Francisco as epitomizing the new totality: "Even the ministers in their opening and closing intonations (over TV) worked in key GOP slogans." What's more, the convention was a professional job, produced by George Murphy, the Hollywood actor who also served as MGM's public relations director (and would be elected California senator in 1964). "Mr. Murphy seemed to regard all the delegates as actors in his super spectacular pageant. Wearing dark glasses, he stood a few feet back of the rostrum. Reporters noted him making the professional gestures for fanfare, stretch-out, and fade. Delegates took their cues right along with the orchestra," Packer wrote. Murphy—whom the *Los Angeles Times* called the convention's "busiest man . . . a combination of Cecil B. DeMille and a paper hanger with the hives"—even used entertainment as a source of control. He needed only flick his hand, *Time* observed, to produce "singers of all shapes and sizes," and he routinely deployed Young Republicans to cut capers in the aisles and thus force delegates into their seats.

A cartoon in the Soviet humor magazine *Krokodil* visualized the 1956 presidential campaign as two rival theatrical shows ("the actors are different but the program is the same: cold war, arms race, positions of strength . . ."), and Stevenson's critique notwithstanding, the Democratic Convention in Chicago also had an entertainment director, Murphy's nominal boss, MGM production chief Dore Schary. The position cost Schary his job. As he wrote in *The Reporter*, shortly before *A Face in the Crowd* opened, the reason given for his discharge a month after the Eisenhower landslide "had to do with my being an egghead. . . . I made too many speeches and wrote too many articles," and, as documented in a single anonymous letter, "my participation in the 1956 Presidential campaign had made for 'irritation and enmity' "—presumably among MGM's Republican stockholders. Still, Schary did take credit for helping introduce the Democrats' next star.

At the suggestion of TV newsman Edward R. Murrow, Schary recruited Senator John F. Kennedy of Massachusetts to narrate the Democrats' keynote film, *The Pursuit of Happiness*. (CBS's failure to telecast this twenty-eight-minute celebration of past Democratic presidents precipitated one of the convention's major controversies.) The thirty-nine-year-old Kennedy was subsequently put forth as a candidate for vice president, and although he lost out to Estes Kefauver, the handsome young senator, author of the bestselling, Pulitzer Prize–winning history *Profiles in Courage*, was tabbed as a political Elvis—another Man of '56 and instant front runner for the 1960 nomination. Another face in the crowd. . . . Such was the process known as Lonesome Rhodes.[5]

Like *The Hidden Persuaders* or *The Golden Kazoo*, *A Face in the Crowd* was an early attempt to represent the new totality. Welcome to Freedomland.

---

5. The size of the TV audience proved disappointing. While some 32 million families (or 85 percent of all TV homes) tuned in for part of the show, less than a third watched most of it. The networks, which had preempted their regular programs, lost money and sponsors rethought their commitment to campaign coverage. The *Nation* commissioned John G. Schneider to provide a postmortem. Terming the race a "show-biz flop," he wrote, "I can't recall a national advertising campaign which was so poorly conceived, so badly written, so clumsily managed and produced, so misdirected and so dishonest as the political campaign of 1956. Maybe if we get some smart, amoral, know-how boys into the act, we'll get a better show in 1960."

Advertising was key—synonymous not so much with publicity as with brainwashing. "We got the feeling that people were manipulating in the crudest way, with humor and whatever you want to call it, [other] people's thinking," Kazan recalled years later. Thanks to Madison Avenue, people were "being made to think in a way they wouldn't ordinarily think." Hollywood had never blamed itself for such chicanery but Kazan's sentiments would scarcely have been out of place at the Beverly Hills Hotel, where, in the flying saucer summer of 1947, a decade before *A Face in the Crowd* opened, the Progressive Citizens of America held their conference "Thought Control in USA." The last hurrah of the Hollywood left before the fall's Un-American hearings, this conclave marked the moment at which the industry's "cultural workers" began to reverse themselves on the product they produced. Suddenly the inherent dangers of horror comics, rock 'n' roll, Mickey Spillane novels, and TV were an issue.

The notion of mass culture as a form of incipient fascism became increasingly common among left and liberal intellectuals once the mission faded. Popular Front sentimentality was demobilized and Pop Front sentimentalists were purged from Hollywood. The former Trotskyist intellectuals of *Partisan Review* worried whether democracy might inherently level intellectual value and thus liquidate Western civilization itself, and—the *Daily Worker*'s nostalgic appreciation of people's hero Davy Crockett notwithstanding—many other progressives, as well as conservatives, reflexively took a similar position. Writing in *Dissent* in 1956, Henry Rabassiere mockingly noted that "the newest fashion in mass culture is to scorn mass culture"—at least among leftish snobs like the men who made *A Face in the Crowd*, former Reds and friendly witnesses both.

However topical, *A Face in the Crowd* had its origins in the radical worldview of the 1930s and 1940s, if only as dialectical corrective to the Popular Front mentality. The movie is easily construed as mocking the liberal flirtation with vulgar Marxism. Lonesome Rhodes is a class-conscious, folk-song-singing exemplar of the Common Man—albeit horribly massified, as though the salt-of-the-earth troubadour Woody Guthrie had been crossbred with the manic juvenile entertainer Jerry Lewis. (No wonder Marcia is intrigued, even after she discovers that this hobo bard is as cynical as the Hollywood version of a CP apparatchik.)

But old habits die hard and so, if *A Face in the Crowd* parodied college-educated fellow travelers, it was also a generic antifascist scare film—stridently dramatizing, in a suitably popular form, everybody's worst fears regarding the American culture industry. Would Adorno and Horkheimer have felt appalled or vindicated by the televised image of Lonesome's seventeen-year-old bride twirling her batons to Beethoven?

Opening in May 1957, *A Face in the Crowd* was a mild sensation, at least with the New York critics—or, a few of them. The *Nation* hailed the movie as "the *1984* of Madison Avenue." Bosley Crowther termed it a "sizzling" piece of work: "Mr. Schulberg has penned a powerful person of the raw, vulgar, roughneck, cornball breed and Mr. Griffith plays him with thunderous vigor."

In Paris, *Cahiers du Cinéma* critic François Truffaut was an even bigger fan, comparing the movie's fierce logic to an essay by Roland Barthes. *A Face in the Crowd*, Truffaut wrote, was "a great and beautiful work whose importance transcends the dimension of a cinema review. . . . In America, politics always overlaps show business, as show business overlaps advertising." But most critics, like the crowd whose mirrored face was shown so unattractive, found the movie distasteful.

As a critique of American democracy, *A Face in the Crowd* was *High Noon* without a hero, *The Searchers* on Tin Pan Alley. Crowther, who shrewdly equated the filmmakers with Marcia, characterized them as men who created a Frankenstein monster and then fell under its spell. "So hypnotized are they by [Griffith's] presence that he runs away not only with the show but with intellectual reason and with the potentiality of their theme." *Time*, which panned the movie as hysterical and obvious, made the same point, concluding its review by wondering if Kazan, "like the villain of his piece, has not somehow mistaken his public for a bunch of 'stupid slobs.'"[6]

The most enthusiastic review, quoted at length by Kazan in his autobiography, was not Truffaut's but the notice that ran in *People's World*.

> When two stool pigeon witnesses before the Un-American Committee conspire to produce one of the finest progressive films we have seen in years, something more than oversimplification of motives is needed to explain it. [Schulberg and Kazan] did not hesitate to betray what both believed in before the witch-hunting House Committee. But they must have learned something during their days in the progressive movement and motion picture audiences will be the beneficiaries. . . .
>
> [*A Face in the Crowd*] will help educate the film audience into an understanding of how public opinion is manipulated in the US and for what purpose. Whether it is the residual understanding Schulberg and Kazan retain from

---

6. The alleged popularity of Lonesome's bleatings—written by Schulberg with folksinger Tom Glazer—is a mortal insult to the taste of the American people. But then, so is the movie, which may be one reason why it was not a popular success. The production cost $1.75 million and, by 1960, had earned back only $1.3 million.

their days in the progressive movement, or whether it is a guilty conscience (or both) that has prompted them to give us this picture, we should be grateful for what they have done.

Comrades after all and forever, or so it would seem.

A Face in the Crowd was neither a hit nor a succès d'estime; it received not a single Oscar nomination. Kazan blamed the movie's failure on its didacticism: "We conceived *Face in the Crowd* as a 'warning to the American people.'" But hadn't America already enjoyed the lecture that was *On the Waterfront*? (Not to mention *High Noon*.) *On the Waterfront* projected a flawed but genuine proletarian hero in contrast to the corrupt crypto-Commie leadership; *A Face in the Crowd* suggested that such heroism was simply a bit of clever acting, a media-amplified fraud perpetrated on the credulous American people. (And yet, which of the two—Brando's Terry Malloy or Griffith's Lonesome Rhodes—would be a theme park's more crowd-pleasing animatronic attraction?)

Did *A Face in the Crowd* tell Americans anything that they didn't know? Samuel Fuller's *China Gate*, which also opened in May 1957, was a bigger scoop—it was set in French Indochina and introduced Ho Chi Minh as the obscure red strongman who might bring the United States to its knees. *A Face in the Crowd* was not news, except perhaps in Hollywood—for which Kazan and Schulberg had proposed a new mission.

Free from the burden of speaking for God, Hollywood might now honestly represent the audience to itself (*Invasion of the Body Snatchers*). The movies might critique old protagonists (*Kiss Me Deadly*) or propose new ones (*Rebel Without a Cause*). Most ambitiously, the movies might offer a new national narrative (*The Searchers*) and articulate an individual political position. It was in late 1956 that John Wayne finally lined up financing for his long-germinating manifesto: *The Alamo*.

Kazan and Schulberg intuited that, in the nation's dream life, media personalities and movie stars would now nominate themselves for the leading role. In the character of Lonesome Rhodes, their movie dramatized the megalomaniacal desire to have one's personal fantasy projected on the screen—an ambition that would become increasingly prevalent during the decade of JFK and *The Manchurian Candidate*, *Bonnie and Clyde* and *Easy Rider*, *Dirty Harry* and "Hanoi Jane" Fonda, until the scenario came to full fruition in 1980 with the election of a second Star-Pol, Ronald Reagan (and was institutionalized fifteen years later in the twentieth century's last decade as the talk-radio opposition to Bill Clinton).

The Berlin Wall fell not long after Reagan left the White House. By then, for many commentators, the Cold War was understood as a struggle between moribund, repressive Communism and responsive, audience-pleasing television. TV prevailed. It was not Brando's wised-up prole but the monstrous winking Lonesome Rhodes who kicked the Commies from the Kremlin. Kazan and Schulberg may have publicly repudiated their youthful politics, but the fear and loathing so forcefully expressed in *A Face in the Crowd* placed them again on the losing side of history.

SOURCES

Abbreviations

AMPAS Library = Margaret Herrick Library, the Academy of Motion Picture Arts and
          Sciences, Beverly Hills, CA

    DW = *Daily Worker*

    LAT = *Los Angeles Times*

NYPL–LPA = New York Public Library for the Performing Arts, Dorothy and
          Lewis B. Cullman Center, New York, NY

    NYT = *New York Times*

Introduction: From God's Mouth to Your Ear

Dore Schary, *Case History of a Movie* (New York: Random House, 1950), 19–20; Schary,
    "Our Movie Mythology," *Reporter*, March 3, 1960; Samuel Goldwyn, "Television's
    Challenge to the Movies," *NYT Magazine*, March 26, 1950.

Hortense Powdermaker, *Hollywood, the Dream Factory: An Anthropologist Looks at the
    Movies* (Boston: Little, Brown, 1950), 39; promotional flyer: *The Next Voice You
    Hear* file, NYPL–LPA; Jacques Ellul, *Propaganda: The Formation of Men's Attitudes*
    (New York: Vintage, 1973), 89, 63–64; Theodor Adorno and Max Horkheimer, *Dia-
    lectic of Enlightenment* (New York: Seabury, 1972), 144.

Thomas Mann, *The Magic Mountain*, trans. John E. Wood (New York: Vintage, 1996),
    31; Bosley Crowther, *NYT*, July 9, 1950; *Life*, April 24, 1950.

Prologue: Mission for Hollywood—Stalingrad to V-J Day

Mission to Moscow production and reception: David Culbert, "The Feature Film as Of-
    ficial Propaganda," in *Mission to Moscow*, ed. Culbert (Madison, WI: University of
    Wisconsin, 1980); Hollywood Canteen: Kevin Starr, *Embattled Dreams: California
    in War and Peace* (New York: Oxford, 2002), 166–68, and Joseph McBride, *Search-
    ing for John Ford* (New York: St. Martin's Press, 2001), 367–68; Zanuck's military
    career: George F. Custen, *Twentieth Century's Fox: Darryl F. Zanuck and the Culture
    of Hollywood* (New York: Basic Books, 1997), 258–61, Starr, *Embattled Dreams*, 159,
    and McBride, *Searching for John Ford*, 378–79; Preminger project: Chris Fujiwara,
    The World and Its Double: The Life and Work of Otto Preminger (New York: Faber
    and Faber, 2008), 30–31; Martha Dodd and Boris Morros: Allen Weinstein and Al-
    exander Vassiliev, *The Haunted Wood: Soviet Espionage in America—the Stalin Era*

(New York: Random House, 1999), 50–71; FBI on Communist activity in Holly-wood: Athan Theoharis, *Chasing Spies* (Chicago: Ivan R. Dee, 2002), 151ff; *Hitler's Children*: *Variety*, January 14, 1943; Edward Dmytryk, *Odd Man Out: A Memoir of the Hollywood Ten* (Carbondale: Southern Illinois University Press, 1996), 8; Breen's concern: Jennifer E. Langdon, *Caught in the Crossfire: Adrian Scott and the Politics of Americanism in 1940s Hollywood* (New York: Columbia University Press, 2008), 52; Hopper's warning: David Platt, "Film Front," *DW*, March 24, 1943; Collins testi-mony, Hearings Before the Committee on Un-American Activities, April 12, 1951 (Washington, DC); Bosley Crowther, "The End of Adolf," *NYT*, March 31, 1943; Patrick McGilligan, *Fritz Lang: The Nature of the Beast* (New York: St. Martin's Press, 1997), 304; Hood-to-Hoover memos, March 19, 1943, and May 29, 1943, in *Communist Activity in the Entertainment Industry: FBI Surveillance Files on Holly-wood, 1942–1958*, ed. Daniel J. Leab (Bethesda, MD: University Publications of America, 1991), vol. 1; see also Gerald Horne, *Class Struggle in Hollywood, 1930–1950: Moguls, Mobsters, Stars, Reds, & Trade Unionists* (Austin: University of Texas Press, 2001), 137–38.

Matthew Low, "Submission to Moscow—A Review of the Davies Film," *New Leader*, May 1, 1943; OWI memo: Clayton R. Koppes and Gregory D. Black, *Hollywood Goes to War* (New York: Free Press, 1987), 205; "'Mission to Moscow' Preview Acclaimed by Press Members," *Washington Post*, April 29, 1943, 1; "The Story of Two Guys Named Joe!": *Mission to Moscow* pressbook, NYPL–LPA; *Variety*, May 5, 1943; David Platt, "Film Front," *DW*, May 2, 1943; Bosley Crowther, "Missionary Zeal," *NYT*, May 9, 1943; notable among the many reports the *Daily Worker* published on *Mission to Moscow* throughout the spring of 1943 are "The Country Votes 'Aye' on 'Mission to Moscow,'" June 4, 1943, "More 'Mission' Comment," June 10, 1943, and "Broadway Fights Censorship of 'Mission to Moscow,'" June 14, 1943; *Variety*, May 19, 1943, and June 8, 1943; Bright in *DW*, June 12, 1943; plans for features dropped: Fred Stanley, "Hollywood Woos Leading Authors," *NYT*, July 11, 1943; "Russ Pro-gram Bowl Event," *LAT*, February 1, 1943.

David Platt, "Film Front," *DW*, June 28, 1943; David Platt, "Film Front," *DW*, August 3, 1943; T.S., *NYT*, July 29, 1943; David Platt, "Warners 'This Is the Army' Is a Terrific War Musical Full of Fun and Vigor," *DW*, August 1943; David Platt, "Film Front," *DW*, August 15, 1943; David Platt, *DW*, August 17, 1943; Robert A. Andersen Jr., "Report: Mikhail Konstantin Kalatozov," November 22, 1943, Kalatozov file, FBI; *LAT*, August 23, 1943; "Party to be Held Sunday for Soviet Film Director," *LAT*, August 26, 1943; Confidential Source A-2, November 22, 1943, Kalatozov file, FBI; Alvah Bessie, *Inquisition in Eden* (New York: Macmillan, 1965), 69; *Watch on the Rhine* premiere in David Jenemann, *Adorno in America* (Minneapolis: University of Minnesota, 2007), 112; Ben Barzman, "Propaganda Trends in Motion Pictures," in *Proceedings of the Writers' Congress: Los Angeles 1943* (Berkeley: University of Cali-fornia Press, 1944), 398; "Writers' Congress Hit by Tenney Committee," *LAT*, Sep-tember 23, 1943; Darryl Zanuck, "The Responsibility of the Industry," in *Proceedings*,

34–35; Schary memo: "At Work With 'Red' Lewis," in Sinclair Lewis and Dore Schary, *Storm in the West* (New York: Stein and Day, 1963), 7–8; Barzman, "Propaganda Trends," 398; John Howard Lawson, "Cultural Changes in America," in *Proceedings*, 473; Tenney testimony: Horne, *Class Struggle*, 68; *NYT*, December 12, 1943; G.E. Blackford, *New York Journal-American*, November 5, 1943; Lee Mortimer, "North Star Is Red Propaganda," *Daily Mirror*, November 5, 1943; *Time*, November 8, 1943; "Canteen Has Birthday," *LAT*, November 1, 1943; "Film Cagers in A.A.U. Play," *LAT*, January 22, 1944; David Platt, "Film Front," *Sunday Worker*, November 1943; "U.S.-Soviet Friendship Day Celebrated Here," *LAT*, November 17, 1943, 1; Randy Roberts and James S. Olson, *John Wayne: American* (New York: Free Press, 1995), 228–29; R.H. Cunningham to D.M. Ladd, "Memo re: M. Kolotozov, Espionage," November 24, 1943, Kalatozov file, FBI; Eugene Gordon, *DW*, December 8, 1943; David Platt, "1943—Hollywood's Greatest Year," *DW*, January 2, 1944.

"Leaders of Film Industry Form Anti-Red Group," *LAT*, February 5, 1944, 1; R.B. Hood to Director, FBI, "Re: The Motion Picture Alliance for the Preservation of American Ideals," February 9, 1944; R.B. Hood to Director, FBI, "Re: The Motion Picture Alliance for the Preservation of American Ideals, Information Concerning," March 22, 1944; see also Hood to Director, May 10, 1944, and Hood to Director, "Re: Communist Infiltration of the Motion Picture Industry," November 23, 1944, in *Communist Activity in the Entertainment Industry*, reel 1, vol. 3; David Platt, "One Good Film Every 10 Days," *Sunday Worker*, May 7, 1944; Frank C. Waldrop, *Washington Times Herald*, May 5, 1944; "Film Axis Stunned," *People's World*, June 30, 1944; on *Wilson*: Custen, *Twentieth Century's Fox*, 160, 275; Frank Antico, "Wilson—Timely Historical Film," *DW*, August 3, 1944; "Leftist Booklet 'Sneaked' into Canteen Here," *LAT*, August 17, 1944; FBI break-ins: Athan Theoharis, *Chasing Spies* (Chicago: Ivan R. Dee, 2002), 155; Morros and FBI, Rosenberg's proposal: Weinsten and Vassiliev, *Haunted Wood*, 117ff, 198ff; David Platt, "Cecil B. DeMille Puts On a Circus for Tom Dewey," *DW*, September 1944; Michael Munn, *John Wayne: The Man Behind the Myth* (New York: New American Library, 2004), 95–96; Norma Barzman, *The Red and the Blacklist: The Intimate Memoir of a Hollywood Expatriate* (New York: Nation Books, 2003), 45–48.

David Platt, *DW*, November 1944; FBI investigating RKO: Horne, *Class Struggle*, 76; Ruth Greenglass visit: Sam Roberts, *The Brother: The Untold Story of the Rosenberg Case* (New York: Vintage, 2003), 88ff; Bosley Crowther, *NYT*, December 16, 1944; David Platt, "Hollywood's Batting Average: 1 Hit in 10," *Sunday Worker*, December 10, 1944; FBI break-ins: Theoharis, *Chasing Spies*, 155; FBI complaint about Communist presence: Horne, *Class Struggle*, 84.

Polonsky in Nancy Lynn Schwartz, *The Hollywood Writers' Wars* (New York: Knopf, 1982), 225; *Life*, July 9, 1945; Maltz meeting reported in letter, July 16, 1945, Ben Barzman FBI file; Bercovici: Paul Buhle and Patrick McGilligan, *Tender Comrades: A Backstory of the Hollywood Blacklist* (New York: St. Martin's, 1997), 36; Collins testimony, April 12, 1951; Barzman, *Red and the Blacklist*, 63.

Art Ryon, "Word of Peace Brings Bedlam in Los Angeles," *LAT*, August 15, 1943.

FN 1: Information on the Communist Party in Hollywood drawn from FBI files, nota-
bly Hood to Director, "Re: Communist Infiltration of the Motion Picture Industry,"
November 23, 1944, and July 19, 1945, and Hearings Before the Committee on Un-
American Activities, particularly Collins, April 12, 1951 (Washington, DC), and
Martin Berkeley, September 19, 1951 (Los Angeles), and interviews in McGilligan
and Buhle, *Tender Comrades*. See also Horne, *Class Struggle,* 60–93, and Theoharis,
Chasing Spies, 139–69. FN 2: J.P. Coyne to D.M. Ladd, "Memo: Johannes Eisler,"
July 30, 1947, Johannes Eisler file, FBI. FN 3: Levitt and Vorhaus in McGilligan and
Buhle, *Tender Comrades,* 450, 674; Stephen Vaughn, *Ronald Reagan in Hollywood*
(Cambridge: Cambridge University Press, 1994), 130; Anne Edwards, *Early Reagan*
(New York: William Morrow, 1987), 304–5. FN 4: Theodor Adorno and Max Hork-
heimer, *Dialectic of Enlightenment* (New York: Seabury, 1972), 122–23. FN 5: *The
Master Race*: Hood to Director, "Re: Communist Infiltration of the Motion Picture
Industry Internal Security-C," March 20, 1945, in *Communist Activity in the Enter-
tainment Industry*, vol. 4.

I. Aliens Among Us: Hollywood, 1946–47

Daniel Lang, *From Hiroshima to the Moon* (New York: Dell, 1961); *Hollywood Atom*,
August 19, 1945, and October 9, 1945; Cynthia Baron, "As Red as a Burlesque
Queen's Garters: Cold War Politics and the Actor's Lab in Hollywood," in *Headline
Hollywood: A Century of Film Scandal*, ed. Adrienne L. McLean and David A. Cook
(New Brunswick, NJ: Rutgers University Press, 2001), 150.

Nelson B. Bell, "A-Bomb Epic Had Roots in Iowa," *Washington Post*, February 9, 1947;
David McCullough, *Truman* (New York: Simon & Schuster, 1992), 475; Robert Jay
Lifton and Greg Mitchell, *Hiroshima in America: Fifty Years of Denial* (New York:
Putnam, 1995), 73; Alice Kimball Smith, *A Peril and a Hope: The Scientist's Move-
ment in America: 1945–47* (Cambridge, MA: MIT Press, 1971), 293.

MGM's Manhattan Project: *The Beginning or the End*?

Ayn Rand, *Journals of Ayn Rand*, ed. David Harriman (New York: Dutton, 1997), 311–
44; Fred Stanley, "Hollywood Atom Race Ends," *NYT*, March 24, 1946; Michael J.
Yavenditti, "Atomic Scientists and Hollywood: The Beginning or the End?" *Film
and History*, December 1978, 73–87; Nathan Reingold, "MGM Meets the Atomic
Bomb," *Wilson Quarterly*, Autumn 1984, 155–63; Lifton and Mitchell, *Hiroshima in
America*, 361; Thomas F. Brady, "Metro's Atom 'Headache,'" *NYT*, June 16, 1946.

"Bikini: Breath-Holding Before a Blast—Could It Split the Earth," *Newsweek*, July 1,
1946; "Test for Mankind," *Time*, July 8, 1946; Lou Cannon, *President Reagan—The
Role of a Lifetime* (New York: Public Affairs, 2000), 428; Bosley Crowther, *NYT*, July
11, 1946; Lang's complaint: Patrick McGilligan, *Fritz Lang: Nature of the Beast* (New
York: St. Martin's, 1997), 340.

Wallace speech: Curtis D. MacDougall, *Gideon's Army* (New York: Marzani & Munsell,

1965), 63; Hayden testimony, Hearings Before the Committee on Un-American Activities, April 10, 1951 (Washington, DC); Ronald Reagan with Richard G. Hubler, *Where's the Rest of Me?* (New York: Duell, Sloan and Pearce, 1965), 174; Marx to Oppenheimer: James G. Hershberg, *James B. Conant: Harvard to Hiroshima and the Making of the Nuclear Age* (New York: Knopf, 1993), 289–90; Lifton and Mitchell, *Hiroshima in America*, 363; "Change Actor Doing Truman in Film," *NYT*, November 25, 1946; Bohnen's letter: Lifton and Mitchell, *Hiroshima in America* 172–73.

Nelson B. Bell, "Nation's Atomic Elite Will See 'Themselves' on Screen Wednesday," *WP*, February 15, 1947; *Variety*, February 19, 1947; *Daily News*, February 21, 1947; *PM*, February 21, 1947; Jack Moffitt, "A Close-up of Democracy," *Esquire*, May 1947; "The New Pictures," *Time*, February 24, 1947; "The Beginning or the End," *Life*, March 17, 1947; *Nation*, March 1, 1947; Bosley Crowther, *NYT*, February 22, 1947; Harrison Brown, "The Beginning or the End: A Review," *Bulletin of the Atomic Scientists*, March 1947, 99; David Platt, "Film Front," *DW*, March 2, 1947.

FN 2: See John Sbardelli, "The 'Maltz Affair' Revisited: How the American Communist Party Relinquished Its Cultural Influence at the Dawn of the Cold War," *Cold War History*, November 2009, 489–500.

When HUAC Came to Hollywood . . .

Picket Line: Gerald Horne, *Class Struggle in Hollywood, 1930–1950: Moguls, Mobsters, Stars, Reds, and Trade Unionists* (Austin: University of Texas Press, 2001) 217; Clifford: McCullough, *Truman*, 553.

"Right of Employer to Fire Red Asked," *LAT*, March 5, 1947; Mayer payoff: Drew Pearson, "Wood's Role in Red Probe Cited," *Washington Post*, June 22, 1950; "Reds Defeated in Hollywood, Johnston Says," *LAT*, March 28, 1947; Hedda Hopper, *LAT*, March 22, 1947; Hedda Hopper to J. Edgar Hoover, Hedda Hopper collection, AMPAS Library; "Charlie Chaplin's *Monsieur Verdoux* Press Conference," *Film Comment*, Winter 1969, 38–39; Bosley Crowther, *NYT*, April 12, 1947; David Platt, "Chaplin's 'Monsieur Verdoux' Bitter Satire on Modern Society," *DW*, April 14, 1947; David Platt, "Two Anti-Soviet Films in Preparation in Hollywood," *DW*, April 20, 1947; Warner's claim: Daniel Leab, "*The Iron Curtain*: Hollywood's First Cold War Movie," *Historical Journal of Film, Radio & Television* 8, no. 2 (1988); Zanuck memo: George F. Custen, *Twentieth Century's Fox: Darryl Zanuck and the Culture of Hollywood* (New York: Basic Books, 1997), 304. See Leab, "*The Iron Curtain*," for a detailed account of the movie's production.

Reagan debriefed: Stephen Vaughn, *Ronald Reagan in Hollywood* (Cambridge: Cambridge University Press, 1994), 148; "US Officials to Figure in Hollywood Red Inquiry," *LAT*, May 10, 1947, 1; "Hanns Eisler Hearing Halts," *LAT*, May 13, 1947, 1; "Screen Stars to Testify in Red Inquiry" *LAT*, May 14, 1947, 1; Gladwin Hill, "Red Film Forced on Taylor; 'Agent' Halted His Navy Service," *NYT*, May 15, 1947, 1; Gladwin Hill, "Hollywood Is a Main Red Center, Adolphe Menjou Tells House

Body," *NYT*, May 16, 1947, 1; "Former Russian Official Surprise Inquiry Witness," *LAT*, May 16, 1947, 1; "Where the Reds Dwell in Filmland," *LAT*, May 16, 1947; *Variety*, May 21, 1947; "Left Wing: Reds Gone Hollywood," *Newsweek*, May 26, 1947; "'Wallace in '48,' Stadium Crowd Yells," *LAT*, May 20, 1947, 1; Macdougall, *Gideon's Army*, 158–59, 545; Warren B. Francis, "Full Dress Inquiry Set on Reds Here," *LAT*, May 29, 1947, 1; Mannix tells Johnston: Larry Ceplair and Steven Englund, *The Inquisition in Hollywood* (Garden City, NY: Anchor Press, 1980), 259; "Eric Johnston Assails US Reds as Traitors," *LAT*, June 5, 1947; "Death Threatened House Un-American Inquiry Pair," *LAT*, June 13, 1947; "Rankin Demands Chaplin Expulsion," *LAT*, June 13, 1947; "What Really Fell from the Roswell Sky," *Albuquerque Tribune*, July 8, 2000; James McAndrew, *The Roswell Report: Fact vs. Fiction in the New Mexico Desert* (Washington, DC: Government Printing Office, 1995); "Cyclist's Holiday," *Life*, July 21, 1947; "Accent on Brass," *Time*, July 20, 1947; *DW*, July 27, 1947, 1; *Esquire*, August 1947, 37; Smith threatens Mannix: Ceplair and Englund, *Inquisition in Hollywood*, 260.

"Chaplin Accepts House 'Invitation,'" *NYT*, July 21, 1947; Welles interview with Hopper in Joseph McBride, *What Ever Happened to Orson Welles? A Portrait of an Independent Career* (Lexington: University Press of Kentucky, 2006), 95–96; Lawson: *Thought Control in U.S.A.* (Hollywood, CA: Progressive Citizens of America, 1947); Edward J. Ruppelt, *Report on Unidentified Flying Objects* (New York: Ace Books, 1956), 34; "Red Scenario," *Newsweek*, August 25, 1947; Twining memo: David Michael Jacobs, *The UFO Controversy in America* (Bloomington: Indiana University Press, 1975), 43.

FN 5: "What Are Films Saying Today?" *People's World*, January 24, 1947. FN 7: FBI home visit: Garry Wills, *Reagan's America* (Garden City, NY: Doubleday, 1987), 249. FN 8: See John Sbardellati and Tony Shaw, "Booting a Tramp: Charlie Chaplin, the FBI, and the Construction of the Subversive Image in Red Scare America," *Pacific Historical Review*, November 2003. FN 10: "Machine Politics Under Fire in Delightful 'Farmer's Daughter,'" *DW*, April 13, 1947; "A Close-up of Democracy," *Esquire*, May 1947, 8; *Tidings* cited in *NYT*, May 25, 1947. FN 11: Berkeley testimony, Hearings Before the Committee on Un-American Activities, September 19, 1951 (Los Angeles); FBI Berkeley file. FN 13: Bellah description: McBride, *Searching for John Ford*, 449; Reagan, commencement address, U.S. Military Academy, May 27, 1981. FN 14: *Fourth Report, Un-American Activities in California 1948: Communist Front Organizations* (Sacramento: California State Legislature, 1948). FN 15: *The Fountainhead* file, Warner Bros. Archives, USC Libraries; FBI report, name redacted (Los Angeles), "Communist Infiltration into the Motion Picture Industry," August 7, 1947, in *Communist Activity in the Entertainment Industry*, vol. 9.

Showtime ("Hooray for Robert Taylor!")

Hood to Hoover, "Contemplated Change in Management at RKO Studios," 14, *Communist Activity in the Entertainment Industry*, vol. 4; Sondra Gorney, "Prizefight Film

Packs Punch," *DW*, August 28, 1947; David Platt, "What New York Movie Fans Think of 'Crossfire,'" *DW*, July 28, 1947; Harold J. Salemson, "Crossfire Irks Anti-Semites," *DW*, August 31, 1947; David Platt, "'Crossfire' Box Office Terrific, Says Variety," *DW*, August 1, 1947; "'Crossfire' Attendance Terrific," *DW*, August 19, 1947; Scott: *LA Daily News*, August 27, 1947; S[pecial] A[gent] name redacted, "Communist Infiltration into the Motion Picture Industry," August 7, 1947, in *Communist Activity in the Entertainment Industry*, vol. 5; Scott: *Thought Control U.S.A.*, 330; *Los Angeles Daily News*, August 27, 1947; Myron C. Fagan, *Red Treason in Hollywood* (Hollywood, CA: Cinema Education Guild, 1948); "Communist Infiltration into the Motion Picture Industry," August 7, 1947; Hood to Hoover memo, "Re: House Committee on Un-American Affairs," August 20, 1947, in *Communist Activity in the Entertainment Industry*, vol. 9.

Edward Dmytryk, *Odd Man Out: A Memoir of the Hollywood Ten* (Carbondale: Southern Illinois University Press, 1996), 33; Alvah Bessie, *Inquisition in Eden* (New York: Macmillan, 1965), 182; Lester Cole, *Hollywood Red* (Palo Alto, CA: Ramparts Press, 1981), 266, 270.

Bessie, *Inquisition in Eden*, 190; Eric Johnson in Gordon Kahn, *Hollywood on Trial* (New York: Boni & Gaer, 1948), 6; I.F. Stone, "The Grand Inquisition," *Nation*, November 8, 1947, 492; Johnston on Warner: Ceplair and Englund, *Inquisition in Hollywood*, 280.

"Communist Infiltration into the Motion Picture Industry," August 7, 1947; Joseph McBride, *Frank Capra: The Catastrophe of Success* (New York: Simon & Schuster, 1993), 544; William Walton, "Kangaroo Court Under Klieg Light," *New Republic*, November 3, 1947; Samuel A. Tower, "79 in Hollywood Found Subversive, Inquiry Head Says," *NYT*, October 23, 1947, 1.

Lardner: "Two Sessions Here Score Film Inquiry," *NYT*, October 26, 1947; Stone, "The Grand Inquisition," 493; Lawson and other prepared statements: Kahn, *Hollywood on Trial*; Lardner: Patrick McGilligan and Paul Buhle, *Tender Comrades: A Backstory of the Hollywood Blacklist* (New York: St. Martin's Press, 1997), 410; "Rogge Says Clark Plans 'Witch Hunt,'" *NYT*, November 8, 1947.

Decision at the Waldorf: The Big Mop-up

Lawson: "Film Group Urges Voiding Contempt," *NYT*, November 17, 1947; Johnston story: Ceplair and Englund, *Inquisition in Hollywood*, 352; Johnston statement: "Movies to Oust Ten Cited for Contempt of Congress," *NYT*, November 26, 1947; Dmytryk, *Odd Man Out*, 94–95; Bogart press release, Committee for the First Amendment file, AMPAS Library; "2 Film Men Say Firing Is Victory for Anti-Semitism," *DW*, November 28, 1947; Joseph R. Starobin, *American Communism in Crisis, 1943–1957* (Berkeley: University of California Press, 1972), 182.

The Fabulous Texan MPAA file, AMPAS Library; *Hollywood Reporter*, November 6, 1947.

II. Fighting for the Ministry of Truth, Justice, and the American Way, 1948–50

Lillian Ross, "Introducing the Black List," *New Yorker*, March 21, 1994; Hughes in Hortense Powdermaker, *Hollywood, the Dream Factory: An Anthropologist Looks at the Movies* (Boston: Little, Brown, 1950), 22; "The Unwanted Spy Film," *Ottawa Citizen*, November 29, 1947; S. Eyman and Allen Eyles, "'Wild Bill' William A. Wellman," *Focus on Film* 29 (1978); "Film 'Iron Curtain' Attacked," *NYT*, February 26, 1948; *Wolnosc* and Zanuck memo: Milton Krim collection, AMPAS Library.

The Iron Curtain Parts and the Campaign Begins

Time, March 22, 1948; classified directive: "A Move by Truman on Italy Revealed," *New York Times*, February 12, 1975; covert political campaign: William Blum, *The CIA: A Forgotten History* (London: Zed Books, 1986); Truman to daughter: Margaret Truman, *Harry S. Truman* (New York: William Morrow, 1973), 359–60; Truman and Marshall: Robert A. Divine, "The Cold War and the Election of 1948," *Journal of American History*, June 1972; LeMay contingency plans: Avi Shlaim, *The United States and the Berlin Blockade, 1948–49* (Berkeley: University of California Press, 1983), 120; Albee "got to chatting": Dore Schary, *Case History of a Movie* (New York: Random House, 1950), 5; Gallup poll: Curtis D. Macdougall, *Gideon's Army* (New York: Marzani & Munsell, 1965), 291; Herb Tank, "'State of the Union' Does Cartwheels," *DW*, April 22, 1948; Alldredge, "Film That Changed History?" *Variety*, January 5, 1949; Truman: David McCullough, *Truman* (New York: Simon & Schuster, 1992), 613; Hollywood Eisenhower for President Committee: "Democrats Boom Eisenhower: Special NR Reports," *New Republic*, April 12, 1948; Myron Fagan, *Red Treason in Hollywood* (Hollywood, CA: Cinema Education Guild, 1949); Cecil B. DeMille, "While Rome Burns: The Right to Work," *Vital Speeches of the Day*, June 1, 1948; *Ninotchka* "licked us": Blum, *CIA*, 27.

Variety, March 29, 1948; *Life*, May 17, 1948; *Time*, May 17, 1948; "Onward with Darryl," *New Yorker*, May 22, 1948.

Variety, May 12, 1948; David Platt, "Thousands Defy Sluggers, Picket 'Iron Curtain,'" *DW*, May 13, 1948; "Communism: Randan at the Roxy," *Time*, May 24, 1948; e-mail interviews with Anatole Beck, August 26, 2005, and Roy Kessluck, September 3, 2005; Wallace in Gladwin Hill, "'Oil Trust' Blocks U.N., Wallace Says," *NYT*, May 17, 1948; for a detailed account of *The Iron Curtain*'s reception, see Paul Swann, "International Conspiracy in and Around *The Iron Curtain*," *Velvet Light Trap*, Spring 1995; Rankin: *Motion Picture Daily*, May 20, 1948; Bosley Crowther, "'The Iron Curtain': New Roxy Film Poses a Question: Is It Being Raised or Lowered?" *NYT*, May 16, 1948; "Zanuck Defends 'The Iron Curtain,'" *NYT*, May 30, 1948.

FN 1: Sidney Blumenthal, *Pledging Allegiance: The Last Campaign of the Cold War* (New York: HarperCollins, 1990), 50.

Fort Apache, Our Home

Emanuel Eisenberg, "John Ford: Fighting Irish," *New Theater*, April 1936; Joseph Mc-
Bride, *Searching for John Ford: A Life* (New York: St. Martin's Press, 2001), 371. My
reading of *Fort Apache* is indebted to both McBride and Richard Slotkin, *Gunfighter
Nation: The Myth of the Frontier in Twentieth-Century America* (New York: Atheneum, 1992), 334–43.

"And Another Redskin . . . ," *Newsweek*, May 17, 1948; Arthur M. Schlesinger Jr., *The
Vital Center: The Politics of Freedom* (New York: Houghton Mifflin, 1949), 190.

Variety, March 7, 1948; *Newsweek*, May 17, 1948; *Time*, May 10, 1948; Robert Hatch,
New Republic, July 12, 1948; André Bazin, "The Evolution of the Western," in *What
Is Cinema? Volume II* (Berkeley: University of California Press, 1971), 150–51; Ford
in Peter Bogdanovich, *John Ford* (Berkeley: University of California Press, 1978), 86.

Rushmore and *New York Sun*: William A. Reuben, *The Atom Spy Hoax* (New York: Action Books, 1955), 138; *Look*, August 3, 1948; Wallace: James Aronson, *The Press
and the Cold War* (New York: Bobbs-Merrill, 1970), 46; Bosley Crowther, *NYT*, October 13, 1948.

Truman: Divine, "Cold War," 107; "Throngs to Greet Truman and Dewey," *LAT*, September 28, 1948; "[Dewey] Speech at Bowl," *LAT*, September 25, 1948, 1; "Dogi Cli-
gin & the West," *Time*, October 4, 1948; Gladwin Hill, "Wallace Demands Curb on
Inflation," *NYT*, October 2, 1948; *Variety*, July 21, 1948; *New York Daily News*, September 27, 1948.

H.L. Mencken, *H.L. Mencken's Last Campaign: H.L. Mencken on the 1948 Campaign*,
ed. Joseph C. Goulden (Washington, DC: New Republic Books, 1976), 133; "Why
They Came Out," *Time*, October 18, 1948.

Polonsky to Wolfert: Paul Buhle and Dave Wagner, *A Very Dangerous Citizen: Abraham
Polonsky and the Hollywood Left* (Berkeley: University of California Press, 2001),
235–38.

FN 6: Slotkin, 722n54; FN 7: "Massacre," in *Reveille* (Greenwich, CT: Fawcett, 1962), 76.

Hollywood Alert: From *The Red Menace* to *Storm Warning*

John Howard Lawson, "The Cold War and the American Film," *DW*, March 28, 1949;
Wood: David Platt, "Big Movie Director Pleads for More Hokum in Hollyw'd
Films," *DW*, March 24, 1949; "Movies: End of an Era?" *Fortune*, April 1949; "Where
the Rainbow Ends," *Time*, June 20, 1949.

Jack Smith, "Taboo of Jingola," in *Wait for Me at the Bottom of the Pool*, ed. J. Hoberman
and Edward Leffingwell (London: Serpent's Tail, 1997), 102; *Hollywood Reporter*,
May 25, 1949; *LAT*, June 10, 1949; Hoover: Daniel J. Leab, "How Red Was My Valley:
Hollywood, the Cold War Film, and *I Married a Communist*," *Journal of Contemporary History* 19 (1984): 71.

Edwin Schallert, "'Fountainhead' Provokes Keen Interest at Premiere,'" *LAT*, June 24,
1949; *Hollywood Reporter*, June 23, 1949; *Variety*, June 25, 1949; *Time*, July 11, 1949;

Cue, July 9, 1949; *NYT*, July 9, 1949; I.F. Stone, "The Grand Inquisition," *Nation*, November 8, 1947; Dore Schary, *Heyday: An Autobiography* (Boston: Little, Brown, 1979), 173; M.A. Jones to L.B. Nichols, "Memo: Dore Schary," October 29, 1951, FBI Dore Schary file; *Variety* (nd) and *Cue* (nd) in *Red Danube* clipping file, NYPL; *People's World* clipping in FBI Schary file; Jose Yglesias, "'Red Danube' Made to Order for J. Parnell Thomas," *DW*, December 9, 1949; Bosley Crowther, *NYT*, May 13, 1949; Jose Yglesias, "'Home of the Brave' Pioneering Film on Jimcrow," *DW*, May 17, 1949; "Letter on 'Home of the Brave,'" *DW*, May 26, 1949; Bosley Crowther, *NYT*, July 1, 1949; Jose Yglesias, "'Lost Boundaries' Shallow, Patronizing Film on Negro," *DW*, July 1, 1949; Manny Farber, *Nation*, June 30, 1949.

Wanger to Youngstein: Matthew Bernstein, *Walter Wanger: Hollywood Independent* (Minneapolis: University of Minnesota, 2000), 231; see also Leger Grindon, "Hollywood History and the French Revolution: From *The Bastille* to *The Black Book*," *Velvet Light Trap*, Fall 1991; Georges Sadoul, *Dictionary of Film Makers*, trans. and ed. Peter Morris (Berkeley: University of California Press, 1972), 167; Feldman sent script to Wayne: Randy Roberts and James S. Olson, *John Wayne: American* (New York: Free Press, 1995), 327–28; Walter Duranty, "Red Square: Russia's Pulsing Heart," *NYT*, September 18, 1932; Edward Dmytryk, *Odd Man Out: A Memoir of the Hollywood Ten* (Carbondale: Southern Illinois University Press, 1996), 115.

FN 19: *DW*, November 20, 1949; T.M.P, *NYT*, June 16, 1950. FN 20: *The Fountainhead* file, Warner Bros. Archives, USC Libraries. FN 22: Joseph R. Starobin, *American Communism in Crisis, 1943–1957* (Berkeley: University of California Press, 1972), 198; V.J. Jerome, *The Negro in Hollywood Films* (New York: Mainstream & Masses, 1950), 8, 22, 62. FN 23: Alvah Bessie, *Inquisition in Eden* (New York: Macmillan, 1965), 33. FN 24: Geoffrey Homes, "New Study of Migratory Workers in California," *NYT*, January 29, 1950; Jose Yglesias, *DW*, June 23, 1950.

"The Saucers Are Real!" (and *Guilty of Treason*)

See Marshall Frady, *Billy Graham: A Parable of American Righteousness* (Boston: Little, Brown and Company, 1979), 198–204; "Trade Papers Rap Red-Baiting Film," *DW*, November 28, 1949; DeMille offered Graham a screen test: Stephen J. Whitfield, *The Culture of the Cold War* (Baltimore: Johns Hopkins University Press, 1991), 78.

"Truman 'Rewrites' H'wood Scripting as Pix Lean to Social Significance," *Variety*, January 19, 1949, 1; Carey McWilliams, "Hollywood Gray List," *Nation*, November 19, 1949, 491–92; *New York Herald Tribune*, November 6, 1949; *Variety*, November 28, 1949; nine Wayne vehicles: Roberts and Olson, *John Wayne*, 317.

Newsweek, November 1, 1949; "Indian Fighting," *New York Herald Tribune*, November 18, 1949; Jose Yglesias, "John Ford's New Western Distorts Indian War History," *DW*, November 18, 1949; *Variety*, July 27, 1949; Lawrence H. Suid, *Guts and Glory: The Making of the American Military Image in Film* (Lexington: University of Kentucky Press, 2002), 117; Zanuck to Vandenberg: ibid., 111; *Variety*, December 1949.

See Donald Keyhoe, *The Flying Saucers Are Real* (New York: Fawcett Books, 1950); *Variety*, January 11, 1950; Tenney Committee on Lavery: *Fourth Report, Un-American Activities in California 1948: Communist Front Organizations* (Sacramento: California Legislature, 1948), 349.

American Cold War Strategy: Interpreting NSC 68, ed. Ernest R. May (New York: St Martin's Press, 1993), 25; I.F. Stone, "The Horrid Word 'Socialism,'" in *The Truman Era* (New York: Vintage Books, 1973), 170; Jacques Ellul, *Propaganda: The Formations of Men's Attitudes* (New York: Vintage Books, 1973), 140.

FN 25: John Howard Lawson, *Film in the Battle of Ideas* (New York: Masses & Mainstream, 1953), 24; Suid, *Guts and Glory*, 109.

Sunset / Panic / In a Lonely Place

Samuel Goldwyn, "Television's Challenge to the Movies," *NYT Magazine*, March 26, 1950; Mayer v. Wilde: Ed Sikov, *On Sunset Boulevard: The Life and Times of Billy Wilder* (New York: Hyperion, 1998), 303.

Parker Tyler, *Magic and Myth of the Movies* (New York: Simon & Schuster, 1970), xxi, xxiv; James Agee, "Sunset Boulevard," *Sight and Sound*, November 1950; Ben Hecht, *A Child of the Century* (New York: Primus, 1965), 467; Diana Trilling, *Nation*, June 25, 1949; "I got my confidence" and "The Doc was a New Dealer": Michel Ciment, *Kazan on Kazan* (New York: Viking, 1974), 64; Samuel A. Tower, "FBI Head Brands Communist Party a 'Fifth Column,'" *NYT*, March 27, 1947, 1; "Evaluation A-2," March 15, 1943, and M.A. Jones to L.B. Nichols, "Memo: Elia Kazan," March 26, 1952, Elia Kazan file, FBI; Gerasimov in David Platt, "USSR Director Contrasts Films of Peace with Films of Force," *DW*, March 23, 1949; Jose Yglesias, *DW*, August 2, 1950.

SAC, LA, to Director, "Memo: Nicholas Ray," September 7, 1962, FBI Nicholas Ray file; Nicholas Ray, *I Was Interrupted: Nicholas Ray on Making Movies* (Berkeley: University of California Press, 1993), 123; Ray on Bogart: Dana Polen, *In a Lonely Place* (London: British Film Institute, 1993), 12.

FN 28: Kazan file, Twentieth Century-Fox collection, UCLA Film & Television Archive. FN 29: Vincent Curcio, *Suicide Blonde: The Life of Gloria Grahame* (New York: William Morrow, 1989), 95–97.

Countdown

H.H.T., *NYT*, May 27, 1950; "Hollywood on the Tiber," *Time*, June 26, 1950; Ridgway and Truman: David Halberstam, *The Fifties* (New York: Villard, 1993), 69; "Schary, the Messenger," *Newsweek*, May 29, 1950; "Something Borrowed, Something New," *Commonweal*, June 30, 1950; John McCarten, "Nearer, My God, to Thee," *New Yorker*, July 8, 1950; Robert Hatch, *New Republic*, July 10, 1950; Schary, *Care History*, 3.

FN 31: Robert Hatch, *New Republic*, July 10, 1950.

III. Redskin Menace from Outer Space: America at War, 1950–52

Hanson Baldwin, "The Cavalry Charges On," *NYT*, July 2, 1950; Pat Ford in Scott Eyman, *Print the Legend: The Life and Times of John Ford* (New York: Simon & Schuster, 1999), 390.

Tim Weiner, "Hoover Planned Mass Jailings in 1950," *NYT*, December 23, 2007; David Platt, "Films Are Owned by Same Gang That Owns A-Bomb," *DW*, April 25, 1951; "U.S. Film in Korea, President Reports," *NYT*, July 20, 1950; *Time*, July 31, 1950.

Hoffman Birney, "A Jovian Redskin," *NYT Book Review*, March 2, 1947.

FN 2: Richard Slotkin, *Gunfighter Nation: The Myth of the Frontier in Twentieth-Century America* (New York: Atheneum, 1992), 361.

Across *Rio Grande* . . . into Manchuria?

Progressive Citizens of America clippings, Southern California Library for Social Studies and Research; Pegler: James Aronson, *The Press and the Cold War* (New York: Bobbs-Merrill, 1970), 107; Choe Sang-Hun, "Unearthing War's Horrors Years Later in South Korea," *NYT*, December 3, 2007; *Time*, August 21, 1950; David Platt, "Impressions of the Apache Indian Film 'Broken Arrow,'" *DW*, October 5, 1950, and "'Devil's Doorway,' a Much Better Film on the American Indian Than 'Broken Arrow,'" *DW*, November 21, 1950.

David Platt, "Films Are Owned by Same Gang"; Thomas F. Brady, "Hollywood Goes More Thataway," *NYT Magazine*, August 20, 1950; Robert Warshow, "Movie Chronicle: The Westerner," *Partisan Review*, November–December 1954; *Daily Variety*, September 8, 1950; Bosley Crowther, *NYT*, October 23, 1950; R.C., "Strand Film Glorifies Confederate Flag," *DW*, November 7, 1950; "Flint Auto Worker Writes About Film 'Rocky Mountain,'" *DW*, December 7, 1950; Gallup poll: David Halberstam, *The Coldest Winter: America and the Korean War* (New York: Hyperion, 2007), 329–30; *Time*, December 11, 1950; *Variety*, November 20, 1950; Slotkin, *Gunfighter Nation*, 361; "Like Custer at the Little Big Horn": in Halberstam, *Coldest Winter*, 390.

Bosley Crowther, *NYT*, November 8, 1950; R.C., "MacArthur Glorified in 'Guerilla,'" *DW*, November 10, 1950.

FN 3: A.W., *NYT*, December 26, 1952.

This Is Korea?

"War Over Hollywood," *Newsweek*, August 28, 1950; "Documentary on Korea," *NYT*, August 15, 1950; J.D. Spiro, "No Interference," *NYT*, September 24, 1950; "Studios Cash in on War Against Korea," *DW*, November 27, 1950; "White House Backs Korea Movie Action," *NYT*, January 27, 1951; J.D. Spiro, "Martial Affairs—Metro and Kipling," *NYT*, September 24, 1950.

Hollywood politics of fall 1950, including conflict within the SDG and Nixon-Douglas campaign, largely drawn from Greg Mitchell, *Tricky Dick and the Pink Lady: Richard Nixon vs. Helen Gahagan Douglas—Sexual Politics and the Red Scare, 1950* (New York:

Random House, 1998), and Kenneth L. Geist, *Pictures Will Talk: The Life and Films of Joseph L. Mankiewicz* (New York: Scribner, 1978), as well as David Platt's interpretative coverage in *DW*, October 18, 1950, October 24, 1950, and October 27, 1950.

The Steel Helmet MPAA file, AMPAS Library; Evans interview: *Film Comment*, May–June 1994.

The Steel Helmet file, AMPAS Library; J. Ronald Oakley, *God's Country: America in the Fifties* (New York: W.W. Norton, 1986), 83–84; "a vehicle would be hit": Halberstam, *Coldest Winter*, 451; *Variety*, January 3, 1951; "War Dep. Withholds Full Approval of 'Steel Helmet,'" *Daily Variety*, January 10, 1950; David Platt, "War Dep't OK's Slaying of Prisoner of War in Coming Film on Korea," *DW*, January 11, 1951; *Daily Variety*, January 12, 1951; Victor Riesel, *New York Daily Mirror*, January 12, 1951.

Helen Gould, "Shoestring Film Jolts Hollywood," *New York Herald Tribune*, January 21, 1951; Bosley Crowther, *NYT*, January 25, 1951; Clair E. Towne, Department of Defense Office of Public Information, to Manning Clagett, MPAA, February 1, 1951, in *The Steel Helmet* MPAA file, AMPAS Library; Samuel Fuller, *A Third Face* (New York: Knopf, 2002), 262; "Controversial 'Helmet' Creates No Incident in Playing Service Dates," *Variety*, February 14, 1951.

MacArthur: Halberstam, *Coldest Winter*, 598; *Newsweek*, April 23, 1951; Zanuck registered title: *Time*, April 30, 1951; "The Crisis: Where Do We Go from Here?" *Newsweek*, April 23, 1951; "A General for President?" *US News and World Report*, April 27, 1951.

FN 5: Joseph McBride, *Searching for John Ford* (New York: St. Martin's Press, 2001), 478f. FN 6: Geist, *Pictures Will Talk*, 173–74. FN 7: ibid., 177–87. FN 8: McBride, *Searching for John Ford*, 483. FN 9: Mitchell, *Tricky Dick*, 197ff. FN 10: David Platt, "'Steel Helmet' Booked to Play Every Army, Air Force Base," *DW*, February 19, 1951; David Platt, "The 'Steel Helmet,' the Bonus March—and Koje," *DW*, July 1952. FN 11: Fore, Cinema Texas Program Notes: *This Is Korea*, November 18, 1980.

The Communist Was a Thing for the FBI!

Hollywood Reporter, December 6, 1950; "Actor Edw. G. Robinson Faces House Red Quiz," *LAT*, February 10, 1951, 1; FBI report, L.A. SAC, December 14, 1950, in *Communist Activity in the Entertainment Industry: FBI Surveillance Files on Hollywood, 1942–1958*, ed. Daniel J. Leab (Bethesda, MD: University Publications of America, 1991), vol. 13.

Variety, January 31, 1951, 1; Mortimer: William Howard Moore, *The Kefauver Committee and the Politics of Crime, 1950–52* (Columbia: University of Missouri Press, 1974), 143; Kefauver and McCarthy: Moore, *Kefauver Committee*, 144–50; Kramer wire: Thomas Doherty, *Cold War, Cool Medium: Television, McCarthyism, and American Culture* (New York: Columbia University Press, 2003), 110; Hedda Hopper, "Drama: Crime Pays Off," *LAT*, March 7, 1951.

Braden: Thomas Doherty, "Frank Costello's Hands," *Film History* 10 (1998): 360; *Time*, March 12, 1951; Jack Gould, "Video Captures Drama of Inquiry," *NYT*, March 13, 1951; Jack Gould, "The Crime Hearings," *NYT*, March 18, 1951; Hill: Doherty, "Frank

Costello's Hands," 367; Jack Gould, "Kefauver Considers Writing Book Based on His Study of US Crime," *NYT*, March 21, 1951; *Life*, April 2, 1951.

"Larry Parks Says He Was Red; Gives Other Hollywood Names," *LAT*, March 22, 1951, 1; Wayne: "Loyal Actors Call for Film Industry Purge of All Subversives," *Los Angeles Evening Herald and Express*, March 23, 1951; Robert Nott, *He Ran All the Way: The Life of John Garfield* (New York: Limelight, 2004), 268; Levitt: Gerald Horne, *Class Struggle in Hollywood, 1930–1950: Moguls, Mobsters, Stars, Reds, and Trade Unionists* (Austin: University of Texas, 2001), 86.

Robert C. Doty, "May Day Marchers Booed and Pelted," *NYT*, May 2, 1951.

I Married a Communist file, Warner Bros. Archives, USC Libraries; *Variety*, January 31, 1951, 1; Art Shields, "Cvetic's 'FBI' Film Incites Violence and Anti-Semitism, *DW*, April 24, 1951; *Hollywood Reporter*, April 19, 1951; *LAT*, April 28 , 1951.

H.H.T., *NYT*, April 9, 1951; Hollis Alpert, "Hokum's Where You Find It," *Saturday Review* (nd), in *The Thing* file, Film Study Center–MoMA; Manny Farber, "Best Films of 1951," *Nation*, January 5, 1952; production history of *The Thing* from Todd McCarthy, *Howard Hawks: The Grey Fox of Hollywood* (New York: Grove Press, 1997), 473–83, and *The Thing* file, RKO collection, Performing Arts Special Collections, UCLA Library; Erskine Johnson, *Los Angeles Daily News*, November 21, 1950; Lasker: *NYT*, November 12, 1950; *Time*, May 14, 1951; T.M.P., *NYT*, May 13, 1951; Harold Cruse, "RKO's 'The Thing' Feeds War Hysteria," *DW*, May 14, 1951.

Bosley Crowther, *NYT*, September 19, 1951; *The Day the Earth Stood Still* file, MPAA collection, AMPAS Library; Wise: Paul Buhle and Dave Wagner, *Hide in Plain Sight: The Hollywood Blacklistees in Film and Television, 1950–2002* (New York: Palgrave Macmillan, 2003), 77; *Variety*, September 5, 1951; Edwin Schallert, "'Earth Stood Still' Advanced Thriller," *LAT*, September 29, 1951; Michael Vary, "'Day Earth Stood Still' Spurs Confusion on Peace," *DW*, October 17, 1951; Kast, "Défense de jouer avec les allumettes," *Cahiers du Cinéma*, May 1952, trans. as "Don't Play with Fire," in *Focus on the Science Fiction Film*, ed. William Johnson (Englewood Cliffs, NJ: Prentice-Hall, 1972).

FN 12: Bercovici testimony, *Communist Infiltration of Hollywood Motion-Picture Industry—Part 2, Committee on Un-American Activities*, May 16, 1951. FN 15: A.H. Weiler, "By Way of Report," *NYT*, April 15, 1951. FN 16: David Caute, *The Great Fear: The Anti-Communist Purge Under Truman and Eisenhower* (New York: Simon & Schuster, 1978), 216. FN 17: *Variety*, April 4, 1951; *New York Herald Tribune*, May 3, 1951; *NYT*, May 3, 1951; Farber, "'Best Films' of 1951." FN 18: *Variety*, September 5, 1951. FN 19: J. Hoberman, "The Cold War Sci-Fi Parable That Fell to Earth," *NYT*, November 2, 2008.

Three Cases: Joseph L., Carl F., and Elia Kazan

Zimet: Patrick McGilligan and Paul Buhle, *Tender Comrades: A Backstory of the Hollywood Blacklist* (New York: St. Martin's, 1997), 730; Zanuck disapproved: Elia Kazan, *A Life* (New York: Knopf, 1988), 396; Reagan: *Hollywood Citizen News*, July 30, 1951.

Jean Rouverol, *Refugees from Hollywood: A Journal of the Blacklist Years* (Albuquerque: University of New Mexico, 2000), 5; Comingore and Barrymore told Losey: Michel Ciment, *Conversations with Losey* (London: Methuen, 1985), 122, 118; Foreman: Jeremy Byman, *Showdown at High Noon, Witch-Hunts, Critics, and the End of the Western* (Metuchen, NJ: Scarecrow Press, 2004), 73; Losey: Ciment, *Conversations with Losey*, 126; Huebsch and Foreman: Victor S. Navasky, *Naming Names* (New York: Penguin Books, 1980), 158.

Partners no longer speaking and Wayne demands meeting: Byman, *Showdown*, 227, 288.

"Menjou and Dmytryk Reunited in a Redbaiting Friendship," *DW*, November 15, 1951; "Mary Pickford Signs for 'The Library,' Her First Film Since 'Secrets' in 1933," *NYT*, November 19, 1951; *David and Bathsheba* as "a Satanic Plot to Destroy Christianity," photograph, William Wyler papers, AMPAS Library; " 'Oliver Twist' Firm Admits Film Is Anti-Semitic," *DW*, October 23, 1951; see also Sid Bernard, "Decision Before Doom," and Dermay Tilleau, "Jewish Stereotypes in American Movies," *Film Sense*, January–February 1952; " 'When Worlds Collide' Carries a Big Spectacular Impact on Screen," *LAT*, November 23, 1951; C.P. Trussell, "House Group Urges Death to All Spies," *NYT*, December 30, 1951; David Platt, "Movie Record for 1951," *DW*, January 1, 1952.

Kazan on Zapata: Jeff Young, *Kazan: The Master Director Discusses His Films: Interviews with Elia Kazan* (New York: Newmarket Press, 1999), 83; Mannix: Lester Cole, *Hollywood Red* (Palo Alto, CA: Ramparts Press, 1981), 264–65; Monroe on set: Peter Manso, *Brando: The Biography* (New York: Hyperion, 1995), 310.

Kazan's initial conception: Paul J. Vanderwood, "An American Cold Warrior: Viva Zapata!" *American History/American Film: Interpreting the Hollywood Image*, ed. John E. O'Connor and Martin A. Jackson (New York: Ungar, 1979), 190; Slotkin, *Gunfighter Nation*, 423; Kazan wanted Harris: *Kazan on Directing* (New York: Vintage, 2009), 169–70; Otis L. Guernsey Jr., "A New Type of Bandit Hero . . . a Thoughtful Rebel," *New York Herald Tribune*, February 17, 1952; Bosley Crowther, *NYT*, February 8, 1952; Skouras and Skolsky: Manso, *Brando*, 317–18; Bosley Crowther, "Viva 'Viva Zapata!' " *NYT*, February 17, 1952; "Tips on Films," *Film Sense*, April–May 1952; Harry Wyllis, "Hollywood's 'Viva Zapata' Falsifies Mexican Revolution," *Sunday Worker*, March 16, 1952; Hollis Alpert, "Kazan and Brando Outdoors," *Saturday Review*, February 9, 1952; Laura Z. Hobson, *Saturday Review*, March 1, 1952; "Elia Kazan on 'Zapata,' " Letters to the Editor, *Saturday Review*, April 5, 1952; Kazan: Young, *Kazan*, 86; Arthur M. Schlesinger Jr., *The Vital Center* (New York: Da Capo, 1988), 228–29; Felix Belair, "Peasants' Revolts Urged by Douglas," *NYT*, April 8, 1952; Steinbeck to Kazan: John Steinbeck, *Zapata*, ed. Robert E. Mosberger (New York: Penguin Books, 1993), 353; Kazan: Vanderwood, "American Cold Warrior," 198.

Samuel Sillen, "Elia Kazan Urges Intellectuals in U.S. to Betray Themselves," *DW*, April 17, 1952; "Kazan Warns Fear Hurts Film Industry," *NYT*, May 15, 1952.

FN 20: John Edgar Hoover to Legal Attaché (London, England), "Carl Nathan Foreman, Security Matter-C," Carl Foreman file, FBI. FN 21: M.A. Jones to Mr. Nichols, "Stanley Kramer," February 7, 1955, Stanley Kramer FBI file. FN 24: Rubin: Tom Weaver, *Earth vs. the Sci-Fi Filmmakers: Twenty Interviews* (Jefferson, NC: McFarland, 2005), 337; *Daily Variety*, October 19, 1952. FN 25: M.A. Jones to L.B. Nichols, "Re: Elia Kazan, Motion Picture Director, Twentieth-Century Fox," March 26, 1952, Elia Kazan file, FBI; Kazan HUAC affidavit, April 10, 1952; Kazan's list: Ralph Rosen, "Inside Looking In," *Film Sense*, July–August 1952, 9. FN 26: *Viva Zapata!* file, Twentieth Century-Fox collection, UCLA Film and Television Archive. FN 28: "'Zapata' Again," Letters to the Editor, *Saturday Review*, May 24, 1952. FN 29: Gordon: J. Hoberman, "A Snitch in Time," *Village Voice*, March 23, 1999.

Campaign '52: Take Us to Our Leader, Big Jim

M.V., "'Fixed Bayonets' Is Dull Stab at Peace Sentiment," *DW*, December 17, 1951; Manny Farber, *Nation*, January 5, 1952; Bosley Crowther, *NYT*, November 21, 1951.

Truman and Eisenhower: David McCullough, *Truman* (New York: Simon & Schuster, 1992), 887; Bosley Crowther, *NYT*, February 20, 1952; Sperling: Lawrence H. Suid, *Guts and Glory: The Making of the American Military Image in Film* (Lexington: University of Kentucky Press, 2002), 138; Michael Wilson, "Hollywood and Korea," *Hollywood Review*, January 1953.

McCarey: Jane Otten, "Some Notes About a Secret Movie Plot," *NYT*, March 18, 1951; David Platt, "'My Son John' an Anti-American Movie," *DW*, April 15, 1952; *Commonweal* quoted in David Platt, "A Leading Catholic Journal Blasts 'My Son John,'" *Sunday Worker*, May 18, 1952; Bosley Crowther, *NYT*, April 9, 1952; *New Yorker*, April 19, 1952; *New York Herald Tribune*, April 9, 1952; Robert Warshow, "Father and Son—and the FBI," *American Mercury*, June 1952; Manny Farber, *Nation*, March 22, 1952; "McCarey Comes to Town to Rebuke New York Critics," *Motion Picture Herald*, April 26, 1952; "Catholic Press Lauds McCarey's 'Son John,'" *Paramount News*, May 12, 1952; "Senator Lauds 'My Son' for Its Pro-Americanism," *Daily Variety*, May 7, 1952; Legion list: *Variety*, May 21, 1952; David Platt, "300 on Legion Witchhunt List," *DW*, May 28, 1952.

Movie's unit publicist: J.Z., "F.B.I. Helps Film 'Walk East on Beacon,'" *Cue*, May 3, 1952; Art Shields, "'Walk East on Beacon' Is Police Culture Product," *DW*, June 6, 1952; Bosley Crowther, *NYT*, May 29, 1952; Manny Farber, *Nation*, June 21, 1952.

Time, June 23, 1952; David Michael Jacobs, *The UFO Controversy in America* (Bloomington: Indiana University Press, 1975), 75–80.

Big Jim McLain file, Warner Bros. Archives, USC Libraries.

Indianapolis Star, August 31, 1952.

FN 30: Harold Cruse, "'Halls of Montezuma,' 'Preparedness' Film," *DW*, January 16, 1952. FN 31: Charles Bartlett, "The Crusading Kefauver," *Nation*, May 3, 1952. FN 35: David Platt, "Hollywood Studios to Persecute 300 on Legion Witchhunt List," *DW*, May 28, 1952; Reagan: "Hollywood Witchhunter Whoops Against the 'Anti-

Anti-Communist,'" *DW*, July 30, 1952. FN 38: *Big Jim McClain* file, Warner Bros. Archives, USC Libraries.

High Noon in the Universe

McCarthy: Fred J. Cook, *Nightmare Decade: The Life and Times of Senator Joe McCarthy* (New York: Random House, 1971), 6; *Variety*, October 1, 1952.

Fred Zinnemann, *An Autobiography* (North Pomfret, VT: Trafalgar Square, 1992), 108; Bosley Crowther, *NYT*, July 25, 1952; Foreman to Crowther: Byman, *Showdown*, 75; Hopper's campaign: ibid., 22; David N. Eldridge, "'Dear Owen': The CIA, Luigi Luraschi and Hollywood, 1953," *Historical Journal of Film, Radio and Television* 20, no. 2 (2000).

Alfred Towne, "The Myth of the Western Hero," *Neurotica*, Autumn 1950; Hollis Alpert, "Yippee-Yi-O-Ky-Id," *Saturday Review*, February 17, 1951; "The Great American Horse Opera," *Life*, January 10, 1949; Wallace Markfield, "The Inauthentic Western: Problems on the Prairie," *American Mercury*, September 1952; Bosley Crowther, *NYT*, October 23, 1952; *Pravda* quoted in "Reds Sneer at Telephones in Broadway Plays; Called Props to Replace Actors," *Variety*, June 17, 1953; Leslie Fiedler, *America and the Intellectuals: A Symposium* (New York: Partisan Review, 1953), 34.

Wayne: Mason Wiley and Damien Bona, *Inside Oscar* (New York: Ballantine, 1986), 229–30; *Playboy*, May 1971; Harry Schein, "The Olympian Cowboy," *American Scholar*, Summer 1955; Herbert L. Jacobson, "Cowboy, Pioneer and American Soldier," *Sight and Sound*, Spring 1953.

Andrew F. Tully, "Ike and Mamie at Home," *Collier's*, June 20, 1953; J. Hoberman, "It's Always 'High Noon' at the White House," *NYT*, April 25, 2004.

FN 39: Ron L. Davis, *Duke: The Life and Image of John Wayne* (Tulsa: University of Oklahoma Press, 2003), 166. FN 43: Hoberman, "It's Always 'High Noon.'"

IV. The PaxAmericanArama: Eisenhower Power, 1953–55

Edward T. Folliard, "Ike Takes Helm in a 'Time of Tempest,'" *Washington Post*, January 21, 1953; Arthur Krock, "Mighty Pageant Is Proof," *NYT*, January 21, 1953; *Episcopal Church News* cited in *MANAS Journal*, October 6, 1954; Hedda Hopper, *LAT*, February 4, 1953.

"No One on This Earth Can Help You": *Above and Beyond* and Fantasies of Invasion

MGM's emphasis: Michael Pressler, "The Making of *Above and Beyond*," *Gettsyburg Review*, Autumn 2002; Lawrence H. Suid, *Guts and Glory: The Making of the American Military Image in Film* (Lexington: University of Kentucky Press, 2002), 215ff. "Pentagon 'Spy' Hunt Fades Out to West," *NYT*, December 31, 1952.

Time, July 6, 1953; Arnold: Dana M. Reemes, *Directed by Jack Arnold* (Jefferson, NC: McFarland, 1988), 24; Alland in Paul Buhle and Dave Wagner, *Hide in Plain Sight:*

The Hollywood Blacklistees in Film and Television, 1950–2002 (New York: Palgrave, 2003), 78; "Film Producer Testifies," *NYT*, November 24, 1953; Bernard Gordon, *Hollywood Exile, or, How I Learned to Love the Blacklist* (Austin: University of Texas Press, 1999), 54.

FN 1: Michael Pressler, "The Making of *Above and Beyond*," *Gettysburg Review*, Autumn 2002. FN 2: Stephen A. Zerby, "Using the Science Fiction Film *Invaders from Mars* in a Child Psychiatry Seminar," *Academic Psychiatry*, July–August 2005.

The Hammer, the Witch Trials, and *Pickup on South Street*

NYT, January 18, 1953; Richard H. Rovere, *Senator Joe McCarthy* (New York: Harper & Row, 1973), 51; McCarthy: Robert Griffith, *Politics of Fear: Joseph R. McCarthy and the Senate* (New York: Hayden, 1971), 189; Welker: Rovere, *Senator Joe McCarthy*, 57; Stone, *The Haunted Fifties* (New York: Random House, 1963), 36; Rovere, *Senator Joe McCarthy*, 198; Thomas Doherty, *Cold War, Cool Medium: Television, McCarthyism, and American Culture* (New York: Columbia University Press, 2003), 128; "America's Voice," *NYT*, March 5, 1953; *Variety*: Doherty, *Cold War*, 132.

Hecht: "Hit Shows Red-Tinged Probe Learns," *LAT*, March 24, 1953, 1; Lang: "Film Writer List Given Red Probe," *LAT*, March 25, 1953, 1; "Actor Tosses His War Medals at Red Probers," *LAT*, October 7, 1952, 1; Dorothy Comingore file, AMPAS Library; "Why Dorothy Comingore, Film Actress, Was Framed," *DW*, March 25, 1953; "Silver City Movie Man Defies Quiz," *LAT*, March 27, 1953, 1; *Hollywood Reporter* et al.: James J. Lorence, *The Suppression of Salt of the Earth* (Albuquerque: University of New Mexico Press, 199), 77ff, and Ellen R. Baker, *On Strike and On Film* (Chapel Hill: University of North Carolina Press, 2007), 224ff; "Congress Witchhunters Blamed for Attacks on 'Salt of Earth,'" *DW*, April 9, 1953. The FBI's Los Angeles bureau put out quarterly "Compic" reports on *Salt of the Earth*, dated March 13, 1953; June 16, 1953; September 15, 1953; December 15, 1953; and March 19, 1954.

Eisenhower to son: Stephen E. Ambrose, *Ike's Spies: Eisenhower and the Espionage Establishment* (Jackson: University Press of Mississippi, 1999), 182–83; Bernard Burton, "McCarthy Seeks to Build a Nazi-Style Mass Movement," *DW*, June 1, 1953; Marion Lena Starkey, *The Devil in Massachusetts: A Modern Inquiry into the Salem Witch Trials* (New York: Time Incorporated, 1963), 292; David Platt, "Theatergoer, Stirred by 'Crucible,' Pleads to Audience for Rosenbergs," *DW*, June 10, 1953; Griffith, *Politics of Fear*, 215–16.

Rovere, *Senator Joe McCarthy*, 49; Hammer quotes: Christopher La Farge, "Mickey Spillane and His Bloody Hammer," *Saturday Review*, November 6, 1954, and Woody Haut, *Pulp Culture: Hardboiled Fiction and the Cold War* (London: Serpent's Tail, 1995), 95–100; "Editorial Statement," in *America and the Intellectuals: A Symposium* (New York: Partisan Review, 1953), 3.

Fuller and Zanuck: Lee Server, *Sam Fuller: Film Is a Battleground* (Jefferson, NC: McFarland, 1994), 33; "half-assed hooker": Eric Sherman and Martin Rubin, *The Direc-*

tor's Event: Interviews with Five American Film-makers (New York: Atheneum, 1970), 136; Samuel Fuller, *A Third Face* (New York: Knopf, 2002), 295; Jacques Ellul, *Propaganda: The Formation of Men's Attitudes* (New York: Vintage, 1973), 107; *Pickup on South Street* MPAA file, AMPAS Library; SAC, Los Angeles, to Director, "Samuel Fuller," May 19, 1952, and Hoover to SAC, Los Angeles, May 26, 1952, FBI Samuel Fuller file; Fuller, *Third Face*, 307–8.

David Platt, "Hollywood Film Once Endorsed by State Dept. Now Suppressed in U.S.," *DW*, June 18, 1953; *LAT*, May 30, 1953; Bosley Crowther, *NYT*, June 18, 1953; Fuller: Sherman and Rubin, *Director's Event*, 137; Sadoul: Fuller, *Third Face*, 304; Bosley Crowther, *NYT*, February 2, 1954; *Hell and High Water* MPAA file and clippings, AMPAS Library; David Platt, "Anti-Communist Films Are Poison at Box Office, Says Variety," *DW*, March 9, 1954; "'Hell & High Water,' War-Monger Fraud," *Hollywood Review*, April–May 1954; Parker cited in David Platt, *DW*, March 9, 1954.

FN 5: Griffith, *Politics of Fear*, 215. FN 7: See Ronald Radosh and Joyce Milton, *The Rosenberg File: A Search for the Truth* (New York: Holt, Rinehart, and Winston, 1983). FN 8: Dassin: Patrick McGilligan and Paul Buhle, *Tender Comrades: A Backstory of the Hollywood Blacklist* (New York: St. Martin's, 1997), 216. FN 9: Rand to Spillane: John Meroney, "Man of Mysteries," *WP*, August 22, 2001; Rand on McCarthy: see George Reisman, *Capitalism: A Treatise on Economics* (Ottawa, IL: Jameson Books, 1996), xiv, and Anne C. Heller, *Ayn Rand and the World She Made* (New York: Doubleday, 2009), 245–47. FN 10: Fuller, *Third Face*, 270. FN 11: Rovere, *Senator Joe McCarthy*, 51. FN 12: *Variety* quoted in David Platt, *DW*, March 9, 1954.

After *Quo Vadis*: Onward Christian Soldier, Watch Out for *The Wild One*

Bosley Crowther, "New Movie Projection Shown Here; Giant Wide Angle Screen Utilized," *NYT*, October 1, 1952, 1; "Scripture on Wide Screen," *Time*, June 14, 1954.

Cecil B. DeMille, *The Autobiography of Cecil B. DeMille*, ed. Donald Hayne (Englewood Cliffs, NJ: Prentice-Hall, 1959), 400; *Variety*, October 18, 1949; Thomas M. Pryor, "DeMille's 'Samson,'" *NYT*, November 20, 1949; Bosley Crowther, "Pair of Spectacles," *NYT*, June 8, 1950; *Quo Vadis* at MGM: Gary Carey, *All the Stars in Heaven* (New York: Dutton, 1981), 286–91; Mervyn LeRoy and Dick Kleiner, *Take One* (New York: Hawthorn Books, 1974), 170; "Letter from Rome," *New Yorker*, October 7, 1950; Peter Ustinov, *Dear Me* (Boston; Little, Brown, 1977), 242; *New York Herald Tribune*, November 4, 1951; "Quo Vadis: Most Colossal Epic Ever Made," *Life*, April 9, 1951; *NYT*, November 9, 1951; *Time*, November 19, 1951; Al Hine, "Pagans and Planets," *Holiday*, November 1951; *Variety*, November 14, 1951.

Daily Variety, November 24, 1951; David Platt, "Ancient Rome's Ruthless and Futile Witchhunt," *DW*, November 1951; *New York Post*, March 27, 1953; T. Jacobs, "'Salome' in Technicolor," *DW*, April 8, 1953.

John Foran, "Discursive Subversions: *Time* Magazine, the CIA Overthrow of Musaddiq, and the Installation of the Shah," in *Cold War Constructions: The Political Culture of United States Imperialism, 1945–1966*, ed. Christian G. Appy (Amherst: University of Massachusetts Press, 2000); "Premier of Iran Is Shot to Death in a Mosque by a Religious Fanatic," *NYT*, March 8, 1951, 1; "The Land Where Anything Can Happen," *NYT*, March 10, 1951; *Time*, April 23, 1951; "Mossadegh Flees His Home as Teheran Mob Attacks It in Demonstration for Shah," *NYT*, March 1, 1953, 1.

"Christmas in Teheran," *NYT*, December 25, 1953; *Pravda* cited in "Moscow Says U.S. Aided Shah's Coup," *NYT*, August 20, 1953; "The Mysterious Doings of CIA," *Saturday Evening Post*, November 6, 1954; "6,500 See Debut of CinemaScope, New Film Process, in 'The Robe,'" *NYT*, September 17, 1953, 1; *Variety*, September 18, 1953; Edmund Wilson, "'You Can't Do This to Me!' Shrilled Celia," *Classics and Commercials: A Literary Chronicle of the Forties* (New York: Vintage, 1962), 205–6; *New York Post*, November 9, 1951; Arthur Knight, "Spectacle, Spectacular, Colossal," *Saturday Review*, November 24, 1951; Zanuck: Jeff Smith, "Are You Now or Have You Ever Been a Christian? The Strange History of *The Robe* as Political Allegory," *Film Studies*, Winter 2005.

Time, January 18, 1954; Rouverol: McGilligan and Buhle, *Tender Comrades*, 166; *The Wild One* MPAA file, AMPAS Library.

"The Day the Motorcycles Came," *Life*, January 18, 1954; *Time*, January 18, 1954; Molly Haskell, "Taking the Rap for the Rest of Us," *Village Voice*, September 13, 1973; Bosley Crowther, *NYT*, December 31, 1953; "The Martians Have Landed" cited in Georges Sadoul, *Dictionary of Films*, trans. and ed. Peter Morris (Berkeley: University of California Press, 1972), 419.

FN 14: Thomas H. Pauly, "The Way to Salvation: The Hollywood Blockbuster of the 1950s," *Prospects*, October 1980, 470; Maltz: David Talbot and Barbara Zheutlin, *Creative Differences* (Boston: South End Press, 1978), 48–49; Dunne: George F. Custen, *Twentieth Century's Fox: Darryl F. Zanuck and the Culture of Hollywood* (New York: Basic Books, 1997), 314–15. FN 18: Martin A. Lee and Bruce Shlain, *Acid Dreams: The CIA, LSD, and the Sixties Rebellion* (New York: Grove Press, 1985), 27–35.

Marilyn Ascends, Joe Goes Down

For a full account of the Ball case, see Susan M. Carini, "Love's Labors Almost Lost: Managing Crisis During the Reign of 'I Love Lucy,'" *Cinema Journal*, Fall 2003, and Doherty, *Cold War*, 49–59; Norman Mailer, *Marilyn: A Biography* (New York: Warner Paperback, 1975), 15; "Monroe as a housewife": Karal Ann Marling, "America's Love Affair with the Automobile in the Television Age," *Design Quarterly* 146 (1989); "Merger of Two Worlds," *Life*, January 25, 1954; C. Roberts Jennings, "The Strange Case of Marilyn Monroe vs. the US Army," *Los Angeles*, August 1966; Hanson Baldwin, "McCarthy and the Army: Senator's Inquiry and Marilyn Monroe's Visit to Korea Show Service's Weakness," *NYT*, February 21, 1954.

Gallup poll: Griffith, *Politics of Fear*, 263; Eisenhower mused: "Fears & Faith," *Time*, March 29, 1954; Jack Gould, "New 'Format' Brings Out the President's Warmth and Charm Before Cameras," *NYT*, April 6, 1954; "Joint Role Hailed in Mending Lives," *NYT*, April 5, 1954.

"A smash hit": Doherty, *Cold War*, 201; Gallup poll: J. Hoberman, "The Movie That First Noticed TV's Grip on Politics," *NYT*, March 29, 1998; Michael Straight, *Trial by Television* (Boston: Beacon, 1954), 239; McCarthy's approval ratings: Griffith, *Politics of Fear*, 263; *Variety*, September 18, 1963.

Jay Starr, "Ruminations of a Film Critic," *Film Sense*, January 1954; Joseph North, "A Film to Shout Hallelujah About," *DW*, March 21, 1954, 1; Biberman telegram: *People's World*, May 24, 1954; Otis L. Guernsey Jr., *New York Herald Tribune*, May 28, 1954; Johnson: Pauline Kael, "Film Chronicle: Night People," *Partisan Review*, January 1955; Bosley Crowther, *NYT*, March 13, 1954; navy brass: "Caine Mutiny Prospers on Slick Half-Truths," *Sunday Worker*, June 27, 1954; Mundt and McCarthy: Doherty, *Cold War*, 202.

Stephen J. Whitfield, *The Culture of the Cold War* (Baltimore: Johns Hopkins University Press, 1991), 61; "delighted okay": Martin Hill, "The Legendary Wake of 'The Caine Mutiny,'" *NYT Magazine*, October 11, 1953.

Kazan: Michel Ciment, *Kazan on Kazan* (New York: Viking Press, 1974), 110; *Time*, August 9, 1954; Lindsay Anderson, "The Last Sequence of *On the Waterfront*," *Sight and Sound*, Winter 1955; Budd Schulberg, "The Inside Story of 'Waterfront,'" *NYT Magazine*, January 6, 1980; Christopher La Farge, "Mickey Spillane and His Bloody Hammer," *Saturday Review*, November 6, 1954.

FN 21: "Monroe Scene: New York's Disgrace," *America*, October 2, 1954; David Platt, "News About Movies, Books," *DW*, July 31, 1953. FN 22: see David Hajdu, *The Ten-Cent Plague: The Great Comic-Book Scare and How It Changed America* (New York: Farrar, Straus and Giroux, 2008), 260; for Wertham's politics, see Bart Beaty, *Fredric Wertham and the Critique of Mass Culture* (Jackson: University of Mississippi Press, 2005). FN 23: Michael Wilson, "Hollywood's Hero," *Hollywood Review*, April–May 1954. FN 24: Robert Nott, *He Ran All the Way: The Life of John Garfield* (New York: Limelight, 2004), 296–98. FN 25: John Howard Lawson, "Hollywood on the Waterfront," *Hollywood Review*, November–December 1954.

Sh-Boom *Them!* (DeMillennium Approaching . . .)

Time, November 23, 1953; "Desert Song," *Newsweek*, August 24, 1953; Dietrich: "Las Vegas: 'It Just Couldn't Happen,'" *Time*, November 23, 1953; Dick Pearce, "After Hours: Pleasure Palaces," *Harper's*, February 1955; Daniel Lang, *New Yorker*, September 20, 1952; "Klondike in the Desert," *NYT*, June 7, 1953.

A "wonderful song title": Alison M. Scott and Christopher D. Geist, *The Writing on the Cloud: American Culture Confronts the Atomic Bomb* (Lanham, MD: University Press of America, 1997), 106; *Time*, April 9, 1956; Roberts and Olson, *Writing on the Cloud*, 412.

Hollywood Reporter, June 1, 1954; *Variety*, June 1, 1954; *Time*, November 23, 1953; *Los Angeles Herald*, October 24, 1953; *Variety*, October 15, 1953; *Brooklyn Eagle*, August 20, 1954; A.W., *NYT*, June 17, 1954.

Todd McCarthy, *Howard Hawks: The Grey Fox of Hollywood* (New York: Grove, 1997) 511–38.

Suid, *Guts and Glory*, 221.

"A Great Event Repeats Itself," *Life*, September 20, 1954; *Life*, August 15, 1955; *NYT Magazine*, January 6, 1957; Lapidus: *New Yorker*, December 25, 1954; *Nation*, June 7, 1958; *Life*, February 16, 1953.

Cecil B. DeMille, *The Autobiography of Cecil B. DeMille*, ed. Donald Hayne (Englewood Cliffs, NJ: Prentice-Hall, 1959), 415; ibid., 411; *Variety*, October 10, 1956; DeMille, *Autobiography*, 417; *LAT*, July 16, 1954; Alan Nadel, *Containment Culture: American Narrative, Postmodernism, and the Atomic Age* (Durham, NC: Duke University Press, 1995), 418; DeMille, *Autobiography*, 426; ibid., 421; ibid., 428.

FN 26: *US News and World Report*, June 28, 1957. FN 29: David N. Eldridge, "'Dear Owen': The CIA, Luigi Luraschi and Hollywood, 1953," *Historical Journal of Film, Radio and Television* 20, no. 2 (2000). FN 30: Bosley Crowther, *NYT*, April 23, 1955; *Hollywood Reporter*, April 1955. FN 31: Horace Sutton, "We're Not Trying to Impress You," *Saturday Review*, June 2, 1956. FN 32: Henry Wilcoxon and Katherine Orrison, *Lionheart in Hollywood: The Autobiography of Henry Wilcoxon* (Metuchen, NJ: Scarecrow Press, 1991), 274–75. FN 33: Frank Rich, "The God Racket, from DeMille to DeLay," *NYT*, March 27, 2005.

V. Searchin': America on the Road, 1955–56

Kiss Me Deadly MPAA file, AMPAS Library; Dale Kramer and Madeline Karr, *Teenage Gangs* (New York: Henry Holt, 1953), vii; "Rumors of Moral Code Quiz Upset Hollywood," *LAT*, June 10, 1955; "Senator Kefauver's Press Book Scrutiny," *Variety*, June 6, 1955; Johnston: "Rumors of Moral Code"; *New York Herald Tribune*, May 14, 1955; Bill Henry, "By the Way," *LAT*, June 15, 1955; *NYT*, May 22, 1955; Mooring: Frank Walsh, *Sin and Censorship: The Catholic Church and the Motion Picture Industry* (New Haven, CT: Yale University Press, 1996), 269–70, 280.

FN 1: Friedlob in *Variety*, June 14, 1955; Batjac in *LAT*, June 17, 1955.

Coonskin Kids, or the Martians *Have* Landed

Jacques Ellul, *Propaganda: The Formation of Men's Attitudes* (New York: Vintage, 1973), 172; *Variety*, March 2, 1955; John Fischer, "Personal and Otherwise: The Embarrassing Truth About Davy Crockett," *Harper's*, July 1955; Mooring testimony, *Hearings Before the Subcommittee to Investigate Juvenile Delinquency*, Committee on the Judiciary, U.S. Senate, June 16, 1955; Labor Youth League and American Legion: James Gilbert, *A Cycle of Outrage: America's Reaction to the Juvenile Delinquent in the 1950s* (New York: Oxford University Press, 1986), 185; Bosley Crowther, *NYT*, March 21, 1955; Thomas M. Pryor, "Metro Pursuing Juvenile Theme," *NYT*, July 12, 1955.

FN 3: Lumen: Albert Goldman, *Elvis* (New York: McGraw-Hill, 1981), 155.

On the Brink of the Wild Frontier: *Kiss Me Deadly, Rebel Without a Cause*!

Thomas Wolfe, *The Electric Kool-Aid Acid Test* (New York: Bantam, 1969), 33; R.S., "Disneyland Dedication from Coast," *NYT*, July 18, 1955; "Davy's Time," *Time*, May 30, 1955.

Kempton and Buckley: "Davy: Row and a Riddle," *Newsweek*, July 4, 1955; Bernard Kalb, "Dan'l, Dan'l Boone," *NYT Magazine*, October 9, 1955; Ben Levine, "Davy's Ghost Still Scares the B'ars," *DW*, May 22, 1955.

David Platt, "'Phenix City Story,' an Unusually Good Movie," *DW*, September 14, 1955; S.M., "Lurid Film About Japan Has Its Redeeming Side," *DW*, August 5, 1955; *Kiss Me Deadly* MPAA file; "Editorial Statement," in *America and the Intellectuals: A Symposium* (New York: Partisan Review, 1953), 5; Claude Chabrol, "Evolution of the Thriller," in *Cahiers du Cinéma: The 1950s*, ed. Jim Hillier (Cambridge, MA: Harvard University Press, 1985), 163.

Bosley Crowther, *NYT*, March 21, 1955; Pauline Kael, "The Glamour of Delinquency," in *I Lost It at the Movies* (New York: Bantam Books, 1966), 39–40; *Rebel Without a Cause* backstory: Lawrence Fascella and Al Weisel, *Live Fast, Die Young: The Wild Ride of Making* Rebel Without a Cause (New York: Touchstone, 2005).

Robert Hatch, *Nation*, December 3, 1955; Kael, "Glamour," 41; David Dalton, *James Dean: The Mutant King* (Chicago: A Capella, 2001), 262; Bosley Crowther, *NYT*, October 27, 1955; Hopper: Fascella and Weisel, *Live Fast*, 126.

Jessel petition: Fascell and Weisel, *Live Fast*, 229; "The Image of the U.S.," *Time*, September 12, 1955; "'Jungle' Appalls Critics in Britain," *NYT*, September 18, 1955; Chris Brunel, "Letter from England About the Movie 'Blackboard Jungle,'" *DW*, October 3, 1955; Bosley Crowther, "Juvenile Misfits," *NYT*, October 30, 1955.

FN 5: Will Perry, "Davy Crockett, the Man and the Legend," *Sunday Worker*, July 10, 1955. FN 7: *Newsweek* and *US News and World Report*: Fascella and Weisel, *Live Fast*, 9. FN 10: D.P., "Case of the Ambassador Who Suppressed a Hollywood Film," *DW*, September 9, 1955. FN 11: François Truffaut, *The Films in My Life* (New York: Da Capo, 1994), 299; Brando interview: Dalton, *James Dean*, 324–25.

Better Red Than Dead: Body-Snatched Prisoners of Comanche Mind Control

Norman Mailer, "The White Negro," in *Advertisements for Myself* (New York: Putnam's, 1959), 313; Walter Wanger, "Excerpts from a Speech to the American Booksellers Convention," in *Invasion of the Body Snatchers*, ed. Al LaValley (New Brunswick, NJ: Rutgers University Press, 1989), 146.

Joost Meerloo, "Pavlov's Dog and Communist Brainwashers," *NYT Magazine*, May 9, 1954; A.W., *NYT*, May 10, 1954; David Platt, *Sunday Worker*, May 30, 1954.

Allen LeMay, "The Avenging Texans," *Saturday Evening Post*, December 4, 1954; Mailer, "White Negro," 312.

For a detailed account of the *Invasion of the Body Snatchers* backstory and production, see LaValley, *Invasion of the Body Snatchers*, which, in addition to an introductory essay, includes production notes, memos, and interviews; *Invasion of the Body Snatchers* MPAA file, AMPAS Library; *Los Angeles Examiner,* May 1, 1955; Haworth: Matthew Bernstein, *Walter Wanger, Hollywood Independent* (Berkeley: University of California Press, 1994), 310; Wanger to Crowther: LaValley, *Invasion of the Body Snatchers,* 163; Ernesto G. Laura, "Invasion of the Body Snatchers," in *Focus on the Science Fiction Film,* ed. William Johnson (Englewood Cliffs, NJ: Prentice-Hall, 1972); *Variety,* February 29, 1956.

"Psychological epic": Joseph McBride, *Searching for John Ford* (New York: St. Martin's Press, 1999), 559; Whitney: Thomas M. Pryor, "Hollywood Newcomer," *NYT,* April 1, 1956; D.H. Lawrence, *Studies in Classic American Literature* (New York: Viking Press, 1964), 63; Herman Melville, *The Confidence-Man* (New York: New American Library, 1964), 153.

Joseph McBride and Michael Wilmington, "Prisoner of the Desert," *Sight and Sound,* Autumn 1971.

The Searchers file, Warner Bros. Archive, USC Libraries; Andrew Sarris, "On *The Searchers,*" *Film Comment,* Spring 1971; *New York Herald Tribune,* May 31, 1956; "Admirable Americana," *Newsweek,* and *Cue,* undated clips, Film Study Center–MoMA; *Look,* June 12, 1956; *NYT,* May 31, 1956; *LAT,* June 11, 1956; *Life,* May 7, 1956; *DW,* July 30, 1956; Robert Hatch, *Nation,* June 23, 1956; Lindsay Anderson, *Sight and Sound,* Autumn 1956; Melville, *Confidence-Man,* 152–53.

McBride and Wilmington, "Prisoner"; Sarris, "On *The Searchers*"; Stuart Byron, "*The Searchers*: Cult Movie of the New Hollywood," *New York,* March 5, 1979; Brian Henderson, "*The Searchers*: An American Dilemma," *Film Quarterly,* Winter 1980–81.

FN 15: See J. Todd, "The Syndrome of Capgras," *Psychiatric Quarterly,* April 1957, and Edward L. Merrin and Peter M. Silberfarb, "The Capgras Phenomenon," *Archives of General Psychiatry,* August 1976. FN 16: Richard Slotkin, *Regeneration Through Violence: The Mythology of the American Frontier, 1600–1860* (Middletown, CT: Wesleyan University Press, 1974), 652. FN 17: Huberman: Randy Roberts and James S. Olson, *John Wayne: American* (New York: Free Press, 1995), 420. FN 18: *The Searchers* MPAA file, AMPAS Library. FN 19: *Godard on Godard,* ed. Tom Milne (New York: Da Capo, 1986), 117, 204. FN 20: Ford in Peter Bogdanovich, *John Ford* (Berkeley: University of California Press, 1978), 86; Wayne: McBride, *Searching for John Ford,* 557.

"That'll Be the Day!" The Spirit of '56

Ginsberg, "America," *Collected Poems 1947–1980* (New York: Harper & Row, 1984), 147–48; Frank to parents: *Robert Frank: New York to Nova Scotia,* ed. Anne Wilkes Tucker (Houston: Museum of Fine Arts, 1986), 14; Ralph Waldo Emerson, "Nature," in *Selected Writings of Ralph Waldo Emerson* (New York: Signet Classics, 2003), 217; J. Hoberman, "Real America," *Village Voice,* September 30–October 6, 2009; "Road-builders on the New Highway Network," *Time*, June 24, 1957; Jack Kerouac, *On the Road* (New York: Viking, 1957), 179–80.

Morgan and King: David J. Garrow, *Bearing the Cross: Martin Luther King, Jr., and the Southern Christian Leadership Conference* (New York: Vintage, 1988), 66, 71; Joseph R. Starobin, *American Communism in Crisis, 1943–1957* (Berkeley: University of California Press, 1975), 308; Joseph North, "Jackie Gleason Rates a Biographer," *DW*, May 16, 1956; Vic Miller, "Finally . . . a Dignified Approach to Indians," *DW*, October 16, 1956; T.S., "'Forbidden Planet,' Good Outer-Space, Comic Epic," *DW*, July 23, 1956; David Platt, "Marilyn Monroe and Don Murray Stand Out in the Delightful Comedy 'Bus Stop,'" *DW*, October 25, 1956; "'Giant' Towers Over Most Hollywood Films," *DW*, October 18, 1956; David Platt, "'Attack' a Hollywood War Film with Guts," *DW*, September 26, 1956; "Comments on Attacks on 'Rock and Roll,'" *DW*, May 25, 1956; Michael Wilson, "Hollywood on the Brink of Peace," *Hollywood Review*, June–July 1956; "Miller Tells Un-Americans He Won't Be Informer; to Wed Marilyn Soon," *DW*, June 22, 1956, 1; "Religious Wedding Unites Arthur, Marilyn," *DW*, July 3, 1956, 1.

Booth, *Rhythm Oil: A Journey Through the Music of the American South* (New York: Pantheon, 1991), 15; "Teener's Hero," *Time*, May 14, 1956.

"Elvis—A Different Kind of Idol," *Life*, August 27, 1956; "Dean of the One-Shotters," *Time*, September 3, 1956; Ezra Goodman, "Delirium over Dead Star," *Life*, September 24, 1956; Sheen: Fascella and Weisel, *Live Fast*, 296; Gerald Weales, "The Crazy, Mixed-up Kids Take Over," *Reporter*, December 13, 1956; Meyer Berger, "About New York," *NYT*, October 22, 1956; *Time*, November 26, 1956; Robert Hatch, *Nation*, December 29, 1956; Jack Gould, "Radio-TV: U.N. Debate Coverage," *NYT*, November 5, 1956.

FN 23: Sarah Greenough, *Looking In: Robert Frank's The Americans* (Washington, DC: National Gallery of Art, 2009), 125–26. FN 24: Sukarno: Richard Wright, *The Color Curtain: A Report on the Bandung Conference* (Jackson: University of Mississippi Press, 1995), 136, 13. FN 28: "Cardinal Scores 'Baby Doll' Film," *NYT*, December 17, 1956; Joseph Kennedy: Philip C. Kolin, "Civil Rights and the Black Presence in *Baby Doll*," *Literature-Film Quarterly*, Winter 1996. FN 29: Mailer, "White Negro," 329.

Epilogue: The Face of the Crowd

Elia Kazan, *Kazan on Directing* (New York: Vintage, 2009), 198; Theodor Adorno and Max Horkheimer, *Dialectic of Enlightenment* (New York: Seabury, 1972), 123.

Raymond Gram Swing, *Forerunners of American Fascism* (New York: Julian Messner, 1935), 88; Schulberg: "Transfer to the East," *New Yorker*, December 1, 1956; "A Guitar-Thumping Demagogue," *Life*, May 27, 1956; Griffith: Gilbert Millstein, "Strange Chronicle of Andy Griffith," *NYT Magazine*, June 2, 1957.

For *Face in the Crowd* backstory, see Michel Ciment, *Kazan on Kazan* (New York: Viking, 1974), 113–19; Mary Ann Callahan, "Comfort Keynotes GOP Parley Clothes," *LAT*, August 3, 1956; Hugh Downs, "TV Brings Out Vanity of Sexes," *LAT*, August

15, 1956; Walter Ames, "Afternoon Shows for GOP Confab on Radio and TV," *LAT*, August 20, 1956; "Eisenhower Nominated by Halleck," *LAT*, August 23, 1956; "The Biggest Studio," *Time*, August 27, 1956; "The Biggest Studio (Contd.)," *Time*, September 3, 1956; W.H. Lawrence, "A Political Production to Market," *NYT Book Review*, January 22, 1956; Stevenson: Edwin Diamond and Stephen Bates, *The Spot: The Rise of Political Advertising on Television* (Cambridge, MA: MIT Press, 1988), 78; Vance Packard, *The Hidden Persuaders* (New York: Pocket Books, 1958), 167; L.D. Hotchkiss, "Convention Had Its High Spots and Flops," *LAT*, August 24, 1956; "The Turn to the Future," *Time*, September 3, 1956; *Krokodil* cartoon: *Nation*, October 20, 1956; Dore Schary, "Hollywood: Fade Out, Fade In," *Reporter*, April 18, 1957.

"We got the feeling": Richard Schickel, *Elia Kazan* (New York: HarperCollins, 2005), 337; Henry Rabassiere, "In Defense of Television," *Dissent*, Summer 1956; Bosley Crowther, *NYT*, May 29, 1957; François Truffaut, *The Films in My Life* (New York: Da Capo, 1994), 114; *Time*, June 3, 1957; *People's World*: Elia Kazan, *A Life* (New York: Knopf, 1988), 556; "We conceived *Face in the Crowd* as a 'warning'": Kazan, *Kazan on Directing*, 200.

FN 5: John G. Schneider, "'56: Show Biz Flop," *Nation*, November 24, 1956.

INDEX

Kramer, Stanley: association with Losey

and Foreman, 173, 175, 177, 207; THE

CAINE MUTINY, 265–66; on crime

commission, 157; FBI file, 175n;

post-HUAC strategy, 177–78; and THE

WILD ONE, 251, 252

Krims, Milton, 39, 143

Ku Klux Klan, 106–8, 154–55

Lamarr, Hedy, 42, 242

LAND OF THE PHARAOHS, 276–77, 292n

Lang, Fritz, 4, 8, 20–21, 26, 27, 286n1

Lardner, Ring, Jr.: and CLOAK AND

DAGGER, 21; and Communist Party, 3n,

18; and THE CROSS OF LORRAINE, 12; at

Fox, 2, 61; and HOSTAGES, 2; and HUAC,

51, 56, 58, 128; move to Mexico, 172,

173; Warner Brothers firing, 41n

Las Vegas, 270–71, 280

The Last of the Mohicans (Cooper), 315

THE LAST OUTPOST, 309n

Lattimore, Owen, 117, 192

Lavery, Emmet, 3, 58, 115–16

THE LAWLESS, 108n, 253n, 309n

Lawson, John Howard: anti-MPA

activities, 13; as Communist Party

member, 2n, 17–18, 23n, 37; contempt of

Congress trial, 70–71; and CSU strike,

21; on Hollywood Ten, 89; and HUAC,

47, 57, 60, 70–71; incarceration, 126; as

screenwriter, 6, 10–11, 14, 41n; Tenney

Committee appearance, 10; on TWELVE

Lay, Beirne, Jr., 219, 277

Leatherstocking Tales (Cooper), 314–15

Lee, Canada, 51, 187

Legion of Decency, 134, 235, 242n, 284,

LeMay, Curtis, 68, 126, 219, 222, 277

LeRoy, Mervyn, 15, 97, 146, 243–44,

Levitt, Alfred Lewis, 7n, 38

Lewis, Sinclair, 9, 210n

Lippmann, Walter, 28, 29

THE LIVING DESERT, 270

Losey, Joseph, 38, 93–94, 173, 174, 253n

LOST BOUNDARIES, 50, 78, 101

LOVE ME TENDER, 327, 328

loyalty oaths: at CBS, 149; Einstein

opposition to, 169; Foreman and, 176;

Lavery support for, 116; Nazi Germany

comparison, 196; SDG and, 145–46

Lucas, George, 263n, 319n21

Luce, Clare Boothe, 241, 303, 304n10

Luraschi, Luigi, 208, 277n

MacArthur, Douglas: firing of, 152–53;

and foreign policy, 45; in Korean War,

137, 148–50; Owen Thursday as

representation of, 78n6; presidential

aspirations, 68, 69, 153, 190–91

Mad (magazine), 253, 261n, 293

MAD AT THE WORLD, 285–86

Maddow, Ben, 101n, 230, 252, 264

The Magic Mountain (Mann), xvii

Mailer, Norman, xiii, 89n15, 256, 323. See

also "The White Negro."

Mainwaring, Daniel, 52, 94, 108n, 309,

Maltz, Albert: blacklisting of, 41;

Party activity, 3n, 17, 106; and HUAC,

52, 57, 128, 161; imprisonment, 135;

movies of, 22, 107, 135, 137, 248n;

relocation to Mexico, 172; Tenney

Committee testimony, 10; "What Shall

We Ask of Writers?", 23n

THE MAN FROM PLANET X, 166

MANCHURIAN CANDIDATE, 55, 338

Manhattan Project, 17, 19, 22–23, 25, 31

Mankiewicz, Joseph, 145–46, 179

Mann, Anthony, 138, 277

Mann, Thomas, xviii, 8, 59, 89n

Mannix, Eddie, 43, 46, 51, 102, 180

Markfield, Wallace , 209–10

Marshall, George, 37, 43, 68, 174

Marshall Plan, 69, 82

Marx, Sam, 22, 24, 28, 29

mass culture/mass media, 288, 299;

Adorno/Horkheimer on, 9n; as

alienating to artists, 234; and A FACE IN

THE CROWD, 330–31, 333, 336; and THE

NEXT VOICE YOU HEAR, xvi, xviii

"mass suckerology," xvii, 47, 223

THE MASTER RACE, 14